HUMANISTS AND REFORMERS

HUMANISTS
AND
REFORMERS

A History of the
Renaissance and Reformation

Bard Thompson

WILLIAM B. EERDMANS PUBLISHING COMPANY
GRAND RAPIDS, MICHIGAN / CAMBRIDGE, U.K.

© 1996 Wm. B. Eerdmans Publishing Co.
255 Jefferson Ave. S.E., Grand Rapids, Michigan 49503 /
P.O. Box 163, Cambridge CB3 9PU U.K.

Printed in the United States of America

02 01 00 99 98 97 96   7 6 5 4 3 2 1

Library of Congress Cataloging-in-Publication Data

Thompson, Bard, 1925-1987
Humanists and reformers: a history of the Renaissance
and Reformation / Bard Thompson.
p.   cm.
Includes bibliographical references (pp. 675-89) and index.
ISBN 0-8028-3691-7 (cloth: alk. paper)
1. Renaissance. 2. Reformation. I. Title.
CB359.T47   1995
940.2′1 — dc20   93-29076
                                  CIP

Maps on pages 91, 95, 98, and 115 provided by Magellan Geographix
6464 Hollister Ave., Santa Barbara CA 93117

Contents

THE AGE OF THE REFORMATION

Acknowledgments

MY HUSBAND, BARD, DIED SUDDENLY AND UNEXPECTEDLY IN 1987, leaving a manuscript he had recently revised to be used as a text by his students at Drew University for his course on the Renaissance and Reformation. After some further supplementing and refinement, he had hoped for the book's eventual publication. I had assisted Bard in assembling the large slide collection he used to illustrate his course lectures, and this aided me in compiling the illustrations for this volume.

Upon Bard's death, the greatest hurdle was finding a publisher who would accept this undertaking in the absence of the author. With determination, patience, and genuine kindness, Wm. B. Eerdmans, Jr., accepted the task. I am grateful to Mr. Eerdmans and to managing editor Charles Van Hof for their roles in seeing this work through to publication. Great thanks is due also to James Doelman for refining and updating some parts of the text as well as the bibliography and to Craig Noll for his careful editing.

I want to express my appreciation to several members of the Drew staff: to Catherine Pappas and Yasuko Grosjean who typed and assembled the manuscript, and to Evelyn Meyer, head of the library's reference department. At Art Resource the help of Jessica Allan and Paul Evans in compiling the illustrations was invaluable. I am grateful also for help in particular ways from Robert Chapman, Daniel Clendenin, Donald Vorp, and Paul Grosjean.

Since his death, Bard's colleagues and students in the graduate school at Drew have offered much encouragement. Three people who never ceased to be supportive of the project were my attorney, Austin J. McGreal, my son, Andrew B. Thompson, and my daughter, Frances T. Ricciardi.

Bard would be pleased.

BERTHA T. THOMPSON

THE AGE OF
THE ITALIAN RENAISSANCE

I. INTRODUCTION

1. *The Mind of the Renaissance*

SCHOLARS SINCE THE EIGHTEENTH CENTURY HAVE AGREED THAT SOME sort of major change took place in western European civilization in the period from 1300 to 1600. However, the extent and nature of this change have been widely debated. Some have seen the period as one in which a radically new sense of the world and humanity emerged, whereas others have seen instead the gradual development of ideas that had long been current. Nevertheless, there are elements in Renaissance thought that recur frequently in comparison to earlier centuries.

In the Middle Ages, people typically yielded some of their identity to corporations — the church, the state, the feudal society, the guild, the university, and the monastic order. With the Renaissance came an increased sense of individuality and a celebration of uniqueness and individual self-determination. The literature of the period is filled with statements such as the following about the dignity, excellence, rationality, and power of individual human beings.

- Human beings are made "in the image of God," meaning that each one has the possibility of being a person of creativity and moral excellence.
- Human beings are free; we are not enslaved by sin or psychological obstructions; we are able to set our own course, determine our own destiny.
- Human beings are actors on the human scene; we are creators, second only to God; we are the God-appointed governors of the world.

- Human beings have immortal souls, which is God's way of verifying the preciousness of humankind.
- Human beings may achieve fame — the personal glory attained by an individual who thrusts himself or herself forward in some important, heroic, or prominent way.

Besides such statements in the literature, Renaissance art was equally powerful in expressing human individuality and dignity. The modern portrait, for example, came into existence during the age of the Renaissance precisely as a means of expressing the uniqueness, importance, and psychological complexity of a human being.

For the fifteenth- and sixteenth-century European there occurred not only a new understanding of the individual, but also an expansion of human horizons — the exploration of the New World, for example, and the scientific conjectures of Copernicus (1473–1543). Such events shook people's confidence in medieval notions of the physical universe and finally began to undermine even the political philosophy and systems of divinity widely acknowledged in the Middle Ages. Older theories of church, state, and society were sacrosanct no longer. In *Utopia,* Thomas More questioned European civilization as he knew it, especially its political corruption, and presented an imaginary vision of a new society. In *The Prince,* Machiavelli (1469–1527) presented a conception of the ruler in which the security of the state might require the machinations of a ruthless Borgia: many readers throughout Europe found his suggestions radical and disturbing. In *The Courtier,* Baldassare Castiglione (1478–1529) proposed a new conception of the duties and opportunities of the individual in society — a conception based not on medieval monasticism or medieval chivalry but on Renaissance humanism. (See the excursus at the end of this chapter.)

A second aspect of discovering the world was the simple discovery by Renaissance people that the world, despite its trials and tribulations, was not as contemptible a place as the medieval theologians and mystics said it was. Rather, it was a scene of such winsome delight and astonishing beauty that God himself was surely present in it and could be worshiped in it. The affirmation and exuberant enjoyment of life on earth dissipated the other-worldliness that characterized some quarters of the Middle Ages. "It is good for us to be here," said the Renaissance humanists. Renaissance art was a veritable celebration of life here and now, and some of its important achievements represented the concern of artists to be faithful celebrants of the world of nature in which they lived. Nudity in art was perhaps the quintessential

4

expression of Renaissance humanism, exulting as it did in the beauty, power, and freedom of human beings. Michelangelo's *David* is triumphantly nude. But not all Italians of the Renaissance shared this exuberance: Savonarola led a public "burning of the vanities" including nude art in Florence in 1497, and Popes Eugenius IV and Hadrian VI both condemned what they saw as licentious and pagan works of art.

The Renaissance acquired a "new" basis on which to reconstruct Western society: the civilization of ancient Greece and Rome. This basis is called classicism because it refers to the cultural archetypes of classical antiquity. If one sought the best possible model for, say, painting or architecture, philosophy or ethics, law or literature, education or town planning, one would refer to the works of the ancient Greeks and Romans. Such an attempt to retrieve classical civilization was not entirely new: to a certain extent the attempted recovery of the ancient world had begun even with the fall of the Roman Empire in A.D. 476. At certain times this retrieval became more intense, and thus historians have seen a series of earlier renaissances before the fourteenth century. However, the thinkers, writers and artists of the Renaissance proper saw themselves as better able to recover antiquity, and contrasted this new culture with the darkness of the ages that preceded their own.

The high value afforded to pagan antiquity led to a certain tension with the traditional faith of Christendom. At times the people of the Renaissance seemed to rather enjoy their idolatrous infatuation with a pagan civilization. However, this aspect of the period should not be overestimated. Individual mysticism as promoted by Joachim of Flora and St. Francis of Assisi continued to have influence through the fourteenth and fifteenth centuries. The students of the renowned humanist scholar Vittorino da Feltre studied Plutarch and the Bible, Caesar and St. Augustine. The single most important question that both Italian and northern humanists asked was, Can Christianity and classicism be reconciled?

The term "Renaissance" has been most often associated with Italy in the fourteenth through sixteenth centuries, and then by extension in reference to other European countries. For this reason, our focus first comes to bear on Italy, where it is usually said the Renaissance began around the year 1300. In that year, for example, the painter Giotto (1266–1337), progenitor of Renaissance art, was thirty-four years of age (a year older than Dante) and in the prime of his career; Petrarch (1304–74), father of Italian humanism, was born a few years later. Geographically, the Renaissance did not spring up everywhere as an indiscriminate impulse but more particularly in the city-states of Italy — Florence being the most conspicuous — in which there was sufficient freedom, wealth, and power to challenge the older authorities and to attempt new expressions of culture.

The fifteenth century — the century that the Italians refer to as the *quattrocento* — is usually thought of as the full flowering of the Renaissance in art, philosophy, and literature. Associated with the quattrocento are the names of such important figures as Masaccio (1401–28), Donatello (1386–1466), Botticelli (1447–1510), Leon Battista Alberti (1404–72), Lorenzo de' Medici (1449–92), and Pope Nicholas V (1447–55).

The 1500s, or the *cinquecento,* brought the so-called High Renaissance of Michelangelo Buonarroti (1475–1564), Leonardo da Vinci (1452–1519), and Raphael (1483–1520) and their illustrious patron, Pope Julius II (1503–17). Titian (1477–1576), a Venetian painter whose life spanned almost a hundred years, also deserves a place among the principal figures of the High Renaissance.

Two important changes occurred in the transition between the quattrocento and the cinquecento: a change of scenery and a change of scale. The center of gravity of the Italian Renaissance shifted from the towns to the city — from Florence, Urbino, Mantua, and Ferrara to Rome itself. And the scale of accomplishments shifted from smaller things suitable to human proportions to colossal things expressive of the infinity of the human imagination — from Donatello's small bronze *David* to Michelangelo's huge marble *David,* from Brunelleschi's small-scaled Pazzi Chapel to the massive St. Peter's Cathedral, from Giotto's quaint *Lord's Supper* to Leonardo da Vinci's vast *Lord's Supper.*

The waning of the Italian states' power in the early sixteenth century culminated in the sack of Rome in 1527. From about this time, cities and states outside the Italian peninsula became the leading cultural centers of the Renaissance.

By that time, many of the same tendencies were evident north of the Alps. In France, where Leonardo da Vinci spent the last years of his life, Renaissance art and poetry flourished at the court of King Francis I (1515–47) and soon transfigured the culture of the country. In Germany and the Low Countries, the Renaissance produced fewer painters, sculptors, and architects, but it did foster a new type of scholar whose zeal it was to discover — actually *recover* — a purer, simpler, more ethical version of Christianity. The most celebrated of these so-called Christian humanists was Erasmus of Rotterdam (1466–1536), known among his contemporaries as the prince of humanists. This tendency was not unrelated to the Protestant Reformation that was to follow. In England, too, the Tudor courts of Henry VIII (1509–47), Edward VI (1547–53) and Elizabeth I (1558–1603) demonstrated a renewed interest in art and learning derived from antiquity. (Mary Tudor, who reigned in England between Edward and Elizabeth, was not noticeably patient with the New Learning.) The English Renaissance opened with the work of three Christian humanists — John Colet (1467–1519), Thomas More, and Erasmus — scholars distinguished by their Christian idealism and utopianism. In England the Renaissance impulse found its fullest expression in the literature of the late sixteenth and early seventeenth centuries, with such writers as Shakespeare, Edmund Spenser and Ben Jonson.

Scarcely a populist movement, the Renaissance made headway in the society of intellectuals, artists, princes, and popes and among people of leisure, wealth, power, and artistic sensibility. One had to be literate even to gain access to some of its treasures. Although the invention of printing during the quattrocento greatly enlarged the scope of its influence, the Renaissance never approximated the vast popular appeal of the two more purely religious movements of the sixteenth century — the Protestant Reformation and the Catholic Counter-Reformation.

THREE FORMATIVE ELEMENTS

THREE developments of the years normally assigned to the Renaissance (1300–1600) are closely related to the essential spirit of the Renaissance. All three contributed to the widely held impression that the Renaissance was an expansive era when the frontiers of the European world and mind were pushed back. All three contributed therefore to the equally prominent impression that the Renaissance was an era of special importance, to be distinguished and separated from the period of time that had preceded it.

One of the three was the appearance of printing. With the invention and manufacture of standard movable type, Johannes Gutenberg (b. between 1390 and 1400, d. 1468) began the printing industry in the Rhineland in the mid-1400s. By 1469 printing was being done in Italy, and by 1475 in England. In Italy, Venice had taken the lead in the printing industry, and among its presses was the famous Aldine Press, operated by the humanist Aldus Manutius (1450–1515), remembered among printers as the inventor of italic type. Beginning in the 1480s, his press published the Greek classics, including Plato, in pocket-sized editions — an enterprise that contributed handsomely toward making the intellectual riches of the Renaissance generally accessible. Mantua, and especially Venice, became centers of Jewish printing, where the Talmud and the Hebrew Bible were published, developments that would be of great importance for the northern humanists and Reformers as well.

The advent of printing made a wide range of material cheaply available: among the earliest printed books were the Bible, psalters and liturgies, the writings of St. Augustine, Cicero, and Boccaccio, and almanacs. No longer was the possession of written material limited to princes, scholars and wealthy noble patrons who could afford the cost of having a work copied by a scribe. Printing intensified the developments of the Renaissance by increasing the speed with which new knowledge and literature could be spread. Also, the numerous copies possible with a printed work greatly increased its chance of survival.

The greatest resistance to printed books came, understandably, from professional scribes, whose living was being seriously threatened. According to the scholar Elizabeth Eisenstein, one noted producer and seller of fine manuscript books, Vespasiano da Bisticci, suggested that printed books were second-rate and unfit for a nobleman like the duke of Urbino's library. However, the duke collected both printed and manuscript books, and even sponsored a press beginning in 1482.

The voyages of discovery beginning with Columbus and Vasco da Gama were the second development that fundamentally molded the Renaissance. While Europeans certainly had traveled and explored in the time before the fifteenth century, the emphasis on conquest and eventually settlement marked a new phase of exploration. Although these were largely undertaken by Spain and Portugal, two essentially medieval nations that were relatively untouched by the Italian Renaissance, they were provoked by societal forces typical of the Renaissance — the economic impetus of capitalism, for example, and the expansive drives of new national states. While much of the technical skill needed for extensive naval exploration came out of Italy, it had been developed there over the previous centuries and cannot be attributed to the Renaissance.

A third formative development was the scientific revolution associated especially with the Italian firebrand Galileo Galilei, although it far exceeded the scope of his work. It occurred principally at the end of the sixteenth century and into the seventeenth and some scholars have argued that it was not part of the Renaissance, that its valuing of empiricism over ancient authority was antithetical to the veneration of the classical past that played such a large part in Renaissance art and philosophy. Even the scientific revolution, however, depended to some extent upon the Renaissance preoccupation with recovering ancient sources — in this case, the scientific texts of the Greeks and those Arabian scholars who had kept Greek culture alive during the Middle Ages.

CLASSICISM

"RENAISSANCE" means rebirth — not of things in general but specifically of classicism. People of the Renaissance believed that the civilization of the Greeks and Romans was an ideal civilization, the golden age of culture, to which all subsequent culture should aspire. The writings of the ancient authors were (and still are) referred to as the classics — they are viewed as standards of excellence against which all subsequent literature and artistic expression ought to be measured. In short, Renaissance society believed that the quintessential expression of human culture — whether literature, philosophy, ethics, law, aesthetics, or architecture — was to be found in the artistic and literary remains of the ancient world. Renaissance people, however, were not antiquarians, proposing that we should live slavishly in the past. Rather than simply wanting to superimpose Greco-Roman civilization on the fifteenth century, they saw classical civilization as an exemplum that they proposed to honor in their own times by means of imitation. In this way the glory of Rome would be born anew in a *translatio imperii,* a transfer of the Empire. That Italy was itself geographically the site of the earlier culture may have given the concept greater force there, but the idea of *translatio* was to be picked up later in France, England, and the German states as well.

The Renaissance fascination with ancient culture is perhaps most clearly expressed in Raphael's *School of Athens* (see plate 70), a colossal painting commissioned by Pope Julius II and completed in 1511; it is still to be seen at the papal *stanze.* In the center of Raphael's picture stand Plato and Aristotle. Plato holds the *Timaeus* and points to heaven, to the world of eternal ideas. Aristotle holds the *Nichomachean Ethics* and points earthward, to the more reliable empirical data. To the left of the main figures stands Socrates, dressed in a white tunic. Diogenes, a Cynic philosopher, sprawls on the steps. Ptolemy, renowned astronomer of the ancient world, holds a globe of the earth, which he took to be the center of the universe. Euclid, a Greek mathematician, describes a circle. Pythagoras, ancient

9

philosopher and mathematician, demonstrates on a slate. Averroës, Moslem philosopher and physician, distinguished by his white turban, leans over Pythagoras to observe his calculations. By including Averroes, Raphael expressed the very great debt that the Renaissance felt toward the Arabian scholars who down through the Middle Ages had preserved Greek astronomy, law, logic, medicine, and philosophy from the destruction of the great library in Alexandria in the third century. In the original cartoon of *The School of Athens,* those were all of the figures represented. When the painting was opened to the public, however, another ancient figure had been included — a single lonely man sitting in the foreground, his elbow resting on a block of marble. He was the philosopher Heraclitus, who saw the world as a single process of becoming.

Raphael's cast of characters personified the intellectual riches of the ancient world, the seat of civilization, which the Renaissance sought to reinstate. The onlookers of 1511, however, would have been astounded by one other feature of this painting. Plato was portrayed by Leonardo da Vinci; Euclid, by the architect Bramante (1444–1514); and Heraclitus, thought to be by Michelangelo. The story goes that Bramante had had a key to the Sistine Chapel and had taken Raphael secretly to see what Michelangelo had done on the Sistine ceiling. Raphael had been so moved at the sight that he had made haste to include Michelangelo, as Heraclitus. It is apparent, therefore, that Renaissance people were not content to look back apprecia- tively upon the ancient authors but actually sought to identify themselves with them.

Such an attitude may help to explain the excitement and emotional intensity caused by the revival of classical studies. Between the humanist Petrarch and the ancient philosopher Cicero (106–43 B.C.) stood almost 1,400 years; Petrarch, however, "knew" Cicero (as he said) intimately enough to write letters to him. Machiavelli, having been banished from political life in Florence, passed his time "conversing" with the ancients. When bones purporting to be those of the Roman historian Livy (59 B.C.–A.D. 15) were unearthed in Padua in 1413, the whole town became excited, and the thrill ran throughout Italy.

To recapitulate, the Renaissance was born out of a profound reverence for classical antiquity — for its wisdom, grace, philosophy, science, archi- tecture, sculpture, painting, literature, laws, ethics, views on education, and ideas on the proper formation of young people for public service. This attitude was not mere sentimentality. Cicero's ethics were actually used. Vitruvius's architectural principles were actually applied. Nowhere is this practical connection more apparent than in the respect paid by the Renaissance to classicism in its narrower sense — respect for order, clarity, rationality, harmonious proportion, moderation, and peace. Those ancient virtues came, not from experience, but from profound philosophical and religious principles — the essential order and harmony of the world, the nature of beauty, and the unity of God. They passed into the age of the Renaissance and were deeply honored by it, although politically the Renaissance was a time of astonishing despotism, brutality, and disorder.

Classical virtues such as harmonious proportion, clarity of purpose, and rationality soon began to make an impression on architecture and painting. The first great architect of the Italian Renaissance, Filippo Brunelleschi (1377–1446), believed that the beauty of a building depended on its harmonious proportion, which was created by the mutual order of each component part attuned to one another according to mathematical laws. The chapter house that Brunelleschi designed around 1443 for the Church of Santa Croce in Florence is considered one of the supreme achievements of his career and one of the most extraordinary examples of Renaissance architecture. Endowed by the Pazzi family of Florence, it is called the Pazzi Chapel.

The first thing one should recognize about the Pazzi Chapel is its scale. It is, like most expressions of the quattrocento, a small building, designed not to express the sense of infinity as Gothic architecture did but to suit and accommodate human beings. Second, this small building superbly illustrates the Renaissance commitment to the classical principles of harmonious proportion. The interior is simple, economical, light, clean, and eloquent (see plate 1). The architectural details are set out in *pietra serena* against white stucco walls, the only decorations being the terra-cotta reliefs by the sculptor Luca della Robbia (1400–1482). In the rational and ordered clarity of this building, which is based on simple geometric principles and dedicated to the principles of harmonious proportion, one might be able to see, as in a mirror, the unity and perfection of God and to sense the rationality of the Christian religion.

The same concern for harmony and proportion led to the reintroduction of perspective in the pictorial arts and therefore to a revolutionary change in sculpture and painting. In its simplest terms, perspective is quite literally a graph of space that enables the painter or the sculptor to achieve the correct relative proportions of every figure, object, and spatial division within the scope of a work of art. To understand the importance of redevelopment of perspective, one must listen to the complaint of Giorgio

1. Pazzi Chapel

Vasari (1511–74) against some medieval painters: "Over and over again they produced figures in the same style, staring as if possessed, with outstretched hands, on the tips of their toes, as can still be seen in San Miniato, outside Florence." Vasari was commenting here on the unreality of the human figures in such works of art. They were flat and unreal; they were "staring as if possessed"; it would be difficult to imagine them speaking; the landscape in which they exist is impossible to walk through; near things and far things, big things and little things are shown without much proportionate relationship to each other.

Perspective had been an important part of classical art and had continued, to a certain extent, in the Byzantine art of the Middle Ages. The revival of it in the West began in the fourteenth century. Leon Battista Alberti, in his book on painting *De pictura* (1435), either introduced the technique of perspective or codified the ideas that previous painters and sculptors had already begun to use. Among the important early fifteenth-century users of the technique were Brunelleschi and Paolo Uccello (1420–92). An excellent example of Renaissance use of perspective, and of the painstaking care with which artists employed it, is Leonardo da Vinci's *Adoration of the Magi,* both in the cartoon of the painting and then in the painting itself (see figures 33 and 34). Perspective brought animated, three-dimensional people to painting and enhanced the ability of Renaissance artists to celebrate real people in a real world.

HISTORY AS DISCONTINUOUS

A SECOND important aspect of the Renaissance may be found in the following inscription on the tomb of Leonardo Bruni (1370–1444), chancellor of the Republic of Florence: "History is in mourning." The Renaissance world was in mourning because it had come to realize that the ancient world, the seat of human culture, had really died. "The Renaissance stood weeping at its grave," wrote the modern scholar Erwin Panofsky, "and tried to resurrect its soul." Petrarch was the very first to speak of the Middle Ages as a "dark age," one that separated him from the riches and pleasures of classical antiquity and that broke the connection between his own age and the civilization of the Greeks and Romans. Giorgio Vasari, a Renaissance historian of art, pronounced medieval art barbaric, declaring that the flowering of painting, sculpture, and architecture could not have occurred in the Renaissance without the rediscovery of the artistic genius of the Greeks and

Romans. Bruni himself made popular and current such expressions as "the decline of classical civilization," the intervention of a "dark age," and, finally, the "rebirth," or renaissance, of culture. Renaissance artists — for example, Andrea Mantegna (1431–1506) and Benozzo Gozzoli (1420–97) — loved to decorate their pictures with orange trees full of fruit; they wanted every-

2. B. Rossellino, tomb of Leonardo Bruni

one to know that they were living in the springtime of history (see plates 10 and 33). These writers and artists were very much attempting to set themselves apart from their forebears, to establish themselves as radically new. Later historians now see much more of the continuity between the Middle Ages and the Renaissance.

The sort of historical perspective adopted by these people of the Renaissance involved a philosophy of history in which history is discontinuous, rather than continuous. That is, from the point of view of Renaissance people, the world of the Middle Ages, although near in time, was remote in sentimental attachment, while the age of the Greeks and Romans, although remote in time, was emotionally near. To begin again, to forge ahead, to proceed, it was necessary first to go back, to a golden age of civilization.

History was in mourning partly because not even the scholars were quite sure what the classical authors meant. The whole extent of classical civilization was somehow obscure, despite the several "renaissances" that had occurred during the Middle Ages. Classical remains had been lost or corrupted or simply left in obscurity. In response, the Renaissance (following Erasmus) urgently cried, *Ad fontes!* (Back to the sources!) It was an era of prodigious scholarship, perhaps unparalleled in the intellectual history of the West. Yet in spite of these efforts much of the culture of Greece and Rome, particularly painting and music, could not be recovered.

It was preeminently an age of book gathering and the making of libraries. Nicholas V, first of the Renaissance popes (1447–55), was quite addicted to books. His apostolic secretaries, instead of saying their breviaries and minding the pieties of the papacy, were dispatched to search for classical manuscripts. One of them, the celebrated humanist Poggio Bracciolini (1380–1459), had an unerring instinct for precious volumes, especially those gathering dust in old monasteries. He could sniff them out with prodigious accuracy like the hog that gathers truffles; his methods of getting them away from poor, unsuspecting monks were scarcely more elegant. Back he came to Rome, laden with works by Cicero, Quintillian, Vitruvius, and many other ancient authors. Manuscripts that could not be bought or purloined were copied with excruciating care. To house his books, Pope Nicholas reestablished the Vatican Library, one of the greatest of all libraries in the West.

Scarcely less prodigious in his search for classical manuscripts was Cosimo de' Medici (1389–1464), ruler of Florence in those glorious days of the quattrocento when Brunelleschi, Ghiberti (1378–1455), Donatello,

3. San Marco library

and Fra Angelico (c. 1400–1455) decorated the city. Cosimo's books were housed in a special library built into the Dominican convent of San Marco in Florence.

Perhaps the most remarkable of all the book collectors was Federigo da Montefeltro, duke of Urbino, whose court in the town of Urbino was one of the most humane and artistically sublime in all of the Italian Renaissance. At Urbino the architect Donato Bramante was born and educated, Castiglione received his inspiration for *The Courtier,* and the middling court painter Giovanni Santi pulled about his young son, Raffaello, amid the extraordinary beauty and rationality of that place. The portrait of Federigo by Piero della Francesca reveals the benign side of that great Renaissance intellect (see plate 2). The other side of his profile would have revealed the scars, including the loss of an eye, from a jousting match with Francesco Sforza.

These libraries were not the dusty preserves of half-asleep scholars.

4. The palace at Urbino

They were, on the contrary, the think tanks of the Renaissance — the regenerative force of a reborn culture. Whatever could be gleaned from the classical texts — in other words, classicism itself — was gleaned in these libraries and was broadcast among all those who had the wits to hear, read, and understand.

Since books require knowledge of their languages, we can understand why the Renaissance was an era devoted to languages, especially to classical Latin, Greek, and Hebrew. Latin had been the dominant international language throughout the Middle Ages, but in style and even vocabulary it had changed significantly since classical times. With the Renaissance came a desire to write in Latin as Virgil and Cicero had written, to retrieve what they saw as its original beauty. Greek had been little known and studied in the West during the Middle Ages, but increasingly in the early fifteenth century Greek scholars from Byzantium migrated westward to Italy.

Throughout the Middle Ages there had been commentaries on such classical writers as Virgil and Cicero, as well as on the Bible. However, with the Renaissance came more zealous and widespread scholarly inquiry. Questions about sources and authenticity came increasingly to be posed. Lorenzo Valla corrected some of the Vulgate's textual errors in his *Annotations on the New Testament* (1444). On the basis of philological evidence, Valla (1407–57) declared *The Donation of Constantine* (upon the basis of which the papacy held the Lateran Palace) to be a forgery. The German humanist Johannes Reuchlin (1455–1522) made significant headway in Hebrew studies, and such early sixteenth-century northern humanists as Erasmus, John Colet, and Guillaume Budé (1467–1540) were to continue the scholarly study of Christian, Hebrew, and classical texts, reacting viciously against the commentaries of the medieval Scholastics.

To recapitulate, the tradition of Renaissance humanism is a book tradition, associated with printing and libraries, with texts and research. Libraries especially are the regenerative force of the humanistic tradition, and those who stand in it must return again and again to the sources, to the classics of the Western intellectual tradition.

Most of this scholarly feat was accomplished without serious disadvantage to orthodox Christianity. Renaissance scholars, however, did complain about and belittle the style in which contemporary Christianity was cast — namely, Scholasticism, the teaching of medieval schools. It seemed too complex, extruded, and speculative; too arid of real piety; too unproductive of real ethical conduct.

HUMANISM

THE THIRD important aspect of the Renaissance is suggested in an often-quoted statement by Leon Battista Alberti: "A man can do all things if he will." Such was the kernel idea of Renaissance humanism. Renaissance thinkers put human beings at the center of all creation, viewing them as creatures who are at the same time creators. They can form or shape the world, completing what God has begun. Even more important, a person can mold his or her own personality, achieving what Alberti called *virtù,* "noble character." Humanism was an affirmation of the freedom, power, uniqueness, and individuality of human beings. Such was the point of view expressed, for example, in Giannozzo Manetti's *On the Dignity and Excellency of Man* (1452–53) and in Pico della Mirandola's *Oration on the Dignity of Man* (1486–87), two of the more pronounced expressions of Renaissance humanism to appear in the quattrocento. Such affirmations of human freedom and power were not made simply in literary form. It is impossible to look at Michelangelo's *David* — fourteen feet tall, with outsized hands and head, triumphantly nude — without being taught the dignity and grandeur of human beings.

Where did Renaissance humanism originate? Alberti suggested that his ideas about human nature were indebted to "the ancient authors," where all "right and relevant thoughts" were to be found. However, contemporary scholars like Charles Trinkaus have pointed out the strong Christian tradition that played a part in this view of humanity.

What gives form and shape to such human potential and puts it to useful purpose? For Petrarch and the Italian humanists who followed him it was *dignitas* and *humanitas* that afforded this potential. In using the term *dignitas* in this way Petrarch was looking back to Cicero's pronouncement on the dignity of humankind: Cicero himself had been echoing the Greeks. Also lying behind this view was the biblical account of creation, particularly Genesis 1:26, and the exposition of this passage by St. Augustine. Having *humanitas* means that one has either attained, or is striving to attain, one's full potential as a human being; it means that one is inwardly composed, in harmony with one's self, trustful of reason and committed to rational pursuits; and it means that one has organized all human faculties in order to become a useful citizen. But — and here is the point — no one attains *humanitas* without insight and study. To be an estimable human being, to arrive at one's full humanity, one must engage in what the Renaissance called *studia humanitatis,* a term that has come down to us as "the humanities."

As the Renaissance used the term, *studia humanitatis* referred not to a block of subjects in a curriculum, but to a means or system for humanizing people. Second, it encompassed not simply the humanities as opposed to the sciences and social sciences but all humanizing knowledge, especially the classics. In fact, one-sidedness in learning had no particular value in the Renaissance. People were deemed capable of knowing at least something about all branches of knowledge. An educated person should have a completely cultured humanity, should in fact be *l'umo universale* (the complete man). We retain this expression in speaking of "the Renaissance man." Furthermore, one should express one's learning with *sprezzatura,* a graceful and effortless manner. Everything that one has acquired with so much travail must be given out with such grace and effortless simplicity that it must seem to have been acquired with no pain at all. Finally, the supreme goal of education was not contemplation but citizenship. Cicero had taught the Renaissance that lesson, and it had been strongly reinforced by such humanists as Leonardo Bruni and Francesco Guicciardini (1483–1540). Genuine human beings are first of all citizens.

In the Middle Ages, men and women were supported by great corporations, including the church, the state, the convent, the guild, the feudal structure, the manor, and the religious society. Renaissance humanism promoted a rather new type of human being: the individual, a person of freedom, self-reliance, and, to be sure, doubts. Nowhere is the individual of the Renaissance seen with greater clarity and greater fascination than in the portraits done by Renaissance artists. In his book *The Portrait in the Renaissance,* John Pope-Hennessy declares: "In the Renaissance, [the portrait] reflects the reawakening interest in human motives and the human character, the resurgent recognition of those factors that make human beings individual, that lay at the center of Renaissance life. It is sometimes said that the Renaissance vision of man's self-sufficient nature marks the beginning of the modern world. Undoubtedly it marks the beginning of the modern portrait." A passing acquaintance with Renaissance portraiture is therefore required of all students of this period of history.

One final detail of Renaissance humanism. In April 1528 the Aldine Press of Venice published a volume by Baldassare Castiglione called *The Book of the Courtier.* It was written, in part, at the court of Urbino, where Castiglione conducted a Renaissance school, in the curriculum of which he included manners befitting humanists. *The Courtier* had immense influence throughout Europe. The Holy Roman Emperor Charles V, surely the most powerful prince of the sixteenth century, was said to have owned three books — the Bible, Machiavelli's *Prince,* and Castiglione's *Courtier.* The book explored the concept of a gentleman or gentlewoman, discussing how one deports one's self, how one treats another, how one speaks and walks. It was based squarely on the humanistic assumption of human worth. If human beings are of inestimable value, as the Renaissance said they were, then one must treat others not as a chorus of alley cats but with dignity, gravity, and kindness, befitting both one's own worth and the worth of another. *The Courtier* ends with a peroration on love in which Castiglione tries to transform the medieval principle of chivalry, using Plato's teaching on ideal love.

EXCURSUS

Castiglione's *Book of the Courtier*

BALDASSARE CASTIGLIONE (SEE PLATE 3) WAS BORN IN 1478 WITHIN THE
territories of Mantua (one of the Italian city-states). After being educated
as a humanist in Milan, he entered upon a life in diplomacy. In Rome,
around 1504, he met Guidobaldo, the duke of Urbino, and entered his
service. For the next four years, until Guidobaldo's death, Castiglione lived
in the splendid palace of Urbino and participated in a court that excelled
all others in Italy. In 1506, on behalf of Guidobaldo, he traveled to England,
to the court of Henry VII, first of the Tudor kings, from whom he received
in his master's name the Order of the Garter.

When Guidobaldo died, Castiglione continued for a while in the
diplomatic service of the duchy of Urbino. He represented Urbino in Rome
at the court of Pope Leo X, where he made or renewed friendships with
Raphael (who came from Urbino), Michelangelo, and several prominent
humanists and churchmen of the day. But when Pope Leo moved against
Urbino in 1516 and papal troops occupied the beautiful city, Castiglione
was not only deprived of his livelihood but dispossessed of his property.

In 1517 with his new wife, Ippolito, he lived briefly in Venice but
soon became permanently employed as ambassador of the marquis of Mantua
to the Holy See. In that capacity he represented Mantua at the courts of
three successive popes: Leo X, Hadrian VI, and Clement VII. Eventually
he became a papal nuncio — a diplomat in the service of the popes themselves. In that august capacity, he represented Pope Clement VII at the
court of Charles V, the Holy Roman Emperor. Apparently Castiglione's
diplomacy was not very successful, at least if we are to judge from the
perfidy and mistrust that characterized the relationship between emperor
and pope. When Pope Clement VII was utterly defeated by Charles in 1527
(the year in which Rome was sacked), the ambassadorial talents of Castiglione were thoroughly discredited; he died shortly afterward, at Toledo, in
1529.

Castiglione sketched out *The Book of the Courtier* in 1508, when the
memory of Guidobaldo was still alive in his mind. The fourth book belongs
to a later period, perhaps 1512–15; the whole work was not completed until
Castiglione's Roman period — say, 1516. It was first printed in Venice in
1528 and thereafter was reprinted again and again throughout Europe. The

first English edition of *The Courtier* was made by Thomas Hoby, English humanist and Protestant theologian, who flourished at the court of King Edward VI. Hoby's English text appeared in print in 1561, at the beginning of Queen Elizabeth's reign; it was among the earliest writings of the Italian Renaissance to be translated into English. Of all of the books written in the Italian Renaissance, *The Courtier* may be the most representative, if not the most important, for at least six reasons.

1. Its humanism: it assumes that human nature, unspoiled by the Fall, is free, rational, and powerful, capable of excellence.
2. Its classicism: it exhibits (as Walter Raleigh put it) "an almost idolatrous reverence for classical precedent."
3. Its agenda is devoted to subjects typical of the Renaissance, such as the correct standards of Italian vernacular literature and the meaning of Platonic love.
4. It expresses the chief moral and social ideas of the period.
5. It redefines the meaning of a gentleman in terms characteristic of the Renaissance.
6. As the very name of the book implies, it locates the center of Renaissance civilization not in the university or in the monastic community but in the court. Graced by painters and architects, poets and philosophers, educators and political theorists, the courts of the city-states of Italy were more than seats of government; they were the highest and finest expressions of Renaissance culture. Anyone who sought political power or social prominence sought a place in at least one such court.

Of all these factors, the one that seems to require some additional interpretation is Castiglione's idea of a gentleman. His model was no longer the model that came out of monasticism, nor was it precisely the model from chivalry. Unlike the medieval scholar of the monasteries, Castiglione's courtier was explicitly a man of the world, skilled at arms, an athlete, well versed in politics, and sufficiently sophisticated to be able to perform perfectly in the elegant society of the court. Unlike the heroes of chivalry, Castiglione's gentleman was not only a knight and a warrior and not only gracious with women and solicitous of the poor and the weak; he also was a lover of learning and accomplished in the arts. Although the pattern for Castiglione's courtier was more pagan than Christian, it was a pattern of such uncompromising morality and self-reliance as to be powerfully appealing to all quarters of the West — to Christians and Jews, to Protestants and Catholics. The figure of the gentleman proposed by Castiglione quickly became a model for continental Europe and the British Isles. Many were to find a living embodiment of it in Sir Philip Sidney, the English courtier, soldier and poet (1562–86).

The fourth book of *The Courtier* opens with a catalog of virtues generally descriptive of the word "gentleman" or "gentlewoman." Noble birth by itself is an insufficient claim to being a gentleman. The real proof of a person's worth involves another set of credentials, which Castiglione identifies as adornment of letters, skill at arms, goodness, courage, knowledge, and virtuous deeds. To such a list, Castiglione invariably adds some quite personal characteristics — good manners, a handsome aspect, physical grace, and a stout and sturdy character. The boorish intellectual was not Castiglione's idea of a success at court. Urbino is unabashedly declared the most exemplary of Renaissance courts, and Eleonora Gonzaga, the new duchess (see plate 4), is cited for her exceptional "wisdom, grace, beauty, intelligence, discreet manners, humanity, and every other gentle quality." It is clear, however, that being a courtier consists not simply in being but also in doing. Praise belongs especially to the person of virtuous deeds. The chief duty of a courtier in fact is to win the mind and favor of the prince, in order to be able to direct the prince in the ways of "justice, liberality, magnanimity, gentleness, and other virtues" befitting a good ruler.

In the conversation among friends that accounts for the preponderance of the fourth book, the question naturally arises: Can virtue be taught and learned, or is virtue to be understood as a gift of God or as an extraordinary endowment of nature? The question was not only interesting but urgent. At stake was the Renaissance assumption that virtue could be taught, that by means of a liberating curriculum, specifically called liberal arts or humanities, people could release their innate goodness and power and achieve their full humanity. Signor Gasparo, one of the disputants, insisted that goodness comes neither from an innate capacity nor from education; it is a gift of God — a point of view not appreciably different from that of conventional religion. Signor Ottaviano, however, strongly demurred: moral virtues are acquired neither as a gift of God nor as some extraordinary endowment of nature; rather, they are learned. We indeed can learn vices too, and habit will eventually confirm us in one direction or the other; we will more and more either to virtue or to vice. Virtue needs a master, said Ottaviano, and that master is education and good teaching. Conversely, the root of evil, or at least the nursery of evil, is ignorance. According to

Ottaviano, "The art that teaches how to distinguish the true from the false can indeed be learned."

The next major topic of conversation around Castiglione's circle was the nature of government. Should human beings be ruled by prince or republic? It was a most timely question. The provocative spirit of the Renaissance stimulated people to ask such questions, to raise the possibility of new forms of government. Many of the Italian city-states (most notably Florence and Venice) had actually gone through experiments, some more permanent than others, of republican government. One of the disputants, Ottaviano, allowed the possibility of *three* kinds of government: first, monarchy, by which he meant the rule of the prince; second, aristocracy — the rule of "optimates," or "the good"; and third, a republic, which he feared always had the possibility of veering toward popular government.

In *The Book of the Courtier,* the argument for monarchy, to which Castiglione is understandably disposed, is an argument from the very oneness of God, as well as from the oneness of great human organizations, such as armies. In most arenas of human experience, obedience to some single authority is seen as a highly salutary virtue. The argument for republican government, in contrast, is based on liberty and on the essential soundness of collegial procedures ("it more often happens that one man's opinion simply is wrong"). The argument moves forward subtly in favor of monarchy, partially on the dubious proposition that, as tyranny is the worst of civic disorders, "it follows that monarchy is the best of the three kinds of government because it is the opposite of the worst." Although Castiglione finally comes out clearly in favor of the rule of the prince, he nonetheless is careful to recommend a system of civic councils from which the prince may solicit advice.

The key to the discussion of government is almost certainly the courtier, whose calling is to surround the prince with such virtues that the prince himself is bound to be "just, continent, temperate, strong, and wise, full of liberality, magnificence, religion, and clemency." Thus it is decided among Castiglione's circle that civil government is to be left to the prince, that "image of God" with whom "God shares his very own righteousness, equity, justice, and goodness." The prince shall be like an architect's square — straight and true, making everything else in the state likewise straight and true. The prince is never quite alone in that awesome undertaking, however, because his courtiers are beside him as his officers of virtue.

In passing, we should not overlook the apparently innocuous statement about architecture. A good courtier, said Castiglione, will encourage his prince to build buildings. As Pope Julius builds St. Peter's in Rome and as Federigo, Guidobaldo's predecessor, built the palace in Urbino, so the prince should build "great edifices." The Renaissance was convinced that architecture was not only an important way to reinstate classical precedents but the quintessential means of displaying the astonishing power and beauty of human achievement that the Renaissance was so determined to proclaim.

The Courtier is most famous for a passage near the end of the fourth book — Pietro Bembo's oration on beauty and love. Bembo (1470–1547), thirty-six at the time, was a distinguished humanist who went on to an important career in the Catholic Church, including membership in the college of cardinals. Bembo's oration is probably not original; it is Platonism of the same sort we hear in a treatise on love by Marsilio Ficino (1433–99) and in a commentary on a canzone of Girolaro Benivieni by Pico della Mirandola (1463–94). It was the intellectual inheritance of the Italian Renaissance as a whole.

I am less impressed by what Bembo says about the several stages of love than I am about the structures of human nature that are crucial to his famous oration. He begins eloquently enough with the observation that "love is nothing but a certain desire to enjoy beauty." Ultimately "beauty springs from God and is like a circle, the center of which is goodness." Bembo here speaks Platonically in saying that ideal Beauty, like all other eternal ideas, has its being in God.

Directly we come upon the structure of human nature that Bembo builds to support his theories. In the human soul, he says, there are three modes of perceiving things: sense, reason, and intellect. To each of these cognitive or perceiving modes, there is joined a power of appetite. In the case of the senses, it is that set of elemental appetites we share with animals, including our fundamental instincts to survive and propagate. In the case of reason, however, the appetite is choice, which is peculiar to human beings. In the case of the intellect, the appetite is will, which is a spiritual appetite that may carry us beyond the human plane to communion with angels and ultimately with God.

If one could diagram a human personality, said Bembo, one would find that sort of scheme. Human beings most truly belong in the middle of the structure. That is, we are *rational* creatures, neither animals nor angels. We can choose how we will live between the two extremes. We may decide to live beneath ourselves, completely bound to the body, or we may decide to live above ourselves. In either case, habit will gradually confirm us in one direction or the other.

5. Pietro Bembo, portrait by Titian

How does such a scheme apply to love? Most of us enter manhood or womanhood preoccupied with sensual love. Sensual love makes the mistake of thinking that the body is the ultimate source of beauty, although, in fact, the body reveals ideal Love very faintly. Believing the body to be ultimate beauty, sensual love tries to join itself as closely as possible to that body.

26

Bembo allows such love, especially on the part of young people, whose hot blood obscures their reason. When youths become more mature, however, and yet remain stalled in sensual love, Bembo becomes embarrassed for them. They should have advanced to the second state; they should have climbed the ladder of love to the stage of reason, in which it is possible to love another in a new mode, by humane love. Humane love is much less preoccupied with the body than with the inner beauty of the person loved and ultimately with a beauty that has no connection with the body.

Bembo imagines a final stage on the ladder of love, when through the faculty of intellect, human beings are able to engage in a love that transcends human nature entirely and fixes its gaze on an ideal Beauty that admits no divisions or particularizations at all. By means of such assiduous contemplation, which Bembo associates with the intellect, human beings are able to enjoy a mysticism that Bembo narrowly stops short of describing as union with God.

2. *Renaissance Historiography*

Renaissance historiography, which began in the renaissance itself, must address two crucial questions: What is the relationship of the Renaissance to the Middle Ages? and What is its relationship to modern civilization?

Italian humanists in the age of the Renaissance believed that the Middle Ages represented a deplorable hiatus between classical antiquity and the revival of classicism that took place in the Renaissance itself. Those humanists were sure that classical civilization fell into decadence in the early Middle Ages just as surely as Adam fell into sin in the Garden of Eden. Flavio Biondo (1392–1463) set the date of that fall in the year 410, when Alaric sacked Rome. According to Biondo, classical civilization expired then and there; what followed in the West was a time of great intellectual decadence down to the time of the Renaissance itself. Petrarch fixed the date at A.D. 312, when the Roman emperor Constantine first embraced Christianity. Thus, between the time of Suetonius, Tacitus, and Cicero, on the one hand, and that of Dante, Giotto, and Petrarch, on the other hand, the arts and letters existed in decadence, from which the Renaissance delivered them. So thought the humanists.

The Renaissance humanists largely ignored something we take for granted — that history is a process, each age evolving from the previous one. They demanded to be delivered from the medieval world, which had been tainted by "modernism," and they proposed to establish a new stage of history, one boasting a renaissance of culture and based upon the golden age of culture, the ancient world of Greece and Rome. In 1460 the architect

Filarete (c. 1400–c. 1469) expressed the prejudices of the age when he wrote: "I ask everybody to abandon the modern tradition. Do not accept counsel from masters who work in that tradition. I praise those who follow the ancient manner of building." By "modern," Filarete meant medieval modern, and specifically Gothic.

With their prodigious feats of scholarship in the recovery and translation of ancient sources, the Renaissance humanists had already stolen from theology the foremost place in intellectual esteem. For that matter, humanism contradicted, or at least seriously compromised, theology in two particulars: by its this-worldliness and by its unabashed assumption of the essential goodness of human nature. Humanism meant (1) an interest in, and commitment to, the ideals of culture expressed in the Greek and Latin classics and therefore illustrative of the golden age of Western civilization, namely, classical antiquity; (2) a consummate intellectual interest, not in God and heaven, but in human beings and their world; and (3) a philosophical belief in the dignity, rationality, freedom, and potentiality of human beings.

How did the humanists explain to themselves this sudden "renaissance" of culture that they had brought to pass? They attributed it to a historical cause: they had been able in their time to revive classical civilization. Why had it fallen precisely to them to achieve such a renaissance of classicism? The humanists offered two explanations: first, the recovery of freedom by the great Italian city-states, such as Florence; second, the elusive quality of individual genius, as it appears, say, in Leonardo da Vinci or Michelangelo.

To summarize, the Italian humanists, in their capacity as historians, contributed three main ingredients to Renaissance historiography: first, the idea that the arts and letters were decadent through a long period of cultural darkness; second, the notion that the great revival, or "renaissance," coincided with the restoration of classical letters and classical art; and third, the claim that the freedom of the great Italian city-states and the genius of the Italian masters and thinkers accounted for the recovery.

ERASMUS AND THE REFORMERS

NORTH of the Alps, the Renaissance produced a variation we call northern humanism or Christian humanism. Its best-known representatives were Erasmus and Thomas More. The agenda of northern humanism was twofold:

to reinstate both classical letters and classical Christianity by reestablishing culture and Christianity upon their ancient sources. When Erasmus cried *Ad fontes,* he was calling for a return to the Greek and Latin classics and to the Bible. He looked back to a supposed golden age of Christianity, namely, ancient Christianity before the popes, to which all issues respecting the arts and letters, faith and morals ought once again to refer. Implicit in what Erasmus said was a repudiation of medieval civilization. The continuity of history was far less important to him than the recovery of that distant age in which *real* culture and *real* Christian authenticity could be found. No one was more vitriolic in attacking medieval Schoolmen and medieval piety than Erasmus. The streak of anticlericalism in his thought occasionally broke into open contempt for popes and priests and especially — despite his own connection with a religious order — for monks and nuns.

The Protestant Reformers, chiefly Luther and Calvin, took their own conception of history straight from the humanists. They believed that the essence of Christianity, which they called the gospel, had been progressively obscured during the Middle Ages by the popes and by the Scholastic theologians. The revival of learning (the Renaissance) and the revival of Christianity (the Reformation) were both to be achieved by the same sort of curious historical procedure of overleaping the Middle Ages to rediscover the golden age of classical antiquity and primitive Christianity. Just as the humanists sought to rediscover the ancient classics, just as the Renaissance artists sought to rediscover the principles of ancient art and architecture, so the Protestant Reformers insisted upon the absolute priority of the one classic that matters — the Bible. Moreover, the Reformers believed that the Renaissance was God's way of getting people ready for the Reformation. God had caused Constantinople to fall to the Turks in 1453 so that Greek scholars would be driven into the West, to teach people Greek and thereby to disclose to the Western world the supreme Christian classic: the New Testament.

Before the end of the seventeenth century, the periodization of history became fixed in the divisions familiar to us: ancient, medieval, and modern, the presumption being that the Renaissance was the first of the phenomena that account for the modern age, but not the only one. We have already cited the two most important bases for such periodization: the Renaissance humanists' perception of the history of culture, and the Protestant Reformers' perception of the history of religion.

To those, we now add three lesser bases. First, the voyages of discovery, including the discovery of the North American continent, which occurred in the fifteenth and sixteenth centuries, reinforced the popular conception that the Renaissance was indeed a distinct age. Second, the rise of the national states, from the fourteenth through the sixteenth centuries, served the same impression. The third basis was a book, Giorgio Vasari's *Lives of the Most Eminent Painters, Sculptors, and Architects,* published in 1550. More than any other intellectual of his age, Vasari convinced the generations that came after him that the period from Giotto to Michelangelo constituted a *rinascita dell'arte* (renaissance of the arts). Giotto, he said, revived "the noble art of painting, which had fallen on evil days."

EIGHTEENTH-CENTURY VIEWS

IF ONE thinks that not much worse could befall the reputation of the Middle Ages, one has yet to examine the hostile opinions of Enlightenment historians. They generally believed medieval culture to have been tarnished by barbarism and superstition, and they were extremely fastidious — one might even say scrupulous — about measuring all culture against classical standards, their zeal on behalf of classicism exceeding even that of the Renaissance humanists. Listen, then, to Edward Gibbon (1737–94) delivering an opinion of the Middle Ages in relationship to the Renaissance:

> Before the revival of classical literature [in the age of the Renaissance], the barbarians in Europe were immersed in ignorance; their vulgar tongues were marked with rudeness and poverty of their manners. The students of the more perfect idioms of Rome and Greece [Gibbon meant the Renaissance humanists] were introduced to a new world of light and science . . . of eloquence and reason.

Before the Renaissance: universal darkness; after the Renaissance: light and science, eloquence and reason.

The opinions of Voltaire (1694–1778) did not differ appreciably, except that he assigned exceptional importance to the genius of the Italians in the rescue of Western civilization: "Barbarism, superstition, and ignorance covered the face of the earth, except in Italy." It neither surprised nor perturbed him that the Italian Renaissance brought with it a certain contempt for religion, which in turn accounted for the boisterous and somewhat immoral temper of Renaissance times.

The Romantics of the late eighteenth and early nineteenth centuries looked at the Renaissance as too much associated with classical decorum, while still admiring its emphasis on individual genius. Romanticism finally delivered the Middle Ages from its besmirched reputation — but only for the time being. The Romantic historians rediscovered the medieval world — the age of Catholic faith, almost infinite in its variety and color, populated by heroic and self-effacing people, magnificently comprehensive in its learning, with cathedral spires punctuating the landscape with exclamations of God. It seemed exceptionally beautiful to them, while the Renaissance, populated with the likes of the Borgias, appeared exceptionally pagan.

BURCKHARDT AND HIS CRITICS

IN THE nineteenth century such scholars as Jules Michelet and Jacob Burckhardt firmly established the Renaissance as a distinct age, or epoch, with a Zeitgeist peculiar to itself.

In the seventh volume of his *History of France,* published in 1855, Michelet described the Renaissance as "the discovery of man," that is, the deliverance of human beings from the loss of human freedom and even the debasement of the human spirit that Michelet associated with the Middle Ages. Individualism, the rediscovery of human freedom and power, the fresh exuberance of the human spirit — these, thought Michelet, were the essential qualities of the Renaissance; they made the Renaissance a distinct epoch, indeed a heroic epoch.

Only five years later, Jacob Burckhardt published *The Civilization of the Renaissance in Italy* (1860), in which the traditional modern interpretation of the Renaissance is cast. (Still readily available in the Harper Torchbook series, Burckhardt's work should be read by all students of the Renaissance.) Burckhardt, who acknowledged that his work was deficient in its treatment of Renaissance art, described his book as an essay, meaning "interpretation," thereby disclaiming any intention to write a conventional history of the period.

Like Michelet, Burckhardt stressed the discovery of the individual and the importance of freedom in the Renaissance: for him these were its defining characteristics. He identifies the Renaissance as a new civilization, discontinuous with the Middle Ages and related instead to classical antiquity. However, more so than other scholars Burckhardt stressed the newness of the Renaissance rather than its links to the past.

By "civilization," Burckhardt meant a complete and consistent culture, involving political life, art, religion, philosophy, literature, and science, as well as a "characteristic stamp on social life." Renaissance civilization, he believed, "is the mother of our own, whose influence is still at work among us." Burckhardt was also prone to seeing similarities between the Italian Renaissance and the burgeoning of German culture and nationalism in his own time.

In Burckhardt's view, the motive power of this great rebirth of culture was the revival of antiquity, coupled with "the genius of the Italian people." Renaissance civilization was shaped by constant reference to the ideas, values, and institutions, not of the medieval world, but of the ancient world. The "mediators" between their own age and the age of classical antiquity were the humanists, who formed a "wholly new element in society." They knew what the ancients knew, wrote as the ancients wrote, thought as the ancients thought, and felt as the ancients felt. By the force of their scholarship and their prejudices, they reinstated classical values in the age of the Renaissance.

Out of this new cultural context came the individual — "firstborn among the sons of modern Europe." Now people found their identity as individuals, rather than as members of one or another of the great medieval corporations. From this individualism came the modern conception of fame or personal glory, as well as a new definition of nobility that depended strictly on personal excellence.

Confident of their own dignity and excellence, individuals of the Renaissance had no intellectual categories that made them especially conscious of personal sinfulness. On the contrary, they believed they had been endowed by God and nature to "make good," as we might say now, out of their own inner resources. Thus, one was more apt to be "saved" by good learning than by good religion. Such shifts in attitude produced Renaissance worldliness, which was "not frivolous, but earnest, and was enobled by art and poetry." This life (not the afterlife), life in this world (not the medieval world), is infinitely beautiful and meant to be lived in its fullest. Ancient writings — Cicero or Plato, to take the prime examples — acquired religious authority commensurate with that of the Bible.

Burckhardt's dazzling panorama and celebration of a new Renaissance civilization did not go unchallenged very long, as scholars soon raised several questions.

- Did not Renaissance individualism actually arise in the Middle Ages upon the inexorable decline of feudal structures or perhaps in the context of medieval mysticism?

34

- Did not the Renaissance love of the world begin in religious movements of the Middle Ages, particularly that of Francis of Assisi?
- Did not the real revival of classicism arise in the earlier renaissances (small *r*), especially that of the twelfth century, rather than in the Renaissance (capital *R*) of the fifteenth?
- Is it not possible that the Renaissance was not an age at all, sharply differentiated from the Middle Ages, but essentially an extension of the Middle Ages?

Had not Burckhardt overemphasized the pagan nature of the Renaissance, and overlooked the attempts of many Renaissance figures to reconcile the classical and Christian traditions?

Among the first to demur against the Burckhardtian analysis were Catholic scholars who thought that the Middle Ages had been too little appreciated. The German historian Thode argued in 1885, for example, that individualism arose from the religious mysticism and subjectivism apparent in such people as Francis of Assisi. Etienne Gilson and Jacques Maritain, formidable figures in the Thomistic revival, insisted that the recovery of classical antiquity, far from being the work of the Renaissance humanists, was the contribution of the medieval Schoolmen.

A new breed of medievalists defended the Middle Ages vociferously against the slurs of Burckhardt. Lynn Thorndike suggested that the Renaissance was, if anything at all, only an unraveling of the great, orderly, rational systems of medieval Scholasticism. Charles Homer Haskins (1870–1937) found the renaissance not at all where Burckhardt thought it was, but in the great intellectual revival of the twelfth and thirteenth centuries. Before Haskins scholars had seen earlier "renaissances" as mere failed precursors to that of the fifteenth century.

Haskins inveighed against two ignorances held by people "who ought to know better." One was the myth that the Middle Ages was somehow uniform. Haskins instead saw the medieval world as one of color, variety, and life, a combination of old and new, East and West, sacred and profane. There were renaissances throughout the Middle Ages — one in the time of Charlemagne (crowned in 800), one in the time of Otto the Great (crowned in 962), one in the time of the Medici. The greatest of them all, however, was the renaissance of the twelfth century — the age of the Crusades, the rise of towns, the development of the first modern European state, the origin of the universities, the finest expression of Romanesque art and the beginning of Gothic, the origin of vernacular literature, and the revival of Latin classics, Roman law, and Greek science and philosophy. The so-called Italian Renaissance came out of the Middle Ages so imperceptibly that historians do not really know when it began.

The Dutch cultural historian Johan Huizinga (1872–1945) of Leyden dealt with the Burckhardtian analysis in a book called *The Waning of the Middle Ages* (1924). Huizinga blurred the separations that Burckhardt had created between the world of the Renaissance and that of the Middle Ages, believing that the transitions of history were not nearly as abrupt as Burckhardt imagined them to be. He argued that rather than the birth of a new age, the period was the death of an old.

Charles Howard McIlwain (1871–1968), a political philosopher at Harvard, also took the side of the medievalists in their dressing down of the Burckhardtians. He argued that modern constitutional history — the conception of limited government against the encroachments of the prince — so far from being the creation of the Renaissance, had its origin in the Middle Ages, particularly in the twelfth and thirteenth centuries, when a revival occurred in the study of Roman law. It is fair to say that McIlwain's opinion is broadly shared by historians of constitutional law.

In reply to McIlwain, we must acknowledge that the Renaissance in Italy flourished in city-states, such as Florence and Venice, where republican governments existed from time to time. (Unfortunately, despotism also existed in the Italian city-states.) What the Renaissance did contribute to modern political history was a heightened sense of citizenship, to which the purpose of education was devoted. Why did one pursue an education? To become fully human and fully a citizen. Thus were humanism and citizenship combined.

Robert S. Lopez, an economic historian at Yale, also took sides with the medievalists. He belittled the Burckhardtians as "poet-historians." They overlooked the fact that the real renaissance occurred, not in the fourteenth and fifteenth centuries, but in the "commercial revolution" of the High Middle Ages, reaching its climax in the time of Dante and Giotto, that is, around 1300. That commercial revolution brought with it a surge of population, advances in technology, increased production and consumption, the development of foreign markets, a vast new exchange of international cultures, the collapse of feudalism, and the weakening of the ecclesiastical structure. Those things, in turn, accounted for a renaissance in the arts and letters, science and law, education and individualism — in short, Haskins's "medieval renaissance." Thus, the Middle Ages closed in "a thoroughly medieval way." The Renaissance, by contrast, was a period of economic depression. Population decreased, technology stood still, inflation climbed, commerce was depressed, and taxation became excessive. So far from being the harbinger of the modern world, the Renaissance was a time of deep depression.

An important feature of mid-twentieth-century scholarship was the research of Ernst Cassirer, Paul Oskar Kristeller, and John Herman Randall, Jr. into the Renaissance philosophy of humankind. They are inclined to find the essence of the Renaissance in its humanism — the philosophy of the dignity, rationality, freedom, and potentiality of human beings. Humanism, they affirm, describes the true character of the Renaissance, verifies its existence, and pervades all of its achievements and expressions.

Debates have raged over whether the Renaissance contributed much, if anything, to modern science. (The suggestion is sometimes heard that if we can prove that it contributed nothing, then we can disqualify it from being "modern.") All parties admit, of course, that the Renaissance humanists popularized the whole body of classical learning and literature, including science, and to that extent contributed to modern science. Hans Baron has attempted to assign most of Galileo's success to figures earlier in the Renaissance — heliocentric thought to Nicholas of Cusa and the Neo-platonic tradition; experimental observation to the Renaissance artists; the mathematical method of validating science to Leonardo da Vinci; and the dynamic view of nature also to Leonardo. It may or may not be far-fetched. Certainly it is safer to say that the Renaissance made no extravagant claims of being scientific.

CONCLUSION

THE LATTER half of the twentieth century has seen not only the continued questioning of the medieval/renaissance antithesis, but also a larger questioning of the validity or usefulness of such broad periodization. Increasingly it has been recognized that any concept that attempts to explain developments that took place in different countries over the space of a few hundred years will inevitably be overgeneral and inexact. Thus, over the past few decades attention has shifted away from discussion of the Renaissance in general, and moved more toward studies of particular aspects of the period. Discussion of Burckhardt's paradigm has thus been shuffled to the sidelines, and at this point no synthesizing paradigm has been presented to replace it.

Another feature of recent scholarship in Renaissance studies has been the shift away from the strict separation between the Renaissance and Reformation that had its roots in Burckhardt's work. Increasingly attention has turned toward the connections between the Reformers and the Renaissance humanists, the similar view they had of the immediate past, and their concern for the restoration of a better ancient past.

In my opinion, the Renaissance deserves recognition as an age (perhaps the Burckhardtian word "civilization" is excessive), but we must relate it properly to medieval history, and we must define the term carefully. By being properly related to medieval history, I mean that the Renaissance must be seen as the outcome of certain economic, social, political, and cultural developments of the Middle Ages. In this respect, I am entirely in agreement with the general historical perspective of Wallace K. Ferguson as expressed, for example, in his book *Europe in Transition.* Ferguson believes that feudalism was the fundamental factor of early medieval life — an agrarian, relatively moneyless economy around which most aspects of social, political, and cultural life were organized. The revival of commerce and industry, the reappearance of a money economy, the rise of the towns, and the development of the modern, centralized, bureaucratic state all represented significant alterations to the feudalistic patterns of medieval life. The first effect of those changes was the so-called medieval renaissance of the twelfth and thirteenth centuries, about which Charles Haskins has already emphatically notified us. The ultimate effect was the Renaissance. In the cities, particularly those of Italy, the growth of capital produced significant changes in the economic, social, and cultural patterns of life. A culture began to appear that was more urban than landed, more lay than clerical, and more secular than ecclesiastical; it was based upon the growing number of urban laymen and women who had the wealth and leisure necessary to achieve a liberal education and to patronize the arts.

I do not suggest that the Renaissance was the summation of all Western civilization or the origination of the modern world. Some of what it stood for was immediately blunted by the periods that succeeded it: the Reformation and the Counter-Reformation. Nor did the Renaissance flourish universally. Spain and Portugal, which sent explorers across the waters, were touched by the Renaissance to a much less significant degree than were Italy, France, or England.

The second obligation of the historiographer is to define the Renaissance properly. As sketched in chapter 1, I find that three formative attitudes define the innermost meaning of the Renaissance.

First, the Renaissance *profoundly revered classical antiquity.* It took the ancient Greek and Latin classics to express civilization in its highest form. The classical values of proportion, harmony, rationality, and regularity became not simply axioms of life but the almost universal norms of excellence by which painting, sculpture, and architecture were judged. It is indeed paradoxical that an age so intellectually committed to a classical sense of moderation and proportion, peace and harmony, could have been so intemperate and violent, but such was the case.

Second, the Renaissance *viewed history as discontinuous.* Instead of possessing our modern consciousness of history as a continuous process, people of the Renaissance preferred to dissociate themselves completely from their medieval forebears — those "modernists" who had corrupted the ancient classical legacy. They disdained the immediate past in preference for a distant past.

Third, the Renaissance *adopted a thoroughgoing humanism.* Through almost every expression of Renaissance culture — philosophy, religion, scholarship, and, not least, art — runs a clear affirmation of human dignity, freedom, and potentiality. Nothing more distinguishes the Renaissance in all its parts than humanism.

EXCURSUS

The Emergence of Printing

THE EMERGENCE AND DEVELOPMENT OF PRINTING IN THE SECOND HALF of the fifteenth century was of immense historical importance; it revolutionized all forms of communication and learning with far-reaching consequences.

We should avoid thinking of printing as an invention of the European Renaissance. Printing with wooden blocks had been practiced in Korea, China, and Japan since the eighth century; metal letters were used in Korea at least three centuries before Gutenberg. The contribution of Johannes Gutenberg was, in the 1450s, to combine a cluster of technological advances — the preparation and use of movable metal type, oil-based ink, and a technologically successful wooden handpress — in the operation of his printshop near Mainz. Paper, which was necessary for printing, had been introduced to Europe in the thirteenth century by the Moors of Spain.

Gutenberg's success led to a revolution in communication. Within fifty years of Gutenberg, the age of the scribe had yielded to that of the printer. "He prints more in one day than could be copied in a year," said an Italian humanist about a German printer who had just set up shop in Italy. By 1500 presses operated in many European towns; they added an important new element to urban culture.

Printing brought into being a new type of entrepreneur — the master printer. More often than not, he was himself a humanist who saw his foremost responsibility to be the procurement of important manuscripts for publication and the cultivation of promising authors. His duties did not stop there. He oversaw a household of assistants, kept an eye on potential markets, set the schedule of production, bought supplies, hired and fired, and raised the capital necessary to sustain such industry. He rapidly became a town celebrity; the literati and foreign scholars congregated in his workshop.

The most famous master printer was the Venetian Aldus Manutius, whose printing company, the Aldine Press, required a staff of thirty to operate. Venice of the fifteenth century contained more printing establishments and produced more books than any other city in Europe. Aldus Manutius, from Bassiano near Velletri, opened shop there in 1494 and began two decades of printing Latin, Greek, and Hebrew books, which were thought the best to be found anywhere. Twenty-eight first editions of classical authors came from his shop — Aristophanes, Thucydides, Sophocles, Herodotus, Xenophon, Demosthenes, Plutarch, and Plato. His editions of the Latin classics — Virgil, Horace, Juvenal, done in the beautiful Latin cursive type that he developed — were extremely well thought of everywhere in Europe. For the convenience of scholar-diplomats and officers of state, Aldus discarded the large folio volume as unwieldy and printed smaller octavo volumes — that is, pocket-sized editions. Around 1500, Aldus Manutius assembled a group of scholars (the Aldi Neacademia) to assist him in the selection and editing of texts; he was by then in touch with the most distinguished European scholars, including Johannes Reuchlin, Conrad Celtis, and Erasmus.

Between 1517 and 1549, Daniel Bomberg (van Bomberghen), lately of Antwerp, operated a printing firm in Venice that specialized in Hebrew books, among them the first complete edition of the Babylonian Talmud in twelve volumes (1520ff.), and a critical edition of the *Biblia rabbinica*

(1525–28). By means of such publications, Bomberg provided the resources for a revival of Western Semitic scholarship and stimulated studies in Hebrew and Arabic, much as Aldus Manutius had stimulated the study of Greek. Italy was the home of printing in Hebrew — the first such book, a commentary on the Pentateuch, was printed there in 1475 — and Padua, Mantua, Ferrara, Naples, Brescia, and Soncino all maintained presses for Semitic publications.

In France there were printshops in at least forty towns before 1501, although the new printing industry was concentrated in Paris, where the needs of the university required books, and in the rich commercial city of Lyons. By the turn of the century, there were sixty printshops in Paris alone, turning out a menu of scholarly books, vernacular editions, and church literature. In 1499 Badius Ascensius moved from Lyons to Paris, where in 1503 he established a printing company of his own — Praelum Ascensianum — which issued seven hundred editions before 1535. The exceptional quality of his work is illustrated by the fact that Badius Ascensius published a new book by one of his friends in 1512 — Erasmus's *Praise of Folly*.

Ascensius's business was taken over in 1535 at his death by his son-in-law, Robert Estienne (1499–1559), the most celebrated printer in France during the reign of the Renaissance prince Francis I. In 1539 Estienne was appointed royal printer for Latin and Hebrew; in 1544, for Greek as well. Many of the choicest pieces of scholarship to come from the French Renaissance came from the presses of Estienne. In 1547, however, after the death of King Francis I, Robert Estienne squabbled with the Sorbonne — a thing not difficult to do — and was forced to flee to Calvin's Geneva (1551), where he died in 1559. He left a legacy of some five hundred publications. His brother Charles continued the business in Paris. More illustrious, however, was Henry Estienne (1528–98), Robert's son, whose editions of the classics were deemed the best of his time.

In Germany and in the German-speaking sections of Switzerland, the Protestant Reformation and the Catholic reaction to it affected printing more than anywhere else in Europe or in the British Isles. It brought forth a deluge of books, pamphlets, and broadsides. In such a context, two printers were outstanding. One was Johann Froben, who was decidedly cool to the Reformation. His printing establishment in Basel, formerly operated by the humanist Johannes Amerbach, became one of the most important centers of humanistic printing in the age of the Renaissance. Here, for example, the Greek edition of the New Testament by Erasmus was published in 1516 — the consummate scholarly achievement of the sixteenth century. If

Froben of Basel was disdainful of the Reformation, there was a publisher in Zurich who was not — Christoph Froschauer, printer of the Reformers. His lifetime catalog of six hundred titles (1521–64) included the works of the Swiss Reformers, as well as twenty-seven complete editions of the Bible.

The father of English printing was William Caxton (1422–91), who spent most of his career in the Low Countries engaged in international commerce and diplomacy. Rather late in life he became interested in translation and publication. In Cologne, he learned to print; from Bruges, in 1473, he bought a press, the type, and all other accessories necessary to run a printing establishment of his own. In 1476, having rented space near the Chapter House of Westminster Abbey, he began an English printshop. From Caxton's press, the following year, there appeared the first dated book printed in England: *The Dictes or Sayengis of the Philosophres.* Caxton's purpose was to provide books in English so that the enjoyment of literature and history might eventually be commonplace. He printed more than one hundred editions, including Chaucer's *Canterbury Tales* (1478), Thomas Malory's *Morte d'Arthur,* the *Chronicles of England* (1480), and the *Polychronicon.*

In the social and intellectual history of the West, printing had at least the following eight effects:

1. It allowed more access to books. The "book and reading culture" to which we ourselves belong depended on the development of printing.
2. It increased the opportunity to consult and compare texts.
3. It stimulated cross-cultural exchange.
4. It provided for a wide and accurate dissemination of the sources of Western civilization — classical, Judaic, and Christian. An important element in this dissemination was the vernacular Bible.
5. It made possible the existence of "standard editions."
6. It enhanced preservation. Printing overcame some of the corruption of texts attributable to scribal error and also countervailed loss by wear, moisture, theft, and fire.
7. It preserved, codified, and furthered the homogenizing of vernaculars.
8. It extended the circle of a lay intelligentsia.

What did printing contribute to the Renaissance and (in Burckhardt's phrase) to the "firstborn among the sons of modern Europe"? Sixteenth-century readers had far greater access to written works than their great-grandparents. Who were these readers and how did printing change reading habits and the constitution of the reading population?

Literacy was not always a feature of Western society. At the beginning of the Middle Ages, at the disintegration of the Roman Empire, illiteracy was common among laypeople. Gregory the Great, first of the medieval popes (590–604), referred to images as the "books of the uneducated." As the chief civilizing agency in the West, the church had a virtual monopoly on learning . The molders of Western monasticism, Benedict (ca. 490–583) and Cassiodorus (died ca. 547), were among the conspicuous educators of the age. Reading and writing, school and library, the copying of books and preservation of manuscripts — those were precious parts of monastic discipline. With the advent of printing literacy was to move beyond the traditional monastic and learned circles, but the process was slow and gradual.

Estimates of literacy in early sixteenth-century Western Europe vary, but it is likely that five to ten percent was the norm; with perhaps some of the better-educated towns like Florence it reached thirty percent.

How did the learner learn? In Victor Hugo's *Notre Dame de Paris,* (1831) a scholar observing the first printed book to occupy his shelves full of manuscripts says, "The book will destroy the building," meaning the cathedral. The Gothic cathedral has been described as an encyclopedia in stone. In it was stored all the memories and teachings that have come down in Christian society since antiquity. Printing may indeed have reduced the importance of the image as a means of communication. One could now learn by reading. Early Protestantism, particularly that taught by Ulrich Zwingli in Zurich and John Calvin in Geneva, included an attack against all secondary means of religious communication — images, ceremonies, the cult of the saints, and some of the seven sacraments — in favor of a direct program of communication based on a word culture of preaching, teaching, and reading. When asked how he would deal with an illiterate constituent, Calvin replied (no doubt with Pope Gregory the Great in the back of his mind): certainly not by giving the person an image, but by teaching the person to read. Martin Luther himself thought it very odd that Protestant iconoclasts who tore pictures off the walls dealt reverently with illustrations printed in Bibles. Evidently, he said, "pictures do more harm on walls than in books" — a tart summary of the shift from an image culture to a word culture.

We may connect the development of printing with the Renaissance in two other ways. Both, however, must be left as questions. First, did the print culture contribute to the individualism that was such a conspicuous feature of the Renaissance? (It is a question of how personal reading is, particularly silent reading. It is also a question of how aggressively personal the entrepreneurs of the printing industry were and how tipped toward individualism the subjects of their printing were. A scribe, in his great humility, put his colophon last; the printer made certain it appeared first — on the title page, where all the individualism pertinent to the author also appeared.) Second, did the print culture with its myriad of books help establish the "feeling of historical distance" between our standpoint in history on the one hand, and classical antiquity on the other — a sense of distance deemed essential to a genuine Renaissance consciousness?

The advent of printing raised new complexities in censorship. Governing authorities, whether of the church or nation-states, could no longer control so easily the spread of written works. Most attempted to establish some sort of licensing or censoring process, but these varied in their effectiveness. Writers found ways to work around censorship by making indirect allusions that might pass by the censors, but be understood or guessed at by readers. Government frustration at inability to completely control the dissemination of controversial works led at times to extreme measures: in 1521 King Francis I of France banned printing altogether for a short time, and in 1579 the English publisher William Page had his right hand chopped off for printing a work that criticized Queen Elizabeth I's consideration of marriage to the French duke of Alençon.

The last major problem we need to consider is the relationship between printing and the Protestant Reformation. The Reformation was the first major movement in history that had the power of the printing press behind it. Luther described the new art of printing as "God's highest and extremest act of grace, whereby the business of the Gospel is driven forward." In 1542 the German historian Johann Sleidan developed the theme that God had conferred a special blessing on the German people — printing — and by that means prepared them to bring true religion to humankind everywhere. Wrote Sleidan: "As if to offer proof that God had chosen us to accomplish a special mission, there was invented in our land a marvelous new and subtle art, the art of printing."

Printing was indeed a major asset to the Lutherans in the dissemination of their ideas. Between 1517 and 1520, as the Reformation got underway, Luther sent thirty pamphlets and broadsides to the printer. They sold 300,000 copies. Beatus Rhenanus informed Zwingli that "sold" was the wrong word; they were *snatched* from the hands of booksellers. In 1517 Luther had written out some propositions in Latin in fairly stiff academic jargon, hoping to provoke a debate among scholars. "They were meant exclusively for our academic circle here," Luther explained to the pope.

"They were written in such language that the common people could hardly understand them. They used academic categories." Scholars stayed away from the proposed debate in droves. Suddenly, though, through the power of the new instrument of communication — the press — German versions of Luther's ninety-five theses were being read by Germans everywhere and were being discussed in the marketplaces of Germany. Soon they appeared in other vernaculars and were being snatched from bookstalls in other countries, especially in central Europe. The sixteenth-century aphorism "printing is the poor man's friend" seems to be an apt description of the dissemination of early Lutheran ideas through the print medium to a wide cross section of society.

Protestant scholars were also beneficiaries of the printing industry. The massive intellectual endeavor to rediscover and interpret the sources of early Christianity — an essential aspect of the Protestant Reformation — could scarcely have been as successful as it was without the texts, lexicons, grammars, and other scholarly apparatus published by the master printers, particularly Aldus Manutius, Badius Ascensius, Robert Estienne, and Johanne Froben.

What did printing mean to Protestant piety? In general, the Reformation idea of the priesthood of all believers — that is, that all people of faith are spiritually powerful and spiritually responsible — would not have worked very well without the support of printing. Luther's German New Testament (1522), for example, was meant to be read at home by simple people; along with two Lutheran catechisms and other standards of doctrine, it was designed to assist people in their common priesthood. Congregational singing came into vogue in Strassburg while Calvin was a minister there, partially because the printing industry had made it economically and physically possible to supply each person in the congregation with a printed hymnal. The Geneva Bible, used in England, carried an admonition to heads of households to preach to their families from the printed Bible, "that from the highest to the lowest they may obey the will of God." On the title page of *Acts and Monuments,* edited by the none-too-sweet-spirited Puritan controversialist John Foxe (1516–87), we are shown two congregations at worship — Catholics with their rosaries, and Protestants with books on their laps. God conducted the Protestant Reformation, said Foxe, not by the sword, but with "printing, writing, and reading." For Foxe, printing was an instrument of discernment: it helped people to distinguish between truth and error; it stirred up their "good wits." This Protestant emphasis on literacy had a demonstrable effect: in the centuries following the Refor-

45

mation such Protestant nations as Scotland and Sweden were to have the highest rates of literacy in Europe.

Even when printing was in its infancy, a prince of the Catholic Church, Cardinal Nicholas of Cusa, called it "this holy art risen in Germany" and advocated its use by the Church of Rome as a religious means. From the vantage point of the Catholic Church, however, printing proved to be a mixed blessing. While the Church of Rome never turned its back on Nicholas of Cusa's "holy art," it began a struggle to contain its abuses as early as the Fifth Lateran Council (1512–17) and employed such means as the index and the imprimatur to control the output of religious literature. The English Protestant John Foxe remarked that either the pope must abolish printing or it would do likewise to him. However, by the end of the century the Roman Church was also producing Bibles in the vernacular, and heavily using the printed word in its theological bouts with the Protestant churches.

II. RELIGION AND
THE ITALIAN RENAISSANCE

3. The Church, 1300–1500

NO ISSUE WAS MORE VEXING IN THE MIDDLE AGES THAN THE QUES-
tion, Where did ultimate power, ultimate authority, reside — in the
church, or in the state? That question provides the starting point of this
chapter, which considers one aspect of the intense religious struggle that
underlay the Renaissance.

In 1294 Boniface VIII became pope at the advanced age of eighty. It
was said of his reign, "He came in like a fox, reigned like a lion, and died
like a dog." His contemporaries accused him of attaining the papacy by
inserting a hollow reed into the cell of his predecessor, Celestine V, and
speaking as a seraph to that old man, inducing him to resign. At any rate,
Boniface was a pretentious pope, given to such outbursts as, "I am Caesar.
I am Emperor." What he did not quite comprehend was the growth of
centralized territorial states, the rise of what we may call nationalism. He
miscalculated in particular the status of France, which was then in the last
stages of transition from a feudal to a national state. Philip IV, known as
Philip the Fair (1285–1314), whose reign marks a particularly decisive stage
in the transition between a feudal and a national monarchy, was the French
king with whom Boniface contended.

Preparing for war against Edward I of England, Philip levied taxes,
one of the French monarchs' favorite methods of accumulating wealth.
Boniface reacted indignantly in 1296 by issuing the bull *Clericis laicos,* in
which he threatened ecclesiastical censures against anyone who presumed
to tax either priests or church property. Philip retaliated by putting an
embargo on the export of church money from France to Rome. In 1301 he

49

6. Giotto, *Boniface VIII between Two Cardinals and a Deacon*

added insult to injury by arresting Boniface's legate. The pope responded in 1302 with the important bull *Unam sanctam*. Not only did he reiterate the proposition *extra ecclesiam non salus est* (outside the church there is no salvation), but he ventured to declare that salvation requires subjection to the papacy — a rather new and strident accent. Boniface located the source of all power, whether spiritual or temporal, in the church — more precisely, in the papacy; spiritual power is to be used directly by the church, temporal power by the several states on behalf of the church. While the papacy itself is not liable to human judgment, it does exercise the right of judgment upon the states.

The debate between the pope and the king of France was extremely acrimonious, as the following exchange illustrates:

> Boniface VIII to Philip the Fair: "Let no one persuade you that you have no superior, that you are not subordinate to the supreme authority of the Church. . . . He who thinks so is a fool . . . he who stubbornly affirms so is an infidel."

> Philip the Fair to Boniface VIII: "To Boniface who gives himself as Supreme Pontiff, little or no greeting. . . . Let your great fatuousness know that We are subject to no one in the affairs of this world. . . . Whosoever believes to the contrary We declare to be a fool and a madman."

In 1303 the Estates General of France passed a series of articles accusing Boniface of a stupefying list of terrible crimes, including the keeping and consulting of demons. At the bidding of Philip IV, the pope was physically attacked by a coalition of French and Italian nobles. He died in humiliation in 1303. It was, by any standards, a staggering blow to the temporal claims of the papacy.

THE BABYLONIAN CAPTIVITY

THEN began a long line of French popes. The first was the archbishop of Bordeaux, a confidant of Philip IV, who became Pope Clement V in 1305. He held court in one French city or another until he settled upon Avignon on the Rhone as the new seat of the papacy. Thus began the Avignon papacy — a period of seventy years that the irreverent referred to as the Babylonian

Captivity, an allusion to the time the ancient Jews were deported to Babylon by Nebuchadnezzar. Altogether there were seven popes, supported by a college of cardinals that was equally Frenchified.

The popes of Avignon lived in unmistakable extravagance. Petrarch, the Italian humanist (see plate 34), passed some of his days there and was struck by the comparison between the "poor fishermen of Galilee" (i.e., the original apostles) and these latter-day successors who lived on the Rhone. He referred to Avignon as "the sink of every vice, the haunt of all iniquities." However glittering Avignon may have been, the Babylonian Captivity worked to the papacy's disadvantage. The English, never overly enamored of French institutions, looked with some skepticism upon this papacy nestled in the heart of France. Being away from Italy, the papacy forfeited much of its control of the Papal States and much of the income that it normally derived from those lands. With the popes away from Rome, the city fell into virtual anarchy. The loss of normal sources of income, coupled with the extravagance of the court in Avignon, required the papacy to find new revenues. Papal taxation now became increasingly burdensome. A host of new devices were introduced, mainly pertaining to control of benefices, which shored up papal finance but did not endear the popes to the common people.

The end of the Avignon papacy was scarcely less dramatic than its beginning. The last of the Avignon popes was Gregory XI. To him goes the credit of returning the papacy to Rome, a move that he did not greatly cherish. He could scarcely ignore the earnest pleading of notable Christians, however, including the formidable mystic and reformer Catherine of Siena. The Italians clamored to have the papacy back and threatened to set up an antipope if their wishes were not honored. In 1376 Gregory XI returned to Rome, although it is not clear whether he really intended to stay there. Evidently the deity intervened, for, quite unexpectedly, Gregory died in a Roman bed.

THE GREAT PAPAL SCHISM

OUT OF these circumstances came an even greater embarrassment to the papacy — the so-called Great Papal Schism. When the college of cardinals met in solemn conclave to elect Gregory's successor, the Romans rioted. "We want a Roman," they shouted — "a Roman or at least an Italian." The cardinals said one to another, "Better to elect the devil than to die." They accordingly elected an Italian, who took the name Urban VI. Urban at once declared Rome as the seat of the papacy and then proceeded to reprimand the cardinals in highly uncomplimentary terms for the manner in which they conducted their lives. The French cardinals, joined by some Italian cardinals, moved at once to undo the pope. In 1378 they declared his election null and void, claiming that it had occurred under duress of a riot by the Roman mobs. In his place they elected a French pope, Clement VII, who promptly struck out for Avignon. Urban VI persisted in Rome. Clement VII persisted in Avignon. So began the schism that was to endure another forty years: two popes, two sets of cardinals, and two papal courts, each supported by its own taxation. The loyalty of Europe was divided between the two, with France as the chief supporter of Avignon, with England and Germany, to say nothing of the Italian states, supporting Rome.

THE CONCILIAR MOVEMENT

IN THIS crisis, conciliarism became an attractive idea. According to this theory, the church was to be properly governed by representative church councils, regularly convened. Such councils now offered a way of ending the papal schism and of making reforms in the church. Conciliarism was neither a new nor a trifling conception. It had been debated by a number of political theorists who lived prior to the outbreak of the schism, for example, John of Paris (1265–1306), Marsiglio of Padua (d. 1342), and William of Ockham (c. 1285–1350) (see Ewart Lewis, *Medieval Political Ideas,* 2 vols. [New York: Knopf, 1954]). Conciliarism was a real threat to the papacy, as it vested ultimate power in the cardinals and, indirectly, the secular powers that supported them.

In Marsiglio of Padua, for example, whose *Defensor pacis* of 1324 was a seminal document in this tradition, a distinction is drawn between the legislator and the executor, a distinction that is applicable in both state and church. The legislator refers to a congress representative of the community of people, whether citizens (in the case of the state) or believers (in the case of the church). Only the legislator can frame law or revise law; the executor (who may be a prince in the state or the pope in the church) is bound to do the will of the legislator. In ecclesiastical terms, Marsiglio's legislator is a general council representative of all believers, while the executor is the clerical order, with the papacy at its head.

So far we have been treating only theorists of conciliarism. When the Great Schism arose, with its twin problems of restoring unity and making reforms, it called forth a new breed of conciliarists who were earnest churchmen, facing a real crisis, and therefore forced to be rather more judicious and reasonable in discussing their point of view. They were Pierre d'Ailly (1350–1420) and Jean Gerson (1363–1429), who were French; Henry of Langenstein (1340–97), Dietrich of Niem (1338–1418), and Nicholas of Cusa (1401–64), who were German. Their opinions differed in degree, those of Dietrich of Niem being the most radical. All agreed, however, on these two propositions: (1) in times of crisis the general council could convene itself and act directly under the headship of Christ, it being understood that the council held the ultimate authority to safeguard the unity and faith of the church when the pope defaults; (2) the council could judge, discipline, or depose an unworthy pope.

The first council met at Pisa in 1409, having been summoned by cardinals of both Rome and Avignon. In the presence of five hundred dignitaries, it declared itself "a general council representing the whole universal Catholic church," and it further stipulated that its only head was Christ. With such impressive credentials, it denounced and deposed both popes, neither of whom appeared to defend himself, and proceeded to elect to the papacy one Peter Filargi, archbishop of Milan, aged seventy, who became Pope Alexander V. That same Alexander, however, was crafty enough to dissolve the council when it began to propose reforms, some encroaching upon papal powers. Neither the pope of Rome nor the pope of Avignon deigned to recognize the legitimacy of such disorderly proceedings as those at Pisa. The papacy, which had been two, thus became three.

The next council, however, was a triumph. Convened by the Holy Roman Emperor Sigismund and the wily Pisan pope John XXIII (successor to Alexander), the Council of Constance opened on November 5, 1414, and endured for five years. John XXIII, feigning self-sacrifice, resigned in March 1415 on the condition that his two rivals do likewise. At such a magnificent gesture, the Holy Roman Emperor took off his crown and kissed the feet of the Pisan pope. Having second thoughts about what he had done, the Pisan pope put on a disguise and escaped, hoping thereby to demoralize the council. He was arrested in flight, brought back for trial, and deposed on May 29, 1415, having been accused of manifold wickedness. Seeing these things, the Roman pope thought it prudent to resign and did so in July. Only the Avignon pontiff persisted. He was finally tried and deposed, and upon the election of Pope Martin V in November 1417, the papal schism was ended. In an effort to make conciliarism normative in the church, the council passed two decrees: *Sacrosancta* (1415), which declared that a general council derived its authority directly from Christ and is subject to obedience by the whole community of Christians, including specifically the pope; and *Frequens* (1417), which guaranteed the perpetuation of conciliarism by requiring the convocation of councils at regular intervals: the first in five years, the next seven years later, and thereafter every ten years.

The next council met on schedule at Pavia in 1423, but nothing of significance was accomplished. The council at Basel, which convened on schedule in 1431, began immediately to exact reforms that touched both papal finance and papal prerogatives. Pope Eugenius IV (see plate 5), who presided somewhat uncomfortably over these affairs, suddenly spied another pressing concern. The Turks of the Ottoman sultanate were now slowly squeezing Byzantium into an ever-diminishing circle around Constantinople. The Byzantine emperor, John VIII Paleologus (see plate 29), and the patriarch of Constantinople, Joseph II (see plate 28), jointly proposed to the Roman papacy that a reunion of Eastern and Western Christianity might occur, which would in turn sweeten the Western sentiment toward the Greeks and would bring Western arms to bear against the Turks.

Accordingly, Pope Eugenius IV and the papal party abandoned the Council of Basel in order to treat with the Greeks, first at Ferrara in 1438, and finally in Florence in 1439. (The plague struck Ferrara, to the delight of Cosimo de' Medici, who brought the whole council to Florence, all expenses paid.) An agreement with the Greeks was struck in Florence on July 6, 1439 — of which great event there is still a memorial tablet on one of the columns of the Florence cathedral. Back in Byzantium, however, zealots of the Greek church denounced the union agreement as a patched-up thing, declaring that they were more prepared to be undone by the Turks than by the pope. The reunion died aborning, as the Turks took Constantinople in 1453.

In Basel, meanwhile, the conciliar party still persisted in their council. In 1439 the Council of Basel presumed to depose Eugenius IV, then, basking in the prestige of the Greek church reunion, elected an antipope, Felix V. It was a fairly inglorious end to the conciliarist movement. The bull *Execrabilis,* which Pope Pius II issued in 1460, forbade forevermore the appeal to a council over the head of a pope. Conciliarism was finished. It did not flourish, I believe, because it entailed a pluralism that was finally impossible in the late Middle Ages — a monarchial papacy on the one hand, and a theory of representation on the other. But conciliarism was not without effect upon Western history. It entered the Protestant Reformation by means of three ideas: the church understood as essentially a community of believers, the idea of representative church government, and the emphasis upon lay religion, which accrues from the populist conception that conciliarism held.

WYCLIFFE AND HUS

JOHN WYCLIFFE (c. 1330–84) and Jan Hus (1372/73–1415), to whom we now turn our attention, were both reformers of prominence. Neither, however, had any connection with conciliarism. Nor did they have any direct connection with the Protestant Reformation, which began a century after their time. Both, however, may be considered precursors of that Reformation. Born in Yorkshire in the early years of the fourteenth century, Wycliffe was educated at Oxford and subsequently taught there, becoming one of the ornaments of that university. Among his idiosyncrasies were two of prime importance. He was a strenuous Augustinian in his thinking; and he much admired the principle of apostolic poverty, which had motivated the Franciscans, the followers of Francis of Assisi, a century before. He proposed to disendow the fat clergy of England. From the ranks of his students at Oxford he created a society of preachers, the Poor Preachers they were called, for they renounced worldly goods, and he dispatched them over the countryside preaching the gospel. Wycliffe's ideal was to form a national Catholic church in England, extricated from papal jurisdiction and thoroughly reformed. He was saved from the full fury of the Catholic establishment for several reasons: (1) a groundswell of popular support, (2) the patronage of John of Gaunt (1340–99), who was the king's brother, and (3) the fact that the papacy was in Avignon and had became identified with French interests. When in the 1380s Wycliffe openly called into question the doctrine of transubstantiation — the official doctrine that described the real presence of Christ in the sacrament of the Mass — his heresy became undeniable, and he forfeited some of his support. Perhaps his death in 1384 spared him a heretic's burning.

Of all his many treatises, two that were entitled *On Dominion* are the most critical. In these he denied the medieval principle of mediation, namely, that sovereignty (in the civil sphere) is mediated, or that grace (in the religious sphere) is mediated. Whatever dominion a person has — that is, whatever civil rights or whatever grace one has — is given to him or her immediately by God. This does not mean that human society is chaotic,

7. John Wycliffe, engraving by Edward Smith

with everyone exercising dominion as he or she pleases. People assign powers to leaders; people delegate power so that society functions properly. There are no proper gradations in society, however, based on the principle of mediation. Furthermore, no one can claim dominion as an inalienable right, as if no responsibilities were attached to it. Dominion is granted by God on two bases: (1) obedience to God, whose will is given in Scripture (by implication, then, everyone must have access to the Scriptures); (2) faithful service to society, church, family, or wherever one's dominion applies. Wycliffe's doctrine of dominion had some pretty heady social implications; he was in fact accused of fomenting the Peasants' Uprising of 1381.

Wycliffe's doctrine also had religious consequences. In his treatise *On the Pastoral Office* (1378), he denied the medieval idea that the priesthood was an office of mediation, and he limited the duties of clergy to two: reforming and preaching. By "reforming" he intended a Franciscan meaning

57

— poverty, simplicity, and service in the world. In his treatise *On the Truth of Holy Scripture* (1378), he declared that "Holy Scripture is the highest authority for every Christian and the standard of truth and of all human perfection." It is therefore no surprise that Wycliffe insisted upon the preparation of an English version of the Bible and that such a vernacular version — the first complete one in the English language — did appear in the course of the years 1382–84, having been translated by a committee of Wycliffe's younger disciples, gathered at Oxford. In his treatise *On the Eucharist* (1381), Wycliffe repudiated transubstantiation, a position that brought him into absolute collision with the church; the body of Christ, he said, is not in sacrament corporally, but "sacramentally, spiritually, and virtually."

The followers of Wycliffe were called Lollards — a word that originated in Holland, where it was applied to sectarian parties. It means "mumbler," someone who does not talk straight and who thus is a heretic. The Lollards arose in Wycliffe's lifetime and persisted in England into the sixteenth century, when they formed one of the parties of the English Reformation.

In 1408 the Catholic bishops of England met at the Council of Oxford. They strictly enjoined the translation of "any text of Holy Scripture into the English language or any other." So began the Catholic resistance to the vernacular Bible, which persisted straight into the Reformation. It was not based on some sort of obscurantism, the simple fear of letting the laity see the Bible in a tongue they could understand; it was based rather on the assumption (correct, as it turned out) that vernacular Bibles would unsettle the critical relationship between the Latin Vulgate text of Scripture and the Latin vocabulary in which church dogma was cast. It is one thing to translate *paenitentiam agite* (Matt. 4:17 in the Vulgate) as "do penance," for such a rendering supports the Catholic sacramental structure, and penance in particular. What is the effect, however, if one chooses to use the equally legitimate translation, "repent ye"?

In Bohemia, meanwhile, and specifically at the University of Prague, interest in church reform began among the Czechs as early as 1350, stimulated perhaps by reforming ideas originating in the University of Paris. The relationship between the universities of Prague and Oxford was destined to become even closer than that between Prague and Paris. In 1382 Princess Anne, daughter of King Wenceslas of Bohemia, married King Richard II of England. Czech students began to study in the English universities. Prominent among them was one Jerome of Prague, the first to introduce

Wycliffe's books to Bohemia. By 1400 the writings of Wycliffe were current and popular in the intellectual circles of Prague; the university had become a stronghold of Wycliffism.

By 1402 Jan Hus had become the chief spokesman of the Czech reform movement. Born in southern Bohemia in 1371, Hus was educated at the University of Prague and entered the Catholic priesthood in 1401. The following year he was appointed preacher of Bethlehem Chapel near the

8. Jan Hus at the Council of Constance, 1414.

university, in the heart of Prague, whose pulpit he soon made famous by his reformation sermons. He was critical of the corruptions of the church — the moral laxity of clergy, papal interference in civil affairs, and unbiblical ceremonies, institutions, and doctrines. In the decade 1400–1410, a reform movement made progress under the stimulus of Hus's preaching. His writings, more pungent and popular than those of Wycliffe, were put into wide circulation. His disciples, as preachers, communicated the Hussite reform principles by word of mouth.

For a while the papal schism sufficiently divided the loyalties of the Czechs, and Hus was spared the fury of either the church or the state. In 1410, however, repression began. Hus's writings were suppressed, and unauthorized preaching was forbidden; Hus himself was excommunicated. The following year Prague was placed under interdict, which effectively curtailed the administration of every ecclesiastical service, from baptism to marriage, from Mass to burial. Hus retired, and in his few years of seclusion he produced his more important writings, including *De ecclesia* (On the church), in which he reiterated and supplemented the ideas of Wycliffe.

Hus was summoned to appear at the Council of Constance. One might have thought that the conciliarists would have looked favorably upon one such as Jan Hus. However, Pierre d'Ailly and Jean Gerson identified him with Wycliffe (correctly so), and they recognized the dangers latent to medieval Christianity in Wycliffe's doctrine of dominion and other radical doctrines that both Wycliffe and Hus shared. Comforted by a promise of safe conduct granted to him by Emperor Sigismund, Hus left the shelter of Bohemia in 1414 and went to Constance, expecting that the issues would be settled by theological discussion. Instead he was sent to prison, placed on trial before a commission headed by d'Ailly, and finally condemned for thirty-nine errors of teaching. When the council ordered Wycliffe's body exhumed to be burned as heretics are burned, Hus could foresee his fate. Called before the council to recant, he refused in the name of conscience to do so. On July 6, 1415, he was deposed from the priesthood, with all the accompanying indignities. The secular authorities then conducted him outside the walls of Constance and burned him at the stake, casting his ashes into the Rhine.

When news of Hus's demise reached Bohemia, a religious revolution occurred. The followers of Hus, however, could not maintain their unity, splitting into a radical and a conservative faction, known respectively as Taborites and Utraquists (or Calixtines). (The terms "Utraquist," from *sub utraque*, "in both kinds," and "Calixtine," from *calix*, "cup," refer to this faction's belief that the laity should receive the Communion cup.) Pope Martin V, first of the popes after the schism, summoned Europe to a crusade against the Hussites. An army of 150,000 soldiers stormed Bohemia — not once but five times. In 1431, when the smoke of the last campaign lifted, the Hussites still remained. The Utraquists survived as the national church of Bohemia, but the Taborites wasted away. The place of the Taborites was eventually taken by people who called themselves *Unitas Fratum,* "Unity of Brethren," who commenced to appear about the middle of the fifteenth century and who survive today as the Moravians.

OCKHAM

THE THEOLOGY of the late medieval church was heavily dependent on the writings of Thomas Aquinas (1225–74), who had systematized Christian thought in a fashion heavily dependent on Aristotle. His work was further developed by Bonaventure (1221–74) and Duns Scotus (1265–1308). The rationally based theological structure developed by these men came to be known as Scholasticism, and it was widely attacked by those writers of the fifteenth and sixteenth centuries who associated themselves with the new thinking of the Renaissance.

While usually grouped with the Scholastics, William of Ockham, an English Franciscan, also refuted many of the bases of Scholasticism, particularly their rational approach to faith. He was born toward the end of the thirteenth century, perhaps in 1285, at Ockham in Surrey. William entered the Franciscan order at an early age and took his bachelor's degree at Oxford and his master's degree at Paris, where he taught between 1315 and 1320. Whether he returned to England to lecture at Oxford is somewhat dubious and of little consequence. It was at Paris that he made his reputation. By 1339 his radical teachings had taken such a hold in Paris that the philosophy faculty saw fit to issue a warning against them.

Oddly enough, the most serious controversy in which he personally got entangled had nothing to do with great philosophical problems, but rather with the question of poverty: how poor should one be? Ockham belonged to the severe branch of the Franciscans, which insisted upon absolute poverty — no goods should be owned by either Franciscan individuals or Franciscan communities. So vociferous did he become about that issue that he fell out with the pope, John XXII, who favored the more relaxed wing of the Franciscans. Ockham had the audacity to accuse the pope of error, and he scandalized Christendom by quoting the Scriptures against the papacy. In 1324 he was summoned to the papal court at Avignon to answer charges of heresy. After four years spent languishing in the papal prison, Ockham escaped and fled to Italy. Deposed and excommunicated, he attached himself to the Holy Roman Emperor Louis the Bavarian, whom he followed to Munich, where he died, probably in 1349, still apparently unreconciled to the papacy. There is reason to believe that he was a victim of the Black Death.

Ockham's life was an unremitting tragedy. For all of his grief, however, he was one of the most powerful forces of his age, not so much because his ideas were completely new, but because he pressed them to their ultimate conclusion with remorseless logic. His historical importance rests upon three achievements: (1) he carried the banner of nominalism; (2) he laid serious challenge to the medieval synthesis, namely, that the Christian religion was susceptible to rational demonstration; and (3) he concluded that religion is something one believes, rather than proves, and that the basis of belief is religious authority, chiefly the authority of the Bible.

A famous example of this tough-minded thinking is called Ockham's razor. This phrase refers to a principle of parsimony or extreme economy in argumentation and explanation. It is the slicing off, as a man does with his whiskers every morning, of all pseudoexplanations. We should not assume that anything is necessary to account for any fact unless it is established by evident experience or evident reasoning or is required by articles of religious faith. According to Ockham: "Plurality is not to be assumed without necessity." Again: "What can be done with fewer assumptions is done in vain with more."

Let us turn first to Ockham's nominalism and its far-reaching effects upon modern Western civilization. The difference between nominalism and its opposite, realism, may be explained as follows. *High realism,* which is associated with the Platonic tradition and which came down in the Western Christian tradition through Augustine and Anselm, assumed that universals, the eternal ideas, are the only realities that exist. The eternal ideas exist in the mind of God and are therefore eternally real — hence, "realism." Particular things that we observe in the world are merely transitory and imperfect manifestations of the universal ideas. What is real is not "this man" but rather "man." In high realism, then, universals, or the eternal ideas, exist prior to the particular: *universalia ante rem.*

The recovery of Aristotelian philosophy and science in the course of the twelfth and thirteenth centuries forced the Schoolmen to give far more attention to particular things than they had been previously disposed to do. Thomas Aquinas and Duns Scotus represented a kind of *moderate realism* that was considerably modified by Aristotelian influence. They held that the universal ideas, while they are certainly what is real, exist in particular things, giving those particular things their identity. We can perceive those universals by a process of active thought that is able to abstract the "universal reality" or "essence" from the mass of particular things. It is important for us to do so in order to understand both the nature of God and the nature of the universe in which we exist. For the moderate realists, therefore, universals, while they are quite real, exist in things: *universalia in rebus.*

Realism, as a way of thinking, pervaded almost every aspect of medieval life. It left intellectuals generally inhospitable to empirical science but disposed instead to ponder the eternal ideas of God. To a considerable extent, it affected social and political theory; it goes far to explain, for example, the subordination of the individual to corporate institutions that was characteristic of medieval life. Corporations were thought to be prior to individuals. Consider the great monastic orders, the schools, the universities, the towns, the manors, the guilds, and the pious fraternities. These and many other corporate personalities expressed the medieval confidence in realist principles.

Ockham, in contrast, denied the reality of universals altogether, maintaining that universals are mere concepts based upon the observed likeness of individual things: *universalia post rem.* Universals, so far from having an objective reality, are mere names; they are nominal — hence, "nominalism." Universals are mere "intentions" of the mind; they do not even exist outside of the mind but are simply creatures of our subjectivity. How does the mind form these intentions, these universals? Things call forth sense impressions in us; these impressions are transmitted by the human intellect into mental images — "universals" — which, as anyone can plainly see, are solely the products of the intellect.

Realism, in Ockham's opinion, was absurd, destructive of all science, truth, and reason. With his attack upon realism, Ockham became the pioneer of modern epistemology. The outcome, so far from being mainly philosophical and theological, was enormously practical. It promoted interest in the individual as alone real; it diverted attention away from universals, which had preoccupied intellectuals since ancient times; and it prepared the way for empirical research, providing a basis for the scientific development of the modern age.

It also raised havoc, however, with orthodox Christianity. A realist can

63

handle the doctrine of the Trinity, for example, rather well — one divinity manifested in three persons. A nominalist, however, having been taught that only the particulars are real, thinks only of three persons and therefore lapses into tritheism, the belief in three gods.

What could Ockham do? Declare Christianity invalid? The English friar was far too devout for that. He took the other alternative — an alternative almost as radical as the first — of disconnecting reason and religion. One must abandon once and for all the attempt to show the rational character of the Christian system. Do not think, said Ockham, that one can prove the existence of God or demonstrate rationally the attributes of God. Reason and revelation stand separated. If one is religious, it can only be on the basis of revelation, expressed in the form of religious authority, and supremely the Bible.

Ockham thereby called into serious question the so-called medieval synthesis of reason and revelation that Thomas Aquinas (1225–74), in particular of all the Schoolmen, had brought to perfection. Aquinas found no necessary conflict between reason and revelation. Philosophy, which is dependent on natural reason, and theology, which is dependent on revelation, do not belong in watertight compartments. Instead, Aquinas proposed to give each one a place in a massive intellectual system in which the things that can be known by reason and the things that can be known by revelation are placed in an ascending hierarchy of essences, reaching from the material upward to the spiritual. This medieval synthesis that Aquinas created — this coherent structure of social theory, moral philosophy, metaphysics, and theology — was the supreme achievement of Scholasticism.

Ockham could not agree. Christianity, in his view of things, is a supernatural system that supersedes human reason. Theology is not a science, as the Schoolmen had supposed, nor is it a form of natural metaphysical cognition; it is based instead on a special mode of cognition that we call faith. This faith answers to certain religious authorities, chiefly the authority of the Catholic Church and the Bible.

How shall we estimate Ockham's importance? Did he dig the grave of Scholasticism? Scarcely. The English friar actually commenced a new scholastic tradition — the *via moderna* (modern way), as opposed to the *via antiqua* (antique way) of the Thomists and the Scotists. Thus, some scholars have seen his work as the highest point of Scholasticism rather than as the destroyer of it. Why was Ockham "modern"? Because of his nominalism; his disconnection of reason and revelation; his insistence that religion is susceptible only to faith and that faith is established upon religious authority, supremely that of the Bible. Ockham was succeeded by a distinguished school — the Ockhamists, or modernists — who numbered among their company the great French cardinal Pierre d'Ailly and the last of the Schoolmen, Gabriel Biel (c. 1420–95).

Biel was the teacher of Luther. The early Luther was an exuberant modernist and referred to Ockham as "my dear master." We shall therefore not be surprised when we hear Luther refer to reason as a whore who has no place whatsoever in religious affairs. Nor shall we be surprised to hear from Luther that the Bible alone is the sole authority of the religious person. The heritage of William of Ockham is to be found, at least in part, in the age that succeeded him: the Reformation.

Finally, note one contradictory aspect of Ockham's thought. We have seen how much importance he placed upon the authority of the church: everything religious finally depends upon that authority. Ockham's nominalism when applied to the idea of the church makes it no longer a divine institution with a life all its own. Instead it becomes merely a convenient designation, a name for the whole body of individual Christians. Ockham, the nominalist, was therefore a conciliarist. Because the church was people, the people should be able to express themselves in its governance through representative councils.

4. The Renaissance Papacy

CHAPTER 3 DESCRIBED SOME OF THE CHANGES THAT OCCURRED IN THE Renaissance papacy, particularly the Babylonian Captivity and then the Great Papal Schism. Because the papacy was so weak, intellectuals proposed conciliarism, a new way of governing the Catholic Church by representative councils, regularly convened. These developments amounted to a grave crisis in the history of the papacy at the opening of the quattrocento, several dimensions of which appear in the following list.

1. Conciliarism profoundly threatened papal power by subordinating the supremacy of the popes to the supremacy of councils representative of the whole Christian constituency.
2. The city of Rome was the greatest victim of the Avignon papacy and of the schism that followed. The capital of Western Christianity was allowed to fall into ruins. It became the battlefield of the barons, over which three or four powerful Roman families fought for control.
3. The kings of France and England, which were now in their final stages of national development, advocated programs of national independence and expansion, without much respect for papal prerogatives.
4. In the Papal States of Italy, the *signori,* or despots, seeing that the popes were absent or impotent, threw off the last vestiges of papal authority and ruled in their own right.
5. The great commercial republics — Venice, Florence, and Milan — pursued their commercial interests relentlessly, whether or not they conflicted with the church's moral and temporal interests.

6. Such a state of affairs required popes of a different order than the popes of the Middle Ages. The Renaissance popes were neither exceptionally pious nor exceptionally learned in the lore of theology. Visual demonstration of the power and majesty of the church and the faith took on a greater importance. Instead of explaining Christianity, they showed it — for example, in Michelangelo's decorations in the Sistine Chapel or in Raphael's Vatican *stanze*. They demonstrated the power of the Catholic Church in the creation of St. Peter's Basilica. Theirs was a sort of pictorial Christianity. On his deathbed, the first great Renaissance pope, Nicholas V, said it all when he said, "There must be something that appeals to the eyes." For good reason, therefore, the Renaissance popes were foremost among the patrons of Renaissance art. Above all, however, the Renaissance popes were chosen for their administrative and political skills. What the papacy needed, and what the papacy got, was a set of popes who were practical, canny, ambitious, tough, decisive, and acutely intelligent — more concerned, frankly, about earthly fulfillment than about heavenly paradise.

REBUILDING THE PAPACY IN ROME

WHEN Pope Martin V (1417–31) returned to Rome from the Council of Constance, which had just ended the three-headed papacy and elected him pope, he found the Eternal City a shambles. Houses had collapsed. The narrow streets were filled with rubble. Sheep grazed over the Palatine Hill. The people of Rome, forgetful that a once-powerful empire had been ruled from there, thought that the grotesque ruins of the forum or the baths of Caracalla had been made by some dark demonic power. Garbage filled the Colosseum several lances deep. Fire had gutted the Church of St. John Lateran, seat of the medieval papacy, and the Lateran Palace, where the medieval popes had lived, was uninhabitable. In 1413 the city had been invaded by the king of Naples. Prominent families — the Colonna, the Orsini, and the Francipani — had seized control of civic affairs. A ferocious bunch they were. Their sport was to hurl one another into the Tiber River. They terrorized the citizens, pillaged the churches, ravaged the nuns, and robbed the monks in this already ruinous city.

Martin V, seeing the Lateran Palace in disrepair, established the papacy on the Vatican hill. Even the buildings there were perishing. An ancient basilica, called St. Peter's, had been built by Emperor Constantine in the

9. Donatello
and
Michelozzo,
monument to
Pope Martin V

10. Monument to Pope Nicholas V

course of the fourth century to commemorate the place where Peter, the apostle, was thought to have been buried. After a thousand years, that basilica was slowly succumbing to rot. Martin was himself a Colonna and was a man of fierce personality and administrative skill. He put a stop to the kaleidoscope of brutality that beset the city; he stimulated trade, beckoned pilgrims, welcomed merchants, and, at long last, collected taxes again.

The early part of the pontificate of his succesor, Eugenius IV (1431–47), was marked by struggles with the powerful Colonna family. In 1434 he was forced to flee down the Tiber by boat, disguised as a monk, eluding his persecutors by a hair's breadth. Eugenius had to maintain his court at Florence, where he bided his time, patronizing the humanists who abounded in that city. It was he who presided over the Council of Florence.

Nicholas V (1447–55), next in the papal line, is often thought of as the first of the Renaissance popes. His name was Tommaso Parentucelli, son of a surgeon, educated in the delights of humanism. Said Pope Pius II, himself a humanist of enormous erudition, "What was unknown to Parentucelli lay outside the sphere of human learning." As we have seen, Nicholas V had an inordinate craving for ancient manuscripts of the Greek and Latin classics. Secretaries such as the renowned book collector Poggio Bracciolini and the upstart Lorenzo Valla were received handsomely into his court. To house his books and his scholars, Nicholas established the Vatican Library, still one of the greatest in the Western world; here all manner of scholars were welcome. As the pope surveyed the city of Rome in its devastation, he resolved to rebuild it. It was he who first conceived of the massive basilica of St. Peter's. With the Florentine architect Leon Battista Alberti at his side — an architect thoroughly committed to the "new" architecture based on classical antiquity — Nicholas prepared a master plan for the reconstruction of Rome. At his death in 1455, the environs of the Vatican had been partially leveled, and trenches had been dug for the huge foundations to support a massive basilica. (See the excursus to chapter 22.) Nicholas's ecclesiastical policies were tepid. He proposed a crusade to deliver Constantinople, which had fallen to the Ottoman Turks in 1453, but could not overcome dissension among the various Italian states. He also envisioned certain reforms within the Catholic Church, being especially attentive to the reformatory ideas of Nicholas of Cusa, bishop of the German diocese of Brixen.

With the elevation of Cardinal Alonso Borgia to the papal throne, as Pope Calixtus III (1455–58), the Borgia family of Spain entered the history of the papacy. The family emblem, the bull, illustrated their hard and rugged traits: pride, energy, fierce temper, and keen intelligence. They were fearless and unscrupulous in politics, sumptuous and violent in their style of life. The family arose at Borja in Aragon; the Romans, mispronouncing the Spanish name, referred to them as the Borgias. Alonso, the first of the family to achieve significant power, became a papal diplomat and prelate, and finally, at the age of sixty-seven, pope. He was elected, in fact, on the assumption that he would not live very long. He lived long enough, however, to promote such an astonishing nepotism that wagging tongues began to speak of the Hispanicization of Rome. Of all the ecclesiastical favors that Calixtus doled out to his family, the choicest went to his nephew Rodrigo, the future pope Alexander VI. At the tender age of twenty-five, Rodrigo became a cardinal. Calixtus's short reign was distinguished by one thing — his enormous anger at the Turks, who in 1453 had overrun Constantinople. "Annihilation of the enemies of the faith" was the central purpose of Calixtus's pontificate. He failed to live long enough, however, to see the launching of a crusade against the Turks, which he announced soon after taking office.

11. Bust of Pope Pius II

Calixtus was followed by Pius II (1458–64), a member of the prominent Piccolomini family of Siena, who came to the papacy in 1458 after a
long career as a distinguished humanist and papal diplomat. As a humanist,
he had written under the name Aeneas Silvius. Upon taking the papacy,
however, he declared: "Reject Aeneas, accept Pius" — rather sage advice,
given the racy nature of some of his literary efforts, especially the comedy
Chrysis (1444). Pius II proved to be a genuine, even heroic, pope. It was he
who denounced conciliarism by the bull *Execrabilis* in 1460. Candid to a

fault, he once told a consistory of cardinals: "The priesthood is looked down upon. . . . Men say we devote our time to pleasure, accumulate money, serve ambition, ride fat mules and fine horses . . . go about town with fat cheeks under the red hat and broad cowl . . . squander large sums on actors and parasites, and spend nothing in the defense of the faith. They do not entirely mispresent the facts." Pius, like his predecessors, was possessed by zeal to undo the Turks and, despite being nearly incapacitated by gout, resolved to lead a crusade against the infidels. His effort failed, and he died in 1464, discouraged but ever dignified, as a few dozen Venetian ships and a poor contingent of crusaders assembled at Ancona, where Pius had planned to embark.

Then followed the indifferent reign of Paul II (1464–71), humanist and inveterate collector. His successor was Francesco della Rovere, who was born in poverty and rose through the ranks of the church to become general of the Franciscan order and finally Pope Sixtus IV (1471–84; see plate 6). Self-indulgent, decisive, a crack administrator, and patron of the arts, Sixtus was typical of the Renaissance popes. He thrashed the Colonna and put Rome firmly under his control. That done, he set about to gain control of the Papal States and to aggrandize the territorial sovereignty of the papacy. The funds to do so came from simony; the personnel to do so, from the ranks of his own family. The beneficiaries of his expansionist policies were mainly his nephews, Pietro Riario and Girolamo Riario. When Lorenzo de' Medici of Florence attempted to block the takeover of the town of Imola, near Florence, by Girolamo Riario, Sixtus lent his tacit support to the so-called Pazzi Conspiracy, in which Lorenzo and his brother Giuliano were scheduled for assassination at High Mass in the Florence Cathedral on Sunday, April 26, 1478. Giuliano died of twenty-nine gaping wounds; Lorenzo escaped with minor injuries. The grave danger of the reign of Sixtus IV was the secularization of the papacy; that is, the papacy became associated with a single family by means of nepotism and heredity, thus reducing the papacy to a princely regime similar to those of, say, Milan, Urbino, Mantua, or Naples.

A pope of ample means, Sixtus was a patron of the arts. He embarked upon the reconstruction of Rome with a holy zeal left unspent in religion. He laid out streets and constructed bridges and hospitals. A simple Franciscan deep down, Sixtus built a simple chapel in the Vatican (named the Sistine Chapel in his honor) and proceeded to bring the greatest living artists to Rome to decorate it: Botticelli, Perugino, Ghirlandaio, and others. It was left to Pope Julius II to complete his uncle's work (Julius was also a della Rovere), and he did so by summoning Michelangelo to decorate the ceiling, for which the Sistine Chapel is so famous.

In the conclave of 1484, the papacy was passed — or, to be more accurate, sold — to Giovanni Battista Cibo, who took the papal name Innocent VIII. His pontificate was not a moral success. Spiritual dignities and favors were unabashedly sold for the garnishment of the papal treasury. The Roman factions, which Sixtus had quashed, rose up again; pilgrims were relieved of their possessions before even setting foot in the Holy City.

FRANCE AND THE PAPACY

SO FAR, what have been the policies of the Renaissance popes? First, to settle the Roman populace and restore the city of Rome to its ancient grandeur. Second, to patronize the arts and humanistic scholarship. Third, to recover and reorganize the Papal States. During the reign of the next pope, Alexander VI, a fourth problem arose: to contend with the French who invaded Italy in 1494. The key to this invasion was Naples. French claims to the Kingdom of Naples went back to 1266, when the papacy had assigned that kingdom to Charles of Anjou, brother of Louis IX of France. The line had run out in the fifteenth century, however, and control of Naples had fallen to a branch of the Spanish house of Aragon. France awaited an opportunity to recover Naples. An occasion presented itself in 1494, when Lodovico Sforza, Lodovico il Moro (the Moor), duke of Milan, fearing the encroachment of Venice, invited Charles VIII of France to intervene in the delicate balance of Italian politics. On September 2, the crops having been harvested in the valleys and plains of France, Charles VIII came south with an army of forty thousand. He reached Pavia, and then Florence, where the fierce reformer Savonarola received him as the agent of God. Then, Siena; next, Rome. Men, horses, carriages, and eight-feet-long cannons poured into the Eternal City, intimidating pope and populace. Finally the army reached Naples. In July 1495 a confederated army of Italians under the leadership of Francesco Gonzaga of Mantua met the French near the village of Fornovo (sixty miles north of Florence, near Mantua), in one of the fiercest battles ever fought on Italian soil. The French suffered heavy losses and withdrew to France. The French menace, however, persisted. Italy, though, as Machiavelli and Guicciardini well understood, would never be the same. The fragile political structure of Italy in the quattrocento had been shattered.

The pope in whose reign these events occurred was Rodrigo Borgia, who procured the papacy by simony on August 11, 1492, and took the papal name Alexander VI. Alexander was a pope of great charm and extraordinary presence, with a genius for administration and all of the fierce intelligence and energy that characterized the Borgias. Driven by elemental human passions, he was devoted to his mistress, Vannozza Catanei, and to the four children she bore him: Cesare, Giovanni, Lucrezia, and Goffredo.

12. Pope Alexander VI, portrait by Pinturicchio

(Alexander also had three other children, born between 1463 and 1471, of an unknown mother.) Born in Spain, a nephew of Calixtus III, Alexander was trained in canon law at the University of Bologna, became a cardinal at twenty-five, and attained the papacy at sixty.

Strange and terrible misfortunes characterized his pontificate, of which the French invasion was only one. In 1495 the Tiber, swollen by rains, overflowed its banks and ran ten feet deep in the streets of Rome. When the waters subsided, the streets were thick with corpses; houses had collapsed, bridges were swept away, and some saw in the cataclysm proof of God's wrath in a time of human depravity. Lightning struck the papal fortress of Sant'Angelo, setting off an immense explosion of powder. Giovanni Borgia was found floating in the Tiber, nine knife wounds in his body, his throat slashed, his hands tied together, a heavy stone attached to his neck. Most people — even Machiavelli and Guicciardini — suspected that he had been dispatched by his brother Cesare. In Florence, the Dominican friar Savonarola excoriated the iniquities of Alexander VI, until the exasperated pope finally excommunicated him, and the Florentines themselves sent him to the scaffold.

Wed at thirteen, Alexander's daughter Lucrezia went through three marriages, each solemnized at the Vatican. One husband was declared impotent; the second was assassinated (again, Cesare was suspected). She endured, nevertheless, until the age of seventy-six as the duchess of Ferrara and was respected for her piety and good works. The pope himself became infatuated with Giulia Farnese, shown in Raphael's *Transfiguration* (see plate 71). Even as the wife of Orsino Orsini, she became the papal mistress; the irreverent Romans lost no time in dubbing her the Bride of Christ.

Alexander was the first pope to recognize the potential dangers of printing. In a bull in 1501, he attempted to impose censorship upon the German press. It was he who drew the line in 1493 that divided the world into zones of colonization for Spain and Portugal. And it was he who dispatched missionaries to the New World on the second voyage of Columbus.

The most crucial event in the reign of Alexander VI derived from the French invasion. It occurred to the Borgias, especially in light of the French invasion, that the time had come to create a vast and powerful state in central Italy that could (1) buttress the papacy, (2) seal the Italian frontiers against foreign aggression, and (3) begin the process of Italian national recovery. The place to begin, obviously, was with the Papal States, which must first be retaken. The one to lead such a campaign was equally obvious

13. Cesare Borgia, portrait by Ignoto Lombardo

— the pope's son, Cesare. Because of this extraordinary political maneuver that the Borgias attempted, Machiavelli saw fit to date the beginning of the modern papacy with the pontificate of Alexander VI.

Cesare, however, as the eldest son, had been destined for the priesthood. Five days after he became pope, in fact, Alexander VI had made Cesare archbishop of Valencia, the primate of Spain. The next year, Cesare became a cardinal. Giovanni Borgia was to have been the family general, the instrument of Borgia aggression. But when Giovanni was found floating in the Tiber River, the role of general was hastily conferred upon Cesare, who was officially defrocked and joined in marriage with a member of French royalty. The cardinal's hat passed to Goffredo, then at the tender age of sixteen. At his marriage, Cesare Borgia received from the king of France the title duke of Valence. Thereafter, everyone called him Valentino.

In 1499 Valentino set out to create an *ordo novus* (new order) for Italy. At the age of twenty-four, with an army of fifteen thousand, he proposed to create the Kingdom of Italy. He would start by recovering the papal territory in the Romagna and the Marche — Imola, Ravenna, Pesaro, and Urbino. Then he would take Bologna, which was destined to be the capital of the kingdom, and finally Florence. In 1502 Leonardo da Vinci became Cesare Borgia's mapmaker and military engineer. In the same year, Niccolò Machiavelli, as an ambassador from Florence, first met Cesare Borgia. Machiavelli became the most accurate interpreter of Cesare's personality and objectives.

By 1503 the Borgias had attained the peak of their success. The despots of the Papal States and the obstreperous Roman families, both of which had eaten into papal prerogatives, had been destroyed. The Duchy of Romagna, an ideal state, had been created. A standing army, the first in Italy, stood ready to defend the state. Cesare conceived of absorbing all of Tuscany into his dominions, thus dominating the entire peninsula.

Suddenly, in August 1503, before Cesare could quite consolidate his power, Pope Alexander VI fell ill of the "tertian fever" and, after receiving the last rites of the church, died of apoplexy on the eighteenth of August. The next day porters used brute force to stuff his great body into a coffin that was too narrow for it. Not until 1889 were the bones of the two Borgia popes, by then mixed together, given even a modest place in St. Peter's Basilica.

Now a landslide of political reverses began, an unstoppable collapse of Borgia power. In the Papal States, the despots returned to their principalities. Giuliano della Rovere, the archenemy of the Borgias, became the next pope. Cesare spent the remainder of his life — a mere four years — in and out of prison, first in Naples, finally in Spain. He died on March 11, 1507.

Despite his terrible reputation, his undeniable ruthlessness, and his cynical political calculations, Cesare Borgia was something of a utopian. In all that he did there was an extraordinary rationality that evoked Machiavelli's admiration. In *The Prince,* Cesare Borgia appears as the exemplary ruler. Yet never in all its history had the papacy come so close to secularization, subject to the personal exploitation of a single family.

THE PAPACY STRENGTHENED

BURCKHARDT pronounced Pope Julius II "the savior of the papacy." Giuliano della Rovere, nephew of Pope Sixtus IV, was elected to the papacy in 1503, without simony, following the short reign of Pius III. Julius had the conviction that papal claims of universal spiritual jurisdiction would ring true in the world of national states only if the papacy was radically independent of all temporal authorities, whether the king of France, the Holy Roman Emperor, the Roman families, or the petty tyrants in the Papal States. The moral and political independence of the Holy See was the cornerstone of Julius's policy. It required moral rigor and a certain political ruthlessness. It required action — diplomatic and military. Erasmus once saw Julius, this vicar of Christ, riding into Bologna on a white charger, fully armed, at the head of his troops. It offended all of Erasmus's humanistic instincts of order and harmony, peace and unity, to say nothing of good taste — but it did not strike Julius as a bit incongruous with the papal office. In his satire *Julius Exclusus,* Erasmus portrayed the pope arriving at the gates of heaven fully armed. In the field he grew a beard, something no pope in living memory had done. They called him *papa barbatus* (the bearded pope) and *pontifice terribile* (the terrible pontiff), for he was fierce.

Julius battled for control of the Papal States, not as a Borgia for family aggrandizement, but for the good of the papacy. He defeated the tyrants of Perugia and Bologna. When the Venetians moved into the Romagna, after Cesare Borgia's demise, Julius joined the League of Cambrai, with Emperor Maximilian of Germany and King Louis XII of France, to deal with the Venetians. That done, he promptly embraced Venice and Spain in what was called the Holy League to drive the French from Italian soil. He was as fierce in the Vatican as he was fierce in the field. No friend of the Roman

14. Pope Julius II, portrait by Raphael

families, he arbitrarily made himself the heir of every cardinal — indeed of every cleric who died in Rome — thus depreciating their wealth while adding to that of the papacy.

No less than Michelangelo or Raphael, Julius II was a creator of the High Renaissance. It was he who summoned the great artists to Rome, supported them, and told them exactly what to build and exactly which themes to paint. From Milan, he summoned Donato Bramante, greatest of the living architects, and had the audacity to instruct him to demolish old St. Peter's — eleven centuries old, encrusted with relics, hallowed throughout the Christian West — and to raise a church in its place. It was to be in the style of a Greek cross and would be the most resplendent building in Christendom. Julius himself set the cornerstone on April 18, 1506, and 2,500 stonemasons commenced to work. The construction proceeded under a succession of architects, including Raphael, Michelangelo, and many others, until its dedication in 1626. The cost was enormous, requiring Julius to offer indulgences to those who would contribute.

The same Julius summoned Raphael from Florence, having heard of his abilities, and ordered him to decorate the walls of rooms now known as the *stanze* of Raphael. And it was Julius who sent for the sculptor Michelangelo and required him to make him a tomb, more marvelous than any conceived. The pope, however, could not suffer the endless doubts and reconsiderations of Michelangelo; they quarreled, and the work came to a standstill. When Julius died in February 1513, his bones were placed inauspiciously in a grave in the Vatican. Long after, what remained of the tomb was erected in the Church of San Pietro in Vincoli (St. Peter in Chains). There one finds the central ornament of Julius's tomb, Michelangelo's *Moses* (see figure 69).

Once more before his death Julius had summoned Michelangelo and required him to decorate the ceiling of Uncle Sixtus's chapel, specifying exactly what he wanted painted — the creation and fall of man (see plates 66-68). The ceiling of the Sistine Chapel required the undivided labor of Michelangelo for four years, 1508–12, as Julius prodded him to hurry, and his unkindly colleagues Bramante and Raphael sniped at his work. They, in fact, were pleased when Michelangelo was commissioned to do the work, for they were convinced that he, a mere sculptor, could not negotiate the tricky angles and vaults of the ceiling. Julius's patronage of the arts, like every other policy he had, was designed to glorify the church and the papacy and to make Rome resplendent as the capital of Christianity.

Julius's successor was Giovanni de' Medici, son of Lorenzo the Magnificent, who became Pope Leo X in 1513 at the age of thirty-seven. Neither as fierce as Julius II nor as virile as Alexander VI, Leo was subtle, sophisticated, and charming, and his private life was veiled in discretion as his father Lorenzo had counseled. His range of interests was as wide as that of Nicholas V. He loved the classics, enjoyed the humanists, and patronized Raphael. The Venetian ambassador at Rome reported an offhand conversation that passed between Leo and his brother, "Let us enjoy the papacy, since God has given it to us."

Leo watched in delight as the construction of St. Peter's Basilica proceeded apace. The cost increased, however, as the vast building grew, and in 1516 the pope was forced to extend the sale of indulgences into Germany. The matter was entrusted to Archbishop Albert of Mainz, who was already in arrears to the papacy. It was agreed, therefore, that half of the proceeds of the sale of indulgences would go directly to the construction of St. Peter's, and half to the repayment of the archbishop's debt to the papacy. The archbishop's agent in the sale of indulgences was the friar Tetzel, who oversimplified the policy of the church and seemed to guarantee the remission of sins generally, rather than simply the cancellation of one's temporal satisfaction. Tetzel's activities in 1517 provoked Luther to post ninety-five theses in a German university town called Wittenberg. Leo X misjudged the seriousness of the German Reformation until it was too late. Luther, in Leo's mind, was just another contentious monk, of which sort the Germans seemed to produce more than other nations.

When Leo X died in December 1521, the Reformation was well established in Germany, and northern Italy had become a battleground between the French and the Spanish. The pope was given a niggardly funeral: he had exhausted the papal treasury.

In 1523 a Venetian humanist, Girolamo Negro, wrote as follows of the status of Rome: "This city stands on a needle's point. . . . I foresee the early fall of this spiritual monarchy. . . . Unless God helps us, we are lost." Sensing something of the same, the college of cardinals proceeded to fill the place of Leo X with no Renaissance pope but with an ascetic Dutchman known for his sobriety and reformatory zeal. Pope Hadrian VI lived but a year in the pontifical office. He succeeded in suppressing simony and nepotism, and he was moving to meet the demands of the Germans for church reform at the time of his death. Many Romans, disgruntled with his ascetic ways, rejoiced at his passing.

Hadrian was the last non-Italian elected to the papacy until John Paul II, over 450 years later. Hadrian was succeeded by another Medici,

15. Pope Clement VII, portrait by Sebastiano del Piombo

Cardinal Giulio de' Medici, the illegitimate son of Giuliano de' Medici, who was slain in the Pazzi Conspiracy. He took the name Clement VII. His eleven-year reign was so overwhelmed by calamity as to make it one of the most disastrous in the history of the papacy.

The struggle between France and Spain, fought out on the soil of Italy, began, as we observed, over which power would control the Kingdom of Naples. The contest grew in intensity during the pontificates of Julius II and Leo X. In the autumn of 1524, in the second year of Pope Clement's pontificate, King Francis I of France led a handsomely equipped army across the Alps into the plains of Lombardy. His foe was the young Holy Roman Emperor Charles V, who combined in his own person the kingship of both Germany and Spain, to say nothing of the Netherlands and Naples, which he also controlled. (In addition to having the title Holy Roman Emperor, Charles V was king of Spain, king of Naples, and overlord of the Netherlands. His mother was Joanna, daughter of Ferdinand of Aragon and Isabella of Castile. His father was Philip, son of the Hapsburg Maximilian I.) The imperial garrison of Charles V was stationed at Pavia, to which the French promptly laid siege. So stubbornly did the French persist at Pavia that Charles V had time to assemble a fresh army of Spanish and German troops. On February 24, 1525, the French found themselves caught between two rings of imperialist forces at Pavia: one within, and one without. The French were crushed between the two, and Francis I was carried off to Spain as a prisoner. By the terms of the Peace of Madrid, which was signed on March 18, 1526, Francis I of France regained his freedom, but only after he had surrendered to Charles V all of his Italian claims.

Scarcely had Francis returned to France, however, than he reopened negotiations with the pope and with the Italian princes, promising to deliver them from Spanish enslavement. Pope Clement, neither very steadfast nor very clever, responded to these overtures with a certain undisguised eagerness. The result was that Emperor Charles V sent an army of Spanish and German troops hurtling toward Rome. He had carefully left the troops unpaid so that, once in Rome, they might be all the more ravenous. On May 6, 1527, they breached the walls of Rome and utterly plundered the city. Clement barely escaped to the fortress of Sant'Angelo; peace was not restored until he agreed to confine himself there at the disposition of the emperor. This event — the sack of Rome in 1527 — many authorities take to represent the decline of the Italian Renaissance.

By the Treaty of Barcelona, June 29, 1529, Pope Clement and Charles V came to terms. The papacy accepted Spanish preponderance in

Italy, while the pope was restored to dignity and given sovereignty again over the Papal States. Early the following year, Pope Clement crowned Charles of Spain Holy Roman Emperor, in splendid ceremonies held at Bologna.

Such was the Renaissance papacy. My own estimate of it is likely more positive than those of most interpreters of the Renaissance. Burckhardt concludes that the gravest peril to the papacy during the Renaissance — secularization — was staved off only by such heroic popes as Julius II and ultimately by the Protestant Reformation, which evoked what Burckhardt calls "a regenerated hierarchy." "The moral salvation of the papacy," wrote Burckhardt, "was due to its mortal enemies. . . . Without the Reformation . . . the whole ecclesiastical state [i.e., the papacy] would long ago have passed into secular hands." Even Lewis Spitz ends his discussion of the Renaissance popes with a certain pessimism: "A tidal wave of moral indignation was sweeping across Europe on the very eve of the Reformation."

III. THE RENAISSANCE
THROUGHOUT ITALY

5. *Italy on the Eve of the Renaissance*

B ETWEEN 1300 AND 1450, EUROPE EXPERIENCED AN ECONOMIC RE-
cession that brought an end to the great prosperity of the twelfth and
thirteenth centuries. The recession was caused by a combination of factors,
not the least of which were the Hundred Years' War (1337–1453), the great
famines of 1315–17, and the Black Death of 1348–50, which reduced the
population of Western Europe by at least one-third. Even with this recession,
the era 1300–1450 was one of decisive economic change, distinguished
especially by the growth of capitalism.

Capitalism, which was fairly well established in Italy and Flanders
before the end of the thirteenth century, came to prevail almost universally
in Western Europe between 1300 and 1450. It was a system of private
business enterprise marked by four characteristics: (1) the accumulation and
reinvestment of capital, (2) the pursuit of profit as an end in itself, (3) a
differentiation in status between employer and worker, and (4) sophisticated
forms of business organization, including bookkeeping, credit, and exchange.

THE GROWTH OF CAPITALISM

CAPITALISM arose in Italy, which, because of its geographic location and its
seamanship, became the center of East-West trade as early as the eleventh
century. Throughout the early Middle Ages, Venice had maintained commercial ties with Constantinople, the center of Near Eastern commerce and

industry. By the eleventh century, Genoa was also fighting for a share of that lucrative Mediterranean trade. Exotic goods originated not merely in the countries of the eastern Mediterranean (the so-called Levant), but from the heart of the Orient. The Tatar Empire (also called Tartar) had maintained overland trade routes through central Asia to China, by means of which Oriental luxuries — silks, ivory, gems, spices, drugs, and dyes — were brought from the Far East to Italian terminals on the Black Sea, whence they were fetched to Italy by Venetian or Genoese ships that regularly plied the Mediterranean. Still other Oriental goods were brought through the Persian Gulf to Syria, or through the Red Sea to Egypt, where the Italian merchants acquired them for the European trade. The countries of the Levant also produced luxury goods for the European market, including cotton, sugar, and alum (with which to set dyes and finish cloth). Once in Italy, such things were either fed into the burgeoning industries of Italy or else transported across the Alps to the headwaters of the Rhine or to the trade fairs of Champagne in northeastern France. The same merchants exported an increasing supply of European goods to the Near East — wine, wool, olive oil, metals, armor, and weapons — where their sale produced the money with which to resupply themselves.

In the era 1300–1450, however, the trade fairs of Champagne were surpassed as the Italians opened direct sea lanes to England and the Netherlands through the Straits of Gibralter. By means of that bold stroke, the Italians could transport Near Eastern wares directly to northern markets, bringing back English wool and unfinished cloth from Flanders that could be fed into the burgeoning woolen industry of such Italian cities as Florence.

Another important change was the appearance of the so-called sedentary merchant. Out of style went the peripatetic merchant, with his goods on his back, his coins in his pockets, his books in his head. Into style came the sedentary merchant, who did business in a counting house in his native city through a network of branch offices and agents, evermore expanding his capital, extending credit, and enlarging his management over his enterprise.

The success of the sedentary merchant depended, however, upon the development of certain new sophisticated techniques in business procedure. Temporary partnerships, called *commenda,* were found to be extremely useful ways of raising capital for some exciting business venture that presented itself on the spur of the moment. Even more usual were family partnerships, which enabled such Florentine families as the Bardi and Peruzzi to organize and maintain a network of international banking. (Both families were

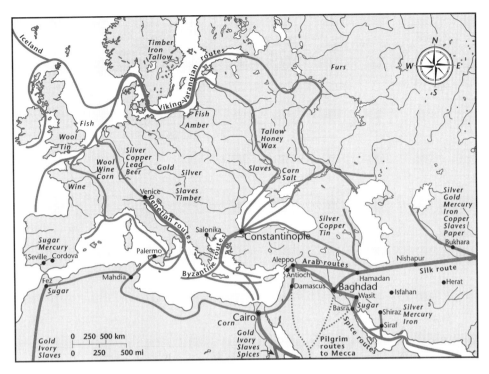

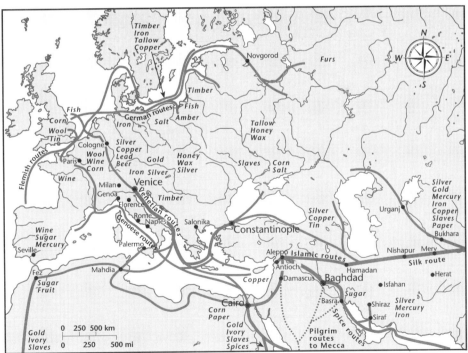

Major Trade Routes A.D. 1028 *(top)* and A.D. 1212 *(bottom)*

patrons of the painter Giotto.) Double-entry bookkeeping came into vogue in the fourteenth century; by balancing both debits and credits, it afforded the merchant the comfort of knowing exactly where he stood on each business venture. Merchants obviously could not trundle sacks of coins from city to city. Besides being unseemly, coins were debased so often that they were not trustworthy anyway. In lieu of payment by coins, Italian merchants organized an elaborate system of bills of exchange and the transfer of credits. To meet the need for sound coinage, both Florence and Venice coined gold pieces in the latter half of the thirteenth century and maintained the coins at a very rigid standard of stability. Florence minted the *florin;* Venice, the *ducat.*

Moneylending proved to be indispensable in the amassing of capital. Usury, however, had been disapproved by the church throughout the feudal age as a practice contradictory to Christian charity; it was strictly forbidden in 1139 by the Second Lateran Council. The demand for working capital was simply too great to be denied, however, and throughout the period 1300–1450 the borrowing and lending of money at interest was increasingly practiced — sometimes openly, sometimes by subterfuge. The law of the church (i.e., so-called canon law) contained loopholes. The simplest of all circumventions was to draw a contract that hid the interest in the principal. Francesco Datini scribbled at the top of each page in his double-entry ledger: "In the name of God and of profit." There was no squeamishness about profit; profit and godliness could be mentioned in the same breath.

During the years 1300–1450, most industrial production continued to be done by master craftsmen who made and sold their wares in their own shops. By and large, "industry" referred to retail manufacturing. The period also saw the origins of "large industry" — that is, industry that manufactured a complex product from beginning to end, that involved a division of labor and depended on skilled labor, and that sold its product on the world market, generally on a wholesale basis. Such was the armor-making industry of Milan or the textile industries of the Italian towns.

In Florence, for example, the manufacture of woolen cloth was a large industry that provided a living to almost a third of the population and became the basis of the city's extraordinary prosperity. That industry brought into being two illustrious Florentine guilds — the *Arte di Calimala,* which imported unfinished woolen cloth from Flanders and finished it, and the *Arte della Lana,* which manufactured woolen cloth from raw wool, generally English. Those guilds represented a new phenomenon; they were not medieval guilds of master craftsmen but modern associations of merchant-industrialists who used the guilds to their own purposes — to maintain monopolies, to work political leverage, and to control workers.

Italian capitalism, such as that of Florence, concentrated immense wealth in the hands of a body of merchants who became the dominant political force of the towns, as well as the patrons of the Renaissance arts. It also created a new class of persons — passive investors, who, by living off their investments, could afford to spend their leisure time in artistic, literary, and philosophical pursuits. Here lies one of the important bases of the Italian Renaissance — the existence of a leisure class and of immensely wealthy merchants who could afford the time and money to pursue the arts and letters.

Over the Alps, the development of capitalism was slower but, thanks to Italian incentive, inevitable. By the middle of the fifteenth century, in fact, the northern merchants were competing with their Italian teachers on equal terms. The decline of the trade fairs of Champagne and the opening of direct sea lanes from Italian ports to those of England and the Low Countries brought both London and Bruges into great commercial prominence. In those two cities, Italian commercial and banking firms made haste to open branch offices. At the same time, the Hanseatic League connected London and Bruges with the commercial traffic that it was promoting in the regions of the North Sea and the Baltic Sea.

The Hanseatic League, already a major commercial power by the fourteenth century, consisted of some seventy cities (Lübeck, Hamburg, Bremen, and Cologne being the most prominent) that conducted trade in the Baltic and in the North Sea. The main Hanseatic routes ran from London and Bruges to Novgorod in northwestern Russia, from Bruges to Bergen on the western Scandinavian coast, and from Cologne to Bruges and London.

Capitalism in the Netherlands developed both around the commercial vigor of the cities, especially Bruges, and the lively export of unfinished woolen cloth produced in Flanders. In the fourteenth-century England lured away many Flemish cloth-workers, and from that point began exporting more finished cloth and less wool. Thus, in the course of the fifteenth century the woolen industry of Flanders was ruined by the simple lack of raw materials, namely, English wool. Only Bruges, as the terminal point of seaborne trade, survived the general disintegration of the Netherlandish woolen industry and the consequent decline of the economy of the Netherlands.

The transition of England from a wool-exporting nation to one of wool-weaving marks the arrival of capitalism in that nation. It is thought to have had a far-reaching effect on the English economy and to have begun the process of industrialization in England, of which the Industrial Revolution was the major epoch.

Meanwhile, the manorial system steadily disintegrated, and the economic context of feudalism thereby collapsed. The manorial system no longer had a reason to exist. The old agrarian economy, in which produce and service were exchanged for land and protection, had yielded to a money economy that proceeded by such new means as rents and wages, buying and selling. To the nobility, the decline of the manorial system brought an inevitable loss of jurisdictional power and a certain loss of political independence — deprivations most keenly felt by the lesser nobles, who still smarted as the Reformation began. For the peasants, the gradual decline of forced labor and the establishment of a monetary relationship between lord and tenant brought some degree of freedom; at the same time, however, it fueled a hunger for still more freedom and a more equitable share of the economic deserts. The disaffection of the peasants would also live to be a factor in the Reformation.

THE RISE OF MONARCHIES

THE ERA 1300–1450 thus witnessed the first stage in the transition from medieval to more modern political forms. The economic conditions that had made local autonomy inevitable — the manorial system, with its feudal economic arrangements — gradually disappeared. The revival of commerce and the rise of the towns increased the circulation of money; money in turn enabled the European monarchies once again to concentrate power. By means of money, kings levied taxes, fattened their treasuries, built armies, and reclaimed their authority over disparate subjects. Whether there is any cause-and-effect relationship between capitalism and the recovery of monarchical power is uncertain, but it can scarcely be denied that the two institutions became entwined. Kings borrowed from the merchant-bankers when military or governmental expenses exceeded their treasuries. The merchant-bankers, in return, served the kings as architects of state financial and fiscal systems. They also supplied the royal court and the royal army when small-scale suppliers could not begin to meet the needs. Royal governments reciprocated such favors by practicing economic nationalism, negotiating trade treaties with foreign powers in pure and unsullied national self-interest. By the year 1300, local autonomy was already a dated idea. In the next

Italy *c.* 1490

two centuries, kings and powerful princes systematically reduced the independent jurisdictions of lesser feudal lords until little of their power remained. It was the age of centralized power, the monarchy, the national state.

In France, the growth of royal power reached a decisive stage around the year 1300, during the reign of Philip IV, Philip the Fair, a remarkable monarch who took exquisite pains to increase the royal power and enlarge the royal domain. Philip levied taxes on property and income, convened the first known meeting of the Estates General, and entered into a monumental dispute with Boniface VIII over the relative powers of church and state. France was quite unlike Italy in a number of crucial respects. French prosperity, which was very considerable in the twelfth and thirteenth centuries, continued to be based upon agriculture; its center of gravity remained the countryside, rather than the towns. It was the most feudalized of all the European nations (Italy, the least so), yet it had an ancient monarchy, hallowed by history and religious sanction, and a sense of national identity, out of which there emerged a strong, modern, national state.

In England, the development of national institutions occurred somewhat earlier and more securely than it did in France. England was much smaller than France and therefore more susceptible to centralized control. Its sense of national identity may be traced as far back as the dissolution of the Roman Empire and to the fact that Britain was the only Christian territory in the West that was not absorbed into the empire of Charlemagne. English feudalism, although imported to England by William the Conqueror after the French model, did not acquire the regional character of French feudalism; it did not, in other words, subdivide the nation into great baronial fiefs. It therefore did not encourage the particularism that, in France, was a noticeable deterrent to the development of royal authority and centralized institutions. It would not be far-fetched to hunt for the beginning of English royal power as far back as the noteworthy reign of Henry II (1154–89), for he was one of the architects of English national institutions, especially of common law. At least we would have to concede that the reign of Edward I (1272–1307) was the occasion of very important changes in the direction of modern statecraft; his reign has indeed been described as the new monarchy.

THE CASE OF ITALY

ITALY immediately presents itself as a conspicuous contradiction to the point that has just been made. Italy had no monarchy to be resuscitated. Medieval Italy was divided into three parts. In the middle of the peninsula, stretching from coast to coast, effectively cutting the nation in two, lay the Papal States — a vast secular state ruled by the popes, the basis of papal finance. The south formed a separate kingdom, the Kingdom of Naples. The northern sections of Italy were nominally under the control of the Holy Roman Empire; now and again a Holy Roman Emperor stuck his head into Italy to see whether anyone was trifling with his overlordship. Frederick I did so in 1154; the Italians, unaccustomed to red beards such as his, called him Barbarossa. He discovered that at least a score of his Italian towns had given themselves republican governments. Indeed, as we have already observed, it was in the towns of northern Italy that the revival of commerce and industry began and the struggle for freedom and self-government was fought. When in the course of the thirteenth century the Hohenstaufen dynasty collapsed, the imperial control over northern Italy for all practical purposes came to an end, and the Italian towns became independent city-states. Feudalism died out much earlier and much more completely in Italy than it did elsewhere in western Europe, owing not to the resurgence of central government but to the rise of the towns.

After the fall of the Hohenstaufen house, Italy, so far from espousing a centralized national state, committed itself almost completely to particularism. It did so, in the first place, because there was no national monarchy in Italy. Second, the entire southern half of the peninsula, called the Kingdom of Naples, was ruled by foreign dynasties. Third, the Papal States, which extended across the middle of the peninsula from shore to shore, cut the nation in two. Fourth, in the northern sections of Italy, political life revolved around the towns, so precocious in their capitalism, which constituted themselves a gaggle of independent city-states. By 1450, however, after the wealthier towns had gobbled up most of their weaker neighbors, there were three great northern city-states: Venice, Milan, and Florence.

Most of the towns began as republics, but the republican governments seldom survived. Economic and social tensions built up in the towns until they exploded in civil strife. Disillusioned by the failures of republican government to keep law and order, on which, after all, the success of business depended, the citizens of one town after another cast their republics to the winds and entrusted their government to the rule of a single strong leader

Italy in the Late 15th Century

whose executive and legislative power was virtually absolute. Republican structures persisted longest in the commercial cities of Venice and Florence, where merchant oligarchies were strong enough to monopolize the government. The rest of the towns settled down to what has been called the age of the despots. "Despot" has an unpleasant ring in English. The Italians preferred a more neutral set of terms. A one-man ruler was simply a *signore,* "lord," of which the plural is *signori.* The government of such a ruler was the *signoria,* "regime." (One must be careful to understand that *signoria* applies to any form of government, not exclusively to one-man despotisms. The government of Florence, for example, was a *signoria.*)

The breakdown of republican government in the Italian towns occurred in a variety of ways. The fashion of the thirteenth century was to turn the town administration over to a *podestà* (literally, he who is in power) — a despot who was by definition an outsider, someone brought in from another city in order to ensure his independence from local skirmishes and family feuds, someone beholden to neither the Montagues nor the Capulets. Some of the great ruling families of the fourteenth century first acquired power as the *podestà.* A striking example is the d'Este family that ruled Ferrara.

When the conception of the *podestà* fell out of favor, as productive of a ranker form of despotism, the towns resorted to a conception that was more popular (in the political sense), that of turning the government over to a *capitano del populo,* "captain of the people," who was far more the creature of the guilds than of the patrician class. As in the case of the *podestà,* however, the office of *capitano* was the breeding ground of despotism; it led inevitably to hereditary lordship. In that very fashion, the Scala family acquired control of Verona; the Carrara, of Padua; the Gonzaga, of Mantua; the Visconti, of Milan.

Once in office, these *signori* renounced their democratic origins entirely and sought an altogether new basis of political power by applying to the Holy Roman Emperor to be his vicars in northern Italy. To take a shining example, in 1395 Gian Galeazzo Visconti, the *signore* of Milan, bought the title duke of Milan from the Holy Roman Emperor Wenceslas for the sum of 100,000 florins. Such instances not only altered fundamentally the basis of political power in the city-states but created a host of hereditary rulers (dukes, marchesi, and the like) and, by freeing those rulers from any popular constraints that the towns might once have imposed upon them, gave them carte blanche to devour one another in territorial expansion. Thus, the consequent political phenomenon in northern Italy was an era of incessant warfare among the towns, promoted by the dynastic ambitions of these *signori.*

The rise of the despots and the consequent decline of republican government brought with it the disintegration of the citizen's militias with which the towns had won and protected their freedom. It was a grievous loss and meant the loss of the power to defend themselves against foreign invasion. When in the course of the fifteenth and sixteenth centuries, Italy was repeatedly ravaged by French, Spanish, and German armies, the Italians found it difficult to resist, so far had they fallen away from their commitment to a standing army. In place of the people's militias, the *signori* relied on mercenary corps, each recruited and directed by a soldier of fortune called a condottiere (literally, a leader, or *duce*). The condottieri were shrewd, tough, often ruthless, and cunning entrepreneurs who contracted with the towns for military service. Stirred by no patriotism, they were moved by a simple self-aggrandizement; Machiavelli has left us with a grim picture of their exploitation of Italy. Two Renaissance sculptors executed magnificent equestrian statues of famous condottieri. In Padua, adjacent to the Church of Saint Anthony, stands the fierce condottiere Gattamelata, by Donatello; in Venice, at the Church of St. John and St. Paul, the equally ferocious Colleoni by the sculptor Verrocchio.

Before turning to consider Venice, Milan, and Florence — the three great city-states of northern Italy in the age of the Renaissance — I summarize here the history of the Papal States and the Kingdom of Naples. The former, known technically as the Patrimony of St. Peter, was "donated" to the church by two Carolingians — Pepin III and Charlemagne — in the eighth and ninth centuries from lands they forced the Lombards to disgorge. Throughout the Middle Ages, they were the primary basis of papal revenue. During the fourteenth century, however, and during a fair portion of the fifteenth, the Papal States suffered grievous exploitation and anarchy. The cause of that condition is not hard to discover. For seventy years (1305–77), the papacy removed itself from Rome to the French city of Avignon. During this "Babylonian Captivity," the popes were physically removed from their Italian possessions. This period was no sooner ended than the papacy suffered an even more serious adversity — the Great Papal Schism, which produced two rival popes, and then three. The crisis was healed only through a series of church councils, which promptly seized the occasion to argue the prerogatives of conciliarism in governing the church — a still further embarrassment to the papacy. Altogether, it was an unhappy era in papal history. Meanwhile, left to their own devices, the major cities within the Papal

16. Verrocchio's monument of Colleoni

States followed the pattern normal in the fifteenth century and accepted the rule of a local despot. By such means, the Malatesta family fastened itself to the town of Rimini; the Bentivoglio family established itself in Bologna; and the Montefeltro family held sway in Urbino. In each of those cities, particularly in Urbino, glittering Renaissance courts arose.

South of the Papal States, in the part of the Italian peninsula less well endowed by nature, lay the Kingdom of Naples and Sicily. It was a feudal kingdom, beset by the rapacity of its lords, both civil and ecclesiastical.

Unproductive of either commerce or industry, the kingdom did not produce towns in the style of northern Italy (except Naples, which was the largest in Italy) and made but a small contribution to the cultural achievements of the Italian Renaissance. However, this view is at least partly due to Naples simply having been overlooked by scholars. King Alfonso the Magnanimous (r. 1443–58), was interested in the revival of the classical arts, and patronized such noted humanists as Lorenzo Valla.

As Holy Roman Emperors, the Hohenstaufens of Germany controlled the Kingdom of Naples and Sicily until 1266, when the papacy, in one of its more scandalous adventures in political supremacy, called in Charles of Anjou, younger brother of King Louis IX of France (Saint Louis) to become overlord of the kingdom. Thus began the French claim to Naples and Sicily. In 1282, however, a revolution occurred in Sicily, in the course of which the Sicilians butchered the French in what became known as the Sicilian Vespers, and transferred their allegiance to Peter III of the Spanish house of Aragon. The two parts of the kingdom were separated. Sicily was ruled by a Spanish dynasty; Naples, by the Angevins of France. When the Angevin line died out in 1382, the Kingdom of Naples became the center of political intrigue between the Spanish and the French, which finally provoked the French invasion of Italy in 1494.

EXCURSUS

Andrea Mantegna

IN THE YEAR 1460, AS THE RENAISSANCE PROCEEDED INTO ITS FIRST principal century, Lodovico III, marquis of Mantua, invited Andrea Mantegna (1431–1506) to become court painter to the house of Gonzaga, the ruling family of the city of Mantua.

Born in the environs of Padua, Mantegna was the son of a poor carpenter whose untimely death left him an orphan; he began life tending sheep in the Paduan hills. When he was ten, Mantegna was apprenticed to a Paduan painter named Squarcione, a man of wretched temper and doubtful artistic ability. In Squarcione's works, faces are abstract, and there is scarcely a hint of perspective. Yet, though he had scant appreciation for the blos-

17. Donatello, *Saint Anthony Healing the Feet of a Young Man,*
bas relief in St. Anthony's Basilica

soming of art in the Italian Renaissance, Squarcione taught Mantegna to
paint and goaded him to succeed.

What changed Mantegna's life was apparently a bas relief that the
Florentine sculptor Donatello made in 1444 for the altar of St. Anthony's
Basilica in Padua. It depicts Anthony healing the leg of a repentant son
who had cut off his foot in remorse for kicking his mother. The scene is set
in an arena that is remarkably like a modern football stadium. It enabled
Mantegna to see the important Renaissance technique of perspective — the
dramatic articulation of space disappearing into infinity. Even in his early
work, Mantegna discloses his lifelong interest in classical architecture and
decorations.

In 1456, when Mantegna painted the San Zeno altarpiece in Verona,
he had quarreled with Squarcione and had become an independent artist,
in the good style of the Renaissance. At twenty-five, he was already a prodigy
and soon became the most important artist of the northern Italian mainland
in the fifteenth century.

On the lower part of this altarpiece, called the predella, three episodes
of biblical history are illustrated. The middle one, a scene of the Crucifixion,
is now in the Louvre (see plate 7). It may be Mantegna's best-known work,
full of tragic emotion and artfully composed. The cracks in the stones
reinforce the painter's pronounced sense of perspective. Both the horse at

right and the reclining soldier playing dice are boldly foreshortened — a technique at which Mantegna excelled. The physical realism of the people is exceptional. The sorrow of Mary, on the left, stands in contrast to the indifference of the soldiers on the right. Christ, deprived of a footrest, seems to evolve from the very juncture of the skyline, his arms flung wide in a heroic gesture of sacrifice. Beyond are the towers of Jerusalem, to which a crowd of spectators is seen to be returning. Everything is etched in an almost excessive hardness of line. Such were the characteristics of this prodigy who was invited to Mantua in 1460.

During the 1400s, the plains of northern Italy teemed with life, supported by an abundant agriculture, the rapidly developing industry of early capitalism, and commerce from the emporiums of Venice, Florence,

18. Andrea Mantegna, San Zeno altarpiece

and Genoa. The cities of Milan, Pavia, Brescia, Bergamo, Vicenza, Verona, Padua, Ferrara, Bologna, Mantua, and Parma lived side by side in comparative wealth and civic pride. Each was an independent and self-governing city-state, yet each was wary of being overtaken by a more powerful neighbor. Parma contributed Parmesan cheese; Bologna, mortadella di Bologna (a spiced pork sausage); Genoa, a type of cotton cloth still referred to as jeans; Milan, fashions for the head called millinery. Here we fix our attention on Mantua.

On three sides of the city of Mantua, the Mincio River overruns its banks to form large, almost impassable lakes. Blessed by such a strategic advantage, Mantua dominated the countryside against its most formidable enemies, and the lords of Mantua manipulated their foreign policy to take advantage of the relentless conflict between the two great northern Italian powers, Venice and Milan. Under Lodovico III (1417–78), of the house of Gonzaga, the city grew to forty thousand, despite desperate seasons of pestilence and flood. Supported by a brisk trade in woolens and silk, a splendid Renaissance court arose under the patronage of that prince. Ruthless in war and cunning in diplomacy, Lodovico was also a man of artistic and scholarly sensibility.

The painter Mantegna was not the only genius whom Lodovico invited to his court. Leon Battista Alberti (see plate 50), perhaps the greatest of all Italian celebrities in the fifteenth century, practiced architecture in Mantua; and Pico della Mirandola, a young man of universal wisdom, precocious beyond any convention, rehearsed the philosophy of Plato in the court of the Gonzagas.

Princes of the Renaissance supported such cultural endowments partly to express their preference for the arts and letters, partly to obscure their upstart origins, and partly to reinforce the legitimacy of their regimes. In Lodovico's case, however, it was rather different: he had been *educated* to appreciate the good things of the mind and eye. In 1423 his father, Gianfrancesco Gonzaga, had invited the most reputable schoolmaster of the age, Vittorino da Feltre (1378–1446), to open a school in Mantua. It soon became the most prominent school of the Italian Renaissance, the training ground of princes including Lodovico, and the model for European education for centuries to come.

The Renaissance held three axioms with respect to education. First, human beings are fit to be educated: we are free, rational, and potential beings; we are educable. Second, education is the only means by which human beings can become fully human. (This view is reflected in our reference to "the humanities" — studies that enable us to attain our full humanity.) Third, the purpose of education is citizenship — service to society; service in the world.

Vittorino educated for a sound mind in a sound body. Wrestling, fencing, swimming, and riding went side by side with Virgil, Homer, Cicero, and the Bible. A devout Christian, he nevertheless believed that virtue, rather than being a deposit from God, was a natural, human resource that we can mine from our own depths, chiefly by means of education. Virtue meant "noble character" — loving the good, hating the evil, disdaining the unworthy, striving toward our own greatest perfection.

The Gonzaga Palace in Mantua illustrates the wealth and power of the ruling families of the Italian Renaissance — the Sforza of Milan, the Malatesta of Rimini, the d'Este of Ferrara, the Scala of Verona, the Gonzaga of Mantua, and the Medici of Florence. Mantegna's most important commission in Mantua was the decoration of the bridal chamber — *camera degli sposi* — in the upper left quadrant of the palace. It was a quite ordinary room, which Mantegna proceeded to transform by creating an imaginary pavilion, with twelve marble pilasters and a roof dominated by a great round aperture (see plate 8).

He reserved the two walls best exposed to the light for his two most important frescoes. The wall to the left portrays a meeting of Lodovico with his son, who had recently been appointed a cardinal of the church. The right-hand wall depicts the Renaissance court of the Gonzaga family. Both subjects may have been suggested to Mantegna by Lodovico himself; they describe the most important political and ecclesiastical connections of the Gonzaga family.

On the ceiling, Mantegna created a pavilion with his brush (see plate 9). He decorated it with the busts of the Caesars of Rome in their canonical order. The "eye" open to the heavens — the *osculus* in classical architecture — suggests the character of an ancient Roman house. These were typical examples of the Renaissance preference for Greek and Roman life: ancient law, ancient philosophy, ancient art and architecture, ancient literature, ethics, and manners were all deemed by Renaissance people to be the most estimable norms for contemporary life that could be found.

If, like Lodovico and Barbara Gonzaga, we were to open our eyes every morning to meet the gaze of some Caesar or other, we would find little difficulty in becoming sentimentally attached to that ancient world. The medieval world, in contrast, although near in time, would recede somewhat in the scale of our attachments. The culture of the Middle Ages seemed too other-worldly to these exuberant people of the Renaissance, who thought better of this world and of the humankind that lived and loved, struggled and suffered in it. By no means did they abandon the church, but they found God also in the beauty of his creation and in the creativity of human beings, particularly in art.

The balastrade around the "eye" illustrates Mantegna's skill at fore-shortening. The maidservants who peek over the balastrade are light-hearted, while members of the court are invariably shown to be solemn, befitting their role as members of the ruling family. One of the maidservants is a Berber woman. Mantegna's people are real people; they illustrate the Renaissance interest in the subtlety and potentiality of human nature. Mantegna delighted in his own virtuosity . . . and in an impish sense of humor.

The architectural arrangement of the left wall of the bridal chamber put Mantegna in a quandary. Lodovico had assigned the painter a subject for that wall — the reunion with his son, Francesco, who had just returned from Rome, having received there the red hat of a cardinal of the church. But someone had cut a door into that panel, making it impossible to place the main episode in the center of the wall. So Mantegna had to place the scene of the reunion in the right-hand section of the wall. On the left, he created a secondary scene. And over the door, he put a plaque in which he dated and dedicated his decorations of the bridal chamber.

The year is 1459 (see plate 10). Francesco Gonzaga, second-born of Lodovico III, has just returned from Rome where Pope Pius II had invested him into the college of cardinals — the first Gonzaga to attain that important distinction. His proud father has come forth from Mantua to meet him. In the background is an ancient villa whose classical features are meant to remind us of ancient Rome. On the right, between two faces in profile, a red-faced man to whom we will return in a moment. The importance of this picture is simply stated: the stability of the princely house of Gonzaga depended on two critical political connections, one of which was to the papacy at Rome.

The right-hand panel is a portrait gallery of the male members of the Gonzaga family and their friends. On the left is the marquis himself. His costume consists of woolen hose, a silk mantle worn over a short jacket with slit sleeves; and a brimless hat — haberdashery typical of fifteenth-century Italian aristocracy.

In the center is the young cardinal, Francesco, his pink cheeks only just beginning to sprout whiskers. Beside him is the fifth son of Lodovico, also called Lodovico, who, in the course of years, became bishop of Mantua. Holding his hand is little Sigismondo, son of the eldest offspring of Lodovico III, who was also destined for a career in the church. As the years passed, he too was named to the college of cardinals. Plainly, the relations between Mantua and the papacy were very cordial. To the left of Sigismondo is his brother, Francesco, whose sweet countenance gives no hint of his future importance as lord of Mantua and husband of Isabella d'Este, incomparable among Renaissance women.

On the right is Lodovico's eldest son, Federigo I, who would succeed him. On the left is thought to be Giovanni Pico della Mirandola, one of the universal geniuses of the Italian Renaissance. Educated at five universities, he claimed to be versed in all of the great literature of the world; he read in Latin and Greek, Hebrew and Arabic; and he quoted with equal authority from Plato, Paul, Zoroaster, and the Jewish mystics. If you want to know what the expression "a Renaissance man" meant, look at Pico; he was one. Between the two is a man who appears to be slightly put off by Pico's erudition and by the hauteur of Federigo. Who is he? Mantegna, the painter.

In the distance (see plate 11) is an ancient villa — a reminder that the Renaissance was a rebirth of classical forms and classical values. Its columns and portico seem to anticipate the great country villas which Andrea Palladio created in northern Italy during the following century. A colossal statue of Hercules guards the villa. And the ancient pyramid, the broken columns, and the colosseum all put emphasis on the indebtedness of the Renaissance to the civilization of the Greeks and the Romans.

Mantegna had an eye for architectural detail. Towers and bridges fascinated him. He recalls for us the houses and streets that made up the landscape of the Italian Renaissance.

The horse on which Lodovico had ridden out to meet his son is being steadied by a groom, while another groom holds four dogs on a leash. By prolonging the leashes of the dogs from one panel to the next, Mantegna manages to connect the panels in a witty way and thus overcome the problem of the door being in the middle of the space.

The horse is an example of a special breed which the princely house of Mantua began to develop in the fourteenth century. The animal's strength and agility was attained by breeding the best of north-Italian horses with Arabian stock.

Behind the horse, amidst luxuriant vegetation, the trees hang heavy with fruit. That was a typical device used by Renaissance painters to remind their viewers that they were living in the springtime of history — a time of optimism, a time of artistic, intellectual, and political renewal. Beyond the trees, there is a natural bridge, carved perhaps by an impetuous mountain stream. On the heights above everything else, architectural structures arise which offer the viewers still further evidence of the startling ingenuity and power of human beings.

These things require interpretation. In the center of the natural bridge, far off in the distance, we see dimly the City of God, made famous in the writings of St. Augustine — a spiritual city, set on a hill and guarded by eight towers.

By placing two man-made structures on the very summit of the earth, Mantegna appears to be deliberately drawing a contrast between what God has done and what man can do.

Creation is God's act, Mantegna seems to be saying. But it has been left to human beings to add to creation, or even, to bring creation to perfection. With what vanity did these Renaissance artists and philosophers express themselves! Yet, it was just such vanity which made the Renaissance what it was and which may have been one of the tell-tale signs of modernity.

Mantegna also seems to suggest that architecture is the supreme achievement of mankind and that Lodovico III has brought his own little world, the city-state of Mantua, to the highest degree of perfection.

Just below one of the towers is a cave from which two tiny figures emerge — affording Mantegna the opportunity to indulge in his taste for painting miniatures. Other miniatures found in these panels offer us glimpses into the common life of the fifteenth century.

Marble is being quarried and cut into blocks and columns; shepherds tend a flock of goats; farm animals graze in a field while the herdsmen sleep; two workers, their tools balanced over their shoulders, walk to work, following a dog; the highways are clogged with galloping commuters; and laborers are at work.

Over the troublesome door which obstructed the left wall of the bridal chamber, Mantegna placed a Latin dedication of his work: "To the most illustrious Lodovico, Marquis of Mantua, the best of princes, a man of unparalleled faith, and to the illustrious Barbara, his wife, of incomparable glory among women, here Andrea Mantegna has offered this modest work in their honor." As you see, the date affixed to the plaque is 1474.

On the right-hand wall of the *camera degli sposi,* Mantegna represented the entire Gonzaga family in their Renaissance court (see plate 12).

The painter was obliged to overcome certain architectural obstacles

— windows on the left and right, and the central fireplace — all of which limited the available space. To accommodate his picture to the fireplace, Mantegna placed the court on a podium, a few steps higher than the plain of the wall.

Lodovico III was both head of the family and chief of state. His government was purely personal, which is to say, he exercised an executive and legislative authority which was virtually unlimited.

Near the seat of authority, one finds the most faithful retainer of all. Lodovico discusses some urgent matter of domestic or foreign policy with his secretary, Marsilio Andreasi. An important dispatch has just been received from one of the Mantuan ambassadors, perhaps the envoy in Venice, or in Verona, or from beyond the Alps. The Renaissance was the first period in history in which diplomacy was conducted by resident ambassadors.

The only other person permitted to be seated at court is the marchesa Barbara, a German princess of the House of Hohenzollern; she had been born and raised in Brandenburg; her Italian was no doubt laced with a German accent. The marchesa's style was decidedly Venetian: her bleached hair, egg-like brow, and richly brocaded outer garment were very chic in Venice.

Next to the cross-looking nurse or nun, there is a single human face, the face of a young girl, whose grace is outstanding in this crowd of cold customers. Is she Barbarina, the next to youngest daughter of the princely couple, or their daughter-in-law, Margaret of Wittenbach?

Two other children of the court are Paola Gonzaga, last of the ten children of Lodovico and Barbara, and possibly young Lodovico, their last son and future bishop of Mantua. The smallest member of the court is the favorite dwarf.

The people at the extreme right are either minor dignitaries of the court, or, more likely, domestic servants. All of them wear the red and white livery of the Gonzaga family. The last of the liverymen supports one member of the household who seems to suffer some handicap of the mind or spirit, his face riven with unhappiness. Records of the frescoes were lost as early as the seventeenth century and historians continue to debate the identity of some of the figures.

The Jews of Mantua referred to Mantua as *Kiriah ha'Alizah,* "the happy city." But Mantegna's portrait of the Gonzagas belies that description. What severe countenances there are in the family circle! Not a smile in the lot! Not a glance in our direction! The medieval world was an age of great corporations — church, state, manor, monastery, university, guild, fraternity

— in which people of all sorts and conditions were sustained. The Renaissance was the age of the individual; and in the individual, as we all know, is the possibility of success or failure, happiness or sorrow, grandeur or misery. Is it the individualism of this new age that Mantegna tries to show on the faces of the Gonzagas?

The well-being of the Jewish people in the Renaissance depended on the goodwill of the prince and his domestic advisers; in Mantua, that goodwill was as generous as anywhere in Europe. Elsewhere in northern Italy, many Jews found persecution increasing in the later part of the Renaissance. In the late fifteenth century they were driven out of Perugia, Vicenza, Parma, Milan, Florence and all of Tuscany; by 1500 they had largely been squeezed out of Italian trade. Nearly two thousand Jews lived in Mantua; it was one of the largest, and surely the most celebrated, of all the Jewish communities in Italy. Mantuan Jews lived together, in their own neighborhood, but at their own choosing. There they maintained a rich communal life, built at least ten synagogues, and grew wealthy through money lending, textiles, and trade in precious metals and stones. Mantua became a center of Jewish music and theater, one of the birthplaces of Jewish printing, and even the site of a Jewish university. Apparently it was in Mantua that the critical scholarship typical of the Renaissance first began to be applied to Hebrew texts. Thus, the idea of free inquiry may have been added to the Jewish legacy in Mantua.

On September 13, 1506, when Michelangelo and Raphael were still young and the foundations of St. Peter's Basilica were only freshly laid, Andrea Mantegna died in his house in Mantua. No painter of the fifteenth century was more caught up in the artistic drama of his time than the high-spirited court painter of Mantua. No artist, philosopher, or statesman more faithfully represented the essential point of view of the Italian Renaissance: that God is also to be found in the beauty of the world and in the infinite creativity of human beings.

6. Venice

EVEN THE ASTRINGENT ERASMUS HAD SOMETHING COMPLIMENTARY TO say about Venice. Venice was, he wrote, "the most splendid theater in all Italy." Indeed the Venetians approved of themselves. They referred to their creation amid the lagoons as *La Serenissima Repubblica*, "the most serene republic." Their maritime power and their city of color and artistic beauty was one of the marvels of the Renaissance.

HISTORY

VENETIA was the name of a province of the Roman Empire situated at the northern end of the Adriatic Sea. When the Germanic tribes gradually overcame the empire in the West, Venetia remained for a while under the rule of imperial officials appointed from Constantinople and stationed at Ravenna. Who were the inhabitants of Venice? The very first Venetians we have any record of were an indigenous population of crude boat-people who fished and made salt among the *lidi* (sandbars) and lagoons of Venice. They were eventually superseded, or at least overtaken, by people from the mainland. The invasion of Italy by the Lombards in A.D. 586 caused refugees from northeastern Italy to seek the safety of the Venetian lagoons. People of wealth and culture, they built a settlement among a cluster of small islands in the lagoons, the chief of which was called Rivoalto, "high bank," from which the famous Venetian place-name the Rialto derives.

In 697 the Byzantine authorities made Venice a separate military command under the leadership of a *dux* (leader). As Latin became ground down by dialectical change, *dux* became *doge,* the Venetian head of state. The long association that Venice enjoyed with Byzantium explains the Byzantine character of Venetian art and, to some extent, of its commercial and political institutions as well.

In 751 the Lombards succeeded in overtaking Ravenna, and the Byzantine control of the Adriatic coast came to an end. Venice survived, however, as an independent city-state. Indeed, throughout the Middle Ages, Venice steadfastly refused to submit to any other power, even that of Charlemagne, whose vast Frankish empire of the ninth century included northern Italy; instead, Venice struck out upon a course of independence, which it maintained through the Middle Ages, into the Renaissance.

Prior to 1000 the Venetians did not venture beyond the rivers of northern Italy, the Po and the Adige, being content to allow the Greeks and the Moslems to transport goods across the Mediterranean. Gradually, however, between 900 and 1100, the Venetians turned from the rivers to the sea and began a lucrative traffic in slaves and lumber. The latter was an essential material of war, eagerly sought by the Moslems. Both the papacy and the empire prohibited commerce in scarce lumber and in slaves, but Venice persisted. When faith conflicted with trade, Venice chose trade: *Veneziani, poi Christiani* (Venetians first, then Christians). Slaves and lumber were essentials in foreign exchange; they brought gold and silver, which could be reinvested in Oriental luxuries. Having acquired access to capital, Venice turned its energies to the other side of its seagoing enterprise: it began to build ships. Trade, capital formation, and ships: these three made Venice an ever-greater maritime power.

As the city grew, the Rialto and the doge's palace became its most celebrated places — the Rialto being the marketplace of Venice, the palace its center of power and of civic pride. The whole city was built upon pilings driven deep into the muck — a technique begun by the first mainland refugees. In 1630, to support a single church, Santa Maria della Salute, the Venetians found it necessary to sink more than a million piles.

Venice developed as a city of almost autonomous parishes, each with a *camp* (square), a *campanile* (bell tower), a parish church, a local saint, some concentration of industry, and a mixture of rich and poor, mansions and hovels. In 1200 there were sixty such parishes. In that year the city encompassed 80,000 persons; in 1300 it had grown to 100,000 — somewhat larger than Paris. Then came the Black Death, which may have been introduced to Europe in 1347 by a Venetian galley returning from the Crimea. It

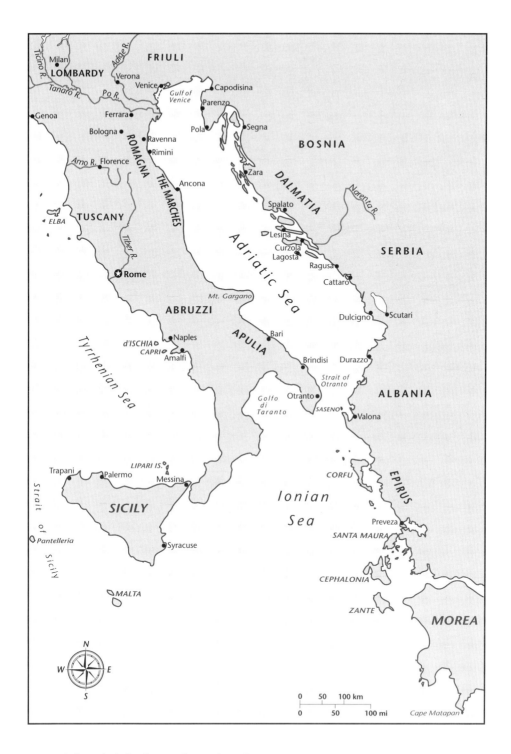

The Adriatic and Ionian Seas

claimed three-fifths of the people of Venice. By 1500, however, the city had grown again to 120,000 inhabitants.

In 828 two Venetian merchants smuggled what were believed to be the remains of Mark, author of the New Testament book of that name, out of the Egyptian city of Alexandria and brought the relics to Venice. To provide for such an important article of religion, the Venetians built a basilica, San Marco, adjacent to the doge's palace (see plate 13). San Marco is the doge's chapel (although not the cathedral of Venice) and the reliquary for the remains of Mark. From the outset, the building was the civic center of the city. Here the doges were sworn to office, the condottieri were commissioned, and victories were celebrated. Next to the basilica a great campanile was raised some 323 feet. Its gilded spire directed ships; its bells told time and notified Venetians of each important event: the arrival of a ship, an execution, the beginning of the curfew. From the top of the campanile, criminals dangled in cages, and Galileo trained his telescope upon the spheres.

The area in front of San Marco was cleared to form the *piazza* (square). From the *Bacino* (harbor), the Grand Canal winds through the heart of the city as a thoroughfare for ships. At the Rialto, a bridge crosses the canal. There the merchants of the world congregated to sell their goods and to exchange the news. "What news on the Rialto?" falls from the lips of a Shakespearean character. National colonies of merchants sprang up in the vicinity of the Rialto. In the *Fondaco dei Tedeschi* (warehouse of the Germans) gathered the Fuggers of Augsburg and the merchants of Nuremberg, Frankfurt, and Cologne.

In 1104 Venice concentrated its shipbuilding industry in the east end of the city in the Arsenal, a remarkable enterprise in which certain modern systems of production were practiced. In its heyday, 4,600 men and women worked there. A hundred galleys took shape at one time. All parts of Venetian ships were standardized in order to speed assembly. As a galley was towed out, it passed the warehouses, from which came successively the cordage, the arms, the supplies, until, at the end of the row of warehouses, the ship was fully equipped, with the men on board. Standardized parts were stockpiled at repair depots all over the Venetian trading empire. Venice never overlooked the importance of ships as the basis of its power.

In the twelfth and thirteen centuries, Venice took steps to expand its commercial empire. It first gained control of the upper Adriatic, then of Dalmatia, and finally, though less securely, of the lower Adriatic. The ambition of Venice did not stop, however, at commercial dominance in the western Mediterranean. It was determined to establish commercial supremacy in the eastern Mediterranean as well. In that respect, the Fourth Crusade, while scarcely a moral success, proved to be a boon to Venice. French nobility struck a contract with Venice to transport an army of crusaders to the Holy Land against a promise of eighty-five thousand marks of silver. In addition, the Venetians made a calculated political deal: in return for an equal share of all the spoils, they would add to the armada fifty armed galleys and the six thousand men necessary to operate them. At the departure of the crusaders in 1202, the nobles still owed Venice thirty-four thousand marks. Thus, the Fourth Crusade began with a substantial indebtedness to Venice. Doge Enrico Dandolo, blind and past eighty, knew exactly how the crusaders might be able to discharge that debt. They would perform a few favors for Venice en route to the Holy Land. The expedition was first directed to subdue Zara, a vexing little sea power in upper Dalmatia that had obstructed Venetian commerce for many years. That done, the crusaders were diverted again, this time to Constantinople itself, on the improbable pretext of establishing a pretender upon the throne of Byzantium who promised to bring the Greeks into submission to the papacy. In April 1204 Venetians and crusaders cracked the defenses of Constantinople and spent the next three days in murder, rape, and sacrilege. The sack of Constantinople yielded to Venice partial control of the city itself, clear title to Crete, and undisputed maritime supremacy in the eastern Mediterranean. To Venice came four bronze horses, created in antiquity, which now grace the facade of San Marco.

East-West trade expanded enormously in the twelfth and thirteenth centuries. The Crusades stimulated a demand in the West for Eastern wares, particularly spices, drugs, and silk, while the West increased its own production of metals and textiles, which could be sold in the East, relieving Venice of the need to deal in lumber and slaves. Venetian merchant fleets plied the seas in well-defined routes, fixed by the state, making calls in ports on a regular schedule. Through the Black Sea ports, commercial avenues were opened to China, owing to the efficiency of the Mongol emperors, who organized roads, posts, military protection, and toll collections from the borders of Hungary to the Sea of Japan. Niccolò and Matteo Polo were among those Venetians, based in Constantinople, who decided to explore the commercial possibilities of the China route, first in 1260, and again in 1271, when Niccolò's son, Marco, also made the trip to the Mongol capital of Peking and, having caught the fancy of the Great Khan, entered his service. An important instrument of trade was the ducat, which the Venetians introduced in 1284 and maintained at 3.5 grams of pure gold.

While it is a caricature to imagine Venice as a tyrannical oligarchy, maintained by excruciating efficiency, spies and informers, tortures and prisons, it is true that Venetian government followed a general movement toward oligarchy. In the early history of Venice, the fundamental authority was the General Assembly, a group of people that met to select the doge and to approve laws. Yet their Byzantine heritage instructed the Venetians in another principle: the integrity of the state. Thus, in the course of time, the following structure of councils evolved to express the sovereignty of the state, as well as a certain distrust of individualism:

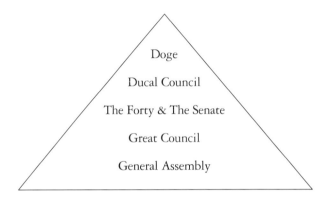

Doge

Ducal Council

The Forty & The Senate

Great Council

General Assembly

The real center of power in this triangle was the Great Council, which contained the Venetian aristocracy; it elected members to the other councils and had broad legislative power. The doge (who held office for life), the Ducal Council, and the three heads of the Forty constituted the *signoria,* the government, the regime — the agency that was responsible for day-to-day administration. By 1300 membership in the Great Council became permanent and hereditary, thus investing some two hundred families with political power. In 1310 the Venetian system added a new institution, *Dieci,* the Ten, designed to suppress plots against the state. The fourteenth and fifteenth centuries saw still further adjustments to the Venetian government that solidified its aristocratic character.

The fortunes of Jewish people in Venetian society varied. On the one hand, those from the Levant lived and traded side by side with the Venetians in all quarters of the Venetian trading empire; some received citizenship and settled in the island of the Venetian lagoon called Giudecca. On the other hand, Jews from Germany were denied the right to participate in international trade but were licensed as pawnbrokers, moneylenders, and dealers in secondhand wares. Admitted to the city, they were confined to an area that had been a foundry and that still carried the name *ghetto-nuova* (the word *ghetto* referring to casting). There they maintained a corporate existence according to Jewish traditions. It was Venice, not the Jewish people, who confined them there; it is hard to escape the conclusion that prejudice was practiced against them by a Christian society.

THE RENAISSANCE IN VENICE

AN UPSURGE of Venetian capitalism in the fourteenth and fifteenth centuries brought the city handsomely into the Renaissance. A producer of ships and textiles, the city acquired fame as a maker of glass and lenses according to carefully guarded techniques. Medieval artisans could stain glass with metallic oxides but had lost the Roman secret of making colored glass clear. Venice rediscovered it. Europe clamored for Venetian crystal and admired itself in Venetian mirrors.

The early years of the Venetian Renaissance were not, however, without hardship. The Black Death decimated the population. Venice was required to fight four desperate wars with its rival Genoa, leading at last to victory in 1381. As international diplomacy became critical in the Renaissance world, the Senate acquired power as the agency of foreign affairs. By the 1450s Venice maintained resident ambassadors at every major capital; they were thought to be the shrewdest in Europe. Venice's man in Rome, Antonio Giustiani, sent 472 dispatches in one year, including news, gossip, character studies, and analyses.

The first change in architecture was not a return to classical forms, as in the case of Florence, but a movement from the Byzantine style of San Marco to a type of Gothic peculiarly Venetian: hence, Venetian Gothic. We see it in the Ca'd'Oro (house of gold), a splendid palace on the Grand Canal built by the merchant family of Contarini in 1420–34; its tall windows and arabesque traceries are typical of Venetian Gothic of the quattrocento. Another quattrocento palace of the same architectural style is Palazzo Bernardo, which is also on the Grand Canal. The doge's palace, extensively remodeled in the course of the 1300s, is another example of the same style. That style is less pronounced in two parish churches built in the mid-1300s: Santa Maria dei Frari (the Frari), constructed by the Franciscans, and San

19. Ca'd'Oro

Giovanni e Paolo ("Zanipolo"), erected by the Dominicans. Neither accen-
tuates the stark vertical lines of northern Gothic, but each uses Gothic
vaulting to create interior spaciousness.

Not until the cinquecento did Venice produce architects committed
to classical forms. The first was Jacopo Sansovino (1486–1570), a Florentine
trained in the Roman environment of Bramante, Michelangelo, and
Raphael, who arrived in Venice in 1527, that fateful year when Rome was
sacked. Deeply committed to the classical style, Sansovino laid down the
principles that governed Venetian architecture for the next two centuries.
His greatest work was the Library of San Marco, opposite the doge's palace,

20. Doge's palace, Venice

which was begun in 1536. The ground story is distinguished by an arcade in the Roman Doric order, based on the Colosseum; the second story, which houses the main reading room, is Ionic, rich in sculptural relief.

Andrea Palladio (1508–80), second of the Venetian masters, has been called the supreme architect of northern Italy. Reared in Vicenza, he spent his formative years in Rome studying the remains of antiquity and the architectural glories of the High Renaissance. In 1554 he published *Quattro libri dell'architecttura,* in which he dealt with the essence of ancient Roman architecture and discussed its application to contemporary buildings. Palladio's work is to be found in the northern Italian cities.

Palladio designed the great villas that wealthy Venetians built on the mainland. Through such intermediaries as Thomas Jefferson, the Palladian villas became models for American civic architecture and inspired plantation houses of the American South. A prime example of the Palladian villas is the Villa Rotunda, which Palladio built at Vicenza in 1550. Another splendid example is the Villa Barbaro, which Palladio constructed at Maser (see plate 14). It was built for Daniele Barbaro, an important member of the aristocracy, who became the Venetian ambassador to England (1548–51) during the reign of Edward VI. Having been trained in classics and philosophy at the University of Padua, Barbaro acquired fame as a scholar; he wrote important commentaries on Aristotle and translated the Latin works of Vitruvius, foremost classical architect, into Italian. Paolo Veronese was commissioned to decorate the Villa Barbaro in 1565. What he produced there may be described as decorative painting. It is full of illusions, or what the French call trompe l'oeil; it is full of imaginative, subtle, humorous inventions that nevertheless work to create a refined atmosphere for the elegant company that gathered at Villa Barbaro.

Perhaps the highest expression of the Venetian Renaissance was Venetian painting. The Renaissance in Venice developed in ways rather unlike that of Florence or Rome. Humanism did not flourish in Venice to the extent that it did in Florence, nor did art become as academic. Venetian

21. Library of San Marco

22. Antonello da Messina, self-portrait

art became ever riper to the pleasures of life. The Venetian masters kept painting Madonnas, but, as Berenson observed, those Madonnas grew more and more like the handsome, healthy, richly dressed Venetians themselves, who did not require a Neoplatonic philosopher to describe for them the metaphysical center of life. As Venetian art developed, the painters discovered that they required more color, more light, more shadows, and more effect of space to express what they wanted to express — the beauty, grace, and comeliness of the human form, the warmth of human emotions, and the enjoyment of the world.

In the quattrocento, Venetian painting was touched by two influences from abroad. From the Sicilian city of Messina came one Antonello da Messina to Venice to 1475; he stayed but a year and a half but may have taught the Venetians how to use oils to serve the Venetian sense of luminosity and color. Oil painting proved a boon to Venetian artists for several reasons. Fresco painting did not work especially well in Venice because of the watery conditions. Venetian artists, moreover, were keen to find some new means of expressing atmospheric and luminous effects in their works, corresponding to the luminous effects given off by the water itself.

One of the greatest portraitists of the Renaissance, with profound interest in the inner psychological experience of his subjects, Antonello may also have been responsible for inspiring the Venetians to portraiture, at which, in time, they excelled (see figure 15). The second impulse came from Florence, namely, the interest in form, perspective, and tactile values that was so apparent in the work of the great Florentine masters. Even as early as 1423–24, these qualities of Florentine art were brought back to Venice by Jacopo Bellini, father of the Venetian school.

The fall of Constantinople to the Turks in 1453 threatened Venetian dominace of the eastern Mediterranean, and increasingly in the late fifteenth and early sixteenth centuries the city turned to mainland interests. However, its power was waning, and the final blow came when Pope Julius II brought together Emperor Maximilian, France and Spain in the League of Cambrai (1509) against Venice. The Venetians were driven back into the lagoon and almost into the sea, spared only by the fact that Pope Julius turned abruptly upon the French — "the barbarians," as he called them — and elected to harry them out of Italy. Although Venice regained some of its mainland possessions through diplomacy and arms, it lost forever the hope of dominance in Italy. Meanwhile, wars and skirmishes with the Turks had seriously taxed Venice's resources and will, depriving *La Serenissima* of some of its important trading cities.

EXCURSUS

Titian and the Other Venetian Painters

TIZIANO VECELLIO, GREATEST OF THE VENETIAN MASTERS OF THE RENAIS-
sance, was born in the village of Cadore, in the Dolomite mountains above
Venice, in either 1488 or 1490. His father was a minor officer in the local
government and a captain of the militia. When Titian was no more than
eight or nine, he was sent to Venice with his brother Francesco to become
an apprentice to the mosaicist Sabastiano Zuccato and by such means to
acquire the craft of an artist. In the Renaissance the artistic craft had
increasingly become an honorable occupation. An artist was a decorator and
a historian of sorts; an artist enabled wealthy clients to express their intellectual and aesthetic values.

When Titian presented himself to begin his apprenticeship, Jacopo
Bellini (ca. 1400–ca. 1470) was the leading painter in Venice; Vasari called
him "first of his profession" in the city. Bellini remains, however, a rather
shadowy and somewhat perplexing figure to us. Although he had been a
student in Florence during the quattrocento, there seems to be something
tentative about his commitment to the Renaissance. Some of his Madonnas
seem remote and rigid; they appear without perspective. It is only when
we begin to study his sketchbooks, one of which is preserved in the British
Museum, another in the Louvre, that we begin to see the new style of
painting emerging from the old. In *St. John the Baptist Preaching* (ca. 1438),
for example, Jacopo Bellini presents figures still molded in the Gothic
tradition. At the same time, the picture contains telltale signs of Renaissance
ideas — the Roman arch as a statement of classicism, the classical orders of
the buildings, and the effort to achieve perspective.

Jacopo Bellini had two sons who worked with him in his studio. The
older was Gentile (1429–1507), who became a celebrity in Venice as a
chronicler of the passing scene, as a storyteller who used art as a descriptive
means and who painted very large narrative pictures. The Holy Roman
Emperor Frederick III made him an honorary knight of the empire (1469).
When the sultan of Turkey required the services of an artist, it was Gentile
who was sent (1479). His most famous work was a large composition,
Procession in St. Mark's Square, Recovery of the Holy Cross (1469), in which, in
the year 1444, that sacred religious object, resplendent in a golden reliquary,
under canopy, was processed around Piazza San Marco in Venice (see plate

125

23. Titian, self-portrait

126

24. Giovanni Bellini, *Pietà*

16). So meticulously did Gentile fill this panorama of Venetian life that we can identify particular people and recognize the architectural details of the buildings in the square.

The younger of the Bellini brothers, and by all odds the more significant, was Giovanni (1430–1516). His poetic imagination, spiritual depth, and extraordinary use of color made him one of the greater European painters of the late quattrocento. He brought Venetian art to the beginning of the High Renaissance and prepared the way for Giorgione and Titian.

Giovanni's early works were done before the arrival of Antonello da Messina (1475). They bear a resemblance to those of Andrea Mantegna, Giovanni's brother-in-law, who was almost exactly his contemporary. The meticulous construction, the hardness of line, and the dull matte finish of Giovanni's early works are reminiscent of Mantegna. Consider, for example, Giovanni Bellini's *Pietà,* which belongs to the period 1468–71. Mary and

St. John the Baptist are shown supporting the lifeless body of Jesus, propping up the dead weight of the Savior for all to see. His face, which has fallen over onto Mary's cheek, has the pallor of death; his eyes are sunken into their cavities. Seldom in Western art has there been a more intense appeal to human emotion.

Upon the arrival of Antonello in 1475, a transformation seems to have occurred in Giovanni's painting — a transformation that may owe at least part of its explanation to the oil medium that the Sicilian apparently brought into vogue in Venice. The chief characteristic of the change in Giovanni's art was the use of color to invest his pictures with infinitely greater warmth and poetic imagination. In *Madonna and Child with Saints* (see plate 17), painted around 1500, we see three remarkably human figures — John the Baptist, the Virgin (with child), and Catherine — stylized only by their stillness; they seem almost transfixed against a landscape of great detail, shown in the fading light of the afternoon. The coloristic effects of this work have always drawn comment, from the stylish orange satin of Catherine's coat to the drab hairshirt of the Baptist.

Venice was the first of the Italian city-states to commission portraits of its chiefs of state, giving stimulus to portraiture. Giovanni Bellini's portrait of Doge Leonardo Loredano, painted in 1501, is a study in simple strength and unobtrusive authority.

To repeat, the sons of Jacopo Bellini represented two distinct traditions in Venetian art. The line of Gentile Bellini led to Vittore Carpaccio, and perhaps to Paolo Veronese, and stopped. The more important line of Giovanni Bellini led to the major Venetian tradition of Giorgione, Titian, and their successors.

The line of Gentile Bellini led directly to the Venetian-born Vittore Carpaccio (1460–1526). The *scuole* (guilds, fraternities) of Venice, as a means of glorifying their existence, commissioned artists to paint impressive canvases commemorating their processions or celebrating the lives of their patron saints. Carpaccio was the painter of the *scuole*. Although he inherited the storytelling gift from his predecessor, Gentile Bellini, Carpaccio was the wittier of the two and far more crisp in his social commentary. He turned every biblical story and every saintly legend into an occasion for showing daily Venetian life as it was actually lived.

The work of Carpaccio that most often draws comment is a series of eight large canvases on the legend of Saint Ursula, done for the Scuola di Sant Orsola, now in the Accademia in Venice. One of these is *The Arrival of the Ambassadors in Brittany* (see plate 18). The Venetians who viewed these

25. Giovanni
Bellini,
portrait of
Doge
Leonardo
Loredano

paintings when they were hung in 1498 saw Venice with gondolas in the
waters, shipping in the background, Venetian architecture, bridges, and
canals as well as passersby in contemporary dress. The wealth, the ostentation, the business, and the religion of Venice were all laid out by Carpaccio
for public inspection.

The young Titian came to such a Venice around 1494, as the quattrocento drew to a close. His first teacher was Sebastiano Zuccato, mosaicist
and painter, into whose house and studio the young apprentice was received.
As was the custom, Titian put in long backbreaking days, washing brushes,
grinding colors, sweeping the floors of the studio, eventually preparing

surfaces for the artist to work on, and finally doing insignificant parts of the artworks themselves. As required by membership in the guild, an apprenticeship lasted from five to seven years; it was the means by which the guild protected its standards. Having survived apprenticeship, a young artist such as Titian was required to spend three more years as a journeyman (a paid assistant to a master) before becoming a master himself.

At the end of his apprenticeship, when he was perhaps seventeen, Titian entered the employ of Gentile Bellini, then in his seventies and the patriarch of Venetian painting. The relationship, however, did not prosper. Titian found Gentile's painting tedious. The old man let him go.

Did Titian at this juncture become an assistant to Giovanni, the younger Bellini brother? Probably. At the time, Giovanni Bellini was overcome with commissions — large commemorative canvases for the chambers of the Great Council; Madonnas and altarpieces for the Catholic clientele; requests for portraits, almost excessive in number. Apparently Titian participated in these activities.

At some point in his early career, perhaps around 1507, Titian became assistant to one of the most interesting but puzzling figures in the history of Renaissance art, Giorgione of Castelfranco (1475–1510). (The root of his name is "Zorzi" in the Venetian dialect. The Italian suffix -one means "big" — hence the meaning "Big George.") Few of his pictures have survived; only some of those can be authenticated. He did not bother to sign his paintings, much less explain their meaning or give them titles. His short life is obscure to us. We do know that he came to Venice from the country at an early age to study painting, was greatly taken by the work of Giovanni Bellini, and became a decorator in a furniture shop on the Rialto. He soon began to make a name for himself by painting in oils. His work struck people as poetic and pastoral, like Giovanni Bellini's, full of light and shadows, rich in color. So popular did Giorgione become in Venice that he required two assistants. One was Titian; the other, Sebastiano del Piombo, who made his name in Rome. When Giorgione died at thirty-five, probably of the plague, he thus left two disciples to carry on his tradition.

Giorgione contributed something to Titian's technique. Giorgione, unlike the youthful Titian, saw no point in making preliminary sketches, whether on paper or on the canvas itself, but proceeded directly to outline the composition with color, continuing to build up the color until the picture took shape. Giorgione painted "with colors only," as Vasari put it, and Titian quickly adopted the same technique. In Titian, however, the style of Giorgione underwent two changes. Titian, disliking Giorgione's abstractions, made all references plain — whether biblical, literary, or allegorical. And Titian transformed Giorgione's idealized nudes into objects of erotic desire.

In 1516 Titian became first painter of Venice. As such, he was expected to do portraits of dignitaries and doges as well as narrative scenes of great battles and other civic events, in recompense for which he received a stipend from the state and certain tax exemptions. But he was in no hurry to do things for Venice: private commissions were keeping him busy. One of those commissions had come from the prior of the Franciscan convent of Santa Maria Gloriosa dei Frari. A great painting was needed for the high altar of the Frari Church, the Franciscan church in Venice. What the Franciscans required was a very large work to fill a very large frame (22 feet high) which was already on order. Titian was given the commission to paint an oversized Assumption of the Virgin (see plate 19), presumably a conventional work with pleasant landscapes and recognizable biblical folk. But when Titian's great work was unveiled in 1519 the Venetians who had gathered at the Frari Church were dumbfounded by what they saw — a beautiful and vigorous woman, not unlike Titian's Venuses, being drawn into heaven by the very plenitude of life within her. She was young. She was beautiful. She was humanity itself, here embodied not in Michelangelo's *David,* but in a woman. Nothing could stay her course to heaven. Both the colossal size of this work and the fact that it has to be looked up to indicate that it was a work typical of the High Renaissance. It was, as H. E. Wethey said, "the first really monumental achievement of the Venetian High Renaissance."

Among Titian's prominent clients from the ruling elite was Isabella d'Este, who, at the age of fifteen, had married Francesco II Gonzaga, marquis of Mantua. Diplomat, stateswoman, litterateur, and patron of the arts, Isabella was unsurpassed among women of the Renaissance. By herself she raised the court of Mantua to the status of those in Urbino and Ferrara, although the wealth of the Gonzagas did not begin to equal that of the lords of Urbino and Ferrara. When she was in her sixties, Isabella commissioned Titian to do her portrait — not as she looked then, but as she did in her twenties (see plate 20).

The ruling families of Mantua, Urbino, and Ferrara intermarried. For them Titian painted portraits, religious work, and poesie, or pleasure paintings based on classical themes, that is, Greek and Roman myths. Among Titian's patrons were Isabella d'Este's brother, Alfonsa d'Este, Isabella's son, Federigo II Gonzaga (1500–1550), marquis of Mantua, and Isabella's daughter Eleanora (1493–1550), duchess of Urbino, who was celebrated in Castiglione's fourth book in his *Book of the Courtier.*

Titian's best-known attempt to capture the perfect image of feminine beauty was *Venus of Urbino* (see plate 21), done for Guidobaldo II della Rovere, grandson of Isabella d'Este, who succeeded to the lordship of Urbino in 1538. Titian's Venus evidently represented the artist's idea of the personification of beauty. This Venus, however, was not an idealized creature. We see her fresh from her bath. She lives in a Venetian palazzo; her attendants busy themselves in the background. She gazes directly at us in frankness, yet not without a certain modesty.

In the middle period of his life Titian acquired his most illustrious patron — the Holy Roman Emperor Charles V. On February 24, 1530, during a respite in the Hapsburg-Valois Wars, Charles, then thirty, went to Bologna to receive the imperial crown from the hands of Pope Clement VII. It was a gesture of peace between pope and emperor, following the disastrous sack of Rome three years earlier. At the time of the coronation, Titian painted a portrait of the emperor in full armor, since lost, and yet another portrait, also lost, done at Bologna in the winter of 1533. So impressed was Charles by these works that he bestowed upon Titian the title Knight of the Golden Spur and Count of the Lateran Palace (May 10, 1533) and declared that he would be painted by no other artist. As court painter to the Holy Roman Emperor, Titian suddenly found that his world had been enlarged: now he was needed in Augsburg; at the same time, they sought his services in Bologna, Venice, and Rome.

Besides being attached to the imperial aspect of the great medieval partnership of church and state, Titian was also very close to its ecclesiastical aspect. The Farnese pope, Paul III, who succeeded Clement VII in 1534, managed to enlist Titian as papal portraitist and eventually to lure him to Rome by holding out the possibility of a benefice for his son Pomponio. In May 1543, at Bologna, a month or so after he had first met the pontiff in that city, Titian produced the first of three portraits of the Farnese pope — *Paul III Seated without Cap.* This first portrait shows the Holy Father by himself, sitting uneasily, heavily bent with age, clutching his purse. His is the countenance of a very old and very frail man, whose crafty eyes alone dispel the imminence of senility and death.

The second portrait, *Paul III Seated with Cap,* was painted between October 1545 and June 1546, while Titian was a guest of the papacy in the Belvedere Palace. That portrait contributed very little to the previous one. From the same period and site, however, came Titian's greatest work for the Farnese family and one of the most remarkable pieces of portraiture in the history of Western art — *Paul III and His Grandsons.* The old pope, his hand tight with tension on the arm of the papal chair, wheels suddenly toward Ottavio Farnese, a young man of twenty-two, who reacts with such revolting obsequiousness that not even the pope can hide his disgust but glares at his grandson with flinty eyes. Standing passively by, oblivious to this suspicious scene, is Alessandro Farnese, a quiet, brilliant papal diplomat at the age of twenty-six. It is possible that the Farnese family put an end

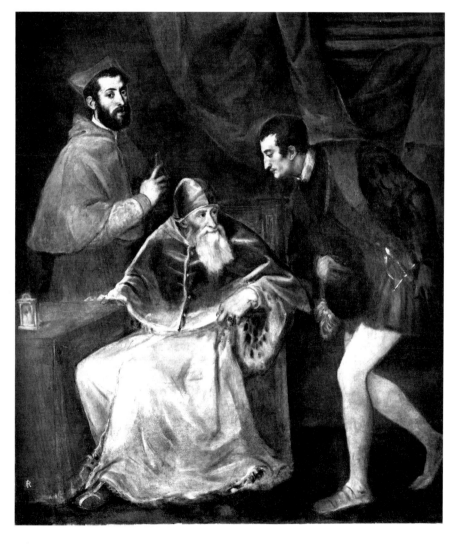

26. Titian, *Paul III and His Grandsons*

to this painting before its completion because its frankness was so disturbing to them.

At seventy, Titian faced the challenge of two rising painters in Venice, two geniuses who were remarkably unlike each other — Tintoretto and Veronese. Jacopo Robusti (1518–94), called Il Tintoretto after the trade of his father, a dyer of woolen cloth, also carried the nickname Il Furioso, descriptive of the furious force with which he worked. He was apt to paint in a torrent of execution, throwing himself into his art, painting with unimaginable speed, spreading paint on the canvas as if in a frenzy. The nineteenth-century art critic John Ruskin once accused him of painting with a broom. Tintoretto was typical of the Renaissance disposition; he wanted to show people who were filled with human energy and vigor. He was deeply, mystically, even piously attracted to the spiritual world, although it is doubtful that he would have recognized himself as a conventional Catholic. Tintoretto's religion was more poetic than dogmatic; he used scenes from the Bible either because they were scenes of high drama or because they disclosed some aspect of human dignity. Briefly attached in Titian's studio, Tintoretto never ceased to think of Titian as his teacher, however impatient he may have been over Titian's deliberateness. For his part, Titian was immediately suspicious of Tintoretto's velocity and impetuosity.

One of Tintoretto's two great cycles of historical paintings was for the Scuola di San Rocco in Venice. Subjects were taken from the Old and New Testaments. This cycle of some fifty pictures has been favorably compared to celebrated cycles by Giotto in the Arena Chapel, Masaccio in the Brancacci Chapel, and Michelangelo in the Sistine Chapel. The most prominent work in Tintoretto's cycle is *The Crucifixion* — an enormous composition, forty feet long,which fills the entire end wall of the scuola's dining room (see plate 22). It is an extensive investigation of the death of Jesus, which Tintoretto evidently took to be a superior example of moral grandeur in religious literature.

Paolo Veronese (1528–88) was of a different sort. His art speaks of unabashed worldliness, happiness, and sensuality. He, best of all the Venetian masters, expresses for us what Venice must have been like at the height of the Renaissance. Born Paolo Caliari in Verona, the heir of a northern Italian art tradition that stretches back at least as far as Mantegna, Veronese (from Verona, his birthplace) came to Venice in 1553 and spent his whole life there, painting the Venetian scene and recording Venice of the late cinquecento. Judging by his habits, Veronese was rather straight-laced and parsimonious. Judging by his art, however, in a painting such as *Feast in the House of Levi* (see plate 23), Veronese lived a life of banquets and processions, in a setting of sumptuous palaces and handsome people.

There may even be something decadent about Veronese's great narrative scenes of Venetian life. They are at least contrived and theatrical. Perhaps they disclose, more than they were meant to, the moral and material decline of Venice toward the end of the cinquecento, when Venetian trade monopolies had been broken by the oceangoing galleons of Spain and Portugal and when the Venetian treasury showed signs of exhaustion.

Titian and his two great friends, Sansovino, the architect of the Library of San Marco, and Aretino, the humanist-poet-playwright, formed a triumvirate, one of the more conspicuous ornaments of Venetian Renaissance society. They preceded him in death.

Titian lived on, enjoying the pleasures of Casa Grande, in almost complete possession of his faculties to the end. In the summer of 1575 a great plague broke out in Venice and took nearly a quarter of the population. Toward the end of the epidemic, on August 27, 1576, Titian died, perhaps of the plague, and, for the sake of public health, was swiftly buried the following day in the Frari Church, where his tomb is to be seen today.

Such were the life and times of the towering figure of Venetian painting. Three things should be written as his epitaph. First, whenever the prominent figures of the High Renaissance are remembered — Michelangelo, Raphael, Leonardo — Titian's name should also be remembered. Second, he lived rather buoyantly through a melancholy era of Italian history — from the 1490s through the 1520s, when Italy was repeatedly overrun by foreign invaders, when Venice declined to a second-class power, and when the Italian Renaissance itself, sapped of its energy by war, was diminished. Third, Titian's career coincided with the beginning of the Catholic Reformation, an all-pervasive principle of moral and spiritual rearmament in Western Catholicism. Of all the prime movers of the Catholic Reformation, Titian was associated with two of the most important — Pope Paul III and Holy Roman Emperor Charles V, yet he continued the artistic traditions established in the quattrocento.

7. *Milan*

SET IN THE MIDST OF THE GREAT FERTILE VALLEY OF THE PO, ADJACENT to the Alpine passes that lead to France and southern Germany, Milan was one of the wealthiest and most populous cities of Italy and was at the center of Lombard politics. Agriculture, textiles, the manufacture of armor, and trade from the emporiums of Venice, Genoa, and Florence were the four sources of the city's wealth and power. The plains of Lombardy teemed with life that its abundant agriculture supported. The cities of Milan, Turin, Pavia, Lodi, Brescia, Bergamo, Vicenza, Verona, Padua, Ferrara, Bologna, Mantua, Parma, and Piacenza all lived in comparative wealth, pride, self-satisfaction, and starchy independence, not overly burdened with sweet charity for one another.

THE VISCONTIS

IN 1262 Ottone Visconti, using the power of his archiepiscopal office, took political control of the city of Milan, which was sorely beset by internal strife among three factions: the older nobility, the rising class of merchants, and a wage-earning proletariat consisting mainly of workers in the armor industry. The Visconti thus became the *signori* of Milan. Ottone's son, Matteo, applied to the Holy Roman Empire in 1299 for the formality of legal power and received the usual title of vicar. Already the expansionist policy of the Visconti was apparent, as certain major cities of the Po valley were brought within the Milanese orbit — especially Brescia, Bergamo, and Parma.

137

The first great Visconti duke was Gian Galeazzo. Born in 1336 of a diplomatic marriage with the house of Savoy, he himself was married at the age of nine to Isabelle, the princess of France, and became a father at fourteen. Political marriage was a Visconti trait. In 1378 he inherited the part of the Milanese orbit of power that his father had ruled from the city of Pavia. That left the city of Milan itself still under the control of his brutish uncle, Bernabó Visconti, who not only presented the inconvenience of existing, but had four ambitious sons who were bound to succeed him. Gian Galeazzo now maneuvered to acquire sole power over the territories of Milan. His child bride having died, he negotiated his own betrothal to the heiress of Sicily, on condition that the marriage be consummated within twelve months. That was a masterful political stroke; as everyone could see; however, its success depended upon Gian Galeazzo being with his bride. Uncle Bernabó, though, saw to it that the Sicilian bride and the Visconti groom were kept at a safe distance — in fact, the whole length of Italy. When twelve months passed and Gian Galeazzo's Sicilian marriage remained unconsummated, Bernabó announced that his own daughter, Caterina, would be Gian Galeazzo's bride, there being not a single logistical problem to stand in the way between the bride and the groom. And so, the marriage was accomplished.

Then occurred one of the most bizarre episodes in Milanese history. In 1385 Gian Galeazzo, with a large retinue, including his bride, set out on a pious pilgrimage to the shrine Madonna del Monte. In the environs of Milan, his Uncle Bernabó came forth to meet him and, having exchanged familial greetings, was forthwith set upon by Gian Galeazzo's retinue and dispatched to his heavenly reward. Each of his sons was also slain. Gian Galeazzo proceeded to enter the city of Milan, his wife smarting slightly at the execution of her father and all her brothers, and took command of the whole Milanese dominion. It was a stroke widely admired, provoking some commentary by Chaucer in *The Canterbury Tales*. Gian Galeazzo proceeded to buy the title of duke from the Holy Roman Emperor. Henceforth, people referred to him as the Duchy of Milan.

In his seventeen-year rule, Gian Galeazzo Visconti created a state out of equal parts of paternalism and despotism. He encouraged the merchant class at the expense of both the nobility and the proletariat. In a word, he sponsored merchant capitalism and in every way promoted the commercial and industrial prosperity of the state. He was the model of a Renaissance prince: ruthless in gaining power, facile in the use of power, unscrupulous in diplomacy, ambitious in every dynastic sense, erudite, and remote.

27. Francesco
Sforza,
portrait by
Boniface
Bembo

It was he who commenced the great Duomo in Milan in 1386, intending it to be the greatest ecclesiastical structure in the Christian world;
it is one of the few notable expressions of northern Gothic in Italy. In two
campaigns, Gian Galeazzo seized all of eastern Lombardy except Mantua
and Ferrara. The Milanese incursion into Tuscany, however, was the boldest
stroke in his career. Bent upon the creation of a great northern Italian state,
the subjugation of Florence was Gian Galeazzo's highest ambition. Florence

and Venice stood side by side in the threat of such a prospect. In fact, the alliance of Florence with Venice against Milanese ambitions seemed to be an eternal pillar of Florentine foreign policy. Gian Galeazzo simply proceeded to surround Florence. Having taken Pisa, Siena, Perugia, and Bologna, there was nothing left except to strangle the enemy. In 1402, however, Gian Galeazzo caught the fever and died.

Upon the death of Gian Galeazzo Visconti, the Milanese empire suffered severe attrition. Not only was Florence spared, but the other Tuscan cities threw off the Milanese yoke. Venice, in a major policy revision, decided to become a mainland power, thereby presenting a grave new threat to Milanese hegemony in northeastern Italy. Gian Galeazzo was succeeded by his sons. Giovanni Maria had the reputation of extreme cruelty. After being assassinated in the Church of San Gottardo in 1412, rumors — likely exaggerated — circulated that he had fed his enemies to his beloved dogs. Filippo Maria then governed until his death in 1447. Florence and Venice, fearing a Milanese resurgence, preserved their alliance, kept vigilance, and hired a condottiere. Milan followed suit. The condottiere employed by Milan to maintain the balance of power was one Francesco Sforza, to whom Filippo Maria Visconti gave his illegitimate daughter Bianca in marriage. Child of the Romagna, the turbulent breeding ground of condottieri, Sforza was a fierce and able general, a man of such magnetism that he could claim both Cosimo de' Medici and Federigo da Montefeltro as his friends. Filippo Maria Visconti died without a legitimate heir. At the time of the duke's death, Sforza, who had entertained every expectation of succeeding to power, was out of the Milanese state. Seeing their chance, the people of Milan proclaimed a republic and named it after their fourth-century saint, Ambrose. The Golden Ambrosian Republic, beset by internal disputes, endured but three years. In 1450 Francesco Sforza reentered the city. The citizens, once weary of despots, were now weary of republicans; they swept Sforza into the Duomo, horse and all, and proclaimed him duke of Milan.

Duke Francesco Sforza, although he had no legal right to that title, established a line and became a major figure in the politics of northern Italy. Both agriculture and industry brought prosperity to Milan. Sforza built the great brick fortress that still dominates the city — the Sforza castle. The duke's friendship with Cosimo de' Medici led to a major shift in the balance of power in the north. To Venice's great discomfort, Sforza struck an alliance with Florence, even admitting a branch of the Medici bank to the city of Milan. In the politics of Francesco Sforza, the chief loser was Venice.

The duke was prolific. When he died in 1466, he bequeathed the state twenty heirs. The two more interesting of his progeny were Galeazzo Maria, who, as eldest son, succeeded his father, and Lodovico, the sixth in the line of succession, but the first of all the sons to have been born after Francesco Sforza had been proclaimed duke. Galeazzo Maria Sforza pursued a reign distinguished by a combination of Catholic scrupulosity and stupefying extravagance, cruelty, and lust. It was fitting that the assassins found him in church. His wife, disconsolate that he had died unconfessed, made out a list of his sins so that the pope would know how to absolve him and thus spare him an undue season in purgatory. She included pillage, robbery, devastation, extortion, injustice, carnal vices, "notorious and scandalous simony," and "innumerable other crimes."

LODOVICO

IN THE scramble for power that followed the assassination of Galeazzo Maria, the reins of government were seized in 1480 by his brother Lodovico, called Il Moro (the Moor) because of his dark complexion. At first, Lodovico served as regent during the minority of the duke's son; then, upon the death of the child, he himself became duke of Milan. Adept at dynastic arrangements, Lodovico il Moro married fifteen-year-old Beatrice d'Este, daughter of the great house of Ferrara, incomparable among the women of the Renaissance, except perhaps for her sister Isabella d'Este. The betrothal of Lodovico and Beatrice set off a season of festivities that included fireworks and spectacles, dwarfs, hunchbacks, and giants, exotic animals, nude gods and goddesses carefully undressed as such. Part of Leonardo da Vinci's commission in Milan was to design the machinery and pageantry for such occasions. Alas, in order to marry Beatrice, Il Moro was required to dismiss his mistress, Cecilia Gallerani. She was sent away — bereft, except for a picture, painted of her own lovely countenance, by Leonardo da Vinci.

Lodovico's court was one of the grandest in the Renaissance. He based his government upon three policies: prosperity, diplomacy, and the patronage of the arts. At no time was Milanese commerce, industry, and agriculture pushed forward so aggressively than in the era of Il Moro. New crops, such as rice, were introduced to the plains of Lombardy. *Risotto,* a culinary speciality of the city, is thus a tribute to the Sforzas. Canals were engineered. It is fashionable to snigger at Shakespeare, who imagined that two gentlemen of Verona could travel back and forth to Milan by boat. In

28. Lodovico and Beatrice Sforza, kneeling in *Madonna Enthroned with Christ Child, Doctors of the Church, and Donors Lodovico Moro and His Wife and Children*, by Bernardino dei Conti.

29. Leonardo da Vinci, *The Last Supper*

fact they could, thanks to Leonardo da Vinci, who extended the system of canals and engineered the locks.

Lodovico's patronage of the arts is sufficient to make his reign memorable. It was he who invited Leonardo da Vinci to Milan and claimed almost twenty years of his life. For Lodovico, Leonardo designed military equipment, built canals, created fantasias, and drew plans for the urban renewal of the city. Two of Leonardo's achievements will live forever in the history of art, although only one of the two survives, and that, precariously. In 1495 Lodovico commissioned Leonardo to do a painting of the Last Supper for the refectory of a Dominican convent in the city — Santa Maria delle Grazie — so that the good friars would have something pleasing and inspiring as they dined. The execution is considered one of the more important exhibitions of the Albertian principle of perspective. Based on the single biblical statement "One of you shall betray me," it is a work of psychological insight and of profound foreboding. The artist does not have the slightest dogmatic interest; his painting, unlike so many on this subject that preceded it, does not treat the Christian sacrament or the sacrificial death of Christ. It is a study of the shock of betrayal. The people are polarized by the announcement. We see Judas. He is the only one who does not need to be told, the only one who recoils, the only one in darkness, the only one who nervously eats.

There is something else interesting about *The Last Supper*. Quattrocento theory — chiefly that of Alberti — decreed that a painting must be an extension of the room in which the spectator stood. Leonardo abandoned that principle. One must look up to see the picture. Its figures are larger than life. They exist on a plane that is greater than our own. This change is one of the most important clues of the High Renaissance, of the cinquecento as opposed to the quattrocento.

For two years Leonardo labored on the commission. The friars, thinking that Leonardo was dawdling, pestered him; he retaliated by making Judas in the likeness of their prior. Instead of using the normal fresco technique, which would have committed Leonardo to quick decisions in execution, the painter chose to experiment with a mixture of oil, varnish, and pigment. As early as 1517, the great painting began to perish. Retouchers worked over it; the friars cut a door through it; steam from the kitchens assaulted it; Napoleon quartered his horses next to it; the Americans bombed it and actually unroofed it. In 1977 a painstaking attempt to restore it was begun.

Gone forever is the great bronze horse that Lodovico commissioned Leonardo to cast for the courtyard of the Sforza castle in memory of Francesco Sforza. Leonardo commenced in 1493 to execute this equestrian statue of such unprecedented size that Michelangelo frankly doubted that it could ever be successfully cast. Leonardo called it *Il Cavallo* (The horse). This colossal statue was to stand twenty-six feet tall and to weigh one hundred tons. Like Lodovico's dreams, Leonardo's horse was spoiled by the French. The bronze was melted to make cannon, and French soldiers used Leonardo's clay model for target practice. Nothing remains of it.

The other artistic genius associated with Lodovico il Moro was the architect Bramante. Donato Bramante was trained in Urbino and spent the formative period of his life, representing the years 1477–99, in Lombardy, first at Bergamo and later at the court of Lodovico il Moro in Milan. With Brunelleschi, Alberti, Michelangelo, Sansovino, and Palladio, he ranks as one of the foremost architects of the Italian Renaissance. After 1506 he devoted his energies toward the construction of St. Peter's Basilica, an enterprise on which he labored until his death in 1514.

In 1492 Lodovico il Moro commissioned Bramante to rebuild the apse and transepts of a Gothic church in Milan — Santa Maria delle Grazie, a church associated with the Dominican convent in which Leonardo painted the Last Supper. As Bramante rearranged the interior masses of the Gothic building, he necessarily remodeled the exterior as well. The result is con-

30. Santa Maria delle Grazie

sidered one of his more important executions. Classical forms are represented in Bramante's design, especially in its exterior columns and decorations. The interior apse and transepts, however, invite our interest (see plate 24). These were designed either with the direct connivance of Leonardo da Vinci or at least according to his principles. Although there is no indication that Leonardo actually built a single building, he drew innumerable architectural plans, especially of churches. What fascinated him were the permutations and combinations of basic geometric figures that might be suitable as ground plans of buildings. Imagine a flower — say, a daisy — with four or five petals. Now imagine a church built accordingly, with a dome as the center of the daisy, and four or five apses radiating away from it. Leonardo's idea was to make a building neither of flat planes nor of inert masses, but a kind of living organism. Bramante tried to realize Leonardo's vision in his own design of Santa Maria delle Grazie. Apses open outward as if pushed by some organic principle. Circles seem to float around great arches (as one scholar put it) like cars on a ferris wheel.

The diplomacy of Lodovico il Moro, however cunning, led to disaster. In 1494, as we have noted, Lodovico invited Charles VIII of France to intervene in the delicate balance of Italian politics. Circumstances gave that diplomatic maneuver some semblance of logic. First, Milan feared the encroachment of Venice. Second, the Visconti had intermarried with junior branches of the French royal house, creating an affinity between the powers. Third, it was well known that Charles VIII was eager to press French claims to the Kingdom of Naples. Finally, France agreed to support the Sforza claim to dukedom — a privilege conferred on the Visconti but never formally upon their successors. The Italian campaign of Charles VIII in 1494 proved successful almost to a miracle. He drove to Rome, rattled the papacy, and overtook Naples. Sensing his miscalculation, Lodovico turned against the French and joined the federation of Italian cities that drove Charles out of Italy in 1495.

So far the unscrupulous diplomacy had worked. Lodovico boasted that the pope was his chaplain; Venice, his treasurer, and the king of France, his courier. His circumstances, however, suddenly changed. Beatrice died in childbirth. Charles VIII also died, to be replaced by a much sterner monarch. Louis XII of France, reviewing the treachery practiced on his predecessor, seized Milan in 1499 and drove Lodovico from power. Most of Italy, even Leonardo, enjoyed the rout of Il Moro. Swiss mercenaries were able to reinstate him briefly, but the French came again to Milan in 1500, and this time they packed Lodovico off to a French dungeon, where he languished eight years and died, as humanists made pious commentary on the fate of tyrants. One Renaissance medalist expressed the popular sentiments of the age that Italy had been dealt a mortal blow by the diplomacy of Il Moro.

EXCURSUS

Leonardo da Vinci

IN ONE RESPECT LEONARDO DA VINCI WAS THE PERSONIFICATION OF THE Renaissance man — *l'uomo universale,* "the complete man." He had a command of disciplines as varied as art, aeronautics, anatomy, hydraulics, military engineering, urban redevelopment, and even the staging of extravaganzas. He also had an extraordinary ambition, not untypical of Renaissance man. "I wish to work miracles," he said. If other people walked, Leonardo was determined to fly.

In another respect, he was a contradiction to the Renaissance. In an age that sought justification in antiquity, that built according to classical models and quoted classical authors, Leonardo was remarkably uninspired by the ancients. In an age that sought to revitalize Christianity according to its own classical simplicity and ethical vitality, Leonardo had little good to say for organized religion. The word "God" did not fall frequently from his lips. Of Catholicism he asked embarrassing questions (Why do Catholics worship the Son when their churches are devoted to his mother?). His religious paintings are not religious; they are neither pious nor of dogmatic value. In an age that put human beings at the center of things and that insisted upon human freedom and human potential, Leonardo was neither unduly optimistic about human beings nor deeply attached to them. They were, he said, "sacks for food" and "fillers up of privies." In a world of sensual delights, Leonardo was strangely immune — at least to the charms of women. Women were enigmas to him; he seemed to see them only through some mysterious veil. Like an ancient Manichaean or a medieval Albigensian, he thought of procreation as evil, or at least unwholesome. Although he grieved at cruelty to animals and bought birds only to release them, when it came to human beings, both love and hate were remote to him. No pangs of conscience afflicted him as he designed engines of war or plotted human destruction at the side of Cesare Borgia.

For Leonardo, authority came neither from classical antiquity nor from Christian revelation; it came from the human eye. Sight and induction from sight were truth, the only truth, and nothing but the truth. Sight was the noblest faculty of human beings. Sight, he said, is the recording angel.

All of these observations must be tempered by the simple truth that Leonardo, trained to be an artist, was not trained to be a classicist or a philosopher, much less a theologian. Genius though he was, he always stumbled over Latin. He was trained in design, painting, sculpture, and engineering. Learning came by sight — by observation and description — not by discussion.

We must therefore comment upon Leonardo as scientist and engineer. His mechanical and scientific ideas were far, far ahead of his time. That, in fact, was just the trouble. His ideas exceeded both the materials and the technology of his age — which explains why so few of his creations ever attained a practical use in his own time. He conceived of the submarine, the airplane, and the parachute; he actually created automation — machines, such as his printing press, in which several steps in the process occurred at the same time. Yet "conception" is the wrong word to apply to Leonardo. For him, science was not precisely a matter of conception, nor engineering a matter of technique. Both science and engineering were important to Leonardo because they taught him how things operated in nature. "How" was Leonardo's greatest word. How does the bird fly? To find out, one must construct a wing or an entire flying machine. In short, Leonardo was far more beholden to the eye than to the intellect, far more preoccupied by the question of how nature functions.

Leonardo was the illegitimate child of a notary, Piero, and a peasant girl, Caterina. According to his grandfather's diary, he was born on Saturday, April 15, 1452, in Vinci, a village some twenty miles west of Florence. Sometime between 1466 and 1469, Piero brought this left-handed boy to Florence, where he was apprenticed to one of the reigning masters, Andrea del Verrocchio. In the Middle Ages, such a boy, precocious but poor, would almost certainly have had to enter a monastic order to pursue a career and realize his ambitions. In the Renaissance, however, the city-state — in this case Florence — became the new vortex of power in which an ambitious young man such as Leonardo could prosper, could even do such a preposterous thing as challenge authority. Each great artist ran a *bottega* (workshop) in which experienced apprentices completed what the master had begun or blocked out. In the *bottega* of Verrocchio, Leonardo worked from dawn to dusk grinding colors, priming canvases, making brushes, learning to cast bronze, and, at last, putting the brush to painting. He signed himself "Leonardo da Vinci, Florentine."

As Verrocchio's apprentice, Leonardo came to the conclusion that painting is foremost of every human calling. One must paint, he said, "all that the eye can see"; through the miracle of sight, the human mind somehow enters into the mind of deity and is able to create animals, plants, fruits, landscapes, and human forms. Not quite true to his word, he made time for many things other than painting. He designed hoists, drills, and machines for the textile industry; he invented staircases inside columns. He made drawings of the human body. He became fascinated by the behavior of water; his notebooks were crammed with schemes for bringing water to cities, making canals, enlarging harbors. He drew endless sketches of the eddies and configurations of flowing water. Hydraulics is the name for it: the study of how water works.

In 1472, the year his name was affixed to the list of Florentine painters, Leonardo painted one of two angels in Verrocchio's composition *Baptism of Christ,* as well as a boy and water breaking over the shoals. Eventually he would far surpass his master in artistic success.

By 1477 Leonardo maintained his own studio, under the patronage, no doubt, of Lorenzo de' Medici. From this period came two of Leonardo's masterpieces. *The Annunciation,* commissioned by a community of friars in the 1470s, depicts the Virgin seated in utmost composure on the threshold of a splendid villa, as the angel Gabriel announces to her that she is to be the mother of the Messiah. When one looks at this work, it is important to realize that darkness precedes light in Leonardo's thought; light penetrates the dark; form and color must compete against the darkness for their existence.

The second masterpiece bore the title *Adoration of the Magi.* Commissioned in March 1481 by another community of monks, the picture was left incomplete when Leonardo left for Milan in 1481 or 1482. Undertaken when he was only twenty-nine and left unfinished, this work nevertheless became a masterpiece in Leonardo's own lifetime and struck awe in the young Raphael when he first beheld it. There remains to us both the cartoon and the painting itself. The cartoon, or underdrawing, is one of the best examples that exist of the Albertian principle of perspective. What interests Leonardo is precisely the excitement generated when the three Oriental potentates, or sages — the Magi — are suddenly brought to their knees by what they took to be the very sight of deity, so that a great psychological reaction runs like an electric current through all the other bystanders.

Having won no particular favor from Lorenzo de' Medici, who in fact preferred other Florentine painters such as Pollaiuolo, Leonardo da Vinci in 1481 or 1482 advertised himself to Lodovico il Moro, duke of Milan, in the following letter: "I have plans for bridges, very light and strong, plans for siege engines, for cannons capable of hurling small stones with an effect almost of hail, causing great terror. . . . I can make armored vehicles which will enter

31. Verrocchio, *The Baptism of Christ*

the ranks of the enemy with artillery. . . . And behind these the infantry will be able to follow. . . . In times of peace, I believe I can give you as complete satisfaction as anyone else in architecture. . . . Also I can execute sculpture in marble, bronze, or clay, and also painting." We have said enough of Leonardo's tenure in Milan to warrant our largely overlooking it here.

1. TOP Pazzi Chapel, interior

2. BOTTOM Federigo da Montefeltro and Battista Sforza, portrait by Piero della Francesca

3. TOP Baldassare Castiglione,
portrait by Raphael

4. BOTTOM Eleonora Gonzaga,
portrait by Titian

5. TOP Pinturicchio, *Submitting to the Pope Eugenius IV in the Name of Federico III*

6. BOTTOM Melozzo da Forli, *Sixtus IV and Bartolomeo Platina*

7. Andrea Mantegna, *The Crucifixion*

8. TOP Andrea Mantegna, Camera degli sposi

9. BOTTOM Andrea Mantegna, pavilion of Camera degli sposi

10. TOP Andrea Mantegna,
The Return from Rome of Cardinal
Francesco Gonzaga

11. BOTTOM Andrea Mantegna,
detail of
The Return from Rome of
Cardinal Francesco Gonzaga

12. TOP Andrea Mantegna,
The Court of Mantua

13. BOTTOM San Marco and campanile

14. TOP Andrea Palladio,
Villa Barbaro

15. BOTTOM Antonello da
Messina, *The Annunciation*

16. Gentile Bellini, *Procession in Saint Mark's Square*

17. TOP Giovanni Bellini, *Madonna and Child with Saints*

18. BOTTOM Vittore Carpaccio, *The Rulers,* detail of *The Arrival of the Ambassadors in Brittany*

19. Titian,
*Assumption of
the Virgin*

20. Titian, portrait of Isabella d'Este

21. TOP Titian, *Venus of Urbino*

22. BOTTOM Tintoretto, *Crucifixion*

23. TOP Veronese,
*Feast in the
House of Levi*

24. BOTTOM
Central nave, Santa
Maria delle Grazie

25. Leonardo
da Vinci,
*Madonna of the
Rocks*

26. Leonardo da Vinci, *The Virgin and Child with Saint Anne*

32. Leonardo da Vinci, *The Annunciation of the Virgin*

There are just two pictures of the Milanese era which require notice. The first is *The Madonna of the Rocks* (see plate 25). Here several things are interesting. First, the composition takes the form of a pyramid, which is typical of composition in the High Renaissance; second, the face of the angel on the right side of the picture expresses Leonardo's skill at chiaroscuro (*clarus* = clear + *obscurus* = dark), the usefulness of darkness and light to define faces and figures; third, Leonardo's use of the primal darkness in this picture may represent human mortality or the melancholy of the human condition, which light penetrates and diffuses, both in the distant background, but especially in the illumination of the central figures of the picture.

The second painting, *The Virgin and Child with St. Anne* (see plate 26), may or may not have been completed in Milan. We do know that it was begun in Florence and that it was carried to France by the aged artist and kept there as one of his few choice possessions until he died. What is interesting about this picture is its composition. Here the principle of the pyramid is compressed upon the figures themselves so that they are actually intertwined, a living pyramid. The women are exceedingly winsome but, as is often the case in Leonardo's work, enigmatic.

The rout of Lodovico il Moro by the French caused Leonardo himself to flee, and he became excessively peripatetic. First he went to Mantua, where Isabella d'Este presided over a brilliant Renaissance court. Wife of Francesco Gonzaga, she collected rare books and good paintings; Leonardo's

33. Leonardo da Vinci, study for *Adoration of the Magi*

portrait of her, painted at this time, does not survive, but there are a number of drawings for it that do. He turned up next in Venice, where from the top of the campanile the anxious Venetians could see Turkish campfires on the other side of the Adriatic. He served briefly there as a military advisor. He then returned to Florence, where he spent his time experimenting. Suddenly he appeared at the side of Cesare Borgia in the Romagna as "General Leonardo da Vinci," mapmaker, designer of military hardware, and engineer of fortifications. His machines included (on paper, at least) armored cars, multi-barreled cannons, artillery projectiles with fins, great rotating scythes that could seemingly cut through whole armies.

Surfeited by war, Leonardo returned to Florence — and to his painting. Thanks to Machiavelli, the *signoria* commissioned him to decorate the east wall of the Great Council in the Palazzo Vecchio. His colleague, commissioned to do the west wall, was twenty-nine-year-old Michelangelo Buonarroti. Leonardo's subject was assigned to him: the battle of Anghiari of 1440, when the Florentines defeated the Visconti of Milan. Once again, Leonardo attempted to use his own medium of oil, varnish, and pigment; the whole brilliant execution began to run, and Leonardo abandoned the mural in disgust. What we might have seen in this painting, judging from Leonardo's

152

34. Leonardo da Vinci, *Adoration of the Magi*

surviving cartoons and copies by such artists as Rubens, is an awesome intertwining of horses and men in the agonies of battles and of death.

About 1503 there came to Leonardo's studio in Florence to pose for her portrait one Lisa di Antonio Maria Gherardini, wife of a prominent Florentine, Francesco del Gioconda. She was then twenty-four. It took Leonardo three years to complete the portrait of Mona Lisa. In defiance of tradition, he painted virtually the whole of her, her hands folded at her waist. The composition of the picture — full-length portraiture — is another sign of the High Renaissance, with its heightened sense of the grandeur and dignity of human beings.

In 1505, also during this Florentine period, Leonardo may have at-

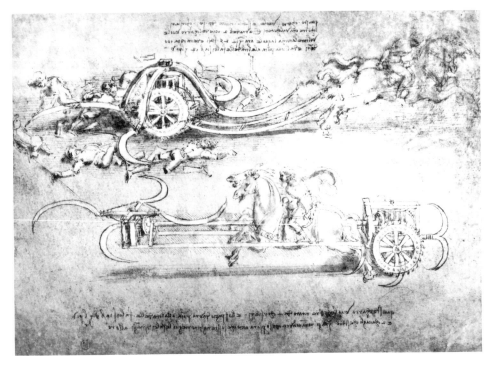

35. Leonardo da Vinci, *Armored Chariot*

tempted to launch a flying device — "the great swan," as he called it — from one of the heights overlooking Florence. An argument from silence would lead us to conclude that he failed. The city fathers now insisted that he complete his commission in the Palazzo Vecchio or return their money. Leonardo elected to do neither. About 1506 he returned to Milan, where the French were now in control. They had cultivated quite a taste for him. He spent much of his time in anatomical study. In 1508, for example, he dissected some fifty bodies of men, women, and children, in an effort to fathom the secrets of the natural world and of human life. The results of these labors were marvelous anatomical drawings of the interior of the body.

The Medici pope, Leo X, collected painters as Nicholas V collected books. In 1513 he brought Leonardo to Rome and established him handsomely in the Vatican Palace. The High Renaissance, however, had passed him by. Michelangelo had painted his ceiling, and Raphael, his *stanze;* the basilica was already going up. When Leo ordered Leonardo to paint, Leonardo started, characteristically, by mixing varnish. Leo accused the old

36. Leonardo da Vinci, *Mona Lisa*

man of beginning at the end instead of at the beginning. In despair, Leonardo left Rome. "The Medici made me," he noted in his diary, "and they have destroyed me." Only one picture is known to have come from Leonardo's Roman period: *John the Baptist*. A somewhat bemused saint points his finger into the sky, perhaps as a reminder of the inevitability of human mortality.

The French themselves had acquired a Renaissance court of no uncertain brilliance. King Francis I, under whose patronage the Renaissance in France now came of age, invited Leonardo da Vinci to France in 1516, established him in the Castle of Clux, near the royal court at Amboise, and pronounced him "first painter to the king." His sight failed, and paralysis inhibited his drawing, but until he died on May 2, 1519, he frequently talked to the king of France. Francis I said of him: "No other man has been born who knew as much as Leonardo."

"Tell me if anything was ever done?" Leonardo reportedly asked himself at the end of his wearisome life. Had he accomplished anything? Few of his engines and inventions either worked or were ever made. Some of his major artistic works melted away before his very eyes. The patrons of Renaissance art oddly failed to patronize him. What is the importance of Leonardo? We could answer this question in several ways: his willingness to challenge all given authority; his reliance on the Renaissance city-state as the new vortex of power in which such a challenge could be legitimately made; his trust in the authority of human sight and in the inductions that one could make from sight; his persistence in trying to discover how nature works (the question that preoccupied Leonardo da Vinci most of all); his grandeur as a Renaissance artist; his acute psychological insight expressed in his art; his consummate ability to execute the Renaissance principle of perspective. These statements together answer the question, Tell me if anything was ever done? Leonardo was a precursor of modern science, a painter of astonishing artistic and psychological depth, and, in some respects at least, the "universal man" of the Renaissance.

Typical of Leonardo were three methods associated with science of the sixteenth and seventeenth centuries: observation, mathematics, and a dynamic view of nature. No more needs to be said about Leonardo's penchant for observation. Data obtained from observation were never fully reliable, however, until they had been verified by mathematical measurement. "No human investigation can be called true science," he said, "without passing through mathematical tests." Forsaking the medieval hierarchy of sciences, with theology at the top, Leonardo graded all sciences according to the degree in which they were verifiable by mathematics. He refused to see

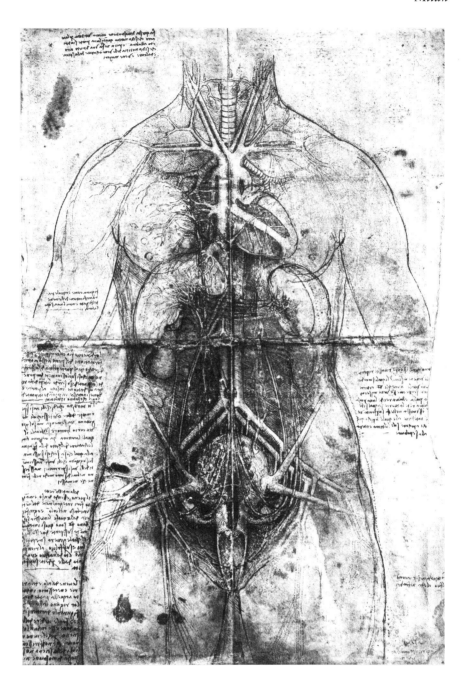

37. Leonardo da Vinci, *Anatomical Study*

nature as static and fixed, whether by laws human or divine. Leonardo's earth was incessantly crafted by oceans, rivers, and winds, a planet in which plants, animals, and human beings grow in one dynamic process of consumption and reproduction. In such ways as these, perhaps, he anticipated Galileo and the world of science that lay beyond.

8. Florence and the Medici

IN 59 B.C., IN THE AGE OF JULIUS CAESAR, FLORENTIA WAS ESTABLISHED as a Roman colony. Never more than a provincial center, the town declined, even as the Roman Empire declined, under the disorder of the Germanic invasions. It was rendered even more obscure by the agrarian system called feudalism that overtook the Roman cities and their urban culture. A revival of the Italian towns commenced around the year 1000, first in the rich plains of Lombardy and then, having overleaped the Apennines, in the hills and valleys of Tuscany. The urban revival owed its life to certain improvements in the towns themselves: greater public security, a rebirth of trade, a renewal of industrial crafts, and a restoration of civic pride. Everywhere the revival produced the same characteristics: an emerging class of merchants who formed protective associations called guilds, craftsmen who formed craft guilds of their own, and the formation of rudimentary town governments — communes — to assume responsibility for common concerns.

In the case of Florence, the first mention of the existence of a merchant guild occurred in 1182; the first reference to a craft guild, in 1193. A commune already existed. In theory, political power resided in the *parlamentum,* the general assembly of people; in practice, the *parlamentum* yielded its power to a *concilium* of some 150 members drawn from the uppermost stratum of society. Florentine aristocracy consisted of merchant adventurers and a landed nobility that more and more staked its future in the town itself. As those classes intermarried, they were fused into a single elite that held the real power in the commune.

The existence of these independent, constitutional, republican communes that dotted Lombardy and Tuscany was legally dubious. Sovereignty belonged to the Hohenstaufen emperors, and as long as the Hohenstaufens could enforce their will upon northern Italy, the existence of the republican communes was precarious. Only when the Hohenstaufen power collapsed in the middle of the thirteenth century could the unmolested towns assert their liberties. It is no accident that the first Florentine republic was declared in 1250, the year of the death of the Hohenstaufen emperor Frederick II.

The demise of the Hohenstaufen house produced in Florence a revolutionary energy that would not be denied. The people themselves, not the aristocracy, established a popular government, which was actually called *il primo populo,* or the First Democracy. Brought into being by an anti-imperial explosion, it was a Guelphic* regime — republican, urban, and papal in its sympathies. The Ghibellines,† on the contrary, were conservative and deeply committed to the principle of empire. In Florence the revolutionary zeal exceeded the boundaries of the city itself; its protagonists would not be content until the whole of Tuscany had been made Guelph. At such a prospect, however, the staunchly Ghibelline towns of Pisa and Siena reacted fiercely. The issue was decided in battle. In 1260, under the walls of Siena, the Florentines were beaten, and their rout was so great that the Sienese were able to enter the undefended city of Florence itself and topple the First Democracy. The Roman papacy could not tolerate such offense to its Guelphic allies; it called upon the French, who swept away the last of the Hohenstaufens and virtually obliterated Ghibelline power in Italy. Florence, once more Guelph, exiled all Ghibellines and ruined them absolutely by distributing their wealth.

---

* "Guelf" (or "Guelph," from the Italian Guelfo, from the German princely family Welf) designates a great political faction in Italy, well formed by the twelfth century, which opposed the authority of the German emperors in Italy. In the long medieval struggle between the empire and the papacy, Guelfs instinctively took the side of the papacy. The party of the new industrial civilization in Italy, the Guelfs were, more often than not, the party of the city republics that were contending against the empire for their rights and liberties.

† "Ghibelline" is from the Italian Ghibellino, a corruption perhaps of Waiblingen, a German estate belonging to the Hohenstaufen family. "Waiblingen" may have become an imperialist (i.e., Hohenstaufen) battle cry. In Italy, "Ghibelline" became the party name of the Italian imperialists — that great class of people, often nobles, whose interests and wealth had been inherited and who found their best advantage to lie in the imperialist idea, as against both the papacy and the new city republics.

GUILDS AND THE GOVERNMENT OF FLORENCE

THE PACIFICATION of Tuscany by the Guelphs was attended by an economic boom, particularly in Florence. Based upon a burgeoning trade in woolen cloth and upon the stable gold florin, which the First Democracy had had the foresight to mint, the boom brought forward the *arti maggiore* (major guilds) in Florence. The members of these seven guilds, listed below, constituted the business elite of the city.

- Arte dei Giudici e Notai — lawyers and notaries, who enjoyed the highest esteem
- Arte della Lana — makers of woolen cloth
- Arte di Calimala — importers of unfinished woolen cloth from Flanders
- Arte di Por Santa Maria — silk merchants
- Arte del Cambio — bankers
- Arte dei Medici, Speziali, e Merciai — doctors; apothecaries; merchants who sold spices, dyes, and medicines; certain artists and craftsmen (e.g., painters) who, buying their colors from the guild, were admitted to it
- Arte dei Vaccai e Pellicciai — dealers in animals skins and furs

In addition to the *arti maggiore,* there were five leading craft guilds, the *arti medie,* representing blacksmiths and shoemakers, carpenters and masons, and nine lesser guilds, the *arti minori,* representing the shopkeepers and artisans. In 1282, without much fanfare, the *arti maggiore,* in cooperation with the leading craft guilds, formed what might be called a guild government. From among their own ranks, they selected an executive branch, a *signoria,* consisting of six "priors," who served two months and were then replaced by six others.

In 1293 that somewhat precarious government succeeded in promulgating a document that became the basis of Florentine constitutional history: "The Ordinances of Justice." A government of six priors was affirmed by these ordinances, and then a seventh was added, the *gonfaloniere,* standard-bearer, the head and spokesman of the six. The ordinances also extended the foundations of the state to include all the guilds then in existence: the seven major, the five middle, and the nine minor. These twenty-one guilds had the political distinction of carrying on their rosters the names of all citizens eligible to be priors. The constitution of 1293 thus bespeaks the

161

parity of the guilds. History teaches us, however, that the rulers of Florence came mainly from the *arti maggiore.* The little people — *populo minuto,* the mass of unorganized workers, a vast proletariat — had no franchise at all.

The government was formed in this way: the names of guild members eligible for election were placed in a leather purse called *Borse,* kept in the sacristy of the Franciscan church, Santa Croce. Every two months, in a public ceremony, names were drawn out at random. Citizens selected were "priors." The government they constituted was *signoria,* the regime. All *priori* were required to leave their homes immediately and move into the Palazzo della Signoria, where they were obliged to remain for their two-month term. Foreign policy, war, internal security, and commerce were all dealt with by this government or by committees elected from time to time to do so. The crucial condition in this procedure was the word "eligible." The roster of the guild members was subjected to *scrutino,* a screening process to discover, for example, whether each was over thirty, or whether each was untarnished by bad debts. Increasingly, however, *scrutino* came to mean political reliability, and it was the means used to control power in the Florentine republic.

It is a curiosity that Florence did not produce a Giorgione or a Titian, who might have celebrated the almost idyllic landscape in which the city is set. The reason may lie in the fact that Florence's physical beauty faded away before the threat of her enemies. Directly west, controlling the single outlet to the sea, was Pisa — prosperous, powerful, and Ghibelline. Blocking the road to Pisa and thus to the sea was Lucca, an indomitable and vexing little power. To the south was pretentious Siena, fancying itself as great as Florence and blocking the road to Rome. To the north was Milan, ravenous for northern Italian power. To the east were the wolves — the petty tyrants in the Papal States or, worse, the greedy popes themselves. The latter half of the thirteenth century and the first half of the fourteenth century were filled with conflict between Florence and her neighbors. It was, nevertheless, an age of great prosperity in Florence. It was based on capitalism and was a time of civic progress and conviviality.

In a single year of 1338, according to the chronicler Villani, the *Arte di Calimala* imported ten thousand pieces of cloth at a value of 300,000 florins, while the *Arte della Lana* manufactured eighty thousand pieces of new cloth from start to finish at a value of over one million florins. In the two hundred shops of the *Arte della Lana,* nearly one-third of Florence's 100,000 people worked.

Those two guilds, plus the *Arte del Cambio* of the bankers, formed the basis of Florentine prosperity, one so pronounced that it enabled its citizens to maintain both hospitals and schools even in the 1300s, as the Renaissance began. Around the *arti maggiore,* all the guilds and professions managed to thrive: the cloth merchants, their wealth manifest in sumptuous clothing and foppish children; the haughty lawyers, stuffed with legal intelligence acquired at Bologna or Pisa; the doctors, Padua-trained in medical lore, yet vexed by toxins and diseases and fearful of some new deadly scourge; the apothecaries, pill-rollers and purveyors of pigments to the painters; the painters, whose ego and poverty alike were assuaged by popular adulation; the barbers, who did minor surgery, bloodletting, and tooth extraction on the side; the rambunctious butchers, who, when arrested for being drunk and disorderly, declared in self-justification, "We feed the people"; the courtesans, outlawed but omnipresent. (These comments are based on the chroniclers. For a few choice phrases, I am indebted to T. C. Chubb, *The Life of Giovanni Boccaccio* [Port Washington, N.Y.: Kennikat Press, 1969], pp. 25–27.)

Florentine capitalism peaked about 1336. Two Florentine merchant companies, the Bardi and the Peruzzi, having been encouraged by swollen profits, made political loans to both England and France. Over a million florins (worth roughly $50 million) was invested in the two sides of the Hundred Years' War. In 1339 Edward III of England defaulted on his debts to the Florentine firms, then repudiated them altogether. The Bardi Bank collapsed. A run occurred on the other Florentine banks. A war with Lucca, then raging, had run up Florence's public debt to a half million florins. A landslide of business failures occurred, with shattering unemployment.

Faced with financial disaster, the Florentine bankers themselves decided to give tyranny a try. In September 1342 they established the French adventurer Walter of Brienne as *podestà* for life. The dim-witted "duke" lasted a year, when the whole populace arose to throw him out. The government of the priors was restored. The economic depression persisted, however, and the misery of Florence was increased because of several factors: (1) the Black Death of 1348, (2) successive famines during the quarter century that followed the Black Death, and (3) the interminable conflicts, now with Milan, now with Pisa, now with the papacy. War expenditures pushed the public debt ever higher, leading to the creation of a state bank, *monte communale,* which sold public shares and kept public books.

In March 1348 the Black Death penetrated the walls of Florence; by May the disease seemed completely insatiable; by June it had run its course, having consumed some sixty thousand Florentines. Boccaccio lived through the plague in Florence. His *Decameron* consists of stories told by ten young men and women who, having isolated themselves against the contagion, found amusement by telling ribald tales. The disease was highly contagious; it could be communicated by the mere touch of infected clothing. It worked havoc on public morality. Mothers abandoned their children; husbands, their wives. Bodies were heaped up in huge burial trenches until the hole had been completely filled. Boccaccio, from whom most of these observations come, has left this description of the plague:

> On men and women alike, there appeared at the beginning of the disease certain swellings, either in the groin or under the armpit, some of which grew as large as an average apple, some larger, some smaller; and these the people called buboes [hence, "bubonic plague"] or plague-boils. From those two parts of the body, the plague-boils spread, until in a short time they appeared on every part of the body; and these, after a while, the course of the plague changed into black, livid blotches, which showed themselves first on the arms and on the thighs, and later in every other part of the body, in some cases large and few in number; in others, small and thickly-strewn. . . . Few recovered, but nearly all died within the third day from the appearance of the symptoms, some sooner, some later, but generally without fever or other complication.

The domestic crisis came to a head in 1378 with the revolt of the Ciompi. The economic disasters that had begun in 1339 called into question the competence of the guild government and of the merchant oligarchy and provoked a demand for representative government. *Ciompi* had come into vogue during the 1300s as a word to describe the lowest-paid wool workers, who wore clogs in the washhouses. In the summer of 1378, following a riotous winter and spring, the Ciompi revolted, aided and abetted by the whole proletariat and members of the lesser guilds. "Down with the traitors who allow us to starve" was the sage observation with which they burned the houses of the merchant oligarchy. The *gonfaloniere,* Salvestro de' Medici, although a merchant, could not disguise his sympathy for the Ciompi. In the autumn, the Ciompi succeeded in establishing a popular government. The priors were routed, and the constitution was reformed. Three new guilds were authorized to represent the disenfranchised and to offset the power of the *arti maggiore.* Nine new priors were selected: three from the major guilds, three from the lesser guilds, and three from the new guilds. Piero degli Albizzi and other leaders of the oligarchy were executed for conspiracy; still others were sent to exile.

This populist government collapsed in 1382. It had proved difficult for the small bourgeoise and the industrial workers to maintain the unity that had made the revolution successful. It took merely four years for the merchants, in collusion with the shopkeepers of the lesser guilds, to crush the democratic regime. The three new guilds were suppressed. Henceforth, half of the priors were to come from the *arti maggiore,* half from the remaining, authorized guilds.

Meanwhile two great states had arisen in the north: Milan under the Visconti, and Venice, a maritime power now encroaching upon the mainland. The threat from the north caused Florence to renew its effort to control Tuscany. In 1384 it took Arezzo on the upper Arno; in 1406 it finally accomplished the feat of capturing the coastal city of Pisa. Only Lucca and Siena eluded the Florentine fold. But Milan, under Gian Galeazzo Visconti, had even bolder designs — to create a great northern Italian state into which Florence itself must be brought by subjugation. Gian Galeazzo evolved a strategy of surrounding Florence, eventually choking it into submission.

Upon the fall of the Ciompi, the Florentine oligarchy passed again into the control of the Albizzi family, members of the *Arte della Lana.* Maso degli Albizzi was head of the family and de facto head of the state. It was he who saw Florence through the crisis of encirclement by Milan, which ended in 1402 upon the sudden death of Gian Galeazzo Visconti. The respite, however, was short. In 1421 the Visconti threatened again, as Filippo Maria Visconti moved against Tuscany. As quickly as that threat had passed, Florence elected in 1429 to subdue Lucca. The public became weary of war. As campaign after campaign against Lucca failed, opinion turned sharply against Rinaldo degli Albizzi, who then represented his family in power and who favored the war effort. Another party, however, had imperceptibly arisen; it was a rather more populist party that believed that foreign policy should be pursued through peace and diplomacy. It was under the conspicuous leadership of one Cosimo de' Medici, who, though not a member of the ruling oligarchy, was the richest banker in the city.

According to legend, the Medici were descended from Averardo, a knight of the emperor Charlemagne, who slew a savage monster while once in Tuscany, his shield being dented by the monster's mace. Charlemagne allowed Averardo to represent the dents on a coat of arms — red balls *(palle)* on a field of gold. Others scoffed at the legend, maintaining that the *palle* were pills which illustrated the name Medici, or coins representing the family business. As early as 1282, when the government of the priors was first constituted, Medicis were enrolled on the lists of the *arti maggiore.* A century later, in the Ciompi uprising of 1378, Salvestro de' Medici, as *gonfaloniere* of Florence, stood with the disenfranchised against the oligarchy and thereby earned a certain populist reputation for the Medicis. Wealth came to the next generation. Giovanni di Bicci de' Medici was born in 1360 in relative poverty. When he died in 1429, he had amassed a fortune, had founded the Medici bank, and ranked first among Florentine capitalists. Never ambitious for political power, he did serve terms as prior and was once *gonfaloniere;* his passion, however, was business, and he was content to let the Albizzi rule. It was Giovanni di Bicci's son, Cosimo, who contended with the Albizzi over issues of war and peace.

On September 7, 1433, Rinaldo degli Albizzi, stung by Cosimo's criticism of his war policies, elected to rid himself of Cosimo by a political trick almost as old as Florence itself. The great bell in the campanile of the Palazzo della Signoria was tolled. The people gathered for the *parlamentum* — an assembly that was hoary with age but, strictly speaking, without any standing in the "Ordinances of Justice." The Albizzi controlled all entrances to the Piazza della Signoria, so that only political desirables were admitted. They shouted for a *balia,* an emergency committee with power to "reform" the government in any crisis, real or contrived. On September 29 the *balia* resolved the so-called crisis by dispatching Cosimo de' Medici into exile. He retired to Venice, grateful to be alive.

FLORENTINE ARTS AND LEARNING

THE ARTISTIC triumph of Florence did not await the advent of the Medici. Beginning in 1250, when the First Democracy was founded, and extending through the 1300s, the government of Florence undertook a series of secular and religious buildings, built in a Gothic style peculiar to Tuscany and therefore referred to as Florentine Gothic or Tuscan Gothic. It employed Gothic structural principles and the Gothic vault, but it softened the vertical character of northern Gothic with a definite sense of harmony and proportion inherited from classical antiquity. Equally important, it did not dissolve the walls, as northern Gothic sometimes did, but proclaimed the quintessence of walls as places of art. It is important to remember that pre-Medicean architecture in Florence was a form of Gothic, not of the Renaissance.

The first of the Florentine buildings in preeminence, if not in age, was the cathedral — Santa Maria del Fiore (see plate 27) — which was begun in 1296 upon the patronage of the *Arte della Lana,* whose emblem of a lamb remains noticeable on its walls. The original design was done by the reigning architectural master of the day, Arnolfo di Cambio. The structure was enlarged several times by later architects and architectural committees, to guarantee to the Florentines that their cathedral would excel those of Pisa and Siena. The Florentines, in fact, almost overreached the limits of engineering possibility; they created a drum for the dome so large that no one knew how to bridge the distance. Pisa and Siena tittered at the gaping hole. It was left to Brunelleschi in the quattrocento to work the miracle of Florence's dome. The painter Giotto commenced the free-standing campanile of the cathedral soon after he became *cap maestro* (architect-in-chief) in 1334. The baptistry of Florence, which stands in front of the present cathedral, and which was the cathedral itself in the early Middle Ages, defies being dated; it belongs perhaps to the eighth century. People of the quattrocento, thinking it to be an ancient temple of Mars, hastened to copy from it as an example of antiquity.

The thirteenth-century religious movements, both Dominican and Franciscan, caused the friars to build churches in almost every Italian town. In Florence, the Dominican church was Santa Maria Novella, a Florentine Gothic structure, begun in 1246 and completed in the quattrocento in time to accommodate the Council of Florence in 1439. Dominicans were preachers; their church was designed for good acoustics and large crowds. The Franciscans, being devoted to the principle of poverty, could not make up their minds whether to build a church or not. They compromised by building a splendid church in a poor neighborhood, and they called it Santa Croce, Holy Cross. It was begun in 1294, according to plans by Arnolfo di Cambio. Scarcely had the nave been built than Giotto commenced to decorate its walls. Such was the preoccupation of the Florentines with walls.

Of the public buildings, the oldest was the Bargello, built by the First Democracy between 1250 and 1260 as the seat of the government. It was replaced by a prominent civic structure variously called Palazzo della Signoria, Palazzo dei Priori, or Palazzo Vecchio. Designed by Arnolfo di Cambio and constructed between 1299 and 1310, the simplicity and force of the Palazzo della Signoria was meant to represent the human capability of governing. A great piazza was cleared in front of this building, partly by the destruction of houses in which Ghibellines had lived. It became the Piazza della Signoria, where all great state occasions occurred, where the *parlamentum* met at the tolling of the bell, and where Savonarola died. In the midst of the piazza, the Florentines completed the Loggia dei Lanzi in

38. Santa Maria Novella

1382 as a setting for ceremonial occasions; today it houses the sculpture of quattrocento and cinquecento masters.

Florence was the home of Italian humanism. Throughout the Middle Ages, intellectuals had entertained the dream of a new Athens, in which the rebirth of learning would occur. Florence, in her own self-conscious estimate, became that new Athens. In its schools, academies, houses of wealthy citizens, and churches and cloisters, humanism was made to flourish. Florence created the first civic libraries of the Renaissance.

Florence also holds a preeminent place in the development of vernacular Italian poetry, having been the home to the three great fourteenth-century poets: Dante, Petrarch and Boccaccio. Dante Alighieri was born in Florence in 1265, and it was in the city of his birth that his earliest poetry, including the important *Vita Nova,* was written. This poetry, like that of Petrarch and Boccaccio, was in the Tuscan dialect, and this helped to establish that dialect as the Italian literary language. During the 1290s

39. Palazzo della Signoria

Dante was also heavily involved in the politics of the city: in 1302 a division within the Guelph faction led to his exile from Florence. He was never to return. Nevertheless, Florence was very much in his mind, and his most important poem, *The Divine Comedy,* is very much concerned with the people and politics of the city.

Should Dante be considered a poet of the Renaissance? He certainly began his writing career at a time before the usual date assigned to the beginning of the Renaissance; however, that his poetry was so celebrated by humanists and fellow poets in the following three centuries while they were busy rejecting as barbarous other medieval works would argue in favor of seeing him as harbinger of the Renaissance. He could thus be seen to stand in relation to it as Giotto did in the world of painting. On the one hand, his intricate portrayal of the levels of Hell, Purgatory, and Heaven in *The Divine Comedy* certainly has a medieval, scholastic feel to it, but on the other it is the supreme classical Latin poet Virgil that leads the figure Dante through the first two-thirds of the poem. Like many works of the Renaissance, *The Divine Comedy* presents a coming together of the Christian and classical traditions.

Dante's literary heir was Francesco Petrarca (see plate 34), born in Arezzo, to which his family had been driven by the same political squabble between White and Black Guelphs that had driven Dante from Florence. From the mid-fourteenth century until his death in 1374, Petrarch would come to dominate the intellectual and literary scene of Florence in the mid-fifteenth century. While Francesco was still a boy, the elder Petrarch, a notary, found business in the French city of Avignon, the seat of the papacy. There, Petrarch had his early education and was exposed to the Latin classics of Virgil and Cicero that would have such an influence on his literary career. At his father's bidding, he embarked on a career in law — the most auspicious calling of the day. He attended the French university at Montpellier and concluded his legal training at the University of Bologna, the most celebrated Italian center for training in law. The law, however, did not satisfy his intellectual curiosity. He was equally indebted to the other side of the legacy from his father — a profound love of the ancient classics, especially Cicero. When his father expired in 1326 and the parental pressure was lifted, Petrarch made haste to Avignon, which was by then the seat of the papacy, a place of splendid learning and rich living. He soon found favor among the princes of the church who were stationed at Avignon and was even admitted to minor orders. Still, he assayed the Avignon papacy with a keenly critical eye; some of the most pungent criticism we have of that institution came from his pen.

Petrarch's literary ambitions were high: he desired to be a public poet in the way in which Virgil had served Rome during the time of Caesar Augustus. Toward this end, and through the patronage of the powerful Colonna family of Rome, he managed to have himself crowned poet laureate in 1341. The splendid ceremony on the Capitoline Hill was modeled on the laureations common in the Roman Empire. As part of the proceedings Petrarch delivered an oration on the nature of poetry. In the same instance, Robert, king of Naples, had commissioned him to "teach, dispute, and interpret the ancient writers, both in the poetic and the historical disciplines, and to compose new books and poetry by himself." His life was an ungainly mixture of activity and passivity. One minute, he was a recluse at Vaucluse, near Avignon, wholly dedicated to contemplation, study, and dour introspection. The next minute, he was wandering through Germany and the Netherlands, or enjoying the patronage of the Visconti of Milan, or of the Carrara of Padua, or of the councils of Venice. A man of the world, Petrarch was nevertheless essentially Italian. He retired at last to a small farm at Arqua, near Padua, where his daughter Francesca attended him until his death.

Petrarch wrote extensively in both Latin and Italian, but for him the Latin work was of far greater importance, for it was the language of Virgil and Horace, and ought to be the literary language of the revived Rome. His Latin poetry includes the epic *Africa* and numerous elegies. Petrarch would be surprised to learn that his posthumous fame depended much more upon his Italian verse, most of which is in the form of short lyric poems. Much of this Italian verse concerned Laura, his ideal love. Like Dante's Beatrice, the biographical facts about Laura are less important than the ideal that she represented for the poet. Both Petrarch's poetic style and his treatment of the figure Laura were to have a profound influence on Italian, French and English poetry of the next few centuries. Poets came to look back on his work as a model in the same way that he had looked to Virgil and Horace. His classical scholarship deserves treatment of its own, and will be considered in the next chapter.

Like Petrarch, the Florentine writer Boccaccio ranged widely in his writings: he was both scholar and poet, and used both Latin and Italian. Exactly nine years after the birth of Petrarch, Boccaccio was born in Paris, where his father, a member of the Florentine bankers' guild, was stationed. His mother was French; he was begotten out of wedlock. Boccaccio was raised in Florence, where he was educated, first in *grammatica,* and then in the more practical *arismetrica,* which outfitted one for banking and business.

40. Boccaccio, shown in detail from a mural painting by Martini Simona in the cloister of Santa Maria Novella

In the fall of 1327 Boccaccio's father was dispatched to Naples as an agent of the Bardi Bank. Boccaccio went along and soon found himself employed as a teller in the Neapolitan branch of the Bardi firm. However, he found much more entertainment in the glittering court of the Anjou kings. Robert of Anjou, called Robert the Wise, reigned in Naples. Out of the medieval squalor, a new Naples was rising — a city of resplendent buildings, a university, and a sumptuous court. Boccaccio happily participated in that world of gaiety and sensuality.

The Bardi Bank collapsed, and in 1340 Boccaccio returned to Florence with his father. There he found solace in reading the ancient classics and in committing his own thoughts to writing. He knew Italian life, and he had made himself a master of Italian prose and verse. Among his early works was *Filicolo,* a prose romance, based on a traditional French story, and

Filostrato, a verse romance which was to greatly influence the English poet Chaucer. Among his most important works in verse was the *Teseida,* believed to be the first epic written in Tuscan.

However, Boccaccio's greatest work was his *Decameron,* which owed its existence to the Black Death of 1348. Seeking to escape the contagion, seven young Florentine women went to the Church of Santa Maria Novella, where they were soon joined by three young men. The ten of them decided to retire to a villa, some two miles beyond the walls of Florence, to wait out the plague. There they amused themselves by telling stories — ten stories by ten narrators, exactly one hundred stories in all.

There are two unmistakable themes in the tales. One is the inevitability and the implausibility of love. Does not love make men and women brave, clever, generous, and even heroic, but at the same time dishonest, unscrupulous, and deceitful? The second theme is the human frailty that seems to attach itself to members of the cloth — to priests, monks, friars, and nuns. For example, one tale describes the amorous adventures of a Franciscan friar, Alberto of Imola, a man of doubtful reputation before he became a Franciscan, who makes his way into the bed of a giddy girl from Venice by convincing her that the angel Gabriel himself proposed to visit her chambers. The *Decameron* was an enormously popular book in the age of the Renaissance: it not only contributed handsomely to the creation of an Italian literary language, but had an influence far beyond the Italian peninsula.

Boccaccio became the very first interpreter of Dante. In the 1350s and 1360s he wrote *In Praise of Dante,* as well as a commentary on the first seventeen cantos of the *Divine Comedy.* On August 25, 1373, when Boccaccio was an old man, the city of Florence appointed him the first public lecturer on the life and literary remains of Dante.

The immediate successor of Boccaccio in the lineage of Florentine humanists was Coluccio Salutati (1331–1406), who became chancellor in 1375 and held that office until his death. Coluccio was a prime example of a civic humanist. Trained in law at Bologna, he used all of his classical education, especially his fine Ciceronian Latin, in the service of the state — which he deemed to be the only proper purpose of humanism. It was he, more than any other, who led Florence safely through the Ciompi uprising of 1378 without political instability or extravagant reprisals. And when Florence was encircled by Gian Galeazzo Visconti in the last decade of the fourteenth century Coluccio pressed the tradition of Florence as a free republic, descended from Rome. In elegant Latin letters, written from the

Palazzo Vecchio, he attempted to form alliances among the free cities against all "tyrants," especially the tyrant from Milan. Furthermore, he appealed to the republican dignity of Florence, "the mother of freedom and . . . the glory of nations." Gian Galeazzo declared Coluccio more potent than the Milanese militia and unsuccessfully sent assassins to remove him.

So far we have seen how Coluccio used his humanistic learning for civic purposes. The connection between the two was rhetoric. Rhetoric is the doctrine or system of the correct use of language — in Coluccio's case, Latin. Rhetoric is therefore the means by which what we know to be true can be made clear and persuasive to others. Rhetoric is the ultimate utility of language; it alone accomplishes the civilizing effect of language. (Contrast the corrupted, modern use of this word in a phrase such as "campaign rhetoric.")

Coluccio wrote a number of moral treatises (e.g., *On the Labors of Hercules; On the World and Religion; On the Tyrant*) that were circulated throughout Italy. In almost every instance, he defined virtue, as Cicero had, in civic terms. Culture, he said, should never be self-sufficient. The true task of a humanist is to participate in the affairs of a republican city where freedom still had meaning and value. Implicit in the things he wrote was the assumption that a human being was fully free to shape his or her own destiny.

Around Coluccio gathered the new generation of Florentine humanists. They assembled at his house or at the *Studium* (university) to exchange ideas or discuss the classics. Even more than Christianity, certainly more than the cobweb divinity of the medieval schools, the ancient classics were deemed the safest guides to moral, civil, and political conduct. In the circle were Niccolò Niccoli, a merchant, who devoted himself to the classics and lived and dressed like the ancients, and Palla Strozzi, the son of a banking family, who collected a precious library of classical works. In 1397, owing to their persuasion, Manuel Chrysolarus was appointed to the *Studium* as professor of Greek. He was a distinguished Byzantine scholar of classical Greek who trained still another generation of humanists, who were distinguished by the fact that they knew Greek and were experts in philology.

The death of Coluccio in 1406 did not interrupt the tradition of Florentine humanism. Coluccio's place was taken by two of his disciples, Leonardo Bruni and Poggio Bracciolini. Bruni, who came from nearby Arezzo, pursued a humanistic education in Florence; he mastered Greek at the instruction of Chrysolarus and entered the intellectual circle of Coluccio Salutati. In 1410, having served both the Medici as family tutor and the papacy as apostolic secretary, Leonardo assumed the office of chancellor of Florence and saw the republic through still more crises of foreign policy.

Bruni is remembered for two things: his civic humanism and his philosophy of education. The former he expressed in two books: *Laudatio urbis florentinae* (Praise of Florence), a work of utmost eloquence in which he sought to enhance the patriotic zeal of the Florentines, and *Historia populi florentini* (History of the people of Florence), in which he tried to establish a critical history of the city on the basis of archival research rather than the medieval chroniclers. In both books, Bruni offered unstinting praise of the republican, the humanistic, and the artistic traditions of Florence, each of which he attempted to pursue back to classical civilization. The real legacy of Athens and Rome was Florence — except that Florence was even more splendid than they were.

Bruni was also a philosopher of education. He believed in the Renaissance ideal of *studia humanitatis:* only by study and reflection can human beings attain *humanitas.* In particular, Bruni believed in the importance of rhetoric. "To enable us to make effectual use of what we know," he wrote in *On Studies and Letters,* "we must add to our knowledge the power of expression."

Through the persistence of Coluccio Salutati, Leonardo Bruni, and their followers, humanism began to permeate all aspects of Florentine life. It became not a curious phenomenon of measurable interest to social scientists but a way of life, a driving force in Florentine culture and civic life in the quattrocento. It affected, for example, the rising artists: Brunelleschi, Donatello, and Masaccio. Through a network of correspondence, the Florentine humanists were in touch with humanistic circles in other cities and lands: Ferrara, Milan, Venice, Paris, even with Humphrey of Gloucester at the court of England.

When in 1444 the body of Leonardo Bruni was lowered into the fine tomb prepared for him by Rossellino in Santa Croce, a copy of his *History of the People of Florence* placed upon his breast and a laurel wreath laid upon his head by Giannozzo Manetti, who gave the eulogy, the happiest age of Florentine humanism was over. Cosimo de' Medici was now the head of state. The era of republican humanism was quite perceptibly slipping away.

Bruni was succeeded, both as the leading Florentine humanist and as chancellor of the republic, by Poggio Bracciolini, doubtless the most famous living humanist, but by now a tired old man. A contemporary of Niccolò Niccoli, Poggio had grown up in Florence, had learned Greek from Chrysolarus, and had been drawn into the circle of Coluccio Salutati. Prolific in many ways, he sired innumerable children — some by less than honorable means — and penned a vast collection of letters. Poggio Bracciolini was kept away from Florence most of his life by his duties for the papacy in Rome. As an apostolic secretary, he was dispatched to search out rare classical volumes by several of the popes, notably Nicholas V. His many letters to Niccolò, asking news of Florence, reported the book findings he had managed to make. In his view of things, classical books were "in prison" in one monastic library or other; by finding them, he had done the whole world a service by "liberating" the books from oblivion. Never mind that he actually purloined them! The victims were unsuspecting monks, for whom he had the lowest possible opinion. By such means, the world of the quattrocento acquired Quintillian's *Institutio,* Lucretius's *De natura rerum,* several of Cicero's orations, several of Tacitus's historical works, as well as the works of the classical architect Vitruvius, upon whose ideas the Renaissance architects depended. In this way the basis of the Vatican Library was laid.

As chancellor of Florence in his old age, Poggio saw the duties of that once-respected office reduced to the job of rendering Cosimo de' Medici's diplomatic notes into Latin. When Poggio was buried on October 30, 1459, Florence also mourned the passing of republican humanism; after Poggio, the center of Florentine humanism shifted from the republican chancellery to the court of the Medicis.

COSIMO DE' MEDICI

IN SEPTEMBER 1434, when the names of new priors were drawn from the *Borse,* the war-weary Florentines had deposed the Albizzi. The new priors were Medicean. Cosimo de' Medici, having been recalled from exile, returned to Florence in triumph. Rinaldo degli Albizzi rattled his saber, but the threat of civil war was averted by the timely intervention of Pope Eugenius IV, who, having been harried out of Rome by the Colonna, graced the church of Santa Maria Novella in Florence.

Cosimo was a complex man. He was a humanist according to education, a conventional Christian, a businessman of vast wealth, a politician who enjoyed power but chose not to show it. "Always," he said, "stay out of the public eye." He traveled the streets of Florence as if he were nobody, riding a mule instead of a horse, allowing the vain and pretentious Luca Pitti to appear as the most powerful man in the city. When the architect

41. Cosimo de' Medici, portrait by Bronzino

Brunelleschi presented plans for a sumptuous Medici Palace, Cosimo rejected them, saying, "Envy is a plant that should not be watered." Yet, power existed in order to be used. "States," he said, "are not well governed by paternosters" (i.e., by prayers, clerics, etc.). However subtly he held the reigns of government, his control of Florence was almost absolute. Aeneas Silvius, soon to be Pope Pius II, described Cosimo as "master of the country." "Political questions are settled at his house. The man he chooses holds office. . . . He it is who decides peace and war and controls the laws. . . . He is king in everything but name."

Politics did not tempt him to neglect his bank. Branches were opened or maintained in almost every capital and commercial center in Europe: London, Naples, Cologne, Geneva, Lyons, Basel, Avignon, Bruges, Antwerp, Lübeck, Ancona, Bologna, Rome, Pisa, Venice, and Milan. In 1470 the average number of men employed at the various branches was between nine and ten.

Three particulars of Cosimo's public career require our notice: ecclesiastical affairs, foreign affairs, and patronage of the arts. In ecclesiastical affairs, the most absorbing issue of the day was the dome of the cathedral — or rather the lack of one. As Pisa, Lucca, and Siena guffawed, Florence gazed with embarrassment at the gaping hole in its duomo — 140 feet from side to side. No wooden beam could be found to bridge such a space; therefore no scaffolding could be built to support the construction of a dome according to conventional methods, that is, until the keystone could lock the arches together. Someone suggested that the cathedral crossing should be filled with dirt, upon which the dome could be built; by the simple expedient of mixing pennies with the dirt, the greedy Florentines would then see to its removal when the dome was up and the keystone in place. In 1418 Brunelleschi, the father of Renaissance architecture, arrived at a solution. In part, it was a classical solution, based upon the construction of the Pantheon in Rome, which Brunelleschi had studied — namely, a series of horizontal courses, each bonded to its predecessor. In part, it was a Gothic solution, with eight major ribs carrying the weight of the dome down to the drum. It was a work of enormous perspicacity, the first great architectural feat of the Renaissance.

With Pope Eugenius in residence and the dome complete, Cosimo elected to consecrate the cathedral on March 25, 1436, the Feast of the Annunciation, and the Florentine New Year. A canopied boardwalk, festooned with banners, was built all the way from Santa Maria Novella to the cathedral. On it walked the pope, turned out in white, tottering under the weight of his jeweled tiara; accompanying him were seven cardinals dressed in scarlet, thirty-seven prelates, the *gonfaloniere,* and the priors. In that duomo, three years later, there was celebrated the reunion of the Greek and Latin churches.

Greek and Latin Christianity had been split for six centuries — a severance that the sack of Constantinople by the crusaders in 1204 did nothing but aggravate. Now the Turks, having encircled Constantinople, threatened to extinguish that city. The Eastern emperor, John VIII Paleologus, appealed to the West for help in the name of Christ; the pope, Eugenius IV, foreseeing a reunion of Greek and Latin Christianity, summoned an ecumenical council to meet in Ferrara on January 8, 1438. Ferrara was cold, and money was short; the Greek and Latin divines fought, and finally the plague broke out. Cosimo was delighted. He invited the council to come to Florence, where, to his way of thinking, it should have been in the first place. It would be good for international business. It would be good for *rinascimento,* "renaissance" — a word now heard more frequently in Florence. The Council of Florence, which met in Santa Maria Novella, concluded an agreement, and the reunion of the two great branches of Christianity was celebrated in the Florence cathedral on July 5, 1439. One of the piers that support Brunelleschi's dome carried an inscription that immortalized the event. But the conservative Greeks at home denounced it, and the reunion finally came to nothing.

The council, as Cosimo suspected, moved Florence into the very forefront of Renaissance humanism. The Greek prelate Bessarion, a classical scholar of great prominence, was prevailed upon to remain in Italy. Gemistos Plethon, thought to be the greatest living authority on Plato, lectured nightly before hushed audiences of Italian scholars, including Cosimo himself; Plato thereby became a living intellectual force in Florence. Moved by the lectures of the aged Plethon, Cosimo endowed a Florentine Academy devoted to Platonic studies and commissioned a young medical student, Marsilio Ficino, to devote himself single-mindedly to the translation and study of Plato.

In the intervals between the sessions of the council, scholars met in conversation. The humanist Vespasiano has left an account of the debates that often occurred in the evening in the Piazza della Signoria. There one might have heard sage comments from Leonardo Bruni or the brittle remarks of Poggio, the scholarly opinions of Tommaso Parentucelli, a near genius who would succeed to the papacy as Nicholas V, the gentle wisdom of Ambrogio Traversari, who had turned the Camaldolese convent in Florence, of which he was prior, into a center of humanistic study, or the eloquent Latin of Giannozzo Manetti. The debaters were men of the church, of the university, and of the state. They were united, perhaps, in one common assumption: that human beings were free, rational beings who were, or at least ought to be, devoted to the classical values of peace and proportion, virtuous character and civic duty.

The humanist who most nearly exemplified Florentine humanism in the age of the council was Giannozzo Manetti (1396–1459), whose treatise *On the Dignity and Excellency of Man* could not possibly be a more forthright declaration of human freedom and potential. To humankind, Manetti ascribes the completion of divine creation. What God "roughed out," as we might say, human beings have brought not only to completion but indeed to perfection, "through the unique and extraordinary acumen of the human mind." All of the achievements of human beings, from the pyramids of ancient Egypt to Brunelleschi's dome, are evidences of human freedom and power. Implicit in almost everything Manetti says in this important book is the viewpoint that human freedom of will is virtually untrammeled.

Cosimo was the supreme arbiter of Florentine foreign policy. The first problem he faced was Milan. Rinaldo degli Albizzi incited the reigning Visconti prince, Filippo Maria, to make war on Florence, expecting thereby to unseat the Medici. In June of 1440, in the battle of Anghiari, Florence routed the Milanese decisively, leaving the Albizzi finally without hope. That was the victory Leonardo da Vinci was commissioned to commemorate in the Palazzo della Signoria.

In 1447, when Filippo Maria died, the issue of succession arose in Milan. Cosimo supported the claims of Francesco Sforza, the Milanese condottiere, with whose splendid bearing and overweening personality he was greatly taken. In 1450 Sforza was in fact proclaimed duke of Milan. That event was attended by a fundamental shift in Florentine foreign policy, as we noted in chapter 7. Heretofore the Florentine alliance with Venice had been sacrosanct; Milan had been the enemy. Cosimo argued the contrary. Venice, with its new pretentions to mainland power, was the more dangerous. In August 1450, shortly after Sforza came to power, Florence signed a formal alliance with Milan. The repercussions were startling. Venice and Naples, having struck an alliance, declared war on Florence and Milan, thus precipitating one of the most momentous crises in Italian history. It ended, however, as suddenly as it arose. On May 29, 1453, the Turks took Constantinople. The shock brought the Italians to terms with one another. At Lodi in the spring of the following year, the great powers — Florence, Milan,

42. Ospedale degli Innocenti

Venice, and the papacy — united in a "holy league" to guarantee the status quo in Italy and to withstand aggression from without. Cosimo henceforth based his foreign policy strictly upon peace and a posture of defense. His son, Piero, and his grandson, Lorenzo, made that policy the Medicean foreign policy.

The tradition of Medicean patronage of the arts actually began with Giovanni di Bicci. He, for example, commissioned new bronze doors for the baptistry in Florence. Lorenzo Ghiberti won the competition to do the doors and literally gave his lifetime to that extraordinary effort — twenty-two years to execute the north doors, twenty-eight more to do the east doors. Michelangelo Buonarroti stood transfixed before the east doors and declared them to be "gates of paradise." It was Giovanni di Bicci who helped to endow a new hospital for foundlings, Ospedale degli Innocenti, which Brunelleschi designed — the first structure in Florence representative of Renaissance architecture. Brunelleschi was also responsible for a radical new design of church interiors. In 1418 he was commissioned to remodel the Augustinian church of San Lorenzo, where the Medicis worshiped. He swept away the whole history of medieval architecture and introduced the classical

43. Brunelleschi, Church of San Lorenzo

form of a basilica. In the Ospedale degli Innocenti and in the Pazzi Chapel, which Brunelleschi built for the rich banking family of that name, one can grasp his architectural principles. He fuses faith and science, Christianity and antiquity. Classical forms and decorations are combined with a profound commitment to harmony and proportion, which is at once both classical and Christian; Brunelleschi is also trying to express divine proportion, the unity and perfection of God.

Meanwhile a twenty-four-year-old painter, Masaccio ("Ugly Tom") was decorating the chapel of the Brancacci family in the Church of Santa Maria del Carmine, across the river. He was painting a series of frescoes on the life of Peter. (Guelphs were partial to the papacy and thus to the first of all popes, Peter.) Though he lived to be only twenty-seven, Masaccio was one of the greatest painters of the Western tradition. It was he who led the Florentine artists deeper and deeper into the new Renaissance world of space, emotion, and action. Small wonder that Michelangelo Buonarroti could be found on many occasions in the Brancacci Chapel studying that work of Masaccio, the father of Renaissance painting.

Cosimo continued his father's patronage of the arts. He lavished funds upon the reconstruction of the Dominican convent of San Marco, spending nearly seven million florins on that edifice in the course of thirty-eight years. The reason is not hard to discover: the guilt of usury. Michelozzo, who designed the new San Marco, made provision in it for Cosimo's collection of books. When the library of San Marco opened in 1444, stocked with Cosimo's treasures as well as eight hundred precious volumes collected by Niccolò Niccoli, it was the first civic institution of its kind in Europe. The same Michelozzo drew rather more modest plans for the Medici Palace than those proposed by Brunelleschi and therefore received the commission to build that structure, which stands in the midst of Florence itself.

Cosimo was particularly devoted to Donatello, the most important sculptor of the early Renaissance. Donatello's bronze statue of David, one of the more perplexing pieces of Renaissance art, was likely the first freestanding bronze executed since antiquity. Cosimo also supported and tried to pacify the obstreperous painter Fra Filippo Lippi. Committed to the Carmelite friars at the age of sixteen, Fra Filippo was scarcely cut out for monastic life. He lied, drank, cheated, and chased women. When he escaped the convent, its officials were relieved; when he was captured by Barbary pirates, they were ecstatic. Once as he executed an altarpiece, he used a nun as a model of the Madonna. Fra Filippo, however, always becoming confused over the various classifications of love, carried her off;

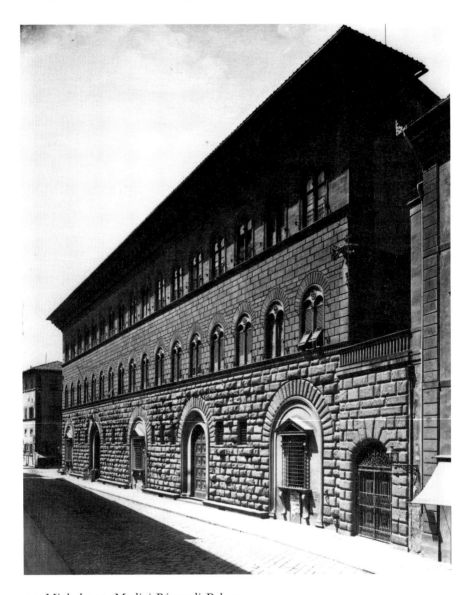

44. Michelozzo, Medici Riccardi Palace

later she bore him a son, Filippino, who became a painter like his father. Cosimo resorted to locking him up in the Medici Palace; he merely made ropes of the bedsheets and escaped.

A much holier "fra" was the precious Fra Angelico, who, at Cosimo's request, began in 1436 to decorate the corridors, cloisters, and chapter house of San Marco. There were other celebrated painters in Cosimo's time, but no evidence that he patronized them. Conspicuous among them were Paolo Uccello, who concerned himself with perspective, and Andrea del Castagno, a turbulent soul whose art was absorbed with the human inner emotional experience, with humankind's terrible dilemmas and tragic destiny.

Before we take leave of Cosimo, let us inquire into the overall fortunes of humanism in his time. An ardent admirer of the new culture, Cosimo intended to make his palazzo on the Via Largo in Florence *the* center of Florentine humanism. But the Medici Palace was not its only site. It flourished also in the *Studium,* which had heretofore been the undisputed preserve of medieval Scholasticism.

The leading humanists of Cosimo's time were Giannozzo Manetti, of whom we have already spoken, and Leon Battista Alberti, whom we consider in chapter 9. Alberti, one of the greater geniuses of the Italian Renaissance, was of Florentine stock, although his family had been banished from the city of Florence before his birth and he himself was drawn away from the city by numerous commissions. His influence, nevertheless, was felt profoundly in Florence. His books *On Building, On Painting,* and *On Sculpture* were definitive for Renaissance art. His lesser-known work *Della famiglia* (1443) was an unabashed apologia for the sort of republican, civic, middle-class humanism of which Florence was the best example. Purposeful work, bourgeois thrift, patriotic duty, usefulness to one's fellow human beings, and the ceaseless, restless pursuit of one's purposes — those were Alberti's recommendations; all of them were based on the premise that the individual possesses the free will to achieve them.

The most exciting feature of Florentine humanism in the age of Cosimo was no doubt the research of Marsilio Ficino into Platonic manuscripts, beginning in 1459. In the Medici villa at Careggi, Ficino gathered around him a group of Platonists who, while they did not despise the vigorous activity of the civic humanists, preferred the superior life of contemplation, based upon the philosophy of Plato. Thus was born the Platonic Academy, from which arose the Florentine tradition of Neoplatonism.

Akadēmia was indeed Plato's word. There were already Florentine academies in existence. One such circle, founded in 1456, called itself *Chorus*

Achademiae florentinae; it included illustrious youth (such as Lorenzi de' Medici) as well as the sages of the city. But Ficino's party was precisely *Accademia platonica* — the Platonic academy. Its members were steadfast in their commitment to the "divine" Plato and to other thinkers in the Platonic and Neoplatonic traditions; they conceived of themselves as "the Platonic family," of which Ficino was "father"; they referred to themselves as "brothers in Plato" and saluted each other with "greetings in Plato." On November 7, the date of Plato's birth and death, they held the "Symposium," at which, after dinner, Plato's *Symposium* was read aloud.

PIERO THE GOUTY

WHEN Cosimo died on August 1, 1464, in his seventy-sixth year, the Florentines buried him in San Lorenzo under a plain slab bearing the inscription *Pater Patriae* (father of the state), a title once ascribed to Cicero. He was succeeded by his eldest son, then forty-eight and afflicted with gout: Piero il Gottoso, Piero the Gouty. Lacking his father's flair, he was nevertheless a fine diplomat and a stickler for detail. Louis XI of France was so taken by him that he permitted the Medici to decorate one of their *palle* with the three lilies of Valois, requiring them to change one *palle* from red to blue.

The chief event of Piero's reign was the manifestation of an opposition party. It was led by Luca Pitti and Niccolò Soderini and certain other collaborators, all of whom believed that the iron rule of the Medici represented too great an infringement upon liberty. They called themselves the Party of the Hill (the Pitti Palace being on high ground across the Arno), as opposed to the Party of the Plain (the Medici Palace being in the city itself). Having failed to make headway in domestic politics, the Party of the Hill turned to Venice for help in unseating the Medici. Piero coolly summoned his soldiers to arms and sent to Milan for help. Luca Pitti lost his nerve and came galloping down the hill to beg Piero for forgiveness. The others were banished; they finally incited the Venetians to attack Florence. Venice dispatched its condottiere, Colleoni, toward the Tuscan frontier, but his forces were turned back, and the crisis ended.

Piero was an ardent bibliophile. He continued Cosimo's tradition of buying books. Particularly he supported the Platonic Academy, which Ficino had inaugurated. Painters, sculptors, and architects continued to enjoy Medicean patronage. Luca della Robbia, who had achieved fame for his *cantoria,* or choir stall, in the cathedral, executed terra-cotta reliefs for Piero

45. Piero the
Gouty, bust
by Mino da
Fiesole

— for which the name della Robbia has ever since been famous. The leading
painters were Pollaiuolo and Botticelli.

Pallaiuolo, or "Chicken Man" (his father sold poultry), was a genius
at depicting the human figure in motion, especially in the strain of struggle
or combat. Botticelli was one of the finest painters of the Renaissance: one
of the most subtle and most withdrawn, he was one of the great masters of
perspective, a genius in linear composition. Piero commissioned Benozzo
Gozzoli to decorate the chapel in the Medici Palace; Benozzo chose to use
the traditional theme of the Magi to depict the arrival of the ecumenical
council in Florence in 1439 (see plate 30). When Piero died in 1469, he
too was buried in San Lorenzo, in a porphyry sarcophagus executed by
Donatello's pupil Andrea del Verrocchio, a solemn, honest, sometimes
clumsy painter and sculptor who was the teacher of Leonardo da Vinci.

LORENZO DE' MEDICI AND SAVONAROLA

BORN on January 1, 1449, educated in humanism, Lorenzo de' Medici, called *Il Magnifico* (the Magnificent), came to power at twenty. Although not handsome, he was virile, energetic, clever, learned, and bawdy. His instincts ran to politics and humanism, not to banking. The Medicean banking empire declined severely under his auspices. He was married to Clarice Orsini, daughter of a great Roman family, after his mother had gone purposefully to Rome to inspect her. Florentines did not take kindly to the marriage; decent people did not look beyond Tuscany for mates. To mollify them, a *giostra* (tournament) was held on February 7, 1469, in the piazza in front of Santa Croce. A succession of pageants, parades, revels, and dances followed.

The first unseemly event in Lorenzo's career was the revolt of Volterra. A dispute arose in that Tuscan village between a group of capitalists who

46. Lorenzo
de' Medici,
bust by
Verrocchio

operated an alum mine and the people of Volterra, who thought they were being defrauded. Lorenzo employed the condottiere Federigo da Montefeltro, duke of Urbino, to quash the revolt and bring the city under direct Florentine control. The much-respected duke was unable to control his unpaid troops, who pillaged the city. Blame for the devastation was laid squarely at the feet of Lorenzo.

The Pazzi Conspiracy of April 26, 1478, mentioned above in chapter 4, must go down as one of the more bizarre and grizzly episodes in European history. It started with Pope Sixtus IV, that toothless della Rovere who had visions of using the papacy to build a family dynasty. In the 1470s the pope tried to buy the town of Imola on the main road from Bologna to Rimini, as a base from which his nephew Girolamo Riario might expand his power in the Romagna. Lorenzo de' Medici resisted. The pope compounded the dispute in 1474 by naming Francesco Salviati archbishop of Pisa without Lorenzo's concurrence. Lorenzo refused to allow Salviati into Tuscany. In 1477 certain aggrieved persons met in Rome to hatch a plot: Girolamo Riario, the would-be despot; Francesco Salviati, the would-be archbishop; and Francesco Pazzi of Florence, who ran the Rome branch of the family bank and believed that the time was ripe for the Pazzi to unseat the Medici. There were also two who doubted that a coup d'état would work. One was Jacopo Pazzi, head of the family in Florence. The other was Pope Sixtus IV. "I do not wish the death of anyone," said the pontiff, "since it does not accord with our office to consent to such a thing." Under persuasion, both doubters gave in. The assassination of Lorenzo de' Medici and of Giuliano, his universally admired younger brother, was scheduled to occur at High Mass in the Florence Cathedral, precisely at the elevation of the consecrated host, when all eyes would be lowered. It was to be a religious — one might even venture to say, papal — event.

The plot was only partially successful. Giuliano was slain by multiple wounds, but Lorenzo managed to escape, although just barely. Archbishop Salviati stormed the Palazzo della Signoria as the Pazzi and their supporters rode through the streets shouting, "Liberty, liberty!" The hostile Florentines shouted back, "Palle, palle," referring to the Medici coat of arms. Once caught, the Pazzi conspirators were hurled from the parapets of the Palazzo della Signoria with nooses around their necks. Poliziano, watching from the piazza below, reported that as Archbishop Salviati gaggled at the end of his rope, his eyes fairly popping out of his head, he sank his teeth into the naked body of Francesco Pazzi, dangling alongside him. Old Jacopo, once they caught him, was treated to the same means of departure.

189

Enraged beyond all endurance, Pope Sixtus excommunicated Lorenzo ("that son of iniquity and foster-child of perdition") and clamped an interdict on Florence, denying the city every churchly administration. The pope, summoning Naples to his side, pronounced holy war on Florence. Lorenzo sought military support from Venice and Milan. Venice, however, was then sorely pressed by the Turks, and Milan was racked by internal disputes over the succession of Il Moro. Under those circumstances, Sixtus IV and King Ferrante of Naples moved against Florence with dispatch and by November 1479 had placed the city in perilous circumstances. The Florentines were stout. The Tuscan bishops met in the cathedral and excommunicated the pope. But Lorenzo knew how dire the situation was, and he therefore made an extraordinary decision. Just before Christmas, he took ship for Naples, delivering himself into the hands of his enemies, suing for peace. The *signoria* of Florence wept. Ferrante was known to have pickled his enemies and put them in showcases. He was hard, vindictive, unprincipled, and shrewd. What could a twenty-nine-year-old Medici do in the presence of such a villain except die? Lorenzo played upon several themes as he treated with Ferrante: the Turkish threat, the possibility that the French would attempt to press their dynastic claims upon Naples, the greatness of classical rulers who pursued the policies of peace. In February 1480 the king of Naples and the Medici came to terms. Florence was required to pay an indemnity, to make rectifications of territory, and to release the Pazzi. Eventually even the pope forgave. When a Turkish flotilla turned up in the harbor of Naples, the Holy Father in Rome was reminded that *all* Italians, including the Florentines, should join hearts and hands in resisting the infidel.

Less than a month after his return from Naples, Lorenzo met the first of several reverses that were to characterize the rest of his career. Financial pressures led to a reconstitution of the government. On April 8, 1480, through the usual legerdemain of a *parlamentum,* Florence acquired a Council of Seventy, which became the center of government, the priors and the *gonfaloniere* being left as ornaments. The Seventy delegated essential powers to two new governmental agencies. The *Otto di Practica* dealt with foreign policy, the *Dodici Procuratori,* with domestic affairs and finance. It was a government that Lorenzo could not fully control, although he remained the first citizen of Florence.

At the same time, the fortunes of the Medici bank were declining, through a combination of Lorenzo's neglect, the incompetence of branch managers, and a European depression. The London branch, exhausted by excessive loans to Edward IV, collapsed. The Bruges and Milan branches

IIERONYMI·FERRARIENSIS·ADEC
: MISSI·PROPHETÆ·EFFIGIES

47. Savonarola, portrait by Fra Bartolomeo

also closed, and the branches in Lyons, Rome, and Naples were all beset by difficulties. To meet his obligations, Lorenzo apparently used public and private funds that, strictly speaking, did not belong to him, and for which either he or his heirs were forced to make restitution.

As the quattrocento progressed to its last decade, a new phenomenon

191

appeared in Florence — Girolamo Savonarola (1452–98), a Dominican friar who preached doomsday to an ever-enlarging circle of Florentines, including the intellectual elite. Savonarola represented Christian values of the Middle Ages — poverty, asceticism, contempt of the world, and anticipation of heaven.

Born in Ferrara, the son and grandson of court physicians, he was as a boy given to introspection and pious undertakings. Disappointed in love, he renounced marriage and gave himself up to strenuous austerity. In 1475, at the age of twenty-three, he became a Dominican friar in order, as he put it, "to stop the devil from jumping on my shoulders." He also declared at that juncture of his life: "I was no longer able to endure the evildoing of the heedless people of Italy." The Dominicans dispatched him to preach in many towns. He appeared in Florence in 1481 and gave the Lenten sermons at the church of San Lorenzo, which the Medicis attended. In those days, he was neither attractive to look at nor easy to listen to. His clothes were patched, and his speech was as hard as steel. His gestures were neither smooth nor civilized; his green eyes blazed fiercely; his body was spindly, his nose, hooked; he was neither pretty nor winsome.

In 1488 Savonarola was stationed at the Dominican convent of San Marco in Florence — the place that Cosimo had rebuilt and that Fra Angelico had decorated — and by 1491, with Lorenzo's approval, he became prior of that convent; one can still see the little cell where he lived, surrounded by his books. By that time his audiences had grown so large (up to twelve thousand persons on some occasions) that no church except the cathedral could accommodate them. Severe fasting and asceticism had sharpened his spiritual faculties. "It is not I who preach," he said; "God speaks through me." The message that tumbled from his lips was simple: unless Florence, unless Italy, unless the Catholic Church repented, they would all be dreadfully scourged by divine agency. Of what were they to repent? Of worldliness, vanity, tyranny, and classicism. Florentines spoke of rebirth. What did they mean? They meant a rebirth of classicism — in a word, of paganism. Christianity also taught that people must be reborn, but it teaches a rebirth of the spirit. And there was that loathsome Ficino, writing books called Platonic theology — what a contradiction in terms! — and arguing seriously that Plato was fit to be read from the pulpit. "Plato, Aristotle, and the other philosophers are fast in hell," thundered Savonarola. "Any old woman knows more about the faith than Plato." In the friar's either-or mind, there was no meeting place between Christianity and classicism.

The struggle, however, was not simply over intellectual loyalties; it was over the manner of life. Souls of Florentines were being destroyed by luxuries, tourneys, sensual pleasures, gambling, cards, carnivals, races, perfumery, powders, paints, dandy clothes, prostitutes, and whatever else the new age spawned or encouraged — even the paintings that made the Virgin Mary appear to be a harlot. At that charge Botticelli cringed; Pico della Mirandola felt his hair stand on end. As long as he lived, Michelangelo could not keep the sound of the preacher's voice from ringing in his ears.

Savonarola and Lorenzo — two who loved Florence so differently — had one auspicious meeting. It was the occasion of Lorenzo's death, on April 8, 1492, in the forty-third year of his life, at which time the friar may or may not have given Lorenzo his benediction. (It depends upon whether one believes the account by Pico, or that by Poliziano.)

Il Magnifico was buried next to his brother Giuliano in the old sacristy of San Lorenzo. In his lifetime, Lorenzo de' Medici had spent his riches upon ancient gems, bronzes, medals, coins, and vases — many of which cost a thousand florins each, in contrast to a Botticelli or a Pollaiuolo, which cost a hundred. He assisted artists but did not often commission their works; he built only one remarkable building, the villa at Poggio e Caiano, which was designed by Giuliano da Sangallo. The leading painters of the Laurentian period were Filippino Lippi (son of the obstreperous Filippo), Domenico Ghirlandaio, and Sandro Botticelli. Lorenzo himself preferred Pollaiuolo, whom he called "the greatest master in the city." He was entirely unruffled when Leonardo da Vinci decided to abandon Florence for Milan or when Verrocchio left Florence for Venice to execute the equestrian statue of the condottiere Colleoni.

Lorenzo's patronage of the boy Michaelangelo Buonarroti was not inappreciable. Born in 1475, the son of a *podestà* of Caprese, a tiny Tuscan village, Michaelangelo was apprenticed to the Florentine painter Ghirlandaio in 1488, at the age of thirteen. He could have found no better teacher from whom to absorb the traditions and techniques of quattrocento painting, especially fresco, at which Ghirlandaio excelled. Ghirlandaio's sense of form and spatial structure became indelibly impressed upon his pupil. When Lorenzo asked Ghirlandaio to provide a list of promising students, the painter had no hesitation in including Michaelangelo among the names. At that point, the boy removed to the Medici Palace, where he lived and worked in the sort of free art school that Lorenzo had established in a garden somewhere between Palazzo Medici and San Marco. His teacher in sculpture was Bertoldo, a middling artist, but a pupil of Donatello, from whom Michaelangelo learned the secrets of that great Florentine master. He went regularly to the Carmine Church to study the work of Masaccio, and to Santa Croce to contemplate the frescoes of Giotto.

Lorenzo was distinguished as a patron of learning. He revived the University of Pisa and transformed the University of Florence into one of the foremost centers of classical Greek learning in the West. Students from all parts of Europe ventured to Florence to study Greek. From England, for example, came Thomas Linacre and William Grocyn in the 1480s. Through the latter's agency, Greek began to be taught at Oxford in 1488; in the age of Henry VIII the names of Linacre and Grocyn were respected as precursors of the Renaissance in England.

Lorenzo also supported the work of the Florentine Academy of Platonists founded by his grandfather — an academy that had few institutional manifestations but consisted mainly of participants: Marsilio Ficino, Pico della Mirandola, Poliziano (the leading classicist of the age), Landino (poet and rhetorician), and Lorenzo himself. In 1477, chiefly as the result of Ficino's labors, the complete works of Plato appeared in Latin — one of the scholarly feats of the quattrocento.

Piero de' Medici succeeded his father, Lorenzo, at the age of twenty-two. The Florentines called him "the Foolish," according to his arrogance, hot temper, and political ineptitude. In the autumn of 1494, shortly after the accession of Piero the Foolish, Charles VIII of France began his invasion of Italy, having been invited, as we have seen, by Lodovoco il Moro of Milan. By October, he and his army had reached the outskirts of Florence, their banners proclaiming *Voluntas Dei* (the will of God). For two years, Savonarola had persistently foretold such an event, predicting that Charles VIII, like Cyrus of old, would cross the Alps to scourge Italy for its manifold sins. The Florentines took him to be a prophet, given to divine revelations; he did nothing to disabuse them of their belief. Suddenly, there *was* Charles. "Behold," cried Savonarola, "the scourge has fallen; the prophecies are being fulfilled."

Piero, having consulted no one in the *signoria,* hastened to the French camp, where he fairly flung himself upon the king's mercy, paid a large indemnity, and gave up key fortresses in the defense line of Tuscany. On November 8 he returned to Florence to tell the government what he had done. The *vacca* (the great bell in the campanile) rang and the *parlamentum* assembled. The Florentines hissed at Piero standing in their midst, spit upon him, and finally stoned him. The next day the Medicis, including Cardinal Giovanni de' Medici, Lorenzo's second son, fled for their lives; the *signoria* sealed their fate by decreeing that they be banished forever. On

November 17 Charles VIII entered Florence and dismounted from his immense black war-horse in front of the cathedral. The people, remembering the preachments of Savonarola, received him as God's agent.

At the departure of Charles, who pressed south toward Naples, Savonarola, with a substantial following at his side, proposed to reorganize the Florentine government along theocratic lines. Florence *would* be ruled by paternosters, Cosimo de' Medici notwithstanding. The model that Savonarola proposed was the Great Council of Venice. Applied to Florence, it invested an aristocracy of three thousand leading citizens with power. In the romanticism of Savonarola, however, the Florentine doge would be none other than God: "God alone will be thy king, O Florence."

By 1495 Savonarola was in serious trouble with the Borgia pope, Alexander VI, whose iniquities he had repeatedly denounced. The friar had also expressed such unconventional opinions as that the pope might err, or that the Bible alone is the norm of Christianity. Alexander first tried to

48. Piero the Foolish, bust by Verrocchio

suppress the friar's preaching; when that failed, he offered to make Savonarola a cardinal. When that also failed, he excommunicated him on May 12, 1497.

Meanwhile, Savonarola had commenced a campaign to destroy the carnival atmosphere of the city that Lorenzo had done so much to foster. In 1496 and again in 1498, young boys, stirred by Savonarola's intense fervor, gathered up all sorts of trinkets, ornaments, jewelry, mirrors, and masks. These were piled in huge pyres in the Piazza della Signoria and set ablaze. It was a famous episode in Florentine history: "the bonfire of the vanities." By now a religious intensity had arisen in Florence that became almost intolerable. Savonarola, at the height of his puritanism, conceived of a sexless society. It became sinful to paint.

Questions of Savonarola's authenticity were raised first by the Franciscans, who wasted no love on the rival Dominicans. An ordeal by fire was proposed for April 7, 1498, in which Fra Domenico was to endure the test as Savonarola's proxy. If he perished, would it not be a sign that the prophet was false? People completely filled the Piazza della Signoria and stood on the rooftops to behold this spectacle, this barbaric test of innocency. The fire was ready, but the friars fell to squabbling. Then it started raining, and the crowds grew surly. When night fell, Savonarola had not withstood the test, and his power slipped away like water through one's fingers. The next day, though it was Palm Sunday, the Florentines hooted and jeered at him. With the pope's encouragement, the friar was apprehended and then tortured by the use of the strappado, an engine employed by the Spanish Inquisition to rack the body with excruciating pain. He made all of the damaging confessions that were wanted of him. On May 23, 1498, Savonarola and his two closest colleagues were hanged in the Piazza della Signoria. The bodies were burned, and lest any relic remain to be venerated, the last dust of Savonarola was swept up and cast into the Arno at the Ponte Vecchio. In his *Diary,* Landucci described the end of Savonarola:

> In a few hours they were burnt, their legs and arms gradually dropping off; part of their bodies remaining hanging to the chains, quantity of stones were thrown to make them fall, as there was a fear of the people getting hold of them; and then the hangman and those whose business it was, hacked down the post and burnt it on the ground, bringing a lot of brushwood, and stirring the fire up over the dead bodies, so that the very least piece was consumed. Then they fetched carts, and accompanied by the mace-bearers, carried the last bit of dust to the Arno, by the Ponte Vecchio, in order that no remains should be found.

Two hard-headed historians of Florence offered judgments of the friar. Guicciardini wrote: "Never was there so much goodness and religion in Florence as in his day." And Machiavelli: "The people of Florence seemed to be neither illiterate nor rude, yet they were persuaded that God spoke through Savonarola. I will not decide whether it is so or not, for it is proper to speak of so great a man with reverence."

EXCURSUS

Giannozzo Manetti

THE DEVELOPING VIEW OF HUMANITY IN THE RENAISSANCE CAN BE demonstrated by a comparison of the writings of the influential medieval Pope Innocent III and those of the Giannozzo Manetti, an early Renaissance humanist. Innocent was the most powerful pope of the high Middle Ages, intellectually the most formidable. He reigned from 1198 until 1216. Shortly before his election to the papacy, he expressed his views of human nature in a book called *On the Contempt of the World.* In 1452–53, in the midst of the quattrocento, Giannozzo Manetti saw fit to repudiate the pope and his book in his work *On the Dignity of Man,* which has become a minor classic of Renaissance humanism.

Innocent took the rather Platonic position that the human soul is imprisoned in the human body, from which the soul longs to be rescued. As long as we live in the prison house of the body, we mortals experience mainly fear and dread, suffering and labor. We might have thought that our souls could put up at least some resistance to such captivity. Indeed, before the fall of Adam, they could. Before Adam disobeyed God in the Garden of Eden, the soul did possess certain faculties to do good and to resist evil — reason (to decide things properly), resistance (to evil), and will (to perceive the good and work for it). Adam's fall, however, has blunted the good effect of all those faculties — not only for Adam but for all of us as Adam's posterity. Human beings have been left defenseless against the attacks of evil (or the devil, if one prefers) and powerless to seek any virtue of their own. Innocent, the Platonist, was apt to connect evil to the flesh, the body, and more specifically to sexual activity: we all inherit our sinful

49. Ciuffag, *Statue of Joshua under the Effigy of Gianozzo Manetti*

condition through the sexual liaison of our parents. Sex is therefore a "tyranny" that accounts for the most profound of human disorders: pride, desire, envy, avarice, anger, gluttony, and every other sort of evil effect. "All are born in this condition; all die in it."

Pope Innocent, however dour, was not totally pessimistic about the human condition. He acknowledged that we retained some ability to struggle for virtue against vice. We too can participate in the struggle of spirit versus flesh. (Notice how the pope defined the struggle.) What is the prescription for fighting that fight successfully? We must "crucify" our longing for the world and all its fleshly habits; we must pass our days in contempt of the world.

Giannozzo Manetti, humanist as he was, found these pontifical musings highly unconvincing. In fact, he wrote *On the Dignity of Man* specifically to rebut the opinions of this great medieval pope. In the first place, Giannozzo repudiated Innocent's suggestion that the body was the prison house of the soul, the flesh having been corrupted by the sin of our first parents, Adam and Eve, and by the sexual union of our parents ever since. For Giannozzo, human nature in all its manifestations is nothing less than excellent, and its excellence is nothing other than an endowment from God. If Innocent chose to dwell on all the less attractive aspects of the body — death, defecation, and all that — Giannozzo preferred to comment on its many sensual pleasures, pleasures of sight, hearing, taste, smell, and touch, of which sexual pleasure is deemed superior.

In the second place, Giannozzo Manetti argued that the soul is the creation of God and that its chief faculties — memory, intellect, will, and affection — are all God-given faculties. He defended that theorem, as one might expect of a humanist, on the basis of both Catholic and classical authorities, chiefly Cicero.

In the third place, Giannozzo refused to believe that this marvelous human creature, with God-given body and God-given soul, has been spoiled by the fall of Adam. He made some passing references to the fall of Adam, as if he believed it, but clearly that biblical event had no intellectual significance for him. In fact he assumed, as the book reaches its conclusion, that our freedom of will is quite intact, quite sufficient to perform the commandments of God and thereby attain virtue by our own undertakings, becoming finally like God himself in our knowing and willing.

As we read Giannozzo, we should not overlook his fine, brief statement on the importance of nudity, which goes a long way toward explaining the importance of the nude in Renaissance art. For Giannozzo, the nude body is the quintessential expression of the beauty, dignity, and excellence of human beings. Giannozzo helps us to understand that the nude is one of the finest expressions of Renaissance humanism that we have and one of the most provocative repudiations of the point of view espoused by Innocent III.

EXCURSUS

Benozzo Gozzoli, *Procession of the Magi*

LIKE HIS TEACHER, FRA ANGELICO, BENOZZO WAS A FIRST-RATE STORY-teller and treated both nature and humanity with an almost religious reverence. Benozzo also acquired from Fra Angelico a range of colors beyond those of his contemporaries, displayed to brilliant effect in his depiction of the procession of the delegates to the Council of Florence in 1439.

The transit of the council from Ferrara to Florence was a huge logistical undertaking involving innumerable persons and animals (see plate 28). First, the oldest of the Magi comes into view — Patriarch Joseph Constantinople, spiritual head of the Greek Catholic Church. If ears mean anything, it is a mule on which the old patriarch humbly rides. A pet panther rides a horse in front of him; no conventional outing is this. The rider of that horse is Giuliano de' Medici, youngest male of the Medici clan.

The second Wise Man to appear (see plate 29) is a more vigorous individual in his middle years, riding a splendid horse. He is the emperor of Byzantium, John Paleologus. Three of Piero de' Medici's daughters, Maria, Bianca, and Nanina, ride in this procession as well. Shown in plate 30, the last of the three kings of the Orient — the Magi, in other words — is Lorenzo de' Medici, still a very young man, not yet in power, yet destined to lead Florence to still greater cultural heights. The rest of the clan tags along behind Lorenzo. Evidently, as Benozzo saw things, Lorenzo would surpass both his father, Piero, and his grandfather, Cosimo, in eminence.

The procession meanders to stupefying extent, from cliff to gorge, from woods to fields. A detail of the painting shows the entire Medici contingent (see plate 31). On the left is thought to be Cosimo de' Medici, founder of the dynasty, whose strategy it was to bring the council to Florence; on the right is Piero the Gouty, Cosimo's eldest son and successor, and the father of Lorenzo the Magnificent. Behind Cosimo and Piero is probably Cosimo's second son, Giovanni. Two unsavory offspring of powerful Renaissance families ride just behind the Medici — Sigismondo Malatesta of Rimini and Galeazzo Maria Sforza of Milan.

The importance of the Medici is unmistakable by their trappings and their grooms. Other grooms transport the gifts which the Magi intend to present to the Christ child.

As we have been taught, a renewed interest in nature was one of the characteristics of Renaissance humanism. To Benozzo and to many other quattrocentro artists, nature meant two things. First, it was the "space," the environment, the habitat of the new men and the new women of the new age called the Renaissance. Second, it was the dwelling place of God. A sincere love of the created order was a legitimate worship of God.

Benozzo misses no opportunity to observe details of the natural order, such as a leopard on a leash, a winding road to a castle and beyond, a distant rider amid cultivated trees, a hunting scene, a hawk and a dove, and birds at a pond (see plates 32 and 33). Although the council met during the winter, Benozzo's orange trees are in fruit and the vegetation is green. The Renaissance is springtime in Benozzo's poetic imagination.

Granted that God is the creator of the world, his creatures — men and women — are the ones who must bring it to perfection; and nothing is more revealing of the astonishing creativity and ingenuity of human beings than architecture. The ultimate testimony to the truth of Renaissance humanism is in the houses, the castles, the buildings. The castle of the Vincigliata punctuates the point (see plate 33).

Among the Wise Men in the Procession of the Medicis (plate 30), toward the back of the group, Benozzo left a picture of himself — the man in the red hat with his name embossed in gold. He is a handsome young man, very self-assured, perhaps even arrogant. A Renaissance man. By no means the Catholic that his teacher Fra Angelico was. He found his God in nature; and even in human beings he found divinity.

IV. RENAISSANCE
LEARNING AND ART

9. *Renaissance Humanism*

SEVERAL OBSERVATIONS MADE IN CHAPTER 1 ABOUT THE NATURE OF the Renaissance bear repeating here. The first is that the Renaissance revered classical antiquity. The relationship that existed between Renaissance thinkers and classical antiquity was based upon *imitatio* (imitation), corresponding to an *exemplum* (an example, a model, an exemplary civilization). The philosophical ideas of the ancients, their ethical opinions, their laws, their architectural principles, and their views on education were deemed exemplary, fit to be imitated, fit to be employed in contemporary society, not necessarily in competition with conventional Christianity, but within its structures.

We use the expression "Greek and Roman classics" with some degree of casualness. The word "classics" is derived from the Latin adjective *classicus,* which refers to something of the highest order, a standard. When Poggio Bracciolini, that indefatigable book collector, discovered somewhere in the cobwebs of a monastic library a copy of Vitruvius, he discovered a classic. Pollio Vitruvius, a Roman architect in the age of Augustus (63 B.C.–A.D. 14), wrote ten volumes of a work entitled *De architectura,* in which he addressed himself to essentials of architecture: the rules of proportion, the "orders" of temples and buildings, town planning, and so on. The work of Vitruvius became the intellectual basis of Renaissance architecture, one of the sources of the Renaissance principle of perspective, and thus, in fact, a classic.

Foremost among the classics were the works of Marcus Tullius Cicero (106–43 B.C.). Cicero's preeminence is not at all surprising, for his purpose was to awaken among the Romans an inclination toward culture. He himself was a humanist; it was he who coined the expression *studia humanitatis* (the humanities) and taught the Renaissance thinkers how to apply that phrase to their own purposes. The range of Cicero's interests was very broad: it included an important treatise *De natura deorum* (On the nature of the gods) that the Renaissance humanists quoted, now approvingly, now disapprovingly; the most important of his writings pertained to ethics in the style of the Stoics. It was he, moreover, who molded the Latin language into an incomparably clear and effective vehicle of thought — Ciceronian Latin.

What did the Renaissance humanists find attractive in Cicero's ethics? To answer that question fully would commit us to an exposition of at least two of Cicero's ethical treatises, *On the Chief Good* and *On Duty.* Here, however, we can make only the most cursory remarks about the constructive value of Ciceronian ethics to Renaissance society.

According to Cicero, the laws of nature distinguish human beings from the rest of the natural order by two characteristics: we are social animals, and we are possessed of a love of knowledge, an intellectual urge. From such assertions, Cicero draws two ethical conclusions. First, a true Ciceronian lives in society, marries, and, as an involved citizen, participates in politics. Cloistered virtue, as in the case of, say, medieval monasticism, flouts the societal character of human nature and appears to Cicero as a form of cowardice. Hence, Cicero had a strong interest in citizenship. Second, in Cicero's proposition that one of the fundamental characteristics of human nature is its intellectual craving, we discover one of the bases of Renaissance educational philosophy: no one can become fully human without having received an education in the liberating arts, in the humanizing subjects, and without intellectual pursuits ongoing through life. In the Renaissance, Cicero's propositions coalesce: the ultimate reason for education is citizenship.

The first point, then, is that the Renaissance revered classical antiquity. That leads to the second observation made in chapter 1: the Renaissance acquired a sharpened sense of historical judgment. In order to go forward, the humanists were forced to go backward — back to the sources, back to the classics, back to a golden age, to an exemplary civilization. To the humanists, therefore, classical civilization, while remote in time, was near in sentiment; and the Middle Ages, while near in time, was remote in sentiment. The ability to see and to understand the continuities and discontinuities of history led the Renaissance to a rebirth of historical perspective and historical judgment. It was a landmark in historical judgment when Petrarch began to talk about a "dark age" that separated his generation from classical antiquity. Leonardo Bruni, the classicist and historian of whom we have spoken, used similar expressions. However unsophisticated those historical judgments may have been, they *were* historical judgments.

A third idea put forward in chapter 1 was that the Renaissance placed the human being at the center of creation. Human beings, said the Renaissance humanists, are both creature and creator. They can form and shape themselves and the world. Such a view affirms human individuality, potential, and free will. And now, the last observation: the Renaissance thinkers seem to say that while freedom may be the birthright of the individual, "humanity" is not. *Humanitas* is acquired only by intellectual pursuit, by insight and study. They meant that, in order to achieve one's full potential as a human being, in order to become an estimable human being, in order to achieve *humanitas* in that sense, one must embark upon a course of studies that carried the congenial name *studia humanitatis.* It referred not to a curriculum in the humanities but to studies productive of full humanity. Such studies included, before all others, the Greek and Latin classics, which were deemed to represent the highest level of human achievement. Equally critical was rhetoric, the science of the correct formulation of language, the doctrine of eloquence. The civilizing effect of language was an idea that fairly possessed the whole of the Renaissance, and it sticks out as one of the essential characteristics of humanism. The issue of whether to include a given item in the curriculum was resolved by asking the question, Does it form human beings and make them whole?

In the rest of this chapter we consider six representative humanists whose works typify these observations.

FRANCESCO PETRARCA (1304–74)

IN ADDITION to his stature as a poet, Petrarch (see plate 34) achieved the reputation of being the premier humanist of the fourteenth century. Leonardo Bruni, the celebrated Florentine humanist who lived in the second generation after Petrarch, observed that "the honors of Petrarch were such that no man of his age was more highly esteemed than he, not only beyond the Alps, but in Italy herself."

Part of Petrarch's importance lies in his historical sensitivity (or, insensitivity, depending upon one's point of view). He rejected his own times in preference for classical antiquity. In his *Letter to Posterity,* he confessed: "Among the many subjects which interested me, I dwelt especially upon antiquity, for our own age has always repelled me." Although the ancient world was a pagan society (at least by Christian standards), it was nevertheless a society of infinite attractiveness. Alas, it was also remote. Petrarch could perceive the historical distance that separated him from classical times. A "dark age" had intervened, disconnecting the late medieval world from that of classical antiquity. He could perfectly well perceive the difference between *antiqua* and *nova,* between ancient times and modern times. How he longed for the former!

His extensive correspondence became an important means by which he expressed his prejudices. Some of the correspondence was fictional, such as *Letters to the Ancient Dead,* addressed to his most cherished friends: Cicero, Livy, Virgil, and Horace. In *Letters to Posterity* (one of which we have already quoted), he staked out a claim for himself in history, being careful to degrade Dante as subtly, but surely, as possible. There he presented himself as the rediscoverer of classicism and the father of a new, purer Latin literature, modeled after the Latin of Cicero. Was he, in fact, the first modern man, as Renan supposed? Part of his modernity was his obvious individuality. He was exceedingly introspective and self-conscious, given to self-analysis and melancholia.

Cicero, whom Petrarch's father had read in the family circle, left an indelible impression upon Petrarch. With Cicero, Petrarch agreed that the purpose of all learning was *ars bene beatque vivendi,* "the art of living well and happily." That meant living a life of moral purpose and of civic purpose. Petrarch was perfectly content to describe himself as a moral philosopher — someone who could teach his fellows how to practice the Ciceronian art.

The other side of this coin was Petrarch's profound antipathy toward medieval Scholasticism, with its Aristotelian base and its accent on logic, natural philosophy, and speculative questions pertaining to the existence of God and to other formal categories of religion. Such sterility he ardently despised. Petrarch sought to disconnect Christian thinking from its link to Aristotelian natural philosophy and metaphysics and to join it instead to a different type of learning, namely, the type of humanism that one finds in the classical authors, particularly Cicero, with its greater accent on ethical vitality and religious imagination. When he made that disconnection and reconnection, he laid part of the intellectual foundation for the Renaissance.

In the treatise *On His Own Ignorance,* Petrarch declares that it was Cicero who first taught him the power of words and the importance of eloquence. He developed an unfailing instinct for literary quality, based upon Ciceronian Latin prose, and he tried to free himself from medieval Latin, which he now described as barbaric. Petrarch did more than anyone else of his age to revive Ciceronian Latin; that accomplishment in itself was a major contribution to Renaissance humanism.

Petrarch's problem was that he had a second mentor: Augustine. In 1342 he wrote a dialogue between Augustine and himself, calling it, quite appropriately, *Secret.* Here we find a remarkably subtle and modern piece of self-analysis. Petrarch's inward turmoil, which came to the surface in this book, ran on two levels. On one level, it was the eternal question of whether learning and goodness are reciprocal or antithetical: do they reinforce each other, or do they destroy each other? At the deeper level, however, the question is whether there can be an accommodation between Petrarch's classicism and his conception of medieval Christianity.

That conflict was expressed in another of Petrarch's writings, *The Ascent of Mont Ventoux.* On the face of it, the piece appears to be an account of a mountain-climbing expedition that Petrarch and his brother undertook on April 26, 1336, while the family still lived near Avignon. Some scholars have mistaken the meaning of this work, calling it the first instance in which a modern person climbed a mountain simply to see the view, and thus an epoch in modernity. At the top of the mountain, Petrarch, the humanist, as he feasts his eyes on the glories of creation and is enraptured by his own humanity, opens Augustine's *Confessions* at book 10 and has the saint lecture him on the dangers of concupiscence and pride. Thus, the piece is an allegory of what might be called the human pilgrimage; part of that pilgrimage, for Petrarch at least, is the tension between love of the things of this world and love of higher things.

The same tension occurred again in the one great intellectual crisis of Petrarch's life. In 1364 four Venetians amused themselves one evening after a good dinner by declaring that Petrarch was certainly a good man but a poor scholar. They were Leonardo Dandolo, son of a doge; Zaccaria Contarini of Venetian nobility; Tommaso Talenti, a wealthy merchant; and Guido da Bagnolo, of whom little is known. Petrarch, then sixty, was the most renowned scholar in the whole Western world. The disparaging remarks of the Venetians came as a severe blow to him. He waited a year, then wrote an elaborate answer in the classical form of invective. It is entitled *On My Own Ignorance and That of Many Others.*

Petrarch begins by explaining the problem. Are goodness and learning antithetical? The Venetians have admitted that Petrarch is a good man, but they do not particularly admire that fact; to make matters worse, they accuse him of being illiterate. Petrarch notes their opinion of him when he says, "Not even virtue can they envy me . . . plain, uneducated fellow."

Petrarch's rejoinder is a case of the pot calling the kettle black: the Venetians are the stupid ones, because their Scholastic education, with its heavy emphasis upon natural philosophy and dependence on Aristotelianism, is essentially unprofitable. In response Petrarch put forward a focus on humanity, one based on traditional Christianity as well as Cicero. These "scribes," as he calls them, have spent their energy on natural phenomena and ignored humanism, namely, the nature of man. "What is the use, I beseech you, of knowing the nature of quadrupeds, fowls, fishes, and serpents and not knowing or even neglecting man's nature, the purpose for which we were born, and whence and whereto we travel?"

It occurs to Petrarch that if he is ignorant, so is everyone else. "How infinitely small, I beseech you, is the greatest amount of knowledge granted to a single mind." In other words, even the greatest minds know relatively little and are ignorant. Much later in the treatise Petrarch returns to the same theme: "A generous soul will realize how meager a portion of knowledge is that which is allotted to all men combined, if we compare it to human ignorance and divine wisdom." He makes a sage observation that all of us should understand: ignorance increases in proportion to knowledge: the more we know, the more we stand in terror of what we do not know.

Petrarch makes a sharp, prolonged protest against Aristotle. It is a protest against medieval Scholasticism, with its Aristotelian base, which Petrarch deems too speculative, too sterile, too unproductive of religious imagination and ethical fervor. It produces people like the four Venetians who despise virtue and babble endlessly about natural phenomena.

The polemic against Aristotle is balanced by an almost ecstatic hymn of praise to Cicero. "I still read the works of poets and philosophers, particularly those of Cicero, with whose genius and style I have been particularly delighted since my early youth." The lavish praise heaped on Cicero leads to the crisis of this essay and its monumental importance in Western intellectual history. The crucial question is simply, Is Petrarch a Ciceronian? Or to put the question another way, Can Cicero and Christ both be believed? Or to put the question decisively, Can Christianity and classicism be married so as to beget Renaissance humanism? At first Petrarch answers no. On the next page, however, his ardor for Cicero increases: "I do not deny that I am delighted with Cicero's genius and eloquence." Finally he proceeds to declare that he is indeed a Ciceronian and, mirabile dictu, Cicero himself would surely have been a Catholic had the opportunity been his.

This section of the work, as well as any other statement of its kind, represents the union of classicism and Western Christianity that is the foundation of Renaissance humanism. Even this crucial passage, however, ends with a question mark, illustrating Petrarch's final uneasiness, tentativeness, and perhaps even doubt about his understanding of the relation between the wisdom of the classical world and that of medieval Christianity.

LORENZO VALLA (1405–57)

THE SECOND representative humanist we consider is Lorenzo Valla, the keenest critical intelligence of the Renaissance. He represents better than anyone of his age the triumph of the historical attitude. While he shared the general antipathy of most Renaissance humanists toward Aristotle, the Schoolmen, and their dialectical thinking, he was not moved, as they were, to replace Scholasticism with some new philosophical principle, whether Ciceronianism or Platonism. He was skeptical of the accommodation sought by many humanists between classicism and Christianity and preferred to think that reason and faith, classicism and Christianity, philosophy and theology were irreconcilable. There was an antiphilosophical, antirationalist streak in his thought. His appreciation for the ancients, which was very real, was almost exclusively confined to their linguistic, rhetorical, and critical faculties. Born in Rome and trained in Mantua by the outstanding Renaissance pedagogue Vittorino da Feltre, Valla was a peripatetic scholar: only in the last decade of his life did he settle down in Rome, as apostolic secretary to the humanistic pope Nicholas V.

Valla's book *On the Elegancies of the Latin Language,* published in 1444, quite soon became the model of the best method in linguistic study and served as the foundation of good Latin style for a whole succession of humanists in all parts of Europe, and most especially for Erasmus. In an earlier work, *On Pleasure* (1431), dealing with pleasure and the true good, Valla, at the age of twenty-six, ventured to attack Petrarch's reconciliation of Ciceronian and Christian ethics. In book 3 of that treatise, Valla specifically called into question Petrarch's assumption of goodness as a moral goal. Three conversationalists — a Stoic, an Epicurean, and a Christian, whose opinions make up the treatise — seem to conclude that happiness or pleasure, understood in Epicurean terms, would be a better method than Stoicism to achieve the bliss that is reserved for Christians. For an Epicurean, pleasure is the state of tranquility or peace that consists in the removal of every painful want. Pleasure can be varied, but it cannot be heightened, for example, by excessive luxury or debauchery. Valla denounced the whole conception and practice of monasticism as a perversion of Christianity. Monks and nuns were, in his view, simply trying to dodge the secular duties demanded of all Christians. There was only one standard of morality, and it was expected of all Christians without regard to status. Valla, no less than other humanists, affirmed the world as the arena of life.

However, the third part of the dialogue clearly shows that Christian pursuit of virtue for the pleasure of heaven is still the highest way.

The work of Lorenzo Valla in disproving *The Donation of Constantine* must stand as an epic event in the history of scholarship. His use of history as an instrument of criticism, his historical-critical method, was the culmination of the rebirth of historical perspective.

It is necessary to begin with the *Donation* itself in order to understand the character of Lorenzo Valla's criticism. At the very opening of the document, we are told that Constantine, "together with all our satraps, and the whole Senate and my nobles, and also all the people subject to the government of glorious Rome," has deemed the "donation" advisable. We are told that the donation consists of the spiritual supremacy of the pope over the whole Christian church and specifically "over the four principal seats [of the church], Alexandria, Antioch, Jerusalem, Constantinople." Furthermore, we learn that the donation also consists of the fullness of temporal power in the West: "Behold, we give over and relinquish to the aforesaid blessed Pontiff, Sylvester, the universal Pope, as well as our palace [the Lateran Palace in Rome], as has been said, as also the city of Rome, and all the provinces, places, and cities of Italy and the western regions." According to section 7, Constantine, lest he intrude upon this new temporal supremacy of the papacy in the West, proposed to remove his empire to the East, to the province called Byzantia; there he would create a new city in his name, thus Constantinople.

At one time this document was accepted as part of the timeless and seamless body of eternal truth. Not so for Valla. He clearly denounces the document as a forgery, and the papacy for complicity in the forgery. He applies the power of historical reasoning to the refutation of the document. Is it not preposterous, he asks, that Constantine, the conqueror of the West, "a man who through thirst for dominion had waged war against the nations," would suddenly in a fit of piety, give it all away to the papacy? He argues that there is no evidence whatsoever of any transfer of power; therefore none likely occurred. Throughout, Valla applies both his philological and his historical tools for critical purpose. The word "satrap" belonged to the middle of the eighth century, certainly not to the middle of the fourth. Who were the so-called nobles in the age of Constantine? Romans were not a subject people but a free people. The grammar of the *Donation* reveals Latin barbarisms that no classical author would likely have committed. Constantinople is listed among the seats of the church, when the very document itself would have us believe that Constantinople had not yet been built but was merely an idea in Constantine's thinking. The forger mistook Byzantium for a province, rather than a city, and he misplaced Thrace — errors that an emperor would scarcely have allowed to stand. Finally, Valla ventures the opinion that the possession of temporal power by the papacy cannot be justified on moral grounds, so associated had it become with crimes, evils, and unseemly wealth.

Valla's refutation of *The Donation of Constantine* was followed shortly by other feats of critical scholarship, based upon his historical-critical method. He demonstrated, for example, that the Apostles' Creed had not been uttered seriatim by the apostles, and that the Latin Vulgate Bible, compared to Greek codices of the New Testament, was full of grammatical errors and bad translations. Most of these observations were made in the text entitled *Annotations on the New Testament,* which Valla completed in 1444, but which remained for Erasmus to publish in Paris in 1505. To those who shook their heads and asked, "Is nothing sacred?" Valla replied, somewhat piously, that he was simply using scholarship to get closer to the mind of Moses, Christ, or Aristotle.

How shall we estimate Lorenzo Valla? Was he skeptic or believer? Do his critical works and his book on pleasure represent an attack on Christianity, or was his purpose rather to cleanse and purify the faith? There is, at the very least, an ambivalence in Valla: a certain worldliness in his motives, a disinterested love of truth, and an intellectual honesty — all of which distinguishes him as a harbinger of a new era.

LEON BATTISTA ALBERTI (1404–72)

AT THE middle of the quattrocento, there appeared two auspicious statements of Renaissance humanism by two very prominent humanists: *Della famiglia* (On the family; 1443), by Leon Battista Alberti, and *On the Dignity of Man* (1452–53), by Giannozzo Manetti. We considered Manetti's treatise in the excursus in chapter 8. Here we focus on Alberti, whom Burckhardt called the first universal genius.

Alberti (see plate 50) belonged to one of the grandest of Renaissance families. It had the misfortune, however, of being banished from Florence in 1402 for political reasons. Alberti was born in exile in Genoa in 1404. He received a thoroughly humanistic education at the University of Bologna, from which he also took a doctorate in canon law in 1428, against the possibility that he might decide to pursue a career in the church. A fellow student at Bologna was Tommaso Parentucelli, the precocious humanist who became Pope Nicholas V.

Alberti returned to Florence in 1434 — the auspicious year of Cosimo de' Medici's return from exile. Already a humanist of astonishing learning, Alberti proceeded to publish a formidable series of Latin works, ranging from poetry and comedy to treatises on law, the horse, the family, and the tranquility of the soul. In all of these writings, he struck the grand themes of Renaissance humanism to which we have become accustomed.

Three of Alberti's treatises were of major importance in the history of art. In 1435, the year after his return to Florence, he published a Latin treatise *De pictura* (On painting), which appeared the following year in an Italian abridgement as *Della pittura.* Around 1450 he published *De re aedificatoria* (Ten books on architecture), an important work that reflected the architectural principles of Vitruvius as well as Alberti's own excursions to the ancient sites of Rome, where he observed, measured, and studied the monuments of classical civilization. His third work, *De statua* (On the statue), was not quite as important as the others and cannot be accurately dated. These writings contain Alberti's artistic principles, including that of perspective.

De pictura was the first treatise on painting of the Renaissance era, likely the first since classical times. The art, or system, of perspective that it teaches — a theory so precious and godlike that it was actually referred to as the divine perspective — may have been conceived, or at least perfected, out of Alberti's own consummate genius, although some scholars have suggested that Alberti merely codified what artists were already doing, while others have attributed the science of perspective to medieval studies in optics. At any rate, the Albertian principle of perspective brought animated, three-dimensional people to painting. It marked a clean break with the flat, floating, somewhat unreal figures of some medieval art. Painting in the new style, said Alberti, had a "divine force" that was capable of making absent persons present and dead persons alive.

When he was not writing, Alberti worked as a consultant in princely courts, giving advice on town planning and architecture. He also offered

50. Alberti,
Palazzo
Rucellai

his services as an architect, even though he was dependent upon others for
engineering skills. Around 1446 he drew the design for Palazzo Rucellai
— a palace to be built in the midst of Florence by the wealthy merchant
Giovanni Rucellai. As he executed that commission, he was able for the
first time to give his artistic principles physical expression. He defined
beauty as follows: "the harmony and concert of all the parts, achieved in
such a manner that nothing could be added, taken away, or altered" — in
short, physical perfection based upon the classical idea of harmony. Palazzo
Rucellai was therefore conceived of according to an overall system of proportion, with classical "orders" and details.

In 1450, a jubilee year, Alberti was in Rome as a consultant to his old friend Pope Nicholas V, who was fascinated by the prospect of rebuilding the city and the Vatican basilica. Among the crowds of pilgrims in Rome, Alberti met Sigismondo Malatesta, the tyrant of Rimini, a man so loathsome that in 1462 Pope Pius II, in a public ceremony conducted on the porch of St. Peter's, consigned him to hell while he was still alive. Among his notorious deeds was to hire Alberti to transform the monastic church of San Francesco at Rimini into a temple dedicated to Sigismondo and to his principal mistress, Isotto. His enemies were to accuse him of incest and of having his wife suffocated. The Malatesta Temple in Rimini, as Alberti reconceived it, has a facade based upon the triumphal arches of Constantine and Septimius Severus in Rome, with a set of proportions corresponding exactly to classical models. Seldom do we have an example as explicit as the Malatesta temple at Rimini of how committed the Renaissance was to classical models.

51. Alberti, Malatesta Temple

52. Arch of Constantine

Alberti, the classicist, referred consistently to "temples," not "churches." He spoke of "the gods," seldom of "God." The ancients, he insisted, would never have used basilicas for churches; basilicas were only for law courts. When Romans wanted temples, they built temples. Three-aisled churches of any sort, whether basilican or Romanesque or Gothic, were unfit for the worship of the gods for one simple reason: the columns obscured the ceremonies at the altar. Thus when Alberti was commissioned to build the Church of Sant'Andrea in Mantua, he wrought a whole revolution in church interiors — the second such since Brunelleschi remodeled the interior of San Lorenzo in Florence. Using the temple of Venus in Rome as his model, Alberti designed a church with a gigantic barrel vault, no aisles, no columns, and with arches opening into the walls and sustained by massive sections of the wall, thereby creating a single, overwhelming spatial effect. He introduced a type of church interior that was to be repeated endlessly in churches throughout Europe, including the central church of Western Christendom, St. Peter's itself.

217

We turn finally to Alberti as humanist. In *Della famiglia,* an elaborate treatise on the Renaissance family, we find a full, but by no means systematic, interpretation of Alberti's philosophy of humanity. There Alberti described a human being as a composite of two parts — the soul, which is of God, and the body, which, although mortal, is noble and beautiful. While the soul is guardian of the body, the body remains in Alberti's eyes as something exceptionally winsome — an idea we hardly need to identify as typical of the Renaissance.

Alberti ascribed "the dignity of man" (a phrase he used as easily as Manetti did) to certain gifts that God has granted to human beings — sentiment, the power of excitement, intelligence, docility (the characteristic of being teachable), memory, reason, moderation, the desire for honor, and, to be sure, a noble and beautiful body. Furthermore, God has endowed human beings with a number of societal attitudes that enable them to live

53. Interior of Sant'Andrea

together and enhance the dignity of their species — justice, equity, liberality, and love. Finally, God has granted human beings certain gifts of courage, enabling them to endure adversity and sorrow.

By "intelligence," Alberti meant both intellectual capacity and the power of moral decision. We have, he said, a "marvelous capacity" to distinguish between good and evil. Guided by one's intelligence, a person is able to love *virtù,* to hate vice, and to attain fame by one's good works. We thus encounter the word that is more typical than any other of the Italian Renaissance — *virtù.* What does it mean? It sounds very much like the Latin word *virtus* and the English word "virtue"; like both, it contains the suggestion of moral power. Alberti, when he used that word, meant that those human capacities with which God has endowed human beings enable us to achieve a "noble character" that is astonishing in its power and accomplishment. We *can* love the good, hate the evil, disdain what is unworthy, hope for worthy ends, and strive toward our "own greatest possible perfection." Insofar as free will means the ability to attain moral or spiritual purposes by one's own capacity, then free will must be seen as a corollary of *virtù.* However, in spite of such comments about free will, Alberti sees individuals as largely subject to the vagaries of fortune, and virtue is simply an aid in combatting these forces. This more pessimistic view comes out most strongly in works other than *Della Famiglia.* The free will necessary to achieve *virtù* is not some quirk of human nature, bestowed on persons who are spiritually elite. It is human nature itself. *Virtù,* said Alberti, is "nothing but nature itself, complete and well formed." But did not human nature suffer at least some degree of moral collapse when Adam fell into sin in the Garden of Eden? Alberti does not deny it. Adam's fall has at least left human beings with a second impulse, an "evil root," the impulse to selfishness and vice. It all depends on which impulse we cultivate. Habit will confirm us in one way or the other, in either virtue or vice.

Humanistic education — *studia humanitatis* — was of importance to Alberti, as to all humanists of the Renaissance, because it informed the intelligence about the proper content of *virtù.* The humanities, in other words, furnish us with the ideals to which virtue ought to aspire. Alberti left little doubt that, as far as he was concerned, the basis of the humanities was more classical than Christian. The "right and relevant thoughts," he said, came from "the ancient authors." As a matter of fact, *Della famiglia* as a whole appears to have been based on "the sayings and authority of the great writers of antiquity."

MARSILIO FICINO (1433–99)

THE LAST two humanists we shall consider — Ficino and Pico della Mirandola — represent the second half of the quattrocento. Both were eminent members of the Platonic Academy in Florence, and both were profoundly affected by Neoplatonism. To help comprehend their thought, we reflect first on Neoplatonism.

Plotinus was an Egyptian, born in A.D. 205 and educated in Alexandria under the instruction of Ammonius Saccas (Ammonius "the porter"), a self-taught philosopher, it would appear, whose principles remain unknown. Ammonius could scarcely have been a cipher, for he produced two geniuses — the Christian theologian Origen and the philosopher Plotinus — both of whom graced his classroom at the same time. Plotinus settled in Rome in 244 and became a teacher there; his house was a schoolroom for noble men and women and their progeny. His biographer, Porphyry, a third-century Boswell, collected his writings in volumes called *Enneads*. Plotinus died in 269.

In his pre-Roman days, Plotinus was thought to have traveled in the Far East. Alexandria was itself a cosmopolitan city where Oriental ideas and Western ideas crossed. It is tempting to ascribe the peculiarities of Plotinus's thought to Oriental influence. He was, at any rate, a philosophical genius who interpreted classical Greek philosophy, especially Plato, in a new way, colored perhaps by intellectual ideas that were current in third-century Alexandria. Neoplatonism became an essential part of the intellectual environment of the Greco-Roman world. Many Christian thinkers knew their Plato, not directly, but through the interpretation of Neoplatonism.

The universe, as Plotinus conceives it, contains a double movement — a way down and a way up. The way down is the eternal process of divine emanation, the outgoing of God from the "center" to the "circumference." At the center of all is God, the One, the Good, a Unity beyond all difference, the Absolute who transcends all thought and being. From God there flows or radiates a succession of emanations, none of which, however, diminishes God's fullness or perfection.

The first emanation from God is Mind, or *nous*. Nous, the highest expression of being, is the world of eternal ideas — the universal principles, the archetypes and patterns after which our world of things is formed. Nous is the Overmind of the universe, of whom all minds partake and in whom everything that is real and intelligible participates. In this very conception of God as Intelligence lies an idea that we will find so striking in Pico's thought, namely, that all truth, even if formulated in different ways, is essentially the same. It was an idea that Ficino shared.

Mind itself overflows into a second sphere of being — Soul. This is the universal Soul, or Oversoul, which enfolds in itself all individual souls, so that all souls are both quite distinct and yet one.

Soul brings us to the outer rim of reality, to the "circumference." Soul makes the world; matter by itself is nothing. As Soul floods the world (a proper image might be many splashing rivulets), it produces a multiplicity of things. Thus, God himself is revealed in creation, in finite things. The world, as Nicholas of Cusa said, is the unfolding of God, the making visible of God. In this idea lies one of the important bases of modern scientific interest.

The human soul, according to Plotinus, has both a higher and a lower side. The lower side desires a body, lives in the world of sensory perception, and deals with all things on a temporal basis. The higher side of the soul, in contrast, seeks to transcend the body. It never completely leaves home, to use the mystical language of Plotinus; "the soul always leaves something of itself above." It is possible for every soul to retrace the process of its descent and to return to its home. That journey was recommended by Pico in his *Oration on the Dignity of Man.* The human being, according to Pico, is free for the purpose of making that pilgrimage.

The first stage of the soul's journey consists of being restored to the unity of the universal Soul. The next step is to rise to Mind. This step, as one might expect, requires one to advance to the world of pure thought, which is the realm of the Mind. Through contemplation, one must withdraw from sensory perception and worldly desires into the world of Mind. Is it not possible to perceive in such a conception the basis of Renaissance intellectualism? As the first manifestation of God is thought, so the summit of human consciousness is thought. And most certainly here is the basis of the *contemplative* humanism of the Florentine Platonists, as opposed to the *civic* humanism of, say, Coluccio or Leonardo Bruni.

Finally, it is within the capacity of the soul to rise above thought and to become one with the One. That step, however, is an exercise that takes us beyond consciousness. Plotinus calls it "a mode of vision which is ecstasy." Such an experience, being beyond consciousness, is also beyond description. One can only succeed in telling what it is not.

Such was the nature of Neoplatonism. It flourished until the opening of the sixth century, when the Christian emperor Justinian attempted to suppress it. Its last great teacher was Proclus, who died in 485. Related to

Neoplatonism, but not to the teachings of Plotinus, were certain secret revelations dating from the second and third centuries, believed to have been uttered by the Egyptian deity Thot, whom the Greeks identified with Hermes. Those revelations of Hermes Trismegistus (Hermes the Thrice Greatest) were referred to as the Hermetic writings. They became an essential part of the Neoplatonic lore in the age of the Renaissance.

We come now to Marsilio Ficino, the most influential exponent of Neoplatonism in Italy during the quattrocento (see plate 35). Born near Florence in 1433, Ficino, a misshapen child of prodigious intellect, was sent to Bologna, where he attended the university, took the conventional Scholastic curriculum, and developed a fondness for Thomas Aquinas that proved to be lifelong. Knowing no Greek, he began avidly to read Latin translations of Plato. Through the boy's father, who was physician to the Medici, Cosimo de' Medici learned of Marsilio's new interest. The stirring events of the Council of Florence (1439), especially the lectures on Plato delivered by Gemistus Plethon to awestruck audiences, had filled Cosimo with great zeal to establish a Platonic academy in Florence. In 1459, under Cosimo's patronage, Ficino embarked upon the study of Greek and began his lifelong work of translating and annotating Plato and the Platonic philosophers. His purpose was to revive Platonism in Italy. Cosimo placed the Medici villa at Careggi at Marsilio's disposal. It housed this peculiar academy, which had no students, but merely enlightened conversationalists, and no curriculum except the annual birthday party for Plato.

As we have noted, Ficino finished the complete works of Plato in 1477 — one of the more important feats of Renaissance scholarship. Published by the Aldine Press of Venice, it attained broad circulation. Ficino also published translations of the *Enneads* of Plotinus, as well as the writings of Porphyry and Proclus.

Ficino's major writings belong to the 1470s, the most important being *On the Christian Religion* and *Platonic Theology: Concerning the Immortality of the Soul.* Ficino had an emphatically Neoplatonic way of looking at the universe. He conceived of God as the Source of all being, as Being itself, from which all things derive and to which all things aspire to return. God is also goodness itself, so that all created things, including human beings, participate in the divine goodness. Ficino taught that a succession of emanations proceed from God, none of which, however, depletes the divine essence. All of the orders of creation, including humankind and nature, are part of the chain of being that proceeds, by emanation, from God himself.

First of the emanations is the angelic Mind, which corresponds to

Plotinus's Mind or *Nous*. Ficino, always careful to draw harmonious relationships between Christianity and Platonism whenever he could, identified the angelic Mind with the Logos of Christianity — the Word, the Son, the expression of divine intelligence, the second person of the Trinity. Next of the emanations is the World-Soul, corresponding exactly to Plotinus's universal Soul; from it proceed both the souls of human beings and the things of the universe. Human beings, who exist at the circumference, or outer limits, of being, are related both to the world (by virtue of having a body) and to the spirit (by virtue of having a soul). We must admit, of course, that human beings have degenerated from the pure idea of Man that exists among all other eternal Ideas in the angelic Mind, because of our dual status — we are of God and of the world.

Ficino understands the fall of humankind in just those terms. We are fallen, not because Adam disobeyed God according to the biblical book of Genesis, but because our soul is sunk in the body, is weighted down by earthly things, has lost its spiritual buoyancy, and no longer wants to fly back to God. Reason may impel us upward to God, but the senses tempt us downward, to the delights of nature. That tension between reason and the senses, pulling us in opposite directions, is our lot as fallen persons. Nevertheless, we as humans remain in a state of genuine ambivalence. Neither our reason nor our will has been destroyed, however defective they may have become in fallen human nature. Both still have the possibility of directing us back to God.

Salvation, for Ficino, means to make one's way back up the ladder of being, finally achieving union with God himself. Salvation is possible for one reason: the spark of the divine is in every soul, which means that in every soul there exists a longing to return to God. Salvation begins when we disengage the soul from the body, the reason from the senses. By such means, the soul regains its buoyancy and begins its flight upward to God, using reason and will as its "wings." At this point Ficino found some usefulness in the Catholic Church. It is the purpose of the church, through its various ministrations, to immerse people in the realm of spirit and to deliver them from their preoccupation with the world. Ficino declared, however, that the church must share this role with the arts and sciences. The liberal arts, properly understood, especially music, painting, history, and scientific observation, all have the possibility of delivering human beings from bodily preoccupations and of stimulating their spiritual appetites.

Every day that a person is in flight back to God, he or she becomes more and more godlike. Our godlike character derives chiefly from our freedom. That is, we have delivered ourselves from bondage to the body in order to exercise a dominion over creation, especially over the animal kingdom, over government, and over the arts. As gods, we can contribute to the very process of creation as we ascend to union with the Creator himself. Such were the excessively optimistic terms in which Marsilio Ficino cast his philosophy of the human being.

Ficino was apparently the first of the Renaissance philosophers to advocate the universality of all truth, an idea common to both Nicholas of Cusa and Pico della Mirandola. Where did such an idea come from, and what are its implications? It arose from the Neoplatonic belief that the very first emanation of God is *nous,* or Mind, which is simply to say that the very first manifestation of God is intelligence. In other words, if the source of all intelligence is God, then it may reasonably be argued that all truth is ultimately one. What are the implications of such a hypothesis? For the past few centuries, we Western people have espoused the idea of toleration as it was taught to us by John Locke and John Stuart Mill.* What is interesting about toleration is that it assumes the opposition of thought, rather than its unity and universality. It assumes that I am right and, in being tolerant, that I forbear what I really believe to be false, evil, or at least unacceptable. Ficino's idea that all truth is essentially one truth, even if we allow for peculiarities in the way that one truth is expressed, appears to be a more profound and peaceful idea than the conception of toleration.

In his *Platonic Theology,* Ficino pressed the universality of truth to an important extreme. He declared that a harmony existed between the Platonic tradition in philosophy and the Christian religion. He proposed to exploit that harmony in his own philosophical system. Furthermore, he believed that the Platonic teaching represented an authority in religion comparable to the authority derivative from divine revelation — human thinking at its best, alongside revealed truth. Ficino declared that the Platonic philosophy is necessary to confirm the Christian religion, rendering it sufficiently rational to satisfy the sophisticated and skeptical minds of the Renaissance. It was not a question of philosophy being the handmaiden of Christianity. In the harmony that Ficino proposed, each was authoritative in its own way; each was required for the sake of the other. Therefore, when Ficino argued that Plato was as fit to be read from the pulpits of Florence as Christ was — a proposition that infuriated Savonarola — he was merely saying the truth as he perceived it.

* I owe this observation entirely to my colleague Professor Charles Courtney.

GIOVANNI PICO DELLA MIRANDOLA (1463–94)

THE GREAT mind of the quattrocento was Pico della Mirandola, Ficino's colleague in the Platonic Academy. Pico was entirely too superhuman to be completely believable. He had everything: noble birth, physical attractiveness, enormous energy, overweening self-assurance, and an insatiable thirst for knowledge left unfulfilled, even though he had attended five universities. At Bologna and Rome he took classics and became adept at Greek and Latin literature and philosophy; at Paris and Padua he was taught the logical and philosophical traditions of Scholasticism; and in Florence he fell headlong under the spell of Ficino and his Neoplatonism. To his mastery of Latin and Greek, which was a common accomplishment in the late quattrocento, he added an uncommon knowledge of Hebrew and Arabic, which led him into Oriental studies and the Jewish Cabala, an important mystical tradition in Judaism.

In the autumn of 1486, when he was twenty-four and bursting with pride, Pico went to Rome, where he proceeded to publish nine hundred theses drawn from the lore of all ages and places, Eastern and Western. A partial list of Pico's authorities included Moses, Plato, Pythagoras, the Cabalists, Mohammed, Zoroaster, Paul, Hermes Trismegistus, and something vaguely defined as "the Arabian books." To the startled scholarly

54. Pico della Mirandola, medallion by Niccolo Fiorentino

225

world, Pico proposed to defend all nine hundred theses before all comers, offering to pay the travel expenses of any impecunious debaters. The contest was scheduled for January of 1487. While Pico may have conceived of himself as a world-class genius, others fancied him as simply an upstart. Pope Innocent VIII grumbled, "This young man wants someone to burn him some day." A papal commission censured thirteen of the theses. When Pico tried to defend the incriminated theses in an *Apologia,* he only made matters worse and decided to scurry off to Paris.

From Paris, where he was imprisoned for a short time as an intellectual deviant, Pico escaped to Florence, where he lived under the protection of Lorenzo de' Medici during the few remaining years of his life. He was, indeed, one of the intellectual celebrities of the era of Lorenzo. His conflict with the Catholic Church, however — first in Rome and later in Paris — unnerved Pico, and he underwent some sort of conversion. He was moved to sell off his hereditary lands and to burn his poetry; he threatened to become a barefoot preacher and fell increasingly under the spell of Savonarola. On November 17, 1494, the day King Charles VIII of France entered Florence, Pico died of a fever at the age of thirty-one.

Pico wrote his most important and best-known work, *Oration on the Dignity of Man,* as the introductory address of the debate scheduled to have been held at Rome in January 1487. It was fashioned after the formal academic speeches that rectors of universities made at the opening of terms.

The *Oration* opens with the praise of humankind. Pico immediately rejects as unsatisfactory the traditional views of the excellence of man, including that advanced by Neoplatonists. A human being's distinction does not come from the fact that he or she is somehow between God and the lower animals, possessed of a superior intelligence. The true dimensions of human dignity derive from creation. According to Pico, God found no archetype for human beings and therefore created them without fixed properties. They have unlimited freedom to make of themselves what they will. They are the only creature whose life is determined, not by nature, but by their own free choice. Man therefore cannot be properly understood as occupying some distinguished place in the hierarchy of being; human beings exist quite apart from that hierarchy, in a new mode of existence characterized by freedom. In sum, Pico assigns the dignity and excellency of humans entirely to our extraordinary endowment of free will.

What may a person do with his or her freedom? One may rise to God or sink to the bestial. Pico rhetorically asks, "Who would not admire this our chameleon?" That is, Pico sees the fall of humankind not in the stark terms of the Bible (Adam's disobedience and expulsion from Paradise), but as the inevitable conflict that exists in a person between spiritual intelligence on the one hand, and the lure of sensuality on the other. Of decisive importance in Pico's thought is the essentially unimpaired freedom that he assigns to human beings.

What is one expected to do with one's freedom if there is truly the wish to make the journey back to God? Such a person is expected to cultivate his or her spiritual intelligence by means of moral philosophy and the liberal arts, disdaining earthly things, in order to exist finally in the untrammeled contemplation of God.

Several things in the *Oration* arrest our attention. First, Renaissance humanists are prone to say that the full humanity of human beings is not something we are born with, but something that we acquire through the process of an education, especially in the liberal arts. "Nature produces man," said Giovanni Boccaccio, "and learning then forms him anew." Pico believes the same.

Second, for Pico, the goal of human freedom and learning is not citizenship, as it was for Cicero and the civic humanists. It is contemplation, a conclusion that is quite understandable, given Pico's Neoplatonic philosophy.

Third, Pico, no less than Ficino, subscribes to the universality of all truth, and for the same Neoplatonic reasons. "I . . . have so prepared myself," said Pico, "that, pledged to the doctrines of no man, I have ranged through all the masters of philosophy, investigated all books, and come to know all schools." For Pico, an idea is rather like a person; it has its own dignity and validity, whether it has come from Zoroaster or from Christ or from Lorenzo de' Medici. Compulsion in matters of belief is neither right nor profitable. Truth really emerges in discourse, debate, and writing. Pico, in particular, and the Renaissance in general, took seriously the freedom of the mind.

Although we can scarcely question Pico's piety, as we once did Valla's, there is some question about his significance as a thinker. His pretensions were as grand as those of Thomas Aquinas, but he ignored the critical tools of scholarship that had been developed by Valla and that might have enabled him to accomplish some new kind of Thomistic synthesis. Pico's detractors have attributed to him merely a jumble of incompatible ideas. The implication is not altogether just. Pico's syncretism is related to the broad humanistic preference for the infinite richness and variety to be found in the world of ideas. The *Oration* of Pico, so far from being trivial, contains conceptions of importance to Renaissance humanism, not the least of which are his extremely optimistic estimate of human nature, based on the idea of human freedom, and the proposition that all truth is essentially one.

10. *Painters and Sculptors of the Quattrocento*

GIOTTO AND HIS TIMES

GIOTTO belongs, not to the quattrocento, but to the trecento which preceded it. Yet it seems difficult to understand the art of the Renaissance without Giotto, and so it is with Giotto that we begin. Giorgio Vasari in his *Lives of the Painters* leaves no doubt that it was Giotto who began the Renaissance in the fine arts. Why was that the case? The answer may lie in an observation once made by Leonardo da Vinci. "The painter who takes as his absolute model the works of other painters will never create anything but mediocrity," said Leonardo. "But if he takes nature as the chief end of his study, he will produce good fruit." That may be the clue to Giotto. Born in the lonely countryside outside the city of Florence around the year 1267, Giotto had no disposition at all to imitate the past generations of artists. Nor, for that matter, did he conceive of reviving classical ideals of art — it was much too early for such a self-consciously Renaissance attitude toward art. He merely wanted to produce pictures which would be faithful to the human, natural, Italian world that he knew.

In that respect, Giotto may have been indebted to Francis of Assisi (1182–1226), who walked the Italian landscape almost a century earlier. What could be the connection between Giotto and St. Francis? Consider two of Francis's teachings. In objection to the pretentiousness of organized religion, Francis advocated a version of Christianity based on poverty, simplicity, and love. If a man really wants to be religious, then let him divest himself of property, live in simple poverty as the apostles of Jesus had done, and spend his life in brotherhood and service toward his fellow creatures. Love was Francis's most potent word. Love expressed in service to the world was an invincible power, capable of cleansing and renewing the world. Perhaps that side of St. Francis is too well known to bear repeating. What is less well known, perhaps, is that when Francis spoke of "brotherhood," he included the whole natural order in that term. Included in the legends of St. Francis is that he once preached a sermon to a flock of birds. Such a story represents his view of *the brotherhood of all nature* which he deeply felt. When we read Francis's "Canticle of Brother Sun" —

> Praised be thou, my Lord, for our Mother Earth,
> Who sustains and rules us,
> And brings forth divers fruits
> And colored flowers and herbs —

we are reading about a worldview which helps to explain the artistic revolution wrought by Giotto and his contemporaries — an artistic revolution on behalf of nature. There is a legend that one day in the countryside near Florence, the painter Cimabue (fl. 1272–1302) came upon a ten-year-old shepherd who was attempting to draw a sheep with a sharp stone on a flat rock. Cimabue, struck by Giotto's talent, offered to teach him to paint. What was the art which Cimabue transmitted to Giotto? It was an art still rooted in the Byzantine tradition, as one can tell in Cimabue's picture of *Madonna Enthroned* in which the figures are symbols rather than persons; their size depends on their moral or spiritual worth rather than on their physical dimensions; and they are shown against a background of gold, representing the omnipresence of God. Yet Cimabue himself had already begun to move beyond the Byzantine tradition into the world of nature, into the world of human beings and human emotions. In *The Crucifixion,* painted by Cimabue in Assisi, we are struck by the fact that drama has replaced moral value as the principal ingredient of the picture. What this picture expresses is grief and helpless protest over the death of a human being. Human passions have reappeared in painting.

Giotto began his career in Rome as a mosaic worker during the reign of Pope Boniface VIII (1294–1303) — the pope who collided with Philip the Fair of France and was finally undone, sending the papacy into a precipitous decline. During his short stay in Rome, Giotto took care to inspect the work of important artists. Arnolfo di Cambio, like Giotto, was a Tuscan. His sculpture moved Giotto deeply. Its very simplicity and the

55. Cimabue,
Madonna Enthroned

intensity of its spiritual quality taught Giotto how to express the essential
qualities of the Franciscan life, which, later on, he was so determined to
express.

The lives of both Francis and Giotto were associated with the town
of Assisi. So moved had the Italian people been by St. Francis that they
built an elaborate basilica at Assisi in his honor during the course of the
thirteenth century. It was almost a repudiation of the things he stood for

— simplicity, poverty, and a ministry of love to the whole created order. The pope, having declared 1300 a Jubilee Year, invited the leading artists to gather at Assisi and to decorate the church in time for the Jubilee. In 1296, Giotto, then in his thirties, joined the convention of artists in Assisi. Cimabue was also on hand. Little by little, the walls of the church became covered by frescoes; and a new style of art began to emerge, so wonderful that Dante saw fit to immortalize it in the *Divine Comedy*. Did Giotto paint any or all of the twenty-eight frescoes depicting the life of St. Francis? It is a hotly disputed issue. Most scholars now believe that the work at Assisi was a collective one which Giotto directed.

Among the fresco paintings in the Upper Church at Assisi is one which shows St. Francis offering his cloak to a beggar — a typical Franciscan act (see plate 36). In the center stands the gentle Francis between earth and sky, the sky having been opened in a V by the mountains. On the left is the secular world, represented by an Italian hill-town with its crenalated walls. On the right is the religious world in which exists a rather humble little church, illustrative of Francis's indifference to pomp and riches.

In the tenth scene of the cycle, entitled *The Expulsion of the Demons at Arezzo* (see plate 37), Giotto returns to the distance between the secular and sacred worlds, the fortified town versus the church. Although Francis is found on the church's side, he appears to be beckoning to the secular world which is alive with demons. The fresco suggests that the pretentious church has cut itself off too long from ordinary life and must return to people through simplicity and honest fervor which are, in fact, displayed in the person of Francis.

Notice the late-medieval hill-town: thick walls, defensive towers, narrow streets, angular, colorful, secure. Despite his gift for observation, Giotto had none of the Renaissance capability of perspective.

The geometrical conception of perspective came only in the quattrocento. Yet, in another fresco in Assisi showing Pope Innocent III confirming the Franciscan Order, *Confirmation of the Rule* (see plate 38), we see Giotto's attempt at perspective. Instead of an infinite vanishing point, such as we saw in the constructions of Leonardo da Vinci, this picture simply stops. A curtain, a blue backdrop, concludes the picture. Giotto overcomes the difficulty by organizing the two groups of characters in perfect balance in an axis around the head of St. Francis.

Francis's belief in the brotherhood of the whole created order is illustrated in the fresco, *St. Francis Preaching to the Birds* (see plate 39). Francis neither spoke much nor moralized much; but his actions and gestures were eloquent — as one can see here in the way Giotto painted his arms.

Around the year 1303, a wealthy money-lender of Padua, Enrico Scrovegni, built a plain chapel in the midst of the ancient Roman Arena in Padua. As Giotto suggests, Scrovegni consecrated the little chapel to God as a means of expiating the guilt he must have felt over the manner in which he had accumulated his wealth.

In 1310, some eight years after the consecration of the chapel, Giotto, who was then working nearby in the Church of Saint Anthony in Padua, was asked to decorate the interior of Scrovegni's structure. Padua was then a free, republican city, in proximity to Venice, the site of a great university, the center of vigorous philosophical debates, and the scene of some of the earliest manifestations of humanism. There is scarcely any mystery why Giotto was invited to decorate the Scrovegni Chapel; he was the leading artist of his day, as even Dante had made clear.

The Scrovegni Chapel is Giotto's supreme accomplishment. On its walls, Giotto unfolds the whole history of mankind's deliverance from the slavery of sin and death (see plate 43). On the top tier of paintings, the story of Mary, the mother of Jesus, is told. The next two tiers in descending order describe the life of Jesus: his infancy, adult career, death, and resurrection. On the lowest tier, Giotto depicts the seven deadly sins and the seven virtues. The entire entrance wall of the building is covered with a huge scene of the Last Judgment.

According to the Golden Legend, a popular thirteenth-century compilation of pious traditions which Giotto followed, Joachim, who would one day become the father of the Virgin Mary, was driven from the temple in disgrace for his inability to conceive children, notwithstanding his twenty years of marriage to Anna, his wife. Here (see plate 40), his head downcast in humility, he has taken refuge with some shepherds. It is clear that Joachim has just arrived. One of the animals in the center is leaping happily at the feet of the newcomer. Another raises his head in curiosity. The shepherds exchange uneasy glances: they have not made up their minds whether to allow the newcomer to stay. Joachim awaits the decision of his hosts.

Joachim dreams of an angel who commands him to return to Jerusalem. There, at the entrance of the city, he will find his wife, Anna, awaiting him at the Golden Gate, to tell him that she is with child. (That child was, of course, Mary.)

In the nativity painting in the Scrovegni Chapel (see plate 41), Giotto shows the birth occurring in a stable, rather than in a cave — which means that Giotto was more in tune with French Gothic iconography than with the Byzantine. The presence of the ox and ass fulfill a prophecy made in the book of Isaiah. Old Joseph, although the father of the new-born child, has fallen asleep; midwives hand the infant to his mother, while angels announce the news to two shepherds. Strange to say, one of the shepherds has turned his back. That indiscretion was tantamount to a revolution in painting: figures may now move and turn in any direction.

The *Kiss of Judas* of this series is as sinister as the others are sweet (see plate 42). By means of an embrace, Judas identifies Jesus for his executioners. The body of Jesus seems almost shrouded in the traitor's cloak. Jesus has realized everything. Judas is doubly a traitor. He has betrayed Jesus. And he has betrayed love itself, of which the kiss is the signet. The startling impact of this scene is increased by the noses and eyes of the Roman soldiers who crowd around the principal figures. Giotto exploits the sinister features of Judas who purses his lips for the kiss which will betray, as if primal good was contending against primal evil. Here is the whole scene of the betrayal of Jesus — the most dramatic scene of the whole Scrovegni series. Giotto, an excellent storyteller, includes two subplots in his picture. As required by iconographic tradition, he depicts St. Peter in the act of cleaving off the ear of Malchus, one of the high priest's servants. Giotto hides most of that grizzly scene behind the back of the hooded servant who is trying to restrain Peter. The second subplot is a character analysis of the high priest, on the right, who points to the embrace of Jesus and Judas, yet vacillates, as if unable to cope with the wickedness of the betrayal. Giotto exaggerates the fierce intensity of the picture by the tangle of tilting spears, torches, and staves.

Giotto attempted to represent the Last Judgment on the entire entrance wall of the Scrovegni Chapel (see plate 43). How different is Giotto's hell from that of his contemporary Dante (1265–1331). Giotto's hell is a place of terrible disorder, without any of Dante's meticulous layers and compartments. In the center of this vast painting is Christ — Christ enthroned as the judge of all men and nations. Beneath the figure of Christ the Judge, the dead rise from their graves and are consigned either to heaven or to hell. Four rivers of red and orange fire proceed from the throne of Christ to engulf the damned.

About the year 1310, immediately after he had completed the Scrovegni Chapel, Giotto was commissioned to paint a great enthroned Madonna for one of the parish churches of Florence, the Church of the Ognissanti, or All Saints' Church. (The picture now hangs in the Uffizi

56. Giotto,
*Madonna
Enthroned with
Child and
Angels*

Gallery.) The throne, with its pointed arches, is Gothic, rather than Byzantine, illustrating Giotto's well-known preference for French-Gothic forms. Here the Virgin actually appears to be seated, rather than suspended. Notice the tactile reality of the Virgin's neck and hand, as well as of the limbs of the child. Art historian Bernard Berenson argues that Giotto was the first great Renaissance master to achieve the ability to stimulate the tactile consciousness of the viewer. "Tactile" means "life-communicating." This Virgin and her child are invested, indeed, with a fine, new sense of humanity, while the angels at the bottom of the picture are among the most human figures Giotto managed to execute.

Compare the Ognissanti Madonna by Giotto with the similar enthroned Madonna done by Cimabue around the year 1280; thereby one may estimate the progress which Giotto made toward the new style of the Renaissance.

After Padua, Giotto did commissions in Rome and Milan. In the 1320s, however, he was recalled to Florence to decorate the Bardi and Peruzzi chapels in the Franciscan Church of Santa Croce. As in the beginning of his life he had painted pictures of St. Francis, so he returned to St. Francis again toward the end of his long career as an artist. Santa Croce became the schoolroom for generations of Florentine artists. To that church came the sculptor Donatello and the painters Masaccio and Michelangelo to study the frescoes of Giotto. Surely there is justification for saying that Giotto was the first great artistic personality of Florence. Why was Giotto so important? First, because he tried to create natural forms, forms with depth, with dimensions, forms which evoke our tactile consciousness. This he did by the simplest means of light, shadow, and functional line. Second, because he succeeded in communicating the significant truth of every scene, the emotional truth, the feelings of his figures; and because in doing so, he enables his viewers to participate in the emotional life of his figures — which is the power of empathy.

In 1330, Giotto was summoned to Naples to work in the service of Robert of Anjou, who then ruled that kingdom. But Florence needed him again as chief architect of the cathedral, and he was recalled in 1334. In his capacity as *capomaestro,* he made the original design of Florence's great, free-standing campanile.

On January 8, 1337, Giotto died in Florence. Much later, Lorenzo the Magnificent had a plaque in the painter's memory affixed in the cathedral of Florence. The Renaissance poet Angelo Poliziano contributed this verse to the plaque: "I am he through whom painting, once dead, was reborn." Giotto's new style influenced all of Italian art from his lifetime afterward. But it did not forcefully emerge for another whole century, when it was renewed by Masaccio.

MASACCIO

MASO DI SER GIOVANNI DI MONE — known in history by his nickname, Masaccio, "Ugly Tom" — was born in the village of San Giovanni in the Valdarno, in December, 1401. He worked principally in Florence and Pisa, and died somewhat mysteriously in Rome, in November 1428, perhaps of malaria, perhaps of poison. Although he lived a scant twenty-seven years, he was one of the outstanding painters in the history of Western art. "To Masaccio especially," wrote Vasari, "we are indebted for the good style of modern painting; for it was Masaccio who perceived that the best painters follow nature as closely as possible." He was a pupil of Ghiberti, a friend of Donatello and Brunelleschi; he graced the streets and guilds and work-shops of Florence in the first quarter of the *quattrocento* when they did. Inspired by the new sculpture of Donatello, he created powerful figures of solid humanity, robust and heroic people indifferent to gracefulness, people who did human things, expressed human emotions, endured human pain. Masaccio's art was sometimes overwhelming in its sense of human suffering; the tragic element of his art even blunted the essential optimism which the Renaissance held toward human nature. The dignity and humanity of Masaccio's figures, their dramatic gestures, their authentic characterization, take us back to Giotto, who worked one hundred years earlier.

In 1427, Masaccio joined his friend Masolino as a decorator of the Brancacci Chapel. On these walls is left Masaccio's essential message. An especially moving fresco here is *Expulsion from Paradise* (see plate 44). Adam and Eve do not stand gracefully under the tree of the knowledge of good and evil as in other Renaissance works. Rather, they are driven out of the garden in shame and sorrow; their suffering is palpable. Adam is naked. He covers his eyes which have seen too much — this mortal creature who has presumed to be like God. Eve's shame is equally unmistakable. Aloft, the angel of justice carries out the sentence of explusion; his sword and pointed finger warning us that there will be no reprieve. The verdict will stand for all time and all human beings.

Above the altar in the Brancacci Chapel is the first fresco painted entirely by Masaccio. It portrays Peter baptizing new converts to Christianity (see plate 45). The neophyte on the right, shivering from the cold, is often held up to illustrate Masaccio's skillful realism. By contrast is the wonderfully vulnerable human being, powerful of body yet touched by religion, about to undergo the sacrament of baptism.

In the panel near the altar that shows Peter healing the sick with his

237

shadow, Masaccio takes the occasion to show us those who have been defrauded of the great prosperity of quattrocento Florence (see plate 46). Great people, even saints, even popes, may parade about doing good, but the poor are always there.

In the panel just right of the altar, Peter is shown distributing money to a woman and child — money fraudulently held back by Ananias (see plate 47). At left is a poor person, too sick to stand without crutches, whose worldly goods fit in a single leather pouch. Behind Peter's outstretched arm is a poor soul who is blind. He begs for any handout that may be forthcoming. Next to Peter is the younger disciple John. Between them stands a person glaring with a certain moral indignation.

Masaccio's masterpiece at the Brancacci Chapel is *Tribute Money* — a great panorama which occupies the main upper-left panel of the altar (see plate 48). At Capernaum, the state tax collector has stopped Peter and his entourage and demanded the payment of the half-shekel tax, diverting the whole crowd of disciples from its normal pursuits. Jesus holds a spirited conversation with Peter over the propriety of paying the tax. In order not to offend the authorities of the state, Jesus requires Peter to cast a fishing line into the sea, in effect, to fish for the money. Peter does as he is told, but without much pleasure.

In the autumn of 1428, Masaccio began the last fresco of the Brancacci decoration, *Resurrection of the Son of the Emperor Theophilus* (see plate 49). Having laid out the picture, Masaccio left for Rome where shortly he died, perhaps of malaria, perhaps of poison. Thirty years later, his work was taken up by Filippino Lippi, Filippo's son, who tried his best to honor the style of Masaccio.

The emperor Theophilus and his court were painted by Masaccio. So was the figure of Peter, shown in the act of raising Theophilus's son. But almost all of the witnesses were painted by another hand — Filippino's. The two splendid monks, so robust, so human? Masaccio! The artist also included himself in the illustrious group of four men standing at the far right (see plate 50). Starting from the right are Brunelleschi, Alberti, Masaccio, and Masolino.

Masaccio died at the age of twenty-seven. But even if, like Titian, he had lived to the age of ninety-nine, his interpretation of reality could not have touched us more profoundly.

THE EARLY SCULPTORS: GHIBERTI AND DONATELLO

In 1401, a competition was held among Florentine sculptors for the commission to do the north doors of the Baptistry, in Florence, in bronze relief. Lorenzo Ghiberti (ca. 1381–1445), then twenty, won the competition, despite the fact that he competed against the cream of Florentine masters, including Brunelleschi. In his *Sacrifice of Isaac,* which he submitted for the competition, he created what is considered to be the first bronze relief of a nude human form which is truly representative of the Renaissance — a new vision of what a human being is. He seemed to possess instinctive knowledge of human anatomy and muscle structure. The picture represents an unpredictable moment when the boy, Isaac, kneels at the altar, as his father, Abraham, puts his knife to his throat. Done with extraordinary skill, the work is distinguished by its soft, curving rhythms.

Ghiberti labored on the north doors until 1424 — some twenty-two or twenty-three years — modeling in wax, casting in bronze, chasing the

57. Ghiberti,
Sacrifice of Isaac

58. Ghiberti, north doors of the Baptistry

bronze, gilding with gold leaf, and finally burnishing the completed work. His subject was the New Testament, organized in twenty-eight quatrefoils, arranged in seven rows up and down, to match the doors done earlier by Andrea Pisano. From each intersection there emerged the head of a prophet from the Old Testament. The quatrefoil shape of the panels, however, limited Ghiberti in his handling of space. It was not until he executed the next set of doors — those which Michelangelo called "the gates of paradise" — that he was able to realize perspective in his bronze reliefs.

Ghiberti was in his mid forties when he was given the commission to do the third set of doors for the Baptistry. The year was 1425. Michelangelo played on words when he described those doors as "the gates of paradise"; he knew very well that the term *paradiso* was traditionally applied to the area between a baptistry and a cathedral. What Michelangelo meant, of course, was that Ghiberti's second effort was truly worthy of paradise. The name stuck. The "gates of paradise" (see plate 51) consist of ten square fields — the quatrefoils having been given up — in which Ghiberti, now power-fully under the influence of Alberti, composed complete pictures of Old Testament scenes, stretching space from the foreground into a more and more remote distance. Foreground figures were projected virtually as statues in the round.

Typical of the north doors is Ghiberti's *Annunciation* (see plate 52). The composition is related to a fair number of late medieval Annunciations, in which the angel Gabriel is seen to fly, rather than walk, into the scene. The background is flat; but the portico is tilted in an effort to indicate depth.

One of the most impressive panels of the "gates of paradise" is *Jacob and Esau,* which Ghiberti has executed according to Albertian principles of perspective. It is thought to be unsurpassed in Renaissance art, according to its values of harmony and space, and even according to the execution of its figures.

For the first time in Renaissance sculpture, graceful, sensuous female nudes are presented. In *Adam and Eve,* Ghiberti devotes more emphasis to Eve, whom the Lord brings forth gently by her wrist; she is upheld by four angels, while still other angels hover above.

Donatello (1386–1466) saw things in his own revolutionary way. Of utmost importance to him were (1) his materials — bronze, stone, wood — with which he worked as though he could see their innate possibilities, and (2) the inner life of the subjects he depicted. The result was an art which, although sometimes careless of surface refinements, was disturbing in its

59. Ghiberti, *Jacob and Esau*

immediacy, able to achieve a level of force and drama hitherto unknown in Italian sculpture.

Scholars refer to the "four epics" of Donatello's career. In his juvenile period (1406–32), he did statues for the Florentine cathedral, including the marble *David*, statues for Orsanmichele (the Florentine granary) including the important *Saint George*, as well as *Marzocco*, the great stone lion of Florence, a beautiful wooden crucifix made by commission for a Florentine family, and a bust of Niccolo da Uzzano. In his so-called ripe period (1433–43), he executed his more famous bronze *David*, as well as the *cantoria*, or choir-gallery, for the

Florentine cathedral. To his Paduan period (1443–53) belong Donatello's great bronze equestrian statue of the *condottiere* of Padua, Gattamelata, as well as bas reliefs for the Church of Saint Anthony of Padua, which introduced the art of perspective to a rising generation of north-Italian artists, notably Andrea Mantegna. In his late period (1454–66), haunted by death, Donatello produced some remarkably poignant pieces, including his *Magdalen.*

Among Donatello's earliest commissions were statues, carved from marble, for the cathedral of Florence. They were to be set in exterior niches, thirty feet above the ground. Using his knowledge of optics, which was very considerable, he was able to calculate sizes and expressions in order to compensate for the great height from which they would be seen. Many of

60. Ghiberti, *Adam and Eve*

those statues were of the Old Testament prophets, for Donatello was quite taken by the fiery intensity of the prophetic temperament.

Intended for a high perch on the facade of the cathedral was a marble statue of David — Donatello's first important work, carved in the period

61. Donatello, *David*, marble

of 1408–9. Donatello's *David* was both proud and remorseful, both triumphant and doubtful. For the first time in the Renaissance an artist had admitted the passing world to that inner world of psychological tensions. In Donatello's *David,* the Florentines suddenly saw themselves — free and

62. Donatello, *David,* bronze

245

63. Donatello, monument of Gattamaleta

proud, yet beset by such enemies as Naples and Milan. They refused to allow Donatello's *David* to leave the ground, where they could see it, but insisted that it be put up in the Palazzo Vecchio.

Donatello's second depiction of David, a bronze David, is considered the first freestanding nude cast or carved since antiquity. Commissioned by the Medici, it is a perplexing work. The cold detachment of this effete, pre-adolescent David, standing smugly with his foot upon the head of the slain Goliath, is in marked contrast to the quite heroic David which Donatello carved in marble at an earlier time.

Around 1443, Donatello was called to Padua to make a colossal equestrian statue, in bronze, of the *condottiere*, Gattamelata. The traveler finds it there today, in front of the Church of Saint Anthony — a picture

64. Donatello, *The Magdalen*

of military force, an image of command, surpassing any equestrian statue of the Renaissance. Donatello remained some ten years in Padua, in which time he managed to change the course of sculpture and painting in northern Italy. Perspective was only one of his contributions; he introduced the whole Renaissance tradition in art to that region.

Donatello's last works were strange and harrowing harbingers of death, such as his wonderful *Magdalen,* carved in wood for the interior of the

247

Baptistry in Florence; that haunting sculpture explores the darker side of human life, its sufffering and death, as well as the melancholy which pervades the whole of the Renaissance civilization, as the counterpart of Renaissance individualism. Emaciated from her long period in the desert, her hair matted, her countenance haggard, her cheeks sunken, her mouth almost toothless, she is the antithesis of the nobility and grandeur of the Renaissance, the other side of the Renaissance coin. This work is typical of Donatello's late period.

THE SECOND RENAISSANCE STYLE: PAINTERS OF THE GENERATION AFTER MASACCIO

THE IMMEDIATE successors of Masaccio were Fra Filippo Lippi (1406–1469) and Fra Angelico (1400–1455). They were followed, in turn, by four painters whose style was indebted to theirs: Veneziano, Uccello, Castagno, and Piero della Francesca. The six together represent what has come to be known as "the second Renaissance style," although the two Fra's were more or less transitional figures. Common to all six was an interest in harmoniously used, properly designed space. In other words, using the Albertian principles of perspective, these six painters attempted to fit together figures, landscapes, buildings, distances, and space into a single, harmonious composition. They were also under great inner compulsion to express the human form realistically — and this in an age which believed so passionately in human individuality and human power.

Filippo Lippi was born in Florence, near the Church of Santa Maria del Carmine. As a boy, he watched Masaccio at work in the Brancacci Chapel. It will therefore come as no surprise that his early paintings betray the strong influence of Masaccio. His early Madonnas, for example, were heavy-featured, plebian types, placed in simple domestic interiors.

Forced by his father to join the Carmelite friars at the age of sixteen, Fra Filippo Lippi soon discovered that he was not cut out for the monastic life. He was constantly in trouble with the monastic authorities over his propensities for wine, women, and song, especially the second. His liaison with Lucrezia Buti, a nun, whom he had persuaded to sit as a model for one of his Madonnas, resulted in parentage for Filippo Lippi; one of his two children by Lucrezia, Filippino Lippi, became an artist in his own right.

Through the intervention of Cosimo de' Medici, Filippo was allowed to leave the order and to marry. That turn of events changed the character of both his life and his paintings. His later paintings reflect the elegant taste of the mid quattrocento: lovely young women, healthy babies, splendid furnishings, handsome costumes, the endless succession of beautiful clouds, fruited plains, lights, and atmosphere which constitute the natural order — and all of this expressed according to the art of perspective. His later paintings glow with warm colors. Gone is the solemnity and heavy volume typical of Masaccio.

Fra Filippo dropped entirely out of sight between 1431 and 1437, during which period *Madonna of Humility* was painted (see plate 53). It is fair conjecture that the painter went into exile with Cosimo de' Medici. At any rate, *Madonna of Humility* is an important work, as it illustrates Fra Filippo's early style, when he was still very attentive to the work of Masaccio. His figures, like Masaccio's, are large and round, people of fairly massive substance and presence.

Madonna and Child with Angels (see plate 54) represents the fully developed style of Filippo Lippi. The Virgin is a new physical ideal, her dress and her hair done in the finest style of Florence in the mid quattrocento. The heavy-featured Madonnas, after Masaccio, are gone.

Fra Giovanni da Fiesole belonged to the Dominican order and served, in fact, as prior of the Dominican convent of San Marco in Florence. His reputation as an "angelic" painter won him the name Fra Angelico. Although he was quite aware of Masaccio's methods of painting, Fra Angelico created wholly different figures — barely corporeal, slender, delicate, refined, and emotionally restrained. He did not share Masaccio's propensity to communicate the intensity of human emotions; or perhaps he was simply too self-constrained to do so. Reluctant to depict evil, he selected religious subjects which would admit us to a world of celestial beauty; and his fresh, brilliant colors served only to heighten that purpose. Yet this painter, whose emotions seem at first glance to have been medieval, reveals his essential character as a Renaissance man in several ways. He was the first Italian to paint a landscape which can be identified. He was among the first to convey the essential pleasantness of nature. He was the first successfully to place a group of figures into a receding landscape, rather than inevitably in the foreground, as in Masaccio's work. He remained abreast of contemporary art theory; his use of perspective and his arrangement of space were as advanced as the books of Alberti. His interest in classical architectural forms, his skillful handling of landscape, and his affirmation of humanity and nature all suggest his commitment to the worldview of the Renaissance.

The work of Fra Angelico was of three sorts. He did many altarpieces which were meant, of course, for public viewing. He decorated the superb little chapel (Niccolo) of Pope Nicholas V in the Vatican. Most of his energy, however, was devoted to the decoration of the halls, cloisters, and cells of San Marco in Florence.

The Annunciation, an altarpiece done for the Church of San Domenico in Cortona, is the first example of Fra Angelico's own style (see plate 55). It is one of his most beautiful creations. Delicate, refined, brilliant with color, it admits us to a world of celestial beauty. At the far left, Adam and Eve are being expelled from Paradise — but it is scarcely the catastrophic event in human history as Masaccio saw it. The angel announces to Mary that she will be the new Eve, and her son Jesus the new Adam. What damage was done to human nature by the fall of the first Adam and Eve will soon be repaired by the new Adam and Eve. Note the classical details of this work and its use of perspective.

The Deposition (see plate 56), commissioned by the wealthy Florentine Palla Strozzi for the Church of Santa Trinità, must have been enormously provocative in mid-quattrocento Florence. For the first time, perhaps, a complicated scene of many figures was arranged against a receding landscape. In the distance is Jerusalem — the very place, albeit in Fra Angelico's imagination. Christ is lowered from the cross by biblical figures painted to resemble Palla Strozzi himself and members of his family.

Coronation of the Virgin is one of a series of forty-four paintings executed by Fra Angelico for the convent of San Marco (see plate 57). Each is six feet in height; each concentrates on one pure image in order to inspire meditation. Devotional images though they may be, none can quite conceal Fra Angelico's interest in genuine human nature.

Fra Angelico spent the years 1446 to 1450 in Rome, painting for the great humanistic pope, Nicholas V. With him was his young assistant, Benozzo Gozzoli. All that remains of their work is a rather precious little chapel in the Vatican called "the Niccolo," decorated entirely by Fra Angelico. His pictures became more complex, less meditative, with greater interest in landscape and in architectural forms. The interior walls of the little chapel are crammed with scenes of the lives of the saints. *San Lorenzo Distributing Alms to the Poor* is considered one of Fra Angelico's very best paintings (see plate 58). Its remarkable fine sense of artistic form made an impression on later artists, particularly on Piero della Francesca. In the background is old St. Peter's basilica, before Pope Julius demolished it.

PAINTERS OF THE LATE QUATTROCENTO

DURING THE last third of the quattrocento, Florentine art was dominated by four masters, Pollaiuolo, Verrocchio, Botticelli, and Ghirlandaio. Interest in spatial composition which had absorbed the painters of the "second Renaissance style" had run its course. But many new aspects of art remained to be explored. The four masters moved forward in three directions. Pollaiuolo and Verrocchio practiced what might be loosely called "scientific" art. They decided that all nature is of one piece — human beings, animals, and vegetation all being worthy of study. They also decided that motion, growth, and decay were more real to the world of nature than the mathematical relationships which artists such as Alberti had supposed. The second trend, represented by Botticelli, could scarcely have been more to the opposite. It sought withdrawal from the world of reality. Poetic and romantic, it led the viewer into a new world of mythological fantasy, religious symbolism, and emotional gratification. The third, practiced by Ghirlandaio, dealt with real types in real situations and to that extent deserves the name of genre painting. Ghirlandaio, unpretentious and by all odds the most popular artist of the four, represented in fresco and oil exactly what he saw, principally Florentines in Florentine surroundings.

The most noteworthy Florentine artist of the late quattrocento was Alessandro di Mariano Filipepi (1445–1510), nicknamed "il Botticello," the Keg. Botticelli was fortunate in the richness of his intellectual formation. He knew and appreciated the tradition from Masaccio, but chose not to follow it. He had been personally taught by Verrocchio and Filippo Lippi. (In Verrocchio's workshop, Leonardo da Vinci had been a fellow pupil.) He had been exposed to the scientific tradition through his close association with Pollaiuolo. He was well acquainted with the Florentine Neoplatonists, Ficino and Pico, by whom he was educated in Neoplatonism and exposed to classical mythology. In the end, however, Botticelli disdained the major dogmas of the Florentine tradition of art and developed a highly personal style, based upon his sophisticated use of the line to describe figures. Above all, we remember Botticelli for his propensity to lead us out of the world of tangible reality into a new world of classical mythology, Christian symbolism, emotional satisfaction, and, finally, when the voice of Savonarola resounded in Florence, religious fervor.

Florentine society in the age of Lorenzo the Magnificent was greatly taken by classical mythology — a conceit which the Neoplatonists ardently inculcated and which the elegant society sought to represent artistically in their houses and villas. Botticelli excelled all others as a painter of mythologies during the Laurentian period.

An excellent example is *Pallas and the Centaur* (see plate 59), which Botticelli painted around 1482 to commemorate the diplomatic triumph of Lorenzo de' Medici over King Ferrante of Naples two years earlier; it had saved the city of Florence from almost certain devastation. Ficino had spun the tale in the salons of Florence — how Minerva (whom the Greeks called Pallas), goddess of reason, having sprung from the head of Jove, was the very essence of intelligence and could tame even the rankest cruelty and irrationality on the part of human beings by the administration of her perfect intelligence. Pallas, bedecked by Medici symbols (the interlocking rings and laurel branches), represents the triumph of reason (Lorenzo) over the sullen beast of cruelty and unreason (Ferrante and Pope Sixtus IV). In case we might have missed the point, Botticelli painted the Bay of Naples in the background. Already the artist's linear style is apparent, as well as his tendency to exaggerate the length of neck and limbs of the women he depicted.

In *Primavera* (Spring), we enter more deeply into Botticelli's world of mythological fantasy (see plate 60). Aside from its mythic themes, the picture is highly illustrative of the social graces, the costumes, the intellectual life, and the cult of classical antiquity as they were practiced and observed in Florence at the end of the quattrocento. Botticelli's interest is spring, the season of love, the season of fertility. The scene is set in an orange grove; the fruit is ripe on the bough. At the far right is Zephyrus, the god of the warm wind; he is chasing the nymph Chlorus, so pregnant with spring that flowers fall from her mouth. Chlorus is transfigured into Flora, goddess of spring, a creature of infinite sensuality and spirituality. Near the center of the picture stands Venus, goddess of love, her hand raised in benediction over these idyllic transports. To her right, three Graces dance in a circle in billowy, diaphanous gowns. Above, Cupid shoots his arrows in their direction. And at the far right, Mercury, the fair youth, turns his back on these revelries, but points to the clouds as if to unveil the mysteries of heaven.

Once again, Ficino may have inspired the picture. Botticelli painted it as the commission of Lorenzo di Pierfrancesco de' Medici (of the cadet branch of the family), to whom Ficino had written letters in praise of Venus, claiming her to be the mother of almost every virtue heretofore assumed to have been Christian — love, dignity, beauty, modesty, temperance, honesty, and so on. The painting may be interpreted as anything between an involved riddle of Neoplatonic truth to a simple allegory of all those good and decent graces which a proper Florentine ought to have. However one interprets the picture, it is surely a mixture of classical and Christian themes, with Venus as Botticelli's version of the Virgin Mary.

A work similarly mythological, and even more famous, is the *Birth of Venus* (see plate 61). It is important first to observe Botticelli's style. Gone is the Renaissance tradition of volume and atmosphere which had been passed down from Masaccio. The picture is a work created principally by Botticelli's extraordinary use of line. Never was Botticelli more willing to exaggerate than in the depiction of Venus, long of neck, with sloping shoulders, and an unbelievable cascade of hair. The picture was commissioned for hanging, as a companion to *Primavera,* on an opposite wall of Lorenzo di Pierfrancesco's salon. Like *Primavera,* it too is a composite of classical mythology and Christian themes — a blend no doubt inspired by Ficino. According to the myth, from which the picture was taken, Venus was born from a sea that had been made fertile by the castration of Saturn. Such grisly business the delicate Botticelli chose not to recall. Instead, he represented two winged zephyrs (Christians might read, "angels") wafting the goddess Venus (Christians might read, "Christ") from the sea (Christians might read, "the Jordan River") on a shell (Christians might read, "symbol of baptism") onto the dry land, where she is met and vested by an Hour who is herself bedecked by the Laurentian laurel. Apparently, the observer of the picture could choose to see either a simple elegant instruction into an ancient myth, or the unveiling of the Christian mystery of the baptism of Jesus.

Savonarola had a sobering influence on Botticelli, although it is by no means clear that he, like his younger brother, Simone, became a participant in Savonarola's political adventures. Still, Botticelli's later art illustrates a growing religious passion and moral intensity. A good example of such fervor is to be found in *The Annunciation* (see plate 62), which Botticelli painted about 1490 for one of the parish churches of Florence; it now hangs in the Uffizi. Mary, who has been reading at a lectern, appears to have been caught aghast by the intruding angel, who has been sent to announce to her that she is to be the mother of Jesus. The angel crouches at the delivery of such stunning news. Mary sways, her eyes closed, her face utterly drained of color, as if she were caught up in some overpowering spiritual force. The emotional exaggeration of this work, which we must admit to be out of keeping with the Renaissance values of peace, moderation, and proportion, points the way toward manners, which evolved into the baroque style of the late sixteenth century.

Domenico Ghirlandaio (1449–1494) represented the taste of the period. His studio took most of the major commissions for public painting, as well as the lucrative trade in portraits. He could not work fast enough to satisfy the demand. If he was a popular artist, Ghirlandaio was on that account no less important. Three artistic qualities enhance his work. He had the best color sense of any Florentine painter of his day — a gift which he managed to convey to his pupil, Michelangelo Buonarroti. A student of architecture, both ancient and contemporary, he acquired thereby the ability to compose figures and architectural spaces into unified pictures beyond the ability of any contemporary Italian painter. In portraiture, he was unsurpassed in the analysis of human character.

Ghirlandaio's major commission, on which Michelangelo may have worked as an apprentice, was the series of frescoes which fill the chancel of the Dominican church, Santa Maria Novella. The frescoes on one side of the chancel narrate the life of Mary; those on the other side, the life of John the Baptist.

Among Ghirlandaio's most important commissions was the decoration of the Sassetti chapel in the Florentine church called Santa Trinità. One of the paintings from that church, *The Adoration of the Shepherds,* is considered Ghirlandaio's masterpiece (see plate 63). It is a statement of both naturalism and classicism. Ghirlandaio's interest in classicism is apparent in the two Corinthian columns, one bearing the date of the painting, and in the classical sarcophagus with its inscription promising resurrection to its occupant. His faithfulness to nature is apparent in both his human representations and in his animals.

11. *Michelangelo and Raphael*

MICHELANGELO BUONARROTI WAS BORN IN 1475 IN THE HILL TOWN of Caprese, where his father, Lodovico, was the *podestà*. Before Michelangelo was quite a month old, Lodovico's term of office came to an end, and the Buonarrotis quit the wilds of the Apennines and moved back to Florence, to the family home near the Church of Santa Croce. The boy, however, was sent off to nurse at Settignano, a village of stonecutters, where the Buonarrotis owned a small farmhouse. Michelangelo was fond of saying that he drank in the stonecutter's art as he drank in his nurse's milk.

He grew up to believe that sculpture was the sublime art. He did not at all share Leonardo da Vinci's passionate belief in the superiority of painting. In fact, Michelangelo declared the contrary when he said: "The nearer painting approaches sculpture, the better it is; the nearer sculpture approaches painting, the worse it is." By sculpture, Michelangelo meant something achieved (as he said) "by the force of taking away." "Sculpture that is done by adding on resembles painting" and is therefore inferior. Vasari explained Michelangelo's intention by using the metaphor of the bathtub, from which water is drawn away, revealing the figure. Michelangelo might have preferred to say, as indeed he repeatedly did, that it is the art of the sculptor to liberate the figure that indwells the stone. As much as he admired the sculpture of his predecessors Donatello and Ghiberti, it was nevertheless achieved (at least to some extent) by the process of adding on, and it was, to that extent, inferior.

The disagreement between Leonardo and Michelangelo did not stop at the relative importance of painting and sculpture but extended deep into their respective personalities. Leonardo was fairly aloof from human affairs; Michelangelo was instinctively attracted to others and longed for their love in return. Leonardo was a skeptic; Michelangelo, a believer. Leonardo was captivated by the mysteries of nature; Michelangelo was much less interested in landscape. Leonardo thought lightly of humanity; Michelangelo saw humanity as a transparency (or veil, as he preferred to say) of God and therefore the very center of his artistic interest.

For three-quarters of a century, the art of sculpture was both Michelangelo's tormentor and his refuge, or, as he himself described it, his "sweet chamber in hell." In 1488, when he was thirteen, Michelangelo prevailed over his father's pretentious scruples against manual labor and became a paid apprentice in the studio of Ghirlandaio. From that Florentine master, he formed a lifelong attachment to the traditions and techniques that fashioned the art of Florence in the quattrocento. In about a year, upon Ghirlandaio's nomination, Michelangelo was invited into the Medici Palace as the guest of Lorenzo the Magnificent and enrolled in the institute of art that Lorenzo had established in a nearby garden for the purpose of training the most promising young artists in the vicinity. There Michelangelo learned the formal techniques of sculpture from Bertoldo, a middling artist, who nevertheless was able to transmit the lessons of his own teacher, Donatello, to his young pupil, Michelangelo. As often as he could, Michelangelo visited Santa Croce to study the frescoes of Giotto and went across the river to the Carmine Church, where he spent hours and days copying the marvelous works of Masaccio. In the Carmine he was once bold enough to criticize the drawings of his classmate Torrigiano and was recompensed by a blow that broke his nose, permanently disfiguring him. At the Medici table, Michelangelo dined with illustrious members of the family, including two latter-day popes, Leo X and Clement VII. He also listened to the Neoplatonists retail their philosophic wares, even though he did not have the benefit of Latin. By such means he may have gained a philosophic basis to his art: the adoration of earthly beauty as a self-disclosure of the infinite God.

When he was seventeen, his benefactor, Lorenzo de' Medici, died, and Michelangelo found himself back again in the modest house of his father near Santa Croce. All Florence was now being shaken by the sobering preaching of Savonarola, whose sermons Michelangelo heard and whose strident voice kept ringing in his ears all the rest of his life. Only three pieces of sculpture belong to Michelangelo's Medicean era, and only two of these require comment: a small marble relief called *Madonna of the Stairs,* the first of all his works, and a wooden crucifix made for the prior of Santo Spirito, who had done him the favor of allowing him to dissect corpses. The Jesus of that crucifix was entirely nude — a scandalous breach of convention — with the languorous beauty of a Greek god.

One of the foremost characteristics of Michelangelo's art is its nudity. We can explain this feature by noting that, for the classical artist and for the Renaissance artist who are interested in human nature and in human life in this world, the nude is the preeminent vehicle in the whole realm of art for confirming and enhancing life itself. It becomes the most significant object in the human world and therefore the most significant object in the artist's imagination. Michelangelo understood this point better than any other artist in the Renaissance.

In 1496 Michelangelo — a lean and wiry man of twenty-one, of medium build and black hair, with a prominent nose noticeably broken — went to Rome. The city was scarcely an inspiration, befouled as it was by human squalor, with the papacy in the hands of Alexander VI, whose dynastic ambitions were widely celebrated. Fortunately, Michelangelo was able to see through the squalor to the mass of Roman architecture, sculpture, and painting that had survived from antiquity, which touched him deeply. "There are many beautiful things here," he noted. His first Roman work was a Bacchus (the Roman god of wine and reveling) of pagan beauty and sensuality that he executed in 1496 and 1497.

The following year a French cardinal in the papal court, who thought to leave a memorial of himself in the Eternal City, commissioned Michelangelo to make a "pietà of marble . . . a Virgin Mary (clothed), with the dead Christ in her arms, the size of a proper man, for the price of 450 golden ducats of the papal mint." In his part of the contract, Michelangelo specified that the sculpture would be "the most beautiful work in marble which exists today in Rome." He went off to Carrara to select the block and set to work. The result of his energies was the Vatican *Pietà,* which depicts the crucified Christ, aged thirty-three, bony of torso and wiry of limb, being cradled in the arms of his mother Mary, who, instead of being fifty-one, as she ought, appears to be younger than her son. Michelangelo's work is seldom anecdotal but rather is dogmatic; it does not tell historical tales but tries to express eternal truths. The age of Mary is therefore irrelevant; it seemed more important to the artist to depict her as the beautiful, ageless woman through whom divinity took on human flesh. The Mary of the pietà is therefore a statement of dogma rather than of historical accuracy. According to Vasari, when the sculpture was first exhibited in St. Peter's Basilica, Michelangelo

65. Michelangelo, *Pietà*

was horrified to hear it attributed to this artist or that; he stole into St. Peter's at night and carved his signature — "Michelangelo Buonarroti, Florentine, made this" — the only one of his works that he himself is thought to have signed.

After five years in the Eternal City, Michelangelo returned to Florence. It was the year 1501; the cinquecento had begun. In Florence he accepted a commission to execute a colossal statue of David for one of the buttresses of the Florentine cathedral. He used a huge block of marble outside the cathedral that had been abandoned by the sculptor Agostino di Duccio in the 1460s; it enabled him to create a statue over fourteen feet tall, quite appropriate for the great height of the buttress where it was intended to be placed. But when in 1505 the Florentines gazed at that extraordinary work, they would not suffer it to be put in such an inaccessible place. The very humanity of the statue led them to demand that it be put in some place where all humankind could be in communion with it. A commission of artists and leading citizens debated its proper location. It was agreed that the colossus should be placed in front of the Palazzo Vecchio as a symbol of the valiant Republic of Florence.

As I have suggested, however, Michelangelo's *David* is not merely a piece of political symbolism. It is a statement about humankind. It is humanity raised to a new power. It speaks the grandeur and nobility of Renaissance man far more eloquently than Pico's *Oration* or Ficino's *Platonic Theology* ever could. The David of Michelangelo is a boy of sixteen, completely and triumphantly nude, with the carriage and muscles of a child of the people, not the effete David of Donatello or the aristocratic David of Verrocchio. For all its magnificence, the statue was immediately stoned by ruffians. In 1527, in the melee that attended the third expulsion of the Medici from Florence, someone threw a bench from the Palazzo Vecchio, shattering the left arm and hand of the statue: it was restored later in the century. In the nineteenth century, after exposure to the elements had rotted the surface of the soft marble, the statue was removed to the Accademia, where it can be seen today.

The third of the High Renaissance masters was Raffaello Santi — Raphael. He was born in 1483, the son of Giovanni Santi, a well-known painter attached to the court of Federigo da Montefeltro, duke of Urbino. Raphael was raised in Urbino, an extraordinary place that was one of the most glorious of all the Renaissance cities, a place of infinite beauty and harmony, graced by the paintings of Piero della Francesca, Botticelli, and other quattrocento artists. It also boasted one of the greatest collections of ancient books and manuscripts in the Western world.

When Raphael was eleven, his father died. Sometime before his seventeenth birthday, he was sent to Perugia and was apprenticed to Perugino, the leading master of that city. He learned quickly what Perugino had to teach him. His first picture, signed and dated 1504, revealed the virtues and clichés, the techniques and coloring typical of his teacher; at the same time, Raphael improved upon them.

Raphael was not a genius on the scale of Leonardo and Michelangelo.

66. Michelangelo,
David

Yet even more than they, he has come to represent the painting of the High Renaissance at its best. He did so because of his extraordinary idealism, which expresses both classicism and the Renaissance itself. Noble figures move through his pictures with utmost dignity and grace in a world that is intelligible and orderly. Everything the Renaissance aspired to — human dignity and rationality, the virtues of order and proportion, integration and harmony — are all expressed in his works. Raphael, however, was more than simply a Renaissance man. A spiritual energy invigorates his figures and affects his compositions, making it difficult for one to believe that his art was contrived intellectually. Some sort of religious force animated his work; in his later art one can catch a hint of the Catholic Reformation.

In 1505, when he was twenty-two, Raphael decided to launch his career in Florence, where there appeared to be an almost insatiable appetite for works of art. Within his first three years in Florence, he painted no less than seventeen Madonnas and Holy Families for Florentine patrons out of his facile religious imagination. Even in these early Madonnas, one can detect the spiritual energy that seems to animate Raphael's otherwise peacefully composed figures. Most of the pictures in this cycle of Madonnas were constructed according to the pyramid that Leonardo had brought into vogue; most entailed a landscape of the Florentine countryside; most revealed Raphael's indifference toward the anatomical precision of Leonardo and Michelangelo. In Raphael's view, the painting consisted, not in anatomical detail, but in the main masses harmoniously composed and properly presented by line and color.

Rather different was Raphael as a portraitist. In painting portraits, he withheld his spiritual proclivities and allowed the pen and the brush to reveal exactly what the eye beheld and what the mind intuited. The result was a tradition of portraiture, reminiscent of that of Antonello da Messina, in which the psychological essence of the subject was fully exposed to public view. Raphael's portraits of the wealthy Florentine wool merchant Angelo Doni and his wife, Maddalena, are excellent examples of the artist's ability to see into human nature (see plates 64 and 65).

In 1505, the year Raphael cast his lot with Florence, Michelangelo Buonarroti left Florence, having been summoned to Rome by Pope Julius II — that *uomo terribile* (awe-inspiring man) — who was determined to revive Rome as the capital of the world. By his colossal dreams and restless energy, by his love of the fine arts and his sixth sense about what art was good and what was not, by his patronage of great artists, and by his insistence that he knew what themes and scenes deserved to be represented in art, Julius

67. Raphael, *Madonna del Granduca*

must be accounted among the half-dozen people who brought the High Renaissance into being.

The pope kept Michelangelo waiting until he could think of a proper undertaking. It would be a tomb — his own tomb, worthy of a pope. Not merely a tomb, but a veritable monument of unprecedented richness and architectural pomp, fit for some prominent place in the old basilica of St. Peter. Michelangelo designed a colossal sepulcher — a freestanding, three-storied pile, surmounted by a sarcophagus, and adorned by no less than forty larger-than-life statues carved in marble. It would, said Michelangelo, surpass any such tomb "ancient or imperial . . . ever built." He left with two helpers for Carrara to find the marble. There he spent eight months wrestling the huge blocks down the slopes at the risk of life and limb. When at last the stones arrived in Rome, they filled up half of St. Peter's square.

Suddenly, in Holy Week of 1506, the pope called a halt to the tomb. He had decided to tear down the old basilica. Funds for the tomb were necessary to build an entirely new basilica, a colossal St. Peter's already being designed by the architect Bramante. Furious, Michelangelo had the servants sell everything that could be sold. In the dead of night and in the black of despair, he stole out of Rome, bound for Florence.

Associated with the proposed tomb of Julius II from its inception were two marble sculptures: *The Dying Slave* and *The Rebellious Slave,* which were among the pieces that the exasperated Michelangelo eventually gave away. Today they are in the Louvre. The beautifully crafted *Dying Slave,* having spent his whole life in bondage, has finally been delivered from the miseries of life by his imminent death. It is even possible to read into this sculpture the Neoplatonic theme of "the way back," as some commentators have done.

Julius, however, had no intention of letting Michelangelo go. Later in 1506 the pope mounted his white charger and led his troops to Bologna, taking this city that rightfully belonged to the Papal States. With a little saber rattling, he easily persuaded the Florentines to send Michelangelo up to Bologna to see him. A reunion occurred. "You should have sought us," said the pope to the artist, using the plural of majesty, "but instead you have waited for us to seek you." Michelangelo declared that he had meant no disrespect. He spent the next months executing an outsized statue of Julius, which, having been cast in bronze, was established in front of the cathedral of Bologna. It had a short life. Within three years, Julius lost Bologna; the people smashed the statue and melted down the bronze in order to cast a cannon, appropriately named La Giulia, which they aimed at the pope.

68. Michelangelo,
The Dying Slave

The year 1508 found Michelangelo in Rome, commencing the most important commission of his career. The Sistine Chapel, begun by one della Rovere, Sixtus IV, was about to receive a new ceiling by another della Rovere, Julius II; Michelangelo received the commission to paint it. He thought little of the idea. He protested that he was a sculptor, not a painter. "The place is wrong," he said, "and no painter am I." Julius persisted. Ascanio Condivi, the sixteenth-century biographer, suggested that Michelangelo's rivals, notably Bramante, egged the pope on, knowing that the vaults of the ceiling presented difficult problems of foreshortening with which Michelangelo was not familiar. Perhaps he would fail! That was a delicious thought to his rivals.

The chapel, built in the 1480s by Sixtus IV, was already magnificently decorated. Quattrocento artists Perugino, Ghirlandaio, Botticelli, and Signorelli had painted biblical scenes on the walls; marble masons had laid a polychrome floor. The flat vault of the ceiling, which was painted blue and dotted with gold stars, now awaited Michelangelo's ministrations. Pope Julius required, and Michelangelo agreed, that the great ceiling show the creation and fall of humankind and the promise of its eventual deliverance. It was decided that he would paint Old Testament prophets and pagan sibyls, alternately, in the spandrels between the twelve arches that supported the vault; the lunettes above the windows would show the ancestors of Jesus; the ceiling itself would be covered with nine scenes from the book of Genesis. The composition of the ceiling can be understood only by understanding its creators: Julius himself and Michelangelo. Julius fancied himself a divinely chosen instrument of God to lead the battle for the survival of the papacy and the renewal of Christianity. He was given to prophetic visions or mystical intuitions that were related to that divine mission. It is probable that the complex structure of the ceiling represents the prophetic visions that Julius was able to express to Michelangelo and that Michelangelo, in turn, was able to realize on the ceiling by his artistic imagination.

Michelangelo brought experts from Florence to retrain him in the techniques of fresco. Having learned, he dismissed them and worked with only a few helpers; together they hoisted a scaffold of eighty feet, especially designed by Michelangelo for the occasion. Lying on his back, he broke off the old plaster, then, day by day, applied a fresh coat upon which the cartoon was laid and the outline traced through by means of a stylus. Within the eight hours that the new plaster was wet, the paint was applied. Paint in the eyes, paint in the beard. The picture of the Flood molded and had to be scraped off and redone. When the money ran out, which happened frequently, Michelangelo had to go begging from the niggardly pope. When he was in Rome, Julius inspected the work himself, climbing the ladder onto the scaffold.

"When will it be finished?"

"When I can, Holy Father."

"When I can! When I can! I will soon make you finish."

Five hundred crowns and an apology tempered Michelangelo's fury. There were worse episodes to follow; tradition has it that once, toward the end of the project, the exasperated pope threatened to hurl the artist off the scaffold.

The first section of the ceiling was completed in September 1509, at which time the scaffold was taken down, allowing Michelangelo to see his work for the first time from the floor of the chapel. This section includes three panels from the life of Noah. The second section assumed a much grander scale, as one can see in the painting of the temptation of Adam and Eve and their expulsion from the Garden of Eden. Standing on the ground in *Creation of Eve*, God creates Eve from the side of Adam (see plate 66). A great kindness passes between Eve and her Creator. At last, the world of faith and love is complete, only to be dissolved by the disobedience of Adam and Eve as seen in the *Temptation and Expulsion* (see plate 67). The tree of knowledge of good and evil divides the Garden of Eden from the barren world into which Adam and Eve are being driven by the angel of justice. In the Fall, both parents reach for the fruit of the forbidden tree. Compared to Masaccio's Adam and Eve in his *Expulsion from Paradise*, Michelangelo is more of a humanist; he softens the suffering of Adam and Eve.

The Cumaean Sibyl painted at this time and the prophet Ezekiel opposite her represent the great age and great wisdom of the Church of Rome, in which are invested and summed up not only the prophecy of the Old Testament but, as the sibyls suggest, the religious lore of classical antiquity.

The third section of the ceiling, completed within the year 1511, reveals a still larger scale of human figures and contains the extraordinary panel depicting the creation of Adam (see plate 68). Here, in a single vision, unprecedented in the history of art, we are shown the majesty of the almighty God — not, however, in the unspeakable holiness that the Neoplatonists would have preferred, but moving before us with a host of angels. We also are shown man — passive, conspicuously impotent, bound to the earth, yet a creature of infinite beauty. The finger of God and the finger of Adam almost touch, as the divine energy passes from God to humankind.

It is a remarkable commentary on the Renaissance philosophy of man — a noble creature who combines in his being the classical ideals of beauty and the Christian ideals of the spirit.

On August 14, 1511, the main scaffolding was cleared away, and Pope Julius celebrated Mass in the Sistine Chapel. Only the lunettes remained to be done; they required but a small, portable scaffold. On Halloween, 1512, the eve of All Saints' Day, the whole of Michelangelo's work stood revealed, and the public was admitted to see it. Vasari reported: "The whole world came running to see what Michelangelo had done. . . . It was such to make everyone speechless with astonishment."

In less than four months, Pope Julius was dead. Michelangelo returned to the creation of a tomb for his papal benefactor. He thought of a more modest, less bombastic memorial for the late pope than the tomb originally conceived for old St. Peter's. In three years, he completed three of the statues that were to grace that tomb. One of the three was a statue of Moses. Today the traveler in Rome finds the grave of Pope Julius II in the obscure church of San Pietro in Vincoli, Julius's church in the days when he was a cardinal. There the traveler sees Michelangelo's *Moses.* Even in the dim light and bad setting, Moses looms as a figure of enormous power, immense vitality, with a countenance not at all unlike that of Pope Julius himself. Moses has two horns protruding from his brow (a long-standing mistranslation of the Hebrew term for "ray of light") and a beard of such magnificent complexity that Vasari thought it must have been executed by a brush instead of a chisel.

While Michelangelo labored upside down on the Sistine ceiling, Raphael arrived in Rome and quickly established himself as one of the foremost artists in the city. Pope Julius found his work pleasing and commissioned him to decorate the *stanze,* or rooms, of the Vatican apartments. In the years 1509 to 1511, he painted the walls of the Stanza della Segnatura, the room in which all important issues of canon law were decided and sealed by papal signature. One rather minor episode in Raphael's decoration of that room immediately catches our eye — his depiction of the fall of Adam and Eve. In comparison with the treatment by Masaccio or Michelangelo, Raphael's version strikes us as a much less tragic event, a much more idealized and classical presentation of the biblical account of the downfall of man.

The main work by Raphael in the Stanza della Segnatura is *Dispute of the Sacrament,* which depicts the history of the central Christian sacrament — the Mass, or Eucharist, or Lord's Supper (see plate 69). The picture is of

69. Michelangelo, *Moses*

70. Raphael, *Adam and Eve*

two spheres. In the heavenly sphere is Christ, whose body is the substance of the Eucharist; he is surrounded by saints and prophets, as well as by the Virgin Mary, and even by God himself. That celestial world is the source of all revealed truth. On the altar below is the consecrated host, in which the substance of the body of Christ has been made to exist by the miracle of transubstantiation. Around the altar are all sorts of learned divines of all ages and parts, discussing the sacrament. Thus, the revealed truth that comes from above is finally submitted to the interpretation of humankind. The connection between the celestial sphere and the terrestrial sphere is the dove, a Christian symbol of the Holy Spirit, who makes the sacrament happen.

Like Leonardo da Vinci's *Last Supper,* this colossal picture is certainly not an extension of the room in which the viewer stands; it is another realm altogether, infinitely greater than that of the viewer. That difference, as we have already observed, is a distinct mark of High Renaissance art.

The *Dispute* shows the learned divines discussing the sacrament. The old man in the foreground — actually Raphael made him to represent Bramante — is careful to consult a book, as if to suggest that we must always cite authorities for the statements we make. The young man in blue — actually a picture of Francesco Maria della Rovere, a relative of the pope — represents the spirit of the new, invigorated Catholic Church which Julius II hoped to create. In the distance, we actually see a new church structure rising — a probable reference to the construction of St. Peter's. In the left-hand corner, in his black Dominican robes, is Fra Angelico.

A bishop is engaged in a discussion with some humble friars — a suggestion that, under Pope Julius's regime, the hierarchy of the church will listen to the lower ranks of the clergy.

Near the altar is Pope Gregory the Great, who was (it is not too far-fetched to say) the founder of the medieval papacy. With him are St. Jerome and other great fathers of the church; they too refer to holy writ and to a pile of learned books around them.

Apparently the church was prepared to listen to an assortment of intelligent people. Here is the poet Dante, recognizable by his laurel wreath; perhaps the *Divine Comedy* has been brought into the discussion. At Dante's side is Sixtus IV, the della Rovere pope who built the Sistine Chapel. More surprising still is the presence of Savonarola, distinguished by his black Dominican hood. Only ten years had passed since the Florentines had burned him at the stake. His appearance here, along with the highest religious authorities, reveals to us the extraordinary degree to which Pope Julius was able to open the councils of the Catholic Church to various shades of opinion. Could Julius have forestalled the Protestant Reformation?

To the left of Pope Sixtus are still other worthies of Christianity: Bonaventure in his brown Franciscan habit, Clement, the first pope after Peter, St. Thomas Aquinas, greatest of all the Dominican teachers, and finally, St. Augustine.

Facing the *Dispute of the Sacrament* is another of Raphael's monumental undertakings — *The School of Athens* (see plate 70). Instead of theologians disputing over the sacrament, here we discover philosophers of classical antiquity engaged in equally important discussions over the nature of truth. Thus, simply by turning one's head, the bystander could pay deference to both classical and Christian wisdom. In Raphael's cartoon, or preparatory drawing, of *The School of Athens,* all of the essential elements of the scene are to be found, except one. If you look carefully you will see an empty space in the center of the steps of the temple. In the final fresco, Raphael placed a figure there, a human figure, bent over a block of marble, a stylus in his hand. Who was he? (We will answer that question at the right time.)

Here, in this magnificent architectural setting, which clearly pre-figures the interior of St. Peter's Basilica, Raphael has assembled the most important philosophers of antiquity. To underline the continuity of the Renaissance with classical antiquity, Raphael has used some of his more illustrious contemporaries as his models for the ancient philosophers.

All one needed to do was to glance up to the ceiling of *The School of Athens* to discover what Pope Julius had in mind. There one saw the statue of a young Greek. It was rather a statement of Julius's intentions to achieve a synthesis of the cultural heritage of antiquity with Christian thought.

In the center of Raphael's *School of Athens,* neatly framed by the arches, are Plato and Aristotle. Each holds one of his major works. Plato, at the left, portrayed by Leonardo da Vinci, holds the *Timaeus.* Aristotle, on the right, holds the *Nichomachean Ethics.* Plato points toward the heavens, in reference to the world of eternal ideas, while Aristotle points earthward, to the more reliable world of empirical observation. To the left of the main figures, in white, stands Sophocles.

At the right, Euclid is teaching his pupils geometry. Raphael depicted him as Bramante, the famous first architect of St. Peter's basilica. By such means Raphael paid tribute to the science of architecture and to his eminent predecessor.

In the group on the left, Raphael painted Pythagoras writing a book, while a young man hands him a slate on which a musical scale is drawn.

The rather enigmatic figure on the right, whom Raphael added to the picture after the cartoon had been drawn, is no doubt Heraclitus, the philosopher who saw the world as a continuous process of becoming. Raphael's Heraclitus is actually Michelangelo. Bramante had taken Raphael secretly to see what Michelangelo had done on the ceiling of the Sistine Chapel. So moved had Raphael been that he made haste to include Michelangelo in this colossal work.

Suddenly Raphael's benefactor, Julius II, was gone. The artist sought some way of paying the old pope honor. He did so in the *Sistine Madonna,* one of his supreme creations. There, in a very large canvas, we see the loveliest of all of Raphael's Madonnas, walking toward us through parted draperies, holding up her child for our inspection and benefit. She was very likely the "baker's daughter" identified by Vasari as Raphael's model on a number of occasions. To her left is St. Barbara. To her right, St. Sixtus. Suddenly we recognize St. Sixtus to be Julius himself, old and frail, the papal crown at his feet. It dawns upon us that we are watching the old curmudgeon as he makes his way into paradise. A picture so rich in color convinces us that Raphael had, by that time, absorbed the color intensity of the artists of Venice.

The new pope, Leo X, was Giovanni de' Medici, second son of Lorenzo the Magnificent. He had known Michelangelo when both were boys in Florence, living together in Palazzo Medici. The pope remembered Michelangelo as being too "irascible," too "intense." Most of the Vatican commissions went to Raphael. Scarcely had the new pope taken his seat upon the ancient throne of St. Peter than he demanded Raphael paint his portrait. Raphael did so with all of the dispassionate objectivity which he customarily brought to portraiture. The pope, at thirty-nine, appears to be excessively corpulent in Raphael's picture of him. At his right is Giulio de' Medici, Leo's first cousin, soon to be pope himself. On his left is a cardinal of the church. Leo does not seem to be the spiritual pastor of millions, but rather a Renaissance connoisseur of ancient manuscripts and fine arts.

The picture pleased the pope nevertheless. At least he fairly overwhelmed Raphael with commissions. At Bramante's death in 1514, Raphael became the papal architect and proceeded to tamper disastrously with Bramante's Greek-cross design for St. Peter's basilica — a fault which Michelangelo later corrected. Raphael was also commissioned to continue the decoration of the stanzas in the Vatican.

Despite the assistance of many helpers, Raphael could not survive the work which was heaped upon him. He died on April 6, 1520, at the age

71. Raphael, *Sistine Madonna*

72. Raphael, Portrait of Leo X

of thirty-seven. As he wanted it, his funeral was held in the Pantheon, which Christians had made over into a church. There, in that classical/Christian place, that classical/Christian artist was buried, in order, as he said, that the light of heaven might shine through the *osculus* (the "eye" or hole in the roof) upon his grave. Suspended above his casket was his last great work, the *Transfiguration of Christ* (see plate 71).

The *Transfiguration* was a work of extraordinary religious intensity. Raphael composed it according to the figure eight. In the upper circle, in an aura of unspeakable divinity, Christ is being drawn into the heavens, with Moses and Elijah at either side, while his own disciples, Peter, James, and John, have been thrown prostrate by the overwhelming power of the spiritual event. In the lower circle are all those creatures who are left spiritually dispossessed, and therefore powerless, when they have no relationship to God. Such was Raphael's last expression of his very pronounced religious intuition.

The last phase of Michelangelo's career (1520–64) ran its course while the Catholic Reformation gained momentum and may be more clearly understood if it is seen from the prospective of a transition from the Renaissance to the Catholic Reformation (see chapter 22 below).

Michelangelo was put off by the attention that Pope Leo X lavished upon Raphael. During the last years of Raphael's life, Michelangelo kept out of the public eye, passing his time quarrying marble. In 1516 he turned up in Florence, where, despite the entreaties of his Roman friends, he remained for almost twenty years. His first commission came, in fact, from the very pope who had paid him no mind in Rome. Leo X asked Michelangelo to furnish the Medici church of San Lorenzo in Florence with a facade. Michelangelo had never attempted architecture before, but he resolved nevertheless to make the facade "a mirror of architecture and sculpture for all Italy." He proceeded to create a wood model of a two-story, free-standing structure — a plastic unity divorced from the church itself — to be peopled by no less than eighteen statues. Having built the model, he set out to quarry the marble. The pope halted the enterprise in 1520, however, and the exterior of San Lorenzo remains as rude today as it did in the cinquecento.

The pope had decided to divert the money to the creation of a funerary chapel in which the deceased Medici could be decently buried. Michelangelo was named architect. Construction commenced in November 1519, on a site symmetrically opposite to Brunelleschi's sacristy at San Lorenzo. In addition to the chapel itself, Michelangelo was required to make fitting tombs for Lorenzo the Magnificent (d. 1492), his brother Giuliano (d. 1478, killed in the Pazzi Conspiracy), as well as two dukes of exactly the same names, Duke Lorenzo (d. 1519) and Duke Giuliano (d. 1516). By 1521 the designs were completed, and Michelangelo was in Carrara buying marble.

Then the project got caught in the vicissitudes of time. In fact, it was not until 1545 that the statues were placed on the Medici tombs by Michelangelo's pupils. And only two of the four tombs were ever constructed.

In 1524 Michelangelo undertook what proved to be his last commission in Florence, the Laurentian Library, designed to house the ever-expanding collection of Medici books and ancient manuscripts. It too was to become part of the complex of buildings at San Lorenzo in Florence. Begun in 1524, the work was suspended in 1526, begun again in 1530, abandoned when Michelangelo left Florence in 1534, and finally brought to completion by the artist Ammanati in 1560. The building is full of deliberate strangeness: the main hall is very high, proportions are everywhere difficult, and columns taper downward. The effect is contradictory and, to that extent, against the grain of classicism with its powerful interest in order, harmony, and proportion.

In 1534, shortly after the death of his father, Michelangelo finally departed Florence and returned to Rome for what proved to be the remainder of his life. Paul III, the first pope of the Catholic Reformation, who took office the same year, commissioned Michelangelo to depict the Last Judgment in fresco, using the entire east wall of the Sistine Chapel. Begun in 1536 and completed five years later, this enormous composition was conceived by Michelangelo as a spiraling movement. Brown human bodies, twisting and turning against a slate-blue sky, rise on the left side of the picture and descend on the right, above the sinister reds that distinguish the mouth of hell. Every figure is shown utterly without rank, most without clothes. The dead rising from their graves and the elect in heaven stand naked before their Judge. In the center of the swirling mass of humanity is Christ the Judge, by no means a benign figure, but the personification of *iustitia,* the divine justice, or righteousness. Only the Virgin Mary, at the right side of Christ, diverts her eyes as a gesture of pity. Michelangelo's *Last Judgment,* given its images of justice, judgment, and pessimism over the human condition, seems to typify the moment when the Italian world passed over from the spirit of the Renaissance to that of the Catholic Reformation.

When Michelangelo had finished decorating the Pauline Chapel for Pope Paul III in the year 1550, he was seventy-five, and his eyesight had failed noticeably. He could no longer accept commissions to paint. Meanwhile, however, he had succeeded Antonio da Sangallo the Younger as chief architect of St. Peter's Basilica. In that capacity, he was able to cast aside the excrescences of both Raphael and Sangallo and to reinstate the Greek-

73. Michelangelo, Laurentian Library

74. Michelangelo, *Last Judgment,* Sistine Chapel

75. Michelangelo, Capitoline Hill

cross plan that Bramante had intended for the great basilica. (See the excursus to chapter 22.) As the architect of St. Peter's, Michelangelo directed his main interest to the dome. Bramante had favored a hemisphere, but Michelangelo conceived of a ribbed dome, with a pronounced upward thrust, modeled after that famous dome by Brunelleschi in Florence. He did not live to see it through to completion; at his death only the drum and the peristyle of the dome had been completed.

Around 1560 the aged artist turned his energies to civic architecture. He undertook the remodeling of the Capitoline Hill, which ancient Romans called the umbilicus of the world. There he restored partially ruined structures, designed new ones, and drew the whole plan together by one of the most beautiful pavement designs in human imagination, graced at the center by the equestrian statue of Marcus Aurelius that had come down from antiquity.

Michelangelo's last works were marble pietàs that prefigured his own

76. Michelangelo, *Pietà*, Florentine Cathedral

77. Michelangelo,
Rondanini Pietà

death. The one that now graces the Florentine Cathedral depicts the relentless power of death. Christ is being drawn downward into the grave, despite the struggle of Mary, his mother, Mary Magdalene, and Joseph of Arimathea to spare him that fate. In the features of old Joseph of Arimathea, Michelangelo depicted himself. Only a few days before his death, he returned to another pietà that he had put aside some ten years earlier. In that work, the *Rondanini Pietà*, we are taught again of the heaviness and inevitability of death. Mary struggles there to support the collapsing body of her son, newly taken down from the cross. In February 1564, as he worked on that pietà, Michelangelo ventured forth in a winter rainstorm, caught pneumonia, and died in his eighty-fourth year. His remains were carried stealthily to Florence, where they were buried in Santa Croce on March 12, 1564. His work, unparalleled in human accomplishment, extended through almost a century of Italian art.

EXCURSUS

Raphael's Vatican *Stanze*

ON THE THIRD WALL OF HIS EXTRAORDINARY ROOM — STANZA DELLA Segnatura — Raphael depicted three cardinal virtues: courage, temperance, law. Courage, on the left side, carries an oak tree — a none-too-subtle reminder that the della Rovere family, from which Julius came, were literally "oaks," people of courage and determination. On the right side is temperance, holding the reins of law in her hand. In the center is jurisprudence, examining herself in a mirror, which is to say, submitting herself to constant self-scrutiny.

Jurisprudence has two faces: hidden in the hair of the young maiden is the countenance of an old man. The wisdom of jurisprudence encompasses both past and future.

On the fourth wall, Raphael treats us to a view of Parnassus — the mountain in Greece sacred to Apollo and the Muses (see plate 72). It is not enough to enjoy the mysteries of Christianity, or to indulge oneself in ancient and medieval philosophy. Poets, musicians, and artists also contribute to Western civilization; and the fourth wall makes that point clear. At the center, Apollo plays a stringed instrument. He is surrounded by poets, writers, and musicians, including the blind Homer (left) and Dante the laureate. How like Raphael's madonnas the Muses are! An inexhaustible stream of poetry flows as water from a mountain spring.

Pope Julius became directly involved in the decoration of Raphael's second stanza, Stanza di Eliodoro, and required Raphael to paint him into the scenery. In the *Expulsion of Heliodorus* (see plate 73), the bearded pope occupies the center of the painting.

Why is Julius there? Heliodorus was a political operative, sent by Syria, who attempted to plunder the temple at Jerusalem. He was stopped, so the story goes, by the intervention of God, who sent two angels and a brave knight, shown here in a gold costume. Together, they drove Heliodorus from the temple. The historical coincidence is clear: Julius, who restored the territories of the papacy by force of arms, is also to be understood as an agent of God.

At right, his cape billowing in the wind, Heliodorus is shown trying to escape. His horse rears, the vase of coins he has stolen spilling its contents on the floor. The avenging angels are suspended in mid-flight, while two youths cling to a column at left to escape the violence of the episode. The ruin of Heliodorus is clear.

In the same stanza, Raphael also presented the Miracle of Bolsena (see plate 74). In 1263, a priest from Bohemia, while on his way to Rome, fell

78. Raphael, *Jurisprudence*

into doubt about the Catholic teaching of transubstantiation in the mystery of the Eucharist. At Bolsena, while he was saying Mass, the doubtful priest saw the consecrated host begin to bleed. At such a miracle, all his doubts gave way and he was restored to full faith in Catholic teaching. Julius insisted again that he be painted into the scenery — as a reminder that he was the no-nonsense guardian of Catholic orthodoxy.

From the Venetian masters, Raphael acquired a fresh sense of color which he used to construct a group of priests, acolytes, and courtiers.

When Julius died (1513), the papacy came into the hands of a Medici prince, the son of Lorenzo the Magnificent, who took the papal name Leo X. Pope Leo, who was as artistically avid as his predecessor had been, suggested to Raphael that he paint a great scene of his namesake, Leo the Great (440–461), turning Attila the Hun away from the gates of Rome (see plate 75). In the scene as it appears in the Stanza di Eliodoro, Leo stands off the terrible leader of the Huns, while Peter and Paul look on, their swords ready, in case their assistance is needed. The event actually occurred near Mantua, but Raphael did not hesitate to move it to Rome to underscore the importance of papal authority.

The Leo whom Raphael painted, however, was Leo X, a Renaissance prince, inclined toward the arts and subtle diplomacy, a gentle soul, nicely turned out, wearing the papal tiara, riding a white mule. Nevertheless the fierce leader of the Huns was impressed; he reacts violently, as if he could detect in Leo some superhuman force.

At any rate, the barbarians are brought up short and turned away — a warning to all who would think of challenging papal authority (including an obscure monk in Wittenberg).

EXCURSUS

Michelangelo's Medici Tombs

AS FREDERICK HARTT HAS OBSERVED, THE MEDICI CHAPEL IS ONE OF Michelangelo's most complete architectural/sculptural fantasies — and one of the grandest. Our eye is caught immediately by the logic of the architectural forms and by the simplicity of the decorative pattern. There are straight pilasters supporting the horizontals — clear, precise definitions of space, reminiscent of Brunelleschi's Pazzi Chapel. Here are two definitions of immortality, the Renaissance "fame" and the Christian "eternal life." How sharply are they separated here.

79. Michelangelo, new sacristy of San Lorenzo

285

80. Michelangelo, tomb of Lorenzo de' Medici

The two tombs face each other. On the left is the tomb of Duke Giuliano the younger, the third son of Lorenzo the Magnificent. On the right is Lorenzo the Magnificent's grandson, also called Lorenzo, duke of Urbino. On elliptical arcs over the sarcophagi, male and female figures recline. They represent Night and Day, Dawn and Dusk. In niches above are shown the two dukes — handsome, beardless young men in Roman outfits.

Part of the meaning of this overwhelming place is the growing sentiment among Italians toward absolutism. The failure of republican governments, the political disasters engineered unwittingly by the papacy, and repeated savagery of foreign invasions combined in the Italian imagination in the form of hope for unity and security in one great prince. Michelangelo made no more attempt to depict the two dukes realistically than they were believable as politicians. (Both wore beards, for example.) Lorenzo was nearly worthless as a leader. Michelangelo idealized him.

As for other interpretations of the Medici Chapel, the menu is full. Neoplatonism may be a good selection. Ever since the Neoplatonist Benedetto Varchi certified the tombs as Neoplatonic, Neoplatonism has been dogma to many interpreters. Between 1520 and 1533 Michelangelo wrote letters on the philosophy of death. The Medici Chapel could be an expression of such thanatopsis. At last, however, this space was primarily a space where Mass for the Dead could be celebrated. More than anything else that purpose gave energy to its design.

From the tomb of Lorenzo we see the figure of Dusk, presented as an aging but still vigorous man. A powerful body sustains the head in which a lifetime of thought is kept. Dusk foresees the approaching night when death will come. The tragic quality is intensified by the technique of the unfinished.

Tragic Dawn, her brow knitted in concern, grieves either over her childlessness or, according to her very time of life, over her unfulfillment. In Dawn we see a humanity beyond the anatomical structure of the sexes, a super humanity capable of bearing greater potential and greater sorrow than most of us could support.

In the figure of Day, Michelangelo created the most powerful and virile of the four allegorical figures. But he left the head unfinished. By the way he sculpted the shoulders and hand, only partially releasing the hand from the mass of the marble, he suggested the enormous, almost brute strength which lies within human capacity.

Night is the most finished of the four figures, and in some respects

81. Michelangelo, tomb of Giuliano de' Medici

the most beguiling, even though she represents the end of things, of day, of light, of life itself.

The Medicis are not looking at us. Something else has their attention: the ineffable love of the Medici Virgin who presses her child to her breast. Michelangelo the Catholic offers us a solution to the questions of life and death, befitting the Catholic Reformation already underway.

82. Michelangelo,
Virgin and Child,
Medici tombs

289

V. THE CLOSE OF
THE HIGH RENAISSANCE

12. The Decline of the Renaissance in Italy

JACOB BURCKHARDT SUGGESTED THAT THE CITY-STATES OF THE ITALIAN Renaissance were the first to achieve a genuine "foreign policy" (meaning a "purely objective treatment of international affairs, as free from prejudice as from moral scruples") and the first to attempt a "balance of power." Burckhardt appears to be right on both counts, although he does not concede how imperfectly the Italian states practiced the balance of power. In fact, it was the collapse of a balance among the major Italian powers (Milan, Venice, Florence, Naples, and the papacy) by the end of the quattrocento that permitted the French to invade Italy in 1494 — an event of disastrous political and cultural consequences.

A self-conscious foreign policy brought into existence for the first time the *ambasciator,* the resident ambassador, as distinguished from the earlier *legatus* (a legate sent on a short-term mission) or the *nuntius* (a nuncio, or ecclesiastical representative). Protected by diplomatic immunity, the *ambasciator* sent daily *relazioni* (dispatches), in which he "related" to his government the political temper of the country to which he had been assigned. Those dispatches are of prime historical importance. Much of what we know about the court of Queen Elizabeth I of England, for example, we have acquired from the dispatches of the Venetian *ambasciator* to the court of England. The more sinister side of diplomacy developed apace — how to cipher and decipher, how to write in disappearing ink, how to poison with discretion, and how to poison over a protracted period of time. We thus can make the case that "foreign policy," "balance of power," and modern diplomacy all had their beginnings in the Renaissance courts of quattrocento Italy.

THE BALANCE OF POWER IN ITALY

A BRIEF history of the attempts by the Italian powers to achieve a balance of power during the quattrocento may enable us to understand the invasion of Italy by the French at the end of that century. At the opening of the quattrocento, the cornerstone of the Florentine foreign policy was the Florence-Venice alliance against the expansionist policies of Milan. Milan, under Gian Galeazzo Visconti, was attempting to carve out a northern Italian state into which Florence was to be incorporated by subjugation. By 1402, Pisa, Siena, Perugia, and Bologna had all been taken by Milan, leaving Florence encircled. Only the untimely death of Gian Galeazzo in 1402 spared Florence almost certain conquest.

At the first quarter of the quattrocento, circa 1425, Venice decided to forsake its time-honored isolationism in the Venetian lagoons and to become a mainland power. The reason? To offset the incursions of Milan into the Romagna. In 1423 Filippo Maria Visconti of Milan encroached seriously upon the Romagna. In retaliation, Venice seized the important mainland towns of Brescia and Bergamo and made deep incursions into Lombardy. As a consequence, Milan concluded an alliance with Naples. The balance of power then consisted of two major forces: Milan and Naples versus Florence-Venice and the Papal States.

At mid-quattrocento, circa 1450, the Florence-Venice alliance came to an end. Cosimo de' Medici of Florence and Francesco Sforza of Milan, largely through their mutual respect and personal friendship, concluded an alliance between their two city-states. That alliance represented an important shift in Florentine foreign policy. Sacrificing the previous arrangement with Venice, it brought into being a new balance of power: Florence-Milan and Naples versus Venice and the Papal States.

Three years later, in 1453, Constantinople fell to the Ottoman Turks — an event that brought considerable sobriety into Italian politics. In the spring of the following year, the great powers concluded the Peace of Lodi, ostensibly to defend the West against the Turks, actually to guarantee the status quo in Italy and thus to withstand aggression from any outside quarter. As such, the Peace of Lodi represents the first attempt, at least in the age of the Renaissance, to achieve a balance of power in the precise, modern meaning of that term.

Three-quarters through the quattrocento (1477–78), when Pope Sixtus IV attempted to aggrandize the Romagna for a della Rovere family dynasty, he was confronted and impeded by the Florentines under Lorenzo the Magnificent. (See discussion of the Pazzi Conspiracy in chapter 8.) A crisis was thereby provoked in which King Ferrante of Naples took the side of the papacy against Florence, while the two great northern powers, Milan and Venice, were too preoccupied with internal disputes to intervene.

Although the Italian states tried repeatedly to achieve balances of power, they pursued policies so clearly quixotic as to court disaster. The ruler who actually precipitated that disaster was Lodovico il Moro, the would-be duke of Milan (1480–1508), who faced three unsettling factors. First, Lodovico feared the encroachments of Venice. Milan and Venice had been intermittently at war since the 1420s, when Venice elected to become a mainland power and began to intrude upon the Milanese hegemony.

Second, Lodovico fretted incessantly over the irregularity of his position as ruler of Milan. The Visconti (who ruled Milan prior to the advent of the Sforza) had been the legal representatives of the Holy Roman Empire in Milan and legally were the dukes of Milan. The Sforza family to which Lodovico belonged, however, enjoyed no such legality; they ruled Milan by a combination of brute power and popular acquiescence. Because the Visconti had intermarried with French royalty, and because of the irregularity of the Sforza rule, Lodovico was terrified that France might make dynastic claims on Milan.

Third, Lodovico was vexed by Naples. At the assassination of his older brother, Galeazzo Maria Sforza, Lodovico il Moro became the regent of Milan, during the minority of Galeazzo Maria's infant son, the dim-witted Gian Galeazzo Sforza. For dynastic advantages, that child was in due course betrothed to Isabella of Aragon, daughter of King Alfonso of Naples and granddaughter of the ferocious King Ferrante. Also for dynastic reasons, Lodovico put aside his mistress, Cecilia Gallerani, and married Beatrice d'Este of the ruling family of Ferrara. Lodovico, however, not content to be regent, was determined to be duke. Such an outcome obviously required the death, or at least the suppression, of the dim-witted boy, Gian Galeazzo. Lodovico's predicament, embarrassment, and frustration increased by leaps and bounds when the dim-witted boy sired an heir to the Milanese throne before Lodovico and Beatrice managed to do so, thereby establishing the legitimacy of his own line. In January 1494, when old Ferrante of Naples finally expired, his son, King Alfonso, exasperated by the sinister proceedings going on in Milan involving his daughter, took the occasion to threaten Lodovico with a coup d'état, in which both Florence and the papacy would be invited to participate.

In desperation, Lodovico il Moro invited Charles VIII of France to invade Italy; he promised Charles the benevolence of Milan in exchange for French guarantees that France would support the legitimation of Sforza power in Milan. (In fact, Charles did appeal to the Holy Roman Emperor to name Lodovico the imperial vicar of Milan.) But why would Charles VIII of France have had the slightest interest in taking sides with Milan against the Neapolitans? His interest was simply to reassert the claim of French dominion over the Kingdom of Naples, which dated from the thirteenth century. (See chapter 5.)

Suddenly, in the midst of these maneuvers, the young duke of Milan, Gian Galeazzo Sforza, died. Lodovico went through the charade of having the duke's infant son, still in swaddling clothes, proclaimed duke of Milan. Neither the people nor the government of Milan would hear of such nonsense while the state was under such dire threats from abroad. A great popular clamor arose to have Lodovico assume power as duke, to which he acceded, with much feigned reluctance and humility.

At the age of twenty-four, Charles VIII was ripe for adventure and planned to invade Italy. His immediate purpose, as we have noted, was to press the Anjou claims to the Neapolitan throne. But he also had some notion of using Naples, once he had acquired it, as the springboard of a new crusade to deliver both Constantinople and Jerusalem from the Turks. His army, one of the largest French forces ever assembled, included Swiss infantry and French cavalry, supported by heavy artillery of the latest design. On October 15, 1494, Charles entered Pavia, where he conferred with his ally, Lodovico il Moro. Venice offered no opposition; neither did Bologna. The way was open to Florence. Charles therefore proceeded to Florence, where the Medici government fell. On November 17, 1494, the Florentines, primed by Savonarola's preaching, received Charles as the agent of God. By Christmas of that year, the French were on the outskirts of Rome. Charles gathered up the pope's son, Cesare Borgia, and swept south toward Naples. King Alfonso abdicated, leaving Naples to the mercy of the French forces. On February 22, 1495, Charles had attained his objective: Naples was his. French soldiers ran riot in the streets of the city. Among the things they passed along was syphilis (the so-called French disease, or, depending on one's standpoint, the Neapolitan disease).

Meanwhile, the Italian will had stiffened. Venice, the papacy, King Ferdinand of Spain, the Holy Roman Emperor Maximilian, and even Lodovico il Moro organized the League of Venice to expel the French from Italy. Charles, realizing that he was overextended, pushed back up the Italian peninsula, harried as he went by Italian forces. A fierce engagement was fought at Fornova, July 6, 1495, between Charles and the united Italians under Francesco Gonzaga. Although the results of the battle were quite indecisive, Charles broke off his Italian campaign and returned to France. Within three years he was dead.

So far, only one government had fallen — that of the Medici in Florence. But many other untoward events were destined to follow in the aftermath of Lodovico's mischief. For the moment at least, the duke of Milan reveled in his cynical politics. Suddenly, however, he lost Beatrice in childbirth, and then Charles VIII of France also died (1498), to be succeeded by a much more resolute and vindictive monarch. The day after Charles VIII expired, Savonarola fell from power in Florence and within a month was hanging from the gallows in the Piazza della Signoria. In 1499, sensing that the dissolution of Italy was at hand, the Roman pontiff, Alexander VI, laid plans with his son, Cesare Borgia, to carve out a vast new state in central Italy ("the kingdom of Italy") to buttress the papacy, seal the Italian frontiers against invasion, and begin a process of Italian unification and national recovery.

The new king of France was Louis XII (1498–1515) of the house of Orléans — a much more grisly monarch than his predecessor. He interpreted the French expulsion from Italy in 1495 as a national disgrace that must be rectified. As far as he was concerned, both Naples and Milan rightfully belonged to France. In 1499 Louis XII appeared at the gates of Milan. Lodovico il Moro, having exhausted the treasury by his many extravagances, could not even afford the mercenaries necessary to make a defense. He did the next best thing: he fled into the Tyrol, where he sought the protection of the Hapsburgs. The following spring, he returned to Milan with a contingent of Swiss mercenaries, bent upon recapturing his dukedom. The Milanese, vexed by the French puppet who had been imposed upon them, threw open the gates of the city and received Il Moro handsomely. The French, however, still held the Sforza castle, and on April 8, 1500, routed the troops of Il Moro and dispatched the would-be duke of Milan to a dungeon in France, where he languished for eight years and died. Thus, a second important Italian regime had collapsed.

Louis XII then proceeded to retake Naples. By the secret Treaty of Granada (1500), the Kingdom of Naples was partitioned between King Ferdinand of Aragon and King Louis of France. The partners, however, soon fell out, and by the beginning of 1504, the Spanish succeeded in driving the French completely out of Neapolitan territory.

The military campaigns of Cesare Borgia led to the creation of the

Duchy of Romagna, achieved in part by French military assistance. Upon the sudden death of Pope Alexander VI in August 1503, however, the whole Borgia scheme to create a northern Italian state dissolved, and thus still another potentially constructive political institution collapsed.

Venice took advantage of the shifting fortunes in Italy. During the invasion of Charles VIII in 1494 and 1495, when Italy was entirely preoccupied with the French, Venice seized certain key cities in Apulia, in southeastern Italy, in order to control the lower Adriatic and Ionian seas. Perceiving the weakness of Florence, Venice supported Pisa in its bid to be free of Florentine control. When Milan reacted in favor of Florence, Venice encouraged the French invasion of Louis XII and, in return for that favor, received the rich city of Cremona, which lies deep within the plains of Lombardy. When the Borgia effort to pacify the Romagna failed in 1503, Venice promptly encroached there also. Italy thus had become fully internationalized. Note that both the king of Spain and the Holy Roman Emperor had participated in the expulsion of Charles VIII from Italy in 1495. It is not surprising, therefore, that in 1509 virtually the whole of Europe united in the League of Cambrai to put an end to the expansionist tactics of Venice. The league included France, the Holy Roman Empire, Spain, Ferrara, and Mantua, as well as the new pope, Julius II, instigator of the league. The Venetian army was systematically driven out of each of its mainland strongholds until it found itself awash in seawater in the lagoons of Venice. Pope Julius administered the coup de grace: he excommunicated Venice. Venice paid no attention. In 1510 Julius II suddenly found it much more worthwhile to expel the French than to punish Venice. The pope organized a new league, the Holy League, of all the major European powers; its purpose was to harry the French out of Italy.

As the cinquecento opened, Venice had been chastened and contained. Milan was controlled by the Swiss, who had beaten the French decisively at Novara in 1513. At the pleasure of the Swiss, Massimiliano Sforza, Lodovico's son, presided as duke over Milanese affairs. After the death of Savonarola, Florence managed to survive under an unwieldly republican government led by Piero Soderini as *gonfaloniere*. In 1512, however, when the Spaniards took Prato, near Florence, the Soderini regime fell, and the Medici returned to power.

Such were the turbulent times in which Niccolò Machiavelli lived and to which he reacted. As Lewis Spitz has observed, almost every important date in his life coincided with some critical event in the ordeal of Italy. The year of his birth, 1469, saw Lorenzo the Magnificent attain power in

Florence. The year he entered public life, 1494, coincided with the French invasion of Italy and the downfall of the Medici. The year of his death, 1527, brought the sack of Rome by the Holy Roman Emperor Charles V and the degradation of the papacy under Clement VII.

NICCOLÒ MACHIAVELLI

THE SON of a notary, Machiavelli was born within the lesser nobility of Florence. There he received a fairly circumscribed education in the Latin and Italian classics (he knew no Greek) and enough of law and grammar to be useful as a public servant. Judging by Santi di Tito's portrait of him, we may imagine Machiavelli as a rather slight man whose sparkling eyes and quizzical countenance suggest a person of keen and critical intelligence. Vain and insecure, he went to considerable lengths to draw attention to

83. Niccolò Machiavelli, portrait by Santi di Tito

himself. His marriage to Marietta Corsini (1502), while amicable, was distinguished by his many infidelities.

At the conclusion of his education, Machiavelli entered the chancery, seat of Florentine foreign affairs and diplomacy. The year was 1494 — the very year in which the Medici were driven from power in Florence at the imminent arrival of Charles VIII of France, that "agent of God" foretold in Savonarola's prophecies. Nevertheless, it was within the structures of the new republican regime that Machiavelli prospered. When his superior, Marcello Virgilia Adriani, advanced to the rank of chancellor in 1498, Machiavelli was also promoted: he became second chancellor of the Republic of Florence and secretary of the *Dieci* (Ten), the branch of the government that directed diplomacy and war at the authorization of the *signoria.*

Foreign policy, diplomacy, and war thus became the staples of Machiavelli's life. He dealt with the Florentine ambassadors, read and responded to their *relazioni;* he inspected the Florentine fortifications and oversaw the military capability of the city-state. Occasionally he himself undertook diplomatic missions. In 1500 he went to France and treated with Louis XII over the status of Pisa, which Florence proceeded to subdue. In 1502 and 1503 he was the Florentine emissary to Cesare Borgia, who was then in the process of carving out the Duchy of Romagna. In 1506 he was the Florentine representative to Pope Julius II and proceeded with the pope in his campaign to retake the Papal States. In 1507 and 1508 he represented his government at the court of the Holy Roman Emperor Maximilian I.

Diplomacy sharpened Machiavelli's wits in the art (or science) of politics; he began to be formed and shaped as a political scientist. It was also an education in military preparedness and tactics. In 1506 he began to organize a standing army for the Florentine city-state. Machiavelli had come to believe that a stronghold within the city, buttressed by fortifications, was less practical than the control of the countryside by a preponderance of infantry. The loss of Prato to the Spaniards in 1512 was therefore a double tragedy to Machiavelli. His new "national militia" collapsed under the assault of Spanish mercenaries — a disaster that also brought down the republican government of Piero Soderini. The Medici returned to power. In the following year, 1513, Machiavelli was implicated in a conspiracy to unseat the Medici; although his complicity was established only on the flimsiest of evidence, he was sent to prison. Fortunately that year also saw Giovanni de' Medici attain the papacy as Leo X. At such a family triumph, the Medici released certain political prisoners, among whom was Machiavelli. He took solitude at his small farm outside of Florence, where he read and wrote and held conversations with the ancients.

Machiavelli's corpus includes three plays, three books, a short story, and some poetry. His plays, some of which verged on being lascivious, enjoyed great popularity in such cities as Venice. Prime examples of Renaissance scholarship were Machiavelli's three books: *The Prince, Discourses on the First Ten Books of Livy,* and *The History of Florence.* The *Discourses,* which purported to be an analysis of Livy's historical works, allowed Machiavelli to express his views on statecraft. As we might have expected of a Renaissance scholar, he advocated the imitation of classical civilization. Roman law and Greek and Roman history should be the stock-in-trade of all people who propose to practice statecraft. He was decidedly unsympathetic, however, to the general Renaissance assumption that human beings are beings of goodness, rationality, dignity, and power. The first principle of statecraft is to assume the worst about people: "Whoever desires to found a state and give it laws must start with the assumption that all men are bad and always prone to display their vicious nature."

Are we to conclude, therefore, that Machiavelli renounced the Renaissance premise that human beings are free to decide and free to achieve their own destiny? Not at all. Most of Machiavelli's political science (especially *The Prince*) is based on the contrary assumption: that we *do* have the possibility of addressing our difficulties and of correcting at least some of them.

The History of Florence was commissioned by the Medici in 1520 but remained incomplete at Machiavelli's death seven years later. Based on archival evidence, *The History of Florence* reveals Machiavelli's sophistication as a historian. In this case, as always, he used history for pedagogical purposes — to teach, castigate, and correct. This book also raises the question whether he was foremost a Florentine or an Italian.

His patriotism for Italy was profound. He despised nothing more than seeing his fatherland overrun by foreigners — barbarians, as he called them. Although he was an ardent republican, he was even willing to sacrifice his republican principles if some prince could be found who could be coached to unite all of Italy against the foreigners. It is noteworthy that Machiavelli dedicated his most important work — auspiciously called *The Prince* — to a sibling of the Medici family, no doubt in the hope that some prince among the Medici might become the savior of Italy.

Note six aspects of Machiavelli's classic work. First, *The Prince* represents a shift in political theory from idealism to realism. "I depart from the views that others have taken," Machiavelli observed in his chapter 15. "It seems to me better to follow the real truth of things than an imaginary view of them. . . . And the manner in which we live, and that in which we ought to live, are things so wide asunder that he who quits the one to betake himself to the other is more likely to destroy than to save himself." By such statements, Machiavelli meant to dissociate himself from political theory based on ideal assumptions, whether theological or metaphysical, ethical or cultural, and to propose a new politics based on observation, experience, and the actual process of political life. (It is interesting to ask how much of this radical, new methodology in political science would have been possible without the nominalism of later Scholasticism.)

Second, if the state is detached from ethics, culture, theology, and metaphysics, we should not expect Machiavelli's treatise to be necessarily ethical, cultural, theological, or metaphysical in its norms and procedures. With a certain indifference toward such considerations, Machiavelli simply describes how political power is acquired, used, maintained, and lost. Cruelty, malice, and deception cease to have ethical equivalences but become simply techniques of political procedures. Thus "a prudent prince cannot and should not keep his word when to do so would go against his interest" (chapter 18); "cruelty can be described as well used (when it is permissible to say good words about something which is evil in itself) when it is performed all at once, for reasons of self-preservation" (chapter 8). The latter quotation illustrates the point that, although Machiavelli was not oblivious to moral categories and certainly did not attack or repudiate such categories, he found them politically useless.

Third, Machiavelli found the very model of his new political realism to have existed in Cesare Borgia, "a man of . . . savagery and courage [who] understood so perfectly how to win men over or to ruin them." What Machiavelli considered so laudable in Cesare were his remarkably unfettered political instincts and activities: "Looking over the duke's actions, then, I find nothing with which to reproach him; rather I think I am right in proposing him, as I have done, as a model for all those who rise to power" (chapter 7).

Fourth, embedded in Machiavelli's thought is a profound suspicion of the general Renaissance assumption that human beings are both good and rational. In fact, all decent political science begins with the opposite assumption, with the recognition that people are perverse. Therefore, politics must be waged with like perversity. The prince must be both human and beast; he, like Achilles, should be instructed by a preceptor who is himself "half-man and half-beast" (chapter 18). "Well-used cruelties" are an important technique of government, and the prince must, among other accomplishments, "learn how *not* to be good," if he does not wish "to come to ruin among the great number of those who are not good" (chapter 15).

Fifth, Machiavelli assumes that evil is a human characteristic and therefore a factor that politics must take into account. "If all men were good," he hypothesized, his political philosophy would be of no account. But they are not good; evil is a human characteristic, one of the ways in which human beings cope with the forces of fortune and circumstance that threaten their existence and their security. Therefore, evil must also be used as a political means; indeed it is an indispensable means of politics unless one wishes to be overcome by "the winds of fortune and the varying circumstances of life" (chapter 18). Such was the greatness of Cesare Borgia; rather than be overwhelmed by evil forces, he, with calculated ruthlessness, used cruelty and deception to his own political advantage.

> This has to be understood: a prince and especially a new prince, cannot exercise all those virtues for which men are called "good." To preserve the state, he often has to do things against his word, against charity, against humanity, against religion. Thus he has to have a mind ready to shift as the winds of fortune and the varying circumstances of life may dictate. As I have said above, he should not depart from the good if he can hold to it, but he should be ready to enter on evil if he has to. (chapter 18)

Sixth, perhaps the real contest seen in *The Prince* is not between good and evil but between human free will and Fortuna, the goddess of the vast and terrible uncertainties of life, of the stars and fates, of financial ruin and catastrophic illness. "I think it may be true that Fortune governs half of our actions, but that even so she leaves the other half, more or less, in our power to control" (chapter 25). Machiavelli goes on to say that when people do not oppose Fortuna with all the vigor of their freedom of will, then Fortuna simply overwhelms them like a rampaging tide. By what means do we stand fast against the terrible incursions of Fortune?

However evil all men and women may be, and despite the role of Fortune, they are not dispossessed of their freedom to decide and act. Machiavelli even appropriated the Renaissance term *virtù,* which he used abundantly, in one or two instances as many as ten times a page. Yet he shifted its meaning to suit his purposes: *virtù* came to refer to human energy, human strength, human ability, human genius and courage, and the will to rule.

Virtù is the means by which people fend off the rampages of Fortuna and therefore express their indomitable endowments of freedom and self-determination. Furthermore, *virtù* affords us the strength of mind and the strength of will to design something worthy, either for ourselves or for society, and to see it through. Again, Cesare Borgia became Machiavelli's model of *virtù:* Cesare had the capacity to see the political problem and the determination to bring about a solution. The person who acts out his or her *virtù* becomes a *virtuoso,* someone who acts forcefully out of one's own inner strength and purpose. The prince, as savior of Italy, must be such a *virtuoso.*

Machiavelli died in 1527, and, as befitting a patriot, he was buried in the Church of Santa Croce, the preeminent place of Florentine honor.

FRANCESCO GUICCIARDINI

NO ONE better illustrates the pessimism that pervaded Italy at the end of the quattrocento and during the first half of the cinquecento than the Florentine historian and statesman Francesco Guicciardini (1483–1540). He has been called the first of the Machiavellians. His career was intertwined with that of Machiavelli. He, like Machiavelli, was both a statesman and a historian. He shared much of Machiavelli's political philosophy and criticism and, like Machiavelli, was an ardent republican.

The son of Florentine aristocracy, Guicciardini was born on March 6, 1483. Lorenzo de' Medici ruled Florence, then unsurpassed among Western cities for its cultural and financial achievements. Alas, Guicciardini was only eleven when Lorenzo's dim-witted son, Piero the Foolish, was driven from Florence with his whole family in the wake of the French invasion of 1494, and the pious regime of Savonarola was inaugurated; he was only fifteen when Savonarola himself was repudiated and hanged in the Piazza della Signoria. At that time, Guicciardini began to study civil law (he always took pains to distinguish civil from canon, or church, law — a streak of anticlericalism ran in the family), first in Florence, then in Ferrara, then in Padua, then in Florence again. In 1505 he took a doctor of law degree from the University of Florence and opened a practice in that city. At that time, Piero Soderini governed the Republic of Florence as *gonfaloniere,* and Niccolò Machiavelli served in Soderini's department of state.

At twenty-six, Guicciardini wrote *The History of Florence,* beginning with the revolt of the Ciompi in 1378 and concluding with his own standpoint, namely, the year 1512. The book was a shrewd historical analysis of the reign of the Medici, especially of Lorenzo, as well as of the invasions of Charles VIII and Louis XII, and the shifting fortunes of the Medici after the expulsion of Piero the Foolish. The prejudices we have had of Piero the Foolish as an arrogant *stupido* were established by Guicciardini. He was the first historian to recognize that the French invasion of 1494 was a turning point in Italian history and that the second French invasion of 1499 left Italy exposed for centuries to the exploitation of "the barbarians."

Most of Guicciardini's political philosophy appears in this early book. As a republican, he believed that the power of the people should be expressed in a Great Council, that the political weight of the aristocracy should be represented in a powerful senate, and that a continuous rule of one man should be preserved either in a Medici prince or in a republican officer such as the *gonfaloniere*. The Medici disease was always the usurpation of all power, coupled with a failure to see that the real weight of political power should lie with the aristocracy.

Like Machiavelli, Guicciardini was a rationalist. The power of the mind, he believed, is capable of deciphering the laws by which history unfolds and thus of shaping the course of history — at least, up to a point. Guicciardini, like Machiavelli, was impressed by the awesome power of Fortuna as a determinant of history. Our best efforts may be quashed by Fortuna. To surrender to Fortuna without a fight, however, is simply to default in human courage.

Guicciardini's political realism was often as cutting as Machiavelli's. In his discussion of the Pazzi Conspiracy, for example, Guicciardini noted that in the death of his brother Giuliano at the hands of assassins, Lorenzo de' Medici got rid of a popular rival and increased his grip on Florentine affairs — a political plus for Lorenzo when most of us thought only to weep over his tragedy.

On January 29, 1512, the *signoria* sent Guicciardini as ambassador to King Ferdinand of Aragon. Later that year, when Machiavelli's militia was routed at Prato by the Spaniards, Soderini resigned, and Cardinal Giovanni de' Medici entered Florence and reestablished Medici rule. While Guicciardini waited to be replaced in Spain, he completed the first two sets of *Ricordi* (political maxims), another important source of his political philosophy, and a prime example of his pessimism. There, he found human nature to be brutish; human life, short and miserable; human accomplishments, imperfect. "We must therefore be content to take things as they are, and to reckon the least evil as good."

When Giovanni de' Medici succeeded to the papacy as Leo X (March 11, 1513), many capable Florentines entered papal service. Thus, in 1518, Guicciardini became the papal governor of Modena, then also of Reggio. In 1521 he was appointed papal governor of Parma. In 1523, under the second Medici pope, Clement VII, he became vice-regent of the entire Romagna. Finally, on June 26, 1526, Pope Clement called Guicciardini to Rome as papal adviser and lieutenant-general of the papal armies.

His later life was affected by the Hapsburg-Valois Wars, particularly by the parts of that conflict conducted in Italy. The contenders were the two most powerful men in Europe — the Holy Roman Emperor, Charles V, and the king of France, Francis I. Convinced that Charles V had designs on the whole of Italy, Guicciardini advised Pope Clement to take sides with the French. In 1526, in fact, Guicciardini was instrumental in forming the Holy League of Cognac to contain Charles V. The league included the major European powers — Francis I of France, the Medici Pope Clement VII, Florence, Venice, and Milan, with the tacit support of Henry VIII of England.

In November 1526 Charles V responded. An army of fifteen thousand German troops crossed the Alps. In February they were joined by an additional five thousand troops, some of whom were Spanish, and some of whom were French dissidents. Ill fed, poorly paid, and mutinous, these imperial armies stormed southward toward Rome, ravaging the countryside for subsistence as they went. On May 6, 1527, shortly before midnight, they breached the walls of Rome, overwhelming the defenses that Guicciardini had managed to mount. For eight successive days, Rome was sacked by riotous soldiers; Pope Clement was driven into the Castel Sant'Angelo. The event is remembered as the instance of Rome's greatest devastation, and many have seen it as a symbol of the close of the Italian Renaissance.

Florence also experienced another upheaval. With the Medici pope virtually under arrest, the Florentines took the occasion to unseat the Medici once again and to restore the Republic of Florence.

In 1529, however, Pope Clement made peace with Charles V. The Treaty of Barcelona, signed by both parties on June 29, 1529, confirmed the imperial claim to Naples, guaranteed free passage of imperial troops across the Papal States, and required the restoration of the Medici in Florence. Guicciardini, despite his many failures as an agent of the papacy, was entrusted with the job of reinstating the Medici. He did so, he said, "with cruel but effective means" in the year 1530. For an ardent republican, it must have been a difficult assignment to put down a republican tradition of three hundred years.

In 1531 Guicciardini became papal governor of Bologna — an assignment he held until the death of Pope Clement. He then retired to write his historical masterpiece, *The History of Italy,* a work comprising twenty books, covering the forty-year period from the death of Lorenzo the Magnificent to the death of Pope Clement VII. He attributed the appalling decay of Renaissance society to a combination of human folly and bad fortune; in his final pessimism, he had come to doubt whether human reason was capable of overcoming either one. It was Florence's fate (as it is the fate of all people and all institutions) to live and to die; Guicciardini had "the infelicity of being born at a time when his country was scheduled to fulfill its doom." In such pessimism, Francesco Guicciardini himself expired in his fifty-eighth year, on May 22, 1540.

13. *The Voyages of Discovery*

EARLY ACCOUNTS OF WORLD GEOGRAPHY

DURING the Renaissance, understanding of the world beyond western Europe came largely from ancient treatises or accounts of contemporary travelers: both of these varied widely in accuracy.

Information about Africa came from the accounts of Arab travelers, inaccurately transmitted through Sicily to Europe beginning in the twelfth century. By similar means, Europeans became convinced that the Atlantic Ocean ("the green sea of darkness") was not navigable and that the equatorial zones of the earth, including major parts of Africa, were uninhabitable. A school of Jewish cartographers, working in Majorca, were much more reliable transmitters of Arabic information about Africa. The Catalan Atlas, developed in Majorca by Abraham Cresques about 1375, was a remarkable effort to represent, by means of a maritime chart, the world beyond Europe as it was known at the end of the fourteenth century.

When it came to Asia, however, Europeans could rely on a fair number of traveler's accounts, written in the thirteenth and fourteenth centuries, when Europeans were drawn in increasing numbers to the Far East in response to the hospitality of the Mongol Empire. That great empire was the creation of Genghis Khan, who led a ferocious Mongol cavalry across the great land masses of Asia and conquered a vast empire including both China and central Asia. The Tatar Khans who succeeded Genghis were tolerant of religions, interested in trade, and curious about cultures other than their own. Europe dispatched a number of travelers to the East. In

1245 the pope sent a Franciscan friar, John of Plano Carpini, to treat with Genghis Khan at his capital at Karakorum. A few years later (1253), King Louis IX of France sent another Franciscan, William of Rubruck, to solicit the conversion of the Mongols to Christianity; Friar William left a detailed account of his pious conversations with Genghis Khan at Karakorum.

In 1256 two Venetian merchants, Niccolò and Matteo Polo, embarked on an extended trip through central Asia and China in the interests of East-West trade. They arrived finally at Peking, which the Tatar Khans had designated their capital; there they held conversations with Kublai Khan on a variety of subjects, including religion. The Polos returned to the Far East in 1271 with Niccolò's son, Marco, a young man of seventeen, and two Dominican friars, with whom Kublai Khan had asked to consult.

Marco Polo, although a young man, had a fascination for observation and detail — qualities that Kublai Khan soon discovered in him. The Great Khan sent young Polo to scattered parts of the Mongol Empire to make and record observations and gather information. Most of Marco Polo's record was based on personal reconnaissance (such as the fact that the Chinese burned "black stones" for fuel); other observations were dependent on hearsay (such as the existence of Cipangu — Japan — off the Pacific coast of China). Marco Polo did not actually write the accounts himself: they were composed in French by Rusticello of Pisa, with whom the traveler was imprisoned in 1298. Scholars believe that Rusticello may have added some of the more graphic battle scenes and tales involving the miraculous and grotesque to Marco Polo's original descriptions.

Captured by the Genoese in 1298, Marco Polo was treated to a long season in prison. Ironically, this detainment afforded him time to write his *Travels,* the most accurate and complete account of Asia available in the Middle Ages. Prince Henry of Portugal, the instigator of Portuguese explorations, owned a manuscript copy of Polo's *Travels.* The work was first printed in 1483. Columbus owned a printed copy, and there is reason to believe that some of Columbus's assumptions — about the extent of Asia, for example, or the location of Japan — were established or confirmed by Polo's *Travels.*

The growing concourse between East and West was abruptly curtailed at the middle of the fourteenth century by the arrival of the Black Death, which devastated the populations of both Europe and Asia, and by the incursion of the Ottoman Turks, who swept down from the steppes of Asia at the middle of the fourteenth century and blocked travel and trade between the East and the West. Farther east, the Tatar Empire disintegrated in 1368, as the descendants of Kublai Khan were driven from their Peking throne by the Mings, a native Chinese dynasty who renewed the ancient Chinese suspicion of outsiders. Thus the West, in the age of the Renaissance, was almost entirely dependent upon thirteenth- and early fourteenth-century travelers for their information about the Far East.

The academic treatises were of two sorts. Some were theoretical works on geography that came from medieval Scholasticism and were based on a conglomeration of biblical evidence, the wisdom of the ancient church fathers, and some partial knowledge of classical authors. Very often, Jerusalem was presented as the center of a universe that was laid out in symmetrical perfection to represent the perfection of God. With few exceptions, those treaties were scientifically worthless. The other type represented the genuine scientific interests of ancient authors, Greek and Roman, transmitted to Western civilization through Arabic translations.

Of the Scholastic treatises, only two are worthy of mention. Roger Bacon included a geographic section in his *Opus majus* of 1264. His work avoided the usual Scholastic errors because he consulted a variety of Arabic texts. From these, he correctly assumed that the continents of Asia and Africa extended considerably south of the equator and that the tropics were habitable. But he extended the land mass of Asia much too far to the east, giving the Renaissance explorers the illusion that by sailing westward a reasonable distance, they were bound to reach Asia. Bacon contributed directly to Pierre d'Ailly's *Imago mundi* (c. 1410), the great compendium of medieval geographic lore, in which the wisdom of the Bible, Aristotle, the classical cosmographers, the Arabic scholars, and Bacon was comprehended. We have already identified d'Ailly as a conciliarist, an Ockhamist theologian, and a cardinal of the church; we meet him now as the most eminent Scholastic geographer of the early Renaissance. His *Imago mundi* was first printed at Louvain in 1483; Columbus's copy, carefully annotated, still exists at Seville. Like his predecessor Bacon, d'Ailly greatly exaggerated the eastern extent of Asia and may have tempted Columbus to believe that a short voyage westward would bring an explorer to the East Indies.

It was a cardinal prejudice of the Renaissance, as we have seen, that the ancient Greeks and Romans had been more civilized than fifteenth-century Europeans; that prejudice extended to geography and cosmography, as well as to art and law and philosophy and all the other parts of culture in which the Renaissance was interested. The earliest known opinion of the Greeks was that the earth was a round disk, tilted to the south, and floating on a vast cosmic sea. Shape aside, it was not unlike the Hebraic conception of "the four corners of the earth." The Pythagoreans were apparently the first to teach that the earth was a sphere — a conception repeated by the philosophers Plato and Aristotle and by the ancient geographers Strabo and Ptolemy. The best opinion throughout the Middle Ages was that the earth was round, like a ball. So said Augustine, Isidore of Seville, the Venerable Bede, and Dante; it was commonly assumed that one could reach eastern Asia by sailing westward.

The most formidable ancient geographer and cosmographer was Claudius Ptolemaeus — Ptolemy. Living in the cosmopolitan city of Alexandria in the second century A.D., that Hellenized Egyptian decided to summarize all known geographic and cosmographic information. After all, the Roman Empire had achieved its greatest extension in Ptolemy's time, and people were demanding to know what the Roman world and the greater world consisted of. Ptolemy addressed those questions in two books: *Astronomy,* usually known by its Arabic name, *Almagest* (The greatest), and *Geography.* Both books were widely known and respected during the Middle Ages, especially among Arabic scholars, who were the principal transmitters of Greek and Roman scientific knowledge to the medieval world.

In *Almagest,* Ptolemy went far beyond Aristotle's fairly simply conception of concentric spheres revolving around the earth and carrying the sun and stars with them. He proposed an elaborate system of "epicycles" to explain the eccentric movements of the planets and other heavenly bodies. The *Almagest* was translated into Latin in 1175 by Gerard of Cremona, a tireless student of Arabic learning who worked at Toledo. In the course of the thirteenth century, it entered the world of medieval Scholasticism and remained the typical medieval academic conception of the universe until the time of Copernicus. The Aristotelian-Ptolemaic system assumed the earth to be the fixed center of the universe, around which the sun and stars revolve, and thus the single, uncomplicated setting for the religious drama involving God and humankind.

Ptolemy's *Geography* made a different sort of impact on Europe than the *Almagest* had made, and at a much later date. It was first translated into Latin in 1406 by one of the disciples of Manuel Chrysolaras from a Greek manuscript brought from Constantinople — a feat of Renaissance scholarship. (Both Pierre d'Ailly and Pope Pius II made digests of Ptolemy's Latin *Geography;* what knowledge Columbus had of Ptolemy's *Geography,* he drew from a printed copy of Pope Pius's compendium.) By dividing the sphere of earth into a grid of 360 degrees of latitude and longitude, Ptolemy was able to pinpoint locations on the earth's surface. He also supplied a set of maps for the world and its regions, including the Mediterranean, Europe, Asia, and Africa. His work, however, contained major errors, some of which proved to be incentives for the Renaissance explorers. For instance, his calculation of the distance around the world was one-fourth too small, and he, like so many other cosmographers, extended the Asian land mass much too far to the east, encouraging the explorers to believe that East Asia could be reached by a short sea journey into the Atlantic.

The writings of Ptolemy are one instance in which the Renaissance was not well served by a "return to the sources." To some extent, both the Ptolemaic astronomy and the Ptolemaic geography had to be challenged and superseded to make way for a modern science and reconnaissance.

CHRISTIANITY AND ISLAM IN SPAIN

THE VOYAGES of discovery have been described by some scholars as a continuation of the Crusades. What sense does that assumption make? As the fifteenth century opened, two Moslem states competed for power in the Levant — the Mamluk Kingdom of Egypt and Syria, established in the course of the thirteenth century by tough and wily Sultan Baybars, and the Ottoman Empire of Asia Minor, a menace to Moslem and Christian states alike. In 1353 the Ottoman Turks crossed the Dardanelles and within four years took Adrianople, effectively encircling the Byzantine Empire. Dramatically, at the end of the fourteenth century, Christian Europe was delivered from the Moslem menace by an unlikely deliverer — Timur the Lame, last of the great Mongol khans, whose cavalry overran both of the Moslem states. In 1400 Timur sacked Aleppo and Damascus; in 1402 he defeated the Ottoman Turks at Ankara and entered Smyrna. Timur died in 1405, however, and his exploits were never to be repeated. The Ottoman Empire rebounded more quickly than its Mamluk rivals. In 1422 the Turks laid siege to Constantinople. In 1453 the city fell to Mehmed II.

The fall of Constantinople was interpreted in various ways in western Europe. The pious saw in it the hand of a providential God, who had emptied Constantinople to furnish Greek teachers and Greek texts for the Renaissance and Reformation. (So thought Luther.) The fretful saw in it the possibility of a Europe beleaguered by the terrible Turks. The astute realized by it that the Ottoman Empire had become the most prominent land and sea power in the Middle East, a power bent upon expansion. The Balkans and the Danube basin became the immediate target of Turkish aggression, which persisted inexorably until the middle of the sixteenth century, when Süleyman the Magnificent was finally stymied at the outskirts of Vienna. Heretofore horsemen, the Turks now inherited the seamanship of Byzantium and emerged as the major sea power in the Mediterranean. By the middle of the fifteenth century it would have been unlikely that any European power could have attempted a crusade by sea; the succession of Renaissance popes who tried to organize such folly might have thanked God for their failure. By the middle of the fifteenth century, the crusading zeal had been entrusted to another breed — to the Spanish and Portuguese of the Iberian peninsula. Only they could still do damage to the Moslems. The Spanish campaigns against Granada and the Portuguese expeditions to northwest Africa may both be legitimately interpreted as continuations of the crusading zeal.

In some respects, these campaigns represent a rather strange turn of events. In the Iberian peninsula, Christianity and Islam had existed side by side since the eighth century, and the civilizing of Christian Europe owed something to that very juxtaposition. What was known of Greek science during the Middle Ages (not to mention many other aspects of Greek learning) was largely acquired through Arabic translations. Arabic art and letters, Arabic industrial and commercial practices, and Arabic technology and cultural habits all made an impression on European societies, not the least, the Spanish. The Iberian peninsula became an ecumenical, or at least intercultural, site, where Islamic, Jewish, and Christian wisdom was treated in concert. In the twelfth century, a Christian prelate, Archbishop Raymond of Toledo, sponsored schools in which Arabic, Jewish, and Christian scholars collaborated, setting off a new burst of scientific inquiry in the intellectual circles of the West. In the following century, two kings of Castile, Fernando III (1217–52) and Alfonso the Wise (1252–84), were particularly hospitable to Judaism and Islam; Alfonso sponsored a secular culture to which the learned of all three major religions were invited to contribute.

But Isabella of Castile (1474–1504), in an abrupt change in Spanish policy, ended the rapprochement and, on behalf of Christian exclusiveness, introduced repression and inquisition. Her policy was based in part upon her own intense zeal for the Catholic faith and in part in reaction to the incursion of the Ottoman Turks in the East. To understand Isabella's policy, let us review briefly the history of medieval Spain.

The Visigoths invaded Roman Spain in successive waves, beginning in A.D. 414. Since they had lived on the borders of the Roman Empire for a while, they were neither barbarians nor infidels; they had absorbed some

84. Isabella of
Castile, portrait
attributed to
Baldome Bermejo

elements of Roman culture, as well as an Arian version of Christianity. King
Euric (467–85) completed the Visigothic conquest of Spain before the end
of the fifth century. In the sixth century, Toledo became the capital of Spain.
The nation included an ancient, indigenous population, mainly Iberians,
some Romans, the Christian Visigoths, and a community of Jews, mainly
craftsmen and traders, who had lived in Spain since ancient times and whose
rights were protected by both secular and canon law.

At the beginning of the eighth century, however, the Moors — that
is, the inhabitants of Mogreb, or Morocco — who had been intent upon
entering Spain for a century or more, invaded in massive numbers and
destroyed the Visigothic monarchy by defeating Don Rodrigo (last of the
Visigothic kings) at the battle of Guadalete, July 711. Spain became a
Moslem emirate, ruled by an emir who was ultimately dependent on the
Moslem Caliphate of Damascus. The Visigothic and ancient Roman and

Iberian populations persisted in Spain. Members of the Spanish Christian population who continued to live in territory conquered by Moslems were referred to as Mozárabes — "would-be Arabs"; they formed a little world of their own in the Moslem cities and towns, with their own churches and cloisters, and their own officials, laws, and justice. They retained their own language, a corrupt version of Latin. Taken together, their customs consti- tuted a "Mozarabic" culture.

The recovery of Spain from the Moors is known as the Reconquest. It was begun in the eighth century, in the Pyrenees Mountains and in the Cantabrian Cordillera by Visigothic nobles, aided by natives of those two regions. As the result of successive military victories, the forces of the Reconquest founded the Kingdom of Asturias. During the next two cen- turies, the forces of the Reconquest succeeded in advancing southward to, and beyond, the Duero River, bringing into being the Christian kingdoms of León and Castile. In the course of the eighth century, the discovery of the sepulcher of Santiago (the apostle James) near Patrón fired the nation- alistic will of Spanish Christians. Alfonso II turned it into a national shrine — Santiago de Compostela — which effectively made St. James the patron of Spain. His shrine became the center of pilgrimage and of Christian revival.

Competition from the Moors, however, continued unabated. In the tenth century, during the government of an extraordinary emir, Abd-er- Rahman III (912–61), the Emirate of Córdova achieved independence; with Abd-er-Rahman as caliph, it became the Caliphate of Córdova. During the caliph's lifetime and for perhaps seventy years after, Córdova was one of the marvels of Western civilization. A city of great beauty, it was the seat of economic and intellectual life for Muhammadan Spain and the source of the social discipline and homogeneity that affected all of Moslem Spain. The caliph was powerful in other ways; his army was considered the strongest in the West; his navy, unsurpassed in the Mediterranean.

The Moors may have been the most highly cultivated people of the European continent during the Middle Ages. The library of the caliph of Córdova included 600,000 volumes. An extensive network of schools and universities was maintained in Spain. Arabic was the language of instruction. The curriculum was based on the Greek and Roman classics, preserved and translated by a succession of Arab scholars from Syria and Persia. Thanks to religious toleration and a generous spirit of intellectual exchange, many Christian scholars came to Spain, and many aspects of Moorish culture found their way into the universities of western Europe. In the tenth century, for example, the French monk Gerbert of Auvergne (later Pope Sylvester II,

999–1003) visited Barcelona and Córdova to study geometry, mechanics, and astronomy. He is thought to have introduced Arabic numerals to western Europe. The Moors developed a distinctive form of art, especially architecture, based in part on the art of Asiatic people — the Chaldeans, Assyrians, and Persians — and in part on Roman and Byzantine art. Very advanced in agriculture, the Moors introduced new orchard fruits to Spain, including peaches, apricots, figs, and dates, and were pioneers in the use of artificial irrigation in farming. They were apparently the first in the West to make paper from plant fibers — a technique imported from China by Asian Moslems. They were also highly sophisticated in the preparation of leather. Córdova in the ninth and tenth centuries was one of the largest and richest cities of the world, with 200,000 residences, paved streets, and piped water. Other important Moslem towns were Seville, Málaga, Granada, Toledo, and Saragossa.

In 1031, however, as a result of internecine conflict among the sheikhs, the centralized authority of the once-powerful caliphs dissolved, and the Caliphate of Córdova split into several independent kingdoms. From the disintegration of the caliphate in 1031 until the end of the thirteenth century, the Reconquest proceeded along three lines: (1) steady military progress southward from the Duero River; (2) the development of various centers of Catholic political power; and (3) the appearance of the Romance languages.

In 1035 Fernando I of Castile (1032–65) first reunited the kingdoms of Castile and León. Fired by aspirations of the Reconquest, he and his confederates managed to conquer the northern sections of the Kingdom of Toledo. Toledo itself fell to his successor, Alfonso VI (1065–1109), in 1085. This event marked a decisive shift in the relative power of Moors and Christians in Spain and permitted the resettlement of Christian populations in cities to the rear — Salamanca, Ávila, and Segovia.

The Cid, a great Castilian warrior who waged the Reconquest and was celebrated in the *poema* and *gesta* of the twelfth century, actually belonged to the court of Alfonso VI. He was Ruy (or Rodrigo) Díaz of Vivar, a town near Burgos. In recognition of his bravery on behalf of Catholic Spain, the Moors called him Cid Campeador, "the warrior lord."

In the course of the twelfth century, Aragon and Catalonia became a single Catholic monarchy. The national unity of *Hispania,* however, was permanently broken during that century by the severance of the Kingdom of Portugal from the rest of the Iberian peninsula. The new nation, from the ancient County of Portucalense, retained the Galician language spoken by its first inhabitants.

The great age of the Reconquest occurred in the thirteenth century at the hands of two extraordinary Catholic executives and commanders — Fernando III of León and Castile (1217–52) and James I of Aragon (1213–76). Fernando retook northern and western Andalusia, including Córdova (1236), Seville (1248), and Jaén (1246). James conquered the Balearic Isles, including Majorca, as well as the Moorish Kingdom of Valencia (1238). Thus, at the close of the thirteenth century, the Moslem holdings in Spain were reduced to the Kingdom of Granada and some few other territories.

From the middle of the thirteenth century until the appearance of Ferdinand and Isabella at the middle of the fifteenth century, the Reconquest was in abeyance, while the power of the Moors in Spain steadily declined. The leading figure of the period was an intellectual — Alfonso X, the Wise, king of León and Castile (1252–84), a patron of the universities, promoter of scientific inquiry, and advocate of a Spanish culture enriched by Moorish and Jewish elements.

On January 19, 1479, Fernando II, better known to English readers as Ferdinand, succeeded to the throne of Aragon, Catalonia, Valencia, and Mallorca. He was already married to Isabella, who had become queen of Castile in 1474. Thus, after 1479, the two great monarchies of Spain were governed

85. Ferdinand of Aragon, bust by the Napolitan School.

318

by royal consorts — Castile by a diarchy (i.e., a joint government of two monarchs), and Aragon by the absolute monarchy of Ferdinand. Ferdinand and Isabella were described as *los reyes católicos,* "the Catholic kings," reflecting their heightened loyalty to the Catholic religion. In the course of their reigns, in the single year of 1492, two notable Spanish accomplishments occurred: the end of the Reconquest and the European discovery of America.

Inspired by intense religious devotion as well as by apprehension of impending danger from the East, the two monarchs, particularly Isabella, were resolved to reduce the Kingdom of Granada. By the middle of the fifteenth century, the Ottoman Empire dominated the Moslem states in North Africa and had already made an entry into Europe, destroying the Byzantine Empire in the process. Early in the sixteenth century, the Ottoman Turks conquered Syria and Egypt and extended their dominion along the whole North African coast. Given their immense power, they would not have found it difficult to invade the Iberian peninsula or to prop up any Moslem regime, whether in North Africa or in Spain. Thus, both Spain and Portugal developed African policies to protect their southern flanks. Spain was determined to control the North African coast, while Portugal was more interested in reducing the Moslem strongholds in West Africa. Spain, however, had a more immediate and more crucial problem — to crush Granada, the last remaining Moslem outpost on its own soil.

The War of Granada began in 1481 and lasted eleven years. It was the last European Crusade, inspired by a mixture of motives — religious exaltation, hatred of unbelief, fear of the Turks, and economic envy. Village by village the Moorish kingdom was overcome. The city of Granada was laid siege to in 1489, and on January 2, 1492, Ferdinand and Isabella entered the Alhambra (the palace of the Moorish kings of Granada) as the Crusade ended. For the first time since the eighth century, all Spain was ruled by Catholic monarchs.

The terms of the surrender of Granada were pacific; they included the protection of Moslem life and property, as well as guarantees of religious freedom. But the crusading spirit could not so easily be contained. Isabella and her fervent religious advisers first directed a policy of proselytizing against the Moors; despite the ardor of the Observant Franciscans who attempted it, the policy failed. With the support of her minister, the influential Spanish cardinal Ximénez de Cisneros, Isabella then resorted to sterner measures. The Moors of Granada were forced to receive baptism or be expelled. Even the Moslems living in Castile and León were required by royal edict (February 11, 1502) to abjure their religion or to leave. Meanwhile, the Spanish attitude toward the Jews, which had steadily deteriorated since the beginning of the fourteenth century, became a policy of persecution under the Catholic monarchs. On March 31, 1492, the Jews of Castile and Aragon were required to be baptized or to leave Spain within four months. Those who left — perhaps as many as a half million — were ancestors of the Sephardic Jews, who still use the Castilian idiom.

The Spanish Inquisition, although it had medieval roots, was essentially a creature of the Catholic monarchs, begun by royal edict of 1477 and later sanctioned by Pope Sixtus IV. It was tied not to the bishops but to the monarchs, who actually appointed the first two grand inquisitors. (The third, Tomás de Torquemada, was appointed by the pope.) Adopting the assumption that error had no right to exist, and outfitted by extraordinary powers, the Inquisition dealt with all sorts of people whose consciences were unsteady, such as baptized Moors, baptized Jews, and, later, humanists and Lutherans. All of these activities may have been out of keeping in medieval Spain, but they were signs of new times, signs of religious fervor and intolerance that appeared in Spain after the fall of Constantinople.

Yet, religious zeal does not entirely explain Isabella's religious intolerance. Part of her policy seems to have been dictated by a deliberate suppression of African and Middle Eastern elements in the culture of Spain and by an equally deliberate decision to align Spanish culture with that of Christian Europe. The signs of that policy were evident everywhere. The Spanish universities were made to flourish; those at Alcalá, Salamanca, and Valladolid were founded during Isabella's reign. The printing industry was begun and encouraged in Spain; printed books were sold and discussed everywhere. Foreign scholars introduced the manners and ideas of the Italian Renaissance to Spain, trimming them to suit Spanish modesty and sobriety. Thus, Renaissance humanism, the cult of the individual and the drive for personal fame, the historical-critical method of criticism, and Machiavellian statecraft all found expression in Spain and were carried into the New World by the *conquistadores*. Isabella's most Catholic minister, Cardinal Ximénez de Cisneros, was himself a composite personality — reformer, disciplinarian, and humanist. By appealing to the anxious spiritual disaffection that existed in Spanish monasticism, by utilizing unabashedly the unsentimental power of humanistic scholarship, and by insisting on the disciplines of poverty and simple preaching, he directed a notable reform of the Spanish church. Some of his followers, it is true, became evangelical sympathizers, susceptible to the ideas of Erasmus and Luther. A great many more, however, formed a Spanish militia to carry Christianity to the New World.

THE IBERIAN TURN TO THE OCEAN

IT USED to be said that the voyages of discovery took place because the conquests of the Ottoman Turks forced the Europeans to find some alternate commercial route to China and India. While commerce did ultimately inspire the Portuguese and Spanish adventurers, it is not true that the Turks had managed to interdict all East-West trade. Some other phenomenon must have occurred to provoke the Spanish and Portuguese.

As the fifteenth century opened, the greatest commercial avenue in western Europe remained the traffic in the Mediterranean, by which food, raw materials, and manufactured goods were transported from East to West and back again. Grain, salt, salt fish, oil, wine, cheese, wool, silk, other raw materials of industry, precious metals, jewels, and some 288 "spices" — pepper from Sumatra, cinnamon from Ceylon, nutmeg from the Banda Islands, cloves from the Moluccas — were shipped across the Mediterranean, often on vessels of Italian registry. In the days of the Mongol khans, goods from China could be brought overland on the backs of camels to ports along the Black Sea or on the shores of the Levatine countries, where they were picked up by Italian merchant companies for transport across the Mediterranean. A succession of political dislocations in China, in central Asia, and in Asia Minor, some of which we have already described, made the overland route increasingly impractical; in the fourteenth century it ceased to be attempted at all. Meanwhile, a sea route between Europe and the Orient had been developed; it ran from China to the East Indies, across the Bay of Bengal to India, and from the Indian Ocean to the Mediterranean either by the Red Sea or by the Persian Gulf, in either case requiring overland portage.

The activities of the Ottoman Turks, particularly their conquest of Constantinople in 1453, indeed amounted to a major inconvenience to the Italian shipping companies, but it did not totally interrupt East-West trade. The Italians managed to keep their Mediterranean trade more or less intact, although each successive political tumult in Asia Minor tended to drive up prices and to encourage Europeans to seek an alternate route to China and India, one free of Turkish interference.

In the 1470s the idea of a direct sea route to the Orient ceased to be far-fetched and became a matter of discussion in the marketplaces of Europe. But who could attempt it? The Italian trading companies, who were quite accustomed to the ups and downs of Mediterranean trade and confident that the ups would prevail, whose crews and ships were unsuited to oceanic travel in any case, made a calculated decision to bend their energies toward a revival of Mediterranean trade and thus a consolidation of their monopoly. (Their decision was well taken: a century after Vasco da Gama, Mediterranean trade continued to exceed that in the Atlantic and Indian oceans.) It therefore occurred that the adventure of oceanic travel fell to ships and sailors specifically accustomed to the Atlantic — those of Spain and Portugal.

Perhaps this small segment of history should be summarized as follows: In the course of the fifteenth century, the beginning of a fundamental shift in world trade seems to have occurred — from a Mediterranean setting to an oceanic setting — in which the Portuguese and Spanish were the chief entrepreneurs and beneficiaries.

PORTUGUESE EXPLORATION

IN PORTUGAL, the Reconquest was completed much earlier than that in Spain; already by 1250 the Portuguese had cleared their mainland territory of the Moors, and an opportunity existed, even then, for Portuguese adventures in Africa and along the African coasts. Portugal, however, was distracted by intermittent warfare with Spain, which persisted until 1411. In any case, an instigator of Portuguese exploration did not present himself until the opening of the fifteenth century. He was Prince Henry the Navigator (1394–1460), who, ironically enough, felt most at home in his chapel and library. Excessively scholarly and excessively ascetic, Henry burned with zeal to disclose the uncharted world and to Christianize it. Henry had yet another side to his personality. He was an inheritor of the crusading spirit of the Middle Ages. As a very young man, he participated in the Portuguese campaign against Ceuta, an important Moorish fortress and trading center across the Strait of Gibralter, which King John I of Portugal seized and plundered in 1415. Henry was knighted on the battlefield (and later became Grand Master of the Crusading Order of Christ). Ceuta became the first overseas center of the Portuguese commercial empire.

Henry's first adventures were inspired by nothing so grand as discovering a new route to India via the Cape of Good Hope (the feat with which history often associates his name, although he died twenty-seven years before that achievement was actually accomplished) but rather the lesser ambition of finding and getting some of the treasures of Africa. At Sagres, on the southwest coast of Portugal, he founded a school of African coastal navigation, to which were drawn the best cartographers, the most skilled naviga-

86. Prince Henry the
Navigator, detail
from polyptych of
Saint Vincent by
Gonçalves

tors, the most learned geographers, and the most experienced seamen of
whom his nation could boast. The voyages down the African coast were to
be made in caravels — not some new marvel of Renaissance technology, but
the best small ships of the day, especially designed for Atlantic coastal trade.
Of Mediterranean ancestry, chiefly Arabic, they were generally two-masted,
lateen-rigged ships of sixty or seventy tons and of seventy or eighty feet
overall.

The expeditions down the western coast of Africa began in 1415 and
met with a surprising succession of achievements: by 1445 Cape Verde had
been discovered, and Madeira and the Azores were explored and colonized;
by 1471 Upper Guinea had been discovered and trade begun in precious
metals, slaves, and ivory; by 1483 the Congo had been reached and a
Portuguese trading post established at the mouth of the Congo River.

The Portuguese explorer who revealed to the world the route into the
Indian Ocean via the Cape of Good Hope was Bartolomeu Dias, who set
sail from Lisbon in 1487 with two caravels and a storeship. (The cape was

so named by King John II of Portugal; Dias himself named it Cape of Storms.) Just after Christmas, 1487, at Walvis Bay, he provisioned his two caravels, left his storeship behind, and sailed south, beyond the sight of land well below the extremity of the African continent, until he picked up prevailing westerly winds, which carried him to the southeast coast of Africa on February 3, 1488. He had sailed around the tip of Africa. Dias's officers and crew, exceedingly anxious at being in such unknown waters, insisted on turning back, although the warm-water currents encountered as they sailed north seemed to indicate that they had found the route to India. Dias retraced his journey, retrieved his storeship, and reached Lisbon in December 1488.

Ten years passed before Vasco da Gama actually achieved India, using the route set by Dias. Meanwhile, Columbus had crossed the Atlantic — a feat of seamanship that made the Portuguese exploits seem pale by comparison. Vasco da Gama was not a navigator; he was a diplomat and soldier. His two principal ships, *San Gabriel* and *San Raphael,* were strongly built,

87. Vasco da Gama

well-armed merchant ships chosen by Bartolomeu Dias, who accompanied the expedition part of the way. The expedition set sail in 1497 from the Cape Verde Islands; it crossed the equator well out into the Atlantic but used the trade winds to carry the ships east again to the African coast. The storms at the Cape of Good Hope proved as violent and intimidating as those reported by Dias. The expedition managed the cape successfully but found many of the ports in the Indian Ocean extremely inhospitable, given the hostility of the Arabs. At Malindi, half-way up the African coast, Vasco da Gama hired a pilot who knew the Indian Ocean; with the assistance of that pilot, Ahmed ibn Majid, the expedition achieved its end, arriving at Calicut on the Malibar coast of India, May 20, 1498. The expedition immediately established a trading post and managed to exchange enough cloth and hardware to assemble a respectable cargo of spices for the trip home. The voyage of Vasco da Gama took two years and the lives of half of his men.

In Portugal, nevertheless, that expedition was deemed a commercial success. King Manuel the Fortunate was resolved to repeat it. In 1500 he dispatched a fleet of thirteen merchant ships, under the captaincy of Pedro Álvares Cabral, to retrace the voyage of Vasco da Gama. In an effort to catch favorable westerly winds to round the tip of Africa, the expedition swung too far out into the Atlantic and touched the coast of Brazil, which Cabral claimed for Portugal. Four of Cabral's captains, including Bartolomeu Dias, were lost at sea. The expedition persisted, however, and managed to maneuver through the dangerous waters at the Cape of Good Hope and, at last, to achieve Calicut on the western coast of India. There the reception given the Portuguese by local Arab merchants was exceptionally hostile; forty of Cabral's men were slain in Indian ports.

In 1505 King Manuel appointed Francisco Almeida viceroy of East India. It was the beginning of the Portuguese empire in that region of the world.

COLUMBUS

IN 1488, as Bartolomeu Dias's expedition sailed back to the port of Lisbon from its adventure around the tip of Africa, a Genoese sailor named Christopher Columbus watched. Columbus (see plate 76) was born in Genoa in 1451, the son of a nondescript wool weaver named Domenico Colombo. The origins of his family, which are, at best, very obscure, have been hotly contested. Some scholars have assumed that the Colón family were Spanish Jews who emigrated to Genoa. Other scholars have proposed that Columbus was a nephew of the French Basque adventurer Guillaume de Casenove-Coullon, an admiral in the French navy. Whatever his origins may have been, Columbus began life as an apprentice in his father's *bottega.* At fourteen, with only a modest education, he put to sea, first on ships that plied the Mediterranean, then in ships that sailed the Atlantic. In August 1476, in a naval engagement at Cape St. Vincent, near Lisbon, his ship was sunk, and he made his way to shore by clinging to an oar. So uncertain are the records of that engagement, however, that we do not know whether he was fighting with the Portuguese against Genoa, or for the Genoese against Portugal. At any rate, he made his way to Lisbon, where his brother, Bartolomé, operated a small shop selling maps. Columbus took ship several times, once to England or Ireland or Iceland, once down the coast of Africa. His marriage to a Portuguese woman in 1478 led to the birth of his first son, Diego.

Apparently during his Lisbon period, Columbus conceived of his adventure across the Atlantic to the "Indies." In preparation, he absorbed Ptolemy's *Geography;* he annotated the *Travels* of Marco Polo and the *Imago mundi* of Pierre d'Ailly; and he may have consulted the world map by the Florentine humanist and physician Paolo Toscanelli, in which a route across the Atlantic to "India and the islands" was actually proposed. What moved Columbus to consider such a journey? Fame and gold, and at least a smidgen of religious zeal. The Portuguese solution to the Moslem interference with East-West trade had been to sail south along the African coast until the extremity of Africa had been rounded, then east to India and China. The Columbian solution was attractively simpler — sail due west.

Columbus proposed his "enterprise of the Indies" (as he called it) to the courts of both Portugal and Spain. King John II of Portugal, having heard Columbus out, referred his plan to a committee, which sent back an unfavorable report. Columbus turned next to the Catholic sovereigns of Spain — to the rather dour Ferdinand and his charming and handsome consort, Isabella. Isabella received Columbus on May 1, 1486. She too referred the matter to a committee, and once again, the committee reacted unfavorably. When the conquest of Granada was completed in 1492, however, the two monarchs found time to review Columbus's proposal. This time they decided in his favor. Portugal had preempted the route to the Orient around the tip of Africa. Spanish participation in the wealth of the Far East seemed to depend on a direct route to the Indies across the Atlantic, such as that proposed by Columbus.

Columbus set sail from Palos on August 3, 1492. Given the title of admiral, he commanded a fleet of three ships — two caravels and a larger vessel of a type between a caravel and a carrack. The larger ship was the *Santa María* (St. Mary), commanded by Columbus himself; the small ships were the *Pinta* (Painted woman), commanded by Martín Alonso Pinzón, and the *Niña* (Girl), commanded by Vincente Pinzón, Martín's brother. Ninety men sailed with Columbus (about forty in the *Santa María*); they were experienced seamen of good reputation, although perhaps down on their luck and eager for the premium wages paid to them by the crown of Castile. The expedition sailed first to the Canary Islands, then due west in the direction of the Orient. On October 10, 1492, when the crews had been out of sight of land for many days, they demanded that Columbus turn back if a destination was not achieved within three days. On October 12, 1492, Rodrigo de Triana of the *Pinta* sighted what is known today as Watlings Island. Columbus and his crew planted the Spanish flag on the shore, named the island San Salvador, and claimed it for Spain. The expedition then proceeded to the islands of the Antilles, to Cuba and Haiti, which Columbus believed to be the coast of China. In Cuba he actually sent a party ashore to present his credentials to the Great Khan.

Soon, winter storms proved damaging to the fleet. The *Pinta* was swept away in a storm on November 21, and on Christmas Day, the *Santa María* foundered on a reef. Leaving forty men behind to settle the Spanish colony of Villa de la Navidad, Columbus packed the *Niña* with the remaining men, as well as curiosities attained during the voyage. On January 4, 1493, he set sail for Spain, bringing with him six Indians, a variety of botanical specimens, including cotton, rare birds, and, above all, gold.

Both the *Niña* and the *Pinta* managed to reach Palos on the same day, March 15, 1493. Ferdinand and Isabella received Columbus at Barcelona, marveled at the curiosities he had brought back from the other side of the Atlantic, and bestowed on him the titles Admiral of the Ocean Sea and Viceroy of the Indies, with suitable monetary rewards.

On September 25, 1493, Columbus embarked on a second crossing of the Atlantic with an impressive flotilla of three galleons, fourteen caravels, and 1,500 men — still under the assumption that his efforts were directed to the discovery of eastern Asia. Finding the colony of La Navidad to have been massacred, Columbus founded a new settlement on the island of Hispaniola, southeast of Cuba. Little else, however, came of the second voyage. Having sailed among the islands for over two years, Columbus returned to Spain in 1496. On the third voyage (1498–1500), Columbus

88. Amerigo Vespucci

managed to reach the mainland of South America but decided against extensive explorations there, in order to return to the colony on Hispaniola. He found the colonists in disorder. They complained of intolerable shortages of food; they clamored for gold, and they railed against the tyrants who governed them. When rumors of the rebellion reached the ears of Ferdinand and Isabella, the sovereigns appointed a governor, Francisco de Bobadilla, who arrived in Hispaniola on August 23, 1500. Columbus and his brothers, Diego and Bartolomé, were caught in the process of putting down the rebellion by heavy-handed measures, including liberal use of the gallows. The governor promptly returned the Columbus brothers to Spain in irons. The sight of the great admiral in chains created a lamentable impression in Spain. On December 12, 1500, the Spanish sovereigns ordered Columbus released, and they invited him to the court. At his trial, on December 17, his dignities were restored, so remarkable had been his services to the crown and the nation. He persuaded the Catholic monarchs to support him in one last adventure — to find a passage through "the islands" to an ocean of which he had heard beyond Panama. On May 9, 1502, he set sail with four caravels and 150 men in search of the Pacific Ocean. It proved a fruitless effort. He returned to Spain in November 1504, ill and despairing. On May 20, 1506, he died: his body now lies in the cathedral at Seville.

The work of Columbus was continued and extended by such explorers as Amerigo Vespucci (1451–1512), a Florentine merchant whom the Medici sent to Spain around 1491. He soon caught the excitement generated by Columbus's voyages and, in 1497, signed on as navigator of an expedition bound for the Indies. In 1499 Vespucci began a succession of independent voyages, in the course of which he sailed along the coastline of Central and South America as far south as the mouth of the Amazon. In a narrative account of those voyages, published in 1504, Vespucci defined Central and South America as a continent and assigned to himself its discovery, arguing that he had actually preceded Columbus. Shortly after, a German geographer and mapmaker, Martin Waldseemüller, published Vespucci's narrative in his *Introduction to Cosmography* (1507) and included a map of the newly discovered lands, labeled "America." The name soon became commonplace in Europe and was used to describe the northern American continent, as well as the southern. Columbus's importance was better confirmed by two other explorers — Vasco Núñez de Balboa, a Spanish adventurer, who crossed the Isthmus of Panama in 1513 and discovered the Pacific Ocean, and Ferdinand Magellan, a Portuguese navigator in Spanish employ, who in 1519 began a voyage around the tip of South America, across the Pacific, that led eventually to the circumnavigation of the earth.

THE AGE OF
THE REFORMATION

VI. THE NORTHERN
RENAISSANCE

14. Erasmus and Northern Humanism

NORTH OF THE ALPS, HUMANISM TOOK ON A SLIGHTLY DIFFERENT cast, as it was devoted more particularly to Christian purposes — namely, the reform of Christian society by intellectual and ethical means. It taught that if one could discover the real sources of Western Christian civilization — the Bible, the church fathers, the classics — one could purify Christianity of its medieval accretions and corruptions, thus restoring it to its pristine form. In addition, by following the patterns of life recommended in those sources, one could generate an ethical force essential to this program of reform. Those assumptions were based upon still another assumption — that each person was sufficiently "free," sufficiently in command of himself or herself, sufficiently unfettered by pride, sin, guilt, or psychological restraint to carry out these activities successfully.

The man who most clearly typified northern, or Christian, humanism was Erasmus. The greatest intellectual celebrity of his age, called by some the prince of humanists, Erasmus was sought after by the crowned heads of state — Henry VIII of England, Francis I of France, and Charles V of the Holy Roman Empire — to say nothing of the popes of Rome and the universities of Europe. A man of exceeding charm, wit, and urbanity, he was distinguished most of all by his prodigious erudition, which he directed to one purpose — the revival of Christianity by means of a humanistic program, at once intellectual and ethical. A true man of the Renaissance, he believed that the way to correct the immediate past was to return to the remote past, to the world of the classics, the Bible, and the early church fathers. Using those classical and Christian sources, the scholar, working in

333

89. Erasmus, portrait
by Hans Holbein
the Younger

tandem with schools and the printing press, could set off a revolution; the scholar could actually generate enough intellectual and ethical force to purge Western Catholic society of its disorders. For Erasmus, therefore, the worst of all stumbling blocks were, first, *obscurantism,* the failure of intellectualism, and second, *pusillanimity,* any faintheartedness in ethical determination.

THE INTELLECTUAL ROOTS OF ERASMUS

To UNDERSTAND Erasmus, we need to understand his roots in a religious movement in what is today the Netherlands. In the course of the fourteenth century, in the midst of the ancient Catholic diocese of Utrecht, there arose a popular movement to give depth and fervor to religious life. It was called *Devotio moderna,* the New Devotion; its founder was a burgher of the town of Deventer named Geert Groote. The overriding purpose of that movement was to inculcate some of the main monastic virtues — sincerity and modesty, simplicity and industry, love of God and charity toward neighbor — making them standards of daily life in the world. Out of the New Devotion came a society of especially devout people called the Brethren of the Common Life, who by and large preferred to live and work in the world but nevertheless determined to follow those monastic virtues as far as it was possible to do so. That brotherhood, although plainly masculine in name, included devout people of both sexes. The Brethren expressed their worldly devotion by a variety of charitable means, but nothing was more typical of them than their schools. Sometimes they established schools of their own; sometimes they planted their members as teachers in existing institutions; and sometimes they simply provided dormitories in which students away from home could live. As Christian teachers eager to shape character, they were greatly interested in the Bible, which they took to be *the* pattern of good living. For the sake of understanding the Bible, they introduced among their schools the study of the Greek language. Soon the Brethren became divided over how much education, and of what sort, should be pursued. Too much learning might wither the spirit. Powerfully moved by the Italian Renaissance, some of the Brethren avidly studied the classics for their ethical content and saw in Cicero and Seneca the kind of erudition that could only be of benefit to the Christian soul. Hence, the New Devotion slowly became identified with both classical and biblical learning.

The most popular expression of the New Devotion was a little book called *Imitatio Christi* (Imitation of Christ). Its authorship is in some doubt, although it is now the consensus of scholarly opinion that the little book was the spiritual diary of Groote himself, edited later by Thomas à Kempis. The essence of the Christian life, proposed by the book, is implicit in its title: to imitate Christ, to live up to the example of Christ.

Erasmus was born in Rotterdam, probably in 1466, certainly in illegitimacy. His father, Gerard, was both a priest and a man of learning. Gerard knew Greek, copied classical manuscripts, and amassed a library. When his pious family harassed him for his concupiscence — which had in fact produced Erasmus and a brother — Gerard fled to Italy. There he attended lectures by Italian humanists. It was thus with full parental blessing that the young Erasmus was enrolled at Deventer, the intellectual capital of Holland, a place impregnated by both the New Devotion and Renaissance humanism. There, as a student in the Cathedral School of St. Lebwin's, he acquired his taste for Renaissance learning. Leading humanists of the day visited Deventer to give occasional lectures. One such was Rudolf Agricola

335

(1444–85), whom Erasmus heard at Deventer when he was twelve. A Netherlander himself, Agricola had spent ten years in Italy (1469–79) and had written a definitive life of Petrarch. Having recrossed the Alps and established himself at Heidelberg, Agricola became the herald of humanism in the North. "It was Rudolf Agricola," wrote Erasmus, "who first brought back from Italy some glimmer of a better literature."

The plague took both of Erasmus's parents within a year of each other. Left without resources, he was withdrawn from Deventer and consigned to guardians who strongly advised monasticism for this poor boy with scholarly ambitions. In 1488 he entered the Augustinian convent at Steyn, where the library was good and where intellectual freedom prevailed in connection with the *Devotio moderna.* At the end of the first year, the novitiate Erasmus took vows as an Augustinian friar. At nineteen, he wrote his first tract, *Against the Barbarians,* a ringing justification of both classical learning and Christian scholarship. (Apparently the "barbarians" included Erasmus's fellow monks, to say nothing of all the other obscurantists of the day, among whom schoolteachers and Christian preachers are prominently mentioned.) Truth, said Erasmus, is of two sorts. For Christianity, truth is revelation, God's own disclosure of himself; truth is a deposit of divine revelation in the Bible. For classical civilization, however, truth is less a deposit than a quest; truth comes by reflection and study, by insight and scholarly struggle. Both sources of truth are useful to Christian society. Erasmus saw no conflict between Christianity and learning; both contribute to virtue. He saw still less conflict between Christianity and classical culture; both teach virtue. Both together represent the *philosophia Christi* (the philosophy of Christ) — a source of ethical power whose chief reference point is the Bible. Erasmus concluded that scholars were far more useful to Western Christian society than martyrs were. Martyrs can only prove their sincerity; scholars, however, can establish the truth.

That little tract was shortly followed by another, *Oration on Peace and Discord.* There Erasmus celebrated the virtue of peace — one of the greatest virtues of classical antiquity. Erasmus realized that peace was essential to his program of ethical and intellectual reform. A revolution by education could scarcely be accomplished in a world of chaos. The *Oration* celebrated Lorenzo Valla, who was already a hero among the Brethren of the Common Life. Valla, although now twenty years in the grave, had succeeded in Italianizing Erasmus. Valla had already taught Erasmus how to use history to recover the sources, how to use the Latin language, and how to employ rhetoric in scholarship and writing.

THE DEVELOPMENT OF ERASMUS'S THOUGHT

ORDAINED to the priesthood in 1492, Erasmus was restless in the monastic life. "Monasticism," he wrote, "is not piety; it is simply a way of living." The very next year, at the suggestion of his prior, Erasmus was assigned as secretary to Hendrik van Bergen, the bishop of Cambrai, an appointment befitting Erasmus's ability as a Latinist and man of letters. Two years later (1495), with the bishop's approval, he departed for the University of Paris, where he proposed to take a doctorate in theology. The Collège de Montaigu, which he entered, educated three great men of the sixteenth century: Erasmus, Calvin, and Ignatius of Loyola. Erasmus found it insufferable. He complained of its stale eggs and stale curriculum. He loathed its Scholasticism. Erasmus supposed that the self-confidence of its theologians in dealing with hell must have accrued from their having been there. Sharp-cornered religion, religion turned into conundrums by philosophy, was bad religion. Simplicity was the hallmark of relevance. It was a point of view not at all dissociated from Renaissance humanism, with its ethical vitality and impatience with obfuscation.

In Paris, Erasmus became acquainted with the work of Jacques Lefèvre d'Étaples, the most influential humanist in the city. Lefèvre was an eminent biblical scholar of considerable originality, as well as an Aristotelian philosopher. His intellectual ties were to the Florentine humanists, particularly Pico della Mirandola. His thought, typical of northern humanists, we consider more fully in chapter 15.

Erasmus was forced by economic circumstances to take on students. His experience as a teacher led him to begin three treatises, each of which had a bearing on education — *Colloquies, Adages,* and *How to Write Letters.* They proposed a philosophy of education based upon the familiar Renaissance ideal of *humanitas* and the Christian ideal of piety, realized in the student through the study of the classics and the Bible.

In May 1499 Erasmus left Paris for England with one of his students, William Blount, the young Lord Mountjoy. His first episode in England was brief, but decisive. He established firm relationships with the two most celebrated men of English letters: John Colet and Thomas More. Colet, who was near Erasmus's age — both were about thirty — was in Oxford giving lectures on Paul's epistles, lectures extravagantly praised by Erasmus and accounted by history to have been among the most important utterances of the English Renaissance. Colet, recently back from a sojourn in Italy, seemed determined to break through the crust of medieval dogma that overlay the

Scriptures to get at the meat of the pie underneath — the meaning of Paul himself. Colet, in other words, was a typical Christian humanist at work, striving to restore the Catholic Church to its true source — the Scriptures. Thomas More moved Erasmus in other ways: by his great piety and great wit, and by his knowledge of Greek. It was More, already celebrated in court circles, who introduced Erasmus to Prince Harry, aged nine, who in the course of time became King Henry VIII.

Three Englishmen had learned their Greek in Florence during the age of Lorenzo the Magnificent — Thomas Linacre, William Grocyn, and William Latimer. Already in the last decades of the fifteenth century, they had managed to introduce Greek to the curriculum of the English universities. Grocyn, in fact, taught Greek to Thomas More at Oxford. Colet himself had been to Florence, where he too had acquired some Greek. (Erasmus was mortified at Colet's lack of that critical language.) He discovered, too, that the English humanists were enthusiastic Neoplatonists. Colet corresponded with Ficino. More translated a biography of Pico for English readers and made Pico's works available. Neoplatonism, with its mystical impulse, strongly reinforced Erasmus's propensity toward a religion of inwardness, rather than a religion of external forms. The English humanists thus Italianized Erasmus a second time.

On his return to the Continent in 1505, Erasmus immersed himself wholly in Greek, the language indispensable for studying the Scriptures, and he began an ambitious edition of the works of Jerome, the great Christian commentator on the Scriptures. At the same time, he edited Cicero's *De officiis* (On duty), always being careful to maintain the balance between classical and Christian undertakings.

There appeared at this time — in either 1503 or 1504 — the book that put Erasmus into the forefront of the liberal Catholic reform. Erasmus's *Enchiridion* was the prime statement of Christian humanism. The word itself is Greek and means "in the hand." It was used to refer to either a dagger or a small book, literally, a "hand" book, a manual of military arms. The double entendre is intensified by the rest of the title: *Enchiridion of a Christian Soldier.* It is therefore a call to arms against the devil and against our own personal vices.

The *Enchiridion* reveals two characteristics of Christian humanism. The reformatory problem, as Erasmus understands it, is both intellectual and ethical. It is an intellectual problem, for what needs to be done is to return the church to its true basis in the Scriptures. The cry of the Renaissance to go back to the sources is heard in Erasmus's insistence that the church be taken back to early Christianity, back to the Bible, back to the church fathers, of whom Jerome is the most literary, the least dogmatic, and therefore the most reliable. The reformatory problem is also ethical. What the Christian soldier must do, once getting back to the sources, is to discern what is the will of Christ for his or her own practical life. That is a very good reason why people should pay attention to the Scriptures, in which the will of Christ is written, just as a soldier studies his military manual to discover what to do.

All people must therefore have access to the Scriptures in their own language. "Do you imagine," Erasmus once asked, "that the Scriptures are fit only for the perfumed?" His rejoinder was that the Scriptures are fit for "the farmer, the tailor, the mason, prostitutes, pimps, and Turks."

Against the whole paraphernalia of medieval religion — dogmas, laws, liturgies, sacraments, bishops, monks, friars, and nuns — Erasmus pits what he calls the *philosophia Christi,* a simple religion of ethical duty, applicable to every Christian. Erasmus assumes that all people — monks and layfolk alike — have the freedom of will to practice such a religion. His attack on the formalities of religion — better, his disregard of them — left him open to suspicion by Catholics and Protestants alike as being somehow detrimental to Christian institutions.

In the *Enchiridion,* Erasmus attempted for the first time to explain human nature. In chapter 4, he conceived of a person as consisting of two parts — body and soul — a dualistic and Platonic way of looking at human nature. In chapter 7, however, he concluded that human beings consist of three dimensions — body, soul, and spirit. Erasmus associated the *body* with visible and fleshly attractions. The *spirit* represented to him the most godly and ethical aspect of human nature. In fact, he associated it with the "image of God," after which, according to the Bible, human beings were fashioned. In other words, the spirit is the source of every inclination we have to be moral and religious individuals. The spirit is inspired and instructed by Jesus, who is, in Erasmus's estimation, the paradigm of virtuous living. The *soul* includes the faculty of reason *(ratio);* and reason, in turn, includes both the intelligence to decide between good and evil and the free will to pursue virtue or not. Much like the Italian humanists, Erasmus thought that human beings, after the fall of their common ancestor, Adam, suffered from a tremendous inward struggle between the upward pull of the spirit and the downward pull of the flesh. Before the Fall, the three aspects of human nature functioned harmoniously and for the sake of virtue; after the Fall, however, they function inharmoniously and in conflict.

In chapter 7, Erasmus dwelt on the struggle between the upward pull of the spirit and the downward pull of the flesh. In that contest, the soul is "neutral" (Erasmus's own word), free to respond in either direction, able to direct us either to virtue or to fleshly affections. The fall of Adam left the soul not as agile as it had been to do the bidding of the spirit but divided in its loyalties and hence neutral. Eventually, habit may confirm the individual irreparably in one style of life or the other. Erasmus was confident, nevertheless, that of the two opposing forces in our nature — spirit and flesh — the spirit is the stronger. Directed by the spirit, and reinforced no doubt by the sacraments of the Catholic Church, the soul, with its servant, free will, always has the possibility of rescuing us from the downward pull and of inspiring us to virtue.

Is the *Enchiridion* a work of the *Devotio Moderna,* or of Italian humanism, or perhaps even of Florentine Neoplatonism? The proper answer may be all three.

In the summer of 1504, while Erasmus was in Louvain, he discovered a manuscript copy of Lorenzo Valla's *Annotations on the New Testament* (see chapter 9 above). It stimulated him to begin a critical edition of the New Testament, with Greek and Latin in parallel columns, and a critical apparatus underneath. Completed and published in 1516, Erasmus's Greek New Testament — *Novum Instrumentum* — was one of the monumental events in the history of Renaissance scholarship. It was the text upon which almost all of the critical scholarship of the Reformation was based.

In 1505 Erasmus returned to England, where he remained a year, mainly in London. This time it was More, rather than Colet, who took up the lion's share of his time. The two embarked upon a translation of Lucian; the electricity that passed between them sparked two important books, Erasmus's *Praise of Folly* and More's *Utopia*.

Suddenly the prospect of a trip to Italy arose — an opportunity no humanist could afford to pass up — and Erasmus was gone from England again. To "see the sacred sites . . . visit the libraries . . . enjoy the fellowship of scholars" — such were Erasmus's declared purposes for his travels in Italy. He arrived in Bologna in time to witness the military triumph of the warrior pope Julius II, a sight that he greeted "with a great groan." In Venice he lived awhile with Aldus Manutius, who agreed to publish his books. From Venice he traveled south through Padua and Siena to Rome, where he was received in Vatican circles as a celebrity.

In the spring of 1509, while Erasmus reveled in the delights of Italy, Henry VII of England died and was succeeded by his son, Henry VIII, who, although scarcely eighteen, already fancied himself a humanist. Erasmus, foreseeing a comfortable living in Henry's realm, made haste over the Alps to Albion. On his way, he mused over the folly of human endeavor and, having arrived at Thomas More's house, hurriedly recorded his reflections in an essay entitled *Encomium Moriae,* which, as Erasmus fully intended, could be translated either as "the praise of More" or "the praise of folly."

Folly enters the scene in this work and proceeds to lecture to a classroom of scholars. She assumes a variety of poses. At first she makes us believe that she is indispensable to the human scene. How could a doctor practice medicine without his sugar pills, or a preacher without humbug? How could the state govern without various sorts of pomposities — honors, ranks, ceremonies, and such? How could a man consign himself to matrimony, or a woman likewise, without the aid of folly? Folly is illusion, recklessness, flattery, and humbug. Folly is that quality of acceptable deception without which life would be impossible.

Suddenly Folly exchanges her mask and now appears in the disguise of all that Erasmus finds revolting, especially those misbegotten pieties of the Middle Ages — saints and their relics, monks and their ignorances, theologians and their cobweb theology. An "ocean of superstition."

Finally, Folly changes her mask again and appears as the foolishness of Christianity, in contrast to the conventional wisdom of humankind, an allusion to the Pauline assertion, "If anyone among you thinks that he is wise in this age, let him become a fool that he may become wise" (1 Cor. 3:18). Erasmus leaves us in *The Praise of Folly* where he left us in the *Enchiridion:* with an exhortation, reminiscent of Neoplatonism, to travel back up the great ladder of being, rising above the things of the body and the sense, and finally, to rise above intelligence itself, to become one with the One.

Does the book amount to anything? As much as we admire it as a satirical achievement, does it contribute very much to the world of ideas? I think the answer is no. In the last section, where Folly discusses the "foolishness" of Christianity, Erasmus had the opportunity to develop one of the important themes of 1 Corinthians — that, in the view of conventional wisdom, the condescension of God to save humankind and the sacrifice of his own Son to accomplish such a feat must appear as consummate folly. Instead of developing that theme, Erasmus takes the occasion to recommend obscurantism. Christians, he seems to say, should forgo most of the enticements of the world, including its wisdom, and become as sheep, as little children, "fools for Christ's sake." Where is the Erasmus who so often decries the failure of intellectualism and faintheartedness in ethical determination?

Erasmus's third period in England lasted from 1509 until 1514. For a while he lived with More, but for the greater part he lectured at Cambridge on divinity, supported by a benefice given him by the archbishop of Canterbury. There he completed the major share of his Greek New Testament — an undertaking that Colet promoted enthusiastically — and put the finishing touches to his critical edition of Jerome. Both of those texts came from the printing press in 1516. In July 1514 Erasmus took his leave of England, never to return as a resident.

For the next seven years Erasmus lived in the Netherlands. During that time, several of his more notable works appeared. In 1517, for example, he published *The Complaint of Peace,* in which one finds his political ethics. The premium that he placed on the classical virtue of *concordia* (literally, a coming together of the heart) led him to attack all war, even the theory of the just war, which was itself classical in origin, having passed from Cicero, through Augustine, into the Western intellectual tradition. A just war was one deemed to be fought for the vindication of justice and the restoration of peace; as far as Erasmus could foresee, however, there was no apparatus for the determination of justice, as each side in war adjudges its own cause just. He saw absolutely no justification for war; all disputes should be settled by arbitration.

ERASMUS AND THE REFORMATION

A SAYING current in the sixteenth century was, "Erasmus laid the egg that Luther hatched." It was intended to identify the debt that Luther and the Reformers owed to Erasmus and the humanists. Luther never failed to acknowledge his debt to the linguistic, textual, and historical work of the humanists and, above all, to Erasmus's Greek New Testament, upon which his own scholarship was based. There were other affinities as well: both parties advocated a scriptural religion as opposed to the sophistry of the medieval Schoolmen; both heaped ridicule on the excesses of medieval piety; both overleaped the immediate past to discover a normative or classical period in the remote past.

Erasmus's problem in the 1520s was what to do about Luther. Letters full of adulation had begun to pass between the two as early as 1518. Erasmus had seen Luther's ninety-five theses, which he approved and for-

27. TOP Santa Maria
del Fiore

28. BOTTOM Benozzo
Gozzoli, *Procession of
the Magi,* detail of
the patriarch of
Constantinople and
Giuliano de' Medici

29. TOP
Benozzo Gozzoli,
Procession of the Magi,
detail of Emperor John
Paleologus VIII

30. BOTTOM Benozzo
Gozzoli, *Court of the
Magi,* detail of Lorenzo
de' Medici and
attendants

31. Benozzo Gozzoli, *Court of the Magi,* detail of Cosimo de' Medici

32. TOP Benozzo Gozzoli,
Adoration of the Magi

33. BOTTOM Benozzo Gozzoli,
Procession of the Magi, detail of
Castle Vincigliata

34. TOP Petrarch
(Francesco Petrarca),
detail from *The Burial of
Saint Lucia* by Altichiero
da Zevio

35. BOTTOM Marsilio
Ficino, shown in detail of
Annunciation of Zachariah
by Domenico Ghirlandaio

36. TOP Giotto,
*St. Francis Donating
His Cloak*

37. BOTTOM Giotto,
*Expulsion of the Demons
from Arezzo*

38. TOP Giotto, *Confirmation of the Rule*

39. BOTTOM Giotto, *St. Francis Preaching to the Birds*

40. TOP Giotto,
Dream of Joachim

41. BOTTOM Giotto,
Nativity

42. Giotto, *Kiss of Judas*

43. Giotto, *Last Judgment*

44. Masaccio, *Expulsion from Paradise*

45. TOP Masaccio,
*St. Peter Baptizing the
Neophytes*

46. BOTTOM Masaccio,
St. Peter Curing the Sick

47. Masaccio,
*Distribution of Alms
and Death of
Ananias*

48. Masaccio,
Tribute Money

49. TOP Masaccio, *Resurrection of the Son of the Emperor Theophilus and St. Peter Enthroned*

50. BOTTOM Masaccio, *Resurrection of the Son of the Emperor Theophilus and St. Peter Enthroned*, detail. Starting from the far right: Brunelleschi, Leon Battista Alberti, Masaccio, and Masolino.

51. Lorenzo Ghiberti, Gates of Paradise

52. Lorenzo Ghiberti, *Annunciation*

warded to Thomas More. He persisted in defending Luther, even while dispelling the idea that either he or humanism was responsible for Luther's opinions. Three matters of dispute, however, developed between the two. One was Luther's rather cavalier attitude toward the unity of the church. As a true humanist, Erasmus believed stoutly that the peace of the church should not be violated. Second, Luther lived comfortably with paradoxes; Erasmus could not, complaining bitterly about the paradoxical character of Luther's thinking. Paradoxes offended his Renaissance instinct for reason and proportion; he could not rest until he had smoothed them all off by the pumice stone of reason. The third was crucial. By ascribing human salvation entirely to God's mercy and not at all to the individual, Luther undercut the sense of human freedom and human responsibility upon which Erasmus's whole program of intellectual and ethical reform depended.

The charged atmosphere of the Low Countries led Erasmus to leave in 1520 and to take up residence in the Swiss city of Basel, where his printer, Johann Froben, made him welcome. By 1523 he was under heavy pressure — especially from his stoutest patrons, Pope Hadrian VI and King Henry VIII of England — to take sides against Luther. At the same time, the letters passing between Luther and Erasmus grew increasingly caustic. In April 1524, for example, Luther wrote to Erasmus thanking him for his linguistic efforts but counseling him to defer to the experts: "We have chosen . . . to put up with your weakness and we thank God for the gifts he has given you. . . . You have neither the aptitude nor the courage to be a Reformer, so please stand aside." On September 1, 1524, came Erasmus's answer — a book entitled *De libero arbitrio* (On the freedom of the will).

Erasmus's attack on Luther is written in elegant style and smart humor. He feels like a fly attacking an elephant — the pachyderm being Luther — and he proceeds in some peril to offer these four observations. First, the Scriptures are by no means clear on the issue of free will — how far God's grace operates in the religious experience and how far human initiative operates. Luther, by declaring humankind religiously incompetent and enslaved to sin and by ascribing everything therefore to God's grace, is indulging in speculation and thus is equally as reprehensible as the medieval doctors whom he dares to attack. Second, by publishing those speculations about the incapacity of human beings, Luther will only confirm the morally weak in their weakness, the lazy in their laziness, the malicious in their malice. Who will reform one's life when told that one cannot? Third, Erasmus prefers to be deliberately noncommittal on the issue of the slavery or bondage of the will; he dislikes dogmatic pronouncements of any sort.

343

Instead of the unprofitable, speculative, tumultuous business of dogmatizing, Erasmus will be content to stress what he himself calls "the morally good life." Finally, it is his personal judgment that some real place must be left in the structure of religion for human freedom of will. It is all well and good to ascribe the greater part of religious incentive to the inspiration of God, but human beings must be accorded enough freedom to strive after the good and true. Thus, in his typical fashion, Erasmus smoothed out the paradoxes, argued for peace over tumult, and pointed toward an ethics-centered religion.

Luther, as one would have expected, answered Erasmus, ferociously choosing words exactly opposite to those of his opponent. To Erasmus's *De libero arbitrio,* Luther replied with *De servo arbitrio* (On the bondage of the will). We will consider Luther's diatribe in chapter 17. It is enough here to say that his repudiation of Erasmus was massive.

Erasmus, the liberal Catholic, lived out the rest of his days in an uneasy relationship with two opposing forces — on the one side, the Protestant Reformation, on the other side, the Catholic Reformation. His works fell under suspicion at the Sorbonne, in the University of Paris, where the Catholic reaction was quite pronounced and where the vigilantes of orthodoxy poked into any sort of liberalism, whether Lutheran or Erasmian. Pope Clement VII actually appointed four Spanish censors to examine his writings. It is ironic that he spent much of his later life in the Swiss city of Basel, which was becoming more and more Protestant with each passing day, due in part to propensities that can be traced directly to Erasmus himself. His own protest against relics, pilgrimages, indulgences, fasting, monastic vows, invocation of saints, and liturgical services; his own lack of concern about the externals of religion; his own strong predilection toward inward religion — those were the things that registered strongly in Switzerland where he lived. Erasmus thought the question of the real presence of Christ in the Mass not worth debating: he spoke vaguely about a mystical presence, a celestial food. That idea was picked up by the Swiss Reformers, notably Zwingli, who declared that when Christ said in the Mass, *Hoc est corpus meum* (This is my body), he really meant *Hoc significat corpus meum* (This signifies my body).

Thus, Erasmus looked out of his Basel window, so to speak, to see the Swiss Reformation unfold before his very eyes, because people had taken him seriously. He was repelled by what he saw. There he was, sitting in the garden of the printer Froben, trying to translate Chrysostom, while the city of Basel seethed with religious tumult. In February 1529 an iconoclastic

344

riot occurred that left the ruins of religious statues and medieval paintings in heaps of rubble. He resolved to leave such a place for the relative peace of nearby Freiburg.

His world seemed to be coming apart at the seams. In his beloved England his own protégé, Henry VIII, had cast aside his wife, Queen Catherine, whom Erasmus adored, in order to marry a lady of her court named Anne Boleyn. Henry proceeded to declare the church *in* England to be the Church *of* England, independent of Rome, with the king himself as its "supreme head." Thomas More resigned as lord high chancellor (1532) rather than countenance the impudence of Henry's displacement of the pope of Rome as head of the church. When More was beheaded, three years later, for his continued recalcitance toward Henry's schemes, both matrimonial and ecclesiastical, Erasmus declared, "By his death, I feel myself to be dead."

Pope Paul III wooed him. Had Erasmus acceded, that pope may have offered him a cardinal's red hat. His thought in his last years took a conservative turn. His criticism of the Protestants grew more strident. They had broken the peace of the church without having achieved any significant amendment of life. He accused the Reformation of the cardinal sin of obscurantism. It was certainly true that the monumental changes of the 1520s had depopulated the German and Swiss universities. In 1521 there were sixty students at the University of Basel; in 1528, one; in 1529, none.

Erasmus returned to Basel in 1535. The Swiss Reformation was then a fact; the French Reformation, just underway. On July 11 or 12, 1536, he died in the ambiguity of having no party and no home. "I wish to be a citizen of the world," he once wrote to the officials of Zurich who had offered him a place. Erasmus lived as the very model of a Christian soldier. His utter impatience with the externals and formalities of religion, which made him even more radical than Luther in that respect, left an indelible impression upon the branches of the Reformation that took their rise in Switzerland. His ideal of peace, his religion of ethical responsibility, and his liberal Catholicism, although obscured by four hundred years of antagonism between Catholics and Protestants, have won him new respect in an age of ecumenism.

15. Renaissance in England, Germany, and France

ENGLISH RENAISSANCE

FORERUNNERS of the English Renaissance were three humanists of great reputation, known as the Oxford Reformers — John Colet, Thomas More, and Erasmus of Rotterdam. All three were Christian humanists, humanists of the northern type — humanists, in other words, who were interested not merely in the revival of classicism but even more profoundly in the revival of a purified and biblical form of Christianity. All three of these men had been Italianized; all three were deeply indebted to the Neoplatonists of the Florentine Academy for their intellectual formation. Theirs, however, was a distinctly biblical humanism, a form of humanism devoted to the recovery of a purer, more biblical Christianity, buttressed both by the study of the early church fathers and by the competent study of the New Testament in Greek.

Having considered Erasmus in chapter 14, we begin here with John Colet, who was born in 1466 and died prematurely at fifty-three in the year 1519. In the course of his career, he was professor at Oxford and subsequently dean of St. Paul's Cathedral in London. Perhaps the finest of all his activities was the founding of St. Paul's School in 1510, an institution related to the cathedral. Modeled after the humanistic schools of Italy, St. Paul's School was unabashedly committed to what was variously called the New Learning (i.e., Christian humanism) or, oddly enough, the Old Religion, namely, the religion of the New Testament and the "old" Catholic Church. It may well have the distinction of being the first Renaissance institution in England.

90. John Colet

As a student at Oxford, Colet had heard the lectures of William Grocyn (1446–1519) and Thomas Linacre (1460–1524), recently back from Italy, and had been inspired by them to begin the study of Greek and to pursue his own education in Italy. There, in Italy, beginning in 1493, Colet fell under the spell of Florentine Neoplatonism.

In 1496, at the age of thirty, Colet returned to Oxford and commenced almost immediately to deliver a series of lectures on Paul's Epistle to the Romans. As we have seen, those lectures are accounted among the most important utterances of the early English Renaissance in that they indicated a shift of religious standpoint and method. Instead of returning with simple Florentine Neoplatonism, Colet brought back from Italy chiefly the *method* of humanistic scholarship, which he now proceeded to apply to the leading work of Paul. Using the historical and philological tools of the Renaissance along with what smattering of Greek he then knew, Colet proposed to break the dogmatic crust that overlay the Bible and to delve for meaning beneath. No longer was the Bible viewed as a verbally inspired arsenal of texts; it

348

was a book whose meaning must be plumbed and whose figures must be understood. Colet applied the Renaissance scholarship to the Bible as fearlessly as to a text of Cicero or Virgil; he used the Latin biographer Suetonius in order to decipher Paul as a historical person.

Colet was among the more outspoken opponents of the medieval schools. He despised the Scholastic neglect of the literal meaning of the text of Scripture in favor of three other methods of interpretation: the allegorical (the description of one thing under the image of another), the tropological (or moral), and the anagogical (the discovery of hidden spiritual or mystical truth in the literal text). Nor did he have patience for the inchworm exegesis of the medieval doctors, which went on endlessly, seemingly without profit. Not even Thomas Aquinas was sacrosanct; Colet accused him of tainting Christianity with profane philosophy.

It is interesting that it was Paul's Epistle to the Romans that initially propelled Luther. Do Colet's lectures constitute a halfway house toward Luther? Colet caught some of the nuances in Paul that Luther seized upon, especially the overwhelming fact of human sin and the utter priority of God's grace in the religious experience. Colet, however, made quite a point of stressing the free will of human beings. Furthermore, he tended to see the evil in people and in the world, not as something inherent in the fallen nature of man, but rather as human failure to achieve the more perfect norm. How does one explain such differences between Colet and Luther, when it is perfectly obvious that both men were interpreting the same text? Perhaps Colet could not overcome the altogether powerful influence of his Florentine mentors, Ficino and Pico, who were so confident of the nobility and grandeur of humankind.

It would be wrong, however, to conceive of Colet as a Protestant. In many respects, he was more conservative than Erasmus of the Catholic tradition. In St. Paul's School, Mass was celebrated daily in the conventional manner. Colet understood the Mass to be a sacrifice; he defined the presence of Christ in the Mass according to the general terms of transubstantiation. Nor did he doubt for one minute the jurisdiction of the papacy. The pope, he said, "is the highest bishop."

Yet a reformer he decidedly was. In a famous sermon that he preached at St. Paul's Cathedral on February 6, 1512, long before Luther even conceived of the ninety-five theses, Colet cataloged the ills of the church with an almost embarrassing thoroughness. His remedial measures, however, were quite Catholic and conservative. Reform, he said, ought to commence in the episcopal office and thus filter down, in good hierarchical fashion, to the clergy and people. Reform must also include a strict enforcement of canon law and a tightening of the recruitment of clergy to exclude the ignorant and licentious.

John Colet was a Catholic with a special place in the history of English Protestantism. It was he before all others, before even Luther and Tyndale, who pointed to the fundamental relevance of the Scriptures for contemporary religious problems — the Scriptures historically, critically, and humanly considered.

Now let us consider the third of the Oxford Reformers, Thomas More. More was born in London in 1478, the son of a barrister of some reputation but of limited means. At the age of twelve, young More was taken into the household of John Morton, archbishop of Canterbury and lord high chancellor of England. There he remained for some two years, acquiring the manners befitting a gentlemen. Morton sent him to Oxford, where, about the year 1492, he entered Christ Church College. There he made great intellectual progress under the instruction of the early Oxford humanists

91. Thomas More, portrait by Hans Holbein the Younger

Grocyn and Linacre, who were famous for their learning in the Greek language and classics.

More's father insisted that he return to London to study law and so preserve the family tradition. He entered the Inns of Court to be trained in the legal profession and was admitted to the bar in 1501. When Erasmus first came to England in 1499, he met More and was fascinated by his piety, wit, and knowledge of Greek. A relationship was struck between them that endured until More's death in 1535. Each reinforced the other in Christian humanism.

Christian humanism evidently brought More to a spiritual crisis. Disdaining the profession of law, he indulged himself in a long period of introspection. Between 1500 and 1503, he lived periodically in the Charter-house of London — the name by which the English referred to monasteries of the Carthusian order — and lavished all his time on the study of Greek and the early church fathers. He thought seriously of entering the priesthood but finally set the idea aside. He nevertheless adopted a severely ascetic way of life, and only the persuasion of his friend John Colet kept him from taking monastic vows. Even in his later, secular life, he persisted in wearing a hair shirt as a penance, when he took a fancy to do so, and tried to maintain the practice of reciting the Divine Office, as one would have done in a monastic community. Although twice married, he conducted his household along monastic lines, with morning and evening prayers, and pious talk at mealtimes. He gave public lectures on Augustine's *City of God*, to which he had devoted his attention for many years.

After 1503, with no uncertain parental encouragement, More regained his ardor for life in society and returned to the profession of law. He entered politics. The next year, he was elected to the House of Commons. Then followed a whole succession of achievements in politics, including embassies abroad to Flanders and Calais, membership on the Privy Council (1518), speaker of the House of Commons (1523), and high steward of Cambridge University (1525). Finally, in 1529, he succeeded Cardinal Wolsey as Henry VIII's lord high chancellor. Having been knighted by Henry, More was known to England as Sir Thomas. During this period, More's wife, Jane Colt, died, leaving him in 1511 with the care of four small children, for whose sake chiefly he married a widow, Alice Middleton. It was she who did not take kindly to that persistent intruder upon the household, Erasmus of Rotterdam. In the course of 1515 and 1516, More completed his *Utopia,* which Erasmus saw through the press at Louvain in 1517.

The fortunes of Thomas More began to change in the year 1529, when

Henry VIII began his attempt to jettison his queen, Catherine of Aragon (see plate 77). Embittered by the lack of a male heir and smitten by the lady-in-waiting, Anne Boleyn, Henry proposed to divorce Queen Catherine in order to marry Anne. More was emphatically opposed to the king's matrimonial maneuvers. He was to be even more stoutly opposed to the principle of "royal supremacy" that Henry VIII and his ministers had brought into vogue in the struggle over the divorce. As Henry was thrown into greater and greater contention with the papacy over the divorce issue, the theory evolved in England of a national English church, freed of papal control, over which the king himself would be the "supreme head." Thus, "royal supremacy" is the theory of the headship of the king over the Church of England. In 1532, with grave doubts about such undertakings, More saw fit to resign as chancellor and passed his time as a Catholic propagandist, directing his polemics not only against Tyndale and the Lutherans but also all Englishmen, in high station or low, who threatened the well-being of the Roman religion in England. More continued to advocate the reform of the church, as one would have expected of a Christian humanist, but only from within, and only under the aegis of regular and competent ecclesiastical authorities.

In April 1534 Thomas More was committed to the Tower of London for his refusal to swear the oath that was required by the First Act of Succession (1534), which stipulated that (1) Henry's marriage to Catherine of Aragon was null and void, (2) Henry's recent marriage to Anne Boleyn was "consonant with the laws of Almighty God," (3) the issue of Henry and Anne would succeed to the throne of England, and (4) the pope would no longer be acknowledged within the realm. At his trial on July 1, 1535, More specifically attacked the Act of Supremacy, passed by Parliament the previous year, awarding Henry the title "supreme head" of the Church of England, as an act "directly repugnant to the laws of God and his holy Church." He declared that a seven-year study of the history of the papacy had left him quite convinced that the papacy existed *de jure divino,* "by divine right." As the trial proceeded, he admitted that he could never, in good conscience, condone the marriage of Henry VIII to Anne Boleyn, which had, in fact, already taken place. More was convicted of high treason and was, by the mercy of his old friend Henry, beheaded rather than disemboweled on July 6, 1535. His head was displayed on London Bridge on the end of a pike, as a warning to others whose loyalties might be divided between pope and king.

Thomas More's most noteworthy book was called *Utopia,* and was a work squarely in the humanist tradition. It belonged to a well-defined type of thought, namely, Renaissance idealism and utopianism. Three books were especially representative of this tradition, all written by humanists, and all written in 1515–16. The three were meant to redress what the authors took to be the skepticism of Machiavelli's *Prince.* The works were Erasmus's *Instruction of a Christian Prince,* written for the education of the future emperor, Charles V, then still in his teens; Guillaume Budé's *Education of the Prince,* written by a preeminent French humanist for the young Francis I of France; and More's *Utopia.*

Utopia (a word coined by More from two Greek words meaning "no place") is an island founded by the conqueror Utopus, some 1,760 years before More. It is an ideal commonwealth and is made to stand in contrast to the failures of English society, as these are detailed in part 1 of the book: the harshness of the criminal code, wars between Christian states, the structures protective of private property, the cruelty and selfishness of kings, and the economic hardships that accrued from the enclosure system. (As English feudalism declined, thousands of acres of arable land were enclosed for pasture and thus for exploitation by major landowners, even while many who tilled the land were dispossessed of their living.) Whether it is fair to commit Thomas More to all of the social philosophy found in his *Utopia* is an interesting question. More as author should not be confused with Raphael Hythloday, the character who describes Utopia. Some scholars have even suggested that Raphael is the object of More's satire. The author does not advocate all that he so agreeably describes. Or does he? An example of this tension between the views of More and the description of Utopia is found in the section on religious tolerance. For instance, the people of Utopia are tolerant of any form of religion that is itself tolerant. When an enthusiastic convert begins to malign other religions, he is promptly arrested and deported "as a seditious person." Such opinions are in no way consonant with those More entertained in his own life. In his *Dialogue . . . Touching the Pestilent Sect of Luther and Tyndale,* he did not hesitate to ask for the vigorous suppression of heretics. Occasionally, More seems to acknowledge that Utopia is a state of life that is, at least in part, unattainable. Raphael, the narrator of the book, once declares: "There are many things in the Utopian community which I may rather wish for, than hope after."

Many of the more practical proposals of Erasmus reappear in More's *Utopia.* There is a strong polemic in both books against international treaties, which, as we have seen, were so facilely made and equally as facilely broken. Listen to More's sarcasm on the subject: "For in Europe, and especially in those parts of it where the Christian faith and religion are professed, the sanctity of leagues is held sacred and inviolate, partly owing to the justice and goodness of princes, and partly from their fear and reverence of the authority of the popes." As topping, he added, "Are not Christians especially designated 'the faithful'?" Erasmus's polemic against war is also repeated in More's book. Injustices to the English laboring classes are carefully examined. The reader is bluntly advised that the poor are daily defrauded of their rights and dues, and this even by common law. By contrast, Utopia is a truer community, a classless society, in which private property does not exist, and for the perpetuation of which public education of all girls and boys equally is seen to be of capital importance. The towns of Utopia are all built according to exact specifications, with wide streets, common halls, hospitals, water systems, and sanitation systems. There is no money. All goods produced and all goods required flow in and out of common warehouses, in what More claims to be an economy of plenty. No one is idle; everyone is working, yet the schedule of work is such that each person is deliberately afforded eight hours of leisure. Leisure is to be devoted to the liberal arts, especially to literature and to music.

The most undesirable aspect about Utopia is the overregulation of affairs, so that spontaneity and originality seem to be forfeited. Housing, education, and even meals are standardized, so that one begins to doubt that there is any place left for the experience of vital thought. The Utopians, however, have generous freedom in the way they live. Thomas More advocated no hair shirts for them. Rather, they live "according to nature"; it is deemed to be a form of ingratitude to God to raise the vanity of asceticism against the natural desires and appetites of the body and against the delights of life.

Indeed, the most important single aspect of More's *Utopia* may be its moral philosophy, which is utilitarian. Pleasure, happiness, and in that sense "utility" is the chief object of life — a conviction that the Utopians have arrived at upon both religious and rational bases. They teach, for example, that the human soul was created by God for happiness. Happiness, therefore, is to be pursued in life for its own sake — not every kind of pleasure, to be sure, but that which is accounted honest and good.

For Thomas More, the root of all human disaffection is pride, which begets selfishness, ostentation, inequality, the exploitation of human beings and animals, injustice, and even war. What can men and women do to offset the pervasive power of pride? Luther would have answered, Nothing! Human nature is corrupt anyway. The very nature of human nature is pride. Only God is powerful enough to intervene. *Sola gratia!* Only by grace are we redeemed from the devastation of pride. A humanist would have answered, Something! The resources available are the reasonableness of human beings, their potentiality sharpened by education, and their freedom to will and act for the good.

In *Utopia,* More accepts neither of those solutions. His is essentially a medieval solution, drawn from the virtues of medieval monasticism — poverty, life in community, a radical equality of persons, and a daily existence of work combined with contemplation. In Utopia those monastic virtues reappear in the form of a classless society from which private property has been eliminated. The means of production, the raw materials of production, and human labor are not left in private hands but are all controlled by the civic corporation. Meals, clothing, and housing are all managed communally. Utopia is a society that despises ostentation, inequality, and excessive individuality. Gold, for instance, is used contemptuously to make chamberpots and manacles for slaves. Utopia is also an agrarian society, although all citizens must necessarily take their turns at jobs to be done in the cities. Its government is staunchly republican. Utopians enjoy a careful balance between labor and leisure — a feature also of monastic life. In Utopia, however, leisure is not used to sing the Divine Office (i.e., to worship God), but to increase the invigoration of the mind and spirit through music, art, and literature. The chief purpose of human existence is neither to make money nor to glorify God but to achieve the happiness that is associated with pleasure — not wanton pleasure, to be sure, but "good and honorable" pleasure, "natural" pleasure, which is associated with the divine purposes of creation. Thus, the monastic virtues of Thomas More are somewhat transfigured in the way they are put to use in his utopian society.

More is particularly a humanist when he subscribes to the humanistic view (also found in Ficino and Pico) of the universality of truth. All truth is one truth. All truth is true, whatever its source — an axiom that cuts against the grain of the exclusivity of the Christian revelation. Thus, as a humanist, More could subscribe to the principle of religious toleration and the freedom of conscience. As a Catholic, however, he could not.

GERMAN RENAISSANCE

GERMAN humanism, which flourished in the first two decades of the sixteenth century, had important antecedents in the late fifteenth century. Rudolf Agricola (1444–85) was the first, according to Erasmus, to have introduced Italian humanism to the regions north of the Alps. Agricola, a

355

native of the Low Countries, spent ten years in Italy and became an authority on Petrarch. When he crossed the Alps in 1497 to establish a humanistic circle in Heidelberg, it was with the intention of making the Germans no less literate than the Italians in the classical culture of the Renaissance. Agricola's intellectual ambitions were realized in his students, the most notable of whom was Conrad Celtis (1459–1508), a lyric poet of considerable reputation in Germany, a sage, and a scholar highly literate in classical literature. Celtis, by virtue of his appointments to major universities, succeeded in introducing humanism into university circles, some of which were hospitable to humanism. Others, entrenched in Scholasticism, proved inhospitable.

German humanism of the sixteenth century, like its counterpart in England, was distinctly northern, or Christian; its intention was to stimulate a reform of medieval Christianity on the basis of a return to the Scriptures. In comparison to the early English Renaissance, that of Germany was rather more satiric and decidedly more nationalistic. Such were the characteristics of the humanist Jacob Wimpfeling (1450–1528), the cathedral preacher of Speier, who attacked certain ecclesiastical corruptions with a wry humor and who was an outspoken advocate of German nationalism. His close colleague, Sebastian Brandt (1457–1521), a citizen of Strassburg, wrote one of the two most famous satires to have originated in German humanism. Published in 1494, Brandt's *Narrenschiff* (Ship of fools) described in lively German verse the various sorts of fools who have assembled to take ship for the Isle of Fools. They included those who buy books never intending to read them, lazy students, pedantic professors, cheating lawyers, retailers of scandal, and so on. The book enjoyed astonishing popularity; it was praised by scholars and read eagerly by the common people, who were delighted to have such a book in their own tongue. The following passage from the *Ship of Fools* affords us some idea of Brandt's satirical style:

> 'Tis not the peasant's pious heart,
> Nor wish to save his better part,
> That bids him send his son away
> Among the priestly ranks to stay.
> Oh, no! 'Tis that he may support
> His relatives; — a thing, in short,
> Full easy for a priest to do,
> Who, though no book he ever knew,
> Could still enjoy his benefice

And lead a merry life, I wis.
For priests no more than monkeys know
Of saving souls from realms below;
I wouldn't trust a cow to one,
Full sure she'd either kick or run;
And as for matins or the mass,
I'd rather hear the miller's ass
Take up the lute and try a song.
But the bishops do the greatest wrong
When they consent to consecration
Without a mite of education.

The major figure of German humanism was Johannes Reuchlin (1455–1522), who is remembered as the pioneer of Hebrew scholarship and one of the few defenders of the Jewish people in the Renaissance era. Reuchlin, a child of the Palatinate in Germany, was educated by the Brethren of the Common Life. It is therefore scarcely surprising that in the 1470s, as a university student in Paris and in Basel, he became an avid student of the Greek language, the Scriptures, and the classics. A lawyer by profession, Reuchlin spent most of his life as chancellor to the duke of Würtemberg. In that capacity, he made three trips to Italy. In the course of the first two, he met the Florentine Platonists Marsilio Ficino and Pico della Mirandola, whose thought and critical scholarship he never ceased to admire. From Pico, particularly, he acquired an appreciation of the Jewish Cabala, as well as willingness to admit that there were many sources of religious truth. During his third trip to Italy, he became the pupil of the learned Jewish Renaissance scholar Obadiah Sforno, at whose hands Reuchlin perfected his already considerable knowledge of the Hebrew language.

Reuchlin's investigations of the Hebrew language, which began in the 1480s, led to publications in the sixteenth century that were of incalculable value to scholarship, including *Concerning the Rudiments of Hebrew* (1506) and *Concerning the Accents and Orthography of the Hebrew Language* (1518). By this time he had become captivated by Jewish mysticism. In a book of 1517, *On the Cabalistic Art*, Reuchlin taught that a secret form of revelation, quite apart from the Scriptures, had been imparted by Moses and the prophets to certain wise men who, in their turn, passed it down in an unbroken tradition, deposited finally in the medieval form of Jewish mysticism known as the Cabala. Reuchlin was certain, moreover, that the Cabala was in essential harmony with Pythagorean philosophy, and he entertained the possibility of stimulating a revival of interest in Pythagoreanism, just as the Florentines had revived Plato and Jacques Lefèvre, Aristotle. Reuchlin's interest in the Cabala, his propensity to see relationships between Judaism and Christianity, and his willingness to admit many sources of religious knowledge seem to be unmistakable signs of Pico's influence upon him.

As he struggled with Hebrew scholarship, Reuchlin became interested in the difficulties experienced by Jews. In 1505 he wrote *Warumb die Juden so lang in Elend sind* (Why the Jews are so long in distress), in which he expressed the hope that God would enlighten the Jews (thus revealing his own attitude of condescension) but also protested their mistreatment. The following year, Johann Pfefferkorn, a Jew converted to Christianity, wrote a tract entitled *A Mirror for Jews,* in which he advocated that the Jews be compelled by law to surrender all books contrary to Christianity and to attend sermons preached for their conversion. On August 19, 1509, the Holy Roman Emperor, Maximilian I, approved of Pfefferkorn's program of confiscation.

Reuchlin entered the lists on the side of the Jews. In an opinion of 1510, he claimed that the Jews were certainly no heretics but could lay claim to all of the protections afforded by law. At that point, Reuchlin ran afoul of the Inquisition. To the side of Pfefferkorn came the Dominican friar Jacob Hochstraten, the grand inquisitor of the province of Mainz. The Inquisition squeezed Reuchlin, intending to make him declare himself a true Christian and therefore an enemy of Jews. He stoutly refused. The emperor, exasperated by the furor, silenced both parties in 1518. The issue, however, remained unresolved and was carried into the universities and ultimately to the papacy. Reuchlin was consistently upheld. The Reformation then unfolded in Germany, and it became convenient to think of Reuchlin as pro-Lutheran. (He was actually quite unsympathetic to Luther.) On June 23, 1520, a decision given in the name of Pope Leo X settled the dispute in favor of the Dominican friar Hochstraten. Reuchlin, under a cloud of disapproval, spent the last years of his life as a professor of Greek and Hebrew at the Universities of Ingolstadt and Tübingen and died in 1522.

Throughout his fight with the Dominican inquisitors, Reuchlin had the undivided support of the German humanists. Two younger members of that community, Ulrich von Hutten and Crotus Rubeanus, attacked the Dominicans in a second classic expression of German Renaissance satire, *Letters of Obscure Men.* In this work the authors assail the Catholic theologians who have taken sides against Reuchlin, parodying their bad Latin, the absurd trivialities they debate, and their hatred of Reuchlin and the other humanists.

Hutten (1488–1523) deserves attention in his own right. He was a humanist, an ardent German nationalist, and a social reformer of some consequence. Social disaffection existed in three classes of German society: (1) the knights, those members of the lesser nobility who had enjoyed status in the feudal structure of society but whose power and wealth had faded in the changing social order; (2) the working people of the towns, who thought themselves exploited at the hands of the middle class; and (3) the peasants, wretched under injustices that princes and landowners practiced against them. Hutten, himself a knight, attempted to coalesce these groups in a social revolution, which entailed a resurgence of German nationalism coupled with a fierce hatred of the Church of Rome.

Hutten's family, who were knights, traced their line back to Frankish nobility. As a boy of eleven, he fled the monastery at Fulda, where he had been sent for monastic training, and struck out upon an education of his own choosing, an education classical and humanistic, at three German universities. He crowned it by a sojourn to Italy, which was the mecca of humanists. By 1517 Hutten had settled down in Germany, where he proceeded to generate a revolutionary spirit, the Roman papacy being the butt of his antagonism. He seemed to envision a kingdom of God on earth, which, rather unlike the biblical model, meant a new Germany in which priests and monks were few and far between, papal taxation reduced, and an era of social justice inaugurated.

The next year (1518), he exercised his humanistic skills by bringing out a new edition of Lorenzo Valla's refutation of *The Donation of Constantine,* thereby hoping to embarrass the papacy. In the following year, he chanced upon an obscure reformer named Luther who was then defending himself at Leipzig. Hutten mistook Luther to be his revolutionary ally in the program of German nationalism and riddance of the papacy, little understanding how loath Luther was to have his religious reformation confused with social revolution. An example of Hutten's nationalism and antipapalism appeared at this time, in the form of a letter, dated 1520, which he addressed to the elector of Saxony, intended of course for public consumption.

By 1520 Hutten was in grave circumstances with the Church of Rome, which demanded his arrest and extradition. As Hutten wrote inflammatory notices of the impending revolution, the knight Franz von Sickingen actually assembled an army of rebels. In April 1523, however, at the walls of the city of Trier, the military effort collapsed in an overwhelming defeat. Stripped of his fortune and suffering from syphilis, Ulrich von Hutten wandered about until Zwingli, the Reformer of Zurich, took him in. There he died at the age of thirty-five, leaving no inheritance except his pen.

FRENCH RENAISSANCE

THE EARLY Renaissance in France coalesced around three remarkable and rather diverse figures; a Greek scholar of exceptional renown, a frail theologian, and the sister of the king of France. The Greek scholar was Guillaume Budé, who was born in Paris in 1467 or 1468, of a family distinguished by governmental service; he died there in 1540. He himself studied law at the University of Orléans, but with scant enthusiasm. At the age of twenty-six, after some years of lighthearted dissipation, he developed an overwhelming passion for classical studies and applied himself to the study of Greek, as well as philosophy, theology, and science. That he conjugated Greek verbs

92. Guillaume Budé

360

on his wedding night, as reported, may be far-fetched, but it is an inescapable conclusion that he knew more about the grammar and syntax of Greek than anyone of his age, including Erasmus, and that his work in Greek represented the counterpart of that of Reuchlin in Hebrew.

Budé was well received in the Renaissance court of King Francis I of France. In 1522 Francis appointed him royal librarian at Fontainebleau, where he proceeded to build a library that became the basis of the Bibliothèque Nationale. In 1530, at Budé's encouragement, Francis established a faculty in Paris devoted specifically to classical, humanistic, and biblical studies — the College of Royal Lecturers, from which grew the Collège de France.

Budé's major works number perhaps ten. Of them all, the most important and substantial was his *Commentarii linguae graecae* (Commentaries on the Greek language), which appeared in 1529. It was an event in scholarship deemed so important that the king caused a special typeface to be cast for the publication of the book. Here the grammar and syntax of classical Greek are examined and illustrated from ancient examples. A Greek-Latin lexicon by Budé was published posthumously in 1554.

Although he was convinced that the church must undergo reforms, Budé shrank from the prospect of participating in its dismemberment. Yet he influenced a generation of students who joined the ranks of French Protestantism. Prominent among them was John Calvin.

The frail theologian was Jacques Lefèvre (1455–1536), a precursor of the Reformation in France. Born in Picardy, Lefèvre became a priest, but quite early in his life he was drawn to the University of Paris by the charms of humanism; there he devoted himself zealously to classical studies and to the Greek language. In 1492, having attained a doctorate at the University of Paris, he set out for Italy, where he accomplished chiefly two things: he read Aristotle at the University of Padua, then the center of Italian Aristotelianism, and he acquired all he could of the Florentine Neoplatonism of Ficino and Pico.

Upon his return to Paris, Lefèvre became a professor in one of the colleges of the university. In that capacity, he commenced a career in critical scholarship, devoted at first to the works of Aristotle and the writings of the early church fathers. He fancied himself a renovator of the genuine Aristotelian philosophy — Aristotle rescued from his entanglements with medieval theology.

In 1507 one of Lefèvre's pupils, Guillaume Briçonnet, became abbot of the Benedictine Abbey of St. Germain des Prés, which still stands on

Paris's Left Bank. He appointed Lefèvre librarian. There Lefèvre remained until 1520, pursuing the career of a Christian humanist.

In 1509 he published *Psalterium quintuplex,* which presented five Latin versions of the Psalms side by side, in order to reveal the variant readings and the problems of interpretation that accrue from the text itself. The work provides us with an excellent example of how critical Renaissance scholarship was applied to the Scriptures with the good intention of discovering what the Scriptures really said. Luther based his lectures on the Psalms — the earliest expression of Protestantism to come from his pen — upon the text of Lefèvre. That work was followed, in 1512, by a decisive piece of critical scholarship devoted to Paul's Epistle to the Romans. It involved Lefèvre's own translation made from the Greek text, set in comparison to the official Vulgate text, and furnished with a commentary. From the commentary particularly, we observe some rather startling conclusions proposed by Lefèvre some five years before Luther posted his ninety-five theses. He seemed to say that the Scriptures must be accounted the sole source of authority in the Christian religion; he questioned whether the Bible required priests to be celibate; he raised objections to the doctrine of transubstantiation, although he did not deny that Christ was really present in the Mass; and he insisted that a reform of the Catholic Church was necessary, not merely desirable. Was Lefèvre also the precursor of Luther on the crucial question of "justification by grace alone" (i.e., forgiveness strictly by God's mercy and not in the least by human activity or merit)?

Lefèvre believed that human beings consist of two parts: a God-given soul, and a body that derives ultimately from the creation of Adam and comes down to us through a long succession of parents. He associated sin with the body, saying, "The sons of Adam are conceived and born with the sin of the flesh." The soul, in contrast, consists of three divinely given faculties that prompt human beings toward goodness. We have a mind to know the good; we have a will *(voluntas)* to will the good; and we have a free will *(arbitrium),* which can do the good. Lefèvre also speaks of a spirit that inhabits every human being; it invests each of us with a moral sense and is closely identified with both the natural law and the moral law (Ten Commandments). The human problem is that our soul has become servile to the flesh. Human willpower, instead of doing the good unambiguously, suffers from a bad case of self-orientation, always curved in upon itself and serving its own selfish interests. Each person is at war with himself or herself, torn between the good impulse of the mind and the will, as opposed to the fleshly and selfish interests of the body.

How are human beings to be delivered from such a predicament? Lefèvre foresees two stages. Through the inescapable pull of the natural law and the moral law, we first become aware of our sinful condition and, using our willpower as much as we can, struggle to obey the law. Although each of us will inevitably be frustrated in our pursuit of the good by the overweening pull of fleshly desires, we have made a good beginning that God will not ignore. Our struggle to fulfill the law is a genuine purgation that enables us to have faith in Christ, receive the sacrament of baptism, and thus obtain forgiveness as an act of pure mercy on God's part. "Man prepares himself," said Lefèvre; "God, however, is the author of justification."

Lefèvre's program reminds us of Gabriel Biel's. (See chapter 17 for a more complete discussion of Biel's thought.) The individual must begin by "doing his very best"; one's own striving is the precondition of God's mercy, just as God's mercy is necessary for the individual's justification. Throughout the process, the individual's will remains active. Lefèvre agrees with Biel that, even in the end, the active will of an individual may accept or turn away from justification.

What is really new in Lefèvre is the idea that justification is by grace alone. That was the very idea that Luther seized upon and made the cardinal principle of the Protestant Reformation. Is there, then, a coincidence between the thought of Luther and that of Lefèvre? Not really. Lefèvre hedged his teaching about justification by grace alone, insisting that human activity is the prerequisite to God's activity. "Neither faith nor good works justify," he wrote, "but they prepare for justification." That is both a very ardent Lutheran statement and a very anti-Lutheran statement. In the final analysis, we must put Lefèvre with the late medieval Schoolmen, such as Biel, and with the Italian humanists, such as Pico.

That critical work on Romans was followed, in 1514, by an edition of the works of Nicholas of Cusa, the German bishop of the fifteenth century whose thought was heavily indebted to Neoplatonism. In 1522 Lefèvre returned to biblical scholarship by preparing a commentary on the four Gospels. King Francis I of France and his sister, Marguerite of Navarre, around whom the humanistic circle gathered, observed Lefèvre's work with satisfaction. As the belief grew that the Bible belonged to Everyman, the king and his sister prevailed upon Lefèvre to make a translation in French. He chose the conservative program of using the official Latin Vulgate text, rather than the original Hebrew and Greek, as the basis of his translation. The New Testament appeared in 1523, the Psalms two years later, and the entire Bible in 1530.

As early in 1517, Lefèvre fell under suspicion of heresy. Certain of his writings were condemned by the Sorbonne in November 1521. Despite the protection afforded him by Francis I and his sister, Lefèvre chose to leave Paris. In 1520 he joined Briçonnet, who meanwhile had become the bishop of Meaux. The bishop had divided his Catholic diocese into thirty-two districts and had proceeded to introduce a program of reform that verged on Protestantism. Lefèvre was appointed vicar-general of the diocese, with the responsibility of uplifting the Catholic priesthood.

In the course of his Italian campaigns, in February 1525, Francis I was defeated, as we have seen, by the emperor Charles V at the battle of Pavia and was led away captive to Madrid. It was a shocking day in the history of France. Louise of Savoy, the king's mother, became regent of France during her son's imprisonment. She found it necessary to make certain concessions to Parliament and to the church. Parliament appointed a commission to discover, try, and punish heretics, who were usually described by the generic name "Lutherans." The group of Meaux fled to Strassburg. Lefèvre's translations of the Bible were burned, and measures were taken to suppress books deemed heretical.

By the Treaty of Madrid, struck in 1526, Francis I was returned to his throne. He promptly recalled Lefèvre and appointed him tutor to the royal children. The old man spent his last years at the court of Marguerite of Navarre, where he died in 1536. Two years before his death, a young French humanist came to see him, seeking advice and a career. His name was Calvin. So close was Jacques Lefèvre to the Reformation, and yet so far away. He was no more willing than Erasmus to suffer an out-and-out breach with the Church of Rome.

In the midst of the circle of French humanists stood Marguerite of Navarre (1492–1549), sister of King Francis I of France. Marguerite was raised in the court of Louis XII and pursued the New Learning with exceptional enthusiasm and competence. She had mastered Latin and Italian in her childhood and later acquired Hebrew and Greek in order to cope with the Scriptures. The most pronounced influence upon her intellectual formation came from two noteworthy exponents of Neoplatonism, Marsilio Ficino and Nicholas of Cusa, in whose writings she was exceedingly expert.

Her court, which sometimes ran to over a hundred distinguished persons, was typical of the French Renaissance. She patronized humanists, sheltered Protestants, and indulged fully in the pleasures and vanities of life. Her *Heptameron,* fashioned after Boccaccio's *Decameron,* was a collection of scandalous, even licentious, tales.

93. Marguerite of
Navarre, portrait
by F. Clouet

She was nevertheless deeply absorbed in religious questions. Besides
reading Ficino and Nicholas of Cusa, she read Luther and Calvin. She aided
and abetted the reformers of Meaux. She not only studied the Scriptures in
Greek and Hebrew but presumed to expound them in public sessions in
her household. Her thought carried her beyond the limits that most French
humanists were prepared to go. Outwardly Catholic, she was in every
essential respect a Protestant intellectual. Her idea of justification, of how
a person attains justice in the sight of God, differs but a hair's breadth from
Calvinism, if at all. Yet when she died in 1549, Marguerite of Navarre died
within the Church of Rome.

EXCURSUS

Art and Poetry in Early Sixteenth-Century France

BECAUSE OF THE ATTENTION DEVOTED TO ITALY, THE ARTISTIC AND literary achievements of the French Renaissance are frequently overlooked. However, France of the early sixteenth century was the first country to be affected by the new learning coming out of Italy, and the solid national state centered around the royal court, especially that of King Francis I (r. 1515–47), helped promote a strong and distinctively French culture.

Scholars have often debated how much the Italian Renaissance influenced France, and how much it developed on its own from medieval sources. Those scholars like Haskins who have argued for an earlier twelfth-century Renaissance have generally found it centered in France, and some scholars have pointed to the influence of medieval Provençal poetry on Dante and Petrarch. Nevertheless, French culture did decline somewhat in the fifteenth century, and the art and literature of the Italian Renaissance clearly was an influence in the early sixteenth century, even if this influence became mingled with traditional French culture.

Ironically, the increased contact between Italian and French culture came about because of the wars of late fifteenth and early sixteenth centuries. Both artists and works of art returned to France with the conquering French leaders. The strong French state promised a degree of stability not possible in the Italian states.

Francis I was an informed and devoted patron of the arts. Early in his reign he lived much of the time in the Loire valley, but from 1528 his court was centered more at his chateaux around Paris. Many of these he had rebuilt at this time, and he took personal interest in the architectural and decorative details. The most noteworthy endeavors in this area were the rebuilding of the Louvre, and Fontainebleau southeast of Paris. Italian artists like Giovanni Battista Rosso and Benvenuto Cellini were invited to France to decorate parts of Fontainebleau.

Francis collected Florentine, Venetian, and Roman art, including such works as Michelangelo's sculpture *Hercules*. He also collected classical sculpture, or had copies made to decorate his court. Titian did a portrait of the king, but declined the invitation to move to France. The influence of these Italian painters and sculptors began to show itself in the work of native French artists. For example, the painter to the king, Jean Clouet, painted in the style of the Italian High Renaissance. With the accession to the throne of Francis's son, Henry II, there was a marked turn to French architects and decorators, who by this time had adopted much of the Italian styles.

Francis I also took a keen interest in the literary arts. He began collecting books early in his reign, adding to the royal collection he inherited. With Guillaume Budé as Master of the King's Library he also began collecting rare manuscripts, especially Greek ones; later he encouraged the royal printer Robert Estienne to publish many of these. He instituted a deposit law in 1537, requiring that printers supply a copy of every work printed in France to the royal libary, but this law seems not to have been enforced or effective. In the last years of his reign he established an impressive library at Fontainebleau: eventually it would become the foundation of the Bibliothèque Nationale.

There was a strong tradition of Romance and lyric verse in medieval French, typified by such celebrated works as the *Roman de la Rose,* but it was still generally conceded that important works of poetry would be written in Latin. However, the early sixteenth century saw a turning to the vernacular similar to that which took place in fourteenth-century Italy. Such poets as Jean Lemaire de Belges (ca. 1473–ca. 1525) were influenced by Dante in this, and called on other French poets to follow them in imitating the Italians. Clément Marot (1496–1544) achieved a high degree of success in writing poetry, including a French versification of the Psalms, translations from Petrarch's sonnets and pastoral poetry that was to later influence the English poet Spenser. At the same time he frequently used such traditional medieval French forms as the rondeau and the ballad. At the court of Marguerite of Navarre, Marot was protected from those who persecuted him for his Protestant leanings.

A renewal of Neo-Latin verse took place at this time as well, but this poetry differed from earlier medieval Latin works in that it strove to imitate the classical models, and asserted individual personality.

The most noteworthy French poets of the Renaissance were La Pléiade, a group that included Pierre de Ronsard (ca. 1524–85) (generally recognized as the leader of the group), Joachim Du Bellay, and Antoine de Baif (1532–1589), Rémy Belleau (1528–77). Using Petrarch as a model, they produced numerous French sonnets, which were in turn to influence English verse. The name "Pleiade" — first used in 1556 — refers to the seven daughters of Atlas who were transformed into stars at their death, and indicates the French poets' attachment to classical sources. Like many Renaissance artists they were reacting against their medieval forebears, among whom they included Marot; they desired to create a new purified French poetry that would be the equal of the ancients. Ronsard and Du Bellay first met in 1545, and four years later Du Bellay wrote the seminal work *La Deffence et Illustration de la Langue Francaise* in which he argued that French poets should use their native tongues, as Petrarch and Boccaccio had written in Italian, and as Virgil and Cicero had chosen to write in Latin rather than Greek. At the same time Du Bellay conceded that there was little worthwhile in the medieval French tradition upon which to borrow. French itself might even have to be reshaped in order to be a worthy literary language. Thus, a new French poetry would be brought to life by a knowledgable reading of the classics and the creative imitation of them. Du Bellay encouraged French writers to attempt the great classical genres of the ode, tragedy, and epic.

The poets of La Pléiade set out to fulfill these lofty goals: Ronsard's chief work was to be his Homeric epic on the founding of France, entitled *La Franciade,* the first four books of which he published in 1573. Similarly Etienne Jodelle (1532–73) composing the tragedy *Cléopâtre captive,* generally held to be the first original French tragedy, but based on a story from Plutarch's *Lives.* Ironically, the poets of La Pléiade are best remembered now for their less ambitious love poetry, particularly sonnets written in imitation of Petrarch. They did much, however, to establish the reputation of French as a literary language. They created a loftier style and ambition for French poetry, and as part of this the Alexandrine (twelve-syllable) line became the French standard. Their concern with Latin and Greek models was to continue in France through to the neoclassicism of the eighteenth century.

VII. REFORMATION
IN GERMANY

16. Introduction to the Protestant Reformation

THE PROTESTANT REFORMATION BEGAN IN 1517 IN THE UNIVERSITY
town of Wittenberg, in the German principality of Saxony. Already by
1521 it had spread to Zurich, in German-speaking Switzerland. From the
French-speaking section of Switzerland, and specifically through the city of
Geneva, it entered France. It traveled northward along the Rhine, into the
Low Countries, into Scandinavia, and into Poland. Even in the 1520s, it
crossed the Channel into England and entered Scotland. Only the staunchly
Catholic nations of Spain and Italy were impervious to Protestantism, and
only the Lutherans' own awkward treatment of the German peasants prevented the Reformation from attaining strength in the southern and southeastern sections of Germany.

Europe began the sixteenth century Catholic; it left the sixteenth
century part Catholic, part Protestant, with a variety of evangelical parties
competing with the old church and with each other, often vociferously, for
a corner on religious truth. Europe began the sixteenth century still under
the overarching umbrella of Christendom, with a more or less common set
of religious and political assumptions; it left the sixteenth century a mass
of new national states and territorial principalities, many with only tenuous
connections to the papacy, if any at all. Europe began the sixteenth century
with a capitalist economy based on the commerce and industry of the towns
and the raw materials furnished by farms; it left the sixteenth century with
a capitalist economy vastly changed and enlarged by colonial expansion into
virtually every corner of the world. Europe began the sixteenth century
already aware of the challenge that the Renaissance had posed to medieval

culture; it left the sixteenth century with the prospects of a modern secular culture, which Protestantism unwittingly made possible, and with the prospects of an age of science, for which the Renaissance was a major preparation.

Unlike the Renaissance, which appealed principally to the elite, the Reformation was a vast popular movement that touched every segment of society. It was the first such movement of the post-Gutenberg era, that is, the first in which the printing press could be used as an instrument of persuasion. From 1500 until the beginning of the Reformation, German printers issued an average of forty books a year; once the Reformation began, however, that number increased to five hundred books a year. Luther's writings were literally snatched from the hands of booksellers. The combination of the Reformation and the printing press produced a great diffusion of knowledge and inaugurated what Oswald Spengler called the modern "book and reading culture." Printing in the service of religion reinforced some radical new ideas such as "the priesthood of all believers" — in other words, the idea that every believer is a priest — suggesting that the combination of personal faith and access to religious knowledge through the invention of printing empowered everyone to be a priest. Printing and the idea of the priesthood of all believers also encouraged literacy and education, including systems of public education, apart from which no one could even begin to acquire religious wisdom, much less become sophisticated in it.

One of the curiosities of the Reformation is that it was a contest between insiders. Ordinarily the great struggles of history have pitted insiders against outsiders — the Frankish Kingdom versus the Visigoths, the Spanish Christians versus the Moors, the Crusaders versus the Moslems. The Reformation, however, was strictly a conflict among Christians — one contingent of insiders who believed that another contingent of insiders was utterly wrong and would go to hell for it.

How radical was the Reformation? While there is good reason to believe that the Reformation was radical *in its consequences,* there is considerable doubt that it was radical *in its intent.* Edward Gibbon, in *Decline and Fall of the Roman Empire,* offered this observation: "After a fair discussion we shall rather be surprised by the timidity than scandalized by the freedom of our first reformers." Indeed, a modern school of German historians called the Tübingen school believes that Luther, because of his great conservatism, staved off a much more precipitous decline of medieval culture and held off the Enlightenment by several hundred years. "Radical," however, is taken from the Latin *radix,* "root." To be radical is nothing more than to return to the root of something, surely not to uproot it. Luther, the passionate insider, only wanted to return to the root of Christianity as it was expressed in the Bible and in the golden age of Christianity. Restoration, not novelty or destruction, was the program of those insiders called Protestants.

Finally, we come to the question of historiography: what was the early Protestant view of history? It was no more and no less the historiography of the Renaissance. The ancient world, while remote in time, was near in sentiment; the medieval world, while near in time, was remote in sentiment. The intellectual problem of the Reformation was exactly that of the Renaissance: to return to the sources, the roots. When Luther, however, said "sources," he meant the Bible; when he said "the golden age," he meant Christianity before there were popes; when he said "dark ages," he meant a medieval world irreparably spoiled by superstition, Scholastic theology, barbarous Latin, and so on.

Was the Reformation aware that it was indebted to the Renaissance in this way? I think it was. In a treatise written in 1523 to the councilmen of Germany, Luther declared that, thanks to God's gracious providence, the Renaissance had prepared the way for the Reformation, just as John the Baptist had been sent by God to announce Christ. Luther ventured the preposterous opinion, in the same treatise, that God himself had caused the fall of Constantinople in 1453 so that the exiles would flood the West, teaching Greek.

WHY THE REFORMATION HAPPENED

IN THIS section I propose four possible reasons why the Reformation took place. Then I discuss the reason given emphatically by the Reformers themselves.

The first possible reason for the Reformation is *nationalism and the rise of national states.* We have considered the beginning of the process of nationalism, just at the turn of the fourteenth century, in the collision between the pope, Boniface VIII, and the king of France, Philip the Fair. Nationalism means the growing national self-consciousness of the several states of Europe. It means also the way taxes are collected and used for national purposes and the way a national militia is formed for national self-aggrandizement. In this sort of process, the papacy began to be seen as an extranational force, an impediment to national development, while papal taxation, which increased enormously with the Avignon papacy, was seen as a grievous and almost illicit burden imposed on sovereign nations. Especially in England and in Germany, the Reformation was worked out in explicitly nationalistic terms and against the extranationalistic pretensions of the papacy.

A second possible reason is *economic disaffection.* The Europe of the Reformation consisted of 65–80 million inhabitants. The prevailing economic system was capitalism. The bourgeois classes, normally associated with capitalist economies, flourished in the towns and cities, which continued to grow in the sixteenth century. New technologies in mining, shipping, and printing invigorated the economy. This setting, however, included two sorts of displaced and disaffected people. The lesser nobility had no place left to them in the exorable erosion of feudalism and were literally a superfluous people. The peasants, especially those of Germany, were an exploited people who sought some better stake in the money economy. Both parties were susceptible to revolutionary tendencies, and both contributed to the course of the Lutheran Reformation and to the emergence of the Anabaptist tradition.

Third is *the weakness of the papacy.* Since 1300, the papacy had suffered a succession of blows that might have toppled a less formidable institution. Consider the list of catastrophes:

- the Avignon papacy, 1305–76
- the Great Papal Schism, 1376–1417
- Conciliarism, 1409–60
- the Reformers Wycliffe and Hus
- the Borgia popes and the threat of secularization, 1455–1503

If one adds to such a list the new nationalism and the more secular agenda of the Italian Renaissance, one may gain some inkling why the Church of Rome was not able to cope at once with the onset of Protestantism.

A fourth possible reason for the Reformation is *the depressed state of the Latin church.* The malodorous accounts of the pontificate of Alexander VI were not the only rumors heard in the taverns and marketplaces of Europe. One German dandy informed another German dandy that ROMA really meant *radix omnium malorum avarita* (avarice is the root of all evil) and that the besetting sin of the Roman church was its greed. It was not hard to believe when one thought of papal taxes (a sore point among Germans) or of the rich lifestyles of the princes of the church.

Another common complaint was the low estate of clergy — poorly paid and living in squalor, poorly trained, sometimes in breach of the vow of celibacy, and almost always consigned to the lowest social status by the rest of society. At the other end of the ecclesiastical scale, the princes of the church were denounced for their extravagances, among which was the practice of holding many church offices but being absent from most. Finally, monasticism, which had been the conscience and invigoration of the Catholic Church through the Middle Ages, had played out as a vital religious force and was in especially low estate in England and Germany. (A revival of monasticism was the first significant part of the Catholic Reformation and got underway as early as 1510, before Luther amounted to anything.)

The Reformers would have been mightily unimpressed with these four reasons. In their mind, the Reformation was a *religious* crisis — not an economic, political, or even moral crisis. In the opinion of Luther and his associates, the overriding question of the Reformation was, What is the gospel? In other words, What does Christianity mean? How does Christianity work? The assumption of such questions put by Luther and his colleagues was that the Roman Catholic Church had lost sight of the essential meaning of Christianity and was teaching something erroneous, a religion of self-help, which Luther characterized by the pejorative term "works-righteousness," as if to say, Catholics are saved by their own activities.

The point of the Protestant Reformation may come down to a single issue, a single question, which we may phrase in the following ways:

- How do I achieve *virtue?* (i.e., the Renaissance question)
- How do I achieve *righteousness (iustitia)* and be saved?
- How can I stand *just (iustus)* before God?
- How can I be *justified?*

These are the same question, put in slightly different terms. It means that *justification* is *the* central issue of the Protestant Reformation.

The late medieval Schoolmen asked the question as well as Luther. The answers they gave, however, were appreciably different, as the accompanying chart indicates.

375

Renaissance	Late medieval Scholasticism	Luther
1. Use your freewill, which, even if impaired, is virtually intact.	1. *Facere quod in se est:* Begin by "doing your very best."	1. We have no such thing as free will; human beings are utterly enslaved by selfishness.
2. Choose *virtù,* noble character.	2. On that account, God will award you the habit of grace.	2. Justification is *sola gratia:* by God's grace entirely.
	3. Then you can earn works of genuine merit and achieve justice before God.	3. How? Through the sacrifice offered by Christ for all sinners.
Assumption: Freedom	Assumption: Some freedom	Assumption: No freedom

CONDITIONS IN GERMANY
FAVORABLE TO THE REFORMATION

THE REFORMATION began in Germany and throughout its first generation was a peculiarly German institution. It will be useful, therefore, to consider briefly the pre-Reformation history of Germany.

In the years after 1300, while France and England were developing into strong, centralized states under royal governments, Italy and Germany were both giving way to political particularism — Italy to the particularism of northern Italian city-states, Germany to the particularism of territorial princes. It is simply inappropriate to speak of a German "nation" before the time of the emperor Maximilian (1493–1519), and not until 1870 was there a national state called Germany.

In other words, as feudal structures were eroded by a money economy and by the vigorous economic life of the towns, there appeared in Germany, not a strong national government, but a system of princely states, or territories, and a gaggle of free cities, loosely federated under a parliament (the Diet) and the sovereignty of an emperor. The German territorial states, being virtually independent, greatly diminished the power of the central government and bred a form of cultural provincialism of which many Germans, including Luther, were ashamed.

One must bear in mind that what we call Germany was only the major power in a still larger political entity known as the Holy Roman Empire. That empire included Italy and Burgundy, and thus all of modern France east of the Rhone. The empire was part of the German predicament. Germany could never afford to concentrate on itself but spent its energies elsewhere. A conspicuous example of that phenomenon was Frederick II (1220–50), who expended the power of the empire extravagantly in Italy, provoking the papacy to wage a war of extermination against the House of Hohenstauffen, while national government slowly disintegrated in Germany.

The election in 1273 of the first Hapsburg, Emperor Rudolf, might have reversed the long German slide into particularism, but it did not. Lacking any means of levying taxes or maintaining a national army (crucial elements in the development of French nationalism, for instance), Rudolf was not successful in establishing a Hapsburg dynasty. On his death in 1292, even his son and heir was denied the imperial throne. Throughout the fourteenth century, the balance of power continued to shift from emperor to territorial princes, in spite of the accomplishments of Albert I (1298–1308), the second Hapsburg emperor, who increased Hapsburg dominions and labored strenuously to establish a hereditary line.

The final triumph of territorialism was achieved at the expense of Emperor Charles IV (1347–78) of the House of Luxembourg, whose policies were firmly lodged in appeasement. In foreign affairs, his reign was noteworthy for a policy of nonintervention in Italian affairs: Charles diminished the empire by abandoning Italy. In domestic politics, he saw fit to confirm German particularism by making it constitutional. Charles himself designed the Golden Bull of 1356 — a document tantamount to a constitution. In it, Charles sought to regulate the often-turbulent struggles among the princes and free cities by assigning the power of electing an emperor to seven carefully defined electors: three princes of the church (the archbishops of Mainz, Cologne, and Trier) and four secular princes (the king of Bohemia, the duke of Saxony, the margrave of Brandenburg, and the count palatine of the Rhine). The Golden Bull guaranteed the power of the seven electors by protecting their lands from division and by requiring the succession of electoral power through inheritance. What the Golden Bull accomplished, therefore, was the more or less constitutional transfer of authority in Germany from emperor to princes, and what followed in the fifteenth century was an attempt by the princes to reconstitute their territories into sovereign states. Not even the reign of two powerful Hapsburg emperors, Albert II (1438–39) and

377

Frederick III (1440–93), diminished the excessive territorialism that characterized German politics throughout the fifteenth century.

When the princes required money to support state governments, they were forced to negotiate for taxes with the three estates of Germany — clergy, nobles, and burghers — and eventually such procedures led to the creation of a *Landtag* (provincial parliament) in one state after another. Such territorial parliaments, where taxes were levied and grievances heard, did not diminish German particularism, however, but tended to reinforce the sovereign governments of the territorial states of Germany by making them more complete.

If the territorial states seemed to add up to a system of political and social security, they did not. Pre-Reformation Germany suffered untold turbulence and lawlessness for the lack of a national government. The princes contended against each other in endless feuds and aggrandizements. Leagues of cities arose to defend the autonomy of the towns against overbearing princes. The knightly class *(Ritterschaft)*, which had been rendered obsolete by the introduction of mercenary armies paid for out of public taxes, manifested great restlessness and resentment and attempted to assert independent power in fiefs still controlled by the knights. Throughout the fifteenth century there were revolutionary expressions among the German peasants, which will be described below. In the absence of a strong, national government, prosecution of crimes and the maintenance of public order was often left to vigilantes; peace making was assigned to the fragile efforts of the so-called *Landfrieden,* local agreements resembling the medieval Peace of God.

Of all of the disaffected classes in Germany, the peasants were the most restless. They arose from the agrarian and feudal organization of the Middle Ages. In the money economy in which they increasingly found themselves, the peasants discovered that most of the time-honored duties expected of them had been converted into money equivalents. Whatever gains the peasants made, whether in prosperity or in personal freedom, were immediately offset by a clamor for more prosperity and more civil rights. In the Rhineland, where the peasants were comparatively better off, the revolutionary sentiment was therefore the most intense. There the *Bundshuh,* the dreaded secret society of peasant revolutionaries, operated with especially awesome effect.

The German world into which Luther was born was a world on the verge of upheaval. It is no wonder that, at first glance, most Germans, even the German peasants, mistook Luther to be a national hero, "the nightingale of Wittenberg," as Hans Sachs said, sent to lead Germans into a new era of hope and national purpose. Much of the resentment expressed by many classes of German society was focused against the Roman Catholic Church. Princes sought to exploit church lands and wealth; cities resented the princes of the church who, in some instances, governed them; town councils disliked the courts of law run by the church and bridled at episcopal control over the religious, moral, and social manners of the burghers; knights blamed the church for draining off the wealth of the empire by taxes, enriching Rome and Italy at the expense of Germans; peasants were convinced that bishops and abbots were among their principal oppressors; and virtually everyone denounced the taxation imposed by the church as a denigration of national dignity and an exploitation of German resources.

Yet, at the same time, largely through the rediscovery of Roman law by Renaissance scholars, the princes of the territories of Germany, by appealing to the absolute power of the *princeps* in Roman law, began to assert their own authority over religious affairs in their realms, the authority of the Catholic bishops notwithstanding. Thus, by the time of Luther, the crucial axiom *cuius regio, eius religio* (who rules the realm, his shall be the religion) could be used to admit the Reformation, or not to admit the Reformation, into the various territorial states of Germany. Meanwhile a quite similar development had taken place in the cities, as town councils began to insist on being able to control religious affairs within their corporate limits.

Aided and abetted by ardent nationalists among the German humanists — Ulrich von Hutten, for example — the chorus of hatred against the Church of Rome grew louder and louder as the fifteenth century yielded to the sixteenth. Almost every imperial diet that met during the century before Luther received a *gravamen,* or formal slate of grievances, compiled by the various classes of German society against the Church of Rome.

17. *Luther*

OUR KNOWLEDGE ABOUT THE LIFE OF MARTIN LUTHER IS BASED largely on his own accounts, given at different times in his treatises and sermons. It must be remembered that these accounts were in the well-established genre of spiritual autobiography, a genre whose chief end was not the precise relaying of biographical facts for their own sake, but the edification of readers and listeners. Thus, the details and developments of Luther's life are at times difficult to piece together, and certain "events" have been questioned by recent scholars. Complicating the "legend of Luther" are the numerous apocryphal tales told about him, by both followers and enemies in his own time, and the attempts of some twentieth-century scholars such as Erik Erikson to compose a psychological biography of Luther.

The Luders were peasants who lived on the edge of the Thuringian forest in Saxony. Luther was to glory in his peasant roots. *Ich bin ein Bauern Sohn* (I am a son of peasants), he said, wanting us to believe that he was party to the sweet simplicity and terrible poverty of peasant life.

Hans Luder married Margaret Ziegler, and the two of them set up housekeeping in Eisleben, a Saxon town of five thousand souls, where Hans Luder found labor in a copper mine. There, on November 10, 1483, Martin Luther was born. Hans was shortly fired, which caused the little family to gather up its pitiful possessions in the summer of 1484 and move to Mansfeld, where Hans Luder again took to the mines. This time he prospered, and in the course of years became nothing less than a small industrialist. When Martin Luther enrolled at the University of Erfurt in 1501, he

94. Martin Luther,
portrait by Lucas
Cranach the Elder

paid his fees in advance and the registrar marked his registration, *in habendo,* which is to say, he came from a family which "had it." So far from being a peasant, Luther was shaped by town life. Despite his attempt to identify himself with the peasants, he may actually have entertained some urban contempt for them.

LUTHER'S INTELLECTUAL WORLD

LUTHER was raised in conventional Catholic piety. His devout mother taught her children the faith and sent them regularly to Mass. Luther never ceased to cherish the Latin Mass. When in the 1520s it fell to him to remodel the liturgy, he refused to abandon the basic structure of the Mass.

Some scholars have suggested that in his childhood Luther absorbed vast amounts of superstition concerning witches and dark powers that no amount of sophistication could ever dispel. What heresy was to the age of Innocent III, witchcraft was to the mid-fifteenth and early-sixteenth centuries. *Maleficium* was its theological name — the cult of the dark powers led by Satan himself. Theologians wrote treatises on the best techniques of "hammering" witches and offered the opinion that, as Adam's rib was crooked, women made therefrom were constitutionally crooked and thus more susceptible to possession by demonic powers. Other scholars, such as Heiko Oberman, have found in his theology a much more Reformational approach to the devil and evil, one in which these powers are consistently contrasted to the much greater strength of Christ. Luther's famous hymn "A Mighty Fortress Is Our God" demonstrates this struggle between Christ and the devil:

> And though this world with devils filled
>   should threaten to undo us,
> We will not fear, for God has willed
>   his truth to triumph through us;
> The Prince of Darkness grim,
>   we tremble not for him;
> His rage we can endure;
>   For lo, his doom is sure —
> One little Word shall fell him.

As a boy, Luther entertained ideas about Jesus Christ that, although conventional in his age, appear curious in ours. Every schoolmaster had a *lupus*, literally "wolf," a student spy who kept records of his fellow students' sins for exposure on Judgment Day. Christ was God's *lupus*. Luther recalled two means by which such an idea became fixed in his imagination. He remembered a painting (or was it a stained glass window?) that surmounted the altar of the Mansfeld Church, depicting Christ as the Awful Judge, dispensing the justice of God from a lofty throne. All we need to do to appreciate what Luther saw is to recall Michelangelo's *Last Judgment* of the Sistine Chapel. There Michelangelo depicted Christ as the Awful Judge, with his hand raised, ominously, almost vindictively, in the gesture of justice. Even more impressive to the young Luther were the *Gerichtspredigten* (judgment sermons) delivered by wandering friars, which dwelt on themes of death and divine judgment. In those sermons, Christ was depicted as the judge who would surely recompense sinners according to their deserts. In the impetuosity of his youth, Luther railed against the Christ of justice: "I knew Christ as none other than a stern judge, from whose face I wanted to flee, but could not, an angry judge, yea, an executioner and a devil in our hearts."

Christ was not the only "executioner" known to the young Luther. Schoolteachers belonged to the same bunch. School was, in his word, martyr-dom. He started school in Mansfeld, transferred in his fourteenth year to the cathedral school at Magdeburg, where the Brethren of the Common Life were active, and completed his secondary education at Eisenach, where the Luder family originated. In later life it occurred to him that the school system suffered from the same tyranny over the human spirit that afflicted religion — too much law, too much repression, and too much fear of justice and judgment. The school, no less than the church, should be overhauled. He was, nonetheless, a staunch advocate of education. Without a vigorous and consistent system of education, Christians could not possibly have access to the Scriptures, let alone attain maturity in them; unless they did, Luther's idea of a common priesthood, of a priesthood of all believers, would have little chance of practical success.

In May 1501 "Martinus Ludher ex Mansfeldt" signed the register of Erfurt University. That university was not well disposed to the New Learn-ing. Luther thus was not formed by humanism; he did not enter the Reformation via northern humanism as both Zwingli and Calvin did. His training was decisively in late medieval Scholasticism. Some contemporary European scholars believe that the Reformation, so far from being the introduction of the modern age, actually forestalled it. Luther's deep roots in medieval Scholasticism may be one of the planks in that sort of argument. That is not to say that he depreciated the importance of the Renaissance. Luther in fact compared the Renaissance to the preparatory work of John the Baptist. Without the linguistic, philological, and historical skills of the Renaissance, the "gospel" — by which Luther always means the essential Christian message — could never have been recovered.

Erfurt was a "modernist," or Ockhamist, university. Late medieval Scholasticism tended to break down into several major schools or traditions, one of which was that of the Ockhamists, the tradition that arose with William of Ockham and that included such notable teachers as Pierre d'Ailly and Jean Gerson. (See chapter 3 above.) They referred to their tradition as the *via moderna* (modern way, hence "modernism"), as opposed to the *via antiqua* of, say, the Thomists. Luther thus was educated within the intel-lectual boundaries of the Ockhamist tradition. For Luther, Ockham was *magister meus,* "my teacher."

384

One of the things he learned from the Ockhamists was how to talk about the presence of Christ in the Mass. In private conversation, Ockham preferred to teach consubstantiation rather than transubstantiation. Why not simply say that the bread and the body of Christ coexist in the consecrated host (hence, consubstantiation) rather than persist in the medieval opinion (Ockham believed, an unscriptural opinion) that the substance of the bread underwent *conversio,* "conversion," and became the body of Christ (hence, transubstantiation). Luther picked up this idea and used it in his early Reformation writings, and probably for the remainder of his life.

The last great Ockhamist teacher was the German divine Gabriel Biel (c. 1420–95), whose thought was stamped on Erfurt University and hence upon Luther himself. To understand what Luther eventually *op*posed, it is quite important to understand what Biel *pro*posed.

One of the main hinges on which Biel's thought swung is the expression *facere quod in se est,* which may be translated for our purposes as "to do one's very best." It means that if one does one's very best, God will surely assist that one in the attainment of eternal life, which is the proper end of the human pilgrimage. Biel wanted to make a place for human moral action: each person should be encouraged to strive after moral excellence. Biel taught that the fall of Adam in the Garden of Eden, which is referred to as Original Sin, had a psychological but not an ontological impact on the free will of human beings. That is, Original Sin may have diminished the pleasure of doing a good act or may have altered or diverted the direction of the will, but it did not change the human status by fundamentally, radically corrupting the freedom of our will. Thus, although Biel conceded that a person's will operates under a certain psychological handicap, he insisted, at the same time, that a person's free choice remains intact.

Biel thus begins with a certain optimism. He then says that "to do one's very best" is the precondition for receiving God's help, God's grace, even as God's grace is the precondition for attaining eternal life. To put it as simply as possible, if I want to solicit God's help, without which my salvation is impossible, then I must begin by doing my very best, knowing that God will be helpful to the pilgrim who begins in that way.

If it is possible for every person to do his or her very best as a preparation for God's grace, we could reasonably expect God to be vindictive to those who refuse or who fail. The punishing activity of God is the *iustitia Dei* of which the Scriptures speak — "the righteousness of God," or "the justice of God," in the active, punitive sense of that expression.

Let us assume, however, that the pilgrim *has* done his or her very best. Then what? God, on his part, finds himself obliged, by an obligation to which, so to speak, he had freely committed himself, to ascribe to that person the merit of congruence *(meritum de congruo)*. "Congruence" here refers to the point at which human effort and God's help coincide. God now proceeds to award that person the *habitus* — the status or habit — of grace, enabling him or her to perform works that God deems to be works of genuine merit, meritorious works that will advance him or her toward the goal of perfection and eternal life. Up to this point, the person has been a sinner, under the impairment of the fall of Adam and unable to perform works that God could deem meritorious. Now, however, given the habit of grace, that person may proceed to do works of undoubted merit and thus pursue his or her course toward eternal life.

LUTHER'S UNDERSTANDING OF JUSTIFICATION

WHAT we have been describing is religious process. The end of that process is what theologians call justification, a crucial word in the controversies of the Reformation. It means that a person has arrived at a position of "justice" or "righteousness" in the sight of God. One's works of merit have fully countervailed one's sins, and one is finally "right" with God.

It is important to notice that the inalienable freedom of human beings continues to be operative throughout this process of justification. To be sure, grace is necessary; grace stabilizes and perfects the human will at the crucial juncture marked by the merit of congruence. Grace, however, does not alter the fundamental requirement that one must *always* — from first to last — do one's very best.

Had Gabriel Biel been consulted by some guilty man who was a distraught parishioner of his, we can almost hear what he would have said to that man: Do your very best, and sometime soon God will bestow upon you the habit of grace. Continue to do your very best, and that habit of grace will enable you to do good works that God will find full of merit, which will finally offset all your sins and make you "right" with God. That distraught parishioner could have been Martin Luther, who, from early childhood, had been searching for a gracious God. For Luther, though, the ultimate question was not simply, Have I done enough? It was, Is it within one's human powers to do one's very best? In the end, Luther denied that very possibility. He therefore redefined justification, changed the meaning of grace, and thoroughly repudiated the teaching of the great Ockhamist master Gabriel Biel.

Having taken his master's degree from the University of Erfurt in February 1505, Luther, under heavy pressure from his father, elected to study law and proceeded to enter the law faculty of the same university. Within a short time, however, he found himself disconsolate. "I despair of myself," he said. Abruptly, on June 20, 1505, he took leave of the university, apparently under pain of some spiritual anxiety, and went home to Mansfeld to see his parents. By July 20, one month later, he had taken a vow to monastic life and was already lodged in the Erfurt convent of the Augustinian order. Luther was later to describe the decision in this way. On July 2 he was on his way back to the university. As he came to the village of Stotternheim, he was caught in an evening thunderstorm. Lightning flashed in a forest of great oak trees through which he was passing. Luther imagined that he saw "the prince of darkness grim." Stunned by lightning or made dumb by fear, he was driven to the ground and shouted out pitifully, "Help, Anna, beloved saint, and I will be a monk." On July 16, after he had sold his books, he gathered his friends together for a farewell dinner. "Today," he said, "you see me. Henceforth, nevermore." Next day they escorted him just down the street to the Black Cloister of Erfurt, to the forbidding convent where the Augustinians of the strict observance lived.

His year as a novice passed. The devil, he noted, does not usually bother a monk in his first year in the monastery. Thus, in the summer of 1506, when he faced the decision whether to withdraw or to profess, he chose to profess the full monastic vows. Soon after he commenced to study for the Catholic priesthood, into which office he was ordained in May 1507. On May 2 he was permitted to celebrate Mass for the first time. His teachers had told him that a priest actually holds "his God" in his hands and "proffers" him to others. Luther doubted his worthiness to do such a thing; in the course of celebrating his first Mass, he faltered at the altar and had to be helped through.

Monasticism did not go well for Luther. There he was, in an extraordinary context; if ever an institution offered people the possibility of achieving spiritual perfection, monasticism did. Luther found, however, that his whole religious orientation began to close in upon him. All he knew was Gabriel Biel's optimism: a man is capable of doing his very best; a man *must* do his very best if he expects help from God. Luther noticed signs all around the convent — "You can do it if you will" — that underscored the point. Biel had also made it clear that God would be vindictive to those who failed to do their very best; that punishing activity of God was what the Bible meant when it used the expression *iustitia Dei.* Luther remembered Christ, the Awful Judge, looming at him from the Mansfeld Church, his arm raised in righteous indignation. The more Luther increased his monastic effort, the more he slipped into despair. Monasticism became to him a circle of ever-enlarging doubt. His later utterances on the subject of monasticism, however irreverent they are, offer us some insight into Luther's condition.

> I was a good monk, and kept my rule so strictly that I venture to say that if ever a monk could get to heaven by monkery, I would have gotten there. All my companions in the monastery who knew me, would bear me out in this. For if I had gone on much longer, I would have martyred myself to death, what with vigils, prayers, readings, and other works.

> For I hoped I might find peace of conscience with fasts, prayer, vigils, with which I miserably afflicted my body; but the more I sweated it out like this, the less peace and tranquility I knew.

> The more holy, the more uncertain I became.

> After vigils, fasts, prayers, and other exercises of the toughest kind, with which as a monk I afflicted myself almost to death, yet the doubt was left in my mind, and I thought, Who knows whether these things are pleasing to God?

> I was deeply plunged into monkery, even to delirium and insanity. If righteousness was to be got by the law, I would certainly have attained it. I was a marvel in the sight of my brethren.

Luther's monastic exertions led, not to satisfaction, but to what he described as *Anfechtung,* "attack." This German word, very prominent in Luther research, refers to an attack of spiritual despair so profound that one can no longer possibly believe that one can be reconciled either to God or to other people.

> For I had no idea except that the "righteousness of God" *(iustitia Dei)* meant his severe judgment. Would he save me from his severe judgment? Nay, I would be eternally lost.

I did not love, but I hated this just God, who punishes sinners; and if not with silent blasphemy, as least with huge murmuring, I was indignant against God.

Then I was the most miserable creature on earth. Day and night there was nothing but horror and despair, and no one could give me help.

When this battle is joined, and a man sees nothing but hell, no escape is evident to him. He believes that what is happening to him must be endless, for it is not the wrath of a mortal man, which would have a limit, but the wrath of the eternal God, which could never have an end.

My heart shivered and trembled as to how God could be merciful to me.

Thus, we see Luther possessed by the need to be justified, to find himself right with God.

In the fall of 1507 Luther embarked upon the formal study of theology, which led him finally to the attainment of the doctor of theology degree, in October 1512. In the meantime, two noteworthy events had happened to him. In the autumn of 1508 he had been appointed to the theological faculty of the University of Wittenberg, where the Reformation was destined to occur. And in 1510 Luther, with another friar, had been dispatched to Rome on an errand by the Augustinian order. Luther perceived Rome as spiritually decayed, which served only to intensify his religious despair. Despite his disillusionment, he was determined to do all the pious things that pilgrims do in Rome. He climbed the *Scala sancta*, the holy stairs that were reputed to have stood in front of the house of Pontius Pilate and that Christ thus ascended in his suffering. Up went Luther on hands and knees. "But when I got to the top," he recalled in a sermon much later, "I thought to myself, Who knows whether it is true?" Still, he was a priest. What priest would leave Rome without saying Mass at one of its altars? He lined up at St. Sebastian's Church, where many priests waited to say Mass. Luther later claimed that he was aghast at the haste with which the Italian priests rattled through the Mass. When he reached his turn, he celebrated Mass with all due solemnity, but the Italians, still waiting their turn, hissed at him from the shadows, *Passa, passa* (get a move on). Luther summarized his Roman interlude as follows: "Some people took money to Rome and brought back indulgences. I like a fool carried onions there and brought back garlic." He meant that he had carted his despair to Rome, hoping to be rid of it, but had come away with an even deeper despair.

In the east end of Wittenberg lay the Augustinian convent, as well as the university itself. Luther was assigned a small room for study in the tower of the convent. There he labored day and night, searching the Scriptures for meaning. And there he experienced what he himself called an illumination, out of which came the crucial ideas of the Reformation. However, because of Luther's own inconsistencies in the recounting of these events, the date of the "tower experience" cannot be determined. Scholars have suggested dates ranging from 1512 to 1519, and many have suggested that Luther overemphasized the one experience in what was actually a gradual change in his thinking.

The critical insight of Luther's illumination, the heart of Reformation thought, is called justification by faith. To understand what that phrase means, we must return again briefly to the teaching of Gabriel Biel, who conceived of the Christian life as a process that depends from beginning to end on human freedom of will, augmented at certain points by God's help. The first step in the process is *facere quod in se est,* "to do one's very best." To the person who does his or her very best, God will eventually award the *meritum de congruo,* which means a habit, or status, of grace. One continues to do one's very best, but now, being in a state of grace, one is able to perform works that are truly meritorious. Finally, at the end of the process, one's meritorious works are sufficient to offset all of one's sins. The person is therefore "right" with God, which is to say, justified. So justification is a process of "making good" (to use jargon that is still current among us).

The more he lived, the more Luther disbelieved this medieval view of justification. How could anybody be sure that one had done enough? How could anybody seriously think that fallen humankind was capable of such a thing? Luther finally denounced it, using a famous but highly pejorative expression — "works-righteousness."

From his study of the Scriptures, from Paul's Epistle to the Romans in particular, Luther discovered another idea of justification, which he believed to have been the idea of Paul, of Augustine, and indeed the gospel itself. In Luther's opinion, justification is not a process at all but an event, an instant, the work of God entirely, for which humankind is not responsible at all.

Luther's first assumption is that we humans have lost our freedom of will to do religious works. Sin has completely enslaved us. We suffer from self-curvature (*incurvatum in se),* which means that even our noblest efforts at goodness and charity will inevitably be spoiled by selfishness.

In Luther's opinion, the medieval church had allowed the New Testament to be obscured and encrusted by dogmas, religious lore, and pious legends. When we break through the crust, we see that the New Testament is really the record of one historical event — the crucifixion of Jesus. What does that event mean? It means that God offered up his own Son as a sacrifice for the sins of all people. Therefore the Jesus who hangs on the cross must be our righteousness. Instead of scrambling around trying to achieve our own righteousness (something that Luther deemed hopeless), we should rather find some means of fastening on to the righteousness that Jesus has gotten for us. We must, so to speak, attach ourselves to him, so that his righteousness covers us both. But how? By means of faith. By having faith in Jesus, I can belong to him and participate in his righteousness. Therefore, justification is *sola fide* — by faith alone.

According to Luther, God reckons us forgiven by our faith. But how do I acquire faith? Faith, as Paul once said, "comes by hearing." Whenever we hear and then believe the tale of how Jesus died in our place, then faith occurs. Normally this happens in church when the sermon is preached. To preach the gospel is simply to tell the tale in terms that make sense to contemporary people. The apostles were the first tellers, and anyone who tells the tale, whether a bishop or not, stands in the apostolic succession. The Christian church is a *Mundhaus,* a "mouth-house." Where there is no preaching, there is no church. In Luther's conception, Christianity thus depends entirely upon the Scriptures — *sola Scriptura.*

But if I am a slave to sin, so that I cannot do any good work on my own behalf, then how am I suddenly able to believe? I cannot. Only as God acts in me through the Holy Spirit am I able to believe. Faith itself is the gift of God; salvation, therefore, is *sola gratia,* "by grace entirely." Although I may believe, my neighbor may not; how does one explain that discrepancy? The answer must be that God chooses some, but not others; God elects some and passes some by; God predestines some and consigns others to damnation. What kind of God is that? He is in fact the *Deus absconditus,* the "hidden God," whose ways are beyond our comprehension.

Let us recapitulate. What has Luther attempted? Christianity is no longer a religion of what human beings should do for themselves, but of what God has done for undeserving humankind despite itself. (That statement has been exaggerated to make the point.) Christ is no longer God's *lupus,* God's spy and avenger, but in fact the only source of a person's righteousness and the prime expression of God's love for humankind. God himself, though his ways are sometimes hidden and include the incomprehensible act of election, comes across to Luther as a loving, forgiving heavenly Father who seeks out wayward and unworthy humans, not the vindictive God of Giotto, of Michelangelo, and of popular religion. Grace no longer carries the connotations of "substance," as it did in the Middle Ages — something "infused" in a person by the sacraments, a *habitus* in a person, a divine vitamin. Instead, grace is simply God's goodwill to undeserving people — *favor Dei,* "God's favor," as Luther put it. Theology itself is no longer *theologia gloria,* "a theology of glory," in which medieval doctors attempt to prove the existence of God; it is *theologia crucis,* "a theology of the cross," in which God is to be seen as partially hidden in the suffering of Christ. This was a religion of enormous security to Luther because it put the question of forgiveness beyond the pale of human effort and consigned it entirely to God. We must not overlook the point that even the stupefying idea of election operated not to intimidate but to console. Those people who had faith *knew* beyond any shadow of a doubt that they were of the elect.

Luther's religion also contained latent diseases. It was a religion of the ear, the intelligence; it lacked the emotional and psychological appeal that medieval religion had to all five senses — in short, to the whole person. Furthermore, because it was based on personal faith, Luther's religion was apt to be subjective; the Protestant tradition has thus had its difficulties trying to maintain the unity and the objectivity that characterized medieval Catholicism.

Let us continue with Luther's thought. Justification by faith simply means that anxious and guilty people find themselves forgiven by means of their faith, or trust, in Christ. That instant in the religious life leads to what Luther calls Christian liberty or Christian freedom — an enormous sense of buoyancy and relief — from one's sense of sinfulness, from the anger and threat of God, and from works-righteousness, namely, the fretful attempt to rescue one's self by good works. Then what? Do Lutherans now simply lie back, content with their forgiveness and Christian freedom? Not according to Luther. Rather, they strike out upon an active life of religious activity that Luther describes as follows.

As far as Luther is concerned, faith means two things. It means trust in Christ. It is *mendica manus,* "a beggar's hand," reaching out for the forgiveness and righteousness that a person can get in no other way. The same faith, however, is also a powerful source of religious energy. Luther refers to it (this time in German, rather than Latin) as *quellende Liebe,* a source of overflowing love that is to be expended by the Christian for the good of one's neighbor. Mind you, Christians are under no constraint to help their neighbor. Nor are they performing works of merit or attempting to earn righteousness, for all of that sort of business is past and gone. Rather, Luther's thought thrusts itself forward from forgiveness and freedom, from relief and buoyancy, toward this new source of religious energy that expresses itself in the form of love to one's neighbor. Luther presumes that we will be able to identify both our neighbor and his or her needs and to deal with the neighbor on a personal basis.

Luther used two metaphors to help us understand how we are to apply this new energy, this "overflowing love." One metaphor is the "common priesthood," or "the priesthood of all believers." This is to say that every Christian, being connected to Christ by faith, shares the priesthood of Christ. Therefore, every Christian is quite literally and fully a priest to his or her neighbor and by that means expresses overflowing love for the neighbor. There is virtually nothing within the sphere of religion that one Christian, as priest, cannot do for others. This conception did violence to the medieval belief in a priesthood of particular persons, out of which the whole medieval idea of hierarchy had its single most important basis.

The other metaphor depended upon the monastic word "vocation," which Luther deliberately appropriated for his own purposes. Someone entering monasticism receives a *vocatio,* literally a divine calling. Luther, who repudiated monasticism as the epitome of works-righteousness, purloined the word "vocation," declaring that every Christian had a vocation, not certainly in monastic seclusion, but in the real world, where love was meant to be shared. The shoemaker, for example, should think of his trade as a vocation; by making good shoes at a fair price, he has the possibility of expressing his love for his neighbor. The same could be said for a mother of five children, or a magistrate, or a member of every other honorable profession. What Luther managed to do was to bring the monastic idea of the sacredness of work out of the monasteries into everyday life in the world; it was one of the sources of the so-called work ethic of Protestantism.

With his doctorate newly in hand, Luther now had the right to expound the Bible, which he proceeded to do for the sake of his students at Wittenberg. He started in 1513 with a series of lectures on the Psalms; Jacques Lefèvre's philological and textual tools were at his side. Already he saw the crux of religion to be Christ suffering in our place. Already he said that it is by faith that we are able to relate ourselves to Christ and be justified. Already he referred to his own theological style as the theology of the cross. Even more important were his lectures on Paul's Epistle to the

Romans, which he undertook in 1515. Luther used, in addition to Lefèvre's work on Romans, the new edition of the New Testament by Erasmus. In his Romans lectures, Luther for the first time described a Christian as *simul iustus et peccator,* "at the same time righteous and yet a sinner." Christians have a double status — righteous in God's sight because God has seen that they stand at Christ's side, under Christ's righteousness, and has forgiven them on that account; but also sinners who must continue to do battle as long as they live against the devil and against their own "domestic" vices. Such a dialectical formula struck Erasmus as being wretched, yet it was quite consistent with Luther's thought.

In 1516, having completed Romans, Luther expounded the New Testament book of Galatians. There for the first time appeared his dialectical interpretation of the law and the gospel. The law of God accuses, and the New Testament gospel forgives; those roles ought not to be mixed. That was a crucial point with Luther. He was convinced that the law of God — let us say, the Ten Commandments — should be used only to convict people of their unworthiness and thus drive them toward Christ. The law of God should never be used as the basis of ethics or as the pattern of religious life. Every instinct in Luther led him to believe that human beings were incapable of performing the law. The whole struggle over works-righteousness had really been a struggle over that principle. The law as a positive force in people's lives collided, moreover, with Luther's strong emphasis upon the freedom or liberty of Christians. The law accuses; it does not edify. Ethics should not be built upon rules, regulations, patterns, or laws, but rather upon the principle of the overflowing love that a person of faith has toward his or her neighbor. A certain antinomianism (indifference or distrust of the law) runs through the Lutheran tradition. There were some very prominent Christians in the 1930s (e.g., Karl Barth) who ascribed the rise of National Socialism in Germany partially to that cause.

THE NINETY-FIVE THESES

IN THE spring of 1517, in the thirty-fourth year of Martin Luther's life, a Dominican friar named Johann Tetzel established himself just across the Elbe River from Wittenberg and commenced to sell indulgences. His activities set in motion the Reformation.

To understand what an indulgence is, we must understand the Catholic view of penance. Penance is a sacrament deemed indispensable to salvation, as it is the means appointed by God to dispense with sins that Christians commit after baptism. Penance consists of four parts: contrition, confession, absolution, and satisfaction. A man who has sinned and who is contrite presents himself to the priest and confesses his sins; the priest absolves him and then lays upon him a temporal punishment for which he must make satisfaction. Every sin involves two things. First is *culpa,* the guilt of sin, which is remitted by God through the whole sacramental transaction of the sacrament of penance. But that still leaves *poena,* the penalty of sin, which the church levies in the name of simple justice, for which the sinner must make recompense either in this life or in purgatory. An indulgence is quite precisely the remission by ecclesiastical authorities of the need to make recompense.

Although the practice of granting indulgences was very old in the Catholic Church, the procedure and theory of indulgences were considerably refined by the bull *Unigenitus* of 1343, which set forth the doctrine of the treasury of merits. It was proposed in that bull that the Catholic Church holds as a treasure the infinitely copious merits of Christ and of all the saints — merits far in excess of any that they themselves may have needed — and that the church may dispense these merits in the inexhaustible treasury to remit *poena,* that is, the recompense owed by living Christians. When the question arose in the quattrocento whether this treasury could be drawn upon for the benefit of souls in purgatory, Pope Sixtus IV delivered a careful but quite subtle answer, which almost everybody interpreted to mean that souls in purgatory could indeed be so assisted. As the sixteenth century opened, money became the normal way of obtaining an indulgence, and the sale of indulgences on a broad scale became a chief means of church revenue. Pope Julius II and Pope Leo X both used the sale of indulgences as a major source of papal finance and specifically to pay for the vast undertaking of St. Peter's Basilica in the Vatican. Great indulgence campaigns were organized in the sixteenth century. The preachers who sold indulgences were seldom as circumspect as they ought to have been when they explained the meaning and scope of indulgences to the pious and well-meaning folk in their audiences. More often than not, they left the impression that an indulgence remitted both the *poena* and the *culpa* of sin (thus, in effect, obviating the need of penance entirely) and that souls in purgatory would surely spring out of purgatory as soon as the coins tinkled in the collection box.

In 1514 Prince Albert of Brandenburg cast his greedy eyes on the archbishopric of Mainz. At the age of twenty-three, he was already bishop of two other dioceses and was in flagrant breach of canon law on account of both his age and his pluralism. He and Pope Leo therefore bargained over the new appointment; Albert agreed to pay the papacy thirty-one thousand ducats to be confirmed archbishop of Mainz. The Fuggers of Augsburg handled the banking arrangement. Leo, for his part, agreed to conduct a jubilee indulgence for eight years in Albert's lands; half of the proceeds would go to remit Albert's debt, half to the construction of St. Peter's Basilica. Johann Tetzel, who led this vast campaign, left nothing to chance. His campaigns were planned to the last detail. Specimen sermons were given out to parish priests to be preached in advance of Tetzel's arrival, depicting loved ones in purgatory with their arms stretched out for help; one would have been extremely callous not to have been touched by such descriptions. The whole town, duly forewarned, would turn out to greet Tetzel — priests and friars, schoolchildren let out for the occasion, the town council and burgomaster, to say nothing of the people themselves. They greeted him with tapers and banners and songs, while the church bells were pealed. Frederick Mecum, an eyewitness from St. Annaberg, recalled that the people's bull that announced the jubilee indulgence was borne into the town on a "satin or gold embroidered cushion." Tetzel himself arrived with all due pomp ("God himself," said Mecum, "could not have been welcomed with greater honor") and was escorted to the marketplace, where the papal banner was unfurled, and the money chest established. Then Tetzel intoned:

> Solbald das Geld in Kasten klingt
> Die Seel' aus dem Fegfeuer springt.

> As soon as the money clinks in the chest,
> The soul springs out of purgatory.

Forbidden to enter Saxony, Tetzel came to the village of Zerbst, across the river from Wittenberg, in the spring of 1517. The Wittenbergers could not contain their curiosity. Over the river they went, to see for themselves what Tetzel was up to, and back they came with their little certificates of indulgence. The trouble started when a stumbling drunkard handed one of the certificates to Luther as a warrant for his stupor. Another one poked through Luther's confessional box in lieu of penance. Luther could not contain himself. He composed ninety-five theses on the subject of indulgences. These he withheld until the great fall festival, All Saints' Day, which fell on November 1, when literally all who counted themselves Christians would get themselves to church. The theses, however, represented no popular stroke. They were cast in academic Latin and were pitched above the competence of the untutored laity. They solicited a debate among intellectuals in the university.

Tradition has it that Luther nailed his theses on the Wittenberg church door on the afternoon of October 31, 1517.

Luther would have known that the academic community gathered for special services on All Hallows Eve (now Halloween), October 31, and he made certain that his theses were posted just in time for that event. About noon on the thirty-first, he left the Augustinian cloister at the east end of Wittenberg, walked through the heart of the town past the marketplace to the Castle Church on the west side next to the river, and posted his theses broadside on the main doors of the church. So goes the tradition account; however, since the 1960s some scholars have questioned whether the theses were made public in this way at all.

The ninety-five theses express Luther's mature thought in provocative form and represent a signal of the Protestant Reformation. Consider, for example, thesis 62: "The true treasure of the church is the Holy Gospel of the glory and grace of God." The purpose of that thesis is to ridicule the idea of a treasury of merit, upon which the indulgence system depended, and to declare that the real treasury of Christianity is the sacrifice of Christ recounted in the Bible. Theses 56–68 expound the same proposition.

The document contains three series of critical theses. The series 26–41 constitutes a direct attack upon the indulgence system. Theses 27, for example, is a rejoinder to Tetzel. The second critical series is 42–51, each thesis beginning, "Christians must be taught." The point of the series is that money paid for indulgences rightfully belongs to the poor. Thesis 50 is illustrative: if the pope knew what his indulgence preachers were doing, he would burn down St. Peter's rather than build it upon the skin and bones of the poor. And 51: the pope should sell St. Peter's for poor relief. Theses 71–89 contain a third series of criticisms, in this instance directed to the more disreputable practices attached to the system of indulgences. In thesis 82, Luther inquires irreverently why the pope does not simply open the gates of purgatory for the sake of Christian love, instead of for money with which to build the church. And in 86 he inquires why the pope, presumably the richest man alive, does not build St. Peter's with his own funds rather than deprive the poor of theirs.

At first Luther's theses circulated privately among friends, but soon found their way into print and circulated widely. Luther's role in this more extended publication is not clear. Archbishop Albert of Mainz, seeing his indulgence revenue dropping off, sent the theses to Rome, but Pope Leo X dismissed them as the work of a drunken German who would think differently when sober. By June of 1518, however, the Luther affair had grown so serious that the papacy decided to begin formal proceedings against the Saxon upstart. He was summoned to appear in Rome within sixty days to answer formal charges devised against him. Luther was in jeopardy. He had only one real bulwark against the papacy, namely, his powerful benefactor, the prince of Saxony, Elector Frederick the Wise, who refused to hand Luther over to Rome or expel him from Saxony.

Germany, despite its exalted status as "the Holy Roman Empire," did not enjoy the concentration of royal power comparable to that in France or even in England in the sixteenth century. The fact worked in Luther's favor

95. Elector Frederick the Wise, portrait by Lucas Cranach the Elder

and eventually shaped the course of the Reformation in Germany. The key elements in German politics may be outlined as follows:

- *Holy Roman Emperor.* The head of state: Maximilian I (1493–1519), of the House of Hapsburg.
- *Secular princes.* Provincial rulers, who offset imperial power: the kings of Bohemia and Denmark, the archduke of Austria, 30 dukes who governed the German states, and lesser princes.
- *Spiritual princes.* Ecclesiastical leaders, who often had political power: 5 archbishops (of Mainz, Cologne, Trier, Magdeburg, and Salzburg), 25 bishops, and 20 abbots.
- *Electors.* Seven of the secular and spiritual princes, designated electors by the Golden Bull of 1356. This office was one of preeminent power in the empire, as it entitled the holder to the exclusive privilege of electing the emperor. The seven were the archbishops of Mainz, Cologne, and Trier; the king of Bohemia; and the electors of Saxony, the Palatinate, and Brandenburg.
- *Free cities.* Certain cities won their freedom by dispensation from the emperor for military service or by purchase from one of the secular princes. They formed themselves into leagues as a means of maintaining their independence against the encroachments of princes or the emperor himself. Each city was governed by a council, which often permitted innovations and freedoms enjoyed nowhere else in the empire. Of the 100 free cities, 28 were in the Swabian League (e.g., Strassburg, Augsburg, Nuremberg), 62 in the Hanseatic League (e.g., Danzig, Hamburg), and 10 in the Rhine district.
- *The Diet.* The parliament. This structure represented a further check upon imperial power. The diet was summoned by the emperor and met in different places. It included the secular and spiritual princes and representatives of the free cities. Diets dealt with the business of the empire in concert; their decisions placed the whole realm under obligation.

As it happened, German politics in 1518 gave Luther a reprieve. The aging emperor, Maximilian I, was making a last-ditch effort to have his grandson, Charles of Spain, confirmed as his successor. The Hapsburgs, in fact, had given out extensive political favors to secure Charles's election, and thus family control of the empire. By August of 1518, when Luther was in real trouble, the situation had crystallized as follows. Five of the electors supported the election of Charles, but two were opposed: the arch-bishop of Trier, and Elector Frederick the Wise of Saxony. The papacy, fearing the Hapsburg pretentions in Italy and, in fact, everywhere, was fiercely opposed to Charles. Suddenly, the supreme pontiff, Leo X, dis-covered that he had an important ally in Germany — Elector Frederick the Wise. As long as the imperial election remained in doubt, Luther was spared.

In the last week in June 1519, the seven electors gathered at Frankfurt to elect the emperor, Maximilian having died in the meantime. The election of Charles, now a foregone conclusion, was swiftly executed, and on the twenty-ninth of that month was officially proclaimed. The new emperor, Charles V, at the age of nineteen, possessed a dominion more vast than Charlemagne's. He was king of Spain, king of Sicily, king of Naples, duke of Burgundy, overlord of the Low Countries, and emperor of Germany. Retiring and inarticulate, with only a smattering of German, Charles was stout in his loyalties and conscientious in his duties; his deepest loyalty was to the Catholic religion.

THE LEIPZIG DEBATE

WHILE the electors were electing in Frankfurt, Luther was debating in Leipzig, where the question of authority was decided. The word "authority" in religion refers to the basis on which sound religious judgments are to be built. In Luther's case, there was still some doubt whether there were legitimate sources of religious authority aside from the Scriptures. Were the decisions of the popes authoritative? Or the pronouncements of church councils?

The Leipzig debate took place in June 1519, in the university town of Leipzig. Luther's opponent was one of the most cunning and competent debaters in Catholic circles: John Eck, professor of theology at Ingolstadt. As the time of the debate grew near, Germany came alive with excitement at the prospect of such a fierce confrontation. On the morning of June 21, Leipzig University was the scene of the opening ceremonies, which consisted of an academic procession, a two-hour oration by the professor of Greek, and an orchestral selection, followed by a luncheon. In the afternoon, the contestants faced each other at elevated desks. On the one side stood Eck, with a great voice and dulcet tones, prodigious scholarship, and a crafty ability at debate. At the opposite desk appeared, not Luther, but the Lutheran divine Andreas Carlstadt, squat, squeaky, constantly shuffling through his papers. When the judges ruled that Carlstadt must put aside his references and cribs, the clumsy Lutheran was stupefied. Luther himself took the rostrum on July 4. The debate then proceeded along the following main lines.

First, was the pope the head of the Holy Catholic Church? Eck certainly thought so. He insisted upon the divine right of the papacy — *de jure divino* — holding that Christ founded the Catholic Church upon the person of Peter, whose successors in the headship of the Christian church are the bishops of Rome, the very vicars of Christ on earth. Luther replied with a thunderbolt: the only head of the Christian church is Christ himself.

Second, how shall one interpret the crucial passage from Matthew 16:18, in which Christ is recorded to have said: "Thou art Peter, and upon this rock I will build my church"? Eck used the passage to bolster his contention that the papacy is head of the Christian church *de jure divino*. When his turn came, Luther declared that the "rock" on which the church is built is certainly not Peter as a person but rather Christ himself and Peter's faith in Christ, and he proceeded to support his point of view with copious quotations from the ancient theologians. Throughout that day Luther taunted Eck about the Greeks. Did not Eck realize that the Greek Orthodox Church, from its inception until the present time, had never adhered to the papacy at Rome? What did Eck propose to do with the host of Greeks over the centuries, including Athanasius and Basil the Great, who may not have subscribed to the papacy? Cast them into oblivion?

Third, as Eck squirmed over the Greek problem, he decided to impale Luther on a dilemma of another sort — the similarity of certain aspects of Luther's thought to the thought of Jan Hus. Eck built his case very slyly, little by little drawing out the similarities between Luther and Hus. At first, Luther resisted the inference: he would be damned if he would allow himself to be classified a Husite or a Bohemian heretic. Over the noon recess, however, he spent over an hour in the university library, reading the record of Hus's condemnation by the Council of Constance. When the debate reconvened on the afternoon of July 5, Luther admitted his sympathy for Hus: many of the teachings of Jan Hus were patently Christian and true. The audience gave out a huge gasp. Eck, convincingly indignant, exploited Luther's admission, implicating him as thoroughly as possible in the Husite heresy. On the following day, he drew the inescapable conclusion that, inasmuch as Luther had repudiated the validity of the Council of Constance (which had condemned Hus), Luther repudiated the validity of church councils in general as sources of religious authority.

As debates are scored, Luther probably lost. Yet the event clarified his thinking on the point of authority. In the course of the debate, he had denied the inerrant authority of both popes and councils, and he left Leipzig more determined than ever to reconceive Christian thought on the basis of scriptural authority alone.

Now that the election of Charles V had been settled, the papacy no longer had reason to curry favor with Elector Frederick the Wise of Saxony. In Rome, Luther's critics urged that action be taken against him: let him be excommunicated. On June 15, 1520, Pope Leo X published the bull *Exsurge Domine* against Luther; it enumerated forty-one instances of heresy in Luther's thought and declared that unless he recanted within sixty days, he would be deemed excommunicated and liable to seizure. (When the grace period elapsed, Luther was in fact excommunicated.)

In anticipation of the papal bull, Luther wrote three especially note-worthy treatises in the year 1520. The first to appear was *Address to the German Nobility* (August 8), in which Luther denied the temporal claims of the papacy, repudiated the status of the pope as the only true "teller" or interpreter of scriptural truth to the Christian church, advocated the priest-hood of all believers, and demanded the reformation of the church, which the German nobility, as members of that common priesthood, ought to undertake. (Notice Luther's willingness to capitalize upon the nature of German politics by appealing directly to the princes of "nobility.") That treatise was shortly followed by *The Babylonian Captivity of the Church* (October 6), in which he proceeded to dismantle the sacramental structures of the medieval church, by means of which, so he claimed, the church exercised a sort of priestly tyranny over the lives of Christians. Of the seven sacraments, he kept only three — baptism, the Eucharist, and penance — although the third had been considerably remodeled by his hand. (Here, by the way, is the point at which Luther renounced transubstantiation for consubstantiation.) Finally, early in November, there appeared the third treatise, called *The Freedom of a Christian,* a short statement of the essence of Christianity developed out of a single, paradoxical statement at the beginning: "A Christian man is a perfectly free lord of all, subject to none; a Christian man is a perfectly dutiful servant of all, subject to all." Christians are free by virtue of their being justified, put right with God, forgiven: they are free from the anxiety over their sins, and they are free from the fretful effort of trying to attain righteousness by their own works. That freedom, however, is only an agility of love that springs from faith and that spends itself with abandon for the good of one's neighbor. The minute we are truly free, then, we willingly become subject and servant to our neighbor.

THE DIET OF WORMS

SUCH was Luther's stature in Germany that he could not simply be consigned over to the papacy without a hearing. Thus, the new Catholic emperor, Charles V, summoned Luther to appear before the Diet, which was scheduled to meet at Worms in the spring of 1521. On that occasion he was promised an opportunity to defend his teachings. On April 17 Luther appeared before that august assembly. On a table in the midst of the Diet were his writings. He was asked abruptly whether they were his, and whether he recanted of them. Luther met this abrupt tactic by one of his own: he demanded a twenty-four-hour stay to consider his answer. The next day he came again to the Diet, where again he was asked whether he was prepared to recant of his writings — yes or no. Luther studied the books on the table. Yes, they were his. He proceeded to give a little review of them. Even the pope had said they were worthless; why, then, should they worry the Diet? Mention of the pope reminded Luther to make a few public remarks on that subject. The consciences of Christians were being enslaved by the papacy on account of its human doctrines. The emperor now broke in to warn Luther to desist. Luther, pretending to be chastened, started out on another line of thought. Could anyone in the Diet show him his error on the basis of the Holy Scripture. Perhaps the emperor himself would do him that singular favor? Luther looked Charles straight in the eye and warned him not to begin his reign by condemning the Word of God in the Bible. The Diet was now in a hubbub. The Catholics in the crowd demanded that he make an unequivocal answer. "I am bound by the Scriptures that I have quoted," said Luther, "and my conscience is captive to the Word of God. I cannot and I will not retract anything, since it is neither safe nor right to go against conscience. Here I stand, I cannot do anything else. God help me. Amen."

The Diet of Worms was of more than casual significance in the history of Western civilization. Luther had challenged the authority of the Church of Rome, rejecting its preeminence in teaching and in jurisdiction, which had endured in the West for over a thousand years. Protestant Christianity had begun. Luther, moreover, had appealed to his own conscience as the human faculty by which a person responsibly determines what the Bible says and what is true in religion. That too was a mark of the subjectivism that has come to characterize the Protestant tradition. Emperor Charles V was quite right when he observed, "It is preposterous that a single monk should be right in his opinion and that the whole of Christianity should be in error a thousand years or more." Viewed historically, Luther's performance at Worms *was* preposterous, and the emperor's judgment of its watershed importance was precisely correct.

The young emperor, seeing that the Diet had failed to bring Luther to terms, proceeded to move against him. On May 25, 1521, when most of Luther's most powerful supporters had left the Diet, the emperor caused the Edict of Worms to be promulgated, as if it were the genuine instrument of the Diet. That edict put Luther under the ban of the empire; it outlawed him and left him liable to seizure; it proscribed his books and threatened his supporters. The Edict of Worms was enforced, sometimes with more rigor, sometimes with less, as long as Luther lived.

For his own safety Luther was now swept into hiding by the agents of Elector Frederick the Wise. At the Wartburg Castle, deep in the forests of Thuringia where he was sequestered, Luther put off his monastic garb and disguised himself as a German *junker* (knight). Whiskers covered his countenance, and he swaggered around with a sword at his side. This was no Martin Luther; this was Knight George. He hunted rabbits with the hounds, but the hounds reminded him of the papacy and the empire, so he took sides with the rabbits. He quaffed beer at the local tavern while absorbed in Erasmus's Greek New Testament; the onlookers marveled at such a queer combination.

This period of Luther's life is called the Wartburg Exile. It was not entirely a frivolous time. Luther proceeded to make decisions and to pursue his scholarly labors. At the Wartburg he translated the New Testament into colloquial German. "I try," he said of his techniques as a translator, "to speak as men do in the marketplace." He did not have any scruples about amplifying the text of Scripture whenever he thought that amplification would serve the German sense. Thus, at Romans 3:28, he added the word *allein* (alone) to the phrase *durch den Glauben* (through faith), so that the whole expression came out in German, "through faith alone." He admitted that his critics stared at such insertions the way "a cow stares at a new barn door." The German Bible — Luther eventually added the German Old Testament to the New — meant two things to the Reformation: it expressed the profound Reformation interest in the Bible as the only reliable statement of Christianity *(sola Scriptura),* and it supported the equally Protestant principle of the priesthood of all believers.

CONFLICT AND THE PEASANTS' REVOLT

WHILE Luther was in exile at the Wartburg, two of his disciples were left in charge of affairs in Wittenberg. One was a sensitive young humanist, Philip Melanchthon, a protégé of Johannes Reuchlin. The other was the fierce, lumbering theologian Carlstadt. It was Carlstadt who elbowed Melanchthon aside and took charge. By Christmas, 1521, the cradle of the Reformation was engulfed in wild iconoclasm under Carlstadt's management. The Catholic Mass was undone and redone. The monks and nuns poured out of the convents and got married. Churches and monastic chapels were scenes of desecration. In the midst of the turmoil, the Zwickau Prophets arrived — three so-called prophets lately expelled from the town of Zwickau. They were enthusiasts in the technical sense of the word; that is,

96. Philip Melanchthon, portrait by Lucas Cranach the Elder

they professed to have received new revelations from God quite apart from the Bible, whose relevance exceeded that of the Bible. They proceeded to deride Martin Luther for his slavish dependence upon the Scriptures. *Bibel, Babel, Babbel,* they taunted — "Bible, Babel, Bubble" — in derision of Luther's biblical interest.

Closely associated with the Zwickau Prophets, yet not one of them, was Thomas Münzer, one of Luther's gravest opponents in the course of the 1520s. Münzer made devastating criticisms of Luther at two points. First, Luther had ignored the social teachings of Jesus and lacked the full measure of courage expected of a Christian. The end of the age was at hand; what Münzer expected and promoted was a great Christian uprising, a revolution directed against the mixture of secular and priestly power that he identified with feudalism and medieval Catholicism. Second, he appealed to an Inner Word, the direct testimony of the Holy Spirit to the believer, genuine revelation itself as a sign of the last days and the impending revolution. Luther, he said, "knows nothing of God, even though he may have swallowed one hundred Bibles." To which Luther replied, "I wouldn't listen to Thomas Münzer if he swallowed the Holy Ghost, feathers and all." (How does a Lutheran answer a Münzer? Most fundamentally, by pointing out that whenever anyone departs from the Scriptures, he or she is in jeopardy of departing from the crucifixion, the historical event upon which the whole structure of justification by faith depends.)

Luther's disenchantment with the Carlstadts and the Münzers of his times provoked him to publish a major statement of political ethics in the year 1523 — *On Temporal Authority.* There Luther specified two distinct realms or powers: *weltliches Regiment* (the kingdom of the world) and *geistliches Regiment* (the kingdom of God). The former was the state; the latter, the church. The former Luther connects with God's continual work of creation; the latter, with God's continual work of redemption. God, who is both Creator and Redeemer of the universe, is therefore the lord of both kingdoms, of both church and state. A Christian, since he or she is both righteous *(iustus)* and a sinner *(peccator),* is a citizen or subject of both kingdoms.

Luther insisted that the two realms are to be left quite distinct and unconfused. It is only the devil who wants to cook and brew the two realms into one. Luther, in making such a reference, was thinking of the revolutionary reformers of his age — Münzer, Carlstadt, and the branch of the Anabaptist tradition that was revolutionary. He was also thinking of medieval political theory, which, in some instances, ascribed all temporal power to its ultimate source in the Catholic Church. (That, surely, was the implication of *The Donation of Constantine.*) Luther, by his separation of church and state, appears to be quite far-reaching. Yet, by making God the lord of both kingdoms and the Christian a citizen of both, he did, in fact, draw the two kingdoms together again.

Luther never doubted that the state was divinely ordained; it was nothing less than the instrument through which God exercises his providential care over creation. Therefore, when political theorists of the early Protestant tradition thought about the state, they did not rush to speak of *human rights;* their first thoughts were rather of *God's prerogatives.* Thus, it was conceivable to them that even a tyrant might be an instrument of God's providence, an expression of God's wrath over human wrongdoing. For Luther, revolution against duly constituted authority was simply and utterly inadmissible. When the great Peasants' Revolution broke out in 1525, Luther thus had no choice except to take sides against the insurgents.

The peasants of Germany had been in a revolutionary disposition since the fourteenth century. As the sixteenth century opened, a revolt by the peasants against the flagrant injustices practiced against them by the landed princes was a highly predictable event. In Luther, the peasants thought they saw a great national hero, someone who stood up against the Church of Rome that they were disposed to regard as the prime symbol of the status quo. In some of Luther's teachings, such as the common priesthood, the peasants were sure they detected important social implications. In March 1525 a prominent segment of the peasants set forth their demands in a document called *The Twelve Articles.* They appealed explicitly to what they referred to as the new gospel — an unmistakable nod to Luther's teaching — and they declared that all their aspirations had been motivated by the hearing of God's word. The last of the articles guaranteed a revision of any or all of the previous articles if they could be shown to be improper according to the Bible.

The revolt actually commenced on the German-Swiss border in June 1523. By spring of the following year, it had spread in all directions, so that virtually two-thirds of Germany was caught in the throes of revolution. Luther, however much he sympathized with the peasants' plight, stoutly held to the conviction that they had no case at all according to the Bible. The best he could counsel them was to lay up their arms and seek arbitration, advice the peasants thought little of. They ignored the great Reformer and turned increasingly to more convincing preachers, notably Münzer. Finally, Luther, in his fear and fury, brought out a fierce pamphlet in May 1525 — *Against the Robbing and Murdering Hordes of Peasants* — in which he authorized the princes of Germany, in God's name, to dispatch the peasants: "Therefore let everyone who can, smite, slay, and stab, secretly or openly, remembering that nothing can be more poisonous, hurtful, or devilish than a rebellious man."

Luther's attitude toward the peasants had three consequences. First, it blunted whatever social advantages might have come from the Protestant Reformation. Second, it seriously impeded the course of Lutheranism in southern Germany. Third, it led directly to the conception of the Lutheran state church and of territorial religion. Luther, appalled by the revolution and by the attendant breakdown of the structures of society, came to the conclusion that his beliefs about the Christian church were no longer realistic. He had once conceived of the Christian church in highly spiritualized, uninstitutional terms. In sharp contrast to Roman Catholicism, the Lutheran churches were simply to be little communities of believers who organized their own affairs, raised up their own ministers from the common priesthood, and sat down together to hear the tale being told, observe the sacraments, and express love for one's neighbor. But when Luther saw the effects of the revolution, including the collapse of the old school system, the breakdown of parish structures, the ruination of church buildings, and the dissolution of episcopal oversight, he came to the conclusion that his older conception of the church was no longer adequate to current needs. On November 22, 1526, Luther went therefore to the elector of Saxony and asked him, as the head of state, to initiate a state church in his principality, on the assumption that the *ius episcopale* (right of episcopal oversight) could be exercised by a Christian prince. (Luther used the activities of the emperor Constantine in the Christian church of the fourth century as an example; it was he, for instance, who called, and presided over, the Council of Nicaea in 325.) Thus began both the idea and the fact of the Lutheran state church.

DEVELOPMENT OF LUTHERANISM THROUGH 1530

A SIMILAR solution was adopted with respect to the politics of Lutheran expansion. Lutheranism did expand in the 1520s, despite the Edict of Worms, or, more accurately, because the Diet was reluctant to enforce that edict. Having originated as a university movement, Lutheranism broke out of the university hothouses into the marketplaces of Germany through a number of means, none more important than Luther's own pamphleteering. The nineteenth-century historian von Ranke declared that between 1518 and 1523 the output of theological literature increased sevenfold in Germany, four-fifths of it on behalf of the Lutheran party, the greater share of that having been written by Luther himself. Another useful instrument of Lutheran expansion was the German New Testament that Luther translated at the Wartburg for publication on September 21, 1522. At the same time, the Reformation was being carried into the key cities of Germany by Lutheran preachers. Luther maintained an extensive system of correspondence. When a clergyman was needed somewhere, he nominated one. When a town council inquired into German forms of worship, he sent samples. When monks asked help in leaving their convents, he supplied that too. By 1524 Germany had become divided into two parts over the question of religion; some states had become Lutheran; others remained Catholic. When the Diet met next in Speier in 1526, it became clear that the political solution of the Lutheran question would have to be arrived at territory by territory. The solution was expressed in the formula *cuius regio, eius religio,* meaning that the prince who rules the territory rules the religion within it. One can easily see how that solution fit the conception of a state church. Two presuppositions latent in this solution were exceedingly important. While the parity and legality of the Lutheran and Catholic churches were recognized in Germany, no other forms of religion enjoyed any such recognition. The Calvinists, the Zwinglians, the Anabaptists, and others had no legal status in the empire. Moreover, religious pluralism within a territory was neither expected nor tolerated. No minority religious parties within a state church were lawful. Saxony, for example, could choose to be all Lutheran or all Catholic. It was the elector of Saxony who determined the outcome. He decided for Luther.

Luther's answer to Erasmus's diatribe *De libero arbitrio* (On the freedom of the will) came late in 1525, in the form of an extraordinary polemic entitled *De servo arbitrio* (On the bondage of the will), which he considered the most important of all his works. (See chapter 14 above.) Erasmus had preferred to be deliberately noncommittal about the more recondite problems of Christian thought such as the question of free will. To Luther, that posture was most irresponsible. "Take away assertions," he said, "and you take away Christianity." There is, in other words, no Christianity without dogma. He always assumed that the crux of the Reformation was a struggle for right doctrine; the Reformation was not a silly issue over loose living or superstition, as if Lutherans were holier than Catholics. It was a question of what the Christian religion really is, and that question is so serious that it holds human salvation in the balance. For all of Erasmus's squeamishness, real, robust Christianity is dogmatic: it asserts the gospel pure and simple. Erasmus had also planted the suggestion that the question of free will is a vain and idle speculation. For Luther, on the contrary, it is the issue before all others. Unless we know how far the mercy of God extends and how far our own will extends, we actually know nothing at all about our situation with God. In his view Erasmus had evaded the fundamental question of all.

The question of free will is very simply the question whether there remains in human beings any power to please God. That possibility Luther denies categorically. A person is unable to do anything but persist in sinfulness, which is what we mean by the expression "the bondage (or slavery) of the will." Salvation is therefore *sola gratia,* entirely by divine grace, apart from any human desire or action.

Erasmus had strewn several thorny question in Luther's path. One asked, "Who will endeavor to amend his life when he is told that he has no free will to do so?" Luther now responds: "Nobody, for nobody can. God has not time for your practitioners of self-reform, for they are hypocrites. The elect, who fear God, will be reformed by the Holy Spirit; the rest will perish unreformed." Erasmus next asked, "Who will believe that God loves him?" Luther responds, "Nobody, for nobody can. But the elect shall believe it, and the rest shall perish without believing it." It galls Luther to think that God must alter his purposes to suit Erasmus's case of nerves.

If ever there was a hard-hitting, sometimes offensive, yet religiously exalted piece of writing, Luther's *Bondage* must be it. It expresses ever so bluntly and profoundly the great maxim of Luther's, Let God be God.

We must bring our discussion of Luther to a conclusion by some passing references to the Lutheran standards of faith. These include two liturgies, two catechisms, and a major "confession," or statement of beliefs.

The liturgies were a Latin revision of the Roman Mass entitled *Formula Missae* (Form of the Mass), published in 1523, and a more radically revised German text of the Roman Mass entitled *Deutsche Messe* (German Mass), published in 1526. Both reveal Luther's great respect for the Latin liturgical tradition of the Middle Ages.

In 1529 there appeared two catechisms by Luther — the Large Catechism and the Small Catechism. Medieval catechisms had been guidebooks for priests, but Luther's were intended to be put into the hands of the laity, befitting the priesthood of all believers. If Luther cried *sola Scriptura,* and if Luther criticized the pope for presuming to be the only true "teller" or interpreter of the Bible, then why does he contradict himself by introducing catechisms that appear to represent a Lutheran teaching authority comparable to that of the papacy? He seems to have detected how dangerous was the subjective tendency in Protestantism, how much it threatened to degenerate into myriad splinter groups and endless private opinion, and thus to have tried by means of such "objective" instruments as catechisms and liturgies to preserve the unity, order, and doctrinal integrity of Lutheranism.

Early in 1530 Emperor Charles V returned to Germany, having attained victory over the French (1526) and having just been crowned Holy Roman Emperor by Pope Clement VII in splendid ceremonies at Bologna. He was resolved to reestablish that great institution of the Middle Ages, the Holy Roman Empire. Such an ambition meant, however, that he had to come to terms with the Lutherans. Charles summoned the Diet to meet at Augsburg in the summer of 1530, in the hope of resolving the religious question once and for all. Although the Diet of Augsburg failed in that attempt, it did manage to solicit from the Lutherans a major statement of religious beliefs. Luther, still under the ban, did not appear at Augsburg but remained at Coburg, some distance north. Melanchthon was therefore the principal Lutheran spokesman at the Diet of Augsburg. He drafted the Augsburg Confession, in collaboration with other prominent Lutherans and with consultation with Luther by correspondence. This confession, presented to the Diet on June 25, 1530, remains today the essential statement of Lutheran thought.

Although Luther approved the text, he did not disguise his apprehension that Melanchthon was, as he put it, soft-pedaling some of the issues. In fact, Melanchthon was. Article 10, on the Lord's Supper, admitted transubstantiation as well as consubstantiation; article 18, on free will, was remarkably understated, with none of Luther's bombast. Melanchthon's article 20, on good works, declared that good works are necessary after faith — an emphasis that Luther, considering how much he prized Christian liberty, would scarcely have made. All were concessions to the Catholics by the milder, humanistic Melanchthon.

Melanchthon's article 4 on justification, however, fairly summarizes the most critical of all questions in the Protestant Reformation. I include it here as a fitting close to this chapter on Luther.

> It is also taught among us that we cannot obtain forgiveness of sin and righteousness before God by our own merits, works, or satisfactions, but that we receive forgiveness of sin and become righteous before God by grace, for Christ's sake, through faith, when we believe that Christ

suffered for us and that for his sake our sin is forgiven and righteousness and eternal life are given to us. For God will regard and reckon this faith as righteousness, as Paul says in Romans 3:21–26 and 4:5.

18. The Hapsburg-Valois Wars and the Expansion of Lutheranism

IN THE 1520S, WHILE LUTHERANISM FLOURISHED IN GERMANY, THE Atlantic powers were ruled by uncommon kings — Henry VIII of England, Francis I of France, and Charles I of Spain, who became, after 1519, Charles V of the Holy Roman Empire. Henry pursued a foreign policy devoted to achieving a balance of power in Europe, Francis was anxious to protect France from Hapsburg encirclement, and Charles, whose ambition outran all the rest, strove for a universal Hapsburg Empire, exceeding even the empire of Charlemagne. These affairs of nations, coupled no doubt by the ever-present threat of Turkish invasion, afforded Lutherans an opportunity to expand and to perfect their institutions.

Charles was born in Ghent on February 24, 1500. His father was a Hapsburg, Philip the Fair, son of Maximilian, the reigning Holy Roman Emperor. His mother was Joanna the Mad, daughter of the Catholic monarchs of Spain, Ferdinand of Aragon and Isabella of Castile. The child of that union, somewhat misshapen by the jutting Hapsburg jaw, was reared in the ascetic piety of the Spanish Netherlands; among his tutors was Hadrian of Utrecht, who eventually succeeded to the papacy as Hadrian VI. Even as a child, Charles dreamed of a universal Hapsburg dominion, a true Holy Roman Empire, closely associated with the Holy Catholic Church and conducted mutually by Hapsburg emperor and pope of Rome. Through his inheritance, Charles was already overlord of Aragon and Castile in Spain and of the Spanish Netherlands, the Spanish dominions in the New World, Luxembourg, Burgundy, Alsace, Naples, Sicily, and Austria. Yet universal dominion eluded him until January 12, 1519,

97. Charles V, portrait by Titian

when his grandfather Maximilian died and the throne of Germany and of the empire fell vacant.

Almost exactly four years earlier, on January 1, 1515, Francis I had become king of France. Francis of Angoulême was an offspring of a collateral branch of the House of Orléans; he succeeded to the throne of France at the

98. *Anthony Marcault Presenting His Translation
of Diodore of Sicily to Francis I and Court*, anonymous

age of twenty-one because Louis XII died without issue. This Valois king ruled with élan. He was handsome, vigorous, proud, and grand. More even than Henry VIII, who had pretensions as a humanist, Francis I was a Renaissance prince; his court included artists, printers, scholars, and such persons of universal genius as Leonardo da Vinci; his palace at Chambord, in the Loire valley, was eloquent of the Renaissance spirit.

As we have seen, the two French kings who preceded Francis — Charles VIII and Louis XII — had both led armies into Italy, in an effort to regain French territories in Italy and Sicily and to establish a French sphere of influence in that peninsula. Francis, a provocative and sometimes impulsive soldier, was eager to take up such causes; he defeated an army of Swiss mercenaries at Marignano in 1515 and, by the Treaty of Brussels of the following year, took control of Milan and established French hegemony in northern Italy, threatening Spanish interests in the region.

The election of a German emperor in 1519 was nothing short of a crisis in European politics. This election would determine whether Charles could achieve a world empire and whether Francis could succeed in Italy or protect France from Hapsburg encirclement. Well in advance of Maximilian's death, both Charles and Francis became contenders for the imperial throne; both maneuvered to attain a favorable outcome of the eventual election. The seven electors of the Holy Roman Emperor represented the chief secular and spiritual officers of the empire. As early as 1517 Charles began to curry favor with the electors, and Francis was in the lists almost as early. Money flowed as copiously as the Rhine. Pope Leo X, who feared the extraordinary strength of the Hapsburgs, supported the candidacy of Francis. He too made bribes unblushingly, offering the red hat of a cardinal to the archbishop of Mainz for an appropriate vote. The archbishop of Trier was also known to be a partisan of Francis. As for Elector Joachim of Brandenburg, Francis would have gladly named him his regent in Germany — if, of course, his vote was right. Luther's patron, Elector Frederick the Wise of Saxony, was also courted by both parties, favorable treatment of Luther being the chief gratuity. On the eve of the election, Frederick the Wise, for reasons known best to him, declared for Charles. Charles was elected on unanimous ballot on June 28, 1519, and was proclaimed in Aachen on October 22, 1520.

As we have seen in chapter 17, the political usefulness of Frederick the Wise came to an end with the election of Charles. Luther, left politically exposed, at the mercy of both empire and papacy, was condemned in 1520 by the papal bull *Exsurge Domine*. In the following year he was called to account before the Diet of Worms and placed under the ban of the empire. One of the chief questions of this chapter is why neither the empire nor the papacy was able to suppress Luther and the Lutherans.

The Diet of Worms (1521) was the last major political event that Charles V attended in Germany for the next eight years. He left immediately for the Netherlands, then settled himself in Spain, which he thought to be the true center of Hapsburg power. Entrusting the eastern regions of the empire to his younger brother, Archduke Ferdinand of Austria, Charles proceeded to consolidate his control over the Iberian peninsula by marrying Isabella of Portugal. He drew the Netherlands culturally and administratively into the Spanish orbit and began to pry the French out of Italy, in such ways redesigning the empire as a formidable *Mediterranean* power. Given the preoccupations of Charles, the Lutherans of Germany were able to revive and flourish in the 1520s, despite their political adversities at the beginning of that decade.

In the Hapsburg-Valois Wars, which followed the imperial election of 1519, Charles V and Francis I fought four campaigns over the issues between them — control of Italy and of the Mediterranean basin, control of the Atlantic and the New World, not to mention the Hapsburg pretension to universal dominion versus the national pride of the French and the French fear of Hapsburg encirclement. In the course of the struggle, the once-grand Italian city-states were more or less ground up in the ceaseless conflict, bringing the Italian Renaissance to a crisis, if not to a conclusion.

The conflict began with a series of political maneuvers in 1521. In August of that year, diplomats of the major European powers met at Calais, each intent on winning the support of Henry VIII of England. England concluded a diplomatic arrangement with the Holy Roman Empire that worked to the disadvantage of the French and actually invited attacks on France from several quarters. At the same time, Pope Leo X also made an arrangement with Charles V to suppress the Lutherans — an arrangement that was also provocative toward France. In response, Francis I stirred up mischief in Navarre and in Castile, both Spanish territories, and encouraged an attack against the western defenses of the empire. Thus, the Hapsburg-Valois Wars began; they lasted a full four decades.

CHARLES'S CAMPAIGNS

IN THE first war, Italy was the site of the most significant battles. An imperial army took Milan from France in November 1521, defeating a formidable host of French, Swiss, and Venetian troops. The next year, Genoa also fell to imperial forces, led by Generals Pescara and von Frundsberg. In 1524 the disaffected French constable Charles of Bourbon, who had come to view the king of France as his adversary, invaded southern France on behalf of the empire and laid siege to Marseilles. Provoked by his losses in Italy, Francis resolved to retake Milan, but his impetuous nature led him to move against Milan too quickly from his redoubt at Pavia. On February 24, 1525, at the decisive battle of Pavia, the French fought a desperate engagement against German and Spanish troops. In a single day, Francis lost ten thousand soldiers and was himself led away to Madrid, a prisoner of the empire. The French nobility suffered egregious losses at Pavia, and French soldiers meandered over the countryside in search of leaders. In France, a stunned people fixed blame not as much on its king as upon the ambitious Queen Mother Louise ("Dame Pride") and upon the French chancellor Duprat. What would the empire do with such an illustrious prisoner? If they sent him to the gallows, the empire would have to endure French hatred forever. If they set him free, Charles V would soon see his old enemy across the field of battle again. By the Treaty of Madrid, January 14, 1526, Charles released Francis, but only on certain conditions — that France renounce all claims to Italy, as well as to Burgundy and the Netherlands; that Francis marry Charles's sister, Eleanor; and that Francis's two eldest sons remain in Madrid as guarantors of the treaty. Francis, however, paid little attention to Eleanor; the marriage was childless and soon failed. He renounced the Treaty of Madrid as having been signed under duress.

The rout of Francis I in the first war electrified the princes of Europe and drew them quickly into the League of Cognac, May 22, 1526, against the ominous prospect of overwhelming imperial power. In union against the empire were the king of France, the king of England (interested, as usual, in a balance of power), the pope of Rome, the duke of Milan, as well as the city-states of Venice and Florence. The emperor was cut to the quick by the perfidy of the pope, Clement VII, and inquired of him, by letter, what had happened to the medieval equation called Christendom, in which the Holy Roman Empire and the Holy Catholic Church had stood together in the Christian West. As for the king of England, Charles wasted no love on that wretched Henry VIII, who wanted to rid himself of his queen, Charles's aunt, Catherine of Aragon.

The second war began in the autumn of 1526, when a large contingent of Germans, led by the veteran Georg von Frundsberg, invaded Italy, bent on establishing an undisputed sphere of imperial influence in that peninsula. He was soon joined by the still-disgruntled French constable, Charles of Bourbon. Together, von Frundsberg and Bourbon led a host of twenty thousand into Italy. Although von Frundsberg died and money ran out, the savage army blundered southward, living off the land. On May 6, 1527, even as the imperial forces began to storm the walls of Rome, Bourbon took a bullet and died on a scaling ladder. Pope Clement scurried down Vatican hill into the fortress of Sant'Angelo. In a scene of utmost devastation, drunken soldiers looted and raped, laying the city to ruin, desecrating sacred places and declaring Luther pope. Charles V had had his revenge against the perfidious pope. The sack of Rome was so awesome that scholars ever since have been tempted to recognize it as the denouement of the Renaissance in Italy.

The defeated made the best of bad circumstances. Francis rebuilt the defenses of France, using the latest technology, and he organized provincial militias. Henry VIII, now smitten by Anne Boleyn and determined to be rid of Queen Catherine, the emperor's aunt, was understandably on bad terms with the empire and more sympathetic toward the French than the English usually were. His courage up, Francis sent an army into Italy, which succeeded in taking Genoa. Then it laid siege to Naples, using the Genoese fleet and its great commander, Andrea Doria, to close off access to Naples by the sea. Doria, however, offended by the excesses of French rule in Genoa, defected to Charles V, and the siege of Naples was eventually lifted. Imperial armies again entered Lombardy and again challenged French hegemony in northern Italy.

The second war was brought to a conclusion by the Peace of Barcelona, June 29, 1529, and the Treaty of Cambrai, August 5, 1529. By the former instrument, Pope Clement VII acknowledged the legitimacy of the empire's claim to the Kingdom of Naples and guaranteed the empire access to Naples through the Papal States. The quid pro quo was a promise by Charles V to Pope Clement that he would now move decisively against the Lutherans in Germany. By the latter instrument, the war was officially ended, as Francis renewed his pledge to stay out of Italy and resolved not to attack the empire again, while Charles, for his part, renounced all claims to Burgundy. The sons of Francis, held hostage in Madrid, were set free on payment of an indemnity. The pope proceeded to crown Charles Holy Roman Emperor in

Bologna, February, 25, 1530, and sent him on his way north to contend with the Lutherans.

Not to be undone by such imperial maneuvering, Francis now arranged the marriage of his second son and heir (the future Henry II) to the pope's niece, Catherine de' Medici, sweetening the relationship between France and the papacy. As if that were not sufficient, the king of France had begun to connive with Sultan Süleyman I, potentate of the Ottoman Turks, encouraging Süleyman to invade Hungary as a means of exerting pressure on the empire from the east. Formal diplomatic relations between Paris and Istanbul followed in 1536. It was risky business, this alliance between France and the infidel Turks, when most of Europe had been taught to believe that the Turks were the scourge of civilization. While Süleyman threatened Hapsburg lands along the Danube, and the Venetians interrupted imperial shipping at sea, Francis attacked Savoy, entered Italy, and sent an army against the Spanish Netherlands. In turn, Charles attacked Provence and made a new incursion into Italy. The third war was brought to an end in 1538 by a new pope, Paul III (1534–39), who found the intervention of the Turks into the political affairs of the West simply too adventuresome and too dangerous to tolerate.

Francis persisted, nevertheless, in his connivance with Süleyman, as the fourth war began. Süleyman moved against Hungary again, while the Turks and the French together prowled the Mediterranean in their fleets, threatening both shipping and coastal cities. In 1542, emboldened by such successes, Francis sent one army into Spain, another into Luxembourg. Supported by Henry VIII, who was once more interested in redressing the balance of power, Charles V was able to crush the rambunctious German prince William of Cleves, a Protestant, who fought with Francis. In June 1544 an imperial army of exceptional power entered France and, as autumn came, threatened Paris. From such an advantageous position, Charles proposed peace to Francis, recognizing that both sides had been exhausted by the conflict. Charles now proposed, and Francis agreed, that the latter's third son would marry the emperor's daughter and would receive from Charles as dowry either the Netherlands or the Duchy of Milan.

Shortly after, in 1547, Francis died and was succeeded by Henry II. Charles retired from public life in 1556 and died two years later. The Hapsburg-Valois Wars were brought to a formal conclusion by the Treaty of Cateau-Cambrésis (1559), which fixed the balance of power in Europe for many years to come. France forfeited all claims to possessions in Italy except five fortresses and renounced sovereignty over Savoy and the Piedmont. Italy was dismembered in still more ingenious ways — Siena went to the Medici of Florence, western Lombardy to Savoy, eastern and southwestern Lombardy to the Farnese and the Gonzaga.

The empire actually fought two wars on two fronts. As formidable an opponent as Francis may have been, he may not have been the most dangerous enemy Charles V was compelled to face. Danger in the east was represented by the ruler of the Ottoman Turks, Süleyman the Magnificent (1520–66). Süleyman resembled Charles in certain respects. Both came to power in the same year (1520); both were military commanders of great ability and courage; both were men of letters; both, although outwardly diffident, even shy, were shrewd politicians and good administrators; both represented important dynasties. Süleyman I followed a succession of powerful sultans to the Golden Throne, including Selim I (his father and predecessor) and Bayezid II (who preceded Selim) — all of whom had the ambition to extend the Ottoman Empire into middle Europe through the conquest of Hungary.

INVASION BY THE OTTOMAN TURKS

UPON the outbreak of the Hapsburg-Valois Wars in 1521, when Charles V was distracted, Süleyman I seized the opportunity to renew the assault on Hungary. Out of Istanbul went a formidable army, technologically up to date; it moved up the Danube to Belgrade, which, having been laid under siege, was forced to capitulate on August 29, 1521. The following year, the Turkish fleet took the island of Rhodes, giving Süleyman unchallenged control of the eastern Mediterranean.

In the spring of 1526, while the Western powers were absorbed by the politics of the League of Cognac, Süleyman struck northward again, this time in an effort to attain complete control of Hungary. At the decisive battle of Mohács, August 29, 1526, the Ottoman Turks engaged the Magyars led by Louis II of Hungary and defeated them in a great slaughter. Those Magyars who were not slain by Turkish heavy artillery and cavalry were driven into the marshes along the Danube by Turkish infantry and drowned. Among them was Louis himself. John Zapolya, the governor of Transylvania, held back an army that could have made the difference for the Magyars; his perfidy won him the title king of Hungary, under Süleyman's suzerainty. By such means, the Danube lands of Charles V, nominally under the rule of Archduke Ferdinand, the emperor's brother, were absorbed into the Ottomon Empire.

421

By 1529 Süleyman was prepared to attempt his greatest ambition — seizure of Vienna. The Ottoman armies, over 200,000 strong, left Istanbul on May 10, 1529, and, struggling against both ever-expanding supply lines and the advent of winter, reached Vienna on September 21. Inside the walled city were 20,000 defenders, including Spanish and German troops. Again and again the Turks breached the walls of the city but could not deliver a blow decisive enough to defeat the defenders. The Turks were sometimes met with point-blank artillery barrages as they stormed the walls; their losses were enormous. Meanwhile, Europe had become aroused by the Turkish threat. Elector Frederick II of the Palatinate, marshall of the Holy Roman Empire, gathered an army at Linz to raise the siege of Vienna, and both the Austrians and the Swabian League issued calls to arms. At the onset of winter, Süleyman thought it prudent to quit Vienna and retreated to the safety of Belgrade. For the moment at least, Vienna was spared.

In 1532 Süleyman sent another great army against Vienna. This time, however, the Christian West had been so thoroughly frightened by the prospect of being overrun by the Ottoman Empire that Charles V was able to engage Süleyman with an admirably equipped army of eighty thousand. The decisive battle was fought at Güns, south of Vienna, where Süleyman was turned back with appreciable losses and retreated to Graz. It was the last serious incursion by Süleyman into middle Europe. With both Francis I and the Lutherans to worry about, Charles did not press his military advantage in the East but turned his attention to western affairs.

At sea, however, the war persisted, as the Turkish fleet engaged the imperial galleys from the 1530s until the end of the century. The prize was not merely control of Mediterranean ports — Tunis, Algiers, and Toulon — but control of the Mediterranean itself. In the thinking of Charles V, the Holy Roman Empire was not as much a European power as a Mediterranean power. In his mind, the Mediterranean must necessarily be a Spanish sea. Hence, the determination with which the two enemies — Turks and empire — contended at sea.

THE SPREAD OF LUTHERANISM

THE VICISSITUDES of the Hapsburg-Valois conflict, coupled with the pressures exerted by the Turks, had a bearing on the fortunes of Lutheranism in Germany. In 1526, the year the Turks defeated the Magyars in Hungary, the Germans met in the critical Diet of Speier. At issue were certain long-desired reforms in the Catholic church, the problem of Lutheranism, and the disunity of Germany, riven by the hostility between the Catholic princes of the Dessau League and the Protestant princes of the Torgau League. In May 1526, barely a month before the Diet of Speier convened, Francis I repudiated the Treaty of Madrid and, with the pope, the king of England, and the Italian city-states, formed the League of Cognac as a counterweight to imperial power. Charles V found himself in a poor political position to act forthrightly against the Lutherans. The Diet of Speier therefore agreed that, pending a meeting of a church council or a national assembly (presumably to enact reforms and settle the issues of the Reformation), each prince in Germany was instructed "so to live, govern, and carry himself as he hopes and trusts to answer it to God and His Imperial Majesty." Although it was meant as an ad interim arrangement, that cleverly worded statement contained the principle of territorial sovereignty over religious affairs — *cuius regio, eius religio* (whose the rule, his the religion) — which would eventually prevail in Germany as the final solution to the religious question. Even in 1526 it was taken to mean that Lutheranism could legally flourish in every territory where the prince was patient with it.

Under the shelter of the Diet of Speier, Lutheran state churches began to appear in one territory after another. As early as 1525, just beyond the borders of the Holy Roman Empire, Margrave Albert of Brandenburg (1511–68) secularized eastern Prussia and initiated a process that eventually saw Prussia evangelized. In the following year, 1526, the Saxon state church came into being, as Luther, disillusioned by the Peasants' Revolution and conceding that "papal and episcopal discipline was gone," begged the elector of Saxony, as head of state, to take matters of religion in hand. The Saxon state church illustrated the general character all Lutheran state churches would take. The old jurisdiction of Catholic bishops having been abolished, the church was governed by superintendents who were directly responsible to the head of state. Monastic property was confiscated. Stubborn or disreputable priests were run out of their livings. Preachers of the gospel were supported out of public funds. The state church conformed precisely to political boundaries, and all citizens within those boundaries were baptized as Christians. Pluralism was disallowed: in a Lutheran territory, all Christians were Lutheran; in a Catholic territory, all Christians were Catholics. Such was the outcome of the *cuius regio, eius religio* principle.

In the same year, 1526, Landgraf Philip of Hesse convened a synod at Homberg that adopted a more radical constitution for the churches of Hesse,

Reformatio ecclesiarum hassiae. The work of Francis Lambert (1487–1530), a convert of Zwingli and disciple of Luther, this *Reformatio* prescribed a form of congregationalism that might have suited the younger Luther. Each congregation in the Hessian church attained its own independence and managed its own affairs, selecting its own ministry. The *Reformatio* required the administration of the strictest discipline in each parish. The minister and a lay brother from each congregation constituted the annual synod of the Hessian church, at which the Landgraf and the chief nobles were also in attendance. In Luther's opinion, however, time had passed these ideas by. In 1527 Luther advised Philip of Hesse to give up such unrealistic proposals and subscribe to the Saxon ordinances. The following year, Philip yielded.

In this period, other territories and cities also become Lutheran. Beginning in 1526, the state of Brandenburg-Ansbach moved definitively toward a conservative form of Lutheranism, and in 1533 the ducal authorities sanctioned the Brandenburg-Nuremberg church ordinance, which became the norm of a conservative family of Lutheran liturgical books, as well as a contributor to the English Book of Common Prayer. The city of Brunswick became Lutheran in 1527 under the leadership of the Lutheran minister, Johannes Bugenhagen. The Lutheran standards used in the cities of Hamburg (1529) and Lübeck (1531) and in the territories of Pomerania (1535) and Schleswig-Holstein (1542) were all indebted to Bugenhagen's Brunswick model.

The good fortunes enjoyed by Lutherans during this period were suddenly eclipsed by (1) the cruelties practiced by Landgraf Philip of Hesse against Catholic bishops, evoking a Catholic reaction, and (2) the victories won by Charles V in the second Hapsburg-Valois War. The emperor plundered Italy and sacked Rome in 1527, reducing the Medici pope to a whimpering prelate and eventually forcing both the papacy and France to terms favorable to the empire (1529). According to the Treaty of Barcelona (June 29, 1529), the pope and emperor came to terms; the treaty stipulated that Charles V would waste no time in suppressing the Lutherans. Under such circumstances, the German parliament met again at Speier in 1529. At this second Diet of Speier, the evangelical princes found themselves sorely pressed by the Catholic majority. Innovations were brought to a halt; Catholic worship and Catholic rights were reinstated in Lutheran territories. On April 19, 1529, the Lutheran delegation at Speier issued a *protestatio* against such repressive measures and on behalf of the freedom of conscience; it was the origin of the word "Protestant."

At this turn of events, the Lutherans weighed the advantages of forming a defensive union under the leadership of Philip of Hesse to offset imperial and Catholic power. The league would have included the Lutheran princes of Germany and the towns, both German and Swiss, that claimed the name "evangelical." The maneuver would have united northern German Lutheran power with that of Lutherans in the south and of the Reformed churches in Switzerland. But serious disputes had arisen in the course of the 1520s between the theologians of Saxony, Luther the chief, and those of Switzerland, notably Zwingli, over the correct Protestant interpretation of the Lord's Supper. In an effort to iron out those differences, thus clearing the way for the defensive union, Philip of Hesse invited both sides to meet in his castle at Marburg. There, on October 1, 1529, the reluctant participants gathered — Luther and Melanchthon for the Germans, Zwingli and Oecolampadius for the Swiss. As summarized below in chapter 19, these three days of debate left the two sides badly divided. Luther denounced the Marburg proceedings by telling Martin Bucer of Strassburg: "Yours is a different spirit." The Swiss Protestants were isolated by the failure of Marburg. Zwingli soon died on the battlefield (1531), fighting with troops from Zurich against the Catholic cantons. The Lutherans likewise were left to their own defenses.

The political advantage gained by Charles V in the second Hapsburg-Valois War (June 1529), coupled with the Protestant embarrassment at the second Diet of Speier (April 1529) and the debacle at Marburg (October 1529), all laid the ground for the Diet of Augsburg in 1530. After Marburg, in spite of further unitive attempts by Philip of Hesse, the Lutherans and Swiss Reformed went their separate ways; a pan-Protestant political league proved politically impossible. In January 1530 Charles V, on the verge of being crowned Holy Roman Emperor by Pope Clement VII (Bologna, February 24, 1530), summoned parliament to convene at Augsburg in 1530. By allowing an expression of "everyman's opinion," the agenda seemed to anticipate an amelioration of religious differences. The evangelicals were required to state the Protestant case in writing. Philip Melanchthon, Luther's foremost deputy, developed a series of affirmative articles, while Luther himself, with Bugenhagen, Jonas, and Melanchthon assisting, compiled a series of criticisms directed at the beliefs and practices of the Latin church. Together, the two texts made up the Augsburg Confession, which was read to the emperor at the Diet of Augsburg on June 25, 1530. The chief theological statement of early Lutheranism, the Augsburg Confession was also a political instrument, signed by the leading Lutheran princes and cities, including the elector of Saxony, the margrave of Brandenburg-

Ansbach, the dukes of Brunswick-Lüneburg, Landgraf Philip of Hesse, as well as representatives of Nuremberg and five other cities.

Catholic theologians present at Augsburg confuted the Augsburg Confession in a document, once revised, which was formally received by the Diet on August 3, 1530. Still unwilling to let go of prospects for reconciliation, Charles V appointed conference committees to attempt to compose the differences between the parties. Lutheran resistance to compromise stiffened; the Catholic majority finally declared the Lutherans to have been confuted and allowed them until April 15, 1531, to conform. Foreseeing this turn of events, Melanchthon, eschewing any further concessions to Latin Catholicism, rushed to defend the Lutheran point of view by a major document of great size — *Apology of the Augsburg Confession* — which, standing alongside the Confession itself, became one of the Lutheran standards. The Lutherans at Augsburg appealed to this apology, insisting that their confession had by no means been confuted.

THE SCHMALKALDIC LEAGUE

DIRECTLY after Augsburg, at Christmastime 1530, the Lutheran princes met at Schmalkalden and, faced with the prospect that their beliefs would be suppressed by force of arms by April, formed an alliance to confront the empire by political and military power. The Schmalkaldic League was formally constituted on February 27, 1531. It included electoral Saxony, Anhalt, Brunswick, and Hesse, in league with such important German and Swiss cities as Strassburg, Constance, Ulm, Magdeburg, Bremen, and Lübeck.

April 15 came and went, and the Lutherans were unscathed. The emperor's forbearance was due, no doubt, to the Turkish incursion into central Europe (1529–32) and to the siege of Vienna. In the same period, Zwingli was killed in the battle of Kappel, releasing the southern German Protestants to swell the ranks of the Schmalkaldic League, which, by 1532, was able to treat with the emperor on virtually equal terms. In July 1532 the empire and the Schmalkaldic League reached an accommodation by the Treaty of Nuremberg: pending either a general council of the church or another meeting of parliament, the Lutherans were allowed a respite from imperial pressure. Thereupon the Mediterranean prince, Charles V, left for Italy and Spain and did not return for nearly a decade.

Pope Clement VII resisted the convocation of a general council, first by procrastination, then by political maneuver — an alliance with France involving the betrothal of his niece Catherine de' Medici to Prince Henry of Orléans. Finally, the pope died (September 25, 1534) and was succeeded by Paul III, who did see some point to having a council but insisted that it be held in an Italian site. In June 1536 he summoned an ecumenical council to meet in Mantua. When that attempt failed, Pope Paul called another council to convene in Vicenza in 1537; it too failed. Meanwhile, the emperor had become preoccupied with other affairs — the Turks again (1535–41), the third Hapsburg-Valois campaign (1536–38), and a revolution in the Netherlands (1539–40).

Given such a reprieve, the evangelical movement spread rapidly into new territories and cities. In 1532 the three princes of Anhalt-Dessau summoned the Lutheran preacher Nicholas Hausmann to preach in Dessau. By the following year, that territory had been converted. In 1534 Nassau became Lutheran, as did the important cities of Hanover, Frankfurt am Main, and Augsburg. The breakthrough of Lutheranism into upper Germany occurred in June 1534 upon the formal conversion of Württemberg to the evangelical religion. That conversion was brought about by two Lutheran preachers, Ambrose Blaurer (1492–1564) and Erhard Schnepf (1495–1558), under the sponsorship of the prince, Duke Ulrich of Württemberg. In December 1534 Pomerania also became Lutheran.

The course of the Reformation frequently took the following form. First came hostility toward officers and institutions associated with the old faith — toward bishops, priests, and monks in particular. Then an evangelical party came into existence. Eventually the prince or, in the case of a city, the town council sponsored Lutheran preaching, usually by some celebrity among the ranks of Luther's associates, sometimes dispatched by Luther himself. Finally the formal conversion would occur, often in conjunction with (1) a visitation of all the churches in the territory or city and (2) the publication of a *kirchenordnung,* "church ordinance," announcing the Reformation and providing, in German, new articles of belief and new forms of worship.

The Münster Rebellion, 1534–35, may have been a serious embarrassment to Protestantism. Actually, however, it may have improved the fortunes of Lutheranism by depriving the Anabaptists of their influence in Germany. In either case, the rebellion was a phenomenon of the left fringe of the Anabaptist movement with its conspicuous revolutionary propensity. The radical Anabaptist Melchior Hofmann, who was given to apocalyptic preaching, won a wide and fervent audience in the Netherlands. His disciple, Jan Mathys, a baker from Harlem, proposed to usher in the new age by means of revolution — a prospect that somewhat exceeded Hoffmann's version of eschatology. To the German city of Münster, where the teachings of Hofmann had already created a furor, came Mathys and Jan Beukels, a tailor from Leyden, who declared that God had chosen Münster to be the New Jerusalem. To participate in the dawning of the new age, thousands swarmed into Münster and, by February 1534, managed to commandeer the city, driving out opponents great and small. The Catholic bishop laid the city under siege. When Mathys died in an effort to lift the siege, Beukelssen was declared king, and a new order was announced, presumably on the authority of Scripture or at least of immediate inspiration, that included both communism and polygamy. Lutheran soldiers joined Catholic soldiers in crushing the revolution (June 24, 1535); the leaders were tortured and executed. The Münster Rebellion brought German Anabaptism into general disrepute. Yet the fact that Lutherans fought side by side with Catholics to put down the revolution tended to dissociate Lutheranism from a taint that might have been attached to Protestantism in general. Lutheranism probably came off the better from the Münster episode. It emerged from that incident as a solid middle-class institution under princely protection. As far as the Anabaptists were concerned, they too regained their composure, especially in the Netherlands and upper Germany under the wise leadership of Menno Simons (1492–1559).

As we have observed, German domestic politics was subject to many vicissitudes — for instance, the third Hapsburg-Valois campaign, the continuing menace of the Turks in middle Europe, and the prospect of an ecumenical council that Pope Paul III could not quite bring into being. Before Charles V could get untangled from such difficulties, Protestantism managed to become established in Albertine Saxony (1539), electoral Brandenburg (1539–40), Macklenberg-Schwerin (1540), and Brunswick-Calenberg (1540). In Albertine Saxony, typically, both a visitation and a church ordinance were employed to inaugurate the Reformation. Saxony and Brandenburg were exceedingly important conquests for Lutheranism.

STRASSBURG AND MARTIN BUCER

IN THE development of the Reformation, no city was more crucial than Strassburg, a commercial hub on the Rhine. Long before Luther attained prominence, Strassburg was a city of humanism and of reformatory zeal. The preacher Johann Geiler von Kaiserberg (1445–1510) used the pulpit of the Strassburg cathedral to inveigh against the evils of the day, especially those associated with capitalism. The circle of humanists in the city, strongly affected by the Alsatian scholar Jacob Wimpfeling and by the satirist Sebastian Brandt, attacked abuses in society and in the church. When the Reformation started, Strassburg printers turned out a stream of Lutheran books. Eventually an officer of the city and an eminent statesman, Jacob Sturm, turned Lutheran. Beginning in 1521, the priest Matthew Zell took courage and began to proclaim Lutheran ideas in one of the side chapels of the cathedral. Two years later, he took a wife who was also well versed in Lutheranism. The Reformation in Strassburg was underway.

In 1523, the year the town council authorized Protestant preaching in the churches of Strassburg, Martin Bucer (1491–1551) appeared in the city. A Dominican since youth, Bucer (or Butzer) had swerved first in the direction of Erasmian humanism. But in 1518, when he heard Luther defend himself before a congregation of Augustinians in Heidelberg, he was converted peremptorily to Protestantism. Of almost no account when he arrived

99. Martin Bucer

in Strassburg, Bucer eventually became a Protestant Reformer of second rank and a figure of great importance in the Reformation. He was (1) the chief Reformer of the city of Strassburg, (2) an important teacher of John Calvin, (3) the preeminent church unionist among all of the Reformers, (4) a Protestant thinker and a designer of Protestant worship of no small consequence, and (5) an important contributor to the English Reformation during the reign of Edward VI. Bucer went beyond Luther when he insisted that the whole of civil society, not just the church, should be brought under the aegis of the word of God in Scripture. Accordingly he set about to re-create the city of Strassburg as a community of love, organized and disciplined according to biblical principles. In 1524 evangelical worship was introduced to the city by means of a German revision of the Roman Mass made by Diebold Schwarz — the beginning of an extremely important liturgical tradition that eventually was carried over into Calvinism. The school system of the city was reorganized by the humanist Johannes Sturm (1507–89; no relation to Jacob), one of the pioneers of the *gymnasium* (secondary school), which prepared students for the university by means of a curriculum both classical and Christian.

Bucer responded to the influence of Zwingli, as well as that of Luther. As the 1520s wore on, he seemed to be grasping for some mediating way of describing the Protestant teaching on the Lord's Supper, neither purely Lutheran nor purely Zwinglian. He appeared at the Marburg Colloquy (1529) as an ambiguous figure, probably more sympathetic to Zwingli than to Luther, yet posing as a mediator between the two schools. In the Tetrapolitan Confession — the confession of the four cities Strassburg, Constance, Lindau, and Memmingen, drawn by Bucer and his colleague Capito for presentation to the Augsburg Diet in 1530 — there is great resistance to Luther's insistence on the real presence of Christ in the Lord's Supper, as well as a stiff reaction to ceremonies and an imperative that all things done in church and society be regulated according to the warranty of Scripture. In the 1530s, however, Bucer came to the conclusion that one *could* speak of Christ's true presence in the Lord's Supper, as long as one meant a spiritual presence, rather than a physical presence received by mouth. Bucer may therefore have been the first to conceive of the doctrine of "the spiritual real presence" of Christ in the Lord's Supper, to which both Melanchthon and Calvin shortly subscribed.

In 1536 Bucer and Capito, on the one hand, and Luther and Melanchthon, on the other, signed a series of accommodations on matters of doctrine, including the Lord's Supper. Called the Wittenberg Concord, the document tended to iron out the differences between Strassburg and Wittenberg. Ever an ardent church unionist, Bucer participated with Melanchthon and Calvin and with certain eminent Catholic theologians — Contarini having been the most prominent — in the colloquies of Worms (1540) and Regensburg (1541) — the last attempts to achieve a rapprochement between Protestants and Catholics before the onset of the Catholic Reformation. In the spring of 1549, discouraged over the political reverses the Protestants had recently suffered at the hands of the Holy Roman Emperor, Bucer fled to England at the invitation of Thomas Cranmer, archbishop of Canterbury, and was appointed regius professor of divinity at Cambridge by King Edward VI. There, with his second wife, the jovial Wilbrandis, he lived out the rest of his life, dying in 1551, just in the midst of the Edwardian Reformation. He contributed substantially to the English prayer book, *The Book of Common Prayer* (edition of 1552), and published *De regno Christi* (The Kingdom of Christ) to teach young King Edward how to convert England into a "Christian commonwealth" under the authority of the Bible.

PHILIP OF HESSE AND LUTHERAN DEFEATS

MEANWHILE the emperor's great strategy of bending Protestant resistance against the moral and political authority of an ecumenical council received an unexpected boost in the bigamy of Philip of Hesse, which seriously compromised the Schmalkaldic League and damaged Protestant solidarity. Philip of Hesse, the mastermind of Protestant politics, was also a human being of unbridled sexual capacity. Although married to Christina, daughter of Duke George of Saxony, and the father of seven children by her, Philip had indulged in so many adulteries that only once between 1526 and 1539 had he ventured to partake of the Lord's Supper. Smitten by Margaret von der Saale, a seventeen-year-old lady of the court, Philip decided to engage in a second marriage as a way of salving his conscience. A serious student of the Bible, Philip had noticed that certain Old Testament patriarchs had practiced polygamy and that the New Testament nowhere prohibited such a practice. His own wife consented. The girl's mother also agreed, but only on the condition that at least some of the princes of the Holy Roman Empire be advised that the marriage was aboveboard and genuine. Still, Philip hesitated. He enlisted Bucer to negotiate with Luther and Melanchthon for their opinions and to present the matter to the elector of Saxony. On December 10, 1539, Luther, Melanchthon, and Bucer joined in a con-

100. Philip of Hesse,
portrait by
Heinrich Giebel

fessional counsel to Philip of Hesse, saying that bigamy, although it had biblical precedent and seemed preferable to divorce, was contrary to one of the fundamental orders of creation. Yet, said they, if Philip could not change his life, it would be better to enter into a second marriage than to persist in his present conduct. The second marriage should nevertheless be kept hidden under the pretext that mistress Margaret was a concubine. Thus advised, on March 4, 1540, Philip of Hesse married Margaret von der Saale in a secret ceremony, attended by Bucer, Melanchthon, and a representative of the elector of Saxony.

When a storm of protest broke throughout the Holy Roman Empire, Luther prescribed telling "a big, fat lie," although Philip repudiated that advice, declaring that lying was against his principles. Of greatest importance was the fact that bigamy was against the law of the Holy Roman Empire. Philip had, in the eyes of the law, thrown both his title and his lands into forfeiture. On June 13, 1541, seeing how precarious his position was, Philip signed a nonaggression treaty with Charles V. Henceforth he could neither come to the aid of the Protestant princes nor negotiate with foreign powers in support of the Schmalkaldic League. As a result of this bizarre episode, Duke William of Cleves suddenly found himself politically isolated and eventually had to renounce Lutheranism; the great archbishopric of Cologne was lost to the Reformation; Duke Maurice of Saxony, Philip's brother-in-law, resigned from the Schmalkaldic League; and the league itself was riven in two. The scandal left Charles in an excellent position to attack his Protestant enemies.

At the emperor's insistence, Pope Paul III summoned an ecumenical council to convene at Trent, an Italian town just inside the borders of the empire; the Hapsburg-Valois Wars, however, delayed the opening of the Council of Trent from 1542 until 1545. (It ran, off and on, until 1563). This famous council certainly began as a political device, designed by pope and emperor, to take advantage of the embarrassment of the Lutherans and the weakness of their Schmalkaldic League. On the battlefield, Charles V entered France in June 1546 with a powerful army; by autumn he threatened Paris. Serious defections to Lutheranism occurred, however, among some of the electors of Germany — Frederick II of the Palatinate, for example — prompting Charles to break off the campaign with Francis I and hastily to conclude the Peace of Crépy with France (September 18, 1544). It marked the end of the French interference, the end of the Hapsburg-Valois Wars. A year later, the Turks also agreed to a truce with the empire.

It did not take a soothsayer to divine the ominous prospects for German Protestantism. Luther himself died on February 18, 1546, after several years of poor health and disillusionment that the Reformation would actually transform individuals and society. In April 1546 the Council of Trent reached its first important theological decision: the Catholic Church "receives and venerates with equal affection of piety and reverence" both Scripture and tradition. In other words, the council had directly repudiated one of the main pillars on which the Reformation had been built — the principle of Scripture alone.

Little stood in the way of Charles's crushing Lutheranism. On June 19, 1546, he proceeded to ally himself with Maurice of Saxony (1541–55), son of the Lutheran Duke Heinrich of Saxony (1539–41). Although the son of a powerful Protestant, the son-in-law of the renowned Protestant leader Philip of Hesse, and the cousin of Elector John of Saxony, another stalwart Lutheran, Maurice seems to have been of a secular mind, with no disposition for religious matters. In trade for Maurice's support, the emperor outlawed Philip of Hesse and John Frederick of Saxony and consigned the electoral

433

dignity to Maurice (October 27, 1546), who thus rose to great political prominence on the ruin of his two relatives. Charles also allied himself with the pope and, together with Duke Ferdinand, Duke William of Bavaria, and Duke Maurice of Saxony, sent a formidable army into the field. The imperial forces swept over southern Germany, requiring the capitulation of many of the Protestant cities there. Saxony, however, became the real battle-ground of the emperor's war on the Protestants. At Mühlberg, on the Elbe River, on April 24, 1546, Charles crushed the forces of the Schmalkaldic League in one of the most important battles in the sixteenth century. John Frederick was captured, and Philip of Hesse, seeing the futility of further resistance, surrendered. Both were arrested. Maurice received the title of elector of Saxony and half of the territory of John Frederick, including the town of Wittenberg. There was very little, if anything, left of Protestant political power. The death of Henry VIII (January 28, 1546) and Francis I (March 31, 1546) left Charles V virtually unchallenged in European politics.

Some means of religious settlement were required if all Germans, including Protestants, were to live peacefully under terms being proposed by the Council of Trent. The emperor therefore appointed a commission of three — an Erasmian (Julius von Pflug), a scholastic theologian (Michael Helding), and a Lutheran (Johann Agricola, court preacher of Brandenburg) to develop a working religious compromise. It appeared on May 15, 1548, and was called the *Interim of Augsburg*. Approved by parliament (June 30, 1548), this Interim was now imposed on Germany at sword's point. Essentially a Roman Catholic statement, it did allow the laity to receive the cup at Mass; it permitted priests to marry; and it made some pretense of limiting the power of the papacy. No one liked this interim arrangement, least of all the pope, who was deeply offended by the infringement of his power. In parts of Saxony, as a favor to Maurice, a less severe *Leipzig Interim* was permitted; it taught justification by faith alongside a generous helping of Catholic customs and doctrines. When the ever-irenic Melanchthon saw fit to defend the Leipzig Interim, he was assailed by Matthias Flaccius Illyricus (1520–75), eventual leader of the so-called genuine Lutheran party. Thus, the bitter theological disputes that preoccupied later Lutheranism had begun.

Germany was deeply aggrieved, both by the religious oppression of Charles V, of which the Interim of Augsburg was eloquent testimony, and by the emperor's growing inclination to evade the constitutional structures of Germany in preference for a Spanish *imperium*. Even the pope (Paul III) bridled at the emperor's clumsy efforts at religious accommodation. The next pope, Julius III (1550–55), although ideologically sympathetic with Charles, was quickly put off by the emperor's efforts to manipulate the Council of Trent, reconvened by Julius in 1551. In the midst of this general dissatisfaction among Germans, Maurice of Saxony made another outrageously self-serving maneuver. Ostensibly to besiege the Lutheran stronghold of Magdeburg in the emperor's behalf, Maurice raised an army. Convinced that his fortunes were more likely to be served as a Lutheran than as a Catholic, Maurice once again abruptly switched sides and, using the power of his army, subtly took command of the Schmalkaldic League, drawing around him the Protestant princes of northern Germany. On January 15, 1552, by the Treaty of Chambord, Henry II of France agreed to take the field in Lorraine on behalf of "the liberties of Germany and its captive princes," in exchange for the frontier bishoprics of Metz, Toul, and Verdun. Thus, in the spring of 1552, both Henry II and Maurice struck against the emperor, forcing Charles to take refuge beyond the Alps at Villach in Carinthia. In the Peace of Passau (August 2, 1552), the Lutherans finally attained peace and freedom to practice their religion, pending the meeting of another diet.

THE PEACE OF AUGSBURG

THE NEXT diet met in Augsburg in 1555. Meanwhile Maurice had died in battle (1553) and Charles V had virtually turned over the reigns of government to his brother Ferdinand, stopping short, however, of committing the imperial dignity itself. After protracted negotiations (February–September 1555), the Peace of Augsburg was signed on September 25. By its terms, equal rights were afforded Lutherans and Catholics in the Holy Roman Empire, according to the *cuius regio, eius religio* formula. No rights were extended to other forms of religion, and no pluralism within a territory would be tolerated. (Toleration was not a sixteenth-century virtue: the Peace of Augsburg was a victory of territorialism, not of toleration.) Anyone aggrieved by such terms had the guarantee of being able to move safely to a more congenial place, including the fair sale of his property. Ecclesiastical property that had fallen into Protestant hands prior to the Peace of Passau was to remain Protestant, according to a special codicil called the ecclesiastical reservation; however, any ecclesiastical prince who was converted to Protestantism after the Peace of Passau would have to forfeit his dignities and possessions — a protection for the Catholic Church against the continuing erosion of its property.

Church bells peeled at the proclamation of the Peace of Augsburg. Lutheranism had achieved legal establishment, but in a divided Germany. It was a compromise that actually blunted the ambitions of the two greatest Germans of the sixteenth century, Luther and Charles V.

Germany was at last at peace and would enjoy peace until 1618, the onset of the Thirty Years' War. The great figures of the sixteenth century were now gone: Luther, Henry VIII, and Francis I. Only Charles V survived, but he had been left tired and fainthearted by his exertions. In 1556, having divested himself of his titles and having made provision for the succession of his several thrones and of the empire itself, Charles retired to the monastery of San Jerónimo de Yuste in Spain, where, two years later, he died. A man of intelligence, force of will, and Catholic zeal, he was the greatest of the Hapsburgs. His starting point — to reawaken the medieval ideal of the Holy Roman Empire, a universal monarchy in liaison with the Holy Catholic Church — ended not at all as he intended, but with the recognition of Lutheranism and the rise of a new Spanish *imperium* in Europe.

VIII. REFORMATION SPREADS
ACROSS THE CONTINENT

19. *Zwingli*

ULRICH ZWINGLI WAS BORN ON JANUARY 1, 1484, SEVEN WEEKS AFTER the birth of Luther, in the Alpine Village of Wildhaus, some forty miles southeast of Zurich. He was the third child of Uly and Margaretha (née Bruggmann) Zwingli, who tended flocks on the steep Alpine slopes and reared a large family in frugality and conventional piety. Compared with Luther's youth, Zwingli's was uneventful. He got by on two inspirations. One was the Alpine grandeur, which supplied him with many theological illustrations, as well as a curious translation of the Twenty-Third Psalm (*In schöner Alp weidet er mich,* "he makes me graze in a beautiful mountain meadow"). The other was Swiss patriotism, instilled in him at the family hearth, which left him an ardent nationalist.

At five, Zwingli was turned over to his uncle Bartholomäus, dean at Wesen, who gave him the rudiments of Latin, upon which all scholarship was based. Noticing that the boy was precocious, Bartholomäus sent him off to the primary school in Basel when he was ten. There, under the pedagogy of Gregory Bünzli, young Zwingli attained proficiency in Latin. About 1496 he was transferred to yet another school, in Bern, where he attended the instruction of the celebrated Heinrich Wölflin (Lupulus), who first set the classics before him — a circumstance of no small importance, as it was from humanism that Zwingli came to the Reformation. By this time, he had also become a promising musician. He had such an excellent voice that the Dominicans of Bern would gladly have enrolled him, had not his father and his uncle put a stop to their designs. In October 1498, having been intellectually prepared for university study, Zwingli ventured

439

to Vienna to take the baccalaureate degree. His name on the university register, however, carries the notation *exclusus:* he was dismissed for some reason now obscure to us, but perhaps on account of his overardent patriotism. The matter could not have been serious, however, for Zwingli re-enrolled for the summer semester of 1500 and pursued his study there until 1502.

THE ROOTS OF ZWINGLI'S THOUGHT

EARLY in 1502 Zwingli returned to Switzerland and entered the university at Basel, which had been founded at the middle of the fifteenth century by scholars and churchmen devoted to the new learning. Basel was the intellectual capital of the Swiss confederacy. With its splendid university and its burgeoning printing industry, the city attracted humanists of the first rank, including the prince of humanists, Erasmus of Rotterdam, who resided periodically in Basel. There his greatest works — the Greek New Testament (1516) and the polemic against Luther *On the Freedom of the Will* (1524) — were published by the famous Basel printer Johann Froben.

The Christian humanists assumed, insofar as they thought alike, that the reform of the church, which they all anticipated, was an intellectual and ethical problem. For them reform involved merely the riddance of medieval dogmatism and superstition and the moral rejuvenation of Christianity. Fundamental to this program was the recall of the church to the legitimate Christian sources: the Bible and the fathers. The humanists were exceedingly zealous both to uncover and to communicate the biblical faith — an enterprise that could not be managed, however, without concern for the texts and skill in language. While Reuchlin labored to supply the lexical tools needed for the Hebrew Bible, Erasmus lavished his energies on the Greek New Testament. The humanists did not take kindly to the medieval Schoolmen, whom they blamed for the burial of the Bible beneath layers of human commentary. The humanistic problem was precisely to break through this dogmatic encrustation and, by using text and language, to reveal again the very sources of the faith.

In this vital environment Zwingli matured as a scholar. He took his bachelor of arts degree from the university in 1502, and his master of arts degree in 1506. Walther Köhler has shown that Zwingli, as a candidate for holy orders, was given very thorough training in the medieval theologians and that he acquired a particular competence in Aquinas and in the Aris-

101. Ulrich
Zwingli

tolian world of thought. Myconius, who was Zwingli's contemporary and
first biographer, left the contrary impression that Zwingli was quite torn
asunder by his intellectual experience and could not seem to reconcile his
theological side and his humanistic side. It was Myconius who had Zwingli
speak disparagingly of the work of the Schoolmen as "the folly of the
Sophists" and who declared that when Zwingli attended lectures in theology,
he felt "like a spy in the enemy camp." There were, at any rate, two eminent
Basel humanists who eventually enabled Zwingli to overcome any disjunc-
ture he may have felt between Christian humanism and Christian theology.
One was Thomas Wyttenbach, who probably came to Basel in November
1505, in which case his unusual style of theology could scarcely have escaped
Zwingli's notice. In his exegetical lectures, especially those on Romans, in
which the skills of humanism were bent to uncover the biblical word,
Wyttenbach pronounced the sale of indulgences "a cheat and delusion" and
professed, in Paul's name, a doctrine of justification by grace through faith.
Zwingli reckoned Wyttenbach a precursor of evangelical theology and did
not hesitate to call him "my master and esteemed and faithful teacher."

The other Baseler who appreciated the importance of humanism for
theology was Johann Ulrich Surgant, who since 1490 had been pastor of

St. Theodore's Church and sometime lecturer in *pastoralia* in the university. To him Christian humanism, with its compelling interest in the Christian sources, meant the revival of preaching, so that the biblical word might resound in the congregations to their edification. When Surgant referred to the "reviving word," he meant the preached word. As a supplement to the Catholic Mass, he actually proposed a vernacular preaching service in his book *Manuale curatorum* (Manual for pastors, 1502), which Julius Schweizer has shown to be the basis of Zwingli's own Sunday service of preaching, introduced at Zurich in 1525.

In the autumn of 1506 Zwingli was appointed vicar at Glarus. On September 29 he celebrated his first Mass in the church of his childhood, having been newly ordained to the priesthood by Bishop Hugo of Constance. Zwingli was a conventional priest. When the parishioners of Glarus complained of wet weather, he paraded the host through the streets of the village on behalf of sunshine. The medieval church in whose structures he served had become inefficient and demoralized in Switzerland, without a real champion either of learning or of moral influence. Zwingli himself suffered his most profound failure in the matter of personal morality. Unable to cope with his own virility, he broke the vow of chastity on more than one occasion. He himself spoke of the shame that overshadowed his life. It is a mistake to suppose that he did not suffer some of the spiritual anguish that beset Luther or share Luther's quest for a gracious God.

The greater part of Zwingli's evangelical awakening was intellectual. The priest of Glarus administered his parish from the first floor of the vicarage, while on the second floor he sequestered his books. His two-storied universe was typical also of his person: he was part pastor, part humanist. Erasmus was the teacher who proved to be decisive for Zwingli. When Erasmus took up residence in Basel in 1514, the hitherto impersonal attachment that Zwingli had felt toward him became both personal and fervent. Erasmus persuaded Zwingli to jettison the medieval doctors once for all, to put aside even the classics in which he honestly delighted, and to commit himself profoundly to the Christian sources, namely, the New Testament and its earliest interpreters, the fathers. It was this reverence for the sources, this rigorous intellectual discipline in uncovering them and this passion to learn the biblical languages, that Zwingli owed to Erasmus. Zwingli, however, overstated his debt to the prince of humanists when he declared in *Auslegen und Bergründen der Schlussreden* (Expositions and proof of the [sixty-seven] articles, 1523) that already in 1514–15 Erasmus had unveiled to him the Reformation theology. Erasmus harbored no such theology, and as there was actually no basic alliance between them, their friendship eventually collapsed and turned to enmity. In the education of Ulrich Zwingli as an evangelical man, Erasmus was nevertheless decisive.

Zwingli was turned out of Glarus, not on account of his moral lapses or his theological irregularity, but on account of his opposition to the Swiss mercenary system. Popes and kings vied with each other to obtain the services of the strong and wily warriors from the Alps. As often as not, Swiss youth found themselves at spearpoint with each other, fighting in opposing armies, without much thought of right and wrong, or much consideration for life itself. The immorality implicit in the mercenary system filtered down into every level of society and cheapened Swiss life. At least twice Zwingli went to battle in Italy as a chaplain to Swiss mercenaries. After the murderous battle of Marignano (1515), in which Swiss dead were strewn over the field, Zwingli wrote an allegorical poem, "The Labyrinth," to denounce the mercenary system as a potential destroyer of the nation. His stout hostility to that traditional and lucrative system cost him his place at Glarus in 1516.

He repaired to Einsiedeln, which in his era, as in ours, was one of the famous Roman Catholic shrines in Switzerland, the site of a chapel that had been dedicated by angels, of a statue of the Black Virgin that had drawn the veneration of pious folk for many years, and of a Benedictine abbey so exclusive that no aspirant was admitted unless he could show so many quarterings of his coat of arms. Pilgrims from all Switzerland and southern Germany swarmed over these holy premises seeking indulgences. The sign over the entrance promised "full remission of all sins."

At Einsiedeln Zwingli was employed by the Benedictines as chaplain to the pilgrims. At first, however, he seemed oddly preoccupied with his own interior development, and his labors were directed largely to his own good. In 1516 occurred one of the momentous events in the history of Christian scholarship — the appearance of Erasmus's Greek New Testament. With that choice volume propped up before him, Zwingli passed his days and nights in the abbey library, searching the depths of Paul, whose epistles he copied out word for word in Greek and annotated according to the commentaries of Origen, Jerome, and Ambrose.

It was in Einsiedeln that Zwingli became an evangelical theologian. He commenced to preach the word of God, the word that is broken out of Scripture, the word that awakens faith in human beings by which they are united to Christ and receive in him the forgiveness of sin. "I began to preach the Gospel of Christ," wrote Zwingli in *Auslegen,* "in the year 1516, before any man in our region had so much as heard the name Luther; and I never left the pulpit that I did not take the words of the Gospel, as read in the Mass of the day, and expound them by means of the Scriptures alone."

In this way Zwingli became a celebrity. To the pilgrims who came to Einsiedeln, he preached in love against the piety that had brought them. To the prelates who visited the shrine — for it was, in fact, an ecclesiastical spa — he gave warning of grave doctrinal errors practiced by the church and prophesied a "great upheaval" if amendments were not made. In August 1518 the Franciscan Bernard Samson arrived in the vicinity selling indulgences by license of Pope Leo X. His slogans and promises were scarcely less extravagant than those of Johann Tetzel, who had recently worked havoc in Germany. Zwingli used his pulpit to denounce this huckster, with such success that Samson fled.

ZWINGLI IN ZURICH

WHEN the office of people's priest at the Great Minster of Zurich fell vacant in October 1518, the celebrated Zwingli of Einsiedeln was immediately considered for the post. (His indiscretions were not overlooked, but his chief rival, a father of six, suffered by comparison.) Zwingli was formally inducted into this eminent post on January 1, 1519, his thirty-fifth birthday. The next day, which was Sunday, he mounted the pulpit to commence a splendid innovation: he would abandon the lectionary of appointed lessons (which he believed to limit the free course of God's word) and would preach a continuous exposition of the New Testament starting with Matthew, and he would preach the word out of the word itself without reference to traditional commentary (which he called *Zwang*, human contrivance and constriction of God's word). As he said in one of his more memorable utterances: "The Word of God will take its course as surely as does the Rhine."

In the course of six years, Zwingli's preaching ranged over the whole New Testament. Solely by the power of that preaching (Zwingli had no other status in civic Zurich), the Reformation came to the small city on the Limmat. Lutheran ideas were also in the air. The books of the German Reformer reached Basel in December 1518 and caused an immediate sensation. Zwingli's correspondence of 1519 was full of Luther, this "Elijah" whom he could not but admire. He would not, however, be called a Lutheran. "Why don't you call me a Paulinian, since I am preaching as St.

444

Paul preached? . . . If Luther preaches Christ, he does just what I do." If there was anything that gave depth to Zwingli's preaching in these early years at Zurich, it was the plague of 1519, which swept away nearly a third of the seven thousand townspeople and brought Zwingli himself face to face with death.

In his sermons of 1520–21, Zwingli declared that certain aspects of conventional piety — fasting, for example — had no basis in Scripture and ought to be curtailed. Opposition to such pronouncements came from three communities of friars in the city. In December 1520 (if the date can be trusted), the Zurich magistrates intervened on Zwingli's behalf. Their quaint mandate guaranteed freedom to preach "the holy gospels and epistles of the apostles" but counseled preachers to "say nothing about other accidental innovations and rules."

Conscience-stricken by Zwingli's sermons, some Zurichers decided to break the Lenten fast in 1522. On Ash Wednesday, according to one eyewitness, the printer Forschauer flouted the fast by cutting up two dried sausages and serving nibbles to certain brazen men, among them Zwingli himself. Zwingli, however, taking heed of Paul's admonition against scandalizing one's neighbor, refrained from eating. Soon the issue spilled out into the streets, where men argued and brawled over the Lenten fast. Zwingli defended those who had eaten meat, in a sermon *On the Choice and Free Use of Foods,* which was written with the same evangelical ardor that one finds in Luther's treatise *The Freedom of a Christian.* Christians, Zwingli, said, must be given freedom to live by their conscience as informed by the word of God. Alarmed at these developments, the bishop of Constance, in whose jurisdiction Zurich lay, sent commissioners to Zurich to counsel obedience toward ecclesiastical laws. Despite this episcopal intervention, the magistrates resolved to do no more than bid the people keep the Lenten fast, until further "elucidation" could be brought to the issue.

Soon the tradition of priestly celibacy was challenged as well. On July 2, 1522, eleven priests met in Einsiedeln, where on their behalf Zwingli drafted a petition to the bishop of Constance: "Petition to Allow Priests to Marry, or at Least Wink at Their Marriage." The signers of this curious piece declared that chastity is a gift of God given to a few. Alas, they confessed, "this gift has been refused to us." Therefore they invoked their scriptural right to marry, in order to be rid of the intolerable burden imposed on their conscience by the tyranny of Rome. Bishop Hugo, already beset by the improprieties of some of his priests, did not find it appropriate to answer. The priests made bold to marry anyway, and Zwingli himself entered into wedlock with the widow Anna Reinhart.

At midsummer of that memorable year, a third issue was provoked by Francis Lambert of Avignon, a Franciscan of some prominence, who was traveling from one Reformation city to another. In Zurich he was drawn into debate with Zwingli on the intercession of saints, but as the basis of argument was declared to be the Bible, Francis was left speechless. He mounted his donkey and rode off to Basel.

At Francis's departure, the local friars took up the cudgels against Zwingli, who had been making sport of their ignorance and sloth. Owing to these trifles of the year 1522, Zurich had been thrown into a crisis over the issue of scriptural authority. When the friars ventured to test this sensitive point, the Zurich Council reacted in Zwingli's favor and resolved to follow the Scriptures in doctrine and worship "to the exclusion of Scotus, Thomas, and suchlike." Now even the convents were thrown open, by the order of the magistrates, to evangelical preaching. Zwingli took this occasion to deliver an important sermon, *On the Clarity and Certainty of the Word of God,* to the nuns of the Oetenbach cloister.

The word of God, said he, is characterized by its "clarity" and "certainty." It is clear, not because it is written lucidly or spoken articulately, but because the Holy Spirit makes it clear by inward understanding. And it is certain in the sense that God in his word accomplishes what he purposes and promises. Zwingli's sermon is ultimately a sermon about the nature of preaching. True preaching is God speaking. Through the work of the Holy Spirit, the esoteric Scriptures and the human discourse of the preacher spring alive in believers and are heard by them as the real, immediate, and effective word of God.

As 1523 opened, it was imperative to consolidate religious opinion in Zurich and to bring the other cantons abreast of events there. The council therefore scheduled a public disputation in the town hall, to which both friends and foes of reform were invited. As the basis for argument, Zwingli prepared *Sixty-Seven Articles,* the first confessional document of the Swiss Reformation. The first sixteen articles were positive in nature; they insisted upon salvation by grace alone and upon the full and final authority of Scripture. Thesis 17 commenced a relentless series of "no's" in which the structure of medieval religion was dismantled, including the pope, the Mass, good works, monastic orders, celibate clergy, penance, and purgatory. Priests and layfolk crowded the hall on January 29 to hear Zwingli defend the *Articles.* Johannes Faber, who represented the bishop of Constance, was reluctant to engage in debate, for he insisted that the meeting was no proper church council. The disputation was nonetheless deemed a victory for Zwingli, whose doctrines met no serious contradiction. The magistrates now issued a mandate, more decisive than the others, declaring that the clergy of the canton should "preach nothing but that which can be proved by the Holy Gospel, and the pure Holy Scriptures." The disputation had the effect of committing Zurich more firmly to Zwingli while weakening the ties of the city to its Roman Catholic bishop.

The tempo of reform now increased. Zwingli found the time propitious to address himself to theological questions. Three of his longer treatises appeared in the months succeeding the January disputation. In *De canon Missae Epichiresis,* he subjected the canon of the Mass, the part of the Mass in which the consecration of the species (the bread and wine) takes place, to exhaustive scrutiny. Aside from his humanistic impatience with its literary imperfections, he was distressed by its bad theology, namely, its doctrine of the sacrifice, which confounded the one all-sufficient offering of Christ on Calvary. He presumed to write four Eucharistic prayers to replace the Roman canon, which illustrate, if nothing else, that his Eucharistic theology was still tentative.

In *Auslegen,* he expounded the skeleton theology of the *Sixty-Seven Articles,* demonstrating his own creativity and integrity as a Reformation thinker, Luther notwithstanding. Scarcely had he finished that work than he dispatched to the printer a sermon entitled *On Divine and Human Justice,* in which his views of church and state are expressed. In Zurich he envisaged a Christian state, the *corpus Christianum* — a single, unified, Christian society in which church and state owe one another a reciprocal relationship of trust, assistance, and freedom. In the Christian state both the minister and the magistrate hold "spiritual offices." The magistrate is invested by God with the ministry of the sword; it is his function to execute human justice, even as Christ himself counseled and practiced obedience to civil authority. Social tranquillity, however, is no end in itself. What is really to be sought is a situation in which human justice will guarantee the preaching of the gospel to maximum effect, a situation devoid of tyranny and tumult in which all members of society are led by preaching to hear and receive God's gracious word of forgiveness. How was that *corpus Christianum,* that Christian society, to be perpetuated? By continuing the Roman practice of baptizing every infant born in Zurich!

But not all of the new believers saw things exactly as Zwingli did. Following the January disputation, a small party of radical reformers arose,

447

dedicated to a more precipitate reformation than Zwingli preferred. They were the nucleus of the Swiss (Anabaptist) Brethren. Incited by Zwingli's own courage as the champion of the principle of *sola Scriptura,* these men saw no reason to temporize, no conceivable justification for delay. Let the "idols" be removed at once! (The word "idols" referred to all unscriptural usages in the church, but especially to physical and pictorial items.) No one contributed to the excitement more than Zwingli's own colleague, Leo Jud, pastor of St. Peter's Church, who on September 1 used his pulpit to denounce pictorial Christianity and to demand the prompt removal of all scenic apparatus from the churches. Iconoclasm ensued. Hottinger the boot-maker led a contingent of overzealous souls in pulling down a great wooden crucifix at which the pious had made devotions for many years.

Iconoclasm prompted the magistrates to sponsor a second Zurich disputation, devoted to the issues of images and the Mass. The problem of the first disputation had been to reconcile old believers and new. The current problem was to discover the proper way between Catholic conservatism on one extreme, and Anabaptist radicalism on the other. The leaders of the Anabaptists appeared for the first time at the second disputation. First among them was Conrad Grebel, who publicly deplored Zwingli's caution in the course of that debate. His closest colleagues were Felix Manz and Louis Haetzer, the author of a recent attack against pictorial Christianity. Associated with these men was the well-known pastor at Waldshut, Balthasar Hubmaier, who claimed to have challenged Zwingli on the subject of infant baptism as early as 1523.

The second disputation opened on October 26 in the presence of some five hundred priests. The bishops, to whom urgent invitations had been sent, were conspicuously absent. In three days of debate it was resolved that images were unscriptural and should be abolished and that the Mass was not a sacrifice but a memorial of Christ's one, all-sufficient offering and should be reconstructed as such. Despite the strenuous objections of the radical theologians, the Zurich Council deferred the execution of these decisions until an orderly program of reform could be worked out and until preachers had ranged over the canton, edifying the people as to the meaning of these changes.

In the course of the second disputation, Zwingli had occasion to preach a sermon on the Christian ministry entitled *The Pastor.* The church, he said, exists among those who adhere to God's word and confess Christ according to that word; the ministry, then, which is responsible for the publication of that word, pertains to the *esse* of the church; those who hold that high office must take the utmost care that they proclaim only the word, to the exclusion of all human doctrines. Zwingli was not content simply to use the word "minister"; the clergyman is also an "overseer," for surveillance is part of the pastoral office. In addition to preaching, the pastor must watch over the moral and spiritual integrity of the flock by exercising discipline in the parish.

The purification of the cultus (the cultic practices of a community, the way it worships, and the furnishings and decorations of its sacred place), which the second disputation had anticipated, commenced in the summer of 1524. In one sweeping action, clergy and craftsmen entered the parish churches, removed the relics and images, whitewashed the paintings and decorations, carted away the utensils, and nailed the organs shut in token that no music would resound in the churches again. To Zwingli these were strokes against ambiguity and superstition and on behalf of simplicity and clarity. It seems inappropriate to define Zwingli's idea of authority as biblical legalism. His policy was really shaped by the seriousness with which he took symbolism. In the church, where the individual's salvation hangs in the balance, one must say exactly what one means, whether by word or by physical symbol. Remnants of the old cultus that are ambiguous or superstitious or sentimental must be rigorously cast aside, and forms must be found that express the New Testament gospel with simple clarity and power.

By Christmas, 1524, only one vestige of medieval religion survived — the Mass. Shortly that liturgy itself came under a sharp final attack in *Commentary on True and False Religion* (March 1525), Zwingli's major effort at systematic theology, in which his doctrine of the Eucharist first appeared in a definitive form. Zwingli and his colleagues supported this written assault on the Mass by vigorous representations to the town council that the Roman rite be abolished. The council acceded to their demands on April 12 — Wednesday in Holy Week. On Maundy Thursday, 1525, the Zurich rite was inaugurated.

VIEWS OF THE EUCHARIST

NEARLY every decision about worship that Zwingli made depended upon his Eucharistic thought. He insisted that faith, which constitutes the new relationship between the believer and God, is not fed by external things, and surely not by anything so crass as the eating of flesh and blood. It was typical of him to say, "None but the Holy Spirit gives faith, which is trust

449

in God, and no external thing gives it." Moreover, an antagonism between spirit and body loomed in his thought. He could not see how material things could participate in the holy or convey grace. They stood, in fact, in contradiction to one another. "Spirit and flesh contradict each other," Zwingli would tell Luther at Marburg. His most compelling text on the Eucharist was John 6, which included the decisive verse 63: "It is the spirit that quickeneth; the flesh profiteth nothing." In any case, Zwingli supposed the glorified body of Christ to be locally resident at the right hand of the Father in heaven. So it is "wrong by the whole width of heaven" to imagine that his body is available on Christian altars so that communicants can feed on him. Zwingli ruled out entirely the possibility that Christians could participate in the substance of Christ's body.

If it was neither possible nor profitable to feed on the body of Christ in the Lord's Supper, it did not strike Zwingli as an enormity if one were to reinterpret "This is my body" to mean "This signifies my body." At that redefinition, the Lord's Supper became a "commemoration of the death of Christ," a memorial of our redemption on Calvary. Thus the bread and wine were reminders of a grace already received rather than vehicles of a present sacramental grace.

As Zwingli conceived it, the Eucharist is the contemplation of the mystery of Calvary. This is no bare memorialism. *Contemplatio* is the critical word. The Supper is an occasion of profound, almost mystical contemplation of the mystery of our deliverance on Calvary, a contemplation so powerful that the worshiper could "grasp the thing itself." The bread and wine serve as powerful stimulants to communicants, reminding them of the body broken and the blood shed on their behalf and enabling them to fix their mind in contemplation more quickly and effectively. In this contemplative sense, Zwingli was even prepared to say, "We have the Lord's Supper distinguished by the presence of Christ." But however ecstatic the Supper might be, it did not include our being nourished by the substance of Christ's body.

Zwingli saw no reason to observe the Eucharist every Sunday. It did not convey grace, mediate the divine life, or remit sin — as these benefits had been traditionally understood. Preaching was the proper center of an evangelical cultus, for it was normally by preaching that people were brought to faith and sustained in faith. The Eucharist as a contemplative event might even suffer loss of effectiveness by too frequent occurrence. Zwingli decided upon a quarterly celebration of the Lord's Supper — a momentous decision that meant the disconnection of the Eucharist from the normal Sunday service and that sundered the unity of word and sacrament that had prevailed in the West since Justin Martyr. Zwingli's decision committed him to the creation of a new type of Sunday service that would feature the sermon. For this use, he borrowed the preaching office that Surgant of Basel had designed in 1502 to accommodate the "reviving word." So, the worship of the Lord's Day came to be called, not inappropriately, "the sermon," and the Eucharist retired from weekly prominence to become an occasional event.

Zwingli also proceeded to create a liturgy of the Lord's Supper, which was used for the Easter celebration in 1525. The church historian Yngve Brilioth has argued that this mean and radical liturgy is a "liturgical masterpiece" of "dogmatic expression." Zwingli resolved to create a liturgy that would accommodate his idea of *contemplatio*. What were chiefly required were stillness and repose, so that worshipers need suffer no distraction but could fix their mind in the contemplation of Calvary, to which all Christian faith referred. Thus, there was no music, no speech except the reading of Scripture. Instead of going forward to the altar to communicate, the people did not stir from their seats. The elements were brought down from the table in wooden plates and cups and delivered to the people where they sat. Each communicated and passed the elements to his or neighbor. No one stirred; no one disturbed the monumental stillness of the Zwinglian Eucharist.

The last phase of evangelical reconstruction pertained to the training of ministers. For this purpose Zwingli inaugurated what he called prophecy (see 1 Cor. 14:29–32), a daily period of rigorous Bible study that commenced in June 1525. Its whole intent was to train theological students and retrain the priests. (By comparison, the Anabaptists might soon appear to be false prophets — untrained and irresponsible interpreters of the Scriptures.) In daily sessions at the Great Minster, the scholars dealt with the Old Testament chapter by chapter (and, after Zwingli's lifetime, with the New Testament as well). The first reader read the appointed chapter from the Vulgate. He was succeeded by the professor of Hebrew, who read and expounded the passage from the Hebrew text. The professor of Greek proposed still other nuances from the Greek Septuagint. The fourth scholar, speaking in Latin, summarized all the insights and suggested how they could be used in preaching. Meanwhile the laymen had congregated. In their presence, Zwingli (or another) took to the pulpit and preached on the passage under discussion. Not only was the Zurich prophecy the means of training evangelical clergy, it also stimulated the production of early Protestant commentaries on the Scriptures, to say nothing of the Zurich Bible of 1529. Some scholars see in this institution the origin of Reformed seminaries.

DISPUTES

In the course of 1525, the Anabaptist problem became acute in Zurich. In their letter to Thomas Münzer of the previous year, Conrad Grebel and his colleagues had said that "infant baptism is a senseless, blasphemous abomination, contrary to Scripture." Zwingli, for his part, had now taken a firm stand on behalf of the baptism of infants. In his newly published disquisition *On Baptism* (1525), he declared that children of Christian parents are born within the sphere of the church; they are accounted heirs of the covenant through the faith of their parents, and the covenantal promises that God holds out to these children of the church ought to be established to them by the sacrament of baptism as a sign of the covenant. The Anabaptists, however, refused to practice this vestige of medieval life. Baptism, as they understood it, was a sacrament of commitment of one's whole life to Christ, which could not possibly be made except out of a genuine conversion that far exceeds the religious capacity of even the most precocious child. The year of the impasse over infant baptism (1525) saw the first rebaptisms and the actual "gathering" of the Anabaptist communities. (See chapter 20.)

As early as 1524, the forest cantons of Switzerland — rural, conservative, and Roman Catholic — struck up an informal alliance to forestall the Reformation. A Protestant organization called the Christian Civic Alliance soon arose to offset the Roman Catholic power; by 1530 the alliance included the urban cantons of Zurich, Bern, and Basel, as well as certain lesser cantons and cities. Thus threatened, the Roman Catholics translated their informal alliance into the Christian Union, which sought and received the support of Roman Catholic Austria. By 1529 the Swiss confederacy was torn asunder over the Reformation. In that year, the First War of Cappel occurred; one cannot say that it was fought, for a negotiated settlement was reached prior to actual battle, in which it was agreed that neither side would persecute the other for the sake of religion and that the treaty with perfidious Austria would be dissolved. The Roman Catholics came slowly to believe that this settlement, which implied the parity of the religions, was to their disadvantage, and they waited an opportunity to win a better decision.

Meanwhile, Philip of Hesse, the leader of the German Lutheran princes, conceived of an international Protestant alliance as a means of extending the Reformation. The inclusion of the Swiss seemed the proper first step. Their participation, however, was made extremely difficult by Luther's undisguised contempt for Zwingli, whose monstrous doctrine of the Lord's Supper exhausted the Saxon's large vocabulary of abuse. It occurred to Philip of Hesse, nevertheless, to attempt a reconciliation of the Reformers. In April 1529 he invited them to confer at his Marburg castle in the autumn forthcoming. The Marburg Colloquy convened on October 1, with Luther and Melanchthon in attendance on the Lutheran side, Zwingli and Oecolampadius representing the Swiss. Other divines were also present, notably Martin Bucer of Strassburg, who, as an advocate of the "true presence," fancied himself a mediator between the schools.

On the first day of the colloquy wide areas of agreement were found to exist between the parties with respect to the chief articles of religion. Conflict arose on the morning of October 2, however, when the discussion was directed to the Eucharist. Luther attributed Zwingli's error to a caprice in his use of the Bible. He therefore insisted upon the literal words of institution, "This is my body," which in fact he had scribbled in chalk on the surface of the great conference table. These words, he said, deserve to be received with wonder, with amazement, but certainly not with a giddy propensity to interpret them symbolically.

Oecolampadius, the venerable Reformer of Basel, responded from the Swiss side. He proposed the classic Zwinglian pericope from John 6:63, "the flesh profiteth nothing," and he ventured to suggest that that verse cast a different light on the words of institution and made allowance for their symbolic interpretation. But the question that Oecolampadius pressed upon Luther was the most profound of all questions from the Swiss standpoint: "Since we have a spiritual eating, what need is there of a bodily one?" If, in other words, our relationship to God is by faith (as evangelical theology declares), and if that relationship is a spiritual one, begun and sustained in us by the Holy Spirit, then why do we need to communicate in the substance of Christ's body? According to some versions of the colloquy, Luther gave a spirited reply: "I don't care what need there is; I am a prisoner of the word of Christ. If Christ should command me to eat dung, I would do it, knowing that it would be good for me." The inelegance of Luther's remark does not detract from the seriousness of his intent. By insisting upon the integrity of the biblical words, he sought to protect the sacramental dimension of Christianity, which Zwingli seemed to jeopardize.

Zwingli himself now interposed the critical text from John, "the flesh profiteth nothing," and insisted that it must be considered very seriously in the way the Eucharist is explained. The words of institution, "This is my body," mean "this signifies my body" — an interpretation no more outrageous than countless examples of metaphoric speech in Scripture. The Lord's Supper is a memorial meal in which Christian people bear witness to the death of Christ as the sole source of their salvation and contemplate this high mystery of their deliverance.

To this line of argument, Luther replied bitterly. "The words *hoc est corpus meum,*" said he, "are not our words but Christ's. The devil himself cannot make it otherwise. I ask you therefore to leave off tampering with the word of God." Zwingli was now infuriated by this persistent appeal to the literalism of the words. Said he: "I remain firm at this text, 'the flesh profiteth nothing.' I shall oblige you to return to it. You will have to sing a different tune with me." Said Luther: "You speak in hatred." Replied Zwingli: "Then declare at least whether or not you will allow John 6 to stand?" Said Luther: "You are trying to overwork it." Replied Zwingli: "No, no, it is just that text that will break your neck." Said Luther: "Don't be too sure of yourself. . . . Our necks don't break as easily as that."

On October 2–3, the issue turned upon another prickly question — whether, as the Zwinglians said, the body of Christ is "in one place," at the right hand of the Father in heaven, so that it "does not come down into the bread of the Lord's Supper," or whether, according to Luther's doctrine of ubiquity, the body of Christ is everywhere present and thus accessible in the sacrament of the altar.

Always Luther came back to the Scripture: "The Word, the Word, the Word, the Word — do you hear? That is the decisive factor." Under this sort of battering, the Swiss slowly retired into silence. Zwingli even wept under Luther's abuse, and the colloquy became a shambles. The ecumenical debacle at Marburg displayed the Lord's Supper as a major point of Protestant contention. The Marburg Colloquy defeated the politics of Philip of Hesse and left the Swiss evangelicals at the mercy of their Catholic foes.

In the course of 1530 the political crisis increased in Switzerland as both religious parties anticipated resumption of the war. The canton of Bern, reluctant to let blood, proposed to bring the Catholic cantons to terms by an embargo on essential supplies. "If you have the right to starve the cantons to death," said Zwingli in a curious Whitsunday sermon (1531), "you have a right to attack them in open war. They will now attack you with the courage of desperation." It was a fair prediction. In the Second

War of Cappel, on October 11, 1531, the army of Zurich was routed, and Zwingli, struck down by the blows of outraged Catholics, died on the field in his forty-eighth year.

The word "Zwinglian" in religious parlance is often used imprecisely and pejoratively. On both counts, the word may be unfair to the Reformer of Zurich. We should see him properly as one of the eminent Reformed theologians, the first of that tradition. His reliance upon the word of God in Scripture as the sole ground of Christian thought, his circumspect use of biblical authority to repair and regulate all parts of ecclesiastical life, his unmistakable accent upon the work of the Holy Spirit, his idea of preaching as the possibility of hearing the divine word, his ruthless purge of ambiguous, weak, and distracting symbols, his interest in discipline as an indispensable part of parish ministry — all of these put Zwingli in the mainstream of Reformed theology. In his idea of symbolism, in his radical doctrine of the Lord's Supper, and in his reordering of the Christian cultus, we see Zwingli's resolve to be responsible to the Bible, to be consistent with his own thought, and to be led by both to the utmost limits of their suggestion.

EXCURSUS

Zwingli's Thought

A SHORT EXCURSION INTO THE THOUGHT OF THIS COURAGEOUS AND unfettered Reformer is appropriate here. Out of convenience we will confine ourselves to the *Commentary on True and False Religion,* his longest and most systematic work. At the outset, Zwingli agrees with Cicero that "religion" (from *religo,* "to bring together") refers to "the *whole* piety of Christians," including doctrine, discipline, and worship. True religion is that which springs from the font of God's word, while false religion is responsive to human tradition and speculation. Zwingli proceeds immediately to the doctrine of God. He concedes that the existence of God is knowable by human reason, as the ancient philosophers bear witness. To the pagan world, however, this partial knowledge is entirely without spiritual profit. The difference between the pagan and the Christian believer is that the latter knows God not merely by rational thought but in faith; the believer has been taught by God himself.

How does God teach us? We might expect the answer to be through the preaching of the gospel, or by the Holy Scriptures. Indeed, Zwingli does direct us to the "divine oracles" (the preaching and reading from the Bible), but what he really intends has a slightly different accent. It is the Holy Spirit who teaches. Did not Paul say plainly that all are ignorant of the things of God except his own Spirit? It is thus rash to expect knowledge of God from any other source. Normally the Spirit teaches us as we listen to the preaching of the Scriptures, but there are places in his theology where Zwingli ventures to say that the Holy Spirit may bring people to faith without any external means at all. Preaching itself is no prerequisite to the Spirit.

Having been directed to the "divine oracles," let us ask what the Scriptures say of God. They say (1) "that he alone is the *being (esse)* of all things"; (2) that he is the "source and fountain of all good"; (3) "that as God is being and existence to all things, so he is the *life and motion* of all things that live and move"; (4) that in God is *prudentia,* by which creation is purposefully ordered; "his wisdom knows all things even before they exist, his knowledge comprehends all things, his foresight regulates all things"; (5) that he is *love,* whose love is freely given apart from any human claim, and is most clearly seen in the delivery of Christ his Son to the cross for our sins. These, however, are not the affirmations of a philosopher; they are the affirmations of God revealed in his word, and they are acceptable only as God himself gives one faith to understand them.

Whenever the doctrine of man is proposed for discussion, people naturally count themselves experts. Zwingli considers this a serious mistake indeed. For a person to comprehend human nature is as unlikely as trying to seize a squid, which emits a cloud of inky fluid to hide itself. Man's camouflage is pride and feigned innocence. To learn of ourselves, we must resort again to Scripture. The God who built the human being knows the secrets of the human heart.

Zwingli proceeds to discuss the Fall, which he attributes ultimately to self-love, epitomized in man's absurd pretension of having equal status with God. "The death that is sin . . . consists in man's unceasingly loving himself, pleasing himself, trusting himself, crediting everything to himself, thinking he sees what is straight and what is crooked, and believing that what he approves, everyone ought to approve, even his Creator." The discourse on anthropology closes on a somber note: "It has now been quite sufficiently shown that man does everything from self-love, and, unless he undergoes a change, will always do so."

In a chapter simply titled "Religion," Zwingli teaches us to distrust our works and to seek our whole help from God. "Religion," he observes, "took its rise when God called runaway man back to himself, when otherwise he would have been a deserter forever." In that very transaction man was shown the deplorable state of his affairs as well as the loyal devotion of this heavenly Father. Piety, then, consists in the despair of oneself, coupled with faith in the generosity of God. "This clinging to God, therefore, with an unshakable trust in him as the only good — this is piety, this is religion." But piety does not stop at that. Having been brought to faith, the Christian is eager to perform God's will; with a devotion like that of a man for his spouse, the Christian is persuaded by no speech except that of God alone.

The next chapter, called "The Christian Religion," establishes the whole of Zwingli's theology upon Christ. To make his point, he finds it necessary to begin by testing the assumptions of works-righteousness, with predictable results. Good works are shown to be vitiated by pride. Pious service is exposed as self-service. The justice of God, which must indeed be satisfied, cannot be satisfied by human merit. It is satisfied by God himself in Christ.

> Wishing . . . to help this desperate plight of ours, our Creator sent one to satisfy his justice by offering himself for us, not an angel or a man, but his own Son, and clothed in flesh in order that neither his majesty might deter us from communion with him, nor his lowliness deprive us of hope. . . . For what can't he do, or what can't he have, who is God? Moreover, being man, he promises friendship and intimacy, indeed kinship and community. What can he refuse who is a brother and shareholder of our weakness?

Zwingli regarded the virgin birth of Jesus to be of critical importance in the economy of redemption. Only thus could it be said that deity took flesh without imperfection. Only with the virgin birth could the sacrifice for man's atonement be unblemished. Zwingli asserted the perpetual virginity of Mary, so that it could be said that virginity was her "quality." His delicate Mariology was expressed in an early sermon *On the Perpetual Virginity of Mary* (1522). It came to light in the Zurich liturgy, which retained the *Ave Maria,* just before the sermon, as a hymn to the incarnation of Christ.

The gospel, which occupies Zwingli's next chapter, is something to be preached. It is the news "that sins are remitted in the name of Christ." When this announcement is truly preached and truly heard, a set of saving events occur in the life of a person. Preaching first elicits repentance. In despair over ourselves, we cast ourselves on God's mercy, which preaching has held out to us. Yet the prospect of God's justice still frightens us, for we know that we are without any justice in the presence of God. Preaching, however, also brings Christ, who has satisfied the divine justice. When we as Christians, by faith, find ourselves in solidarity with Christ, we know that we are forgiven and indeed "just," and we begin to live in newness of life. But is there a possibility that this theology of the gospel leads to antinomianism — a disdain for the moral law? It is an unlikely prospect, according to Zwingli. No one who has felt the terrible disease of sin and the marvelous health of forgiveness will resort willingly to the disease again. The person newly recovered from a broken limb does not say, "I have found a splendid physician; I must break my leg again."

In the succeeding chapters (entitled "Repentance" and "Law"), Zwingli conceives of the Christian life as properly double-sided: it is a life of peace and war, of joy and sorrow; it is unremitting struggle against the weakness of the flesh and the ravages of self-love, broken now and then by the satisfaction of having loved and trusted God and done his will. Zwingli's point is that both sides pertain to the believer. It is the Christian's reasonable expectation to undergo both the comfort and the struggle that the gospel entails.

Zwingli's doctrine of election establishes a secondary line of development in his thought that includes the doctrines of the church, the ministry, and the sacraments. Election is most fully treated in the sixth chapter of the Reformer's treatise *On the Providence of God* (1530). As far as Zwingli is concerned, election is to be seen as the expression of God's undivided justice and mercy; the accent in Zwingli's thought falls on God's disposition to gather humankind into the church: God elects in order to save. "Election," wrote Zwingli, "is the free disposition of the divine will in regard to those that are to be blessed."

If election is the sole ground of our salvation, how can the structures of grace in the visible church make any conceivable difference? Calvin found a plausible way of dealing with that dilemma so that he could affirm the "treasures of grace" in the visible church. Zwingli, however, was far more apt to depreciate the traditional structures:

> Since faith is a gift of the Holy Spirit, it is clear that the Spirit operated before the external symbols were introduced.

For if the celebration [of the Eucharist] could do anything of this kind, [that is, convey grace] Judas would have returned to his senses.

Election precedes faith, and faith follows election as a sign of it. For Zwingli, faith is a state of being that is created in us by the Holy Spirit; it is a new relationship between us and God; it is the "light and security of the soul," by which we are delivered from anxiety and defended against adversity; and it involves a spiritual union with Christ, although that union is not so clearly defined as Calvin's *mystica unio,* or union between Christ and the believer. When Zwingli says that election precedes faith, he is tempted again to minimize the structures of the visible church. Infants and sundry pagans are chosen by God quite irrespective of those structures, "for his election is free." Thus, Zwingli is sure that Socrates and Seneca will be among the saved.

In Zwinglian thought, the term "church" is used in two ways. In the first instance, it applies to the whole company of the elect, which, because its constituency is known only to God, is properly called the invisible church. The term "church," however, also pertains to the visible institution, which includes all who are rated as Christians, all who are enrolled in the name of Christ and who participate in parish activities. This church is visible because its constituency is recognizable. How can we be sure that the visible church is a true church of God? Melanchthon and Calvin refer to the marks of the true church, according to which such a determination can be made. Where the word is preached and the dominical sacraments are administered according to Christ's intention, one may speak confidently about the church. Instead of marks, Zwingli foresees certain indications that the saving work of God is being done in the congregation. Where the people are gathered around the word of God, where discipline is practiced, where the sacraments are correctly celebrated, and where Christ is confessed, there are trustworthy indications that the will of God is being served. In these instances the visible church somehow transcends its empirical existence, its sociological reality, and participates in the *una sancta*.

20. *The Anabaptists and the Left Wing of the Reformation*

IN THE COURSE OF THE 1520S, IN THE SWISS CITY OF ZURICH, A HANDFUL of devout people established the first Anabaptist community. Having been inspired by Zwingli, the Reformer of Zurich, and having been conscience-stricken by Zwingli's insistence upon *sola Scriptura,* they nevertheless became impatient with Zwingli's own policy of prudence and delay and distrusted certain aspects of his thought. They therefore proceeded, over his bitter opposition, to create their own community and ultimately drew upon themselves persecution at the hands of the Zurich magistrates.

As we saw in chapter 19, the year 1523 brought two public disputations to Zurich. In the first one, held in January 1523, Zwingli defended his *Sixty-Seven Articles,* in which he promised to reform the religious institutions of the city strictly according to the Scriptures, and in which he dismantled the whole structure of medieval Catholic piety. Some fervent souls in the city took heart from this reform and began to press for immediate and radical changes. They were the nucleus of the Swiss Brethren, which is the correct name of the early Anabaptist community in Zurich. Incited by Zwingli's own stout courage, these people saw no reason to temporize, no justification for delay. A wave of iconoclasm ensued, and some of the more zealous members of the Swiss Brethren were consigned to jail. The distraught magistrates of Zurich then sponsored a second disputation, held in October 1523, in which some attempt was made to allay the religious crisis that had boiled up over the use of images and the continuance of the Roman Mass. The Anabaptist leaders first came to prominence at that disputation. Chief among them was Conrad Grebel, the son of a distinguished Zurich family who had been educated in humanism and lately trained by Zwingli himself in the Scriptures. His associate was Felix Manz, who had also read the Scriptures under Zwingli's direction. Associated with these men was Balthasar Hubmaier, a gentle clergyman in the nearby mountain community of Waldshut, who had taken a doctorate in theology and was a very respectable theologian. He had already tackled Zwingli on the question whether infants should be given the Christian sacrament of baptism. He thought not.

The second Zurich disputation accomplished its business in the course of three days. It was agreed that images were unscriptural and should be abolished and that the Mass was not a sacrifice (as Roman Catholics thought) but only a memorial of Jesus' crucifixion and must be remodeled accordingly. Then, to the consternation of the Anabaptists, the Zurich magistrates, with Zwingli's approval, deferred the execution of those decisions until the people of Zurich had been prepared to receive them with unanimity and peace. To the Anabaptists, such prudence was intolerable. So began the tradition of Anabaptist dissent.

Such tensions were symptomatic of a far more serious disagreement. Zwingli conceived of Zurich as a Christian state according to the medieval idea of *corpus Christianum,* namely, a single, unified Christian society in which church and state find themselves in a reciprocal relationship of assistance and trust. Zurich, according to Zwingli, was to be an Alpine Israel into which the *whole* of society would be incorporated and in which church and state would reciprocate support and favors. Implicit in this design was the continuation of the Catholic practice of baptizing infants, because the primary way by which such a society perpetuates itself is by the baptism of every infant who comes to life within it. When the Anabaptists trifled with Zwingli's grand design of a *corpus Christianum,* when they demanded the immediate destruction of the Roman Mass, they threatened the order and stability of that Christian state. When Zwingli saw the danger of Anabaptist radicalism, he developed a policy of delay. He insisted upon the competence of the state, as the divinely ordained agency for the well-being of society, to delay the demands of Scripture long enough to allow the people to receive them without offense.

In the eyes of the Anabaptists, it was clear that Zwingli had raised a second norm alongside that of the Scriptures, the norm of governmental delay. He was merely the pretender of *sola Scriptura.* They began to distrust the idea of a *corpus Christianum* into which *all* of society, even those lukewarm in the faith, would be gathered. They began to doubt the integrity of the

Magisterial Reformation, that is, the reformations of Luther, Zwingli, Calvin, or the Church of England, in which magistrates were allowed to play a decisive role and in which the state was understood to be God's divinely appointed instrument, the expression of God's providence over his creation. It now occurred to the Anabaptists that all those who were seriously committed to the religious standards of the New Testament would have to be *drawn out of society,* not into it, would have to be *drawn out of the historic church,* not into it, gathered into little communities of the saints, into little righteous remnants, admission to which was exclusively by the baptism of consciously true believers, which meant inevitably adults, not children. That was a most shattering, far-reaching conception indeed.

Anabaptist dissent did not touch the basic Christian doctrines as we find them expressed, for example, in the creeds of the Christian church. It pertained, rather, to three matters that require our attention: the definition of Christian life, the definition of the Christian church, and the relationships of Christians to the world.

THE CHRISTIAN LIFE AS DISCIPLESHIP

IN THE first place, the Anabaptists insisted that Christianity is a discipleship — *Nachfolge Christi,* our discipleship to Christ. The terms of that discipleship — what we are expected to do to fulfill it — are laid out for us in the Bible, particularly in the four gospels, and essentially in the Sermon on the Mount. The Swiss Brethren were plainly dissatisfied with the viewpoint of justification by faith, as it was taught by the major Protestant thinkers. It seemed to *interiorize* Christianity too much (too much emphasis, in other words, on such ideas as faith, forgiveness, freedom, and security), even as medieval Catholicism had *institutionalized* Christianity too much. As a consequence, Reformation thought was unproductive of a vigorous ethical life, a life of genuine holiness. What the Swiss Brethren intended to stress was not the Reformers' emphasis upon faith, but rather the transformation of life. They were highly put off by Luther's description of a Christian as *simul iustus et peccator.* Their whole point was that a Christian must *advance;* he or she must go forward to the status of a *disciple;* he or she must show evidences of having been reborn. To sum it up: while Luther and Zwingli and Calvin speak of faith, the Anabaptists speak of discipleship; while Luther and Zwingli and Calvin speak of believers, the Anabaptists speak of disciples.

What are some of the particulars of such teaching? Baptism is the badge of this discipleship. As only an adult can make such a religious commitment, only an adult can legitimately be baptized. Obedience *(Gehorsam)* is the foremost obligation of discipleship — obedience to the teaching and the example of Jesus, of which the very epitome is the Sermon on the Mount. There the great Anabaptist virtues are set forth: radical love, self-surrender, and suffering. The Swiss Brethren do not argue that these values pertain to the secular world (they might even have agreed with Luther that fallen humankind is incapable of obeying the Sermon on the Mount); they pertain to another dimension of existence, namely, to the gathered communities of the saints, drawn out of the world. One cannot do these things unless one is reborn and undergoes a radical change and subsists in a community of elite Christians. Nor can these values be sustained without *Absonderung* — a great Anabaptist word that refers to separation from the secular world and from the church of history. The disciples are gathered out of the world, into a separated life of great holiness (a lifestyle still practiced by contemporary Amish and Mennonites). That does not mean that the saints are excused from making a witness to the world. On the contrary, evangelism in the world is the responsibility of every disciple. Baptism for the Anabaptists, just as baptism was for Jesus, is the beginning of a public ministry in the world. Witness to the world may mean, however, to suffer at the hands of the world, if by that means the truth of Christianity may thereby be vindicated. Thus the Anabaptists developed a whole theory of martyrdom, pertaining to both individuals and whole communities. The true church of Christ is the suffering church.

THE SEPARATION OF THE CHURCH

WE ARE now in a position to understand how the Anabaptists functioned as historians. In their view of history, the emperor Constantine stood at the watershed of Western civilization. Before Constantine, church and state were separated, and the church was persecuted by the state. After Constantine, church and state were united, and the suffering church ceased to suffer. Thus, the Christian church "fell" in the reign of Constantine. The correct Christian procedure is therefore to abandon the church of history, to abandon every society in which church and state are joined, and to restore the "pre-Constantinian" church — a feat that the Anabaptists described by their well-known word *restitutio*, "restitution." It means literally to reinstate the primitive Christian church.

According to Anabaptist thought, the Christian church is neither the sacramental ark of the Middle Ages ("outside of which there is no salvation") nor the *Mundhaus* ("mouth house") of Luther in which preaching resounds; the church is the society of the elite; the church is a gathered community, coterminous with neither society nor the state nor the historic church but living in radical separation from the world in order to practice the perfection prescribed by Jesus. Entrance is by baptism, called believer's baptism, which depends upon the decision of an adult; infant baptism to the Anabaptists was both meaningless and without support in the Scriptures. The structures and practices of the church must be ordered strictly, legally, according to the Scriptures, to which, as Conrad Grebel once said, "nothing must be added, nothing taken away." The church, in fact, must be rebuilt after apostolic patterns; that type of renovation also belongs under the term *restitutio*.

The idea of *Absonderung* had several important implications. Taking their lead from certain passages in the New Testament, the Anabaptists developed a theory of "two worlds." They looked upon the secular world, with all of its economic, political, and cultural structures, as a highly demonic reality, with which one should not compromise an inch. Opposed to the secular world was another world, a world without end, a kingdom of God, of which the gathered communities of the elite were anticipations. The secular world, as we have said, is not to be left to its destruction — it is to be evangelized. Every disciple is by definition an evangelist. And evangelism will inevitably involve suffering at the hands of the world. Part of the Anabaptist disposition toward biblical literalism accrues from a profound suspicion of culture. To admit the world to the realm of the church, even to the slightest degree, is to run the risk of encumbering the saints with elements of the demonic (thus the modern Amish hostility to such things as cars, telephones, and electricity). Life in the other world, in the kingdom of God, involves the ethics of love, nonresistance, and pacifism, applied to all human relationships. Life within the kingdom of God also involves intense corporate discipline, designed to protect the elite from the encroachments of the world.

THE SPREAD OF ANABAPTISM

ON THE night of January 21, 1525, the Anabaptists of Zurich assembled in the house of Felix Mantz. It had been their custom for some time to meet in conventicles for the study of the Scriptures. On this occasion, however, an episode occurred that marks, as well as any other, the beginning of sectarian Protestantism. The Catholic priest, George Blaurock, who had had sacramental hands laid upon his head at least three times as a Roman Catholic — once in the sacrament of baptism, once in the sacrament of confirmation, and once in the sacrament of holy orders — suddenly demanded to be *rebaptized* as a sign of his newly acquired rebirth. The deed was quickly done by Conrad Grebel as the spiritual leader of the little society. What an episode! It amounted to starting all over again, as if the medieval structures of religion counted for nothing. The very word "Anabaptist" traces to that event, for the word means someone who rebaptizes.

Anabaptism grew through the process of rebaptizing little groups of would-be disciples. At first this was done by sprinkling or pouring water over the heads of recipients. At Easter of 1525, for example, Hubmaier proceeded to rebaptize some three hundred members of his congregation at Waldshut, drawing water from the fountain in the marketplace and administering it from a milking pail. But in February 1525, one zealous soul insisted upon being plunged into the icy waters of the Rhine, and that was the beginning of immersion in the Anabaptist tradition.

The suppression of the Swiss Brethren at the hands of the Zurich magistrates began in 1525. That year, Hubmaier was roughly expelled from Zurich after he had been forced to recant his Anabaptist teachings. On March 6, 1526, the town council passed an edict that anyone who ventured to baptize another would be drowned. That stroke of gruesome irony goes back to the code of Justinian: he who dips shall be dipped. In the following November, the council decreed death to any who attended Anabaptist preaching. Grebel, weary of the hardships he had suffered, fell victim to the plague and died in the summer of 1526. Manz, having been found guilty of the edicts just recounted, was trussed up and unceremoniously dumped into the Limmat River, which courses through the middle of Zurich. The date was January, 5, 1527 — the beginning of Anabaptist martyrdom. Blaurock was scourged through the streets of Zurich and sent on his way to banishment; only the fact that he was not a citizen saved him from execution. The leadership of the Swiss Brethren having all been dispatched, the Anabaptist movement was eradicated from the canton of Zurich by the year 1531.

Elsewhere the movement enjoyed considerable expansion. Beginning in 1525, it proceeded north along the Rhine, into Germany, and established itself in the cities of Augsburg and Strassburg. Hubmaier carried it into

Moravia, where, in the course of time, it became transformed into the Hutterite movement, a fellowship of communistic societies welded together by the Tyrolean Anabaptist Jacob Hutter. Communism in the Anabaptist movement was fairly complex in its motivation. It was based in part upon certain texts of the New Testament (e.g., Acts 2:44), in part upon the contempt of the world, and in part upon the heightened sense of brotherhood that existed in the elite Anabaptist communities. The Anabaptist movement, as it expanded, behaved as all other parties to the Reformation did; that is, it held meetings (synods) and produced statements of belief (confessions). The Schleitheim Confession of 1527, one of the more noteworthy statements of the Anabaptist viewpoint, represented the beliefs of the surviving communities in Switzerland as well as those of southern Germany. The movement actually profited by the debacle of the Peasants' Revolution, which brought profound distrust of the Magisterial Reformation on the part of oppressed peasants and townsfolk and thus induced many to form Anabaptist communities. By virtue of its acceptance of suffering as something indispensable to the Christian experience, the movement was peculiarly adept in absorbing persecution, which it received from all sides, from Lutherans and Catholics alike. It is an interesting fact that Anabaptists were persecuted, not so much on charges of heresy, but rather for sedition, that is, for the threat they posed to the civil order.

One of the more colorful episodes in Anabaptist history was the Münster Rebellion. It is fair to observe, at the outset, that that rebellion was not the work of mainline Anabaptists but rather of a distinctly revolutionary party within the Anabaptist tradition. The episode began when one Melchior Hofmann, who fancied himself a prophet, the new Elijah in fact, prophesied the imminent return of Christ, when the saints (i.e., the Anabaptists) would reign on earth. He designated Strassburg as the city elected by God to be the scene of that great event. Strassburg rewarded Hofmann for his prophecies by consigning him to life imprisonment. Yet Melchior Hofmann had been clever and resourceful enough to set forth his views in writing, so despite his imprisonment, Melchiorite Anabaptism began to spread. It blossomed with new prophets, and its constituency grew strong in northern Germany and in the Netherlands. The thought of this revolutionary tradition had three interesting characteristics. First, the eschatological hope — the hope of the end of the age and the return of Christ — which preoccupied most of the Radical Reformation, was here reconceived in literal, political terms: a revolution was about to occur, and the saints would actually reign. Second, the idea of the church as a gathered community of true disciples drawn out of the world was also reconceived as an actual Christian commonwealth brought into being by revolutionary means. Finally, in contrast to the normal Anabaptist preference for the New Testament as a pattern, the Melchiorites favored the Old Testament for what we may describe as its prophetic fierceness.

In the early 1530s, political affairs in the city of Münster had gone awry, and it seemed ripe for a takeover by the Melchiorites as the New Jerusalem, as the scene of the great revolution. They concluded that Hofmann had simply not gotten the name right: it was not Strassburg, but Münster. Into the city came Jan Mathys and Jan Beukels, both of the Low Countries, both steeped in Melchiorite ways. In 1534 they managed to seize control of the city affairs. Lutherans and Catholics ran for their lives as the prophets threatened to kill all of the "godless" who refused to engage in rebaptism. In a rare show of ecumenism, the Catholic bishop of Münster rallied Lutherans and Catholics alike against the monstrous regiment of Anabaptists. To offset that challenge, the prophets sent out an urgent call to all of the Melchiorites to gather quickly in "the holy city of Münster." On Easter Sunday, 1534, Mathys lost his life on the ramparts. His rule had lasted merely six weeks, in which short time he had managed to remodel the city after Anabaptist principles, including a form of communism. Beukels then established himself as "the king of righteousness over all." He proceeded to appoint twelve elders of the tribes of Israel. The elders published a new code of moral law in which the problem of postbaptismal sins was neatly solved by not allowing any. In that code, the saints of Münster were specifically referred to as the Israelites. Polygamy was introduced after the model of the Old Testament patriarchs. The "king of righteousness" set the example by maintaining a harem. In the course of 1535, however, the continuing siege by Lutherans and Catholics, with its attendant famine, brought the Israelites to their knees. On June 25 the city fell and the saints were slaughtered almost to the last man. King Jan and the elders were cruelly tortured until they expired, whereupon their bodies were suspended from the steeple of St. Lambert's Church.

The Anabaptists in northern Europe reorganized themselves in order to overcome the dreadful reputation of Münster, and in doing so, they returned again to the mainline tradition that commenced in Zurich. The man chiefly responsible for the renaissance of Anabaptism was Menno Simons, a Dutchman born in 1492 and educated for the Catholic priesthood, into which he was ordained in the year 1524. Even in the early years of his priesthood, he entertained certain doubts about the Church of Rome, having been touched first by the attitudes of the major Reformers and later by the teachings of the Anabaptists. After 1531 he was, for all intents and purposes, a nondescript Protestant preacher, although he retained his Roman orders and persisted in doing his priestly duties. But in 1536 he experienced a rebirth and quit the Church of Rome. He then received formal instruction in the tenets of the Anabaptists, probably from one of their leading lights, Obbe Philips, who proceeded to rebaptize him. In 1537, at the hands of this same Obbe, he was ordained a second time as an Anabaptist elder. His importance to the tradition is clear enough. Two years after the Münster debacle, he came to prominence as a leader; he was greatly helped by not being implicated in the Melchiorite fanaticism, and he was firmly committed to the scriptural and pacific type of Anabaptism that had arisen in Zurich. He proceeded from place to place preaching, rebaptizing, and gathering together the disorganized remnants. Menno was also a major theologian of the Anabaptist tradition — not that he said much that was new, but merely that he said it in a systematic way, and in writing. His *Foundation of Christian Doctrine,* written in 1540, was especially important in establishing his authority over the Anabaptist communities in northern Europe. Already in 1545 the saints were being called by his name — *Mennisten,* or "Mennonites."

Such was the disdain for the Anabaptists in the age of the Reformation that only in the nineteenth century was there any serious effort to understand them. Nineteenth-century interpreters typically attempted to explain the Anabaptists as leftovers from the Middle Ages. Some hitched them to the tradition of medieval dissent, which included the Waldenses, the Lollards, and the Hussites. Others assigned them to the monastic tradition of the Middle Ages, especially to such ardent groups as the Spiritual Franciscans or the Brethren of the Common Life. Others attempted to demonstrate the continuity of the Anabaptists with the mystical tradition of the Middle Ages. Contemporary scholarship, however, especially that coming from the Mennonites themselves, eschews the effort to connect the Anabaptist tradition to medieval tendencies. The Anabaptists were indeed radical Protestants, even as the term "Radical Reformation" implies. They were intent upon carrying the principles of the Reformation to their furthest logical conclusion. The actions of the Swiss Brethren in Zurich, in the face of Zwingli's timidity, is cited as a case in point.

21. *Calvin*

THE GREATEST AND MOST SUBTLE MIND OF THE PROTESTANT REFOR-
mation belonged to John Calvin, who was born, educated, and converted in France. Such a great gift by France to the Reformation is hardly
to be ignored or left unacknowledged. Neither is it to be interpreted as a
quirk of history. The nation was then ruled by a renaissance prince, Francis I
(1515–47), a sovereign sufficiently beloved by his people and successful in
war to deserve the epithet "the Great." A man of letters, enchanted by the
culture of the Italians, whom he repeatedly tried to overrun, Francis cultivated French arts, letters, and language and yet at the same time did his
best to Italianize his court and country. For example, he founded the Lecteurs
Royaux (College of Royal Lecturers), a remarkable Renaissance endowment,
to advance the interests of French humanism, while, at almost the same
time, he paid the Italian legal scholar Andrea Alciati twice the stipend
given to him in Milan to come to France and lecture at the University of
Bourges, to inspire the youth of France in Italian ways. The king's sister,
Marguerite, was a conspicuous patron of the French Renaissance. Poet and
philosopher, she read Greek, Latin, and Hebrew and spoke Italian, Spanish,
English, and German. At her court she surrounded herself with poets,
painters, philosophers, and musicians. The intellectual force called John
Calvin entered life as a Frenchman in the midst of such an awakening. His
earliest ambition was certainly not to be like Luther but to be like Guillaume
Budé, the eminence of French humanism.

Luther was already in a Saxon convent, suffering from attacks of
spiritual despair, when Jean Cauvin was born at Noyon, in Picardy, on July

471

102. John Calvin

10, 1509. His birthplace, northeast of Paris, was an old cathedral city, an episcopal seat since 531, a place hallowed by Carolingian and Capetian coronations. The twelfth-century cathedral dominated the landscape, casting shadows of Catholic culture over the town. One of the twelve peers of France, the bishop of Noyon was at once the spiritual leader and secular ruler of the town, as well as the most prominent member of the local aristocracy. Since 1501 the episcopal office had been held by Charles de Hangest — a not unpredictable circumstance, since members of the de Hangest family had held that bishopric for generations. Calvin went off to Paris as a student with three younger members of the de Hangest family, to one of whom, Claude, he dedicated his commentary on Seneca's *De Clementia* in 1532. There he spoke of having been "brought up in your house." Young Calvin attended the Collège de Capettes, a private academy for boys in Noyon, with those aristocratic schoolfellows. Unabashed, persistent, and logical, Calvin also betrayed certain aristocratic manners and prejudices acquired from his childhood associations with the de Hangest family.

His own family had just risen to the petty bourgeoisie through the clever and indefatigable efforts of his ambitious father, Gérard Cauvin, a plebian (as Calvin once said) whose ancestors not so far back had been boatmen on the Oise. In 1481, having acquired some kind of practical legal experience, Gérard won an appointment as registrar of the town. Later he acquired a succession of offices that took either financial or legal experience, including secretary to the bishop and attorney to the cathedral chapter. In 1497 he was admitted to the petty bourgeoisie and became a citizen. It must have been just at that time, or shortly after, that Gerard married Jeanne LeFranc, also of the petty bourgeoisie, a beautiful and devout woman who died when Calvin was no more than three; he remembered only that she took him to the shrines of the neighborhood, including a relic of St. Ann, which, as a mere wisp of a child, he kissed. To this family, which lived in the center of town near the granary, came five sons, two of whom died in their youth. Jean was the fourth. Charles became a priest but died excommunicate in 1537. Antoine assisted Calvin in Geneva.

CALVIN'S EDUCATION AND EARLY THOUGHT

TWO MONTHS before he reached the "regular" (i.e., canonical) age of twelve, Calvin was appointed chaplain to the altar of La Gésine in Noyon Cathedral — a nominal office, whose functions were performed by clerics paid to do so. Such a benefice, negotiated by his father, afforded young Calvin a modest income to defray his educational expenses, paid in this instance by local farmers in the form of a grain tax. In 1527, for the same purpose, he attained the curacy of St. Martin-de-Martheville, which he later exchanged for that of Pont l'Evêque, the town in which the Cauvins had arisen. In the meantime, in 1523, decently endowed by such benefices, Jean Cauvin (Latinized to Joannes Calvinus, from which we have "Calvin"), age fourteen, had been registered in one of the colleges of the University of Paris. He was dispatched to Paris in the company of three younger members of the de Hangest family, schoolfellows from the Collège des Capettes in Noyon, although his circumstances were not as affluent as theirs. At first he lodged with one of his uncles, Richard, a Parisian blacksmith. Soon, however, he was admitted to the Collège de la Marche, an excellent college of letters and liberal arts, where he was taught by an illustrious pedagogue, a priest of Rouen named Mathurin Cordier. Although Calvin had access to Cordier only a little while — three months at most — the learning he obtained was decisive. Cordier, an excellent Latinist and an elegant writer in French, established Calvin's prose style for life, equipping him in both languages and giving him his first good taste of French humanism. Calvin dedicated his commentary on 1 Thessalonians to Cordier as a means of expressing the debt he owed to Cordier's instruction.

Admonished, no doubt, by the church establishment at Noyon, which supported him, to get more seriously interested in the priesthood, Calvin shortly transferred to Collège de Montaigu — as austere, orthodox, Scholastic, and intimidating as any institution of which Catholic France could boast. Erasmus, who had endured Montaigu as a student, complained (as students do) of its stale eggs, but equally of its stale divinity. Rabelais, who also attended Montaigu, denounced its inhumanity and advocated burning it down. However disagreeable Collège de Montaigu may have been, it was yet a respectable, even celebrated, seat of conservative Catholic learning. Its former principal had been John Standonck (1483–1504), a member of the Brethren of the Common Life, who believed that the discipline of the cloister was also proper to schools and who gave Montaigu its conspicuous severity and asceticism. A reformer of sorts, Standonck had no interest whatsoever in the French Renaissance, not to mention the revival of the classics or the new philosophy of humanism. His efforts to reform the Catholic church ran in the direction of strict Catholic orthodoxy, reinforced by rigorous asceticism and a deep, somewhat subtle educational system, sweetened by particular attention to the Catholic mystical tradition.

On Standonck's death in 1504, the direction of Montaigu passed to his protégé, Noël Béda, persecutor of Christian humanists, whose mind was sincerely narrow, whose soul burned with sincere zeal to regenerate Holy Mother Church through a Standonckian program of orthodoxy and asceticism. He once declared Greek to be "the language of all heresies." Béda presided over a school of 525 students, some of whom were said to "perish with despair" over the severity of life at Montaigu, and all of whom were the butt of endless guffaws from the up-and-coming young humanists of Paris. In 1514 Béda was relieved of his duties at Montaigu to devote himself single-mindedly to the harassment of Christian humanists. A suitably ferocious replacement was found in the person of Pierre Tempête (whom Rabelais satirized as *horrida tempestas*), under whose regime young Calvin endured at Montaigu.

The experience at Montaigu, however, was not without profit to Calvin. Where else did his knowledge of Augustine and the fathers, so striking in his early publications, come from, except the classrooms of Collège de Montaigu? Of particular usefulness to Calvin may have been John Major (Mair), an Ockhamist of reputation, who rejoined the faculty soon after Calvin's own arrival. A commentator of the *Sentences* of Peter Lombard, Major may have educated Calvin in the very grist of decent Catholic theological thinking, to say nothing of the nominalist method and of the Ockhamist tradition. During Calvin's term in Paris, Major prepared a commentary on the four gospels (it was published in 1529), defending Catholic thought and practice against the criticisms of detractors — Wycliffe, Hus, and Luther. Calvin's first exposure to Luther may have occurred in the classroom of John Major.

The myth that young Calvin was called "the accusative case" has long been exploded; there is no evidence at all that the fourteen-year-old freshman was either morose or austere. On the contrary, he had many friends who were decisive for his intellectual formation. Humanists all, they offset the severe Catholicism of Montaigu. Heirs of French conciliarism of the preceding century, of Pierre d'Ailly and Jean Gerson, who longed for genuine reform within the church, heirs of the Italian Renaissance and of northern humanism, the French humanists trusted in the integrity of scholarship to cut through the tangle of medieval doctrine and religious lore and reestablish the Catholic Church on a scriptural and patristic footing.

One of Calvin's earliest acquaintances in Paris was an erudite cousin, Pierre Robert Olivier, better known as Olivétan, whom he had known also at Noyon. Already taken by Lutheran opinions, Olivétan was intellectually indebted both to ancient authors, classical and Christian, and to such modern writers as Rabelais.

Still another Picard in Paris was Fourcy de Cambrai, rector of the university (1510), who introduced Calvin to his circle of friends. By such means Calvin was received in the houses of two of the greatest figures of the University of Paris — Guillaume Cop and Guillaume Budé — whose credentials as humanists probably surpassed those of any others in France. Cop, who had come from Basel, was a medical scholar, professor of medicine at the university, and attended the king. He had three sons with whom Calvin was on especially close terms. In Cop's household, where Calvin was always welcome, the eminent figure of French humanism was also frequently a guest — Guillaume Budé, the most learned Hellenist in France. To be a Lutheran had scarcely entered Calvin's mind. To be a Budéan — that was an idea worthy of consideration.

Meanwhile the Latin works of Martin Luther had begun to be published in France by the printer Simon du Bois; they were promptly condemned by the Sorbonne (April 5, 1521), which, by that time, had been given surveillance over printed matter. No one did more to make Luther appealing to the intellectual community in Paris than a nobleman from Picardy, Louis de Berquin. The very month that Calvin entered the university, de Berquin had been given royal reprieve from a sentence of death for trafficking in Lutheran ideas. (Very likely de Berquin had translated something of Luther's.) The Sorbonne had accused him before Parlement, his papers had been confiscated, and he had been locked up, awaiting execution.

Elated by the deliverance of de Berquin, students of the university (including perhaps freshman Calvin) celebrated the occasion by staging a morality play, *La farce des théologastres,* in which both the Sorbonne and Montaigu were sorely ridiculed, while Luther, Erasmus, and Lefèvre were held up for approval. One of the six characters of the play was "Le Mercure d'Allemagne." The messenger from Germany was none other than de Berquin, harbinger of Lutheran ideas in Paris. Like a cat with nine lives, de Berquin managed to survive repeated confiscations of his books and papers (1523, 1526), thanks chiefly to the intervention of Marguerite, the king's sister. In the end, however, he met his death in the flames (April 1529).

The tensions in Paris, of which the de Berquin incident was typical, came partially from royal absolutism, which held the church under tight subservience and rendered it innocuous. France was a monarchy, in which a succession of Capetian and Valois kings had gradually increased the royal prerogative. Neither Parliament nor the church could claim much independence. By the Concordat of Bologna (1516), Francis I had forced Pope Leo X to yield over to the Crown the appointment of bishops and abbots and to surrender some of the gains made by the church nearly a century earlier in the Pragmatic Sanction of Bourges (1438). Francis presided over a vast system of patronage and power that left the church considerably demoralized and often neglectful of its proper discipline and duties. In other instances, however, it bred repression such as that exercised by the Sorbonne.

From such circumstances came a fresh movement of religious reform. It originated from yet another remarkable Picard, Jacques Lefèvre of Étaples (Faber Stapulensis), discussed above in chapter 15. A Christian humanist, Lefèvre used his knowledge of languages and his considerable interpretative skills to present the Bible as an expression of reform. He thought that a new age was about to overtake Western society, based on a return to ancient sources, the Bible and the fathers, and to ancient civilization, classical and Christian. His Latin translation of the Pauline epistles (1512), which followed by three years his work on the Psalms, had many refreshing characteristics and, in some instances, revolutionary ones. Having been a student in Italy and indebted especially to Pico della Mirandola, Lefèvre represented one of the more tangible links between the Renaissance humanism of Italy and the Christian humanism of the north.

In Paris, Lefèvre lived at the abbey of St. Germain-des-Prés on the left bank of the Seine. The abbot of that convent, Guillaume Briçonnet, had become a staunch advocate of the Fabian principles (i.e., those of Lefèvre). When he became bishop of Meaux (just beyond Paris) in 1516, he invited a number of learned men from the University of Paris to join him there, to assist him in a program of diocesan reform. Lefèvre, who was already being heckled by Noël Béda, was among them. The others were his colleagues and kindred spirits — William Farel, Gérard Roussel, and the Hebraist François Vatable. Lefèvre, humanist that he was, cherished peace and eschewed controversy almost excessively. Goaded, however, by Farel, a fiery little red-bearded rascal, Briçonnet moved boldly to reform the diocese. In March 1523, in the year of Calvin's arrival in Paris, repression first struck the reformers of Meaux.

Briçonnet, however, was not without influence in high places. He had been confessor to the king's sister, Marguerite, a thoroughgoing humanist who quite admired her confessor and his doings at Meaux. Her *Dialogue en forme de vision nocturne,* written the following year (1524), was eloquent of progressive religious ideas as conceived by a Catholic humanist.

In 1528 Calvin, at eighteen, took the master of arts degree. At that point his father authorized him to make an abrupt change of course: he would give up philosophical studies preparatory to the priesthood and undertake a career in law. Calvin attributed this change of strategy to Gérard Cauvin's belief that the law offered a more lucrative career. Behind it, however, lay Gérard's difficulties with the canons of the cathedral in Noyon. In the course of settling an estate of benefit to the church, Gérard Cauvin either could not or would not make a full disclosure of the accounts, in recompense for which he was finally excommunicated. In the face of such difficulties, the benefices used to support young Calvin in his education seemed likely to dissolve.

At nineteen, therefore, Calvin struck out for the University of Orléans, where the science of jurisprudence was the intellectual speciality. The faculty of law consisted of eight professors, of whom the most celebrated was Pierre Taison de l'Estoile, the keenest legal mind in France. A devout man and a conservative interpreter, l'Estoile formed Calvin's legal intelligence for all time. Calvin wrote appreciatively of his "penetrating mind, his skill, his experience in the law."

Once again Calvin surrounded himself with young humanists — Nicholas Duchemin, for example, with whom he boarded for a while, and François Daniel, who could conceivably have introduced him to Rabelais. Already taxed by the rigors of law school, Calvin put his health at risk by undertaking the study of Greek, probably at Orléans. His teacher was Melchior Wolmar, a young German-born, Swiss-trained scholar who had learned Greek at the University of Paris and would have continued to teach there had not his Lutheran sympathies brought him into disrepute. He was appointed to the faculty at Orléans in 1527. Calvin dedicated his commentary of 2 Corinthians to Wolmar, acknowledging his debt to Wolmar, not as a Lutheran, but as his instructor in Greek.

On Monday, April 29, 1529, Andrea Alciati gave his first lecture at the University of Bourges, where he was to remain for the next five years. The French legal establishment, including its law students, were titillated. Calvin, Wolmar, and Duchemin all joined the general migration of students and scholars to Bourges to bask in the eminence of the greatest Italian legal celebrity. Milanese by birth (1492) and early training, Alciati had been instructed in jurisprudence at Pavia and Bologna and had taught law in Italian and French universities. A humanist with excellent literary credentials, he had attained an even greater reputation as an interpreter of Roman law. At the University of Bourges, founded in 1463 by Louis XI as a center for the study of Roman law, Alciati was given a professorship in that subject.

Roman law, which held the state to be real, supreme, immutable, permanent, and objective, was far more in accord with French royal absolutism than the Augustinian, papal, and Germanic legal strands that made up medieval political theory. By expounding the *Code* and *Pandects* of Justinian, in which he was expert, Alciati offered an alternative to conventional jurisprudence.

In the main, however, Calvin was greatly put off by Alciati. The large crowd of students whom Alciati had drawn to Bourges soon began to grumble at his turgid commentary, delivered in medieval Latin — a ploy, no doubt, to prepare the students for the introduction of a new, humanistic method. So, when the students protested, Alciati shifted to a more elegant, although superficial, sometimes comic, often irreverent discourse, radical in its advocacy of Roman law and contemptuous of French jurisprudence. Alciati was too much for Calvin — too vain, too pompous, too fond of wine and victuals. When Alciati poked fun as their sainted l'Estoile, Calvin's group reacted with a printed defense of their teacher, *Antapologia* (1531), written by Duchemin with a preface by Calvin.

Calvin left Bourges in haste to attend his dying father, who expired excommunicate on May 26, 1531. The death of his father released Calvin from parental obligation and set him free to pursue his own purposes. He went straightway to Paris, intending to devote himself to humanistic studies, and enrolled in the College of Royal Lecturers, which Francis I had founded the previous year. What a triumph for French humanism the new college was! What a personal achievement for Budé, who had used the preface of his monumental *Commentaries on the Greek Language* to beg the sovereign for such an establishment! Completely independent of the University of Paris, based on a precedent set at Louvain a few years earlier, the college offered instruction in Latin, Greek, and Hebrew. Consisting simply of professorial chairs, the college had no building, suffered no curriculum, grades, or tuition, and afforded its lecturers freedom in research and teaching. During the summer and autumn of 1531, Calvin subscribed to Greek courses given by Pierre Danès and may have begun the study of Hebrew under instruction by François Vatable.

On April 4, 1532, there appeared on the bookstalls of Paris Calvin's *Commentary on Lucius Anneas Seneca's Two Books on Clemency.* Calvin had paid for the publication himself. It was a work of pure humanism, intended to illustrate the young scholar's humanistic credentials to the Paris intelligentsia — despite the fact that he had just taken pains to complete his doctorate in jurisprudence at the University of Orléans. Seneca, an important Roman

Stoic — Calvin placed him "next after Cicero" — had written on clemency, hoping to mitigate the distemper of the emperor Nero. Calvin's interest in Seneca was related to the general revival of Stoicism in the Renaissance, beginning with Francesco Petrarca in the fourteenth century. He attempted exactly what Petrarca had attempted earlier — to bring Stoicism into some sort of relationship with Christianity. Calvin referred to "our Seneca" and "our religion." Erasmus had twice published the works of Seneca, but he was dissatisfied with his work and invited others to improve on it. With overweening self-confidence, young Calvin eagerly took up Erasmus's challenge, declaring that he had discovered things in Seneca that had gone completely unnoticed by Erasmus. It did not sit well with the Erasmian crowd.

Written in chaste, yet sophisticated Latin, Calvin's Seneca commentary drew prodigiously on Greek and Roman sources, on the fathers of the church (Augustine is cited fifteen times), and on humanists of the fifteenth and sixteenth centuries, including Valla, Erasmus, and Budé. There are only three citations to Holy Writ, and very inconsequential ones at that. The suggestion that Calvin was writing out of Protestant sympathies is preposterous.

Why *did* Calvin write the Seneca commentary? A work of political ethics, Calvin's Seneca commentary addressed (whether it was specifically designed to or not) the statecraft of Machiavelli, whose *Prince* (and other writings of a political nature) must certainly have come to the attention of a young man who prided himself on being both a lawyer and a humanist. It is true that Calvin interpreted *princeps legibus solutus est* to mean that the prince is above the law, as the Roman jurists did, as Alciati and Budé also did, maintaining that the prince is himself *lex animata,* the living law. Against the statecraft of Machiavelli, however, Calvin interposed, as Seneca and the Stoics had done before him, the crucial qualifications of justice and equity. The difference between a king and a tyrant is that the king acquires his realm legitimately and promotes the public good, being responsible to the moral world order, while the tyrant rules without the consent of the governed or abuses his power in some other way.

CONVERSION TO PROTESTANTISM

SOME time before May 21, 1534, Calvin became an evangelical Christian by means of a sudden conversion. In the preface to his commentary on the

Psalms written in 1557 — and therefore long after the fact — he explained that having been "stubbornly addicted to the superstitions of the papacy," God had made his heart teachable, presumably by the Bible, and although not yet fully Protestant or willing to forsake his literary studies, he "burned with great zeal to go forward." The words "stubbornly addicted" suggest that Calvin had indeed been exposed to Lutheran opinions but had "stubbornly" rejected them. Olivétan and Wolmar may have tried to persuade him of the legitimacy of Lutheran teachings. Louis de Berquin had only recently been burned at the stake (April 17, 1529) — a martyr to Lutheran ideas. While he wrote the Seneca commentary, Calvin lived with Étienne de la Forge, a robust cloth merchant and devout Waldensian, who made no effort at all to hide his advocacy of Lutheran principles.

In *Reply to Sadoleto* (1539), Calvin put an interesting interpretation on his conversion. A new breed of theologian, he said, had arisen in his time, reformers who had no desire "to turn away from the profession of Christianity, but to reduce it to its own source and to restore it, as it were, cleansed from all filthiness to its own purity." So, as late as 1539, Calvin still used the language of Renaissance humanism to describe the Protestant Reformation. Nevertheless (as he goes on to say) he was at first offended by such novelty and, due chiefly to his "reverence for the church," valiantly resisted it.

The year 1533 opened as a good one for the partisans of reform. The Fabians enjoyed the good humor of the French Crown. At the pleasure of the king's sister, evangelical sermons were delivered in the Louvre. Christian humanism, after being sorely threatened in the era 1525–26, appeared to have resumed its ascendancy; Calvin may have considered the possibility of passing his life in Paris as a liberal Catholic scholar in the tradition of Lefèvre and Budé. Suddenly, however, a crisis occurred. The Sorbonne saw fit to condemn Marguerite's *Mirror of a Sinful Soul.* On All Saints' Day, 1533, when the new rector of the university, Nicholas Cop, arose to give the customary rectorial address to the faculty, he took the occasion to denounce the Sorbonne and to laud the partisans of reform, basing his testy discourse on the beatitude "Blessed are the poor in spirit." The exegesis of Matthew 5:3 that Cop used was heavily indebted to a sermon by Luther (1522) that Martin Bucer of Strassburg had translated into Latin in 1525; it rang with the sounds of free grace and with the dialectic between law and gospel. The opening of the address, in which the oppressors of evangelical religion were laid low, bears a resemblance to the *Paraclesis* of Erasmus found in the preface to the third edition of his New Testament.

No one now believes that Cop's address was written by Calvin, although Cop was his close friend and although part of the draft exists in Calvin's hand. Neither is there any reason to suppose that Calvin was out of sympathy with Cop's oration. It probably was a fair representation of his own opinions in the autumn of 1533.

Cop's rebuke of the Sorbonne did not sit well with the French Establishment. The Sorbonne and the Parliament began proceedings of heresy against the upstarts Cop and Calvin, and in December the king ordered "Lutherans" expunged from the French body politic. By that time Cop had fled to Basel. Calvin, whose crime was complicity with the rector, temporarily left Paris as well. By early 1554 he had returned, but then moved to the home of his friend, Louis du Tillet, canon of the cathedral at Angoulême and curé at Claix — a liberal priest of Lefèvre's persuasion who gave him shelter and put a library of perhaps four thousand volumes at his disposal.

Since 1527 Marguerite had maintained her court at Nérac as queen of Navarre. There she protected Jacques Lefèvre, who had been defeated at Meaux and was now in the extremity of his very long life. Sometime in the spring of 1534, Calvin went to Nérac specifically to see Lefèvre, seeking some sort of clarification from the old man of what his own life should be. We do not know what words passed between the ancient sage and the troubled young man. We do know, however, that Calvin set out for Noyon, clear across France, and having got there resigned his benefices on May 21, 1534.

John Calvin thus became a Protestant in 1533 or 1534. If, at the same time, he rejected some of the assumptions of French humanism — the freedom and autonomy of human beings, for example, their rationality and power — he did not repudiate all things humanistic. He did not repudiate the historical perspective of humanism, for example, or its reverence for the sources or its respect for education and languages as means of entering the sources. It was Calvin who labeled the Genevan liturgy "according to the custom of the ancient church," as if to underscore where he thought the historical basis of Western Christian society lay. It was Calvin who warned that one should not "follow the philosophers further than is profitable" (*Institutes* 2.2.4) — which is to say, one may agreeably follow in the way of the humanists until the humanists presume to teach us about the nature of humankind or the way to God. Furthermore, Calvin never quite managed to resign from the classic pose of the French humanist, namely, to be a scholar. The book-lined study was his lifelong temptation. Peace, tranquility, seclusion, and scholarship were the virtues of the Christian humanist. Calvin discovered them to be the refuges in which God persistently found him and called him out.

Released from Noyon, Calvin traversed the nation, gathering the first French Protestants. In Paris, as the guest of Étienne de la Forge, he met craftsmen, military officers, professors, students, and members of the nobility — earnest inquirers each one. At Poitiers and Angoulême, he may even have attempted to organize congregations; at least at Poitiers he celebrated the Eucharist without canonical orders. (Calvin was not ordained.) At Orléans he completed *Psychopannychia* (1534), a curious work in which he disabused some Anabaptists of the notion that the souls of the dead go to sleep at death and remain so until the Last Judgment.

Calvin's peripatetic career was brought abruptly to a close by an incident of October 18, 1534. Placards were attached that night to the doors of public and private buildings, both in Paris and elsewhere in France, defaming the Roman Mass. The authorities reacted with unexpected fury against all manner of "Lutherans" who might have been responsible for the affair of the placards. With du Tillet, Calvin beat a hasty retreat, going first to Metz, then to Strassburg, finally to Basel, the city of Erasmus, an important center of European printing. There, to escape detection, he lived under the assumed name of Martianus Lucanius (the latter an anagram for Calvinus).

The preface of the first edition of Calvin's *Christianae religionis institutio* (Institutes of the Christian religion) is dated August 23, 1535. That means that between the affair of the placards (October 1534) and the end of summer in the following year Calvin had conceived of, and written, one of the monumental works in the history of theology. To be sure, the first *Institutes* was a small work (relative to the 1559 edition) in six chapters, one each devoted to the law, the creed, the Lord's Prayer, the sacraments, the miscalled sacraments, and Christian liberty. In an introduction addressed to Francis I of France, "John Calvin of Noyon, Author," explained the purpose of the book eloquently and respectfully to the sovereign. It was twofold: to vindicate the Protestants in France who were even then being imprisoned, tortured, and burned by "cruel persecutors"; and to afford French Protestants a catechism, a book of religious instruction responsible to the word of God.

In the course of two years at the most, Calvin had thus managed somehow to advance from sophistication in French humanism to sophistication in Protestant intellectualism. Scarcely more than a neophyte himself, Calvin exhibited a certain familiarity with the Protestant Reformers, some competence in the ancient fathers, and enough learning in the medieval doctors to be their critic. The book was immediately popular, and the first supply from the printer, Thomas Platter, was soon exhausted. A second, enlarged edition appeared in Strassburg in 1538; the first French edition, in 1541. The third Latin edition was published in 1543 and four times reprinted. The definitive edition, greatly enlarged, came in 1559. All editions after the first were specifically designated for "the preparation of candidates in theology." The French edition, *Institution de la religion chrétienne,* although burned at Notre Dame in February 1544, contributed handsomely to the French literary tradition.

CALVINISM AND LUTHERANISM COMPARED

THE Calvin of the 1536 *Institutes* may not have been the Calvin for all time. This may be the appropriate place, nevertheless, to ask whether Calvin was a "Lutheran," as so many of his early detractors insisted. Of course he was. He admitted as much in *The Necessity of Reforming the Church* (1543), where he wrote, "God raised up Luther and others who held forth a torch to light us into the way of salvation and on whose ministry our churches are founded." On the crucial question of whose righteousness makes us just in God's sight — Christ's or ours or a little of both — the two great Reformers spoke with one voice: Christ's alone. Both Reformers, in other words, were ardent advocates of the doctrine of justification by faith alone, which Calvin called, in the 1559 *Institutes,* "the main hinge on which religion turns" (3.11.1). Both subscribed (inescapably) to a doctrine of predestination that, in Calvin, became a formal doctrine of great prominence and power.

We can also say that of course Calvin was *not* a Lutheran. The Reformed tradition, of which Zwingli, Bucer, and, above all, Calvin were the primary teachers, had characteristics of its own, which distinguish it from the Lutheran churches.

We begin to detect differences between the two Reformers as we examine what each teaches about how the Christian life evolves. Luther and Calvin agree that the law of God is extremely important in its accusatory role. The law convinces us that it is utterly hopeless for us human beings to attempt to earn righteousness for ourselves. The law therefore makes us acutely aware of our depravity and helplessness, and as a schoolmaster, it directs us to Christ. Such is the usual way Christian life begins.

Luther and Calvin also agree that we are justified by faith alone —

that is, forgiven, put right with God, and taken into God's care, only through faith in Christ, in the manner fully described above in chapter 17.

At that crucial juncture, however, the thought of the two major Reformers diverges. As we have seen, Luther's thought moves from forgiveness (i.e., from "justification by faith") to freedom, and from freedom to a life of spontaneous love *(quellende Liebe),* expended for the good of one's neighbor, either in the course of one's worldly vocation or, more particularly, in the priesthood of all believers. In Luther, the accent falls emphatically on such terms as "freedom" and "spontaneity," "relief" and "consolation." Luther would not allow the law of God to be used as the basis of Christian ethics or as the structure and goad for Christian living because he was convinced that such a use of the law (1) would then blunt the emphasis on freedom and spontaneity and (2) might lead back again to all of the wrongheaded notions about works-righteousness.

Calvin's teaching is altogether different. For Calvin, forgiveness (i.e., "justification by faith") leads not to freedom but to an intense, heroic life of fulfilling the will of God as stated in his law. The *rigor* of the law (i.e., the demand of the law that we obey it completely) may have been discharged by Christ, but the *claim* of the law survives. In other words, the law of God is nobly and properly used as a pattern and stimulus for Christian life and as a basis for Christian ethics.

Such is the *tertius usus* (third use) of the law in Calvinism. The first role of the law is accusing us and directing us to Christ. The second role is the usefulness of the law when applied to civil society. The third and principal use of the law, however, is for Christians — it is a structure and goad for Christian living, following the experience of justification by faith.

For Luther, grace brings consolation and comfort — the joy of being forgiven and the trust in God's unfailing mercy. For Calvin, though, grace brings demand — the obligation to live in great holiness of life according to the law of God. In Calvinism, therefore, the idea of sanctification comes to loom as large as the still-critical doctrine of justification by faith alone. For Calvin, justification and sanctification were collateral doctrines; he would not suffer them to be separated. Calvinism is religion *soli Deo gloria,* "to the glory of God alone." It is a life of intense, heroic holiness, shaped according to the law of God and stimulated by the important ideas of discipline and obedience.

The *Institutes* of 1536 had not yet been offered to the public by the printer when their somewhat sinister author disappeared from Basel as Martianus Lucanius and reappeared in Ferrara alias Charles d'Esperville. He had gone to Italy to consult Princess Renée (1510–75), daughter of Louis XII of France. Renée was a cousin of the king's sister Marguerite and an early partisan of Lefèvre's; at the moment she was living unhappily as duchess of Ferrara. Her husband, the duke, was Ercole II d'Este, son of Lucrezia Borgia, and enough of a conventional Catholic to resent his wife's efforts to turn the court of Ferrara into a refugee camp for displaced evangelicals from France. Calvin spent April and May with Renée, hoping perhaps that Ferrara could become the center for Italian Protestantism. Evidently the idea got a bad reception, and Calvin beat a hasty retreat over the Alps under the twin threats of the Inquisition and Ercole's repression.

FIRST STAY IN GENEVA

TAKING advantage of a temporary amnesty granted by Francis I to religious exiles, Calvin returned to Paris, where, with a brother and sister, he settled the estate left to them at Noyon. From Paris, he intended to go directly to Strassburg, which seemed a likely place to find a scholar's retreat. (He had now had quite enough of the reforming business.) But the Paris-to-Strassburg highway was closed on account of troop movements — Francis I and Charles V being again at war — and he had to go the long way around, by way of Geneva, where he stayed overnight. There he was discovered in a hotel by his old friend du Tillet. Later, a knock came on the door of Calvin's chamber, and there was William Farel (1489–1565), the fierce, diminutive evangelist and Reformer of that city, who, after almost superhuman efforts, had finally managed to get the place Protestantized. Still it had little enough that could be called Protestant — no creed, no school system, no ecclesiastical organization to speak of, and no parochial structure. The city newly redeemed from Roman Catholicism teetered on the verge of demoralization, and suddenly there was Calvin! Farel was certain that God had arranged it. Calvin recalled, "Burning as he was with a marvelous zeal to promote the Gospel, Farel instantly put forth all of his efforts to detain me." Calvin, however, failed to see the point; hemming and hawing, he recited for the first time what was to become a standard list of excuses — his youth, his dyspepsia, his failures as a reformer, his true vocation as a scholar.

Farel, who knew how to use his flaming red beard to good advantage, pronounced divine wrath over this reluctant Calvin: "If you refuse, God will unquestionably condemn you." Calvin capitulated, although he never ceased to detest his reformatory labors. "This I can honestly testify: not a day passed in which I did not long for death ten times." He received the menial title "reader in Holy Scripture" from the magistrates of Geneva. When Farel tried to get him a small stipend, the Little Council refused; the secretary even failed to catch his name, referring to him in the minutes as "that Frenchman."

"When I first came [to Geneva]," wrote Calvin at the end of his life, "there was almost nothing there. They preached and that was all." We must take care, however, not to diminish the accomplishments of William Farel. Uncomplicated, unsophisticated, but full of zeal and a provocative preacher, Farel had been one of Lefèvre's more vociferous followers. After 1523, when he first fled from France, Farel associated himself with the Swiss Reformation, particularly that of Bern. He introduced Neuchâtel to the Reformation and finally entered Geneva on October 4, 1532, and staked out the ground for the work Calvin was yet to do. His liturgical handbook, written at Montbéliard in 1525, was excessively didactic and plain; it may indirectly reveal the nature and scope of Calvin's challenge in Geneva.

For a century and a half, the city of Geneva had struggled to attain autonomy in political affairs by gradually casting off the control of the Catholic bishop, while rebuffing the political encroachments of Savoy. In 1527 the prince bishop of Geneva, Pierre de la Baume, fled in a cloud of disfavor; eventually (1534), the Genevans declared the episcopal office vacant. In 1528 the patriots expelled the *vice dominus* who represented the political interests of Savoy, preferring instead an alliance with Bern (which survived) and with Fribourg (which did not). The bishop, aided by Savoy, persisted in trying to subdue the patriots of Geneva until Bern finally intervened in January 1536 and would have assumed political control of the city had not the Genevans resisted. Even if it could not control the city, Bern would continue to claim influence over Geneva's political and religious affairs. By the time Farel began his work in Geneva, the role of the bishop had been assumed by the magistrates. Protestant worship started in the home of one of the patriots, Jean Beaudichon, until Farel managed to secure the use of a Franciscan chapel (March 1, 1534). After two disputations (winter 1534 and spring 1535), at which the Catholics made a poor showing, the crowds swept Farel into the cathedral of St. Pierre (August 8, 1535) — he had already attained access to the two other principal churches of Geneva, the Madeleine and St. Gervais — where he preached with great emotion, provoking some iconoclasm and, very shortly (August 10), the end of the Roman Mass. Farel introduced the Protestant forms of worship he had written at Montbéliard. Repressive sumptuary laws and regulations governing church attendance followed in February 1536.

The city was governed by a succession of four councils. The Little Council took care of the day-to-day administration of the city. It drew its immediate authority from the Council of Sixty, a more substantial authority from the Council of the Two Hundred, and ultimate authority from the General Council, which consisted of all citizens. When the city decided to accept the Reformation in May 1536, a preliminary determination to do so was first made by the Little Council; that decision was then referred by the Two Hundred to the General Council and ratified by that communal body in the cathedral of St. Pierre on the twenty-first of the month.

In January 1537 Calvin and Farel submitted a proposal to the magistrates entitled "Articles concerning the Organization of the Church and of Worship at Geneva." This plan for the edification of Geneva, which purported to be "as nearly as possible" in conformity with Scripture, was conceived around two foci: the weekly celebration of the Eucharist and, inseparable from it, parish discipline, including the act of excommunication. We may think to ourselves, What a curious way to edify anyone! In fact, however, the "Articles" takes us very close to the crux of Calvinism.

The proposal begins with an argument for Holy Communion "every Sunday, at least as a rule." Calvin's insistence on a weekly Eucharist is finally theological and is expressed in this key sentence: "Then we are really made participants of the body and blood of Jesus, of his death, of his life, of his Spirit, and of all his benefits." Calvin thus appears to say that the Holy Communion increases our participation in Christ, on the basis of which we are justified — forgiven, set right with God. The idea that Christians are actually joined to Christ in a spiritual union forged by faith exists in the thought of both Luther and Calvin but is more prominent in Calvin, who describes it as "the mystical union" (*Institutes* 3.11.10; see also 3.1). Therefore Calvin took the opportunity afforded him by these "Articles" to repudiate two other current conceptions of the Mass — the Zwinglian idea of commemoration and the Roman Catholic idea of sacrifice — neither of which was capable of expressing the idea of the mystical union between Christ and the believer that Calvin took to be the raison d'être of the sacrament. Considering the "frailty" of the people, however, Calvin and Farel conceded that for the time being the Holy Communion might be celebrated only once a month in the three principal churches, yet on a staggered schedule, allowing the city at large to have access to the sacrament more often.

Directly connected with the weekly celebration of the Holy Communion was parish discipline — a highly organized, seriously intended system of moral and spiritual rectitude. What could possibly be the connection between discipline and the sacrament of Holy Communion? Those who took the discipline lightly or disobeyed it altogether were to be excommunicated in the most literal sense of that word — prevented from taking Holy Communion. They would be unable to experience, at least in this sacramental reference, their communion with Christ and would therefore be unable to identify themselves any longer as members of the church. In short, failure to keep parish discipline meant that one's whole sense of churchmanship and participation in Christ would be lost, since one would be prevented from attending the sacrament of Holy Communion.

We must not fail to see that Calvinism, which directs the individual to a life of intense holiness, incited by and structured according to the law of God, falls easily into the pattern of parish discipline as a means of reinforcing that conception of the Christian life. Calvin referred to discipline as the ligaments of the church (*Institutes* 4.12.1). In the "Articles" of 1537, he and Farel insisted that without a system of discipline, and specifically without the God-given right of the church to correct people up to and including excommunication, "a church cannot retain its true condition."

To manage the disciplinary system, Calvin now proposed to "elect and ordain" a corps of lay elders, selecting the most responsible, upright laymen, who would represent all quarters of the city, charging them to administer what he later called "fraternal corrections," up to and including excommunication. In this manner, discipline, the Holy Communion, the law of God, and the idea of sanctification were fitted together to form the basis of the Calvinist experience. What a marvelous antipathy exists between the sacrament that draws us into communion with Christ and a church-managed system of discipline that denies that very participation to those who are manifestly disrespectful of it according to the manner of their lives.

The Genevan magistrates accepted these "Articles," but with serious reservations. Holy Communion was allowed only four times a year, and the specifications for discipline remained unsettled — a point of contention between magistrates and pastors for years to come. The magistrates assumed that the regulation of public morals was an affair of state, as it had been for generations, and they were particularly wary about vesting the right of excommunication in the hands of clerics, knowing how heavy handed church-controlled discipline had been in the past. The pastors were just as convinced that without disciplinary powers, including excommunication, they could not maintain the church in its integrity. Finally, on January 4, 1538, the government denied the pastors the right to excommunicate anybody, bringing the issue between the two parties into utmost tension.

Meanwhile Calvin and Farel labored to get a confession of faith approved by the people of Geneva, as if it were both a sacred and a civic obligation to witness to such an instrument. In 1537 Calvin published *Instruction in Faith*, a summary of the *Institutes* made useful for layfolk. Alongside it went a "Confession of Faith," written perhaps by Farel, and offered to the government on November 10, 1536; it was promptly tabled. The "Confession" declared — indeed "protested" — that in Geneva, religion would be arranged according to "Scripture alone . . . without mixing it with any other thing which might be devised by the opinion of men." Among the twenty-one articles was one devoted to excommunication — "a thing holy and salutary among the faithful." Calvin intended to make submission to this "Confession" a test of citizenship. In the spring of 1537, starting with the magistrates, who were the first signatories, various strategies were tried to get the people to subscribe. Such attempts, however, seemed only to stiffen the resistance of the Catholic party. Meanwhile the free spirits of the town, including some of the Reformed, bridled under the Calvinist discipline. The disapproving named their dogs "Calvin" and poked fun at the pastors in outrageous ways. In the elections of February 1538, the parties in opposition to the new religious regime were swept into power.

The issues of discipline and creedal conformity were made still more vexing by theological disputes. Dutch Anabaptists arrived in Geneva in March 1537 and troubled the waters; after a two-day debate, the magistrates turned them out. Then Calvin was accused of Arianism by Pierre Caroli, a preacher at Lausanne who had earlier been one of Lefèvre's disciples at Meaux. When Calvin visited Lausanne to come to the assistance of Viret, who was already being assailed by Caroli, that brilliant but unsteady preacher turned on Calvin himself and, basing his case on evidence drawn from Calvin's writings, including the *Institutes*, accused the Genevan Reformer of being an Arian. Would Calvin justify himself by subscribing to the Athanasian Creed? Calvin would not! The reasons for his reluctance are obscure; apparently he did not want to qualify in any way his allegiance to Scripture alone. At any rate, enough suspicion of Calvin's Trinitarian orthodoxy had been aroused to send the dispute into the custody of two synods, one at Lausanne, one at Bern, in the spring of 1537. There Calvin defended himself successfully and was exonerated, while Caroli, having been eviscerated by his none-too-pleasant opponent, was thrown out of office.

Was Calvin inconsistent in refusing to subscribe to a nonscriptural instrument (the Athanasian Creed) at the same time that he was trying to impose just such a text (his "Confession of Faith") on the people of Geneva?

Taking advantage of the squabbles of Geneva, Bern, ever eager to extend its political influence, demanded that both Geneva and Lausanne bring their cultic practices into conformity with those used by the Bernese. The new government in Geneva, eager to consolidate its power, even if it meant appeasing the Bernese, agreed to use the Bernese ceremonies, specifically the Bernese costume, without having even consulted the pastors. In the furor that followed, Calvin and Farel resisted, and their constituency joined them in their defiance. Not that the issues themselves were so great — what harm is there in using a baptismal font? — but that the infringement upon the church was so great! The magistrates responded by forbidding the pastors to preach on Easter Day. Being at liberty, they simply ignored their suppression and preached — Calvin in St. Pierre, Farel in St. Gervais. They refused to celebrate the Eucharist, however, and for very good reason: no discipline, no Communion. The pastors had, in effect, excommunicated Geneva. The town quickly returned the favor. On April 23, 1538, the several councils ratified the Bernese ceremonies and dismissed the pastors on three days' notice.

IN STRASSBURG

THE EXILED Reformers retreated to Basel, where Calvin, more certain than ever that he was unsuited for public life, expected to find a book-lined study for a withdrawn life of Christian scholarship. About the end of July, Farel was recalled to Neuchâtel, where he remained for the rest of his career. About the same time, from Strassburg, Bucer and Capito began to pester Calvin to assume the responsibilities of pastor of a congregation of French refugees in that city. An on-site inspection by Calvin in July set off extensive hemming and hawing, in the course of which the young Reformer produced again his standard list of excuses — dyspepsia, repeated failures, and the like. Bucer finally inquired of Farel how to deal with such an obdurate human being. From Neuchâtel came the advice: pronounce the wrath of God. Bucer proceeded to pronounce judgment on Calvin in a thunderous letter: "God will know how to find a rebellious servant, even as he found Jonah." Appalled by the example of Jonah, Calvin yielded once again to the remonstrances of his friends. As September began, he took ship down the Rhine to Strassburg. There he spent three years, which were perhaps the most formative of his life.

Strassburg was one of the great cities of continental Protestantism. Its theologians — Martin Bucer and Wolfgang Capito — although signators of the Wittenberg Concord (1536) and to that extent Lutheran, were widely acknowledged for their independence as thinkers, for their importance as theologians and exegetes, and for their subtlety as negotiators. So far from being Lutheran, Bucer had many of the characteristics of a Reformed theologian and may even be counted among the founders of that tradition. His inclinations toward a pastoral ministry, expressed especially in his book on the cure of souls, put him in the forefront of those Reformers who gave character to a distinctly Protestant pastoral theology.

In Jacob Sturm the city boasted a political genius who was successful in giving Strassburg a place of eminence among the cities of the Holy Roman Empire, probably beyond its deserts. A proponent of the Reformation, Jacob Sturm was also a proponent of public education, which surely reinforced the Reformation by bringing literacy and liberal studies to bear on the new Protestant intellectualism. Jacob Sturm founded a system of primary Latin schools in Strassburg. Another important Strassburger was Johannes Sturm, who complemented Jacob's work by establishing a *gymnasium* conceived in the best traditions of Renaissance humanism, that is, devoted especially to classical studies, Ciceronian in particular, and designed to make young human beings more truly human. Johannes, rector of the *gymnasium* and a friend of Calvin's since their days together in Paris, promptly appointed Calvin "lecturer in Holy Scripture," giving him occasion to see how a Renaissance school operated.

On September 8, 1538, Calvin preached his first sermon to the "little French church" *(ecclesiola Gallicana),* a refugee congregation of five hundred souls attracted to Strassburg by the openhanded policies of Jacob Sturm. The site of their gathering shifted from place to place until, in 1541, they settled in the old Dominican church in the center of town. On July 29, 1539, Calvin applied for citizenship and, as the constitution of the republic required, subscribed to one of the guilds; henceforth he was listed as a tailor.

In November 1538 the church celebrated Holy Communion, and that occasion must have called into being one or two important contributions to the Calvinist system of worship. Calvin commissioned some skillful person to translate from German to French the liturgy that had come into use in Strassburg in 1524, when a young priest of Lutheran persuasion, Diebold Schwarz, had introduced a German version of the Roman rite.

492

Bucer had revised Schwarz's Mass over the years, making it expressive of Reformed liturgical and sacramental opinion. Now Calvin revised it again (but not significantly) and caused it to be cast into French. It was published in 1540 as *The Form of Prayers and Manner of Ministering the Sacrament according to the Use of the Ancient Church,* and it stands as one of the most important and conspicuous debts Calvin owed to Bucer. In its own way, Calvin's liturgy *was* the Mass, constructed according to the shape of the Western Catholic rite and on the assumption that word and sacrament were inseparably joined. (Calvin wanted the Eucharist every Sunday; the Strassburg magistrates limited it to only once a month.)

Some characteristics of Calvin's liturgy, however, were classically Reformed. The Ten Commandments, for example, were to be recited *after* the prayer of confession and the announcement of absolution — which reflected Calvin's "third use" of the law, as the basis and incentive of the reconstruction of one's life. In the so-called Great Prayer, Calvin took a page from Farel and "fenced" the communion table against unworthy participants — not by physical barricades, but by an unedifying recital of the sorts of persons ("idolaters, blasphemers, contemners of God . . .") who were not wanted. In so doing, Calvin gave striking liturgical expression to the inseparable relationship between parish discipline and Holy Communion on which he and Farel had always insisted.

As a lecturer in Sturm's *gymnasium,* Calvin resumed the exegetical labors he had begun in Geneva. Late in 1539 he published *Commentary on Romans* — the first of an extensive list of exegetical works that would eventually include all of the books of the New Testament except Revelation, and all but eleven books of the Old. In the previous summer, he had overhauled the *Institutes,* making it a substantial textbook of dogmatic theology intended chiefly for the training of young ministers. Bucer's *True Cure of Souls* had appeared a year earlier; it is not far-fetched to suppose that some of Bucer's ideas found their way into Calvin's own exposition of the Christian life and of the pastoral office. Such was the happy relationship that existed between Bucer and Calvin.

In French, rather than scholar's Latin, Calvin published *Short Treatise on the Lord's Supper* (1540), in which he took pains to clarify his thinking on Eucharistic issues that had vexed Protestants for almost twenty years. On finding a Latin copy of this treatise in a bookstore late in life, Luther said of Calvin, "I might have entrusted the whole affair of this controversy to him from the beginning. If my opponents had done the like, we should have soon been reconciled."

In the *Short Treatise,* more elaborately in *Institutes* 4.17, and more precisely in a reply to Heshusius, Calvin gave his thinking on the Lord's Supper. Both the Catholic and Lutheran view of the Mass involved a real participation of the Christian in the substance of Christ's body. The technical words "tran*substan*tiation" and "con*substan*tiation" were attempts to express that crucial consideration. Zwingli, at the other extreme, gave up any attempt to say that Christians participate in the substance of Christ's body. For him, such an idea was both absurd and irrelevant. The sacrament was important enough as a mystical contemplation of Christ's sacrifice on Calvary. Calvin, standing between the extremes, attempted to redefine the term "substance" in order to keep it.

Calvin argued that when we attempt to define the essence of a human life (whether Christ's or anyone else's), we do not normally hold a discussion about the person's chemical properties, which, in any case, change from moment to moment, year to year, and are therefore scarcely a reliable index to the person anyway. What is real about a human being is the inner force that constitutes personality. Both Catholics and Lutherans appeared to Calvin to be wide of the mark when they defined "substance of Christ's body" in terms of its literal composition. Would it not have been better to say that the "substance of Christ's body" is the inward, animating power of Christ's life? Therefore what comes to us in the mystery of Holy Communion is not the physical substance of Christ but the inward, animating power of his life. It is not literal food for the mouth and stomach but spiritual food for the soul. Calvin's view of the sacrament has been called the spiritual real presence. It offers an interesting example of Protestant conservatism: Calvin attempted to redefine an important medieval category in order to conserve the Western religious tradition.

Calvin's literary activity in his early months in Strassburg included *Reply to Sadoleto,* an apologetic work addressed to one of the ablest Counter-Reformation cardinals. Jacopo Sadoleto (1477–1547), bishop of Carpentras, wrote to the magistrates of Geneva, now that Calvin and Farel were gone, and invited them to return their city to Roman obedience. Calvin replied in the name of Geneva. He insisted on the sufficiency of Scripture — "the Lydian stone by which [the church] tests all doctrines" — and refuted Sadoleto's appeal to tradition by the observation that the Church of Geneva, being honorable to Scripture, is closer to ancient religion than the Church of Rome is. He also defended most vigorously the companion doctrines of justification by faith, alien righteousness, and the mystical union that unites believers in Christ.

As a citizen living on a florin a week, so poor that he was forced to sell some of his books and take in boarders, Calvin yet found enough courage to think about marriage — to someone modest and obliging, thrifty and patient, likely to take care of his health and relieve him of emotional distress. Friends came up with two candidates, neither worthwhile. From his own parishioners, Calvin himself chose Idelette de Bure, widow of an Anabaptist whom he himself had converted. In August 1540 Farel arrived from Neuchâtel to bless the union. Idelette de Bure was already the mother of a young woman, Judith, who lived in Calvin's house until her marriage, and a son, somewhat older, who was a student. To the new couple a son was given in 1542, but he died in infancy. Soon infirm, Idelette herself died in 1549. In Calvin's correspondence are expressions of deep attachment to his wife and equal sorrow over the vicissitudes of his life, tempered with an overriding concession to God's providential care.

TRIUMPHAL RETURN TO GENEVA

MEANWHILE the church in Geneva suffered from a combination of bad leadership, low morale, and political strife, to say nothing of the incursion of the Bernese, who exploited the town's disarray, or the attempt of Roman Catholics, incited by Sadoleto's letter, to regain control of the city. Two hostile parties came into being. The Artichauds favored a liaison with Bern. The Guillermins, so called from Farel's Christian name, resisted the new ministry of the Genevan church and worked actively for Calvin's recall. The Guillermins were led by the aristocrat Ami Perrin, the regent Antoine Saunier, and Mathurin Cordier, none of whom were easily mollified, not even by Calvin's entreaties not to disturb the unity of the church in Geneva. Matters deteriorated to the point that, on September 21, 1540, the Little Council voted to recall Calvin. A month later, an embassy was dispatched to secure Calvin's concurrence. That set off a flurry of activity. Calvin began hemming and hawing, offering again his standard list of excuses. Bucer and the Strassburgers protested, hoping to keep Calvin where he was. Zurich and Basel joined Geneva in importuning Calvin, declaring that Geneva would never know peace without him. Farel intruded and made a special trip to Strassburg to exercise his now-customary liturgy of pronouncing divine wrath on poor Calvin. (Said Calvin: "I would do anything rather than yield to you in this matter.") Finally he relented. At the beginning of September 1541, he took leave of Strassburg, retaining his citizenship in the likely prospect that he would soon be back. Eleven days later he was acclaimed in Geneva. "There is no place under heaven," he said, "that I am more afraid of."

At thirty-two, Calvin pitched in to do the work necessary in Geneva with a gritty resolve. On the day of his arrival he went to see the magistrates, demanding that a commission be appointed to write an ecclesiastical constitution for this town of twelve thousand. The Sunday following he preached from the Bible exactly where he had left off in 1538, as if nothing had happened. Something, however, *had* happened — happy years in Strassburg with good colleague Bucer. Back came Calvin with a plan for the Genevan church that would cross oceans and cultures to become the pattern of Reformed church-life everywhere.

Working with a commission appointed by the Little Council, Calvin prepared a draft document that, when submitted to the magistrates for their approval, was adjusted significantly by the Little Council, modified again by the Two Hundred, and ratified by the General Council (on Sunday, November 20, 1541). The document was called *Ordonnances ecclésiastiques* (Ecclesiastical ordinances), which, with admirable perspicacity, the syndics declared to be "taken from the gospel of Jesus Christ." The fact that none of the changes made by the magistrates was sent to the ministers for their instruction, much less approval, was a harbinger of church-state tensions that persisted in Geneva after Calvin's return.

The document opens with a discussion of church officers: "There are four orders of office instituted by our Lord for the government of his church." Officers are by no means functional extenders of the priesthood of all believers as Luther thought; rather, they belong to an *order* established in the Holy Catholic Church by Christ himself. They are pastors, teachers, elders, and deacons. François Wendel imagines that Bucer unveiled this constellation of church officers to Calvin in Strassburg. Clearly, however, the *Ordinances* is an amplification of ideas and plans Calvin expressed in the "Articles" of 1537.

By the order of elders, Calvin meant to establish a corps of lay councillors, distinguished by their spiritual and intellectual bearing, to assist in the ministries of discipline and the cure of souls. This was scarcely a new idea to Calvin, for he had proposed it quite clearly in his "Articles." In the 1539 edition of the *Institutes* he distinguished between preaching elders and ruling elders (5.26), the latter to lead in matters of discipline. Bucer's system of lay curators in Strassburg may also have encouraged Calvin in his own design for the office of elder. Upon reading the evidence, however, it becomes apparent to us that what Calvin wanted (as distinguished from what he got)

496

was an independent spiritual jurisdiction, based on scriptural precedent, operated by twelve elders chosen or nominated by the pastors, and enforced by the powers to summon, to censure, and to excommunicate members of congregations who breached morality or offended against doctrine. In short, Calvin wanted a system of ecclesiastical discipline by divine right to exist alongside the civil administration.

The civil power, however, would never admit such a challenge to its authority. The twelve elders were to be chosen by, and from, the several councils — two from the Little Council, four from the Sixty, and six from the Two Hundred. Elders were required to face an annual review conducted not by the church, but by the seigneury, which reserved the power to discharge them. Some clever linguist or lawyer among the magistrates shaded the language of the *Ordinances* so that "elders" ceased to be divinely authorized officers of the church, becoming instead "deputies of the seigneury."

The Consistory, consisting of elders and pastors who met on Thursday mornings to administer discipline, was intended to be the core of Calvin's spiritual jurisdiction. The *Ordinances* allowed the Consistory certain powers necessary to make the disciplinary system function — the power to summon recalcitrant persons, to make "friendly remonstrance," to admonish, and, in the extremity, to excommunicate — that is, to inform obdurate people that "as despisers of God, they must abstain from the Supper until a change of life is seen in them." The magistrates, however, saw fit to add rejoinders to the draft text, as follows:

> All this is to take place in such a way that the ministers have no civil jurisdiction.
>
> Nor is the Consistory to derogate from the authority of the seigneury or ordinary justice.
>
> The civil power is to remain unimpaired.
>
> Even where there will be need to impose punishment or to constrain parties, the ministers . . . are to report the whole matter to the Council, which, in their turn, will decide to order and do justice as the case requires.

In such formulations, Calvin saw one thing, the civil authority another. Calvin presumed that the right of excommunication was guaranteed to the church; the civil authority, that it was withheld for the exercise of magistrates alone.

What is the theological root of Calvin's system of church discipline? He described the work of the elders as "fraternal correction" — a description taken from Hebrews 3:13. In the *Ordinances* he defined discipline as a medicine useful for bringing sinners back to health — a means toward repentance, in other words, that would not work very well if too harsh and purgative. Calvin repeated endlessly the observation that discipline was essential if the church was to preserve its integrity. While all of these observations may not be beside the point, neither do they ever get to the point. Calvin's preoccupation with discipline serves two theological purposes: the third use of the law and the doctrine of sanctification. If the outcome of the Christian life is to be holy and if the law of God is principally useful by providing us the form and incentive of such holiness, then we can finally imagine how all of these "corrections," "medicines," and "integrities" offered to us in the form of parish discipline serve our best interests as religious people.

Beginning December 6, 1541, when it met for the first time, the Consistory began a surveillance and correction of Genevese habits. Apparently there was much to correct. The medieval city of Geneva had gained a certain perverse distinction for its unseemly conduct, including drunkenness, obscenity, and the corruption of priests and friars. It harbored a licentiousness so flagrant that, long before Calvin, the city government had made it a point to try to regulate public morals.

The minutes of the Consistory indicate that nearly every Thursday morning saw a procession of offenders, each brought before that ecclesiastical tribunal by the police. Some had not been to church, and others had acted badly in church or had insisted on performing like Catholics in church. Others had been caught in the usual array of social disorders — drunkenness, gambling, adultery, family feuding, and wife beating. No one was exempt, not even, for example, the wife of Ami Perrin, one of the most distinguished citizens in the city. In every instance, the Consistory heard the case and imposed penances, some of which were deliberately reminiscent of those used in the early Christian church.

The civil government, with Calvin's concurrence, also tried to shape character by regulating amusements through legal enactments. Dancing, gambling, and the theater were all severely curtailed. In 1546 the saloons were replaced by neighborhood centers *(abbayes),* where drinking and card playing were scrutinized and bawdy songs forbidden. Instead, the customers were encouraged to make pious conversation and to gaze upon a French Bible that was displayed on a pedestal. People were not to be served before they had been observed saying grace. The Genevans stayed away from these places in large numbers. In three months' time, the taverns were back in business.

Now that the Consistory was in operation, the liturgy and catechism were in use, preaching was being done on a daily basis, and a church of full integrity was coming into sight, Calvin turned his attention to a system of general education for Geneva. In 1542 he picked a Savoyard humanist, Sebastian Castellio, to be rector of the system under church control. Among the refugees who now came to Geneva in increasing numbers, Calvin found many intellectuals, some of whom he appointed to his staff, permitting him time to write. In 1542 he wrote an essay against the Catholic theologian Albert Pighius, an advocate of free will, and prepared a Latin text of the *Institutes,* which appeared the following year.

None of Calvin's writings of this period was more important, however, than an explanation of Protestantism written at the request of Bucer for submission to the German Diet of Speier scheduled to meet in 1544. By the end of 1543, Calvin, already acknowledged the foremost spokesman of Protestantism, had finished a major treatise, *The Necessity of Reforming the Church,* to be used by the Protestants at Speier. The question here was simple, and not so simple: What is the Reformation? Calvin began by extolling Luther and his foundational role. That, however, was a historical answer, not a conceptual one. Reformation means to preach the Bible without care for the consequence; it means to restore the doctrine, sacraments, and government of the church "according to the exact standards of the word of God." But those were procedural answers. What was the conceptual answer? For Calvin, the Reformation ultimately meant to restore Christ to the center of Christian thought. It is "to tell a man to seek righteousness and life outside of himself, that is, in Christ only, because he has nothing in himself but sin and death." (Such a thought was simply the idea of "justification by faith alone," sharply stated once again.) It appeared to Calvin that medieval religion was full of particular requirements that, in one way or another, compromised that fundamental fact of biblical faith. Works-righteousness did so. The veneration of the saints did so. The idea of the Mass as a sacrifice and a good work did so. Reformation was therefore an attempt to "restore the church" by restoring Christ to the center of Christian thought. Reformation was waged in the name and interest of the Holy Catholic Church itself.

The years 1545 and 1546 saw an intensification of the Consistory's activities, including a certain delight in the darker side of surveillance, involving informers, intrigue, and such. Whether he deserved the reputation or not, Calvin was considered the moving spirit behind what the public perceived to be the Consistory's excesses, and he became the target of popular indignation. In January 1546 a distinguished member of the Little Council, Pierre Ameaux, manufacturer of playing cards, chose a dinner party to announce that John Calvin was nothing more than a Picardian pip-squeak who preached foul doctrine. (Bad feeling had existed between the two, stemming chiefly from the doubtful character of Pierre's wife, an advocate of free love.) Imprisoned, Ameaux was sentenced to beg Calvin's pardon on bended knee in the presence of the Two Hundred. Calvin's sense of outrage now swelled up to unimaginable proportions. Because Ameaux had impugned the very word of God, he was required on April 5, 1546, to walk all around the town, dressed only in a shirt, carrying a lighted torch, pleading on his knees for mercy at three designated locations. The Genevans were appalled at the humiliation demanded by Calvin of one of their magistrates.

Ameaux may have been something less than a blueblood, but the Perrins and Favres were Genevan elite — patricians whose social station seemed surely to guarantee them exemption from the penalties Calvin exacted for easy living. Both families, furthermore, had been among Calvin's early supporters. Ami Perrin had been a leader of the Guillermin party, which had managed Calvin's return to Geneva. Both Perrin and François Favre, his father-in-law, bridled however at the repressive machinery of the Consistory, of which both had personal experience. In February 1546 Favre was excommunicated — kept from Holy Communion — for moral offense. Garpard, his son, underwent a similar disgrace. Franchequine, his daughter, the wife of Ami Perrin, was arrested for dancing at a wedding reception and was sent to the Consistory for suitable recompense. She responded with a shower of insolence. While the Favres and Perrins demanded to know where the Consistory got its competence to act so, Calvin demanded to know whether the Favres and Perrins were above the laws of God and man. The Favres fled Geneva. Perrin was sent as Geneva's ambassador to the court of Henry II, who acceded to the throne of France in 1547. In the February elections of that year, the Calvinist regime experienced a serious erosion of its political base.

The elections of 1548 were of critical importance. By that time, two political factions existed, sharply defined and opposed. One party consisted of the old Genevans, led by Ami Perrin; they were probably less interested in

ousting Calvin than in controlling him. Deeply resentful of Calvinist discipline, they nevertheless did not deserve the name "Libertines," which the
Calvinists gave them. On the other side were the "Calvinists," whose constituency included large numbers of French and Italian refugees. In the elections
of 1548, the old Genevans, the so-called Libertines, achieved a clear-cut
mandate to govern. For the next six years, Calvin labored under the political
handicap of a new majority that, although Protestant and even Calvinist, was
not sympathetic toward the prevailing church-state relationship, especially
church regulation of public morality. The elections of 1548, moreover, set off
a wave of hostility against the refugees, as well as much personal abuse directed
toward Calvin and his associates. One circumstance that neither side counted
on was the increasing stream of religious refugees to Geneva, reinforcing
Calvin's constituency by both numbers of persons and intellectual power. In
the summer of 1549, for example, Théodore de Bèze (Calvin's eventual
successor) arrived in Geneva, as well as the children of Guillaume Budé.

In the elections of 1554, the Calvinists elected three of the four syndics;
in the following year, they achieved a majority in the several councils. The
city belonged to Calvin. An ascendant Calvinism provoked renewed discussion of excommunication. In January 1555, to Calvin's satisfaction, all three
of the councils of Geneva voted to adhere to the provisions for excommunication in the *Ecclesiastical Ordinances* of 1541. On the face of it, that was an
ambiguous decision: the *Ordinances* had for years been the very subject of
dispute. In fact, the ministers were now allowed to interpret the *Ordinances*
to mean that the power of excommunication was vested in the Consistory.
At last, Calvin achieved the aspect of the disciplinary system that would
make it work — the power to excommunicate obdurate sinners from the
Lord's Supper. As the years passed, and especially in the revision of the
Ordinances made in 1561, the Consistory acquired more and more constitutional power, including the authority to call witnesses and examine them
under oath, as well as the explicit prerogative of admitting persons to, and
excluding persons from, Holy Communion.

The overthrow of the Libertines invigorated Calvinist Geneva. The
English bishop John Bale, an exile from Marian England (i.e., England after
the accession of Mary Tudor in 1553), called Geneva "the wonderful miracle
of the whole world," and the Scottish Reformer John Knox, who lived in
Geneva, described it as "the most perfect school of Christ that ever was in
the earth since the days of the Apostles." In that Christian society, so
thoroughly reformed according to God's will, lived all manner of people
peacefully and in religious exultation. Many were French, driven from

France by the "exterminations" of Henry II (1547–59). Some were Marian exiles, some Italian Protestants of great reputation (e.g., Barnardino Ochino) or of radical opinion (e.g., Lelio Socinus); others were Germans, Spaniards, or Scots. In the ten-year period, 1549–59, over 5,000 refugees were admitted to Geneva; over 1,700 came in the single year 1559. At the same time, Geneva could no longer contain the Reformed religion as Calvin taught it; it began to take root in France (1555), was established in Scotland (1560), and made inroads in the Palatinate region of Germany (1563).

Humanists, of whom Calvin was one, insisted on the education of young men and women, according to classical curriculums and procedures, as preparation for citizenship and participation in Christian society. Both in the "Articles" of 1537 and even more conspicuously in the *Ecclesiastical Ordinances* of 1541, the establishment of a college to serve the purposes of citizenship and religion was required.

Toward the achievement of that purpose, the elementary schools of Geneva were reorganized into a central system and reduced in number to four. In 1557, as we know, Calvin visited Strassburg, where, although rebuffed as a preacher, he was allowed to inspect Sturm's *gymnasium.* On his return, a school site was selected and a building begun with money raised by public subscription. Meanwhile the Genevan Academy was inaugurated on June 5, 1559, in the cathedral, at which time Théodore de Bèze, lately of Lausanne, become rector, and Calvin's statutes for the school — *Leges academiae genevensis* — were proclaimed. The Genevan Academy invested its students handsomely in liberal studies — in Greek and Latin languages and literature — and was in every respect a Renaissance school, respectful to both Cicero and Christ. Begun with 162 students, the academy grew rapidly in numbers. Those who acquitted themselves with distinction in the preparatory grades were permitted to advance to the *schola publica,* the academy proper, where instruction in law, medicine, and especially divinity, was given. It would be hard to exaggerate the importance of the alumni of the Genevan Academy to the advance of Calvinism on the continent of Europe and in the British Isles.

Stricken with tuberculosis, Calvin preached his last sermon on February 6, 1564. In April the magistrates visited him to make their farewell; soon after, Farel came bounding from Neuchâtel to see his old friend. The fierce and godly man died on May 27, 1564, in his fifty-fourth year; his remains were deposited in an unmarked grave. His legacy was much more than Geneva; it was a whole constituency of Reformed churches, everywhere indebted to his doctrine, his discipline, and his worship.

22. *The Counter-Reformation*

BY THE MIDDLE OF THE SIXTEENTH CENTURY, AND SURELY NO LATER than the death of Calvin (1564), the Protestant Reformation had made significant headway in Europe. Parts of northern Europe had already been lost to the papacy. In Germany, the religious issue was being decided state by state; according to the Peace of Augsburg (1555), each German prince was permitted to decide the religious disposition of his territory according to the formula *cuius regio, eius religio.* The same year, the nobility of Poland received from Parliament substantially the same privilege accorded the German princes. In Scotland, the year 1560 saw the introduction of a Calvinist ecclesiastical regime. Three years later, Elizabeth I perfected the English Reformation in what has come to be called the Elizabethan Settlement. Switzerland had been cleft by the Reformation and now was half Catholic and half Protestant. Lutheran state churches had arisen in Scandinavia. Only in France and the Netherlands was the religious outcome still in doubt, and only in Spain and Italy could one find unambiguous loyalty to the Catholic religion on a grand scale. From those two countries, the Counter-Reformation would come.

The revival of the Catholic Church in the sixteenth century goes by the name "Counter-Reformation," or "Catholic Reformation," which refers to the Western Catholic Church's girding its strength (1) to meet the critical challenge of the Protestants, (2) to set aright its own spiritual disorders, and (3) to collect, define, and publish its doctrines, disciplines, and worship. As we will see, the Counter-Reformation took the Catholic world one important step beyond the Renaissance — to a new age of religious fervor and determination. Unlike the Renaissance, which was fundamentally elitist, the Counter-Reformation was a vast popular movement that touched all segments of Catholic society. The age of Catholic triumphalism had begun. The art that expressed its powerful emotion was baroque. The Counter-Reformation consisted of four easily definable parts, in the following order:

1. A revival in the religious orders of the Catholic Church
2. The revival of the Inquisition
3. The founding of the Jesuit order
4. The Council of Trent

THE RISE OF RELIGIOUS ORDERS

ACTUALLY, the religious revival in the Catholic Church began *before* the Protestant Reformation, giving some Catholic historians every justification for saying that reform would have come to the Catholic Church, Luther or no, and that what we should be talking about is not "Counter-Reformation" but "Catholic Reformation." In 1517, the very year Luther nailed up his ninety-five theses, a group of about sixty distinguished churchmen founded the Oratory of Divine Love in one of the churches of Rome for purposes of religious renewal centering on the frequent and devout celebration of the Mass. Soon, chapters of the Oratory were organized in other towns of northern Italy — Verona, Vicenza, Brescia, and Venice. Adherents to this movement were some of the up-and-coming churchmen of the day, including Bishops Giovanni Pietro Caraffa and Jacopo Sadoleto, the British exile Reginald Pole, and the Venetian aristocrat Gasaro Contarini. They became four of the most prominent participants in the Counter-Reformation.

Not that they always agreed. Caraffa was ferociously conservative. Pole, stunned by the unfolding of the Reformation in his native England, espoused his Catholic religion militantly. Contarini was both learned and liberal; some suspected him of Lutheran leanings. Sadoleto was a brilliant controversialist; he and Calvin were destined to do literary battle. Pope Paul III (1534–49), last of the Renaissance popes and first pope of the Counter-Reformation, took these young prelates under his wing, made them cardinals, and authorized them to work out a scheme of reform for the Catholic Church as a last attempt to find accommodation with the Lutherans. In 1537 they presented Pope Paul with a document called *Consilium de emendanda ecclesia.*

This "strategy for correcting the church" advocated strict observance of canon law against prevailing abuses: no longer should the papal powers be used for gain, or the privileges and prerogatives of the higher clergy to turn a profit; no longer should unfit and unlearned men be admitted to the priesthood; no longer should the religious orders be left undisciplined; no longer should frivolous writers (Erasmus, for example) be allowed to pollute the places of Catholic learning; no longer should apostate monks or passionate priests hankering to marry be given dispensations. Given the damaging nature of its recommendations, the *Consilium* was never officially made public. (Luther, however, published a pirated German edition of the *Consilium,* including many retorts of his own.) Part of the significance of the *Consilium* consisted of its omissions; it represented no attempt to address the crucial theological differences that divided Lutheran from Catholic, most notably the question of justification.

Contarini was dispatched, nevertheless, to treat with the Lutherans one more time. When the German diet met at Worms in 1540 and at Regensburg (or Ratisbon) in 1541, conversations ensued between the Catholic and Lutheran parties. At the colloquy of Regensburg, Cardinal Contarini and Philip Melanchthon managed to fuzz the question of justification by the creative use of words, as bystanders waited breathlessly for the possibility of the reunion of Western Christendom. But talks foundered on other issues, such as transubstantiation and papal authority, neither of which the Lutherans could abide. When Melanchthon reported to Luther back at Wittenberg, he met with a cold reception for having trifled with the crucial issue of justification, and when Contarini returned to Italy, he was accused of heresy and expired the following year. With the failure of Contarini's mission, the Catholic church turned resolutely away from the strategy of accommodation to the strategy of reclaiming its own inner integrity and power and rightness as the true religion of Christ. The impasse at Regensburg brought forth the Counter-Reformation in the strict sense of that word.

The pope in whose reign this transition occurred was himself a transitional figure. Paul III began life as Alessandro Farnese, son of an elegant Renaissance family, a Renaissance prelate in the grand tradition. He was *papa* in both senses — pope and parent. One of his early papal deeds was to create cardinals of his grandsons, Ascancio Sforza (age 14) and Alessandro Farnese (age 15) as "props for his old age." Yet he, above all men, eventually turned the Catholic Church in a new direction: from Renaissance to Counter-Reformation. It was he who confirmed the Jesuit order (1540), sanctioned the Roman Inquisition (1542), and convoked the Council of Trent (1545).

Meanwhile, the fervor generated by the Oratory of Divine Love had begun to affect the religious communities of the Catholic Church. Old orders were revived; new orders were established. It is a simple axiom, but an important and reliable one: revivals of religion in the Catholic Church have often been preceded by revivals of Catholic monasticism.

Considerably before Luther attained prominence, Baptista Mantuanus had worked to revitalize the *Carmelite* order. In 1522 Paolo Guistiniani of Venice restored the *Camaldolese* order to its primitive existence as an austere company of hermits. In 1525 Matteo de Bascio, son of Italian peasants, advocated a return to the strict poverty and simplicity practiced by Francis of Assisi. Called *Capuchins,* the strict Franciscans who followed Matteo wore the four-pointed hood *(capuce)* that Francis had worn. Sons of Italian peasant stock, the Capuchins proved to be good, plain preachers; they performed the important service of keeping the Italian masses close to the Catholic religion. Paul III confirmed the Capuchins in 1536. Two years later, women of the Franciscan tradition established the *Capucines,* devoting themselves strictly to the rule that Francis had given in 1224 to St. Clare and her followers, the "Poor Clares." Later in the century, Peter of Alcántara attempted to invigorate the Spanish Franciscans by establishing an *Order of Barefoot Friars* in 1555; seven years later, Teresa of Ávila sought to revive Spanish Carmelite fervor by founding the *Discalced* (unshod) *Carmelites.* Both of those Spanish foundations were confirmed by Pope Pius IV in the 1560s; both produced classic expressions of Spanish mysticism. (See Peter of Alcantara's "golden book," *Prayer and Meditation,* 1560.)

Teresa of Ávila (1515–82) grew up in the walled city of Ávila, in an age when the national and cultural glory of Spain was at its height. Precociously religious, she set out as a child with her brother, Rodrigo, to convert the Moors, with some romantic prospect of being martyred in the process. At twenty (1535), she enlisted in the Carmelite order, which, beginning in the winter of 1560, she proceeded to reform. The first convent of Discalced Carmelites was organized at Ávila on August 24, 1562. With the help of her protégé, Father John of St. Matthias, better known as St. John of the Cross, she succeeded in establishing seventeen foundations of nuns, fifteen of friars. However important she was as a monastic reformer, Teresa of Ávila attained prominence as one of two outstanding representatives of Spanish mysticism. Three of her writings deserve attention. In her *Life* (1563–66), she provided an important psychological interpretation of the life of mysticism that she practiced. In the *Way of Perfection* (1565), written as a practical manual for her nuns, she dealt with a variety of topics important

103. Bernini, *Ecstasy of Saint Theresa*

to the life of contemplation, always with "perfection" as the ultimate goal of the monastic vocation. Her masterpiece was *The Interior Castle* (1577), in which she attempted, as far as words would allow, to discuss the outermost limits of the mystical experience, even the soul's communion with God.

Teresa's most celebrated disciple was John of the Cross (1542–91), whose mystical writings *The Ascent of Mount Carmel* and *The Dark Night of the Soul* rank among the greatest in the history of Western mysticism. *The Ascent of Mount Carmel* prepares the seeker after God by purging his or her soul of its sensual part. The sequel — *The Dark Night of the Soul* — finds the seeker ready to be "purged," "stripped," "subdued," and "made ready" in his or her spiritual parts "for the union of love with God." This is "darkness" because God extinguishes *all* human activities, even our own human efforts at loving him. What matters now is the utter passivity, even "aridity," of the soul, into which God himself can begin to infuse his love. Just as a log of wood becomes transformed by being immersed in fire, even taking on some of the properties of fire, so is the passive and arid soul enkindled by God's love. "This dark night," wrote John of the Cross, "is an inflowing of God into the soul."

So far we have dealt with the revival of older monastic communities, but new orders were also created in this effervescence of religious fervor in the Catholic Church. Gaetano di Tiene, a noblemen of Vicenza who had spent his energy establishing chapters of the Oratory of Divine Love in some northern Italian cities, finally reached the conclusion that the Catholic malaise was due to the low estate of the clergy. He therefore proposed to establish a new sort of monastic community, one of "clerks regular" — priests (or "clerks") who would continue to work in the world but live in a community under a rule (*regula;* hence "regular") and assume the monastic vows of poverty, chastity, and obedience. Caraffa, then bishop of Teate (or Chieti), became superior of this new organization upon its confirmation by the pope in 1524. The members called themselves *Theatines,* after Caraffa's diocese. Drawn mainly from aristocracy, the Theatines represented a strange combination of poverty and wealth, humility and power. The order soon became the nursery of Catholic bishops. The fact that the Theatines were aristocratic and did work in the world furnished the Catholic Church with an agency to deal effectively with institutions that mattered, such as the universities, the courts, and the aristocracy. The Theatines and later the Jesuits, who were patterned after them, began to pose a formidable threat to Protestant intellectualism.

Three orders of clerks regular followed. The *Barnabites* began in Milan in 1532 as the Clerks Regular of St. Paul and took their nickname after the Milanese Church of St. Barnabas, which was assigned to them as headquarters. They professed a responsibility for teaching the young and for pastoral care but attained notoriety for popular evangelism in open-air missions in the regions of Milan. A similar order, the *Somaschi,* began in 1528, at Somasca, near Bergamo, in northern Italy. It was devoted to the care of the more pitiful victims of the Italian wars, particularly the children. Equally unpretentious was the beginning of the *Oratorians.* In 1548 a devout Florentine, Philip Neri, established the Brotherhood of the Holy Trinity in Rome to care for pilgrims, often desperately poor, who flocked to that city. In 1551, having been ordained a priest, Neri invited students and young priests to gather regularly in his rooms for prayer *(oratio),* conversation, and music. His colleague was Giovanni Pierluigi da Palestrina, master of the papal choir, one of the most respected musicians of the day. From Neri's oratory came the oratorios of Palestrina, as well as a new religious congregation, the Oratorians, authorized by Pope Gregory XIII in 1575. Renowned for scholarship, seriousness of purpose, and musical sophistication, the Oratorians succeeded almost immediately in raising the level of the Catholic priesthood, starting with the clergy of Rome.

REVIVAL OF THE INQUISITION

BY THE fifteenth century, the medieval Inquisition had run its course and had ceased to be effective. In 1477, however, Ferdinand and Isabella of Spain obtained the permission of Pope Sixtus IV to revive the Inquisition in Spain as means of curtailing the Moors and the Jews and thus as an instrument of national consolidation. The Spanish Inquisition was therefore both papal and national. It was surely born out of the long and bitter contest between Spanish Catholicism and the Moors, which left the Catholic Church of Spain auspiciously severe in its dealings with dissenters, whether Moors, Jews, or Protestant Christians. Thomas de Torquemada was appointed third grand inquisitor; under his regime some 2,200 people were dispatched to the flames. His second successor was Cardinal Ximénez (1508–16); he extended the surveillance beyond the Moors and the Jews to Catholics of all sorts, even the regular clergy. Ximenez was succeeded as grand inquisitor by Cardinal Hadrian, who, in 1522, was elected to the papacy as Hadrian VI. By that time the Spanish Inquisition was being used to repress the heretical opinions of Erasmians and Lutherans. Even such august Catholics as Teresa of Ávila and Ignatius of Loyola fell momentarily under suspicion as deviants from acceptable Catholic teaching.

Cardinal Caraffa, who served in Spain as papal nuncio, was greatly taken by the success of the Spanish Inquisition, and he was determined to install it in Rome as a universal, permanent, centralized department of the papal government to suppress heresy everywhere. Having no understanding of the freedom of conscience, Caraffa simply believed that error had no right to exist. In the twilight between the Renaissance and Counter-Reformation, the Farnese pope, Paul III, hesitated. But when he beheld the spread of Lutheran opinions in Italy itself — at Lucca, for example — and when he witnessed the failure of Contarini's efforts at accommodation with the Lutherans, he yielded to Caraffa. On July 21, 1542, the year following the ecumenical debacle at the Regensburg colloquy. Paul III sanctioned the Roman Inquisition by the bull *Licet ab initio* and extended its authority throughout the Christian world.

The bull appointed six cardinals to oversee the Inquisition as "commissioners of the pope" and as grand inquisitors. Chief among them was Caraffa. It gave the inquisitors power to overrule bishops in their own dioceses, to degrade priests, to administer censures and punishment, to invoke the assistance of secular government, to delegate their investigative and punitive powers to other church officers as they saw fit, and to hear appeals without offering the accused access to ecclesiastical courts. Whatever the inquisitors might legitimately do in the discharge of their inquisitorial duties, said the pope, "we decree to be completely valid and to be observed in perpetuity."

Caraffa lost no time in setting the Inquisition into motion. His strategy was one of severity, particularly toward the rich and powerful, to whom the poor and untutored looked for their standards. Particularly irksome to him were the Calvinists, for whom he promised awesome punishment. Soon the highways were clogged with galloping heretics, making their getaway over the Alps to the safer reaches of France, Germany, the Low Countries, and England. Many were tried and imprisoned; many abjured their heretical opinions, and indeed some stood their ground and died in the flames.

Throughout the 1540s the Inquisition moved effectively forward in Spain and Italy. In the mid-forties, it was introduced to France, where King Francis I struggled to contain the Huguenots; there it claimed victims in Rouen, Toulouse, Grenoble, and Bordeaux. The diocese of Meaux, once a sanctuary for evangelicals in France, was suppressed in October 1546; sixty-one evangelicals were arrested, of whom fourteen were eventually burned for heresy. Yet the Roman Inquisition was curtailed in every place where secular government became jealous of its own prerogatives. Venice, for example, used its own jurisdictional rights to blunt the full force of the Inquisition. Henry II of France (1547–59) insisted upon the competence of his own civil and ecclesiastical authorities to deal with domestic heresy.

In 1555 Cardinal Caraffa was elected to the papacy as Paul IV (d. 1559). As one might expect, the activities of the Inquisition were accelerated. Four years after his accession, Paul IV issued the first official *Index librorum prohibitorum* (Index of prohibited books). The idea was not new. Problems presented by the printing press had been addressed already in the Fifth Lateran Council (1512–17), and lists of prohibited books had appeared as early as 1521, the university faculties of theology having taken the lead in making the compilations. But the *Index* of 1559 was the first official, churchwide list. As the full title suggests, it was part and parcel of the Inquisition: "Lists of Authors and Books against which the Roman and Universal Inquisition orders all Christians to be on their guard, under threat of censure and punishment." Several classes of writings were proscribed: Protestant writings, of course; works of Renaissance humanists deemed morally unfit, such as Boccaccio's *Decameron;* and works disrespectful of the Church or of Catholic teaching, such as those of Erasmus. Vernacular editions of the New Testament were proscribed — not that Catholic eyes could not be shown Holy Writ, but because vernacular versions inevitably undermined the Latinity of the Vulgate Bible in which Catholic teaching was traditionally cast. Printing thus proved a mixed blessing.

THE JESUIT ORDER

THE GREATEST impetus toward the Counter-Reformation was contributed by the Society of Jesus, the Jesuit order, whose members took a special fourth monastic vow of absolute obedience to the pope. Jesuits were the elite of the Catholic religious: only the most intelligent, attractive, energetic, athletic, educated, dedicated, and morally correct were admitted to the ranks of the Society of Jesus. The Jesuit order arose out of the militant Christianity of Spain, which, as we have already observed, acquired its character through the long struggle of Spanish Catholicism against the Moors. It was equally indebted to the mystical propensity of Spanish Catholicism, which, as we have seen, came to flower in Teresa of Ávila and John of the Cross. Although it posed a most formidable resistance to Protestantism, the Jesuit order was not essentially defensive; its mission was to revive the Catholic faith in Europe and to extend the Catholic faith to non-Christian lands. It was the last great expression of monastic heroism in the Western world.

The founder of the order was a Basque nobleman, Don Inigo de Onez y Loyola (1491–1556) — Ignatius of Loyola — a knight in the court of Ferdinand and Isabella of Spain (see plate 78). In the first war (1521–23) between the Holy Roman Emperor Charles V (also the king of Spain) and King Francis I of France, Ignatius defended the city of Pamplona. His right leg was shattered by a French cannonball on May 19, 1521, rendering him unfit for military service. During his convalescence at Loyola, he asked to read some romances of chivalry but was given instead Ludolph the Carthusian's *Life of Christ* as well as a pious classic called *Flowers of the Saints.* Too lame to fight as men conventionally fought, he resolved to begin a spiritual knighthood on behalf of Jesus and the Catholic Church, to establish a righteous army to serve a righteous King, in a righteous cause against the devil and the enemies of the faith.

In March 1522, when he was up and around, Ignatius made a pilgrimage to a shrine near Barcelona; there he retired to a cave at Manresa where he spent the next ten months in solitude. A spiritual crisis ensued, not unlike that of Luther some years before. The question uppermost in the minds of both men was, How can I be at peace with God? Luther's answer involved a denial of human effort and the abandonment of one's self wholly to the mercy of God — in short, the doctrine of justification by faith alone. Ignatius came to a quite different conclusion. Without doubting the importance of God's grace, Ignatius believed that one's human freedom enables one to decide between God and the devil. People remain free to choose and desire those things for which they were chiefly created, namely, to seek God and to praise and serve him, "and by this means to save his soul." (How could a Christian soldier have decided otherwise?) The classic expression of Ignatius's faith, his *Spiritual Exercises,* was apparently worked out in some preliminary form in the cave of Manresa. Luther could not have written such a book, doubting both its premise (freedom) and its purpose (a highly structured spiritual life). Luther was also hidebound to the Scriptures. Ignatius was not; he had the Spanish mystic's propensity for visions of God, in which he ardently trusted.

In February 1523, back in the world again, Ignatius made a pilgrimage to Jerusalem — a conventional gesture among the religiously ardent. On his return to Spain in 1524, he decided that the moral rearmament to which he had been called required a much better education than he had received at court. At thirty-three, therefore, he started to learn Latin. Then he proceeded to the Universities of Alcalá and Salamanca. But the Inquisition misconstrued some of his public utterances in 1527 and treated him to a season in jail. At his release, he found it prudent to resume his education in Paris. Beginning in February 1528, he spent several years in two colleges of the University of Paris — Collège de Montaigu (where Erasmus and Calvin also studied) and Collège de Sainte Barbe.

In Paris, the Jesuit order gathered. By 1534 there were ten, including Pierre Lefèvre (or Faber) of Savoy, Francis Xavier of Pamplona, Diego Lainez of Almanza, and Alfonso Salmerón of Toledo. The ten spent the next five years in Italy attempting to persuade the Vatican to sanction their new order. Although he accepted the Theatine pattern of clerks regular as a proper model for the Jesuits, Ignatius did not get on well with Caraffa, who led the Theatines and who shaped Vatican policy. Certain curiosities in Ignatius's teaching may have offended Caraffa and the Vatican authorities; he insisted, for example, that good Catholics go to confession and take communion every Sunday. Finally, however, he succeeded in drawing a constitution that proved acceptable in Vatican circles. Pope Paul III confirmed the new order on September 27, 1540, by the bull *Regimini militantis ecclesiae.*

A Jesuit, said the bull, shall be "a soldier of God under the banner of the cross." His duties shall include (1) "the advancement of souls in Christian life and doctrine"; (2) "the propagation of the faith by public preaching, spiritual exercises, and works of charity"; (3) "the Christian education of the young and unlearned"; and (4) "the hearing of confessions." Each Jesuit, abandoning his own will, shall subscribe unconditionally to do the will of the pope and of the general of the Jesuit order. Ignatius was elected general on April 7, 1541, and held that office until his death on July 31, 1556.

Like an army, the Society of Jesus depended upon its mobility. In 1545 Pope Paul licensed the order to preach and administer the sacraments everywhere, without first obtaining the permission of either bishops or parish priests — an exceptional privilege of access that the pope confirmed by the bull *Licet debitum* of 1549.

The interior strength of the order depended upon an extraordinary spiritual vitality, of which Ignatius's *Spiritual Exercises* is the finest expression. That manual, published in 1548, consists of a series of meditations, prayers, and examinations of conscience designed to be used under the guidance of a skilled director over a period of four weeks. Toward the end is a prayer of self-surrender that illustrates the Jesuit temperament:

> Take Lord, and receive all my liberty, my memory, my understanding, and my entire will, all that I have and possess. Thou hast given all to me. To thee, O Lord, I return it. All is thine; dispose of it wholly according to thy will. Give me thy love and thy grace, for this is sufficient for me.

The *Exercises* close with eighteen *Regulae ad sentiendum cum ecclesia* (Rules for thinking with the church), in which obedience, the soldier's virtue, appears as the highest of all virtues. Included in the *Regulae* is this statement: "What seems to me white, I will believe black if the hierarchical church so defines." Every year, every Jesuit puts aside his duties to "make the *Exercises*" and thus renew the commitment on which his vocation was originally made. Highly educated themselves,* the Jesuits pursued their purposes by means of education. They established schools — at Padua, Venice, Bologna, and Messina and Palermo in Sicily — each with the distinctive Jesuit *ratio studiorum* (order of studies, curriculum), which is humanistic, yet (for purposes of religious argumentation) dialectical. In 1550 Ignatius himself established *Collegium Romanum* (Roman College), which soon occupied space in the great Jesuit Church of Rome, the Gesu. By 1584 it had dispatched over 2,000 students into the fray. Side by side was the *Collegium Germanicum* (German College), founded in 1552 as the training ground of Jesuits destined to confront the Protestants of Germany. By 1700 the order sustained 769 colleges and university establishments in which approximately 200,000 students were enrolled. Many of those students became rulers of nations or framers of public policy or makers of opinion. By such means, the Jesuits attained a not insignificant influence over European political affairs.

The order flourished in Italy, Spain, and Portugal. When John III, king of Portugal (1521–57) asked Pope Paul III to authorize a Portuguese mission to the East Indies, the enterprise was entrusted to the Jesuits. Ignatius designated Francis Xavier and Simon Rodríguez as fit to go. Xavier (see plate 79), born of Spanish nobility in 1506, had met Ignatius at the Collège de Sainte Barbe in Paris and had been enrolled by him as one of

---

* The complete Jesuit regiment required two years as a novice, a year of general studies, three years of philosophy, four years of theology, followed by ordination to the priesthood and a year of practical divinity, two more years of trial, followed by full admission to the order.

the charter members of the Society of Jesus. Winsome, intelligent, constructive, and dedicated, Xavier was deemed by Ignatius a suitable Jesuit for the Portuguese mission. He left Rome for Lisbon on March 16, 1540. From there King John dispatched him to evangelize the Portuguese possessions in India; he arrived in Goa on May 6, 1542. After an effort of three years in southern India, he passed over to Malacca, Malaya, the Moluccas, and other East Indian islands, where he preached for another term. On August 15, 1549, he landed in Japan; there he labored with some success for several years. Francis Xavier died on November 17, 1552, in his forty-sixth year, just as he had entered China to begin yet another ambitious campaign. Historians assess the importance of Jesuit missions in other than religious terms. First, the missionaries furnished the West with accurate accounts of the history, geography, religion, philosophy, and art of Asia (later, of Africa and America also), unsettling some of the exclusivity that had been attached to the Western intellectual tradition. Second, European imperialism — an imperialism of soldiers and merchants — was sweetened by the more generous nature of the Jesuit intent, namely, to save souls.

In France, the Jesuits were met with stout antipathy, being viewed as a Spanish affair, beneath the French dignity, unwanted, and unnecessary. In Germany, however, Pierre Lefèvre (Faber) and his disciple Peter Canisius (1521–97) waged the toughest intellectual warfare against the Protestants with unquestionable success. Every conceivable means was used in the unending struggle to recover the allegiance of the followers of Luther, including schools, libraries, seminaries, monasteries, and catechisms. Canisius and his Jesuit colleagues stemmed the progress of Protestantism in Bavaria, Austria, Bohemia, and many other territories and towns. At the death of Ignatius in 1556, the Jesuit order was organized into fourteen provinces and consisted of 1,500 members.

THE COUNCIL OF TRENT

THE LAST aspect of the Counter-Reformation, and perhaps the greatest, was the Council of Trent (1545–63), which defined and published Catholic teaching in the face of the Protestant challenge. Councils, by their very nature, are threatening events; they close some doors, and they open others. The church has been appropriately wary of councils. After Trent, three hundred years passed before Vatican Council I (1868–70) occurred; another hundred years, before Vatican II (1962–65). We should not be surprised to discover, therefore, that out of the intense furor of the Council of Trent came decisions that shaped the Catholic mind in the early modern world.

Why was such a council even permitted? Did not the bull *Execrabilis* of Pope Pius II outlaw conciliarism? What Pius II actually condemned was not the holding of councils but the attempt by conciliarists to use representative church councils as a means to subvert the authority of the papacy. Indeed, the Fifth Lateran Council (1512–17) was convened by Pope Julius II and conducted by Pope Leo X fifty years after *Execrabilis.* Alessandro Farnese got elected Pope Paul III in 1534 on the platform that he would immediately convoke a Catholic council to make reforms and define doctrine. The Protestants indeed took particular delight in referring to the ideas of conciliarism, being fully aware that conciliarism had been outlawed. Ulrich von Hutten took every conceivable occasion to clamor, "Consilium! Consilium! Consilium!" Luther appealed for a *representative* church council in 1518, again in 1520, and continued to do so until 1539, when he wrote a whole treatise *On the Councils and the Church,* in which he said, "We cry out and appeal for a council."

True to his word, Paul III summoned a council to meet in 1536, but war between Charles V and Francis I prevented it. Undaunted, the pope issued another call to gather at Vicenza in 1538; the same war intervened. In 1542 the pontiff tried again: Catholic prelates were to gather at Trent (Trento) in northern Italy — a small town, Italian in character, but situated just inside the borders of the Holy Roman Empire. The site was a concession to Emperor Charles V. Charles generally favored the convention of a council, believing that it afforded him the pretext of making the German Protestants knuckle under. In 1544, by the Peace of Crépy, Charles had finally brought the French to bay. From his standpoint, therefore, conditions were ideal for the beginning of the council. The pope responded accordingly, issuing a summons to begin the Council of Trent in March 1545. He appointed three legates whose duty it was to make sure that the council remained firmly papal: Giovanni Maria del Monte (later Pope Julius III), Marcello Cervini (later Pope Marcellus II), and Reginald Pole. As the princes, prelates, ambassadors, and their entourages all arrived in Trent, the local bishop, Cardinal Madruzzo, was suddenly undone by unforeseen problems of a most mundane sort. Wine jumped 30 percent; room rents became exorbitant; meat and grain became almost impossible to obtain.

Under such circumstances, the Council of Trent got underway on December 13, 1545. Besides the three papal legates, there was only one other cardinal in attendance — Christopher Madruzzo of Trent, the only bishop representative of the German Catholics. In fact, there were only four archbishops at Trent, only twenty bishops, only four heads of religious orders — a minimal representation for such a significant event. Princes, ambassadors, and theologians were also present, but they were without franchise. The only voting members of a Catholic council are bishops and heads of religious orders. They vote *placet* (yes), *non placet* (no), or *placet iuxta modum* (yes, but with reservations). No Protestants were there, neither were there any representatives from the Orthodox churches of the East. As one might expect, Italy sent the largest delegation: twelve prelates. There were five from Spain, two from France, and Cardinal Madruzzo of Germany. The politics of the Council of Trent were both complex and intense. Some delegates were conservative; others liberal. Some were "conciliarist" as opposed to "curialist" (i.e., apt to argue the rights of the council in opposition to the pretenses of the papal curia). Some were ultramontanists (i.e., "over the Alps") in their sympathies — somewhat jaded in their opinion of the papacy.

The Council of Trent opened uneasily. Cardinal del Monte, its president, made an opening "intervention" in which he proposed two items for the agenda: the grievous corruptions in the church and the loss of theological clarity, not to mention downright heresy. The two improvements needed were thus a new definition of Catholic doctrine and the reform of the more flagrant abuses. But which should be given precedence: doctrine or reform? The papal party thought that the time had passed when it was appropriate to pamper the Protestants with talk of reform; the proper business of the council was dogma! But Charles V (for political reasons) and the Spanish bishops (for religious reasons) insisted that priority be given to reform. Out popped all the prejudices, as one by one the ultramontanists, the curialists, and the conciliarists had their say. Bishop Campeggio saved the occasion by proposing that doctrine and reform should be treated concurrently. His resolution carried, and tension subsided, but the papacy had lost the initial skirmish.

Thus, reforms were made apace. Session 21, for example, struck at the ignorance and illiteracy of the clergy. The first substantial decision of the council, however, was one of doctrine. Session 4 (April 8, 1546) declared that the Council of Trent "receives and venerates with equal affection of piety and reverence" both Scripture and tradition. As the whole Protestant Reformation had been based on the principle of *sola Scriptura,* such a statement left the gulf between Catholics and Protestants impassable. Seven or eight bishops, led by the bishop of Chioggia, expressed sympathy for the

Protestants and warned of the uncharitable implications of this decree. Cardinal Pole redressed them. "The church," he said, "is an army drawn up for battle. She cannot proceed to the attack unless her equipment is complete. We have first to prepare our weapons and then to engage the enemy. . . . Our beliefs and our worship in their entirety depend upon Tradition." Pole carried the day, and the decree was enacted. Reconciliation with the Protestants was henceforth unlikely, if not impossible.

Meanwhile, the political fortunes of Emperor Charles V greatly improved. On April 24, 1547, the year after the death of Luther, Charles defeated the Protestant military alliance at the battle of Mühlberg, and the two principal Protestant captains, the elector of Saxony and the landgraf of Hesse, were both taken prisoner. A month earlier (March 31), Francis I of France had expired. Thus Charles was at last the master of European politics. The Council of Trent took heart at these events and proceeded to attack Protestantism in its vitals. Session 5 (June 17, 1546) defined original sin in terms that contradicted the Protestant insistence upon total depravity. When the council stated, for example, that Adam "was changed for the worse" by virtue of the Fall, it muted the strident tones of Luther and Calvin that the human will was in complete bondage to sin. Furthermore, the council maintained that what remains in human beings after they have received the sacrament of baptism is not sin but "of sin and inclining toward sin," which certainly allows human beings to contribute something to their own justification.

The following session of the council, session 6 (January 13, 1547), treated the crucial doctrine of justification. The preparatory debate was long and intense. Cervini and Pole, representing the papal faction, observed that most of Luther's errors accrued from his mistaken notions about justification, and they urged the council to take a firm Catholic stand on that subject. Moderates, such as Jacopo Seripando, general of the Augustinians, wished to adopt a statement that would not be so completely offensive to the Protestants — one saying, for instance, that good works, while necessary, were less important than faith. Sanfelice, the bishop of La Cava, made bold to argue for justification by faith alone (Luther's view of the matter), whereupon he was set upon by the ultraconservative bishop Zannetini of Chironissa (in Crete). In the argument that ensued, Sanfelice plucked Zannetini's beard. At Ignatius's instruction, the Jesuits Lainez and Salmerón now intervened energetically to insist upon the absolute necessity of good works by human beings as a condition of their justification. When the decree on justification was finally promulgated (January 13, 1547), the Council of Trent had grown to two papal legates, two cardinals, ten archbishops, forty-seven bishops, five generals of religious orders, and two abbots.

The decree opens by saying that Christ alone is the salvation of the world. By his sacrifice on the cross, he achieved "justice" sufficient to offset all the "injustice" of human beings. Human beings have been left "unjust" by the fall of Adam, their willpower having been "attenuated and bent down" but "by no means extinguished," as Luther had said. But this "justice" of Christ does not apply to everyone; it applies to those who are "born again in Christ," the sign of which is the sacrament of baptism. Justification begins therefore with baptism, at which time the first fundamental connection with Christ is made. Baptism, however, is not enough. When the Catholic child becomes an adult, a process of justification begins. God calls again to the baptized adult through "prevenient" grace (i.e., the grace that "goes before"). Christians may assent or may resist that prevenient grace out of their own free will. If they choose to cooperate, however, no one should doubt that God has encouraged them to do so by means of another sort of grace, "assisting" grace.

According to the Council of Trent, justification is not a once-for-all *event,* an experience of forgiveness as the Protestants thought; justification is a *process* that proceeds throughout life in which the believer is actively involved, a process that the decree describes as "advancing from virtue to virtue." It is literally the transformation of the soul, which theologians refer to as sanctification. In this struggle to attain to justice, still another sort of grace is helpful, "sacramental" grace, which comes to people through the seven sacraments.

Therefore faith is not enough to become just — despite what Luther thought. To advance from virtue to virtue requires both faith and works, as well as the mortification of the flesh and the observance of the commandments of God and the church. Finally, by all of these means, "the man of injustice becomes just" and attains the possibility of eternal life. Take special notice of the word "becomes."

The two parties to Western Christianity used the same words to mean different things. For the Protestants, justification meant a *once-for-all event;* for the Catholics, an *enduring process.* For the Protestants, that event was the forgiveness of sins — a moment of unspeakable relief out of which the whole religious life flowered; for the Catholics, the process of justification included both the forgiveness of sins and the renewal of life. For the Protestants, "justification" meant to *be reckoned just* in God's sight on account of what Christ did; for the Catholics, "justification" meant to *become just* in God's sight through the combined powers of God's grace and human effort.

519

The political successes of Charles V filled the Spanish and German prelates with such zeal that the papacy increasingly feared imperial intimidation in the affairs of the council. An epidemic at Trent, which caused the death of one bishop, provided an excuse to move the council to Bologna (a little closer to Rome) on March 23, 1547. When Charles V protested staunchly against such trifling maneuvers, the embarrassed pope prorogued the council on February 15, 1548. On the death of Pope Paul III the following year, Cardinal del Monte emerged from the conclave as Pope Julius III (1550–55). Preferring peace with the emperor, Julius reconvened the Council of Trent on April 29, 1551. By choosing the Jesuits Lainez and Salmerón to represent him, Julius cleverly neutralized the Spanish preponderance. In Session 13 (October 11, 1551), the council issued a complicated decree on the Eucharist, specifically redressing the errors of Luther, Calvin, and Zwingli with respect to that sacrament and proposing the time-honored doctrine of transubstantiation, yet without using the scholastic distinction between "substance" and "accidents."

At the emperor's insistence, some Protestants were invited to Trent at this time, but no one of prominence attended. Those who did were disgruntled that no important issues remained to be discussed. The council seemed to languish in a loss of direction. Pope Julius prorogued it on April 28, 1552. Nine years passed before it reconvened. Meanwhile the Peace of Augsburg (1555) guaranteed the rights of Lutherans in Germany. The death of Charles V on September 21, 1558, led to the Treaty of Cateau-Cambrésis the following year, in which an international settlement among the French, Spanish, and Germans was finally achieved. Death in 1559 also ended the imperious pontificate of Paul IV (Giovanni Pietro Caraffa), who succeeded Julius III in 1555.

The third and final assembly of the council was convened by Pope Pius IV (1559–65) on January 18, 1562 and lasted until December of the following year. As the balance of power among the European monarchies was now at equipoise, Pius attempted to remove the council from all political considerations, in effect disconnecting the bishops from their national interests. The upshot of that change of strategy was to enhance enormously the power of the papacy. The papacy emerged from the Council of Trent with a more vigorous authority than ever before.

In Session 22 (July 17, 1562), the council defined the Mass as a sacrifice. The question that had been before the council was whether Christ offered himself as a sacrifice to God only on the cross (the Protestant opinion) or whether Christ also offered himself as a sacrifice to God in every Mass (the Catholic opinion). It was another touchy issue for Protestants. Protestants denounced the idea that every Mass involved the sacrifice of Christ because, aside from the possibility that it was not biblical, they were sure that it denigrated the sacrifice of Christ on Calvary — that one, great propitiatory event on which the whole Protestant scheme of justification of faith depended.

The decree teaches that each Mass *does* involve the sacrifice of Christ, which we should understand as a sort of sacramental extension out into time of Christ's unique sacrifice on Calvary. Each Mass thus has a propitiatory value of its own, applicable to those sins that Christians commit after their baptism. Embedded in the decree are four rather obscure words, *sicut hominum natura exigit* (as human nature requires), which make all the difference in the world. In other words, it is fundamentally human to want to treat with God through sacrifices. Religion and sacrifice are inextricably connected. Few Protestants have the intellectual and emotional conditioning to subscribe to that premise. The four Latin words, almost a parenthesis in the affairs of Trent, may represent another irreconcilable difference between the two Western Christian traditions.

The toughest rebuff to Trent was written into the liturgy of the Church of England in 1549 and is still recited each Sunday by hundreds of thousands of Anglicans and Methodists and sundry other Protestants, without their knowing how polemical it is:

> [Thou] didst give thine only Son to suffer death upon the Cross for our redemption, and made there, by his one [sacrifice], once offered, a full, perfect, and sufficient sacrifice, oblation, and satisfaction for the sins of the whole world.

On December 4, 1563, the Council of Trent closed forever, as 255 constituents signed the various decrees and canons. It had arrived at three decisions that made impossible any accommodation with Protestants: (1) Scripture and tradition as the joint bases of religious authority; (2) justification as a process, involving both faith and works; and (3) the Mass as a sacrifice. The positive benefits of the council were enormous. It clarified Catholic teaching, improved the efficiency of church organization, cured abuses, left the papacy stronger than ever, and filled the Catholic world with confidence and religious zeal. It is appropriate now to refer to Tridentine Catholicism, in respect to the Council of Trent.

Three heroes of the Counter-Reformation had careers that were particularly illustrative of the Tridentine spirit: Peter Canisius, Charles Borromeo, and Robert Bellarmine. Of Canisius, we have already spoken. A

521

Jesuit, he became the foremost teller of Catholic truth to a Germany sorely divided between Catholics and Protestants. "He stemmed the Reformation" in Germany, said Pope Pius IX of Peter Canisius at Canisius's beatification. His reputation came from two cogent and beautifully written cathechisms — *Catechismus major* (1555) and *Catechismus minor* (1556) — which were expressive of Tridentine Catholicism and specifically designed to rebut Luther's larger and smaller catechisms. Borromeo, a nephew of Pope Pius IV, became the archbishop of Milan (1560–84) in the aftermath of the Council of Trent and proceeded to enact Tridentine Catholicism by a series of practical steps. He intensified Catholic discipline, making it effective for both clergy and laity; he rebuilt churches, reformed the religious orders, and founded schools and colleges. His *Collegium Helveticum* (Swiss College) in Milan dispatched scores of students into Switzerland to excite the Catholic cantons of the Swiss Confederacy with the new Tridentine faith. Bellarmine (1542–1621), an Italian Jesuit, nephew of Pope Marcellus II, became the foremost controversialist of the early Counter-Reformation. In 1576, after a distinguished beginning as an educator, Bellarmine began to teach courses in controversial theology in two of the Jesuit colleges of Rome, *Collegium Germanicum* and *Collegium Anglicanum* (English College), for the benefit of Jesuit missionaries being prepared for service in those countries. Beginning in 1586, those lectures were published as *Disputationes de controversiis Christianae fidei adversus hujus temporis haereticos.* Bellarmine's *Controversies* became the stock-in-trade for all sorts of persons, great and small, fierce or tepid, who wished to do battle with the Protestants.

Everywhere the Renaissance in Italy crumbled under the weight of foreign invasions, economic depression, and the increasingly sober nature of the Counter-Reformation. A failure of nerve overwhelmed the Renaissance humanists, who did little to stave off the sobriety of the Counter-Reformation. The Italian Renaissance persisted longest in Venice, where humanists were few but where artists continued to flourish, where civic pride was fierce, the papacy thought little of, and the Inquisition given almost no quarter at all. There, in Venice, was one of the "universal men" of the Renaissance, Paolo Sarpi, a priest who knew about optics and mathematics and who, like Pico, had informed himself about Oriental religions. In 1618 he published *History of the Council of Trent,* the first such account of the council. In Sarpi's *History,* the papacy appears as a conniving and manipulative power, cleverly using the council to protect and augment papal prestige. What Sarpi was, and what he wrote, stand among the final expressions of the Renaissance in Italy.

EXCURSUS

St. Peter's Basilica

THE GREATEST OF ALL RENAISSANCE BUILDINGS WAS BUILT ON THE ROMAN hill called *Mons Vaticanus*. The building is St. Peter's Basilica, the largest ecclesiastical structure in the West.

Mons Vaticanus was associated with the mystery religions of the Greco-Roman world long before it became a place of Christian veneration. There the cult of Cybele held its mysterious rites celebrating the dying and rising of the god Attis. *Mons Vaticanus* means "the hill of prophecy," and the prophecy referred to was that of the ancient cult of Cybele. The Romans thought little of the place. Pliny the Elder said that it was ridden with

104. St. Peter's Basilica, panorama

105. Early St. Peter's

mosquitoes. "Poisonous" was the word that the satirical poet Martial used to describe the Vatican wine.

Suddenly the fortunes of the hill changed. The boisterous Emperor Caligula (A.D. 37–41) built a circus on the slopes of the Vatican in the third decade of the first Christian century. His successor, Nero, constructed a bridge over the Tiber, the better to get to Caligula's circus, where he conducted a variety of sports, including the execution of seditious persons called Christians. Around A.D. 67, perhaps to distract attention from a fire in Rome that he was alleged to have started, Nero executed certain Christians in Caligula's circus; among them may have been the Peter upon whom the papacy was founded. The tradition soon arose that Peter, having been crucified upside down, was buried in a lower-class cemetery adjacent to the circus.

In the opening years of the fourth century, the Roman emperor Constantine espoused Christianity and proceeded to make that hitherto illegal religion legal. In fact, he ardently promoted it by a variety of means, including the construction of churches. (Before Constantine's time, Christians had thought better of building houses of worship, which merely served to advertise their whereabouts and thereby invited persecution.) About the year 322, anticipating new revenues from the eastern half of the empire, Constantine began the construction of a massive church dedicated to Peter. He had it built on Vatican hill over the site of what he believed to be the grave of that apostle. The building was completed prior to Constantine's death in 337.

It was a basilica. It was, in other words, patterned after the Roman halls of justice, which were invariably rectangular, divided by rows of columns into a central nave, with an aisle on either side. At the front was an apse, in the midst of which sat the chief justice on a marble throne. It took little ingenuity to transform the secular basilica into a place of religion. The worshipers kept to the nave. The bishop sat in the apse on a chair called *cathedra* (hence, the expression *ex cathedra*). The ambo, the box where witnesses gave their testimony and where lawyers advocated their case, became a reading desk for reciting the Scriptures.

The interior of St. Peter's was massive. The columns, from their base to the architrave, were thirty feet; they had been pulled down from pagan temples and were of several sizes and sorts. Instead of a vaulted ceiling, which was costly and required time to build, Constantine ordered exposed wooden rafters, locked at the middle by iron bands.

In front of the basilica, Constantine cleared away an enormous space for an atrium, which, in the course of time, was enclosed by galleries and outfitted with a campanile. Penitents, denied permission to the church itself for some sin of great magnitude, languished in the atrium.

Although this church was not the seat of the papacy in the Middle Ages — that honor fell to the Church of St. John Lateran — it was nevertheless a place of historical importance, the sentimental center of Western Christianity. It was here that Charlemagne received his crown at the hands of the pope on Christmas Day in the year 800. Here also many of the artistic achievements of the West — mosaics, sculptures, and frescoes — were displayed.

The bronze statue of St. Peter, for example, graced the old basilica. No one knows where it came from. Some authorities are sure that it is an ancient statue of Jupiter brought down from the Capitoline Hill. More likely it was executed by Arnolfo di Cambio in the thirteenth century. Its foot has been worn by the kisses of the faithful.

During the Avignon papacy and the Great Papal Schism that followed, the old basilica was left to tumble into disrepair. Wolves foraged amid the wreckage. When Pope Martin V returned to Rome in 1420 after the schism was ended, he found the building partially in ruins and took pains to restore

106. Bronze
statue of
St. Peter

it. It was Nicholas V, first of the Renaissance popes, who reached the grave
decision to tear down the old basilica and raise a building in its stead that
would express the style of the Renaissance. Why did Nicholas, a humanist
who revered antiquity, arrive at such a rash decision? Three reasons are
probable. First, Nicholas's architect, Leon Battista Alberti, warned the pope
that the south wall of the old basilica leaned six feet out of perpendicular.
"I am convinced," he wrote, "that some slight shock or movement will cause
it to fall." Second, the old basilica had become a hodge-podge of monuments
and accretions, put there no doubt in the name of piety, which nevertheless
spoiled the sense of symmetry that the Renaissance people found seemly

and decent. Third, Nicholas had arrived at the principle, typical of the Renaissance popes, that people must be taught about Christianity through the eye, and specifically through the grandeur of great buildings and great works of art. He wrote, "To create solid and stable convictions in the minds of the uncultured masses, there must be something that appeals to the eye." He resolved therefore to create a great new Renaissance structure. But no sooner had he got a few of the footings laid than he died.

In 1308 fire had destroyed the Lateran Palace of the popes. All of the popes beginning with Gregory XI therefore lived on Vatican hill. Nicholas V, if he did not survive long enough to see the new basilica rise, succeeded, at least, in building a new palace on Vatican hill.

The popes who succeeded Nicholas were either too timid or too short-lived to continue the new basilica. Pius II and Innocent VIII actually resorted to mending the old basilica. Not so Julius II. Julius II was cast into a gigantic mold. Nothing tickled his fancy more than the idea of building the most splendid edifice ever conceived in the Christian West. It was in the spring of 1505 that he resolved to build a new basilica on strictly contemporary lines and on the grandest scale imaginable. The Romans thought it insufferable that a pope would take it upon himself to sweep away a building hallowed by 1,200 years of history. But he did. Some 2,500 workmen invaded the old basilica and, without even making an inventory, demolished enough of the old building to make way for the new. Julius laid the cornerstone on April 18, 1506.

The first architect of St. Peter's was Donato Bramante. Would it not be a fair assumption that such Renaissance men as Julius and Bramante would refer to some classical model of architecture — to the Roman basilica, no doubt? They did not. Bramante proposed, and Julius agreed, that the new St. Peter's would take the form of a Greek cross, so massive that it would exceed the length of the old basilica by two-fifths, the width by three-fifths. Why, of all things, did Bramante propose a Greek-cross design? One look at that design will tell us why. It involves a series of lesser domes around a great central dome, a series of lesser geometric forms around a single great geometric form. It is therefore the perfect embodiment of the Renaissance ideal of unity, proportion, and harmony, which was, in turn, the highest expression of beauty and a mirror of the perfection of God.

How had Bramante thought of these things? He was fifty-five when he left his native Lombardy in 1499 to strike out for Rome. He had worked in the city of Milan in the days when Leonardo da Vinci was in residence there. Leonardo conceived of geometric figures as suitable ground-plans for buildings. Imagine a daisy, with four or five petals. Imagine a public building built accordingly, with a great central dome, and four or five apses radiating from it. Leonardo's idea was to make a building a living organism. His ideas, transfigured by Bramante into the Renaissance virtues of order, harmony, and proportion, found their way to Rome and St. Peter's.

But even before Bramante's time, people conceived of the Greek cross as an ideal Renaissance conception of architecture, as one may judge by the painting which Perugino executed for the Sistine Chapel in 1482, during the pontificate of Julius's uncle, Sixtus IV. Similar structures appear in the

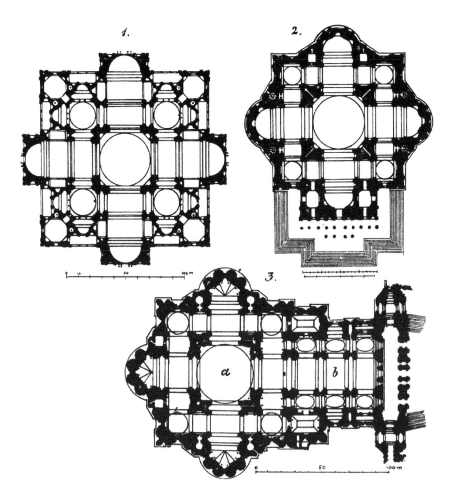

107. Three plans for St. Peter's Basilica

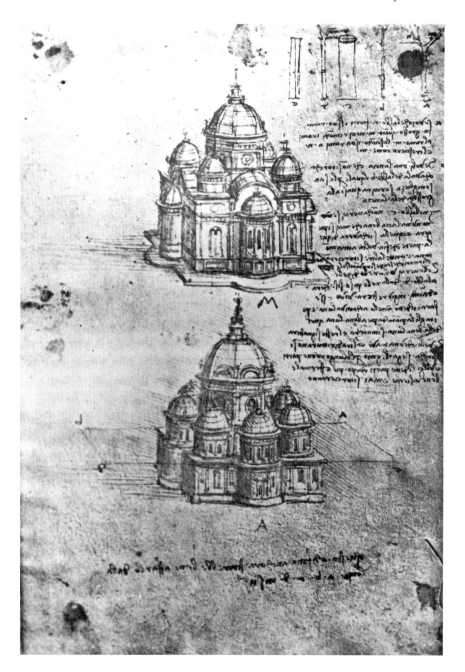

108. Leonardo da Vinci's daisy design for domes

paintings of Raphael. Their classical model may be found in such buildings as the Temple of Vesta.

When he first came to Rome, Bramante accepted a commission to build a tiny temple in the courtyard of one of the city's churches. Bramante's Tempietto of 1502, although on a very small scale, illustrated his ambitions for St. Peter's Basilica. The peristyle and the dome of the Tempietto were

109. Bramante, Tempietto

to become, in Bramante's imagination at least, the drum and dome of St. Peter's.

In 1513, not long after he had promised indulgences to those benefactors who would contribute to the construction of the great building, Julius II died. Bramante followed him to the grave the following year. At their death, four gigantic piers that supported the crossing were complete, and the connecting arches were in place. Raphael, as he painted *The School of Athens,* provided an idealized conception of what the basilica looked like.

Leo X, the Medici pope who succeeded Julius, inherited a partially demolished ancient basilica and a new one scarcely begun. The crossing lacked a roof. Debris and dust were everywhere. Leo appointed a committee of three architects, of whom Raphael soon became the sole survivor. Lionized and at the height of his fame, Raphael was overwhelmed by honors and commissions. He was not, however, adept as an architect. What he knew he had learned from Bramante. He nevertheless proposed a plan in 1514 that would have been Bramante's undoing. What Raphael proposed was to change the Greek-cross design into that of a Latin cross. He did not survive to see his radical plans for St. Peter's mature. One afternoon, in the spring of 1520, he dashed from the Villa Farnesina on foot and arrived at St. Peter's in a great fever. Within six days, the vastly overworked young artist was dead. He was thirty-seven years old.

In 1534 Alessandro Farnese, son of one of the great Roman families, became Pope Paul III. Paul III was the first pope of the Counter-Reformation. The popes of the Counter-Reformation toughened the moral fiber of the Catholic Church, resisted the Protestant advance, and presented their church as a triumphant, militant force here on earth. Imperceptibly, therefore, the fundamental purpose of the great basilica began to change. Its importance as a statement of Renaissance grandeur diminished; its importance as a statement of Catholic triumphalism increased.

The first of Paul III's architects was Antonio da Sangallo the Younger. Sangallo had the good sense to revert to Bramante's Greek-cross plan, having rejected Raphael's drastic revision, but he proceeded to produce an exterior design full of towers, pyramids, bumps, and assorted protuberances. It was vastly overwrought, utterly lacking in the Renaissance care for economy of expression.

In 1546 Sangallo died from the fever. Paul III turned to Michelangelo Buonarroti, then seventy-two years old, to take up the responsibility of building the basilica. Michelangelo conceived it to be the crowning achievement of his life. Although he denied that he was an architect, he has been deemed one of the great architects of all time. In that riddle lies one of the most important shifts in the history of art. Michelangelo, the architect, approached St. Peter's as a sculptor would; he was apt to see the building as he saw a piece of sculpture, as an organic form capable of being molded and carved, expressing movement, and forming symphonies of light, shadow, and texture — in short, the building became a dynamic force to be released by the artist's imagination. The back of St. Peter's remains just as Michelangelo built it. It illustrates his approach to architecture from the mentality of a sculptor.

This may have been the first moment of baroque art — when the bonds of classical art that had hitherto held the Renaissance artists so tightly to the classical idea of geometric perfection were broken, allowing for a greater sensuousness and emotion, and a luxuriating in endless entrancing fantasies.

Michelangelo held tightly to Bramante's Greek-cross plan, which he found to be luminous and beautiful. Thus Michelangelo, if he was the father of baroque art, was himself held captive to the classicism of Bramante and of the Renaissance. It was only when he treated architecture as sculpture that the first, primal examples of the baroque style began to appear.

Michelangelo died on February 18, 1564, in his eighty-ninth year. What did the building look like at his death? The north and south transeptal arms of the Greek cross were almost complete, both inside and outside, as far up as the entablature, and the drum of the dome had been set in place.

He died, however, before his final design for the dome had quite been settled. The idea that one massive dome would one day surmount the tomb of Peter was an idea as old as the Renaissance itself. But what sort of dome? Michelangelo was displeased with the rather squat conception of Bramante. His ideal was the great elliptical, ribbed dome that Brunelleschi had designed for the cathedral in Florence. Although his successors altered his design in some detail, it was the dome of Michelangelo in its basic features that was finally constructed.

Giacomo Della Porta served as chief architect of St. Peter's in the feverish days of Pope Sixtus V (1585–90). A man of enormous energy, determined to see the building go up, Sixtus ordered shifts of eight hundred workers to work around the clock. By such means Della Porta managed to complete Michelangelo's dome, making only minor adjustments as he proceeded.

It was Sixtus V who ordered the removal of the Egyptian obelisk from Caligula's circus to the middle of St. Peter's Piazza — a task so stupendous that Michelangelo had pronounced it impossible. In his *Natural History,* Pliny the Elder reported that the obelisk had been transported from Egypt to Rome by Emperor Caligula in A.D. 37 on a barge so huge that the arms of four men could not encircle its main mast. It stood in a single piece, more than eighty feet high, weighing more than a million pounds. Sheer weight had driven half of its length into the ground. In 1586, however, Sixtus ordered it removed. More than five hundred mathematicians, engineers, and doctors of science submitted plans for its removal. The job fell finally to Domenico Fontana, second-ranking architect of St. Peter's.

On April 30 of that year, by means of an ingenious wooden crane of Fontana's design, eight hundred men managed to lift the obelisk one foot off the ground, as virtually the whole Roman populace watched. On May 17 the obelisk was lowered horizontally to the ground by the same means and was conveyed to its destination on rollers. On September 14, when the summer heat had subsided, the eight hundred workmen, having been to early morning Mass, stood ready to reerect the obelisk in the midst of the vast square. Pope Sixtus had promised instant death to anyone in the multitude of bystanders who dared utter a sound; a gallows stood conspicuously in the square. Fontana, standing on a podium, directed operations as a conductor might a modern orchestra. The horses strained; the windlasses turned; the obelisk quivered and slowly rose. The ropes, however, began to

110. Raising the obelisk

smolder from the friction. According to a tradition, a sailor from Liguria risked his life by shouting, "Water them!" — for which bravery and common sense Pope Sixtus both pardoned and rewarded him. By nightfall the obelisk was safely in its cradle, as the Romans danced and drank and shot off fireworks at such a feat.

On Della Porta's death in 1602, Pope Clement VIII appointed Carlo Maderno in his place. It was he who brought the building to a conclusion and, in so doing, brought an end to the age of Bramante and Michelangelo. Maderno made a daring, perhaps ominous decision. In order to provide more space for people on the great papal occasions, he decided to attach a nave to the Greek-cross church of Michelangelo. Approved in 1607, the nave was completed eight years later. There is a slight kink in Maderno's nave; it inclines slightly to the south. Why? Because Fontana had failed to set the obelisk axially with Michelangelo's east arm of the church.

What had Carlo Maderno done? He had disturbed the Greek-cross conception that the Renaissance architects had favored because of its perfect spatial proportions. By virtue of his nave, he had increased the longitudinal sense of the building, the illusion of infinite distance, leading to a far-off holy of holies beneath the dome. His conception is mysterious, dramatic, and baroque. On the one hand, therefore, Maderno had curtailed the classical sense of the structure; on the other hand, he augmented its baroque character. It was Maderno who created the facade of St. Peter's, which is generally criticized as being too congested or busy, too heavy, too broad. Among its many disadvantages, it obscures the dome.

Pope Urban VIII (1623–44) was the first, and perhaps the greatest, of the baroque popes, during whose reign St. Peter's Basilica received most of its baroque ornamentation and thus most of its present character. Urban was the son of a distinguished Roman family, the Barberini, a man trained in music and the arts, a distinguished scholar who knew Galileo and who spared him imprisonment when the Inquisition ventured to denounce his scientific findings. Most important of all, it was Urban VIII who appointed Gian Lorenzo Bernini chief architect of St. Peter's. Thus, for forty years, Bernini, greatest of the baroque architects, a genius of boundless energy and religious enthusiasm, was able to embellish the building.

There are two ways in which a work of art can depart from the normal by way of exaggeration. One way is typical of classical art. The exaggeration here is idealism — ideal proportions, ideal harmony, ideal beauty — which in fact does not ordinarily exist. Think, for example, of Brunelleschi's Pazzi Chapel with its perfect geometric shapes (plate 1), or Bramante's Greek-cross

53. TOP Fra Filippo Lippi, *Madonna of Humility*

54. BOTTOM Fra Filippo Lippi, *Madonna and Child with Angels*

55. TOP Fra
Angelico, *The
Annunciation*

56. BOTTOM
Fra Angelico,
The Deposition

57. TOP Fra Angelico,
Coronation of the Virgin

58. BOTTOM Fra Angelico, *San
Lorenzo Distributing Alms to the
Poor*

59. TOP Sandro Botticelli,
Pallas and the Centaur

60. BOTTOM Sandro
Botticelli, *Primavera*

61. TOP Sandro
Botticelli, *Birth of Venus*

62. BOTTOM
Sandro Botticelli,
The Annunciation

63. TOP
Domenico
Ghirlandaio,
*Adoration
of the Shepherds*

64. BOTTOM LEFT
Raphael,
portrait of Angelo
Doni

65. BOTTOM
RIGHT Raphael,
portrait
of Maddalena Doni

66. TOP Michelangelo, *Creation of Eve,* Sistine Chapel

67. BOTTOM Michelangelo, *Temptation and Expulsion,* Sistine Chapel

68. TOP Michelangelo, *Creation of Adam,* Sistine Chapel

69. BOTTOM Raphael, *The Dispute of the Sacrament*

70. TOP Raphael, *School of Athens*

71. BOTTOM Raphael,
Transfiguration of Christ

72. TOP Raphael, *Parnassus*

73. BOTTOM Raphael, *Expulsion of Heliodorus*

74. TOP Raphael, *Mass at Bolsena*

75. BOTTOM Raphael, *Leo the Great Repulsing Attila the Hun*

76. Christopher Columbus

77. Catherine of Aragon, portrait by Michiel Sittow

78. TOP *Saint Ignatius before Pope Paul III*, anonymous

79. BOTTOM Francis Xavier, detail from *The Miracle of Saint Francis Xavier* by Peter Paul Rubens

80. TOP Bernini's baldachin,
St. Peter's Basilica

81. BOTTOM Bernini's colonnades,
Vatican Square

82. Elizabeth I

111. Carlo Maderno's nave of St. Peter's Basilica

design. The other way of exaggeration is the way of fantasy. Baroque art, while it did not abandon the Renaissance concern that the materials of art be handled properly, broke the bonds of classicism and allowed the human spirit to express itself in fantasy. It enabled Bernini, for example, to express states of great spiritual exaltation and psychological depth, to depict heroism, human emotion, and religious ecstasy. Because it so well expressed the Catholic Church's own rising sense of religious resurgence and power, baroque became the art form par excellence of the Counter-Reformation.

The first commission that Bernini undertook for Pope Urban was the construction of a baldachin, or canopy, over the main altar of St. Peter's, over the place, in fact, where Peter was thought to be buried (see plate 80). That work occupied Bernini from 1626 until 1633. The baldachin was cast entirely of bronze that had allegedly been purloined from the Pantheon. The scale of the whole basilica makes the scale of Bernini's canopy quite deceptive; it is actually as high as the Farnese Palace, the largest palace built

535

in the Italian Renaissance. Its enormous weight required special, deep foundations that even intruded upon the sacred precincts below the altar where the remains of Peter were thought to be. Bernini's baldachin stands as one of the masterpieces of baroque art.

Innocent X, who succeeded Pope Urban in 1644, remained aloof to Bernini, until the architect executed three fountains in the Piazza Navona,

112. Bernini, monument of Alexander VII

opposite the pope's family palace. Alexander VII, in contrast, who succeeded to the papacy in 1655, was immediately devoted to Bernini and commissioned him at once to execute a system of great colonnades in front of the basilica (see plate 81). The first stone was laid in 1651, and the work was completed in 1666. The colonnades of Bernini have a symbolic purpose: to gather in the Catholic faithful, to beckon to the Protestant outsiders, to extend the faith to non-Christians. It was a statement in stone that could not have been more representative of the resurgent spirit of Catholicism in the Counter-Reformation.

It was also Alexander VII who required Bernini to build the *Cattedra Petri* (see plate 80). For many centuries the chair thought to have been used by Peter as bishop of Rome was kept on view at the Vatican. Vandals, worms, and relic collectors, however, had made off with chunks of it, and in 1656 Bernini was ordered to enshrine it. His accomplishment does not impress one as particularly beautiful, but it is typical of the church's triumphalism as expressed by the baroque. The chair is held by two Latin fathers, Ambrose and Augustine; they are joined by two prominent Greek fathers, Athanasius and Chrysostom, as if the unity of all Christianity came to focus at the *cathedra* of Peter. It is a work of dogmatic importance, as well as an expression of intense religious fervor.

In commemoration of the last great pope under whom he served, Bernini executed a monument for Alexander VII. High on a pedestal, the white pope kneels on a cushion, his vision fixed on celestial things, while baroque figures of Charity and Truth languish below. It is a fitting conclusion of our study of Bernini and of the 1,300-year history of St. Peter's.

IX. THE ENGLISH
REFORMATION

23. *The Tudors to 1558*

AT BOSWORTH FIELD, ON AUGUST 22, 1485, HENRY, EARL OF RICH-
mond, routed the royal forces of King Richard III of England. Richard
died in the battle, and Henry took title to the throne of England as
Henry VII. Thus ended the Wars of the Roses, which had sapped the vitality
of England for over a quarter of a century. And thus began the age of the
Tudors.

Conflict had been the staple of English life since 1337, when Edward III of England, in the tenth year of his reign, laid claim to the French
crown and declared war on France. The Hundred Years' War that then
ensued between England and France may be plotted in three parts: a period
of continuous fighting from 1337 to 1380, including the important battles
of Crécy (1346) and Poitiers (1356); a respite from 1380 until 1415, broken
by the decisive English victory at Agincourt in 1415; and a final period of
war from 1415 until 1453, in which the tide of English victory was
eventually turned by Jeanne d'Arc, enabling Charles VII of France to recover
the English-held territories in France, until only Calais remained of all of
England's continental possessions.

The conclusion of the Hundred Years' War, however, did not bring
peace to England. In fact, that war had sapped England's resources in various
ways, leaving the Crown tottering precariously under the heavy intimidation
of the English barons who scoffed at royal institutions and generally raised
havoc across the countryside. During the minority of King Henry VI (1422–
61), the Crown was exceptionally weak, impoverished, and stigmatized by
the defeat in France. Even when that righteous, although slightly mad king

achieved manhood, he proved incapable of administering the realm. The barons managed to control both Parliament and the council. Popular exasperation with the poor estate of public affairs finally led to a serious uprising in southern England in 1450, known as Cade's Rebellion. Three years later, upon the English defeat in France, Henry VI lapsed into a fit of insanity. Those seizures recurred throughout his life, leaving him virtually unfit to rule.

Conditions were thus excellent for mischief. During Henry's incapacitation, control of the council was taken by the Beaufort family, successors of John of Gaunt, fourth son of King Edward III, and the founder of the Lancastrian line. After 1447, for example, Edmund Beaufort, duke of Somerset, controlled the government. A faction of the barons bridled at this Beaufort ascendancy. They were led by Richard, duke of York, who was also a descendant, on both his mother's and his father's side, of King Edward III. (One of the English predicaments in this era was the fecundity of King Edward III.)

When dotty King Henry sired a child, it became apparent that Richard of York, heretofore the heir apparent, would not succeed to the throne of England. Henry's queen, fearful that the York family might do harm to her infant son, persuaded her husband, in one of his rare rational moments, to exclude Richard of York from the council and to invest the Beauforts with control of the government. Richard of York acted predictably: he began a civil war that eventually acquired the name Wars of the Roses — the white rose being the sign of York, the red rose, of Lancaster.

The Wars of the Roses included some of the more disreputable and undignified episodes in English history. If they had been fought over some constitutional principle, or over some social grievance, they might have deserved a better reputation, but they were not. They were exercises in wanton violence. The fortunes of the two houses, Lancaster and York, shifted with stupefying treachery. Finally, when the Yorkist monarch Edward IV died prematurely in 1483, leaving the realm to his twelve-year-old son, Edward V, the stage was set for the final mischief. Richard of Gloucester, who was at first content to be protector of the realm during Edward's minority, claimed the throne for himself and was crowned Richard III (1483–85). A succession of reprisals followed Richard's accession, attended by various rumors and alarms, including the report that Richard had murdered his nephews in the Tower of London, namely, the sovereign, Edward V, and his royal brother, the duke of York. As suspicion of Richard grew in England, Henry Tudor in Brittany prepared to invade England with

French support to press his own dubious claims to the throne — claims established in a lineage through his mother, Margaret Beaufort, to certain illegitimate offspring of John of Gaunt. In August 1485 Henry Tudor landed at Milford Haven with an army heavily French. Shortly after, he met Richard at Bosworth Field, and in the course of that engagement, Richard was killed. The English, now full of dread over civil war, were prepared to support a strong monarchy — one of the more obvious characteristics of the Tudor age.

HENRY VII

THE ISLAND kingdom, which had a shrinking population of three million, suffered from a number of ills at Henry VII's investiture, including the violence of public life and the weakness of the Crown. It has been fashionable to describe the government of the twenty-eight-year-old king as "the new monarchy" and as "the beginning of modern English history," although it is perfectly clear that Henry undertook no radical departure from constitu-

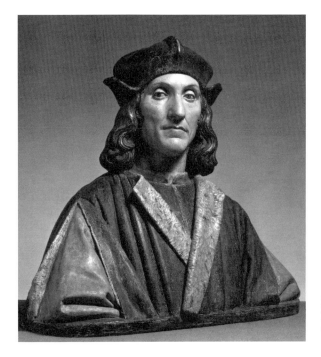

113. Henry VII, painted terracotta bust by Pietro Torrigiano

tional precedent; he simply restored to effectiveness those political institutions that the kings of England had used to govern throughout the later Middle Ages. He neither diminished the powers of Parliament nor made exaggerated claims of royal prerogative. He simply managed a strong government, using the institutions bequeathed to him. At the heart of his domestic policy was (1) political stability, which meant that it was important to quash the lawless barons and curtail the civil wars, and (2) financial solvency, which required a variety of levies, short of direct taxation, and a tight-fisted approach to fiscal affairs. Henry was a shrewd and dispassionate man, well-endowed with political savvy.

His first move was dynastic. As a Lancastrian (his mother being a Beaufort), he saw fit to marry Elizabeth of York in January 1486, firmly establishing the Tudor line and pacifying the realm. The birth of a son (auspiciously called Arthur) in the following September served to secure the dynasty even more. The rambunctious barons, however, remained to be quashed, which Henry managed to do through the Court of the Star Chamber, which was simply the royal council acting in its judicial capacity. Once the barons had been broken, the shires were returned to the administration of sheriffs and justices of the peace, carefully monitored by the Crown. The peace of the realm was enhanced by the support of the middle classes — the burghers of the towns and the gentry of the countryside — whose interests were greatly served by Henry's policies.

Henry's diplomacy was based upon peace and the improvement of England's international reputation. (Both saved money and fostered trade — great virtues in Henry's scale of values.) He therefore struck an entente with France, established friendly relations with the Hapsburgs, and arranged a marriage between his eldest son, Arthur, and Catherine of Aragon, daughter of the Spanish monarchs, Ferdinand and Isabella. When Arthur died within months of the wedding, Henry pestered the pope, Julius II, to grant a dispensation, permitting his second son, Harry, to marry the widowed Catherine.

Henry VII died on April 21, 1509, in his fifty-second year, the twenty-fourth of his reign. He left to his son Harry, who took the name Henry VIII, an abundant treasury, a prosperous island, a functioning government, a safe throne delivered from rivals, and a dynasty recognized as legitimate throughout Europe.

Although Henry VII had been a respectful son of the church, certain circumstances existed during his reign that beckoned the English Reformation. The expression "Church of England" was, strictly speaking, a misnomer. There were actually two "provinces" of the Church of Rome in England — that of Canterbury in the south of the realm, that of York in the north. The ecclesiastical establishment suffered a number of inconveniences. Some of the dioceses were led (one could scarcely say administered) by nonresident bishops, usually Italians. Of the fifteen bishops who *were* resident in England, all but five attained the episcopate through civil service. The classic example was Thomas Wolsey, who rose to ecclesiastical prominence as a servant of the Crown. In the course of his career, he was archbishop of York (1514), then successively bishop of Bath and Wells (1518), Durham (1524), and Winchester (1529); he was lord high chancellor of England (1515) and virtually governed the realm between 1515 and 1529; and he was the pope's legate to England and the one cardinal allotted to England. What is the more astonishing, he held many of those offices all at once. A contemporary accused him of being the spiritual father of nearly one-third of all the Catholics in England. At the same time, however, he was dubbed the unpreaching prelate: people perceived that he was more interested in worldly pursuits than in God's worship.

There were perhaps eight to ten thousand clergy in England to serve the nearly three million Catholics. Anticlericalism was rampant. The humanists, particularly, denounced the English clerics for their unconscionable ignorance. In 1551 Bishop Hooper discovered twenty-seven priests in his diocese who were unable to identify the author of the Lord's Prayer. The seven or eight hundred monastic communities in England possessed nearly half of the ecclesiastical wealth in the realm and had become therefore one of the mainstays of the economy. But the monastic houses, however venerable, had suffered a grievous decline in personnel — sometimes as few as four to a house. Henry VIII began dissolving the monasteries in 1536, with the money from the sale of the lands going to the crown. Their wealth tempted such an outcome; their weakness made it possible.

One voice out of the past returned to haunt the Tudors — the voice of John Wycliffe, through his followers, the Lollards. Wycliffe, as we saw in chapter 3, proposed to snatch the Church of England away from papal jurisdiction and, having thoroughly reformed it of its many ills, to establish it as the *national* church. He objected to monasticism on principle; he ridiculed the sloth and wealth of English clerics; he insisted upon the supreme authority of Scripture in the church and doubted that transubstantiation was scriptural; above all, in his two treatises *On Dominion,* he upset the medieval principle of mediation, cutting the intellectual ground from beneath the priesthood and the ecclesiastical hierarchy.

545

Followers of Wycliffe were called Lollards, a word that came to mean a heretic. Lollardy arose around 1382, toward the end of Wycliffe's life. There were cells of Lollards among the younger priests at Oxford. Those were apparently the men who cast the Scriptures into English in the 1380s, largely under the direction of Wycliffe's protégé Nicholas Hereford. Lollardy also made progress among middle-class laypeople, especially in the Midlands. By the end of the fourteenth century, Lollard burghers and country gentry had attained a respectable representation in the House of Commons. Repression began in 1401 with the act of Parliament *De haeretico comburendo,* which exposed the iniquities of that "sect" and entrusted to the episcopal courts the suppression of the Lollards, including, in the extremity, their burning. When John Oldecastle, whose zeal outran his common sense, led a Lollard march on London in 1414, Henry V smashed the uprising, and Lollardy was driven underground. There it remained, a fairly unheroic institution, until the opening of the sixteenth century.

In the late fifteenth century Lollardy began to revive, particularly in the southwest of England. By the 1520 it was difficult to distinguish between longstanding Lollards and the new Reformers, as their thinking and activities overlapped in many ways. The Reformers found in old Lollard texts a way of thinking that frequently reflected and supported their own, and a number of these texts were printed in the early 1530s — and suppressed by the religious authorities.

A strong, new intellectual current was also furnished in the early Tudor age by the Oxford Reformers — John Colet, Thomas More, and Erasmus of Rotterdam, discussed above in chapter 15. All three were northern humanists; that is, they were interested in a revival of classicism but even more profoundly in the revival of a much purified, simplified Christianity, reestablished on its true footings of the Bible and the church fathers. All three were well-read in Italian humanism, particularly in the writings of the Florentine Platonists Marsilio Ficino and Giovanni Pico della Mirandola. All three believed that the preoccupation of a Christian scholar should be the classics and the Bible, treated by means of the classical languages and all of the scholarly apparatus one could command. Whether or not the Oxford Reformers were forerunners of the English Reformation is a greatly contested question. I think they were. They taught the Church of England to honor the Holy Scriptures, as interpreted by the Greek and Latin fathers ("the old authors," as Archbishop Cranmer liked to say), against what Anglicans took to be the doctrinal exaggerations of both the Latin church and the churches of the Reformation.

If Oxford was the scene of the first gentle scholarship of the English Reformation, Cambridge furnished its more brash proponents. In St. Edward's Church of Cambridge, the earliest Reformation sermons were preached and Luther's ideas were invoked for the first time. It was the Cambridge pub the White Horse Tavern, however, where the intellectuals gathered to discuss the latest Reformation intelligence. The pub soon acquired the name "little Germany." By 1520 or 1521 the Cambridge group included Thomas Bilney, a priest; Robert Barnes, prior of the Austin Friars in Cambridge; and Hugh Latimer, a divinity student at Christ's College. All three were remarkably indebted to the Oxford Reformers, as well as to Luther. They fancied themselves preachers of the Reformation, took the Eucharist often, and engaged in spiritual exercises. All three spent their energies in works of charity. Such was the character of the earliest Anglicanism. Other young people were known to have been in Cambridge at this time include William Tyndale, Thomas Cranmer, Nicholas Ridley, Matthew Parker, and Miles Coverdale. Their names are a roster of very prominent officers of the Church of England in the Tudor age.

Beginning in 1525, the Cambridge movement was suppressed. Barnes's Christmas Eve sermon, 1525, in St. Edward's Church drew Cardinal Wolsey's ire. (Small wonder: it contrasted the poor, little baby Jesus with the big, fat, rich Wolsey.) Barnes was tried, convicted, and incarcerated but managed to escape to Luther. In 1535 he was allowed to return to England and promptly took up the cudgels again. This time fate was not so kind: he was burned for heresy in 1540. Meanwhile, Bilney had been arrested (1527) and sent to the Tower. At his trial, one hostile witness claimed to have heard him preach that "Mary Magdalene was a stewyd hoore, howbeit she afterward turned to grace." Bilney's life ended on August 19, 1531, in the Lollard Pit of Norwich, where he was burned at the stake.

The foremost figure of the early English Reformation was William Tyndale. His importance was twofold: he was a translator of Scripture into the English language, and he was the first important advocate of Lutheran opinions in England.

Tyndale was born in Gloucestershire circa 1490 and at some precocious age entered Magdalen College, Oxford, where he read in the liberal arts, mastered seven languages, including Greek, and became addicted to the Scriptures. After a brief tour at Cambridge, where he may or may not have conspired with Bilney, Barnes, and company, he became tutor in the household of Sir John Walsh in Gloucestershire and spent his spare time preaching to people in the vicinity on the virtues of the Reformation. When the

114. William
Tyndale

ecclesiastical authorities tried to silence him, Tyndale resolved to translate
the Bible into English so that the people could see the truth for themselves.
Such an effort, however, took money and episcopal approval. In 1523 he
applied to the bishop of London, Cuthbert Tunstall, for permission to make
an English translation but was met with a chilly reception. Undaunted, he
turned to a wealthy London merchant, Humphrey Monmouth, who
belonged to a society of Protestant propagandists and book smugglers called
the Augmentation of Christian Brethren, or simply the Christian Brethren.
They either were Lollards or were closely related to the Lollard movement.
Monmouth's house in London was a beehive of illicit religious activity,
conducted mainly by merchants who moved back and forth easily between
England and the Continent. There Tyndale labored unremittingly for six
months, in the course of which he completed most of the translation of the
New Testament.

In May 1524 Tyndale embarked for Hamburg in Germany, where
large amounts of money had already been sent for printing the English New
Testament. Apparently, Tyndale met Luther at Wittenberg at this time. A

quarto edition of the New Testament was eventually struck off, part of it at Cologne and part at Worms, and was smuggled into England in bales of cotton when the Rhine thawed enough for navigation in the spring of 1526. Its arrival produced a spate of book burning in England, beginning with a notable bonfire outside St. Paul's in London on February 11 of the next year. Nevertheless, many copies of the English New Testament got into circulation, and it became one of the first instruments of the English Reformation.

Tyndale remained abroad, writing religious treatises and preparing an English version of the Old Testament. In the year 1534 or thereabouts, he settled in Antwerp, where he lived and worked in a house owned by English merchants. There in May 1535 he was betrayed to local authorities by an agent of the English crown. He was consigned to the dungeon at Vilvoorden, where he endured confinement for over a year without candles, books, or writing materials. On October 6, 1536, Tyndale was strangled and burned for obstinate heresy.

How shall we assess Tyndale? He was, in the first instance, a Renaissance scholar of the northern, or Christian, tradition. His English New Testament, which required great sophistication in the Greek language, was based upon the perfected Greek text established by Erasmus's critical edition of 1516. Tyndale knew that translations of the Bible had an unsettling effect on the Latinity of Catholic doctrine. He deliberately chose English words that would unsettle the precise Latin language of Catholic dogma. Instead of "grace," he used the more Protestant "favor"; instead of "charity," "love"; instead of "confess," "acknowledge"; instead of "penance," "repentance"; instead of "priest," "elder"; instead of "church," "congregation"; instead of "salvation," "health."

Second, Tyndale was not an original thinker. He was considerably indebted to Luther, at times bordering on outright plagiarism. Tyndale's *Pathway into the Holy Scripture,* for example, is a replica of Luther's *Preface to the New Testament.* Furthermore, the character of Tyndale's thought was, and remained, consistent with that of Luther. He was an ardent advocate of the essential Protestant teaching of justification by faith alone, although he may have allowed the law a more constructive role in religious life than Luther would have preferred. Tyndale's political ethics were also patently those of Luther. His was the first important voice in England to sound the crucial words *sola Scriptura, sola fide, sola gratia.*

The last gasp of William Tyndale was reported (by the martyrologist John Foxe) to have been, "Lord, open the king of England's eyes." Tyndale had fallen oddly out of date. By 1536, when Tyndale died, the king of England's eyes were fully open. How that aperture occurred remains now to be discussed.

HENRY VIII

ON April 21, 1509, Henry VIII succeeded his father, Henry VII, as king of England. He was just shy of eighteen, but even then a great giant of a man, handsome, virile, skilled in arms, untiring in hunting, riding, wrestling, and tennis. He was intelligent and a fair scholar. Henry was an accomplished musician, was modestly versed in Scholastic theology, and fancied himself a patron of the New Learning (by which name England designated the Renaissance). Erasmus, then in Italy, scurried back to England, never doubting that a new age would blossom at the court of Henry VIII. It was an opinion widely shared and generally trumpeted.

Shortly after his father's death, Henry fulfilled the older monarch's dying wish by taking to wife Catherine of Aragon, widow of his late brother Arthur. The Spanish alliance — Catherine was the daughter of Ferdinand and Isabella of Spain — had been a critical part of Henry VII's foreign policy. Unfortunately, Arthur had died just five months after his marriage to Catherine, leaving in doubt whether the marriage had even been consummated. At any rate, that marriage had created a first degree of affinity between Catherine and Henry VIII, which had to be set aside before Henry's union with Catherine could legitimately have taken place. Pope Julius II had done so in November 1504, but with considerable doubt about the propriety of such a dispensation and only under duress by Henry VII.

It is scarcely surprising that Henry VIII's first adventure was war. In October 1511 Pope Julius II created the Holy League with Spain and Venice to unseat the French from Italy. It was assumed that England would certainly participate in those hostilities against her ancient enemy, the French. At least Julius lost no time in prodding Henry to action. The queen, acting on orders from Spain, also counseled action. Parliament voted the Crown a military subsidy in February 1512, although the royal treasury already bulged at the seams, thanks to the policies of Henry VII. The young king scarcely needed to be thus cajoled. In 1512 he dispatched an English expedition to Bayone, to coincide with a Spanish thrust at Navarre. The outcome was an embarrassment to the English. The next year, Henry personally led an expeditionary force to Calais, which achieved some unpretentious success. Meanwhile, the Scots, who invariably took sides with the French in such military tests, had invaded England from the north in August 1513 and had been routed on September 7 at Flodden by an English army under the command of the earl of Surrey. Ten thousand Scots died at Flodden, including King James IV himself. Henry VIII returned to England from modest success in France to find the Scottish border quite secure and the

115. Henry VIII, portrait by Hans Holbein the Younger

551

116. Thomas Wolsey

Scottish throne in the hands of his own sister, Margaret, during the minority of the child-king James V. Aside from fastening down the Scots for a good long time, the war had been a success in establishing England's claim in the arena of European politics, to say nothing of Henry's own fame.

The man who had managed Henry's war in France was Thomas Wolsey, the preeminent figure in the early reign of Henry VIII. Born in 1472 or 1473, the son of a butcher of Ipswich, Wolsey attained the A.B. degree from Magdalen College, Oxford, when he was fifteen and was ordained to the Catholic priesthood on March 10, 1498. Already by 1501 he displayed a remarkable talent for bilking the church: he applied for a dispensation to hold three benefices and be absent from all three. In 1507 he became chaplain to Henry VII, who sent him on minor diplomatic missions to Scotland and the Netherlands and took notice of the dispatch with which he carried out such duties. In 1509 he was appointed chaplain to Henry VIII and, a little later, the royal almoner and a member of the royal council. It was Wolsey who drafted and equipped the army that

Henry VIII led to France in 1513. By that time, Wolsey's gifts for administration were recognizable to the whole court, and together with his insufferable self-confidence and huge capacity for work, they enabled him to eclipse all other younger civil servants surrounding the king. In 1515, when Archbishop Warham resigned as lord high chancellor, Wolsey was appointed to succeed him; he thereby attained command of the whole English civil service. From that date until his demise in 1529, Thomas Wolsey was the king's first minister and responsible for much of the day-to-day business of governing.

Meanwhile, Wolsey had begun to clamor for higher and higher preferments in the church. In 1509 he was consecrated bishop of Lincoln, apparently without much intention of carrying out his episcopal duties. Already by that time, he had sent Polydore Vergil to Rome to negotiate on Wolsey's behalf for the cardinalate. In 1513 Wolsey became bishop of Tournai, later, bishop of Lincoln, and finally, in 1514, archbishop of York. By that time, Henry VIII himself was addressing letters to Pope Leo X, recommending Wolsey for election to the college of cardinals. In 1515, the year he became chancellor, Wolsey finally achieved the cardinalate. This was not the end of his ambition for church preferments, however. In 1518, after suitable pressure had been applied, Pope Leo designated Wolsey papal legate to England — not *legatus natus* (an ordinary legate, usually a native of the country to which he had been sent), but *legatus a latere* (an extraordinary legate, virtually a foreigner sent to England). As if church-state relationships had not been unsettled enough by that designation, Pope Leo later compounded the matter by naming Wolsey *legatus a latere* for life. Still his ambition was not quenched. Although he was not a member of any religious order, Wolsey became abbot of St. Albans, the richest abbey in England, and exchanged several wealthy bishoprics for their revenues — Bath and Wells (1518), Durham (1524), and Winchester (1529).

Some scholars have argued that Wolsey's chief motivation in this period was his desire to be pope. His legateship gave him a power that no individual had ever before possessed: control over both of the provinces of the church in England. Yet he also contained in his own person all of the chief ills of the Church of England: pluralism (the holding of more than one high preferment), nonresidence, simony (the exploitation of church offices, for which he was notorious), and the breach of celibacy (his entourage included at least one son and two daughters). As far as the church was concerned, Wolsey accomplished two ruinous things: he himself by his own moral excesses weakened the church in England irreparably, and because he was the pope's man, *legatus a latere,* he also weakened irreparably the loyalty of the English to the see of Rome.

What is fascinating is the almost total reliance Henry placed in his chief minister. Wolsey, for his part, flouted the king's patronage to the utmost, and lived in unspeakable pomp. He built palaces, founded colleges, maintained an elaborate household, dressed lavishly, and ate and drank copiously.

Despite his great intelligence and enormous capacity for greed, Wolsey had little head for the fiscal affairs of the state. He could manage neither to live within the budget nor to increase the revenues. His direct tax on land and wages — the "subsidy" of 1513 — was all too soon absorbed in governmental expenses. He did not know how to exploit trade. He did not deal well with the price rise that occurred just after Henry VII's death; it led not merely to general inflation, but to rent gouging and to the practice of "enclosure" — the reduction of arable lands for sheep grazing. The levies demanded by Wolsey for the support of wars began to produce popular resistance approximating rebellion. Henry stepped in to call a halt to such levies and for the first time allowed himself to question the competence of his first minister.

The first French war of Henry's reign ended in victory (1514), both in France and on the Scottish border. The outcome boded well for Wolsey as the architect of Henry's foreign policy. The question was whether Wolsey's policy favored the interests of England or those of the papacy, to which Wolsey aspired. Whom did Wolsey really wish to serve?

Louis XII of France died in 1514, the year the war ended, and was succeeded by Francis I, a young monarch every bit as winsome, vital, robust, and brash as Henry himself. Henry was enormously put off by such a rival. Francis immediately proceeded to stir up trouble in Scotland, where he unseated the regency of Henry's sister, Margaret. At the same time, he sent an army over the Alps. At the fierce battle of Marignano (September 1515), he defeated the Swiss and Milanese and retook northern Italy. Henry VIII seemed to fall under the shadow of his French rival.

Wolsey maneuvered to deliver both the papacy (under Leo X) and Henry VIII from the political and military intimidation of Francis I. But in the shifting sands of European politics in this period, his diplomatic achievements were largely illusory. Finally, in 1519, at the death of the emperor Maximilian, the Holy Roman Empire passed to the young Charles V, whose dominions extended from Spain to the Netherlands. Suddenly the rivalry between Charles V and Francis I became the preeminent political fact of the age. Henceforth all diplomacy had to account for the contest between Hapsburg and Valois. That was a preoccupation made all the more inscrutable by the fact that the Ottoman Turks were steadily advancing into the underbelly of Europe and, by 1529, had reached the outskirts of Vienna.

Whatever power Wolsey had in this period came from the fact that both parties to the great rivalry, both Hapsburg and Valois, sought England's friendship, or at least her neutrality. In 1520 Henry and Francis met near Calais for jousting and pageantry in a most splendid setting known as the Field of the Cloth of Gold. Later, Henry and Charles also met — in that instance, in Burgundy. In 1521 Pope Leo X died. Perhaps by allowing him to think he had some chance of being elected pope, Charles V inveigled Wolsey into swinging English foreign policy decisively against France. Thus, in 1522 England was preparing for war with France. The English campaigns in Normandy and Picardy (1522–23) were of no great account. The nation had no great enthusiasm for a war in which England's interests were scarcely involved, one that, at any rate, cost money. By 1524 the popular clamor against Wolsey's war policy and the taxation that attended it was very serious indeed. In February 1525 the French were crushed at Pavia; Francis I of France was taken prisoner to Madrid, and Italy fell under the control of the Holy Roman Empire. Wolsey took what advantage he could of this great embarrassment of France, forcing the French to pay an indemnity against another English invasion.

Suddenly Wolsey reversed the English policy. By the Treaty of Cognac (May 1526), England subscribed with France and the Italian powers in a common effort to drive the Hapsburgs out of Italy. Was Wolsey attempting to redress the balance of power? Or was he really playing the politics of the papacy, now beset by the overlordship of Charles V in Italy? Whichever it was, it was a blunder. In 1527 the ravenous armies of Charles V retaliated against such maneuvers by the seizure and sack of Rome itself. Pope Clement VII, held prisoner by the Holy Roman Emperor, lost all control of Italian affairs, to say nothing of the oversight of the church.

Meanwhile, by 1527 Henry VIII had come to the conclusion that his failure to sire a male heir accrued from the illegality of his marriage to Catherine of Aragon. (Besides, he was in love with a lady at court named Anne Boleyn.) Catherine of Aragon posed the inconvenience of being the aunt of Emperor Charles V. Thus, Wolsey's foreign policy left Henry, the woebegone pope, and the ferocious emperor locked in an incredible entanglement over the matrimonial problems of the king of England.

In 1529, without giving Wolsey the slightest hint, France and Germany signed the Peace of Cambrai, making relations normal between the two powers but leaving England isolated and embarrassed. Two months later, Wolsey was finished.

Marriage to Anne Boleyn

At first the marriage of Henry VIII and Catherine of Aragon had been happy. Except for the child Mary, however, born in 1516, Catherine had experienced a long succession of stillbirths, infant deaths, and miscarriages. By 1525, when the queen was forty, all hope of issue was given up, seven years having passed without a pregnancy. The question of a male heir loomed as a very critical matter in Henry's mind. It was taken as national consensus, as a de facto law, that a woman could not rule successfully. If she married a subject, she risked another civil war. If she married a foreign prince, she invited overlordship from abroad. Beside himself, Henry consulted the doctors, vowed a crusade against the Turks if given a son, and finally unveiled his illegitimate son, Henry Fitzroy, whom as "the duke of Richmond," he commenced to groom as his heir apparent. In 1527, however, Henry and Wolsey agreed to overturn Henry's marriage to Catherine of Aragon on the basis of moral scruples.

How was this question first raised? We have two versions of the matter. One version is by Henry himself. He declared that he had been reading the Bible devoutly and his conscience had been stricken by Leviticus 20:21: "He that marrieth his brother's wife doth an unlawful thing; he hath uncovered his brother's nakedness; they shall be without children." That text, said Henry, explains why such a pious man as himself would be bereft of a male heir. Thus, a bad case of the scruples accounted for the annulment proceedings, which history records as "the king's great matter."

The other account is, to say the least, different. It was written by the English Catholic cardinal, Reginald Pole, in his book *De unitate ecclesiae* (On the unity of the church). According to Pole, Henry was enslaved by his lust for a girl who refused to be merely the king's mistress, knowing that the king got tired of his mistresses, but who insisted on being his wife. How did that girl know that the king got tired of his mistresses? Because her very own sister, Mary, had been one of his royal mistresses. Thus Pole caught Henry invoking Leviticus against Catherine of Aragon, although Henry never imagined that his new alliance with Anne Boleyn was tarnished by the same impediment. In short, Henry was about to enter upon a second relationship forbidden by Leviticus.

117. Anne Boleyn

The girl in Cardinal Pole's account was Anne Boleyn, whose sister Mary, Henry had known before her. The daughter of Sir Thomas Boleyn, Henry's courtier and minister, Anne claimed distant relationship to Edward I. Not yet twenty, she joined the court of Henry and Catherine. Her charms were debatable, but her determination to have Henry was beyond dispute.

The campaign to undo the marriage was based on the fact that a legitimate doubt existed among canon lawyers whether or not it lay within the competence of Pope Julius II to make the dispensation, overriding the impediment of the first degree of affinity. The strategy became almost as important as the basis. The tactic was to have the matter of the annulment remanded to England and decided in England by one or more papal legates in a legatine court. By such a tactic, the Crown could counteract the political pressure of the Holy Roman Emperor, Charles V (nephew of Catherine), upon the weak Pope Clement VII.

How, we may ask, was it possible for the king of England to lead his Catholic nation so successfully against the papacy on an issue as dubious as an annulment of his marriage with a beloved queen? The answer is not hard to discover. (Part of it, in fact, has already been disclosed in the activities of the Lollards, the English humanists, and the Cambridge reformers.) The English had a low opinion of the clergy and the religious, whose ignorance and moral clumsiness were widely celebrated in both popular literature and humanistic satire. They resented the concentration of land and wealth in the ecclesiastical establishment. They complained of the never-ending succession of exactions that the church managed to wheedle out of people from the cradle to the grave — in fact, even after the grave. (It took a mortuary fee to get the grave dug and another fee to have a will probated.) They recoiled at the unseemly luxury of the prelates and at their brazen disobedience of the strictures against pluralism and absenteeism, against simony and nepotism.

More than any other European power, England fretted over the ambiguity of dual allegiance — to the king and to the pope. In the course of the fourteenth century, Parliament passed a series of statutes, called the Acts of Provisors and Praemunire, designed to circumscribe papal interference in the affairs of the Church of England and, thus, of England as a whole. Infringement of these laws against papal encroachment was seen as a form of treason that made one liable to imprisonment and the forfeiture of property. The statutes of provisors and praemunire made Wolsey's performance all the more outrageous — and ominous. By being, in effect, the prime minister of both the pope and the king in England, Wolsey both flaunted his great power and courted disaster.

At first, however, Henry sought an annulment directly from the pope, the competent authority, whose granting of annulments was commonplace. In May 1527 Wolsey therefore summoned Henry to appear in his legatine court to answer allegations that he was living in sin with his brother's widow. If Wolsey could thus establish Henry's guilt, would not the pope move with alacrity to dissolve such a marriage? The strategy did not work. Queen Catherine, always touching in her innocence, reacted to the news with great moral indignation. Late in the same month, the troops of Charles V sacked Rome and took the hapless pope, Clement VII, into confinement. Such a pope was not likely to trifle with the marriage of Charles's Aunt Catherine.

The next attempt by Wolsey and Henry was to have the case remanded to Wolsey's legatine court and decided there. To this proposal, the pope eventually agreed (April 1528), promising that the decision handed down by that court would be irrevocable. Cardinal Lorrenzo Campeggio, the nominal bishop of Salisbury in England, was also appointed to serve with Wolsey as judge. By July 1528, however, Queen Catherine had begun to put pressure on the pope through her nephew, Charles V. She offered the pontiff the perfectly valid observation that her rights could scarcely be defended if the matter were settled in Henry's England. She demanded to have the case revoked to Rome.

Campeggio arrived in England with secret instructions from the pope; they required him to procrastinate as long as possible, keeping Henry below the boiling point without committing the pope. Campeggio's first initiative was to attempt a reconciliation of the parties. Henry was furious at such trifling delay. When the Italian cardinal proposed to Catherine that she solve the problem by retiring to a convent, he was met with a frosty reception. Henry had an imperative that no celibate pope could quite perceive. Wolsey, for his part, had the commendable foresight of being able to see his own downfall in Henry's frustration. Thus, the pressure on Rome was increased by the English monarch and his prime minister, even while Catherine was keeping up her own pressure on the pope, through Charles V, to have the case recalled to Rome and settled there.

In October 1528 the Spanish announced the discovery of a hitherto unknown document, purported to have been written by Pope Julius II to Queen Isabella of Spain to convince her of the complete sufficiency of his dispensation. That document delayed the proceedings again. Finally, sensing the imminent peril of schism in England, Wolsey and Campeggio agreed to open the legatine court on March 31, 1529, in Blackfriars Hall, London, while Henry's ambassadors in Rome deliberately disguised that event. The queen, defended by the prominent English humanist and bishop John Fisher, appeared in the tribunal and made a profound impression by her fine bearing and determination. She questioned the competence of the court but was overruled, whereupon she appealed from the competence of that court to the pope himself. She implored Henry to acknowledge that she had come to him as a virgin bride — which meant, of course, that there had been no marriage to Arthur, no impediment, no need for the papal dispensation of Julius II, and no question at all about the legitimacy of her marriage to Henry VIII. Henry disputed her at every turn.

On July 23, 1529, Campeggio produced the ultimate Roman weapon. Announcing that the legatine court was merely an extension of the Roman Consistory, which never deigned to labor during the summer's heat, Campeggio adjourned the court until the first of October. The king's counsellors were stunned. Wolsey gave in to the adjournment, as he knew nothing better to do. He had already learned that earlier in July Pope Clement had buckled under the pressure of Charles V and had revoked the case to the Roman See. On July 19, 1529, Pope Clement wrote twice to Henry VIII, first informing him that Catherine's appeal had been granted, and second begging him not to rend the English bonds with the Holy See. Campeggio left England.

Wolsey was doomed. Scarcely had the legatine court adjourned than writs were issued by Henry VIII summoning Parliament. The Parliament that convened in November 1529 and met on and off until 1536 brought an end to papal jurisdiction in England and is therefore referred to as the Reformation Parliament. At the opening of Parliament, Sir Thomas More, Henry's new lord high chancellor, delivered a rebuke to Wolsey, who had been ousted from that office scarcely a month before.

On October 9 the attorney general indicated Wolsey for praemunire in the king's bench. He was to be tried on the charge of the illegal exercise of his papal powers; he was to be tried in the king's court, under common law. Wolsey might have protested that the king had no jurisdiction over him. Instead, he pleaded guilty and threw himself on the king's mercy. On October 18, 1529, Thomas Wolsey surrendered the great seal of England. His capitulation was one of the first great strokes of the English Reformation.

Wolsey endured only another year. He resolved to visit York, of which he was the archbishop, having never been in residence there before. Rumors circulated about his designs against Henry. In November 1530 the royal council ordered him arrested and brought to London. That great lord, foreseeing his end, died en route, at Leicester, on November 24, 1530.

The fall of Wolsey led to the rise of two Thomases — or three, if we count Thomas More. More attained the chancellorship after Wolsey was forced to relinquish that office, but he made it a condition of his acceptance that he would have no part in the annulment proceedings, which he found disreputable. He passed his few years in office making adjustments to the English legal system and penning polemics against sundry heretics, Tyndale in particular. The conduct of government was left to Henry himself. Parliament also pursued its own interests. Commons, the scene of the more important matters, consisted heavily of middle-class representatives — country gentry, city merchants, and lawyers — who were noticeably anti-clerical and quite put off by church exactions.

In the matter of the annulment, however, Henry was stymied. His frustration was soon alleviated by two Thomases whose careers were bound up with the Reformation in England: Thomas Cranmer and Thomas Cromwell. It was Cranmer who advised Henry in August 1529 to solicit opinions on his annulment from the major theological faculties of the European universities, to which issues of that sort had typically been referred. One well-chosen English representative was dispatched to every quarter of the Continent to make sure that the king's interests were made clear. Oxford and Cambridge, as one might expect, decided for Henry. So did the French universities, there being no love in France for either Charles V or his Spanish aunt. The universities in northern Italy — Bologna, Padua, and Ferrara — also took sides with Henry, but the other Italian universities did not. The universities in Spain and Germany generally declared against the king of England. Those opinions were to be used in Rome against a recalcitrant pope, along with a dark threat of calling a general council of the Catholic church if the pope did not behave as Henry wanted.

Cranmer, who thought up that scheme, was born of lesser gentry of Nottinghamshire in 1489. As the second son, he was, by tradition, assigned to the church, for which purpose he entered Jesus College, Cambridge, about the year 1502. He spurned a degree in canon law, which was the shortest route to high preferment, but took a degree in pure theology, including competence in Greek and some in Hebrew. John Fisher was chancellor of Cambridge in those days, having been elevated to that office from the famous Lady Margaret Professorship of divinity. Erasmus was also in Cambridge after 1511, giving courses in Greek exegesis of the New Testament. The Cambridge movement got underway still later, after 1516, when Erasmus's Greek New Testament appeared. Cranmer took his bachelor's degree and then his M.A., whereupon he was elected to a fellowship and looked forward to a career as a don. So far he had not taken holy orders. He enjoyed the reputation of being a good scholar and a cautious, conventional man. In 1515 or 1516 Cranmer married, thus losing his fellowship. His enemies were later to claim that his wife, "Black Joan," was the barmaid at the Dolphin Tavern. Although she did live there for the first part of their marriage, it seems likely that she was of somewhat higher stature. Joan, as well as the baby she was carrying, perished in childbirth. The authorities of Cambridge, believing that Cranmer had acted honorably in a difficult situation, reelected him to his fellowship. After a decent interval, he was ordained, probably in 1519 or 1520, when he was in his thirtieth year. Soon after, he attained the degree doctor of divinity.

In the summer of 1529 Henry VIII was hunting near Waltham. Cranmer was also in that area, tutoring students during a Cambridge recess. He

118. Thomas
Cranmer,
portrait by
Gerard Flicke

suggested to Henry's advisers, whom he chanced to meet, that they refer
the question of the king's divorce to the universities. He commended that
approach for two reasons. First, Pope Clement might accept the judgment
of the universities and thus relieve himself of the responsibility; second,
Charles V might bow to an overwhelming presentation of learned opinion.
When Henry heard of Cranmer's plan, he said, "That man has the right
sow by the ear." Cranmer returned to Jesus College, little expecting that a
mere table conversation would shape his whole career. Suddenly he was
summoned to see the king, who ordered him to develop the plan.

In 1530, with many favorable opinions from the universities in hand,
Henry summoned the nobility to London to sign a letter to Pope Clement VII, in which the favorable decisions of the universities were invoked
and "extreme remedies" were threatened if the pope did not now serve the

king's justice. Dukes, earls, barons, bishops and abbots, and members of Commons affixed their names.

Pope Clement met this ploy by insisting on the technicality that the annulment case was now pending in the papal court. He admonished Henry under no circumstances to remarry until the case had been settled, threatening the possibility of excommunication if he did.

Meanwhile, Henry maneuvered to stifle the English clergy by using the statutes of praemunire. Who could doubt the power of such a tactic? Had it not recently brought down Wolsey? In December 1530 the whole clergy of England suddenly found themselves indicted in the king's bench for having violated the laws of praemunire. The following February the two provinces of the Church of England — Canterbury and York — met in convocations; they declared their guilt and agreed to pay Henry an indemnity of 100,000 pounds and 18,000 pounds respectively to obtain a royal pardon. Henry was not satisfied; he demanded the clergy acknowledge him to be "Protector and Supreme Head of the English Church and Clergy." The stunned clerics finally agreed, making only one qualification proposed by Archbishop Warham, "as far as the law of Christ allows."

Still, Henry did not know what to do next. Forbidden to remarry by the pope, he was confined to Catherine, who refused to let go, and in love with Anne, who would not afford him the amenities of marriage without marriage. Enter the other Thomas. Thomas Cromwell, who attained prominence in 1531, knew exactly how to proceed: disconnect England from papal jurisdiction and settle the annulment in England.

Born at Putney in 1485, the son of a blacksmith and brewer, a self-confessed ruffian in his youth, Cromwell went abroad at the age of eighteen, served in the French army, worked for an Italian banking firm, and finally settled at Antwerp as a market analyst in that key center of European commerce. In 1512 he returned to London, married a wealthy woman of good family, and, after a period of study in jurisprudence, became a solicitor, with side interests in commerce and banking. Although he lacked any sort of Renaissance education, Cromwell was a man of formidable intelligence. He returned from Europe, expert in many languages, worldly wise, cool, and dispassionate.

A. G. Dickens has shown how this man was shaped by his European experience, which was urban and secular. He was unfettered of all usual prejudices, whether ecclesiastical or political. "He learned," wrote Dickens, "to think in terms of function and efficiency, to disregard hidebound traditions and all-embracing philosophical systems."

Already in 1520 Cromwell was attached to Cardinal Wolsey's household as a solicitor and by 1525 was prominent among the cardinal's business associates. He managed to survive the fall of Wolsey without dishonor either to Wolsey or to himself, and he soon emerged as one of the king's favorites and as a member of the Reformation Parliament. With the backing of the Boleyns, upon whom he had had occasion to show financial favor, he was named to the Privy Council in 1531; each year thereafter he managed to attain some new royal appointment: chancellor of the exchequer (1533), principal secretary (1534), and lord privy seal (1536).

The Cromwellian solution — to oust the pope from English affairs — evolved slowly, beginning in 1532. It was conducted by what G. R. Elton has called an almost finicky constitutionalism, that is, by a succession of bills, carefully enacted by Parliament. Small wonder, therefore, that Thomas Cromwell is accredited with having contributed to the making of England as a modern constitutional monarchy.

The first issue to arise was the constitutional independence of the

119. Thomas Cromwell

church in England. Did the church have the right to make ecclesiastical laws without the consent of the Crown? In 1532 a bill was introduced in the House of Commons by the member from Taunton (Thomas Cromwell) entitled Supplication of the Commons against the Ordinaries. It decried the fact that the church makes laws without the knowledge or consent of the king or of his subjects. Stephen Gardiner, bishop of Winchester, put up a spirited defense on behalf of the "ordinaries" (i.e., the bishops). But Henry VIII managed to erode the unanimity of the bishops by accusing the prelates of being of two loyalties. Did not they swear allegiance to a foreign power? The bishops could sniff their own treason in Henry's remarks. Gardiner retired to his diocese in disgrace. All but one of the rest of the bishops knuckled under. On May 15, 1532, the convocation yielded to the Crown in a formal document called *The Submission of the Clergy.* By that instrument, the bishops and the clergy of England granted two concessions: they agreed not to make new laws unless licensed by the king to do so and unless those laws had received royal approval; they agreed to submit the corpus of canon law to the judgment of a royal commission that had power to determine which laws, if any, should be stricken.

The next day, May 16, 1532, Thomas More resigned his office, conscience-stricken by Henry's presumption of royal supremacy over the Church of England. It was the end of his political career. Henceforth he resolved to defend by his bearing and his writings the Catholic faith that he had not been successful in defending while he was in office. More was succeeded as chancellor by Sir Thomas Audley, crony of Cromwell's and lately speaker of the House of Commons.

The year 1532 saw the development of still other aspects of royal supremacy. In the first months of the year, Parliament passed an act entitled Conditional Restraint of Annates, in which the payments normally paid by benefice holders — bishops in particular — to the pope on their succession to office were to be withheld, for the time being or permanently, as a means of bringing pressure on Rome. Aside from curtailing the papacy's chief source of revenue from England, the bill warned the Holy See that any act of retaliation by the papacy, including excommunication and interdict, would be met by the continuance of the Church in England under *national* auspices.

The archbishop of Canterbury, William Warham, expired on August 23, 1532. In the autumn, Cranmer, who was abroad doing the king's business, received an urgent dispatch from Henry VIII, directing him to return at once to assume the see of Canterbury. By ordinary standards,

Cranmer was not the logical choice to succeed Warham. At Nuremberg, where he had been stationed, Cranmer fell in love with Margaret, a niece of the Lutheran preacher Andrias Osiander, and, canonical prohibitions notwithstanding, had married her. Furthermore, he was no bishop, but merely an archdeacon. The obvious choice would have been Bishop Gardiner of Winchester, who had already fallen out with Henry. Cranmer returned to England in January 1533. By that time, anyone could see that Anne Boleyn was badly in need of the benefit of clergy: her imminent offspring might arrive illegitimate. On January 25, 1533, Henry secretly married Anne Boleyn. Even Cranmer testified to the secrecy of that event: "For I myself knew not thereof for a fortnight after it was done." Pope Clement VII, ignorant of these bizarre happenings, yet anxious not to work any more damage in England, confirmed Cranmer's appointment as archbishop in January and sent the necessary bulls the following month. On March 26 Cranmer vowed obedience to the Holy See, without which he really could not have been invested, then proceeded to disavow it for conscience' sake. On March 30, he was consecrated archbishop of Canterbury.

The see of Canterbury was not prepared to take Henry's annulment case under its own jurisdiction. Only one thing remained to be done: stifle any possibility of an appeal by Queen Catherine to the papal court in Rome. That was done in March 1533 by an act of Parliament entitled Restraint of Appeals, which, as finally enacted, prohibited appeals to Rome in testamentary and matrimonial cases.

Archbishop Cranmer's court was opened at Dunstable on May 10, 1533. The site was chosen because Queen Catherine lived nearby and could not plead that the hearing was inaccessible. She refused, nevertheless, to acknowledge the court's competence to judge her case and did not honor the summons to appear. The verdict, therefore, came swiftly. On May 23 Cranmer pronounced the king's first marriage null and void on the grounds that Pope Julius II had illegally dispensed with an impediment by divine law. But the child of that union, Princess Mary, was not adjudged to be illegitimate because her parents were deemed to have acted in good faith at her begetting. A few days later, upon his return to London, the archbishop scrutinized the king's new alliance with Anne Boleyn and declared it "good," given the illegality of the union that had preceded it. The new queen was solemnly invested in Westminster Abbey on Whitsunday, June 1, 1533. Three months later, on September 7, the royal birth occurred; to everyone's dismay, the issue was female. The child was called Elizabeth. Cranmer stood as godfather at her baptism.

Henry as Supreme Head of the Church

The Restraint of Appeals act was a logical extension of the laws of praemunire. It attempted to relocate all ecclesiastical jurisdiction within the kingship of England. Therefore, the act began with a new interpretation of history: "Where by divers sundry old authentic histories and chronicles, it is manifestly declared and expressed that this realm of England is an empire." Here the word "empire" *(imperium)* was being proffered as the basis on which to establish the king's spiritual jurisdiction. One could no longer conceive of England in medieval terms. Rather, the imperial title devolved upon the kings of England in a direct line from Emperor Constantine, in whom was vested all jurisdiction, both spiritual and temporal. (Histories appeared at this time suggesting that King Arthur was directly related to Helena, Constantine's mother and herself a Briton.)

The second line of the Restraint is a rehearsal of the first: "This realm of England is an empire, and so hath been accepted in the world, governed by one supreme head and king." "Empire," as it is used in this document, means a conception of political authority that takes its sanction from no other source except itself. Thus "empire" meant that England was a sovereign state free from every foreign authority and discontinuous with medieval traditions and from medieval theories of church and state. It amounted to a new conception of the state of England, based on somewhat dubious historical precedents but established upon a strict constitutionalism, that is, a succession of parliamentary acts.

The Restraint proceeds to reach the perfectly logical conclusion that the Church of England, as a self-contained spiritual authority under the king's headship, is sufficient unto itself to settle all cases in England and will brook no appeals to Rome, either in matrimony or divorce, wills or testaments.

The year 1534 brought the issue of royal supremacy to a conclusion. On March 23 the Roman Consistory reached a unanimous decision: the marriage of Henry VIII and Catherine of Aragon was perfectly valid. Parliament, with a certain foresight, had already reacted to meet the new challenge. It had convened on January 15, 1534, and had proceeded to ratify or reinforce the acts of 1531–34, fashioning the whole body of legislation into a consistent legal statement of royal supremacy. The most important acts were the following:

> *The Submission of the Clergy and the Restraint of Appeals* made statutory the submission that the clergy had made in 1532 and incorporated the Restraint of Appeals into these enactments of 1534.

- *The Ecclesiastical Appointments Act* made irrevocable the withholding of annates (i.e., the firstfruits of a benefice) from Rome. In the absence of Roman jurisdiction, it prescribed new procedures for the election of bishops and abbots, under quite close supervision of the Crown.
- *The Dispensations Act* stopped all payments to Rome, declaring that dispensations from canon law could no longer be referred to Rome. Parliament assigned that power to the archbishop of Canterbury, who was deemed to act in the king's name.
- *The First Act of Succession* declared the union of Henry and Catherine null and void, declared Catherine of Aragon no longer queen of England but dowager to Prince Arthur, declared the marriage of Henry and Anne "consonant with the laws of Almighty God," and established the heirs of Henry and Anne in the line of succession to the Crown. Elizabeth would rule if there was no male heir.

The last bill included several announcements. Those who attempted to tamper with the succession would be guilty of high treason. Nobles, princes of the church, and all other subjects would be required to swear an oath to uphold the specifications of the act; refusal to do so would also make one liable of high treason.

On March 30, 1534, Henry gave his consent to that series of bills and prorogued Parliament until November. Before the members returned to their constituencies, however, they swore the oath to uphold the Act of Succession. As G. R. Elton has suggested, that oath really amounted to "a political test of obedience to the new order and of adherence to the royal supremacy."

Shortly after Easter (April 5, 1534), Archbishop Cranmer called Bishop John Fisher to London and bade him swear the oath. That venerable bishop refused — not indeed because he quibbled with the right of the Crown to establish succession, but because he could not countenance royal supremacy. Fisher was sent to the Tower (April 17). Among the first laymen to whom the oath was offered was Thomas More. He refused to swear it for reasons of conscience similar to those of Fisher. He too was sent to the Tower, on the same date.

In November, Parliament reconvened and proceeded to pass the following additional bills, which brought the matter of royal supremacy to a conclusion:

- *The Supremacy Act* declared that Henry VIII "justly and rightfully is and ought to be Supreme Head of the Church of England."

- *The Second Act of Succession* included for the first time in statutory form the oath that the king's subjects were expected to swear.
- *The Treasons Act* made it treasonable to deprive the king of any dignity or title that he possessed, even when that is done by the use of such words as "heretic," "schismatic," or "tyrant."

The parliamentary acts of 1534 completed the establishment of the Church of England, settled the definition of royal supremacy, and brought papal jurisdiction in England to a close. Two characteristics of the process deserve notice. First, it was accomplished without much reference either to continental Protestantism or to the dissenting tradition in England. Second, it was constitutional — done by the government, specifically by the Parliament, by the consent of the governed.

At the opening of 1535, Henry named Thomas Cromwell vicar-general for the administration of the king's prerogatives in spiritual affairs. Cromwell proceeded at once to make a visitation of the Church of England, taking particular note of church revenues. In February the bishops were required to surrender the papal documents requisite to their appointment and to reapply to the Crown for royal commissions to hold the episcopal office. (The commissions of Cranmer and Gardiner were dated February 10, 1535.) The summer of 1535 saw the execution of two recalcitrant Catholics of uncommon stature.

John Fisher, who had been born in Yorkshire about the middle of the fifteenth century, became bishop of Rochester (1504) and a distinguished educator associated with the university at Cambridge. As chancellor of Cambridge, he had brought Erasmus to that university — a sign of his partiality for the New Learning. It was he who encouraged the mother of King Henry VII to endow one of the most famous tenures at Cambridge — the Lady Margaret Professorship — and to found two colleges at Cambridge — Christ's College and St. John's. Fisher courted favor with no one. Wolsey's easy morality drew stinging rebukes from Fisher. Nor did Henry VIII escape his wrath over the matter of the king's annulment. As confessor of Catherine of Aragon, Fisher defended the queen at the legatine court on June 18, 1529, and vigorously opposed every effort by Henry to put her away. Fisher stoutly resisted the notion of royal supremacy, which he found preposterous. His "treason" in that respect led to his incarceration. On May 20, 1535, the new pope, Paul III, did Fisher the dubious favor of naming him to the college of cardinals. That deed threw Henry into a fit of temper and sealed Fisher's fate. Henry threatened to send Fisher's head

120. John
Fisher, portrait
by Hans
Holbein the
Younger

to Rome by itself to receive the cardinal's red hat. In June, Fisher was put on trial, charged with treason, and convicted by a jury of twelve freeholders. On June 22, at the Tower of London, Fisher's head was struck off and displayed on a pole on London Bridge.

On July 1, 1535, Thomas More was brought to Westminster Hall for trial and, although he defended himself brilliantly, was convicted of treason and sentenced to be disemboweled. Henry graciously commuted the sentence to beheading — which, in fact, was done on July 6.

The year 1536 brought the beginning of the suppression of all the monastic institutions in England. Recent scholars have generally agreed that the monasteries were dissolved largely because Henry desired their wealth. That the good name of monasticism had been badly tarnished made the process much easier; people had lost respect for the institution, as monks and friars evoked almost no respect for intellectual acumen, charitable works, or religious sanctity. Also the monks and friars were less "national" than the secular clergy; people perceived them to be papal agents; even Cromwell referred to them as "the pope's spies." Ever since the days of Edward I, the kings of England had never shrunk at confiscating monastic property when it served some national emergency or charitable purpose. It did not occur to Henry VIII that he was without precedent, and that he was now head of the Church gave him much greater power in this area than any earlier English monarch. Cromwell inherited from Wolsey a national deficit that he could not correct. Expenditures exceeded income. Wool customs had fallen off badly. Military expenditures, given the threat posed by Spain and France, increased steadily. Cromwell knew that the value of monastic property ran into the millions; the annual income alone from that property exceeded 200,000 pounds. Such a revenue promised to correct many of England's financial problems. The only theory that we have to dismiss is that proposed by nineteenth-century historians, notably von Ranke, that the Crown dissolved the monasteries and redistributed their riches to nobles, merchants, and corporations as a means of binding influential classes to the revolution being conducted by Henry and his prime minister. Henry and Cromwell in fact had only one object in mind: to enrich the Crown.

Prior to the dissolution was a visitation of the monasteries, conducted under the aegis of Cromwell as the king's vicar-general. Cromwell, in turn, appointed inspectors, who made their way around the monasteries with the ill-disguised intent of compiling an unfavorable report on monastic life. Their findings were sufficiently scandalous to bring up the scruples of Parliament. In February 1536 Parliament passed legislation dissolving the lesser monasteries, where most of the vulgarity was thought to be. Throughout the year, officers of the Crown proceeded to dissolve the three hundred convents affected, made inventories of all their goods, and attempted to make a decent disposition of the two thousand religious who lived in those communities. Some ten thousand tenants and servants were thus deprived of their livelihood.

As the dissolution proceeded, Cromwell's survival and Henry's throne were suddenly challenged by an uprising in northern England known as the Pilgrimage of Grace. By the end of 1536 Lincolnshire, Yorkshire, and most of the north were in a fever of resistance to the religious policies of the Crown. Agrarian interests and religious interests coalesced. In the north, the old faith was more stubbornly held than anywhere else in England; Henry's attack on the monastic establishments, numerous in Yorkshire and Lincolnshire, was perceived as an attack on the ancient religion. Moreover, northerners were fearful that dissolution of the monasteries would bring about some sort of revolution in agriculture — the redistribution of vast tracts of land, the eviction of tenants, the acceleration of enclosures, and the like.

The revolution began at Louth, in Lincolnshire, on October 1, 1536, when a riot occurred that soon spread throughout the county. A conglomeration of fifty thousand rebels assembled outside Lincoln, poorly armed, led by a collection of priests, friars, and monks. They entered Lincoln, displaying a banner on which was depicted the chalice and the host of the Eucharist. They fancied themselves not rebels but pilgrims; their enterprise was "a pilgrimage of grace." By October 19 the pilgrimage had been throttled by royal arms, under the duke of Suffolk, and by a direct appeal to Henry to the deep-seated patriotism of these people.

No sooner had the Lincolnshire rising been suppressed than a more serious one broke out in Yorkshire, Cumberland, and Westmoreland. Rebels there began to assemble around October 9. They too conceived of their enterprise as a pilgrimage, and they too carried a religious banner — in this instance, displaying the five wounds of Christ. If anything, this second rising was more overtly Catholic than the first. The rebels protested against the new laws that were detrimental to the old faith, demanded the suppression of heretical books and the removal of heretical bishops, and advocated the restoration of papal supremacy over the church in England. They even had some notion of a constitutional monarchy, that is, of a Parliament independent of Crown control. If they could detect an enemy of Christ's church, it was not the king, however, but his agent Cromwell, whom they asked to be sequestered.

The leader of the second rising was the Yorkshire solicitor Robert Aske. His followers were strong enough to take the city of York, which they designated the capital of a northern state. They established ordinances of government, recruited an army of twenty thousand, and won the allegiance of such dignitaries as the archbishop of York and of such nobles as Lord Darby.

Norfolk was the king's chief agent in dealing with Aske and his followers. On December 6, relying on royal concessions and a pardon — neither of which Henry had the slightest intention of keeping — Aske dissolved the pilgrimage. The following year saw retributions throughout the north, in the course of which both Aske and Darby were executed.

The Pilgrimage of Grace had the unfortunate effect of hastening the dissolution of the greater monasteries. Many monks had participated in the rising, and many distinguished abbots and priors had been implicated with Aske. The pilgrimage provoked Henry to root out all of the religious who had participated; in fact, he now resolved to make a radical clearance of the last traces of monastic life in his realm. At the end of 1536 the great abbeys of England were still intact. By the end of 1538 all but a few of the noblest abbeys had been dissolved. They were made to surrender by one means or another — excessive taxation, royal intimidation, or bribery. Between 1537 and 1540, some 150 large abbeys were closed forever, as well as 30 convents for women. The great abbeys of Glastonbury, Colchester, and Reading collapsed in the autumn of 1539. When Waltham Abbey in Sussex surrendered on March 23, 1540, the process was completed.

To make these activities constitutional, Parliament passed the Dissolution Act in 1539. The preamble, written perhaps by Henry himself, attempts to justify the dissolution of the monasteries. They have been taken from "slothful and ungodly" religious and "turned to better use," namely, the instruction of children, the support of professorships in the biblical languages, a system of old-age relief, and the establishment of new dioceses. Some of these objectives were realized. Six new episcopal sees were soon forthcoming. Endowments were increased at many cathedral schools. At Oxford, Christ Church College was brought to completion by monastery funds, and at Cambridge, Trinity College was so founded. At both institutions, Henry endowed regius professorships in divinity, medicine, law, and the biblical languages.

With the suppression of Waltham Abbey, monasticism virtually ceased to exist in England. The monastic houses, now desolate of people, were swiftly entered by local citizenry, who used the stone for construction, the lead for shot, and the wood for kindling. Royal agents were also quickly on hand to salvage things of value. Silver utensils alone brought in an estimated eighty-five thousand pounds; the revenue gained by the sale of monastic gems, metalwork, images, and paintings exceeded a million pounds. Henry managed to save portions of the monastic libraries through the efforts of his book agent, John Leland, but many books and irreplaceable manuscripts were doubtless lost. With the passing of monasticism, the Church of England lost one of its primary ties to the papacy and to Western Catholicism; it lost an institution that had always conserved art and education, sacramental life and piety, theological scholarship and teaching.

The dissolution destroyed the refuge of Henry's stoutest opponents to the religious settlement. It enriched the Crown by well over 100,000 pounds a year, twice the income achieved by Wolsey, and it secured the well-being of the land-owning classes, to which, in 1538, Cromwell commenced to auction the monastic property.

Henry VIII probably expected England to hew to the Catholic faith, of which he considered himself something of a champion, despite his anti-papalism and despite his breach with Rome. There is slight evidence, if any at all, that he cherished very much of continental Protestantism. Yet Henry's chief ministers, Cranmer and Cromwell, both of whom had Protestant leanings, led the king into unexpected alliances, while the king's own matrimonial adventures diverted his attention and wasted his moral leadership in a time of religious tension. Such was the story of the years 1536–40.

To Henry's great delight, Catherine of Aragon died at the beginning of 1536. Anne Boleyn also rejoiced at her passing, believing that her own position as queen was now unassailable. She was again with child, and she hoped that the child she was carrying would be Henry's devoutly hoped-for male heir. However, the much-awaited miscarried. From that moment, she was doomed. Henry was tired of her. In May she was packed off to the Tower, while rumors of incest and adultery surrounded her sudden disappearance from the court; one of her alleged lovers was said to be her own brother. Cranmer interceded with Henry on her behalf, but to no avail. On May 19, 1536, seven days after five of her accomplices in love were executed by due process of law, Anne Boleyn was beheaded, the first queen's head to fall from the chopping block. Henry was determined to have the marriage annulled, so that the child Elizabeth could not succeed to the throne. Scarcely forty-eight hours after Anne's demise, Cranmer declared the marriage void. The grounds of annulment were never published, owing, no doubt, to their delicacy. Henry's affair with Anne's sister had created an impediment of first affinity. Did Cranmer rule on the basis of another marriage that was forbidden by Leviticus?

On May 30, 1536, after an interval of only ten days, Henry married Jane Seymour, a circumspect young woman who had been lady-in-waiting to Queen Catherine. To this union, a son was born on October 12, 1537 — the future Edward VI. Nine days after that joyful event, however, the queen perished from the travail of childbirth. Henry's next matrimonial adventure was a marriage of diplomatic convenience, arranged by Cromwell. It was Cromwell who suggested that Henry marry Anne of Cleves, sister of the duke of Cleves, a German prince of Lutheran leanings. By the marriage, Cromwell hoped to cement an Anglo-Lutheran alliance to offset the strength of two continental powers, France and the Emperor. Cromwell pictured Anne to Henry in glowing terms. Holbein who was sent to paint her portrait, was admonished by Cromwell "to improve her," but he could find nothing more than a well-fed German hausfrau with rather crude

121. Jane Seymour,
portrait by Hans
Holbein the Younger

manners. Henry was enormously put off by her. He knew no German; she, no English. The marriage was celebrated nevertheless, on January 6, 1540, with Henry never more reluctant to do his nuptial duties. When the German emperor threatened reprisals on the duke of Cleves and his new English ally, Henry had had enough. Thomas Cromwell lived just long enough to assist Henry in obtaining an annulment. Then he dutifully laid his head on the chopping block (July 23, 1540) and died, so it is said, in the Catholic faith.

There were two other wives of Henry VIII, whom we will consider later in this chapter. Catherine Howard was beheaded for adultery. Catherine Parr had the good fortune of outliving Henry.

122. Anne of Cleves,
portrait by Hans
Holbein the Younger

Catholics, Protestants, and Henricians

In the 1530s three theological parties existed in the Church of England. The first was a Roman Catholic party, one still loyal both to Catholic teachings and to the pope. Two of its most prominent members — John Fisher and Thomas More — were beheaded in 1535. A third, Reginald Pole, was in exile. Pole had been born in 1500, the son of a distinguished Straffordshire family of royal lineage. The Poles were, in fact, the last remnant of the old Yorkist faction left in England. Henry VIII took a personal interest in Reginald Pole's upbringing. By means of church pensions and benefices, Pole was able to afford an education in Italy, where he made friends among the elite young churchmen and humanists and became accustomed to the sort of Catholic piety soon to be expressed in the Catholic Reformation. He returned to England in 1527, in the midst of the annulment proceedings. With his Catholic conscience pulling him in one direction, his debt to King Henry in another, Pole was in conflict with himself. When Wolsey died, Henry offered Pole the important see of Winchester or the eminent archiepiscopal see of York. When he refused them both, he fell from the king's grace and left England in the spring of 1523 for an extended exile, not to return until the reign of the Catholic queen, Mary Tudor. He passed his exile mostly in Italy, in the forefront of the young movement known as the Catholic Reformation. In 1536 Pope Paul III named Pole to the college of cardinals. In the same year, at Padua, Pole wrote his work on the unity of the church, in which he both dismantled the principle of royal supremacy as attempted by Henry VIII and demonstrated the legitimacy of the papacy in Rome by scriptural and historical evidence. The following year, Pope Paul attempted to send Pole to England as the papal legate. So vociferously did Henry VIII rebuff the pope's overture that the mission was scrapped. In August 1538 Henry took out his revenge on the members of the Pole family still living in England. Reginald Pole's mother and brothers were arrested for treasonable activities in defense of the pope and the old

123. Reginald Pole, portrait by Sebastiano del Piombo

religion, and some members of the family were actually executed in 1541. Pole, undaunted, proceeded to an important career in the papal service. At the Council of Trent, for example, he sat as a distinguished cardinal and papal legate.

The second party was the Protestant party, led by Cranmer and Cromwell and a number of bishops — Nicholas Shaxton of Salisbury, Hugh Latimer of Worcester, and Edmund Foxe of Hereford. The Protestants were partial to the principle of royal supremacy and to the nationalization of the English church that Henry had carried out in the early thirties. Their disdain for the Roman papacy was ill disguised. "From the tyranny of the bishop of Rome and all his detestable enormities," wrote Cranmer in his English litany, "good Lord, deliver us." The Protestants, moreover, were persistent advocates of the English Bible as the basis of a Christianity reformulated on the basis of Scripture. (That was a legacy from the English humanists, who cherished the Bible and the church fathers above all other learning.) Cromwell and Cranmer threw their support to successive editions of the Bible in English, since the government, under Cromwell's aegis, ordered the universities to reconceive theological education around a biblical center. The Protestants found it agreeable to negotiate with the Lutherans of Germany during the thirties, as we shall see, but it is difficult to estimate just how much of English Protestant thought may have been imported directly from Germany. Cranmer, by his own testimony, adhered to the Catholic view of the Mass until 1538, at which point he subscribed to an opinion that may have been Lutheran. The Protestants were excessively finicky over what they took to be the remains of Roman superstition still left in England. In 1538, for example, the shrine of St. Thomas at Canterbury, hallowed since the Middle Ages, was completely reduced, the gems and gold being consigned to the royal treasury, while Thomas à Becket himself was formally discredited for having sided with the papacy against an English sovereign.

The third party was a party of conservative bishops called Henricians — aptly named, for they entertained the thoughts of Henry VIII. They accepted the constitution of the Church of England as set forth in the parliamentary acts of 1534, including the principle of royal supremacy. They nevertheless fancied themselves (as no doubt Henry did) as staunch defenders of the Catholic faith, particularly the seven sacraments, the real presence of Christ in the Mass, and the apostolic succession of bishops (of which they believed themselves a part). They were Catholics, if not *Roman* Catholics, and they stoutly resisted the inroads of Protestant teaching in the Church of England. They denied the Lutheran doctrine of justification by faith alone, rejected the assumption that anyone could interpret Scripture, resisted the production of the Bible in English, disliked fraternization with the Lutherans of Germany, and favored stiff measures against any breach of Catholic orthodoxy in England.

Foremost among the Henricians was Stephen Gardiner, bishop of Winchester, perhaps the ablest theologian and canon lawyer in England. In 1535 he wrote *De vera obedientia* (On true obedience), in which he defended the constitution of the Church of England as it had been conceived by Henry VIII. Other prominent Henricians were John Stokesley, bishop of London, whom Erasmus called the most learned man of the age; Edmund Bonner, bishop of Hereford, then of London, who left the most galling memories of his hostility toward heretics (to get one's children to go to bed at night, all one needed to do was say, "Bonner"); and Cuthbert Tunstall, bishop of London, then of Durham, whom Erasmus considered among the leaders of the Renaissance in England.

The Henricians had the advantage of a political sponsor who more than offset the political power of Thomas Cromwell. He was Thomas Howard, earl of Surrey, third duke of Norfolk. In the years 1536–40, England was riven by the struggle between the party of Cranmer and Cromwell and that of Gardiner and Norfolk.

As the year 1536 proceeded, both Catherine of Aragon and Anne Boleyn had been gotten out of the way, and the relationship between France and Germany had gotten noticeably worse. Henry therefore decided upon a foreign policy of isolated neutrality: he proposed to conduct himself so that he would be left alone in his island kingdom. Cromwell fretted, nonetheless, over a papal bull, issued by Paul III, August 30, 1535, threatening Henry with excommunication and the forfeiture of his throne, which would require a crusade against England on the part of Charles V of Germany and Francis I of France. Such papal mischief goaded Cromwell to seek an alliance with the German Lutherans. Negotiations with the Lutherans, which had been in the wind since 1533, took a serious turn in 1535, when an English delegation was sent to Wittenberg to treat with that accommodating Lutheran, Philip Melanchthon, and his associates. While the theologians in Wittenberg, strongly led by Melanchthon, worked out a set of religious principles called the Wittenberg Articles, the various parties in England produced a similar document called the Ten Articles, whose purpose was to match up the teachings of the Anglicans with those of the Lutherans to the greatest possible extent.

124. Thomas
Howard, duke
of Norfolk,
portrait by
Hans Holbein
the Younger

The Ten Articles of 1536, the first of the Anglican statements of faith, is a compromise between the Henricians and English Protestants. Henry himself tinkered with the title, to clear away any misunderstandings; it read: "Articles devised by the Kinges Highnes Majestie." The first article declares that the Anglican faith shall depend on the Bible, the three ecumenical creeds, and the first four ecumenical councils (but not, presumably, on papal teaching or the traditions of the Middle Ages). Only three sacraments are discussed: baptism, the Mass, and penance. The other four traditional sacraments are neither accepted nor rejected. Article 4 expresses the real presence of Christ in the Mass, without explaining how that occurs: "Under the form of bread and wine . . . is truly, substantially, and really contained and comprehended the very self-same body and blood of our Saviour Jesus Christ." The statement on justification, found in article 5, is thought to have been borrowed from Melanchthon — for the sake of diplomacy, no doubt — but someone among the English theologians doctored it, obscuring the Lutheran meaning. The last five articles all pertain to ceremonies and customs of the church (regarding images, saints, prayers for the dead, and such); those articles are not only patient, but actually conservative, of the piety of the medieval Latin church.

In August 1536 Cromwell, as Henry's vicar-general for religious affairs (a title he received some time before January 1536), issued royal injunctions requiring every priest to publish the Ten Articles in his parish once a quarter and to expound them publicly twice a quarter. The injunctions also required an English Bible to be placed at the disposal of parishioners in every parish in England. A translation by William Tyndale and Miles Coverdale, called Matthew's Bible, had already been prepared, although the printed copies of that work would not be available for another three years.

Whatever hopes the Ten Articles may have aroused that the policy of the Church of England was being bent in the direction of Wittenberg were soon dispelled by the appearance, in 1537, of *The Institution of a Christian Man* — the so-called Bishops Book — which became the second of the Anglican standards of faith. In it, the Church of England rediscovered not only the four lost sacraments of 1536, but other aspects of medieval divinity.

The reason for such a shift in policy is not hard to discover. Late in 1536 war had broken out between Francis I and Charles V, releasing Henry VIII from any anxiety over being threatened from abroad. His disdain for Lutheranism came back in spades. The Pilgrimage of Grace may have convinced Henry that the persistence of Catholic opinion in England was much stronger than he had supposed. And the birth of a son (Edward) in October 1537 no doubt convinced him that, in the eyes of heaven, he was at last doing things correctly.

Completed in July 1537, the Bishops Book was, as the name implies, the result of conversations among the Anglican bishops, Henrician and Protestant. The Anglicans here conceive of the Christian church as a composite of many free and equal national churches, none of which has any sovereignty over the others — a rebuff, of course, to the papacy at Rome. They subscribe to all seven of the Catholic sacraments, although only three — baptism, the Eucharist, and penance — are believed to have been instituted by Christ, while the remaining four — confirmation, matrimony, holy orders, and extreme unction — are apparently of lesser origin and significance. The "sacrament of the altar" (i.e., the Mass, or Eucharist) receives a very conservative, Catholic definition, just short of transubstantiation. The article on justification falls far short of the Protestant doctrine of justification by faith alone; contrition, faith, charity, hope, confidence, and something called spiritual grace are all declared prerequisites to justification.

Late in 1537 the relations between France and Germany improved to such an extent that the Peace of Nice, ending the hostility between the two powers, was signed during the summer of 1538. Suddenly, Henry's foreign policy of isolated neutrality seemed inadequate. All of Cromwell's anxieties returned. New overtures were made to the Lutherans, and new strictures were laid against the remnants of Catholicism in England in order to make the entente with continental Protestantism seem legitimate. These maneuvers of 1538 set off a crisis in England powerful enough to crush Cromwell, strong enough to persist beyond Henry's lifetime until the reign of his third child, Elizabeth, and pervasive enough to survive in Anglicanism to the present day. It was the clash between the old religion, as represented by Gardiner and Norfolk, and the new religion, as expressed by Cranmer and Cromwell, with Henry in tethers between the two.

In the summer of 1538, at Cromwell's instigation, Lutheran delegates appeared in London to resume the discussions begun in Wittenberg in the fall of 1535. Because of Henry's reluctance to commit either himself or his subjects to the Lutherans out of hand, the conversations amounted to very little, and the Lutherans went away disgruntled. Those conversations, however, did lead to a document, Thirteen Articles, which, while it attained no validity in either Germany or England, contributed to the development of Anglican doctrine as finally expressed in the Forty-Two Articles of Edward VI and the Thirty-Nine Articles of Elizabeth I. The crucial article among the thirteen is article 4, on justification, which, with astonishing clarity and forthrightness, declares in favor of the Lutheran doctrine (or more probably the Melanchthonian doctrine) of justification by faith alone.

Meanwhile, in new injunctions issued in September 1538, Cromwell, as Henry's "vicegerent" for religious affairs, heated up the campaign against popish superstitions and pressed the availability of an English Bible in every parish of England. Throughout the year, agents of the Crown demolished the scenic apparatus of Roman Catholicism, especially shrines and other places of pilgrimage, heaping ridicule on what was left of medieval piety. Included in that purge was the world-famous shrine of St. Thomas à Becket at Canterbury. In August 1538 Henry arrested most of the Pole family, as well as other prominent people believed to be implicated in their propapal schemes.

Foreign affairs turned even worse in 1539. In January of that year,

France and Germany renewed their treaty of peace and friendship. Henry, by then a widower, tried first to placate Francis, then Charles, by offering to take a wife from their midst, but both of those sovereigns rebuffed him. Meanwhile, Cardinal Pole traversed Europe, calling on all Christians to implement the papal bull of 1535 and deprive Henry of his realm.

In the Parliament that met from April until June of 1539, the chief issue was religion. It was clear by that time that England was being torn in two by the contention between the Henrician and Protestant factions, and that before further damage was done, the "supreme head" and his Parliament would have to bring some resolution to the question. On May 16, 1539, less than a year after the Lutherans had gone home, the duke of Norfolk proposed a discussion in the House of Lords on six questions of religion. Four theologians of the Protestant party and four of the Henrician party were appointed to address the questions. When deadlock ensued, Henry himself invaded the discussions and threw his weight to the conservative side.

Parliament passed the Six Articles Act in June 1539. These articles — the most conservative expression of the Anglican religion to be published in Henry's reign — bound all England to (1) transubstantiation, (2) communion in one kind only (i.e., the bread), (3) the celibacy of priests and the illegality of priestly marriage, (4) the sanctity of monastic vows, (5) the legitimacy of private Mass, and (6) the necessity of private confession to a priest. That document was a rank repudiation of Protestantism in England. It should have squelched the Protestants, but curiously, it did not. Bishops Latimer and Shaxton were forced to resign their sees. Cranmer sent his wife home to Germany. Some five hundred Protestants were rounded up in London, accused of disavowing the Six Articles. For the most part, however, the English Protestants took their defeat in good grace. Cranmer survived. Cromwell, who had almost been unseated by Norfolk, regained most of his power within a month.

Worse times were just ahead for the Protestant party. In the midst of the great fuss over religion, Cromwell renewed his attempt to bring Henry VIII into alliance with the German Lutherans. As early as March 1539, Henry, at Cromwell's prodding, began to entertain the possibility of an alliance with the duke of Cleves, who was associated with the German Lutheran defense organization known as the Schmalkaldic League. In October 1539 Cromwell cajoled Henry into a marriage with Anne of Cleves, the duke's daughter, as a means of cementing the alliance. But when Henry spotted her in January 1540, he loathed her at first sight and married her in spite of himself. Even in the marriage bed, Henry must have realized that he did not care much for Anglo-Lutheran coziness.

The Henricians almost immediately picked up strength. Norfolk, who had teased Henry with one of his nieces (Anne Boleyn), now brought forward another niece for royal inspection — Catherine Howard. Henry, smitten at once, demanded of Cromwell that he unload Anne of Cleves by means of an annulment. Cromwell, although he was an expert in wife removal, could scarcely have done what Henry wanted without installing the Howards in power. It was a bitter dilemma. On June 10, 1540, Thomas Cromwell was arrested in the midst of the Privy Council and was accused of heresy and treason — that is, of having violated the Six Articles Act and of having forced Henry to marry Anne of Cleves without his will and consent. He

125. Catherine Howard, portrait by Hans Holbein the Younger

was condemned without trial and, having supplied enough evidence to ensure Henry an annulment, was beheaded on July 23, 1540. It is said that he died a Catholic.

How shall we assess Thomas Cromwell — that rather unsympathetic figure, whose ability seems undeniable, whose cunning, apparent? Was he merely one more poor soul used up by Henry VIII or caught in the snares of religious rancor and matrimonial intrigue that characterized the age of Henry? No, there is more to be said. Of Cromwell, the Tudor historian G. R. Elton has written, "In eight years he engineered one of the few successful revolutions in English history, and he achieved this without upsetting the body politic." Elton means that when Cromwell died in 1540, the state of England and the English monarchy were remarkably different institutions than they had been when Wolsey died. A revolution had occurred, carefully justified on ancient prescription. Of what did that revolution consist?

First, England had become a sovereign national state. The matter was settled in the preamble that Cromwell affixed to the Restraint of Appeals (1533):

> Where by divers sundry old authentic histories and chronicles, it is manifestly declared and expressed, that this realm of England is an Empire, and hath so been accepted in the world, governed by one Supreme Head and King, having the dignity and royal estate of the imperial Crown of the same, unto whom a body politic, compact of all sorts and degrees of people divided in terms and by names of Spirituality and Temporality, be bounden and owe to bear next to God a natural and humble obedience.

What does that text suggest? In Wolsey's time, England, then a respectful member of the Holy Roman Church, was entangled in medieval political perceptions that, more often than not, ascribed the fullness of all power, both temporal and spiritual, to the papacy in Rome, by whom it was divested upon the several sovereign states. By using the word "empire," Cromwell appealed to the ancient claim of *imperium,* namely, lay authority over the state bestowed on a king directly from God. (The case of the emperor Constantine would be exemplary.) The preamble of the Restraint of Appeals therefore means that the state of England is disconnected from medieval political theory; that England governs itself without any superior on earth; that England's sovereign possesses, *by a direct, personal grant from God,* authority over both church and state; that England is an independent, sovereign state, governed by a sovereign who is both "supreme head" in affairs spiritual and king in affairs temporal. The theory of *imperium* explains the interest among the English in a possible connection to Constantine, through King Arthur (fifth or sixth century), who was thought to have been in direct lineage to Helena, Constantine's mother and a Briton.

Second, the English church became "the Church of England," to quote Cromwell's preamble to the Supremacy Act (1534), with the king of England as its "supreme head." That meant that the *Anglicana ecclesia* (English church) had attained its own, independent, national unity, and a new authority directly from God. As supreme head — a benefit conferred directly and personally by God upon the sovereign — Henry could exercise the "power of jurisdiction" (*potestas jurisdictionis*) over the temporal affairs of the church, but not the spiritual or sacerdotal functions (*potestas ordinis*), which required priestly ordination. As vicar-general, Cromwell carried out the jurisdictional powers that Henry gladly exercised over the Church of England.

Third, Cromwell, by establishing this revolution by statute and protecting it by law, brought Parliament into partnership with the king; he reassigned sovereignty, not simply to the king, but to the *king in Parliament* — perhaps the first instance of a constitutional monarchy. Henry VIII chose a parliamentarian as his leading adviser. Cromwell entered Parliament in 1529 with every intention of exploiting it; he knew how to use Parliament to sanction and protect a constitutional revolution, and he was apparently able to educate Henry in the advantage of a representative institution.

This sovereign, national state of the Tudors, however, was never understood to be a creature of Parliament. It was an act of God: Henry was king by divine appointment, and supreme head, by the same. What Parliament did was to legalize the revolution by means of statute, giving it the protection of law and the means of prosecuting those who disobeyed. Henceforth, it was understood that *Parliament made laws* — a power that gave that institution new eminence in the state.

The death of Cromwell left Henry without a principal minister and severely decreased the efficiency of his administration. There being no apparent successor to Cromwell, the responsibilities of government were assumed by Henry himself and by a Privy Council badly divided over the question of religion. Norfolk and Gardiner continued to lead the conservatives. Direction of the English Protestants fell to Archbishop Cranmer and to Edward Seymour, earl of Hertford, whose rise to power was associated with the fact that he was the uncle of Edward, Prince of Wales.

In August 1540 Henry married Catherine Howard, niece of the duke of Norfolk — a circumstance that seemed to guarantee the triumph of the Howards and of the conservatives generally. In November of the following year, however, the Privy Council discovered that Catherine had been promiscuous before and after her marriage to Henry. So conspicuous had her indiscretions been that Parliament accused her of treason and sent her to the scaffold in February 1542. Even the self-righteousness of Bishop Gardiner lost its luster in that episode. Norfolk survived by taking sides against his own niece. Two years later, in June 1543, Henry ventured into matrimony again, with another Catherine. He married the widow Catherine Parr, a woman of Protestant leanings, as experienced in marriage as she was disinterested in politics. So she survived.

126. Catherine Parr, from a painting by Holbein

127. Mary,
Queen of Scots

In the summer of 1541 the fragile arrangement between Francis I and Charles V broke apart when two French foreign officers were murdered by the Spanish governor of Milan. England was courted by both contenders — a luxury Henry VIII did not often enjoy. He decided to vex the French by making an assault on Scotland, where sympathies were traditionally pro-French and papalist. In October 1542 Norfolk led an English army into Scotland, in a maneuver to attain English dominance over that nation. In November, James V of Scotland counterattacked in force, but his formidable army, disconcerted by internal disputes, was destroyed by a much smaller English contingent at Solway Moss. The Scottish succession passed to an infant, Mary Stuart, Queen of Scots, the daughter of James V and his French wife, Mary of Guise; Mary Queen of Scots was therefore the personification of the Franco-Scottish alliance. In July 1543 Henry VIII forced the Scots to accept the onerous Treaty of Greenwich, which required the marriage of Mary Stuart to the Prince of Wales and therefore anticipated, if not the

588

union of the two realms, the subservience of Scotland to England. At that prospect, Scottish nationalism improved to a fever pitch; Archbishop Beaton, the militant Catholic cardinal of Scotland, escaped from prison and soon succeeded in restoring the pro-French and papalist sentiments in Scotland. Henry VIII had no option except more military power. Hertford, who was sent north, burned the city of Edinburgh and scorched the countryside. So the matter remained until Henry's death. His Scottish policy was a failure.

Henry's military adventure on the Continent was not much better. In 1543 he entered the European war on the side of Charles V and the empire. In the following year, an English expeditionary force of forty thousand, led by Norfolk and Surrey, invaded France from Calais, while the imperial forces moved simultaneously on Paris. Henry appeared on the field in a litter. The campaign, which was directed at the conquest of Picardy, resulted in the capture of a single town (Boulogne), which the French eventually bought back. It was a minuscule accomplishment at a staggering cost. By the time a treaty had been concluded with France in June 1546, Henry had spent two million pounds for the campaign, 650,000 of which had been raised by unprecedented taxation. To pay for his military expenditures, he was also forced to sell crown lands, including monastic properties, and to debase the coinage. He weakened, and almost destroyed, the financial foundations of the realm that his father, Henry VII, and his minister Cromwell had worked so hard to establish.

Meanwhile, the contest over religion remained a stalemate. The Six Articles proved unpleasant to Protestants. Latimer was finally imprisoned for nonconformity, while Shaxton was tried and condemned for the same offense and finally forced to abjure. Three times, Cranmer was cited for heresy in the early forties and each time rescued by Henry himself. In 1543 the canons of Canterbury Cathedral complained of the heretical opinions of their bishop. Henry simply remanded the case of Cranmer to Archbishop Cranmer. Soon after, a member of Parliament from Bedfordshire named Gostwick complained to the House of Commons of Cranmer's heresy. Henry warned him that he would be "poor Gostwick" if he continued. In 1545 Norfolk accused Cranmer of heresy in the midst of the Privy Council. Said Henry on that occasion: "I would you would well understand that I count my Lord Canterbury as faithful as a man towards me as ever was prelate in this realm." That settled the matter once and for all. It may explain the survival of the English Protestant party in the dangerous forties.

In 1543 the Henricians managed to get a bill through Parliament (the

Act for the Advancement of True Religion) that restricted the right to read the English Bible by class. Common folk and most women could not read the English Bible at all. Those who could — noblemen, gentlemen, merchants, scholars, and politicians — were those apt to be interested in reformation. In other words, the bill may have been a miscalculation on the part of the Henricians.

The doctrinal history of Henry's reign came to a conclusion with the publication in 1543 of *A Necessary Doctrine and Erudition for Any Christian Man* — the so-called King's Book. This work was the finest and fullest expression of Anglo-Catholicism as practiced by Henry and the Henrician bishops. Even Cardinal Pole pronounced it true religion and ordered it read from the pulpits of England during the reign of Mary Tudor. Cranmer and Gardiner both contributed to its production (although the terms of the book greatly exceeded Cranmer's personal convictions). Henry himself kept close watch over the project and decorated the book with a preface of its own.

Some aspects of the book were certainly not pleasing to the English Protestants. It subscribed to all seven sacraments, making no distinction among them, and affirmed transubstantiation. Those who clamored for Communion in both kinds were called "a pestiferous and devilish school." Luther's assumption that, following the fall of Adam, the human will is enslaved to sin was frankly repudiated: "We conclude that free will is in man after this fall." Justification was described in correct Catholic terms as a *process* "of attaining [one's] own justification." Beside these crucial Catholic affirmations, the few Protestant touches seem insignificant. It was, in sum, a book of stout Catholic doctrine, with only a few concessions to the Protestant sentiment.

As the forties wore on, the older generation gave way to a new, more liberal generation. Suffolk died in 1545. Norfolk ended his career in disgrace. Hertford and Lisle, who replaced the old dukes, were known to have Protestant leanings. Even the Prince of Wales was being brought up by his Protestant mother (Catherine Parr) and Protestant tutors, at whom old Henry seemed to wink. The collapse of the Howards occurred in the mid-forties, when Norfolk's son, Henry, earl of Surrey, committed a major indiscretion. A descendent of Edward I, he rashly displayed the royal arms of Edward the Confessor, implying his own legitimacy in the line of succession to the throne of England. Father and son were both arrested for treason in December 1546. Surrey was executed in January. Norfolk was scheduled for the same fate on the twenty-seventh of that month. In the early hours of that day — January 27, 1547 —

Henry VIII died in his fifty-seventh year, as Cranmer held his hand. The demise of Norfolk was therefore interrupted. According to the Succession Act of 1543, sovereignty passed to nine-year-old Edward VI, and after him, to Mary; after Mary, to Elizabeth.

EDWARD VI

AT Henry's death, Edward VI's minority would continue another nine years, in keeping with custom and with his father's will. Parliament acclaimed him on January 31, 1547; Cranmer crowned him in Westminster Abbey on February 20, using the ancient ritual from which all conspicuous reference to the pope had been expunged. (Pope Paul III, for that matter, recognized the succession, not of Edward, but of Mary Tudor, daughter of Henry and Catherine of Aragon.)

128. Edward VI, portrait by Hans Holbein the Younger

Who was Edward? His mother was Jane Seymour, who had died in childbirth. He had been raised by Catherine Parr, whose evangelical sympathies were easily attested. The boy's Protestant upbringing, however, did not stop at that. Three tutors of evangelical leaning were given charge of his education — Richard Cox, John Cheke, and Anthony Cooke. The boy was precocious, and his Protestant sympathies were well understood both at home and abroad. Cranmer, at Edward's coronation, referred to him as the second Josiah (the first Josiah having been a distinguished king of Judah, 639–608 B.C.). Calvin, in a letter to King Edward in 1551, acknowledged that Edward had read Calvin's biblical commentaries at the tender age of fourteen.

Henry intended to leave the government of England, during Edward's minority, to a number of executors, each equal in power, who would form a council of regency. He deliberately excluded extremists from both sides. Both Gardiner and Bonner were on that account left out; so was the earl of Essex, Catherine Parr's brother, who was a hot gospeler. But Henry's plan for Edward's minority miscarried. He had underestimated the ambition of Edward Seymour, earl of Hertford, Edward's uncle. While the death of the old king was being withheld momentarily from the public, Seymour sped to Hertfordshire, where Edward was staying; he took his young nephew into custody and brought him to London. Under such circumstances, Seymour was able to persuade the council of regency to breach Henry's last will and testament and to proclaim himself lord protector (January 31, 1547). Soon after, he acquired the title duke of Somerset. Although he spared Norfolk's life, Somerset made sure that the old duke passed his life in the Tower, deprived of all his titles and dignities. Somerset's only serious remaining rival was Lisle, now earl of Warwick.

Somerset was born in 1505 and had risen to prominence as a soldier in campaigns against the French and the Scots. The marriage of his sister, Jane, to Henry VIII (1536) led to his election to the Privy Council. Upon the birth of Edward, he was made earl of Hertford. The death of his sister did not deter his ambitions. In 1542 he commanded the English forces that defeated the Scots at Solway Moss. Thus, at Henry's death, he was able to present himself to the nation as conqueror of the Scots and guardian of the boy-king. His theological opinions were noticeably Protestant; his teachers, however, were not Lutherans but oracles of the Reformed branch of the Reformation, notably, John Calvin of Geneva and Heinrich Bullinger of Zurich.

Somerset faced severe problems. The exchequer had been exhausted;

129. Edward
Seymour, engraving
after the painting by
Hans Holbein the
Younger

the coinage, debased. The church had been despoiled; the people, badly divided over religion. The Scots were infuriated, and only a thin truce kept the French at bay. The good administration of Cromwell had all but disintegrated. As far as religion was concerned, Somerset maneuvered to unseat the last remaining conservative from the council — Chancellor Wriothesley — leaving the council pliantly Protestant. Meanwhile, at Archbishop Cranmer's invitation, Protestant theologians of the Reformed persuasion began to trickle into England. Somerset conceived of a "Great Britain" consisting of England, Scotland, Ireland, and Wales, but he could not imagine how to bring the Scots to heel, short of military action. In September 1547 he routed the Scots at Pinkie but then failed to take political advantage of his victory. The next year, Mary Queen of Scots was sent off to France for her upbringing, and thereupon the Scottish policy of Henry VIII dissolved.

In November 1547 Somerset put an act through Parliament that repealed or softened many of the old statutes that penalized religious nonconformity — including the Six Articles Act and all restrictions against the printing or use of the English Bible. "Nothing," wrote Somerset in the preamble to that act, is more becoming of a prince than "great clemency and indulgency and rather too much forgiveness." Such liberalism brought on a spate of religious curiosities, sects, and controversies that were characteristic of Edward's whole reign. The same month, Parliament passed the Act against Revilers and for Receiving in Both Kinds, which gave assurance to conservatives that disrespect of the Mass would not be tolerated, while guaranteeing to Protestants that they could receive Communion in both species. The New Injunctions for Religious Reform was issued in July, under the protector's name; these laws cracked down hard on the pomp and circumstance of medieval religion, outlawing candles, images, shrines, and processions. (The English in Edward's reign worried a great deal about such things.) The Great Bible and Erasmus's *Paraphrases* of the Gospels were required to be available in every parish, and the clergy were enjoined to read one homily from Cranmer's *Book of Homilies* every Sunday, to abate the "ignorance and blindness" of the people.

In the course of the forties, Cranmer had assembled twelve sermons, including six of his own, and tried unsuccessfully to have the collection approved by the Convocation of Canterbury in 1543. Now that the *Book of Homilies* was needed, Cranmer had it published. It had the effect of instilling Cranmer's growing evangelical conviction into the Anglican church. The "Homily of Salvation," for example, which Cranmer wrote, teaches the doctrine of justification by faith alone with great candor, clarity, and power, as if there were no other admissible point of view. Likewise, the "Homily of Faith," also by Cranmer, resounds with Lutheran meaning, although it comes down harder than Luther might have preferred on the necessity of good works as a consequence of faith. The same point is made in the "Homily of Good Works," the third sermon in the important trilogy by Cranmer. No book was more apparent of Cranmer's evangelical disposition than the *Book of Homilies;* none was more effective in shifting English opinion in the Protestant direction.

Still another blow was dealt to English Catholicism in the course of 1547. Parliament passed the Act Dissolving the Chantries, which affected the thousands of small foundations for religious, charitable, fraternal, and educational purposes that flourished in medieval England. Included were 2,300 chantries (in which Masses for the dead were said), colleges, over a hundred hospitals, fraternities, guilds, and other endowed institutions. The act declared that true religion required the dissolution, since, for example, purgatory was an unscriptural superstition and Masses for the dead were founded on ignorance. Income from the confiscation would be turned to "good and godly uses" — to create more grammar schools, to endow the universities, and to make pensions for the poor. There is not much evidence, however, that education was much advanced or the poor much relieved. Mainly, the spoils garnished a depleted royal treasury.

At the opening of 1548 Cranmer sent around a query to the bishops, asking whether they could support an English version of the Mass. The result was inconclusive, but Cranmer argued that something must be done in any case, in order to permit the people to receive the sacrament in both kinds, as Parliament had recently required. Thus, over the winter of 1547–48, he and a committee of seven bishops and six doctors of divinity met at Windsor Castle and prepared *The Order of the Communion,* which was published in March 1548. A small pamphlet of ten pages, it contained an English form for the administration of Communion in both kinds, designed to be inserted into the Roman Catholic Mass at the proper place. Evidently, the word "Communion" had come to be preferred to the more traditional word "Mass"; the new document gave no credence at all to the traditional assumption that the sacrament involved a sacrifice of Christ. Some scholars have suggested that Cranmer and his Windsor committee had swung all the way over to the Zwinglian side, but that accusation is far-fetched. It is at least of some sentimental importance that certain liturgical pieces from *The Order of the Communion* — Confession, Absolution, and the Comfortable Words — have survived in the Anglican and Methodist liturgies to this day; they were written by Cranmer and his colleagues on the basis of two liturgical texts developed at Cologne in the forties.

The Book of Common Prayer

The Order of the Communion was an interim arrangement. In September 1548 the Windsor committee began work on a new prayer book that was destined to become the single most important expression of the Church of England. A completed text, called *The Book of the Common Prayer,* was sent to Parliament in December of the same year. Parliament approved it in January; Edward gave his consent in March, and the book was appointed for use in the parishes on Pentecost, June 9, 1549. All of the matter from *The Order of the Communion* was included.

The first and most obvious thing to be said about the new prayer book is that that it is profoundly related to medieval life. It is a very careful, reverent adaptation, in English, of the Sarum Missal, that is, the medieval Catholic missal used in the diocese of Salisbury. Virtually every prayer in the Roman Canon — that section of the Mass in which the consecration occurs — received a counterpart in the new prayer book, often with literary affinities. So, the structure of the prayer book became part of the Catholic substance of the Church of England.

Second, the prayer book was designed to be as comprehensive as possible of all parties in the Church of England. The very titles of the book contained traditional ideas and phrases, such as the term "Mass," which invited the sympathy of conservative people. The Roman Catholic doctrine of the sacrifice, however, was completely read out of Anglican worship in a polemic, written by Cranmer, which appeared originally as follows: ". . . by hys one oblacion of hymselfe once offered a full, perfecte, and sufficiente sacrifice, oblacion, and satisfaccion for the synnes of the whole worlde." Some of the most characteristic ceremonies of the Roman Mass were abolished, including the elevation of the host.

Third, as its title says so eloquently, the new book was a "book of common prayer," that is, an instrument not simply for priests, but for the whole people. It was therefore cast in the English language and ruled by the English Bible.

The chief problem with the new prayer book was its ambiguity about the Lord's Supper. It could be interpreted any which way — which is apparently what its editors wanted. But Gardiner, who had decorated the Tower of London since June 1548, proceeded to kill the new prayer book by declaring that it was a Catholic masterpiece, thereby convincing the Protestants that it was worthless.

Parliament passed the Act of Uniformity to go with the new prayer book. It abolished the Roman Catholic cultus in England and impressed the new book of liturgical services on the whole realm in uniform usage. The "established" Church of England, in other words, was to have an "established" liturgy. Persons reluctant to use the new book, whether clerical or lay, could expect to find themselves in jail.

Meanwhile, Somerset's administration was being severely pressed by economic difficulties. The Tudor inflation flared up excessively in the forties and brought with it very oppressive poverty. As trade in wool increased, so did the practice of enclosure, that is, the condemnation of farmland for sheep pasture by the lords of manors, who were themselves driven by economic necessity. Whole villages disappeared before the vast regiment of sheep. Enclosure riots broke out with ever greater frequency as the forties wore on.

When the new prayer book was imposed upon England at Pentecost, 1549, it received a poor reception all around. The laity mocked it as a frivolous novelty. Parish priests tried to turn it back into the Mass. Protestant theologians denounced its ambiguity, while Bishop Gardiner advanced five reasons why the book was suitably Catholic, thereby confounding the Protestants even more. By Whitmonday, Somerset's decrepit government faced a serious rebellion in Cornwall and Devon, as parish after parish rallied to the defense of the old faith. The insurgents, who numbered at least ten thousand, stated their complaint in fifteen articles; they demanded that England be taken back to the religion of the Six Articles, with the Mass in Latin, Communion in one kind, the restoration of ceremonies and images, and the recall of the English Bible.

A second uprising occurred in the eastern counties, specifically Norfolk, where resistance to the government's agrarian policies came to a head. It was led by a tanner named Robert Ket, who commanded a force of some sixteen thousand insurgents. Their hostility was not directed toward the Protestant establishment of Edward VI, but rather toward the Norfolk gentry, that is, toward the ruling class of a county that was conspicuously exploitive and indifferent to social suffering.

While Somerset stood frozen in uncertainty, the outraged gentry took matters into their own hands; they suppressed the two uprisings with a certain savagery. Russell and Herbert put down the religious rebellion in the west, while Warwick quelled the agrarian disturbance in Norfolk. By the fall of 1549, peace had been restored all around.

Somerset's administration was profoundly embarrassed by these political, social, and religious difficulties, contributing to the popular perception that Somerset was incompetent to govern. His programs to cope with the agrarian crisis were no more successful than his foreign policy. Instead of "the Empire of Great Britain," cemented together by a common Protestantism, Somerset had managed to place England between two hostile Catholic powers — Scotland to the north and France on the Continent. (In France, in fact, the siege of Boulogne was underway.) Warwick, conqueror of the eastern rebels, asserted himself openly in 1549 and led a coup d'état that was planned in September and completed in October; the lord protector was arrested and imprisoned in the Tower of London. Almost no one of importance stood up for him.

After some months, Warwick arranged for Somerset's release; on April 10, 1550, he was even readmitted to the council of regency. In June his daughter was married to Warwick's son, which seemed to seal the reconciliation. Warwick was the governor of England, although he eschewed the title of protector, preferring to manipulate the council and instruct the young king. This new set of arrangements, however, proved fragile. The young king's frailty was now widely recognized; people whispered that he did not have long to live. It was no time for powerful men to be nice. Somerset, whom the English called the Good Duke, enjoyed immense popularity, despite his failures. It soon became apparent that Somerset might even be able to recover a following in Parliament. Thus, in October 1551, Warwick struck. He consolidated his own power by assuming the title duke of Northumberland, and he allowed his cronies to be invested with similar ornaments of nobility. Immediately after, he caused Somerset to be arrested on a far-fetched accusation of treason. On January 22, 1552, the day before the Parliament was scheduled to reconvene, Somerset suffered the ax. The next day, amid an outpouring of public sorrow, Parliament was presented with the fait accompli.

John Dudley, earl of Warwick, was the second of the young soldiers to achieve power in England after the fall of Cromwell. He made his reputation at Dussindale in 1549, when he put down Ket's rebellion. Unlike Somerset, who could charm the spots off a leopard but had no clue about administration, Warwick had a loathsome personality, yet a will to rule and an administrative brilliance that led him to see the evils in English public affairs and to cure them. He was determined to restore the administrative and fiscal structures of the English government, left dilapidated by Henry VIII and by Somerset.

At first, no one knew where Northumberland stood with respect to religion. At Oxford, the Roman Mass was reinstated, and Protestant mail to the Continent was full of lamentations that the duke might be a papist. However, it soon became obvious that he was not merely a Protestant but an extreme one. Bullinger, the successor to Zwingli in Zurich, described him as "the shining light of the Church of England." What motivated him? It is generally assumed that Northumberland's reservoir of piety was slight. Perhaps he was afraid of the power of the Henricians, particularly that of Norfolk and Gardiner. Perhaps he had designs on church revenues and property in a time of financial crisis. Perhaps he was moved by the young king's own Protestant zeal. At any rate, he began to pursue a Protestant policy with great vigor and consistency.

First, he got rid of the Henricians, whom he turned out of their sees and excluded from government. Second, in the dioceses left vacant by that housecleaning, Northumberland installed Protestants, having wrung from

130. John Dudley,
earl of Warwick,
after a painting by
Hans Holbein the
Younger

them as many financial concessions as possible. John Bale (with wife) took up the Irish See in 1551, declaring that he was no "Mass merchant." Miles Coverdale (with wife) assumed the see of Exeter at the same time. John Knox (the father of Scottish Presbyterianism) was offered the see of Rochester but declined it because he could not suffer the "popish fooleries" that remained in the Church of England. John Hooper, lately returned from Zurich, was invested with the see of Gloucester (1551). John Ponet received the see of Rochester in 1550. Divines such as these constituted a minority wing of the Protestant party in England, to the left of Cranmer and his closest colleagues. Third, Northumberland promoted a certain orderly iconoclasm by parliamentary acts. Liturgical books were ordered destroyed; scenic apparatus (statues, paintings, vessels, and ornaments) was removed from the churches and surrendered to the Crown.

The Reformed Influence

Perhaps no circumstance was more important to the evolution of Protestantism in England than the infiltration of some twelve theologians from the Reformed churches of the Continent, including three of conspicuous importance — Martin Bucer, Peter Martyr, and John à Lasco. In 1547, the year Edward succeeded, the German Lutherans suffered a crushing defeat, delivered to them by Emperor Charles V at the battle of Mühlberg, and were forced to accept the Augsburg Interim (1548), a religious settlement generally detrimental to the Protestant cause. Theologians went to England out of a sense of hopelessness for the future of Protestantism on the Continent. They also went because Archbishop Cranmer importuned them to come. Cranmer was then possessed with the idea of holding a great synod of Protestants, on English soil, to attempt to forge a consensus among all of the parties to the Reformation. Cranmer was a conciliarist; he held consistently to the idea that a general council was the supreme reality of the church universal, the only means by which the church attains unity and doctrinal harmony. He proposed to hold such a council in England.

In October 1547, within the first few months of Edward's reign, Cranmer sent invitations to Philip Melanchthon, leader of the Lutherans now that Luther had died, and to John à Lasco, a Polish theologian of Reformed sympathies who was then superintendent of the Reformed churches in East Friesland. The fact that Melanchthon finally declined Cranmer's invitation meant that, while foreign influence on the English Reformation steadily increased, it came not from Wittenberg but from Zurich and Geneva — in other words, not from the more conservative Lutherans, but from the more radical Zwinglians and Calvinists.

The first of the continental divines to arrive in England was Peter Martyr Vermigli, an Italian theologian, lately of Strassburg, who reached England in 1547 and was appointed regius professor of divinity at Oxford. He was soon followed by Martin Bucer, the well-known Reformer of Strassburg, who despaired of his future in that city after the imposition of the Augsburg Interim and fled to England in the spring of 1549; he too was appointed to a regius professorship of divinity, but at Cambridge. Finally, in June 1549 John à Lasco arrived and the following year became superintendent of the Strangers' churches of London. No more curious institution ever existed. The Strangers' churches consisted of several congregations of religious refugees ("strangers"), organized along presbyterian lines, with presbyterian forms of government and worship, yet situated in the very midst of Bishop Ridley's Anglo-Catholic diocese of London.

In 1552, stimulated perhaps by the resumption of the Council of Trent the previous year, Cranmer renewed his effort to convoke a great Protestant council in England. On March 20, 1552, he wrote to Bullinger, proposing "a synod of most learned and excellent men" that might devote itself to a consensus among Protestants. A letter to Calvin went out the same day, beseeching Calvin's attendance. A week later, Cranmer invited Melanchthon, assuring him that Edward VI "places his kingdom at your disposal." In their replies, Calvin begged to be excused on account of the smallness of his ability, while Bullinger stated bluntly that the project was ill timed. Melanchthon did not bother to answer.

Despite its failure, Cranmer's ecumenical project was not without results. It stimulated the flow of continental Protestants into England. Those theologians contributed to the evolution of the Anglican "standards" of faith — the Ordinal (1550), by which priests were ordained and bishops consecrated; the Book of Common Prayer (revised in 1552), which we have already seen to be particularly expressive of the Church of England; and the Forty-Two Articles of Religion (1553), the official theological text of the church. They participated in the highly contentious dispute over how the Lord's Supper should be interpreted in the Church of England. And some of them, at least, were accountable for the appearance of a "Swiss party" in England during Edward's reign — a fraternity of more radical theologians indebted to the policies, not of Calvin, but of Zwingli and Bullinger.

At the head of the Swiss party was John Hooper, formerly an English Cistercian, educated at Oxford, who could not subscribe to the Six Articles and fled to the Continent. At Strassburg he acquired a wife. In 1547 he moved his family to Zurich, established himself in Bullinger's household, and learned from Bullinger all there was to know. In 1549 Hooper returned to England and rose rapidly to the leadership of the Swiss party. Northumberland nominated him in 1550 for the see of Gloucester, but Hooper refused to be consecrated in the traditional vestments, which he denounced as unscriptural and "papistical." In the so-called Vestiarian Controversy, which he thereby set off, he was opposed by both Cranmer and Ridley, and by both Bucer and Martyr. The furor persisted until 1551, however, when he was at last consecrated. For a long time historians presented a caricature of Hooper, highlighting his obstinate biblicism, conspicuous sincerity, scrupulous attention to small points, and disdain for polite behavior. However, recent studies have noted his popularity among the common people of the time, and his concern for social reform.

There remains now to describe the impression made by Peter Martyr, Martin Bucer, and John à Lasco upon the English Reformation.

Born in Florence in 1500, Pietro Martire Vermigli joined the Augustinian order against the wishes of his aristocratic family; he studied at Padua and Bologna and attained the doctorate in the classics, philosophy, and Holy Scripture. By 1540 he had risen to be visitor-general of his order. Two years later, as the Roman Inquisition closed in on the evangelical activities of the humanistic circle to which Martyr belonged, he crossed the Alps, remained awhile with Bullinger in Zurich, and settled finally in Strassburg, where he became professor of theology. In the winter of 1547 Archbishop Cranmer received him handsomely in England and shortly assigned him to Oxford as regius professor of divinity; his instructions were to consolidate Protestant thought in that university, which still harbored a

131. Peter Martyr

vexing regiment of Roman Catholics. He scandalized the university by bringing along his wife, Catherine, the first woman ever to reside in an Oxford college, a liberated nun of such heroic proportions that the irreverent students at Oxford referred to her as Flaps. In May 1549 Martyr was drawn into a public disputation on the Lord's Supper with prominent Roman Catholics at Oxford. He might have taken that important occasion to clarify the Anglican perspective on the Eucharist. Yet, Peter Martyr spoke very obscurely on the subject and only contributed to the impression that the Church of England was veering off from its Catholic heritage in the direction of Zwinglianism. He participated in the Vestiarian Controversy, taking sides against John Hooper, and was asked to criticize the new prayer book and did so, once again raising doubts whether any of the sacraments carried or conveyed spiritual reality. Attempts have been made to connect Peter Martyr to the Forty-Two Articles of Religion. At least Bishop Jewel, who held the see of Salisbury in Elizabeth's reign, informed Martyr in a letter of 1562 that he and his party "do not differ from your doctrine by a nail's breadth."

On October 2, 1548, Archbishop Cranmer invited Martin Bucer to England: "Come therefore to us and become a laborer with us." Bucer was a veritable patriarch of the Reformation on the Continent. Once a member of the Dominican order and fluent in the thought of the greatest Dominican, Thomas Aquinas, Bucer was first captivated by Erasmus and then converted by Luther (1518). Beginning in 1523, he conducted the Reformation in the city of Strassburg. He was Melanchthon's friend and Calvin's tutor, the most ardent church unionist of the sixteenth century, and a liturgical scholar of exceptional learning; some of his liturgical ideas had already been used in the English prayer book of 1549. Everyone was delighted at his coming except members of the Swiss party, who thought him too conservative; they thought it would be better for England if Bucer "were called up by the Lord."

In December 1549 he was assigned to Cambridge as regius professor of divinity. On hearing that Bucer was feverish and impoverished, King Edward sent twenty pounds toward the purchase of a stove. Of Edward, Bucer wrote: "He is godly and learned to a miracle; he is well acquainted in Latin, and has a fair knowledge of Greek; he speaks Italian, and is learning French. He is now studying oral philosophy from Cicero and Aristotle; but no study delights him more than that of Holy Scriptures, of which he daily reads about ten chapters with the greatest attention." Bucer did not survive the fever, which he had incurred during his Channel crossing. After a long and increasingly severe illness, he died at Cambridge on March 1, 1551.

Before he died, Bucer completed a radical treatise addressed to Edward VI. Entitled *De regno Christi* (On the kingdom of Christ), it was one of the most auspicious pieces of Protestant idealism to be written in the age of the Reformation. Bucer was convinced that the whole of human life, both individual and social activity, must be ordered according to the will of God as expressed in the Bible. That is what the Reformation meant to Bucer. Reformation did not mean tinkering with the church. Reformation meant redoing the whole of the social order. England under the precocious Edward had the possibility of becoming a "Christian commonwealth," or "kingdom of Christ," in which all of common life, individual and social, could be brought into conformity with the will of God. Such a program required a joint administration of both church and state. While one uses persuasive force, the other coercive force, there is no difference in their final purpose — to establish the kingdom of Christ here on earth, in this island kingdom called England. "All classes of men in [this] realm [shall] thoughtfully, consistently, carefully, and tenaciously . . . work toward this goal, that Christ's kingdom may as fully as possible be accepted and hold sway over us."

When Bucer arrived in England, the prayer book had just come into use. Asked for his opinion, he offered a *Censura,* or criticism, in January 1551. In the course of fifty pages, he urged the English authorities to remodel their prayer book, eliminating those customs that still permitted a Roman Catholic interpretation; he particularly urged a revision of the part of the book in which the elements of bread and wine were consecrated. In the Vestiarian Controversy, Bucer generally supported Cranmer against Hooper, arguing that tradition was of immense value to the ceremonial and devotional expression of Christianity. Not everything had to be justified on the basis of Scripture (as Hooper insisted), as if the Bible were a spare-parts catalog, in which every conceivable item either was, or was not, in stock. Of all of the continental divines in England, Bucer most clearly expressed the view of the Lord's Supper held by Calvin — the spiritual real presence. That meant that while Christians do not receive the chemistry of Christ's body, his flesh and blood, they do receive, as a kind of nourishment for the soul, the life-giving virtue of Christ — the power of his personality and of his being.

John à Lasco (Jan Laski: 1499–1560), son of Polish nobility, entered the Catholic priesthood in 1521 and could have advanced rapidly to the episcopal office in Poland. Instead, he fell under the influence of Renaissance humanism and in 1524 withdrew to Basel and became Erasmus's pupil.

132. John à Lasco

After leaving the Church of Rome in 1538, he became an adherent of the Reformed branch of the Reformation and, in the course of the 1540s, assumed leadership of the Reformed churches of East Friesland. It is probably fair to say that he subscribed to a mild form of Calvinism (from which the bristles of predestination had been plucked), although his view of the Lord's Supper was Zwinglian. Around June 1550 he settled in England, having been invited repeatedly by Cranmer to come. In July of that year he was appointed superintendent of the Strangers' churches of London. Most of the "strangers" were craftsmen and artisans, weavers in particular. The intention of à Lasco and his associates (Martin Micronius and Jan Utenhove) was to establish a little Geneva in the midst of Bishop Ridley's London diocese. It was a clear case of nonconformity already in 1550. Bishop Hooper pushed through a license for à Lasco's activities (July 1550), as King Edward and Northumberland winked at such an indiscretion. À Lasco proceeded to draft a constitution for the church, *Forma ac ratio,* which included a presbyterian form of government and a mild version of Calvinist doctrine. The experiment collapsed at Edward's death (1553); the strangers beat a hasty retreat, and à Lasco himself returned to Poland in 1556 to establish a Reformed church in that country.

Anglican Standards

In the last three years of Edward's reign, the government published three standards of Anglican doctrine: the Ordinal (1550), a revised version of the prayer book (1552), and the Forty-Two Articles of Religion (1553). The Ordinal, containing formulas by which priests and bishops were set aside for religious duty, was the work of a committee of twelve; it was indebted also to a book that Bucer had written in 1549 on ordination (De ordinatione legitima). It was designed to replace the ordinal of the Church of Rome and was therefore involved in the sensitive issues of how priests were ordained and bishops consecrated. As early as 1554 the Church of Rome declared that Anglican orders were invalid because the new ordinal observed neither the intention of the Roman Catholic Church when it ordained priests nor the form of the sacrament of holy orders as correctly prescribed. The issuance of the new ordinal was a pretext for getting rid of more of the stubborn Henrician bishops. Bonner had already been removed from the see of London in 1549 and replaced with the more tractable Nicholas Ridley. Gardiner and Day were both prosecuted in 1550; the former was deprived of the see of Winchester in 1551. Tunstall was also prosecuted in 1550 and finally removed from the see of Durham in 1552. Heath of Worcester was deprived in 1550 for failure to subscribe to the Ordinal and was sent to jail the following year.

Meanwhile, the Vestiarian Controversy kept the nation stimulated. In April 1550 Hooper refused the see of Gloucester because he would not swear "by all the saints" or be consecrated in episcopal vestments. Edward himself took up his pen and struck out the offensive words "by all the saints," exclaiming, "What wickedness is here, Hooper!" But the unseemly squabble went on and on until Hooper was finally arrested and eventually committed to the Fleet prison. He finally agreed to wink at his scruples long enough to be consecrated bishop in the "rags of Antichrist" (i.e., the vestments); the deed was done on March 8, 1551.

At the same time, Bishop Ridley moved boldly to Protestantize the diocese of London. On May 5, 1550, he required his clergy either to remove or to obscure every altar in every parish church of the diocese and to replace them with communion tables. (People were to be taught the difference between sacrifice and communion!) On June 11, 1550, he set the example by installing a communion table in the nave of St. Paul's Cathedral, obscuring the altar by a huge drapery.

Besides Bucer's *Censura,* these turbulent years also saw Gardiner and Cranmer trading treatises on the correct understanding of the Eucharist. And Edward VI, who was exceedingly superstitious about superstition, received a thundering letter from Calvin (January, 1, 1551), saying, "God does not allow anyone to sport with his name, mingling frivolities among his holy and sacred ordinances." Under such provocation, it was agreed by both Crown and Canterbury that the original prayer book would have to suffer a more radical revision.

The revised prayer book was completed in the spring of 1552 and was impressed on England by a parliamentary act of April 14, 1552 — the Second Act of Uniformity. We notice immediately that a change of language has taken place. The word "Mass" is stricken. The word "altar" has been replaced by "table" or the quaint phrase "God's board." Ceremonies have been reduced, and the use of vestments severely curtailed. The new book was even more radically purged of elements that might have suggested that the Eucharist is still a sacrifice. The intercessions were relocated under a new label, "For the whole state of Christ's Church here in earth," to forestall any possibility that Anglicans still intercede for the dead. As Bucer had recommended, the prayer at the consecration of the Communion elements was remodeled, and a new formula was invented for the administration of Communion that had something of a Zwinglian ring: "Take and eat this in remembrance that Christ died for thee, and feed on him in thy heart with thanksgiving." (Similar words were already in use in à Lasco's congregations.) Ordinary household bread was deemed sufficient for sacramental use. When consecrated, it was administered directly into the communicant's hands — a practice discouraged in the first prayer book.

While the book was being printed, a storm arose over the medieval custom of kneeling to receive Communion. John Hooper seized every occasion to warn King Edward of that sort of idolatry, his court sermons being suffused with such exhortations. Soon, John Knox began to sound the same alarms, insisting that kneeling was a sign of transubstantiation. The council of regency, at Edward's prodding, had a special rubric appended to the Book of Common Prayer, a rubric printed not in red as rubrics (from *ruber,* "red") usually are but in ordinary black ink — the best the printer could do so late in the printing process. The famous Black Rubric stated that, while the Church of England continued to require kneeling at the reception of Communion, no one should imagine that rule to mean that the church subscribed to transubstantiation or countenanced the adoration of the elements. Indeed, the consecrated elements "remain still in their very natural substances."

In his *Censura,* Bucer had chided the English for the lack of a confession of faith. In 1551 Edward and his council requested Cranmer "to frame a book of articles of religion." The council approved the articles, which numbered forty-two in the final draft, on November 24, 1552; the king formally authorized them on June 12, 1553, three weeks before he died. Thus, the importance of the Forty-Two Articles cannot be fully measured in terms of Edward's reign; their importance lies rather in the fact that they became the basis of the Thirty-Nine Articles of Queen Elizabeth.

The Forty-Two Articles confirm a shift on the part of the Church of England toward the doctrines of the Continent, especially those of the Reformed churches. For example, in article 11, on justification, the Church of England defers to the teaching of Archbishop Cranmer in the *Book of Homilies:* justification is by faith, apart from any human merit; yet it does not occur without sincere repentance, the fear of God, and subsequent good works. The possibility of free will is denied in article 9, while article 12 describes works done prior to justification as having "the nature of sin" — in other words, they are spoiled by innate human selfishness. Article 17, on predestination, teaches a milder form of the Calvinist doctrine (God elects some to save some) and treats the doctrine of election as a source of comfort.

Some articles are antithetical to Roman Catholicism. Article 23 is a repudiation of purgatory and of the cultus devoted to the saints, as having been "vainly invented" without the warrant of Scripture. Article 20 contains an attack on the primacy of the pope; article 22 denies the infallibility of church councils; articles 12, 13, and 22 renounce unscriptural accretions to the body of Christian doctrine; article 30 forbids the interpretation of the Eucharist as a sacrifice. Article 36 advocates the principle of royal supremacy: "the King of England is the supreme head under Christ of the Church of England and Ireland, while the pope of Rome hath no jurisdiction in this realm." In article 31, the law of clerical celibacy is abolished.

The sacraments are discussed beginning with article 26; the Eucharist is interpreted in article 29. That article will not countenance either the Roman Catholic or the Lutheran perspective on the Mass, which leaves two possible interpretations: Calvin's or Zwingli's. The Forty-Two Articles declares for Calvin — a subscription that the Thirty-Nine Articles of Queen Elizabeth confirms.

608

In one instance, the Anglican articles are noticeably respectful of the past, namely, in the deference they pay to tradition, both as an honorable means of interpreting Scripture (article 21) and as the source of legitimate ceremonial and liturgical forms.

With what astonishing speed had this religious progression taken place! No more than five years had passed since Henry's death. Yet, the Henricians had been thoroughly turned out; the dioceses of England were administered by Protestants, who were, in turn, administered by Zurich and Geneva, or else by Cranmer and Northumberland. This exuberance, however, depended on Edward VI, but the king was mortally ill. Throughout his life, he had suffered from tuberculosis. In the spring of 1552, an attack of measles, compounded by smallpox, enfeebled him still more. By March 1553 he was too ill to open Parliament.

If Edward died, his sister Mary would succeed, according to the several acts of succession (1536, 1543) and according to Henry's will. As a staunch Catholic, Mary could be expected to put an end to the Reformation and to the people who had lately engineered it. In some desperation, Northumberland persuaded Edward to set aside his father's will, to cast both of his sisters (Mary and Elizabeth) out of the line of succession on the alleged grounds that they were illegitimate, and to bestow the crown on Lady Jane Grey, a gracious young girl in her teens, daughter of the duke of Suffolk, to whose heirs Henry had bequeathed the throne should all of his children die without posterity. On May 21, 1553, Lady Jane Grey was married to Guilford Dudley, Northumberland's son. Thus, if Lady Jane Grey reigned as queen, with Dudley as her consort, Northumberland would rule England.

Edward agreed to this wildly illegal plot under Northumberland's withering insistence that Mary would surely bring back the Roman religion to England. In June the king signed the legal instrument that changed the line of succession. While Cranmer was the first of a hundred or more to sign this instrument, it is by no means sure that he approved of the plot. In any case, the council failed to gain custody of Mary — a crucial step to the success of the plot. Forewarned, she escaped into Norfolk and thus into the protection of the Catholic Howards. On July 6 Edward expired, saying, "My Lord and God, save this realm from popery, and maintain it in true religion."

MARY I

ON July 11 Lady Jane Grey was proclaimed queen in London, but her reign was short lived. Mary, with an army of supporters, marched on London. It was not by any means zeal for the old religion that rallied England to Mary's support. Her base of operations was in the eastern counties, where Protestantism was strong. Rather, her real power lay in the prevalent disgust that the English felt over the self-seeking of Northumberland (who was even accused of having poisoned Edward) and in the profound English sentiment in favor of a hereditary monarchy. Northumberland, with an army of ten thousand, set out to confront Mary, only to find himself engulfed in ill will. He retreated to Cambridge with remnants of his army. There, in the square, he threw up his cap and led his troops in three cheers for Queen Mary, a generous deed that failed to avert his doom. With the hapless girl he had

133. Queen
Mary I
(Mary Tudor)

used to serve his ambition, he was thrown into the Tower of London. The plot had been undone. Mary was queen.

The reign of Mary Tudor lasted a mere five years, yet it created an impression on England never to be forgotten. For the first time in that nation's history, a queen regnant ruled the realm. Two things seized her mind and determined her policy: the Catholic religion and her Spanish descent.

In 1557 the Venetian ambassador to the English court made a routine analysis of Mary's character for his government. He began by observing her origins: she was the daughter of Catherine of Aragon, the Spanish-born queen, whom Henry VIII has labored so arduously and so publicly to jettison. He noted the unhappiness of her youth, that she had been made ignominious by being officially described as a bastard. He reported her unswerving dedication to the Catholic religion, her mother's faith, which she herself had practiced throughout Edward's reign, often at personal risk. He described her as "of short stature, well made, thin and delicate, and moderately pretty." Of her intellectual capacity, he wrote: "She understands five languages — English, Latin, French, Spanish, and Italian." Yet, "as to the qualities of her mind, it may be said of her that she is rash, disdainful, parsimonious rather than liberal." He observed that she suffered from some affliction that the doctors treated by copious bloodletting, leaving her perpetually frail. Finally, he commented on her conspicuous melancholia, which he attributed to four causes: the evil disposition of her subjects toward her, the financial straits of the Crown, the unhappiness of her marriage, and her hatred for her sister Elizabeth. "She is, moreover, a prey to the hatred she bears to my lady Elizabeth, and which has its source in the recollection of the wrongs she experienced on account of her mother [i.e., Anne Boleyn] and in the fact that all eyes and hearts are turned toward my lady Elizabeth as successor to the throne."

In August 1553, one month after she came to power, Mary issued a proclamation on the subject of religion, in which she set forth a policy based on tolerance and persuasion. She did not propose to hide the fact that she was a Roman Catholic, and she would be pleased if her subjects would embrace the old religion in quietness and with charity. For the time being, however, no compulsion would be tried with respect to religion. There were thus almost no reprisals at first. Northumberland was the only notable exception. Although, in the end, he recanted and embraced the Church of Rome, he suffered the ax for the enormity of his crime. But Lady Jane Grey and her husband, Guilford Dudley, and Archbishop Cranmer — all of whom had been implicated in the plot — were merely arrested, on charges of treason. Mary did redecorate her prisons. Out of the Tower, blinking in the sunlight, came the old Henricians: the duke of Norfolk and bishops Gardiner, Bonner, Tunstall, and the others. Gardiner was named lord chancellor and chief minister in the new government. Into prison went most of the Edwardian prelates: Latimer, Ridley, Hooper, Coverdale, and the rest. The foreign theologians — Peter Martyr, John à Lasco, and the others — were now noticeably nervous and hastily applied for permission to leave.

Illustrative of Mary's early policy was the case of the so-called Marian Exiles. In the first two years of the new reign, upward of eight hundred Edwardian Protestants were given passports and allowed to leave the country. The exiles lodged themselves in the centers of the Reformation on the Continent. There were eight colonies in all: Emden, Wessel, Zurich, Strassburg, Frankfurt, Basel, Geneva, and Aarau. In those cities, the Edwardian Protestants lived in the midst of the Reformed branch of the Reformation. When they returned to England in Elizabeth's reign, they brought back their Reformed propensities; it is believed that these people were the nucleus of Tudor Puritanism.

That maneuver brought two enemies into collaboration — on the one hand, Bishop Gardiner, whose policy it was to encourage dissidents to leave, and, on the other hand, William Cecil, mastermind of this well-planned migration of leading Edwardian Protestants. To both Cecil and Gardiner, the maneuver offered the promise of practical results. To Cecil, it meant the survival of English Protestantism; to Gardiner, the survival of Anglo-Catholicism. The exodus was well planned and financed, leadership having been undertaken by a ways and means committee called the Sustainers. By December 1553 the Sustainers had underwritten the first stage of the project; they sent abroad a company of Protestant divinity students to be educated in the continental universities. The second stage of the exodus occurred in 1554, when the main body of prominent Protestants was sent abroad.

By 1553, the Hapsburg-Valois Wars had again reached an impasse, and both powers were forced to look for allies. Mary Tudor was deeply attached to Spain, both by blood and by sentiment. Her mother was the daughter of the Catholic monarchs, Ferdinand and Isabella; Charles V was her cousin. The idea of an English alliance with Spain by means of marriage had been fixed in the English imagination by Henry VII and was renewed by Henry VIII. From the beginning of her reign, Mary was determined to marry a Spaniard. Charles V now proposed his own son and heir, Philip, archduke of Burgundy. From the outset of such negotiations, however, most of Mary's unwieldy council (it consisted of fifty members) was stoutly opposed to the Spanish match for a simple reason: it threatened to reduce England to a dependency of Spain. Gardiner was particularly opposed.

The irony of Mary's reign was that she was forced to use her position as "supreme head" of the Church of England — a title she abhorred — in order to undo her brother Edward's mischief. Her most ardent desires in terms of religion were (1) to restore the primacy of the pope over the Church of England and thereby the "Roman" sense of Catholicism, and (2) to return to the church all those properties confiscated since 1536 so that monasticism might once again flourish in England. Such matters, thanks to Cromwell, could be accomplished, if at all, only by parliamentary action.

The first Parliament of the new reign met in October 1553. After vigorous debate and some dissent, Parliament passed the Act of Repeal, which annulled most of the religious legislation of Edward VI and effectively restored the Church of England to its status of the year 1547, the last year of Henry VIII. That meant that the Book of Common Prayer was abolished, as well as the Ordinal and the Articles of Religion. In contrast, the heresy laws, repealed by Somerset, were not reenacted. No encouragement was given to the queen that she could ever expect to return church lands to their previous owners and thus restore English monasticism. Although she was allowed to omit "supreme head" from her titles of royalty, she was instructed to cover up the omission by using "etcetera" wherever "supreme head" used to be. What Parliament really did was to restore the Henrician, not the Roman, version of Catholicism. To make matters worse, Commons sent deputies to express its displeasure to the queen at the very thought of her marrying a Spanish prince. Extremely put off at that sentiment, Mary rushed headlong into the marriage, which was arranged by proxy even in the same month of October 1553.

When that decision was made known, it set off a series of demonstrations and conspiracies during the winter of 1553–54. The most serious of those conspiracies originated in Kent, where Protestantism was strong. It was led by Sir Thomas Wyatt, a man of Protestant sympathies, and it reached London before it was crushed — a rare instance in which the capital itself was beset by conspiracy. In the repression that followed, Lady Jane Grey and Guilford Dudley were both sent to the block. Princess Elizabeth, who barely escaped the same fate, was committed to the Tower of London. Some ninety participants in Wyatt's rebellion were executed.

In March 1554 Parliament met again, but without measurable improvement in its disposition toward Mary and her ministers. When Gardiner attempted to revive the heresy laws and reinstate the Six Articles, he was rebuffed in the House of Lords. Parliament did pass a set of injunctions that had the effect of sanctioning many Catholic customs, including the Latin language. Bishops were required to dismiss married clergy, or else see to their return to a celibate state, with suitable penance. "Zwinglians" were to be dealt with harshly. The same Parliament made it clear that, as Mary's husband, Philip could never be considered king regnant and could not retain the crown if Mary died. In July 1554 Philip arrived; the marriage was celebrated on July 25, and the English disapproved.

The most decisive event in Mary's reign was the Spanish match. It threw England into confusion and alarm, and it cost the queen a fair share of her popularity. No queen had ever ruled England. Mary wanted a consort to assist her and to give her a male heir to perpetuate her line and forestall the succession of Elizabeth. Her subjects agreed, but they assumed that she would marry an Englishman (such as Edward Courtenay, earl of Devonshire). This queen, however, who had never tried to hide her Spanish preference, selected Philip of Spain, son of the Holy Roman Emperor. With such a mate, Mary could count on her own security in England, to say nothing of the restoration of Catholicism in her realm. Mary's matrimonial designs, however, met with the hostility of her subjects. It was axiomatic among the English that foreign entanglements were dangerous, but this entanglement was simply inconceivable; it promised Spanish domination.

In the spring of 1554 Parliament gave grudging consent to the marriage, but when Gardiner proposed, on Mary's behalf, that Elizabeth should be disinherited and that the throne of England should be committed to the line of Philip and Mary, Parliament refused. Thus, the Spanish match increased the probability of an Elizabethan succession and, to that extent, contributed to the endurance of the Anglican church.

Having got her way in the Spanish match, Mary proceeded to do everything she could to end the schism that had torn the Church of England from the papacy at Rome. At first, she had to depend on two resources: her own powers as "supreme head" and the repeal by Parliament of the Edwardian religious legislation. In 1554, acting on the parliamentary injunctions of the same year, the government ejected from their livings nearly a quarter of the English clergy on the grounds that they had broken their vows of celibacy and taken wives. Such activity suddenly deprived nearly two thousand parishes of priestly services and created an underground network of shifty priests who moved from parish to parish, taking care to

134. Philip II,
portrait by Titian

cover their tracks. Most of the Edwardian "novelties" had, by this time, been cast aside, as England returned to the religion of the Latin Mass.

Still, some means remained to be found to restore the realm to papal obedience. That means was Reginald Pole, whom Mary had designated to be Cranmer's successor in the see of Canterbury. But Charles V had detained Pole for a time, being frankly afraid of his blazing sincerity and determination. Pole was not unlike Mary in temperament. He did not care for

615

diplomacy. What mattered was principle; expediency be damned. Although he, like Mary, was personally kind and considerate, he was just as resolute as she to disinfect England of the Protestant disease and restore the realm to Roman obedience.

Finally, in November 1554, Cardinal Pole landed at Dover and was admitted to England as the papal legate, bringing with him the pope's absolution of England and instruments of England's reconciliation to Rome. Upon the cardinal's arrival, both houses of Parliament petitioned the queen for a reunion with Rome. The queen, with her consort, then addressed a formal intercession to the papal legate, asking him to absolve the nation of heresy and schism. On November 30, 1554, the absolution was solemnly given.

Two acts of Parliament served the reconciliation. The Revival of the Heresy Acts put into force again most of the ancient statues against heresy; the Second Act of Repeal retracted in detail all of the antipapal legislation that Parliament had passed since 1529. Yet, this legislation offered no possibility that the church could ever recover its monastic property, and the Second Act of Repeal subtly but carefully hedged against any diminution of royal prerogative. The Elizabethan bishop John Jewel remarked that Mary had given England a "Parliament pope."

The question was, How far had England really come from the anti-clerical, antipapal nationalism of Henry VIII? Mary and her cardinal must have asked the same question, for at the turn of the year, 1555, the persecution of dissidents began. The responsibility for the Marian persecution cannot be laid to the Spaniards, for both Philip and Charles V urged upon Mary a policy of leniency. Nor was Gardiner the instigator; he said publicly that the heresy laws should be allowed to stand *in terrorem,* that is, without being administered. When the burnings began, none occurred in that bishop's see (Winchester). "Bloody Bonner" burned half of the martyrs because his London diocese contained them. Even John Foxe, the Puritan martyrologist who recorded these events, admits that Bonner, so far from being an instigator of repression, was merely the one on whom the burden fell. The highly respected historian of the English Reformation, A.G. Dickens, argues that Mary herself was responsible for the persecutions. She was doubtless encouraged by her Spanish confessors and her English archbishop, who was, in the words of his successor (Matthew Parker), *carnifex et flagellum ecclesiae anglicanae* (tormentor and scourge of the Anglican church).

The trials began in January 1555, and before Mary's reign was over, 275 (according to John Foxe) or 282 (according to William Cecil) men and women were burned for heresy. Well over half of those people came from the lower classes of society. (That fact is scarcely surprising when we recall that most prominent members of the Protestant constituency had gone abroad in the Marian Exile.) It was this consignment of simple, humble people to the flames — and not so many, at that — that established the persecutions of "Bloody Mary" deep in the national consciousness, created a classic of John Foxe's *Book of Martyrs,* and stirred up a virulent anti-Catholicism that persisted in and after the reign of Elizabeth.

That is not to say that there were no great men who perished. The first prominent member of the Protestant establishment to die was John Rogers, a cleric at St. Paul's in London, well known as the translator of Matthew's Bible. He was burned in the notorious "fires of Smithfield" on February 4, 1555, in the presence of his wife and ten children. The Swiss partisan John Hooper died in the flames at Gloucester the same month. Two other Edwardian bishops, Ridley and Latimer, were tried and excommunicated at Oxford on October 1, 1555, and, fifteen days later, were fed to the flames in the courtyard of Balliol College. Said Latimer to Ridley as the pyre was ignited: "Be of good comfort, Master Ridley, and play the man; we shall this day light such a candle by God's grace in England, as I trust never shall be put out."

Cranmer watched the execution of his old colleagues from the Bocardo Prison in Oxford but proved much less resolute than they. Torn between his religious convictions and his obedience to royal supremacy, he made a series of recantations, finally confessing the pope's headship over the Christian church, as well as the real presence of Christ in the Mass, and accusing himself of the divorce of Henry and Catherine. On March 21, 1556, however, when it came his turn to die, he retracted his recantations. When the faggots were lighted, Cranmer held his right arm into the flames until the hand that had signed the recantations was burned to the stump.

Any satisfactions Queen Mary may have known were short lived. In September 1555 Philip, who had never reciprocated her love, left England to assume duties in Spain. His departure, coupled with the queen's childless state, caused Mary both embarrassment and grave disconsolation. She now despaired of the child that might have perpetuated her line. In November, Gardiner died. So far, no real structures had been built to support and extend the new Catholicism. No provision had been made for the training of priests. Monasticism, which had traditionally provided the church with scholars, enjoyed a very limited revival. Only six houses had been restored; in those six, scarcely a hundred religious lived. Mary and her ministers did not even bother to fill the vacant dioceses, of which there were ten by the end of 1558.

By 1556 the Spanish match had begun to cause mischief between England and the papacy. Paul IV, who had attained the papacy the previous year, was a quarrelsome man, given to an assortment of prejudices. The pope, who harbored animosity toward Spain, first fell out with Philip; the dispute grew so intense that the pope found it necessary to excommunicate Mary's husband. Then he fell out with Cardinal Pole, revoked Pole's legatine commission, and summoned Mary's archbishop to Rome to answer for heresy. By 1558 the English were profoundly dispirited by these squabbles.

Meanwhile, as the Hapsburg-Valois Wars were resumed in 1557, England found herself being drawn into war with France at Philip's prodding (June 1557), an involvement that cost England the city of Calais (1558), the last of her medieval possessions on the Continent. That expensive and useless war, coupled with the loss of Calais, crushed the spirit of Queen Mary and extinguished whatever spark of loyalty toward her that still burned in her people. In this abject poverty of success and affection, Mary mistaking even her final illness as a symptom of pregnancy, died on November 17, 1558. Pole's death followed hers within twelve hours. Neither the Catholic reaction nor the Spanish connection was destined to survive Mary, for her sister Elizabeth found it prudent to shape a policy out of Mary's mistakes.

24. *The Reign of Elizabeth I*

ON NOVEMBER 17, 1558, ELIZABETH, THE THIRD CHILD OF HENRY VIII, ascended the throne of England; she was twenty-five (see plate 82). Nearly everyone who treats Elizabeth starts with her personality. She was a woman of high spirit — imperious and willful, with steely courage and a capacity to understand human affairs as great as her father Henry's. She did not hesitate to display herself to her subjects, who found her both proud and affable and who thus responded to her with a fitting mixture of fear and love. Those who beheld her did not fail to comment upon the ostentation of her jewels and overdone apparel — which dazzled her subjects and in her later years disguised the signs of age. The glory of her physical self, as the Virgin Queen, corresponded in Reformation England to the resplendent Virgin Mary in the now discredited Catholic cultus. Her intellectual gifts, which were substantial, she used to full advantage. She knew and used Latin, French, and Italian, all of which she employed regularly in dispatches to her ambassadors. When it came to defending the rights of the Crown, she was every inch a Tudor, true child of her father Henry.

It was her piety, however, that caused the first speculation: what were her religious leanings? If one takes the word "piety" in its base meaning, as loyalty or affection to something, then one could say that Elizabeth's piety was English. The unity and safety of her realm were of foremost importance. A fable has come down to us from the Elizabethan era that illustrates the nature of the queen's religious policy. As mentioned in chapter 23, the theologian Peter Martyr had brought his wife to Oxford, an over-plump lady who scandalized that celibate community. There she died on

February 16, 1553. According to the fable, room was made for her mortal remains in the Church of St. Mary's by removing the bones of St. Frideswide, which had lain there in holy repose since the year 1180. Four years later, during the reign of Queen Mary, the body of Mrs. Martyr was unceremoniously dug up by the papists and flung on the dungheap in the stables of the dean of Christ Church College. The bones of St. Frideswide were returned to their appointed place. At Elizabeth's accession, the question arose: Whose bones belonged at St. Mary's? The issue having become a cause célèbre, the queen herself was called upon to make a decision. Said Elizabeth: "Mix 'em." Which being done on January 11, 1561, the united bones of a virgin saint and a Protestant's wife were solemnly reinterred in a common receptacle in St. Mary's of Oxford. The story would seem to imply that the so-called Elizabethan Settlement of religion was a middle way between the religion of Rome and that of Geneva. We shall have to see to what extent that was the case.

Three days after her accession, Elizabeth appointed Sir William Cecil (in 1571 to become Lord Burghley), a courtier of Henry VIII and civil servant of Edward VI, to be her first secretary; it was an association, one might even say, a collaboration, that endured for forty years, until Burghley's death in 1598. Although a Protestant, and one of the organizers of the Marian Exile, Cecil was not really a religious man; his virtues were rather to be rational, cautious, correct, and cool — to be administratively stunning (in spite of Elizabeth's dilatoriness) and conservative of the queen's finite resources.

As the daughter of Anne Boleyn, for the love of whom Henry had broken England's tie to Rome, Elizabeth was expected to renounce her sister's Catholic religion and sever once again the connection between England and the papacy. Not that the English cared very much; Mary had managed to destroy what was left of their sentimental attachment to the Church of Rome. The papacy, in return, was decidedly cool to Elizabeth, refusing to accept the legitimacy of this child of the adultress Anne Boleyn. Elizabeth and Cecil found little solace in foreign affairs. In Scotland, Mary of Guise ruled as regent for her daughter, Mary Stuart, Mary Queen of Scots, who was also dauphiness of France and who represented in her very person the union of two of England's most formidable and enduring opponents. Confronted by the combined enmity of France and Scotland, Elizabeth and Cecil saw some virtue in prolonging the Spanish alliance. Such an alliance, however, was unseemly unless England were prepared to remain Catholic. Would the English public put up with such a thing? The tumultuous welcome that Elizabeth received at her accession seemed to invite an end to the Roman connection. From the Continent, an even greater threat loomed in the possible accommodation of France and Spain, enabling both of those Catholic powers to confront apostate England and her illegitimate queen. Elizabeth's initial strategy was therefore as follows: (1) placate the Spanish as much as possible, (2) disengage England from the Church of Rome as unobtrusively as possible, and (3) avoid at all costs some dramatic blowup in religion, which would surely preclude the success of policies (1) and (2).

Elizabeth's hope for an unobtrusive settlement of religion was soon dashed by the return of the Marian Exiles — the elite members of the Protestant establishment who had gone abroad during the reign of Bloody Mary. In 1558, as intelligence of Mary's death reached the Continent, the exiles began to drift back to England. With them, they brought very definite opinions about religion — opinions forged in their minds in the Protestant, and more precisely, Calvinist, centers of Europe. The Marian Exiles, being people of considerable standing in English society, were able to obtain

135. William Cecil, portrait bust by School of the Clouets

decisive power in the House of Commons. That power was controlled and manipulated chiefly by Richard Cox, head of the so-called Prayer Book Protestants. Before the Marian Exile, Cox had been dean of Christ Church College, Oxford, as well as chancellor of the university. He had helped to write the Book of Common Prayer and had been tutor to Edward VI. In Frankfort, where he spent most of the exile, he led a group of English people who staunchly upheld the use of the English Prayer Book of 1552. Hence, they were known as the Prayer Book Protestants. Fortunately or unfortunately for Elizabeth, the Marian Exiles were not all of one mind and soon fell to squabbling among themselves.

A second faction of the exiles was led by John Knox, the Scottish Reformer, lately chaplain to Edward VI. He and his followers, who had passed the exile in Calvin's city of Geneva, preferred Calvin's simplified mode of Christian worship over that of the English prayer book. Knox said that the Book of Common Prayer contained "things superstitious, impure, unclean, and imperfect."

So, there were Coxians and Knoxians. The Coxians got off to a good start. They returned to England and seized positions of influence. The Knoxians got off to an exceptionally bad start. Knox had written a diatribe entitled *First Blast of the Trumpet against the Monstrous Regiment* [rule] *of Women* (Geneva, 1558). It was aimed at Mary Tudor. Mary, however, had died at the inopportune time of the book's utterance, and Elizabeth, who succeeded Mary, was sure that the book had been meant for her. So, Knox was persona non grata in England. He went directly from the exile to Scotland, where he contributed to the development of Protestantism in that country. His point of view, though, was indeed represented in England.

Both Coxians and Knoxians believed that the Christian religion, as observed in England, should be "purified" of most, if not all, of the popish characteristics that remained in it from medieval times. In that respect, they deserved the name "Puritans," as they were called. The Knoxians were the more radical of the two parties. Given their way, they would have radically remodeled the Church of England, using Calvinist structures and forms of worship. Knox and his colleague Christopher Goodman also conceived of government as a commonwealth, in which both the sovereign and the people would be limited by social contract or covenant mutually arrived at.

The presence of the Marian Exiles in England seemed to deprive Elizabeth of the option of refashioning the Church of England according to the character it had under her father, Henry VIII — very catholic, yet not papal. Why, then, did Elizabeth allow herself to fall under obligation to the Coxians and Knoxians? Because she needed bishops. Mary, as we have noted, had not bothered to fill the vacant sees of England. There were ten such vacancies at the end of 1558 — ten episcopal appointments, including the archiepiscopal see of Canterbury, that fell to Elizabeth. Moreover, of all the English bishops whom Elizabeth inherited from Mary, only one managed to survive the religious tests imposed by Parliament in 1559. Thus, the English hierarchy literally had to be rebuilt. Elizabeth faced the prospect of having to create twenty-five new bishops. Where could she find the talent except among the Marian Exiles? The names of the new bishops — Parkhurst, Pilkington, Sandys, Grindal, Jewel, Scory, Cox, Horne, and Aylmer — were the names of Marian Exiles.

A much more ominous portent for Elizabeth was the appearance of Puritanism in Parliament. Beginning in Elizabeth's very first Parliament, a strong Puritan contingent appeared in the House of Commons; it was led by the Marian Exiles, particularly Francis Knollys and Anthony Cooke. In league with the Puritan theologians outside of Parliament, the Puritan faction saw fit to challenge Elizabeth's prerogative of setting religious policy by herself. It was scarcely a new struggle. After all, both the church reforms of Henry VIII and the reformation of Edward VI had been carried out with parliamentary sanction and enforced by parliamentary statute. Yet, Elizabeth took the position that she alone legitimately defined religious policy; Parliament could only establish penalties for the disregard of such policy. The struggle between queen and Parliament was intensified by the fact that, while the Puritans were hell-bent to move forward vigorously with reforms, Elizabeth was persuaded that extreme caution was the best policy. Moreover, the contest soon became associated with the issue of free speech. If the Puritans were to have a hearing, they required the freedom to express their views in the House. But when Puritan members of the Commons attacked Elizabeth's religious policies or challenged her sole prerogative in matters of religion, she was something less than tolerant of their untrammeled right to speak their mind. Freedom of speech became one of the touchy issues of Elizabeth's reign.

Within forty-eight hours of Mary's death, Elizabeth issued a proclamation forbidding "the breach, alteration, or change" in the Catholic religion of her realm, thus putting a stop to religious tumult, at least for the time being. She also borrowed Mary's use of "etcetera" to obscure her own view of religion. That is, she was queen of England, France, and Ireland, defender of the faith, etcetera. Whether she was Protestant, Catholic, or supreme head of the Church of England was left to everyone's imagination. At stake, of course, was not only the tranquility of England but very likely Elizabeth's retention of her own throne. A ceaseless threat to Elizabeth was Mary Stuart of the reigning house of Scotland; she had excellent credentials to be queen of England, should Elizabeth default, and her unabashed Catholicism delighted the popes of Rome as well as the Catholic powers of Europe.

Subtly, however, Elizabeth began to tip her hand. In 1558, when old Bishop Oglethorpe of Carlisle, as he celebrated Christmas Mass in her chapel, persisted in elevating the host, as Catholics had done in the Middle Ages, Elizabeth left. She received a copy of the Bible in English with such relish that it seemed almost evangelical. And when, at her coronation on January 15, 1559, Bishop Oglethorpe again had the impudence to heave up the host, the queen stomped out.

THE ELIZABETHAN SETTLEMENT

THE FIRST Parliament of the new reign met on January 25, 1559. The monks of Westminster who greeted Elizabeth with tapers in the broad daylight met with a stern rebuff: "Away with those torches; we can see well enough." She informed the two houses of Parliament that their chief responsibility was to establish "a uniform order of religion" in England. An Act of Supremacy was the first order of business for the new Parliament — an act that would repudiate the jurisdiction of the papacy in England, restore royal supremacy over the Church of England, and ascribe to the sovereign some such title as "supreme head" of the church, putting an end to the "etcetera" and its ambiguity. It took four drafts of such a bill to satisfy all parties and allay the tensions that then existed in England. The first draft was introduced in Commons on February 9. An expression of Elizabeth's own wishes, it would have taken England back to the religious situation of 1547 — the last year of Henry VIII. When the Protestants denounced its timidity, the bill was remanded to them for revisions. A fresh draft was prepared by Anthony Cooke and Francis Knollys, in collaboration with the Coxian theologians — Cox himself, Jewel, Sandys, and Grindal. Attached to this Protestant draft, which the Coxians introduced on February 21, was some sort of prayer book, no doubt the 1552 version of the Book of Common Prayer.

The House of Lords, in which the old Catholic bishops continued to sit, gave vigorous opposition to this radical bill, which Elizabeth also distrusted. Said Archbishop Heath of York: "By leaping out of Peter's ship [i.e., the Roman Catholic Church], we hazard ourselves to be overwhelmed and drowned in the waters of schisms, sects, and divisions." The Lords had their way; the bill was again referred to committee — this time, however, a committee of more conservative propensities. From that committee came a third draft of March 22. The House of Commons, rather than vote this bill down, decided to face the issues, accept the necessary compromises entailed in the bill, and pass the Supremacy Act. Still, it was necessary to have the queen's assent, which was not forthcoming by the time Parliament was prorogued for Easter. On April 10, 1559, after Elizabeth had had time to listen for public reaction, a final text of the Supremacy Act was proposed to Parliament and was passed; it is distinguished from the preceding only by the queen's ecclesiastical title, which is "supreme governor" rather than "supreme head" of the Church of England. The reason for the alteration was patently sexist: it was deemed inappropriate to speak of a female "head" of anything.

The Act of Supremacy of 1559 struck down the Marian statutes that had reinstated the jurisdiction of the pope of England: papal jurisdiction was once more abolished. The statutes of Henry VIII in the critical years of 1532–34, by which the principles of royal supremacy were worked out and first expressed, were put into effect again; Elizabeth thus became "supreme governor" of the church.

In April 1559, the month that saw the passage of the Supremacy Act, Parliament also approved (narrowly, in the case of the House of Lords) the Act of Uniformity, which reinstated the 1552 Book of Common Prayer for "uniform" usage throughout England. That Act of Uniformity was the outcome of several earnest conversations among Elizabeth, Cecil, and the Protestants. Elizabeth hoped to have the first (1549) Book of Common Prayer adopted, for it was the more Catholic of the two versions. The Protestants insisted stoutly upon the second (1552) version, which scarcely went far enough in the evangelical direction to suit their pleasure. Elizabeth came off worse in the scuffle, although three modifications were made in the 1552 prayer book as concessions to her. First, the so-called Black Rubric was deleted as unnecessarily offensive to Catholics. Second, vestments and church ornaments were to conform to those that were customary in "the second year" of Edward VI (1548) — approximately as they were in the last quarter of Henry VIII's reign. Third, the "Words of Administration" for Holy Communion in the 1549 book were prefixed to those of the 1552 book, shifting the emphasis back again upon the real presence of Christ in the sacrament. Offensive references to the pope were also removed. The prayer book was enjoined throughout the realm, beginning June 24, 1559 (the Nativity of St. John the Baptist); strict penalties were provided for clergy who refused to use it and fines for laity who avoided church.

Thus, in the propitious month of April 1559, two acts of Parliament were passed that created a new Anglicanism. On May 8, 1559, Elizabeth gave her consent and dissolved Parliament. Half of the Elizabethan Settlement of religion had been accomplished.

John Jewel complained "that it is no easy matter to drag the chariots without horses, especially uphill." He referred to the lack of bishops in the Church of England. Through the summer of 1559 the bishops who had survived the vicissitudes of English religion refused one by one to take the oath of royal supremacy required by the Act of Supremacy and were therefore deprived of office. By January 1560 only Kitchin of Llandaff survived. Twenty-five English sees were vacant, either through deprivation or through Mary Tudor's carelessness. It fell to Elizabeth to reconstitute the English hierarchy.

She began with the highest ecclesiastical office in the realm, that of archbishop of Canterbury, the primate of England. The man she had in mind for that post was Matthew Parker, her own tutor, who was known to be modest and judicious, a believer in the English monarchy, and a subscriber to the moderate religious opinions of Thomas Cranmer. He was foremost a scholar, a Cambridge don. In fact, he had attained such prominence in that university that he became its vice-chancellor. He was a historian rather than a theologian. His sense of history enabled him to feel the weight of tradition and to appreciate the increment that the Church of England could have from its Catholic past.

On September 9, 1559, letters patent were issued appointing a royal commission of bishops to confirm the election of Parker and to proceed with his consecration. Required to consecrate him legally were an archbishop and three other bishops, each of whom was in possession of a see. As Secretary Cecil observed, however, "There is no Archbishop or four bishops now to be had." Even Kitchin refused to participate. Nevertheless, Parker was consecrated archbishop in the chapel of Lambeth Palace on Sunday, December 17, 1559, at the hands of four bishops — Barlow, Scory, Coverdale, and Hodgkins — three of whom were Edwardian bishops who had resigned or been deprived when Mary Tudor came to power.

Gradually the other vacant dioceses were filled, some with bishops created in the era of Edward VI but subsequently deprived of their office by Mary, and others by prelates whose preparation included the Marian Exile. Cox himself became bishop of Ely; Edmund Grindal presided over the diocese of London; James Pilkington was assigned to Durham; John Jewel received the see of Salisbury; Edwin Sandys was sent to Worcester, and so forth. The 8,000 clergy of the parishes of England managed these transitions without much apparent difficulty; only some 250 were deprived. Some of the new bishops, however, were exceedingly uncomfortable with the trappings of Roman Catholicism that had survived in the Church of England. Wrote Bishop Pilkington in 1573: "We endure, I must confess, many things against our inclinations." In the southern and eastern countries of England, where Protestant sentiment was very strong, some of the prescribed vestments were discontinued. In Kent there was suspicion that Calvin's Genevan form of worship was being surreptitiously used instead of the Book of Common Prayer. Secretary Cecil complained of the "nakedness of religion" that prevailed in Bishop Parkhurst's diocese of Norwich.

In 1562–63, three important writings appeared in defense of the new Anglican establishment. The first was Bishop John Jewel's *Apology of the English Church* (1562), in which he justified the Church of England on the grounds that it had broken away from a corrupted institution (i.e., the Roman Catholic Church) and had returned to Christianity of the golden age (i.e., the first three centuries). "We have called home again to the original and first foundation that religion which has been fouly foreslowed and utterly corrupted." Jewel also made a point of discrediting the Council of Trent, then in session, declaring it unrepresentative of Eastern Catholics, Anglicans, and Protestants, and therefore illegitimate. He defended the competence of the civil magistrate to oversee religion in his or her realm, ascribing such competence to God's wishes as explained in the Bible.

In the following year (1563) there appeared one of the supreme expressions of Anglican and, more precisely, Puritan lore — John Foxe's *Book of Martyrs* — which, alongside the Bible and the Prayer Book, formed the indispensable library of every pious English home. Here is the story of the English Reformation told from the standpoint of its martyrs — from Tyndale to Cranmer. Here is the storehouse of Puritan polemics against the Church of Rome, the testimony to the exceeding power of martyrdom in the success of a religious movement. (See the excursus to this chapter.)

Also in 1563 the Edwardian articles of religion, forty-two in number, were revised and republished as the Thirty-Nine Articles of Religion. Approved by the church in 1563 and imposed by law in the Subscription Act of 1571, the Thirty-Nine Articles mark the completion of the Elizabethan Settlement.

These articles, which we have already discussed in their Edwardian form, represent an essentially Calvinist system of religious thought, set over against Roman Catholicism, on the one side, and Anabaptism, on the other. They express a Protestant side of the Church of England, as distinguished from the more Catholic features of that church — its respect for tradition, its inheritance from the Middle Ages, its interest in liturgical worship and the sacramental side of Christianity, and, above all, its hierarchical character epitomized by its bishops. Thus, Elizabeth's "settlement" brought forth an established church of both Protestant and Catholic manifestations.

The pluralism of American society in the twentieth century would not have been appreciated — or understood — in Elizabethan society. It was taken for granted that all Elizabethans were solemnly united to their queen in two aspects — a secular aspect called the state or commonwealth, and a spiritual aspect called the church, whose doctrine, organization, and rituals were established by law. Religious nonconformity, however well intended, was no more tolerable than treason against the state. The English Puritans prospered because they had no idea of changing the established church from a position outside of it. Puritans did not separate. They took the Church of England as it was, stayed within its ranks, and proposed to purify it. The classic Puritan point of view was simply that the Elizabethan settlement (1559–63) had not gone far enough: "popish fooleries" still surviving in the Church of England remained to be gotten rid of.

English Catholics, on the other hand, did run the risk of being seen as nonconformists. At the beginning of Elizabeth's reign, they existed in such preponderant numbers as to make a difference. By 1570, however, bereft of priests and generally abandoned by their friends abroad, the English Catholics had dwindled to 150,000 members.

Meanwhile, the English foreign policy being conducted by Elizabeth and Cecil depended upon nothing so conventional as military power or economic strength; rather, it consisted mainly of stirring up mischief for France and Spain. The treaty of Cateau-Cambrésis (April 1–3, 1559), while it confirmed the legitimacy of Elizabeth in the eyes of the continental powers, patched over the animosity between France and Spain on which Elizabeth's foreign policy had so sorely depended. The queen could not count on England's military establishment, which her sister Mary had allowed to run down into dilapidation. Nor was the financial condition of England of much account — thanks again to Mary. Elizabeth and Cecil therefore proceeded by stirring up trouble among the Huguenots in France and among the revolutionary parties in the Spanish Netherlands. Both were essentially religious conflicts upon which England played. In 1559 a third religious quarrel presented Elizabeth with yet another opportunity in foreign policy — the Reformation in Scotland.

REVOLUTION IN SCOTLAND

AT THE death of Henry II (1559), Francis II, at fifteen, became king of France. His wife, two years his senior, was Mary Queen of Scots. Her relatives, the Guise family, eminent Catholics, ruled both France and its satellite, Scotland. Mary of Guise, widow of James V of Scotland, presided over Scottish affairs as regent for her daughter, Mary Queen of Scots. Yet the Scots, who were fiercely nationalistic, waited for some good opportunity to turn the Guises out. It came in a rather unexpected form — the appearance of Protestantism in Scotland.

Lutheran ideas had begun to penetrate Catholic Scotland in the early 1520s through the importation of contraband religious books, which the Scottish Parliament banned in 1525. Three years later, the Lutheran preacher Patrick Hamilton was burned at the stake, setting off a spate of riotous religious activity. In 1546, in the university town of St. Andrews, the fiery Reformed evangelist George Wishart was dispatched to the flames by a worldly prelate and papal legate, David Cardinal Beaton. The Protestants took their vengeance on the cardinal by executing him in his own palace in St. Andrews three months later. Wishart's bodyguard was a tough little peasant priest named John Knox, who attended Wishart's sermons carrying an oversized sword. Upon Wishart's demise, Knox joined the Protestant defenders of the Castle of St. Andrews against the French troops in the service of Mary of Guise. In August 1547 the castle fell to the French, and Knox was indentured as a galley slave in the French navy. For a year and half, he was chained to a rowing station on a French vessel, his hatred of France and Catholicism increasing with every stroke. In April 1549 Knox finally reached England, where he ministered to, and preached at, the Protestant boy-king, Edward IV. At Edward's death (1553), Knox, foreseeing the Marian reaction, fled to Frankfurt and eventually to Calvin's Geneva, which he pronounced "the nearest perfyt school of Chryst that ever was in the erth since the dayis of the Apostillis."

In December 1559, in the second year of Elizabeth's reign, a group of

136. John Knox,
facsimile after a
copper engraving by
Hendrik Hondius
the Younger

Scottish nobles, calling themselves "the lords of the congregation," swore a covenant to cast out the Guise regime and introduce the Calvinist religion to Scotland. Knox was summoned home from Geneva. He had already called Mary of Guise an unruly cow and had offended Elizabeth by his *First Blast.* Elizabeth had the perspicacity to pipe Knox straight through England (where he was not wanted) to Scotland (where he was), knowing that the Scottish Reformation was likely to bloom under his not so subtle care.

The expected revolution, however, achieved little more than a stalemate, despite the preachments of Knox and the presence of an English army, sent by Elizabeth. The decisive event in the revolution was the death of Mary of Guise, which signaled a pervasive decline of French Catholic influence in Scotland. By the Treaty of Edinburgh (July 1560), the French were expelled from Scotland, and the government was committed to the lords of the congregation, led by Maitland of Lethington, and to the Calvinist religionists, led by Knox. On August 24, 1560, Parliament outlawed Catholicism in Scotland. The animosity that had festered for centuries between England and Scotland was suddenly dissipated by the simple circumstance that the same religion, albeit in somewhat different forms, existed north and south of the border.

Knox preached the Reformation with such vigor that one bystander, James Melville, reported that "he was like to ding [pound] the pulpit in blades [pieces] and fly [jump] out of it." Three texts of the Scottish Reformation illustrate the Calvinist and Presbyterian character that Knox gave to the Reformed Church of Scotland: (1) *First Book of Confession* (1560), which affirms the Calvinist religion entirely; (2) *Book of Common Order* (1564), Calvin's Genevan liturgy revised for Scottish use; and (3) *First Book of Discipline (1560 or earlier),* in which the governmental structure of this Presbyterian church is partially described.

When Francis II of France died in December 1560, his mother, Catherine de' Medici, widow of Henry II, became regent of France during the minority of Charles IX. Mary Stuart, a queen dowager of France at the age of eighteen, and the entire Guise faction were maneuvered aside by Catherine. Although she loved France and was halfhearted about Scotland, Mary Stuart had little choice except to return to the Scots and to her Scottish realm. Mary was beautiful and passionate, intelligent but foolish, Catholic but wanton. Her claim to the English throne, should Elizabeth die childless, be deposed, or otherwise default, was impressive; it lay through Margaret Tudor, daughter of Henry VII, sister of Henry VIII, who had married James IV of Scotland.

Mary reached Leith in Scotland on August 19, 1561. The Sunday next, she ordered Mass to be celebrated in Holyrood Castle in Edinburgh — an event that provoked Knox to utter one of his fiercest sermons in St. Giles Cathedral. In France, the first wars of religion were just beginning between the French Catholic establishment and the Huguenots. England was desperately afraid that Mary would undo the Reformation in Scotland and would subdue the Scots once again to France and the papacy. In 1562 Elizabeth took the occasion to intervene in the French wars of religion on the side of the Huguenots. The English occupied Le Havre, a maneuver that succeeded only in arousing the patriotism of both French parties. The English were ousted by the combined efforts of French Catholics and Huguenots, ending one of the more conspicuous diplomatic blunders of Elizabeth's reign.

MARRIAGE AND SUCCESSION

MEANWHILE, Mary Stuart was under heavy persuasion to remarry. Elizabeth proposed that she take the Englishman Robert Dudley, designated earl of Leicester just for the occasion, but the Scots, suspecting that Dudley was Elizabeth's own used vehicle, rejected the suggestion with aplomb. Mary decided upon Henry Lord Darnley, son of the Earl of Lennox. It was a risky business. Darnley had been born in England. He actually shared with Mary Stuart a common grandmother (by a second marriage) in Margaret Tudor. The fact that Darnley could inherit in England (by virtue of his English birth) and had ancestral ties to Henry VII simply enhanced Mary's claim to the English throne and frightened and enraged Elizabeth. Indeed, the marriage of Mary Stuart and Lord Darnley eventually put the Stuarts on the English throne: the child of that union, James, born in 1566, became James I of the combined realms. The immediate outcome of the Scottish nuptial was to intensify pressure on Elizabeth herself to marry, lest England fall into the hands of foreigners and Catholics.

England expected that Elizabeth would marry. Elizabeth expected that she would not. The difference between the two expectations was that Elizabeth did not propose to tell. Why should she forgo one of her most strategic advantages in the game of international politics? Besides, she much enjoyed her romantic sports, even if they kept her realm well supplied with gossip and consternation. From the standpoint of her subjects, the queen's marriage was a serious business. If she did not marry and have issue, the succession would become a matter of dispute, even civil war, among the Stuarts, the Suffolks, and the Hastings; there was even the abominable possibility of a Catholic monarchy.

Among the queen's early suitors was Philip II of Spain, who thought so well of himself, and of England, that he offered himself to the second Tudor sister. The earl of Arran was inspected, but quickly dismissed. Archduke Charles of the Holy Roman Empire and Eric of Sweden were both considered as diplomatic candidates, but both were passed over. Meanwhile, Elizabeth had begun a liaison with Robert Dudley, son of the duke of Northumberland. Unfortunately, he had the inconvenience of a wife. The wife died suddenly, raising suspicions of foul play. Elizabeth regained her composure, and the infatuation cooled. The queen offered Dudley, as the new earl of Leicester, to Mary Queen of Scots as a suitable husband. Mary declined, and Dudley persisted in England as merely the queen's favorite. In the fall of 1562 Elizabeth caught smallpox and narrowly survived. Her health was the occasion of vigorous debate in Parliament, beginning January 1563, over her single estate and the problem of succession.

In the House of Commons, the Puritan constituency had grown to a choir of fifty vocal participants, led by Thomas Norton. The chief issue of the second Elizabethan Parliament, which opened on January 12, 1563, was the queen's marriage and the line of succession. As early as the twenty-sixth, the two houses petitioned the queen to marry and to permit Parliament itself to declare the succession — extravagant requests, indeed, yet honestly based on fear of the queen's untimely death. Elizabeth received the Commons' petition on January 28 and a similar one from the Lords, on February 1. She cloaked her anger under vague promises of compliance. In April, when still no answer had been forthcoming, Elizabeth prorogued Parliament, having delivered herself of a final speech on the subjects of marriage and succession that no one seemed to catch the meaning of.

Parliament stood prorogued for three years. By the fall of 1566, however, money was so short that Elizabeth had no choice except to recall Parliament to session on September 30. When the queen presented her request for money in the form of a subsidy bill (October 18), the Commons made the passage of such a bill conditioned on the receipt of a suitable response from Elizabeth on the subject of the succession. The Lords eventually joined the Commons in a united stand. Elizabeth managed to work off her fury by adept political maneuvers. On November 5 she summoned representatives of both houses and, having dressed them down, informed them that she *would* marry but that the subject of succession was not a "convenient" subject at that time. She might be a "petticoat" monarch, she said, but she would be damned if she would bend under pressure from Parliament. She described her subjects in the two houses of Parliament as a bunch of feet trying "to direct the head in so weighty a matter." When the Commons still refused to be quiet, Elizabeth, on November 9, ordered that body in effect to shut up and be content with her promise to marry. Two days later, Commons accused her, at least by implication, of having abridged that house's free speech and of having bound that house against the exercise of its legitimate parliamentary privileges. The breach between Crown and Parliament had grown very wide indeed. On November 25, seeing that she had gone too far, Elizabeth backed down. A jubilant Commons quickly passed a subsidy bill, taking note in a preamble to that bill that her majesty had agreed to marry and to settle the succession. Elizabeth fumed: "I know no reason why any of my private answers to the realm should serve as prologue to a subsidies-book."

Elizabeth had come out best. The Parliament that she dissolved early in 1567 and that, at its closing, she rebuked for its impudence, never managed to discover when the monarch would marry, or to whom, and never got the satisfaction of settling the succession. For its part, the English Crown encountered a more or less new phenomenon: organized and quite skillful opposition in Parliament over a matter of state.

THE VESTIARIAN CONTROVERSY

IN THE same Parliament, the second Elizabethan, a variety of ecclesiastical disturbances were brought up for discussion, including a lack of uniformity with respect to the use of vestments. The Elizabethan Settlement required the Church of England to adhere to the vestments that were in use during the second year of Edward's reign, but the Puritans eschewed those vestments (the surplice, in particular) in favor of the plain "Geneva" gown — the gown of John Calvin, fashionable in Geneva. Meanwhile the clergy in the southern province of England had met in convocation at Canterbury. That convocation approved the Thirty-Nine Articles of Religion, but when it turned its attention to matters of rites, ceremonies, and ecclesiastical haberdashery, a furor arose involving the Puritans and their opponents. The Vestiarian Controversy had begun.

At that time, Puritanism enjoyed two prominent spokesmen — Lawrence Humphrey and Thomas Sampson — both Marian Exiles, both associated with the English universities, which were then the most fertile grounds of Puritan ideas in England. It was said of Humphrey, who was regius professor of divinity at Oxford and president of Magdalen College, that he "did stock his college with a generation of" Puritans. In the convocation of 1563 a Puritan campaign, designed by Sampson, was directed against wearing the surplice, making the sign of the cross in baptism, and other activities deemed idolatrous, and a strenuous effort was made to have the use of the Genevan gown approved. It was preoccupied by the importance of symbolism, believing that one must take great pains in religion to express, whether in words or in symbols, exactly what one means and that one must jettison everything ambiguous or contradictory that might confuse people or obscure the true nature of religion.

Elizabeth, alarmed by this split in her clergy, decided to move decisively against the Puritans. She notified the whole lot of them that she would insist on uniformity in worship and vestments. Archbishop Parker got instructions from her to do his duty. Late in 1564 he tried to treat reasonably with Sampson (the dean of Christ Church College, Oxford) and with Humphrey, only to be told by them that the vestments proposed by her majesty had been irreparably spoiled by their association with Roman Catholicism; they were the garments of Antichrist.

Determined to put a stop to the increasing instances of irregularity in the Church of England, Archbishop Parker drew up a set of regulations entitled *Advertisements,* which appeared in March 1566; they regulated preaching, prescribed the correct vestments to be worn by clergy of all sorts, specified correct observances of worship, and gave admonitions about the style of life proper to clergymen. Although Elizabeth egged her archbishop on, she refused, in typical Elizabethan fashion, to lend her name to his *Advertisements,* lest she suffer some political disadvantage by doing so. The rules concerning preaching were very explicit and were designed to curtail the effective use of the pulpit by Puritan propagandists.

As the Vestiarian Controversy heated up, Sampson was deprived of his deanship at Oxford as an illustration of what could happen to obstreperous Puritans. A Puritan outburst at Cambridge was quashed. Knowing that Bishop Grindal had Puritan sympathies and could not be trusted, Parker himself convoked the clergy of the diocese of London — 110 all told — and forced them to subscribe to the *Advertisements.* Thirty-seven refused and were suspended.

The Puritans counterattacked. They resorted to a war of pamphlets, of which Anthony Gilby's *Pleasant Dialogue* was typical. Its purpose was "to roote out the wedes of poperie" in the Church of England; it included a list of one hundred instances of such corruption in the church — "crossing, coping, surplessing, kneeling, with pretty wafer kakes and other knacks of Poperie." The remedy for all this, according to Gilby, was to return the Church of England to "the pure simplicity of Christ's worde."

At the same time, the Puritans attempted to garner support from abroad. In 1566 Humphrey and Sampson wrote to Bullinger, Zwingli's successor at Zurich, soliciting his endorsement of the Puritan position. The Anglican bishops, however, who enjoyed Bullinger's friendship no less than the Puritans, had anticipated such a ploy and had already obtained an opinion from Bullinger in which he counseled all Christians of England, lay and clerical, to submit to the religious authorities. The bishops saw to it that Bullinger's response was printed and broadly distributed. That blow to Puritan prestige, plus Archbishop Parker's grim determination to ride out the storm, brought the capitulation of the Puritans one by one. By the autumn of 1566 or the spring of 1567, the Vestiarian Controversy was over.

The controversy was most damaging not to the Puritans but to the Anglican bishops. Denounced by Elizabeth for being ciphers and assailed by the Puritans for compliance with policies widely perceived to be popish and for toadying to the queen, the bishops emerged from the contest in a state of embarrassment. The Puritans, smarting at their defeat in the ecclesiastical arena, returned to the offensive in Parliament, where they managed to throttle no less than eleven government bills in the session of 1566.

RELATIONS WITH SPAIN AND THE CATHOLIC CHURCH

THREE events happened at the turn of the year 1567–68 that were to require Elizabeth's attention for the next twenty years. First, Mary Stuart was driven from Scotland into England. Second, at Douai, in the Spanish Netherlands, William Allen founded a seminary to train Catholic priests for service in England. Third, Thomas Cartwright returned to Cambridge to become the latest mouthpiece of Puritanism. Within a year Darnley was being excluded from any political role, and he and Mary had little contact. Mary took out her unhappiness on the Protestants of Scotland, driving into exile the leader of the Protestant lords, the earl of Murray (1565). She turned for solace increasingly to her Italian secretary, Riccio, who was a clever musician and able to handle Mary's foreign correspondence. In a fit of jealousy, Darnley and a group of accomplices invaded the queen's chamber — she was then with child, the future King James, whose name decorates the King James Bible — and stabbed Riccio to death (March 9, 1566). Intent upon avenging Riccio's murder, Mary banished all of Darnley's cronies from the places of power and recalled Murray, the Protestant earl. When Darnley fell ill toward the end of 1566, Mary had him carted to Kirk o'Field, a house in the environs of Edinburgh, and left him there to be obliterated in an explosion set to destroy the house. The perpetrators of that plot were none other than a band of Scottish lords, led by a wild man, James Hepburn, earl of Bothwell, who was apparently willing to do the most extraordinary things to please Mary. Darnley was not blown up, however, but was found strangled in the garden outside the house, as if he had been forewarned of the plot. Bothwell, implicated by popular opinion ("Here is the murderer of the king," read the placards) as well as in a court of law, was duly tried and found innocent of Darnley's murder. At that stroke of good fortune, he swept Mary away to Dunbar (with her connivance, no doubt), where they lived together in sin until he could get a divorce. On May 15, 1567, Mary Stuart was married to Bothwell in Protestant rites.

Mary had finally undone herself. The Queen of Scots appeared before the world as utterly unseemly, tainted by murder and adultery, bad taste, and religious inconsistency. Scots of all sorts and conditions turned against her. Imprisoned at Loch Leven, she was forced to abdicate in favor of her infant son, with Murray as regent during the child's minority. Bothwell fled to Denmark. Having escaped from Loch Leven, Mary made one last attempt to regain her crown, but her militia was crushed at Langside on May 13, 1568. She retired to England in despair, appealing to her sister queen,

Elizabeth, to protect her and assist her in her struggle against those she persisted in calling rebels.

At first, Elizabeth kept Mary at Carlisle under the surveillance of Sir Francis Knollys. What were Elizabeth's options with respect to Mary? If she struck at Mary, she would be perceived as disloyal to monarchy. If she assisted Mary in Scotland, she would subvert her own best politics for Scotland. If she allowed Mary to stay in England, she would aid and abet Catholic agitation in her own realm. At the turn of 1568–69, first at York and then at Westminster, commissioners representative of (1) Mary Stuart, (2) Elizabeth, and (3) the earl of Murray met to hold an "examination" into Mary's supposed crimes — murder, adultery, rebellion, and the like. Murray brought out into the open the famous Casket Letters, which, whether forgeries or not, purported to implicate Mary herself in Darnley's murder. The hearings did nothing to dissolve Mary's bad reputation. Murray returned to his regency in Scotland. Mary, brought south, began twenty years of confinement in a succession of English castles and country estates, an ever-present threat to Elizabeth.

The arrival of Mary Stuart in England brought an end to the pro-Spanish foreign policy that England had pursued with sometimes more and sometimes less enthusiasm since the very beginning of the century, when Prince Arthur had married Catherine of Aragon. Not that the so-called Spanish amity had existed without complications over the intervening years. In recent times, Elizabeth had meddled in the affairs of the Spanish Netherlands on the side of the Dutch rebels. Philip of Spain had offered clandestine aid to English Catholics. England had presented an ever more serious challenge to Spanish preponderance in the New World.

Early in 1569 a group of disgruntled noblemen, led by the duke of Norfolk and the earl of Arundel, and distinguished by nothing more substantial than their common hatred of Cecil, began to treat with the Spanish ambassador in London, Guerau de Spes, a man whose chief talent was mischief. Using a Florentine banker, Roberto Ridolfi, as their intermediary, these men offered Spain a plan to bring Elizabeth to bay, get rid of Cecil, restore Catholicism to England, and declare Mary Stuart successor to the throne. When the duke of Alva, Spain's principal agent in the Netherlands, refused to act in support of this revolution until the Catholics of England arose en masse in its support, the plot collapsed and the Norfolk faction became as docile as Elizabeth could please. Norfolk himself was sent to the Tower.

In the north, about the same time, a group of fairly independent nobles along the Scottish border harbored grievances against the Crown, which, although probably far more economic than religious, were cloaked in a revival of Catholicism. In November 1569, in Durham Cathedral, the earls of Northumberland and Westmoreland and their colleagues celebrated Mass as they enthusiastically tore the English prayer book and Bible to shreds and smashed the Anglican Communion table, which they called a "trestle of bordes." Leaving that Norman cathedral, the rebels marched south in a crusade dedicated to the restoration of Catholicism ("God, Our Lady, and the Catholic Faith"), the removal of Cecil, and the fixation of Mary Stuart as Elizabeth's successor. Elizabeth dispatched three armies to crush this "Northern Rebellion," which dissolved in fear in the presence of her armies, its leaders disappearing into Scotland. The queen's retribution was swift and severe: some eight hundred conspirators, mainly common folk, became Catholic martyrs.

Cecil was now persuaded that Spain had proved an unreliable partner in foreign affairs. In 1570 he sent Sir Francis Walsingham to France to seek a rapprochement with Charles IX and to investigate the possibility that the bargain might be sealed by the marriage of Elizabeth to the duke of Anjou, Catherine de' Medici's second son. Although nothing came of the proposed marriage, Walsingham managed to arrange the Treaty of Blois (April 1572), in which the two powers pledged mutual defense.

Meanwhile, the release of Norfolk from the Tower in August 1570 was enough to whet the conspiratorial instincts of Ridolfi all over again. By shuttling back and forth from England to the Continent, he managed to hatch a plot to assassinate Elizabeth and to assign the English throne to Mary and her would-be consort, the duke of Norfolk. Cecil's agents soon discovered all of this nefarious business, including its principal players: Mary Stuart, Philip of Spain, the duke of Norfolk, and the pope. A second Ridolfi plot had been quashed. Norfolk was sent back to the Tower and sentenced to death (January 1572); Mary herself was in imminent danger. Elizabeth hesitated until, in May 1572, Parliament forced the issue; Norfolk lost his head (June 2), and Mary was spared.

As nonseparatists, the Puritans could afford to be both vocal and visible. The English Catholics, in contrast, were forced to practice their religion surreptitiously. In 1559, the year after Elizabeth became queen, Pius IV took the papal throne. His policy toward England was one of conciliation, based on the possibility that the new queen might yet be recovered to Roman obedience. In 1562 some English Catholics appealed to Rome through the Spanish ambassador, asking for a concession to attend

Anglican services as required by law. They were rebuffed, but the pope did authorize the papal emissaries still active in England to give absolution to those who attended Anglican services against their conscience.

In January 1566 a sober Dominican assumed the papacy as Pius V. He took a much more severe position with respect to the Church of England. At once, he dispatched agents to England to absolve and reconcile the Catholics who had compromised their faith under duress of English law. In the north of England, the activity of those commissioners, coupled with the arrival of Mary Stuart (1568), contributed to the outbreak of the Northern Rebellion (1569). Among the leaders of that rebellion was Nicholas Morton, a Catholic priest of York, who had been trained in Rome for surreptitious service in England. With the rank of apostolic penitentiary, he moved among English Catholics, absolving and reconciling those who had been forced to abjure; also, as a son of Yorkshire aristocracy, he was adroit in drawing the northern nobility into the rebellion.

Timed to reinforce the Northern Rebellion came an important bull from the hand of Pius V in February 1570 — *Regnans in excelsis*. By this instrument, Elizabeth was excommunicated, deprived of her throne, and disallowed the obedience of English Catholics, the presumption being that one or more of the Catholic powers of the Continent would execute the terms of this bull. *Regnans in excelsis* contained some technical errors that were to prove useful in the course of time. For example, it allowed Elizabeth no possibility of defending herself, contrary to canon law. The bull also contained some errors of fact, for example, that Elizabeth claimed to be "head" of the church. Pius fancied that the bull would give dramatic encouragement to the northern rebels. Its appearance actually coincided with the collapse of the rebellion. Pius also imagined that the continental powers would enforce the bull with alacrity. In fact, the Catholic princes of Europe, so far from trying to enforce the bull, would not even allow it to be published in their realms. *Regnans in excelsis* was a serious miscalculation in the papal designs for England.

The bull did have two outcomes. First, it set off the succession of plots by the Spanish ambassador de Spes and the merchant Ridolfi, taking advantage of the presence of Mary Stuart in England. Of these plots, we have already written.

Second, the bull had the unhappy effect of implicating English Catholicism with treason. For ten years, English Catholics had been able to temporize, affirming both their loyalty to the queen and their loyalty to the Church of Rome. But no more. The pope's bull absolving English

Catholics from allegiance to the queen of England saw to that. English Catholics must henceforth choose between country and religion. Most chose country, citing the technical, legal flaws in the papal bull and thus suggesting its illegitimacy.

The third Parliament of the reign (1571), stunned by the treasonous nature of *Regnans in excelsis,* passed a succession of bills designed to protect England against such mischief. It was henceforth treason to publish the bull of Pius V, to introduce any papal bull in England, to deny the queen's title, to intimate that she was a heretic, to support any movement against her rule, or to make clandestine trips abroad, failing to return within the year. Despite such strictures, Anglican bishops made alarming reports of Catholic gains. "I marvel what it means," wrote Archbishop Parker to Cecil in September 1572, "that they grow so fast." In truth, the number of English Catholics did not increase, even to the end of Elizabeth's reign.

Although English Catholicism did not grow, it at least survived and maintained itself through an important institution of 1568. In that year William Allen founded a seminary at Douai in the Spanish Netherlands, the sole purpose of which was to educate English priests for service in England. Allen was born in Lancashire in 1532 and died in Rome in 1594 as a cardinal and as prefect of the Vatican Library. He entered the church during the reign of Mary Tudor. In 1561 Allen left Oxford, where he had been principal of St. Mary's Hall, and took up residence at Louvain, where a colony of English Catholics lived in exile. Several years later he founded the English College at Douai, which offered an education to English Catholics comparable to that of Oxford and Cambridge and gave training for the Catholic priesthood. The Douai institution was generously endowed by Catholics in the north of England. Soon, more than 150 English students were studying divinity at Douai. In 1575 the first of these seminarians arrived back in England. Mendoza, the Spanish ambassador, reported in December 1579 that "these priests go about disguised as laymen, and, although they are young, their good life, fervency, and zeal in the work are admirable."

The seminarians, whose mission was spiritual and who were forbidden to discuss politics or ridicule the queen, managed to arrest the decline of English Catholicism and to prepare the Catholic minority in England for a permanent existence alongside the established church. Such an accomplishment dashed Elizabeth's intention of creating a single Church of England, comprehensive of all of her subjects. It is not surprising, therefore, that the seminarians met persecution. Cuthbert Mayne, son of Devonshire, educated at Oxford and Douai, was drawn and quartered for high treason at Launceton on November 29, 1577 — the first of the seminarians to be executed. He was not the last. In 1581 the government laid heavy strictures on the Catholic faithful. Attendance at Mass brought a stiff fine (about $2,000) as well as imprisonment. To convert another or to be converted oneself was treason: it withdrew a queen's subject from allegiance to her.

In 1572 Gregory XIII attained the papacy as successor to Pius V. He allowed his English policy to be defined by William Allen, who persuaded the pontiff to send Jesuits to England. In 1579 a college of the Society of Jesus was opened in Rome, the sole purpose of which was to prepare missioners for English service; the following year, the first contingent of Jesuits arrived in Elizabeth's realm. They were led by two Oxford men who had once held holy orders in the Church of England — Edmund Campion, a man of uncommon ability and saintly character, and Robert Parsons.

At their departure for England, Campion and Parsons inquired of Pope Gregory how they should interpret the bull of Pius V. The pope replied that *Regnans in excelsis* could not bind the consciences of English Catholics until some foreign power could be found to execute it. It was a shrewd bit of casuistry that relieved the consciences of English Catholics. Campion made sure that all Englishmen and women understood the unpolitical nature of the Jesuit mission. In the disclaimer known as Campion's Brag, he declared, "I never had in mind, and am strictly forbidden by our Father that sent me [i.e., the pope], to deal in any respect with matters of state or policy within this realm, as things which appertain not to my vocation and from which I gladly restrain and sequester my thoughts."

The government of Elizabeth was unconvinced. On a summer Sunday in 1581, as he celebrated Mass in the chapel of the Yates family in Berkshire, Campion was betrayed and was eventually (December 1, 1581) executed for treason. Parsons made good his escape to the Continent. Altogether, some 250 English Catholics in this era died for their faith.

PURITANISM STRENGTHENED

THE EIGHTEEN years between the bull and the Spanish Armada (1570–88) were the heyday of English Puritanism of the Tudor era. It is not difficult to understand why. Elizabeth and her ministers were locked in struggle with the English Catholics, relieving the Puritans of governmental pressure and convincing many nonpartisan people in England that the Puritans were more nearly right in their outlook about religion in the state than the Catholics were. By 1570 (the year of the bull), most of the older generation of Puritan leaders had either died or had passed into obscurity. Even the center of Puritanism had shifted — from Oxford to Cambridge. Emmanuel College, Cambridge, under the leadership of Edward Dering, had been restaffed as a training center for Puritan clergy, while at Christ's College, Cambridge, there were in attendance such forthcoming Puritan intellectuals as William Ames and William Perkins, not to mention John Milton. Both the press and Parliament aided and abetted Puritanism. The nation was virtually awash in Puritan propaganda (primarily pamphlets), until the authorities diminished the flood of publications in 1586. Parliament was almost, but not quite, a forum for Puritan opinions and Puritan schemes for church reform. To be a Puritan in the 1570s meant to believe that the current halfway house called the Church of England — somewhat Catholic and somewhat Protestant — would soon give way, and must give way, to a more perfect form of Christianity, one that bore a striking resemblance to Calvin's Geneva. Not even Elizabeth's Privy Council was without Puritans. Leicester, Knollys, Walsingham, and Mildmay were all of that persuasion, despite the queen's downright opposition, even hatred, for Puritanism and its sympathizers.

Up to this time, Puritanism had not been noticeably profound or constructive. Like a petulant child, it had proceeded mainly on vexation over the popish remains in the Church of England — vestments and such. In 1570, however, a new and fresh generation of Puritan thinkers arose who were not content any longer to fret and squabble over the small points of religion, but proposed quite in earnest to presbyterianize the Church of England in all essential respects — in its doctrines, in its polity or government, and in its worship. In other words, they would solve the problem of the Church of England by a fairly radical change of its nature. In place of the Anglican bishops, the Puritans hoped to install a system of church government featuring ministers and elected elders, presbyteries (regional councils), and synods — an apparatus that bore similarity to those of the Reformed or Calvinistic churches in Scotland and on the Continent. It was soon evident that this presbyterian system, with its representative overtones, did not rest comfortably with either the divine right of kings or the monarch's presumption of being "supreme governor" of the church. That point was not lost on Elizabeth either.

The prophet of Presbyterian Puritanism was Thomas Cartwright, (1535–1603) who used his important Cambridge professorship — he had been appointed Lady Margaret Professor of Divinity in 1569 — to attack the nature and government of the Church of England and to inculcate Presbyterian ideas, thereby throwing the university into tumult. Dismissed from his post in 1570 by John Whitgift, the master of Trinity College, Cartwright took up residence in Geneva, where he observed firsthand how a Calvinist community organized and expressed itself.

The Parliament of 1571 included several bold spirits who seemed to have caught the ideas of Cartwright. Peter Wentworth, who represented Barnstable in the House of Commons, asserted the right of Parliament, over that of the bishops, to determine religious matters. Walter Strickland, another Puritan protagonist in Commons, proposed alterations to the Book of Common Prayer — an indiscretion deemed so rude that he was forbidden to attend the House. When Parliament met again in 1572, Cartwright was called home to press the Puritan opportunity. Serious consideration was given to a bill that would have winked at Puritan nonconformity. Specifically, the Act of Uniformity would have been applied more rigorously to papists than to Puritans, who, by their bishops' leave, would have been allowed to tinker with the official prayer book or to use the books of worship of the continental Reformed churches. The bill passed three readings before Elizabeth quashed it.

In addition to their attempts in Parliament, the Puritans also made use of the proven power of the pamphlet. In June 1572 there appeared the first *Admonition to the Parliament,* for which two young London ministers, John Field and Thomas Wilcox, were deemed the culprits and were cast into Newgate Prison. The *Admonition* set forth a "true Platforme of a church reformed," according to the teachings of Cartwright and, to be sure, of the Reformed churches abroad. The clergy of the established church were assailed for their ignorance, covetousness, popish attire, and abject dependence on the English prayer book. Anglican bishops were denounced for their pomp, idleness, and rich livings. The Anglican prayer book, described as being full of Catholic remains, was shamefully compared to the simple, sufficient worship of the ancient church. The admonitioners proposed to divest the Anglican bishops of the government of the Church of England and to turn it over to the joint rule of "ministers, seniors, and deacons," according to the custom of Calvin's Geneva. Attached to the pamphlet was a truculent piece entitled "A View of Popish Abuses Yet Remaining in the English Church." Here a voluminous criticism was launched against the Book of Common Prayer, which was described as having been "culled and picked out of that popish dunghill, the Masse book, full of all abominations."

Thus began an era of pamphleteering called the Admonition Controversy, in the course of which Cartwright affirmed the scriptural warrant for Presbyterianism against the written rebuttals of the Anglican champion, Bishop John Whitgift. The controversy included Whitgift's *Answer,* Cartwright's *Reply,* and a second *Admonition,* the Puritan pieces being turned out on a secret press, despite the government's attempt at censorship. Cartwright argued that the presbyterian form of church government alone had the sanction of Holy Scripture; it alone was *de jure divino,* "according to God's law." Puritanism was momentarily ascendant. It intrigued the court, titillated London, and gained admirers in the East Midland. Toward the close of 1573, however, Elizabeth's resolve to undo the Puritans stiffened. The queen prodded her bishops to enforce the Act of Uniformity. Prominent Puritan preachers were silenced, including Edward Dering, who had been preaching at St. Paul's in London with almost magical effect. The Puritan press was discovered and put out of commission. Cartwright fled to the Continent (1573) before a warrant for his arrest caught up with him. His chief associate, Walter Travers, followed within the year. Together, they continued to flood England with pro-Puritan books and pamphlets printed abroad. The most conspicuous of these was Travers's *De disciplina ecclesiastica,* a detailed proposal of presbyterian church government that quickly became catalog, textbook, and bible of English Presbyterians.

Having been archbishop of Canterbury for sixteen years, Matthew Parker died in 1575. He was succeeded, not by the eminent Elizabethan prelate Richard Cox, who was then out of favor with the queen, but by Edmund Grindal, archbishop of York, a prelate notorious for his Puritan sympathies. It was one of Elizabeth's conspicuous mistakes. When Grindal went to Canterbury, Sandys moved to York, and Aylmer to London; the three most important English sees were thus in the hands of Marian exiles.

Meanwhile, the Puritans were quietly, steadily, and systematically working out their own system of parish life within the structures of the established church. In many parishes, psalm singing gradually supplanted the use of choir and organ. On Sunday morning, worship according to the Book of Common Prayer was followed directly by evangelical preaching. On Sunday evening, after Evening Prayer, the young were rehearsed in Calvin's Genevan catechism. And so on. The most typical of all the Puritan devices was "prophesying." The Puritans were used to scoffing at the "dumb dogs" and "bare readers" of the established church — clergy too ignorant or too indifferent to do very much except read what was put in front of them. The Puritans proposed to correct this scandal among the clergy, and to exercise the laity at the same time, by using a technique called prophesying, imported from the Reformed churches of the Continent, in particular the Swiss church of Ulrich Zwingli. The so-called prophesying was a weekly exercise attended by both clergy and qualified laypeople. It was devoted to a detailed exposition of an assigned passage of Scripture by learned clergy, one after the other. The moderator — "one of the gravest and most learned among them" — finally gave his judgment of the true sense of the text under discussion, after which questions were posed by the audience.

The approximation of these prophesyings to meetings of a presbytery (ministers and lay elders for purposes of church government) did not escape notice. It occurred to Elizabeth that these exercises were Puritan cells, and she ordered Grindal to suppress them. Grindal, however, finding the prophesyings to be harmless and even beneficial, refused: "Bear with me . . . madam, if I choose rather to offend your earthly majesty than to offend the heavenly majesty of God." Elizabeth was not impressed. In June 1577 she sequestered old Grindal, and sequestered he remained until his death in 1583. For almost six years, Canterbury was for all intents and purposes vacant.

Given this administrative snarl in the established church, Puritanism enjoyed another burst of progress. Prophesyings abounded. Here and there, local authorities allowed the Puritans to establish little Genevas within the Anglican framework.

The weakness of the Crown in controlling Puritanism during Grindal's administration soon led to a much more ominous phenomenon — the appearance of separatism. So far, Puritanism had been stoutly nonseparatist, that is, very reluctant to surrender its participation in the Church of England. Now in the 1580s, however, separatist churches began to appear — religious groups that were willing to forgo membership in the established church if separation would lead to a more purified version of Christianity. In 1581, for example, Robert Browne and Robert Harrison led a secessionist movement at Norwich; a parish, nominally Anglican, left the Church of England to form an independent religious organization, espousing congregational principles. Congregationalism means that the seat of religious authority is deemed to reside neither with bishops (as in Latin Catholicism and the Church of England) nor in presbyteries and synods (as in mainline Puritanism and Scottish Presbyterianism) but in the local congregation. The Brownists did not, however, sweep the day, as Browne and Harrison had hoped, but merely drew the dislike of Anglicans and Puritans. In 1582 they were driven into exile, to Middleburgh in Holland, where they

proceeded to squabble. Browne, having thought better of separatism, returned to England and to conformity, dying in 1633. Despite Browne's
personal change of heart, separatism became more widespread. The
Brownists were soon joined in separatism by the Barrowists, followers of
Henry Barrow of London, who even recruited separatists from his prison
cell until the government extinguished him for good (1594). In the Elizabethan age, the separatists did not accomplish very much, except to make
separatism conceivable. As Independents in the seventeenth century, however, the separatists became powerful enough not merely to dominate Puritanism, but to win a civil war and control the government.

On Grindal's death (1583), the see of Canterbury fell to Whitgift,
Cartwright's opponent, who had been bishop of Worcester since 1577 and
had acquired a reputation for his stout defense of Anglicanism against its
Puritan detractors. Whitgift lost no time in giving battle to the Presbyterian
Puritans. In the very month of his confirmation (September 1583), he
decreed that no one would be permitted to exercise ecclesiastical functions

137. John Whitgift,
portrait after an
engraving by
G. Vertue

without subscribing to three religious tests — (1) royal supremacy, (2) conformity to the Book of Common Prayer (1559 edition), and (3) assent to the Thirty-Nine Articles of Religion, and all three as agreeable with Scripture. The more Whitgift turned the screws on the Puritans, the more John Field, one of the Puritan leaders, urged resistance to Whitgift's three tests. The outcome remained in doubt.

A new era of Puritan resurgency began in 1582 — the last, in fact, in the reign of Elizabeth. A concerted effort now began to introduce a presbyterian form of the Protestant religion within the Church of England on the basis of two standards: (1) the Calvinist forms of worship as they had been fashioned into English by John Knox, and (2) a formal system of presbyterian polity that was then being put down on paper. Chiefly through correspondence, Field encouraged those prophesying to conceive of themselves as classes ("classis" was a synonym for "presbytery") in a national presbyterian organization that would include provincial synods and a national assembly. Where prophesyings did not exist, Field designated some Puritan preacher to organize a classis. Provincial synods began to meet two or three times a year, and a general assembly was convened in London. Meanwhile the preparation of a formal Presbyterian book of government was underway. A decade earlier (1574), Walter Travers had written a long exposition of presbyterian principles — A *Full and Plain Declaration of Ecclesiastical Discipline.* Now, in 1586, a new, brief manual of presbyterian polity, written apparently by Travers, was being circulated among Puritans for criticism. It entrusted the government of a local parish to a consistory (session) and prescribed other graded assemblies: the classis (presbytery), consisting of delegates from twelve parishes; the provincial synod, consisting of delegates from twenty-four classes; and the national assembly.

This "Classical Movement" actually began in 1582 with the appearance of the Dedham Classis. In the Parliament of 1586-87, Anthony Cope attempted to persuade his colleagues in Commons to abolish all existing laws touching ecclesiastical government and to introduce Puritan standards of government and worship. When Elizabeth quashed Cope's bill, Peter Wentworth took the occasion to deliver another of his speeches against infringing the liberties of that house. Both Cope and Wentworth were sent to the Tower. Even by that time, however, the Classical Movement had begun to collapse. The death of Field in 1588 cost the movement its chief organizer; the deaths of Leicester (1588) and Walsingham (1590) deprived Puritanism of its remaining champions in the Privy Council. The national assemblies of 1588 and 1589 were remarkably unedifying. And the defeat of the Spanish Armada in 1588 ended the threat of Catholic resurgency and robbed Puritanism of its peculiar patriotic appeal. Meanwhile, the Puritans took to squabbling among themselves. Disputes arose among Puritans whether Travers's new discipline was agreeable with Scripture, whether it damaged the peace of the English church, and whether it should be installed with or without the approval of Parliament. Over such issues, the Puritans quite lost their unanimity.

The year 1588 was also the year of the so-called Martin Marprelate tracts — amusing but scurrilous attacks on the English bishops written by Puritan propagandists. So outrageous were these tracts that they cast a pall of disfavor over the whole Puritan movement, provoking Elizabeth to full-scale hostility toward Puritanism. Even Thomas Cartwright was moved to denounce these latest Puritan tractarians for their "disordered proceeding."

Archbishop Whitgift, sensing his advantage in the Puritans' disarray, commenced to apply the repressive machinery of the established church against the Puritans with mounting severity. Especially useful in the suppression of religious nonconformity was "the regular court of the high commission for ecclesiastical causes" — the High Commission — pieced together in 1580 from innumerable agencies established since 1559 to deal with religious pluralism. Equally successful against the Puritans was a new breed of Anglican propagandist, such as Thomas Bilson, who argued the "divine right" of episcopacy, and the tough-minded Richard Bancroft, chief snooper of the High Commission, who denounced the Classical Movement as a vast scheme of Puritan sedition.

The Parliament of 1592–93 passed the Act against Puritans, which, although directed specifically against the Separatists, marked a general rout of Tudor Puritanism. The leaders of Presbyterian Puritanism were taken into custody and were released, only to deprive them of the advantage of martyrdom. Elizabeth and her archbishop had finally prevailed over the pesky Puritans. Puritanism would not reassert itself again until the accession of James I in 1603.

Throughout this period, the Puritan representation in Parliament continued to be formidable. The most conspicuous of the "Parliament men" — Puritan protagonists during the middle years of Elizabeth's reign — was Peter Wentworth of Northamptonshire, who first took his seat in the House of Commons in 1571. The issues raised by Wentworth's prickly conduct were two: freedom of speech, and the right of the House to conduct its constitutional affairs. The issue between Wentworth and his queen was joined in 1571, when Walter Strickland, another Puritan protagonist in

Commons, proposed alterations to the Book of Common Prayer. Elizabeth took the position that, as supreme governor of the Church of England, she alone could make alterations to the established religion. At her bidding, Strickland was summoned to appear before the Privy Council, where he was rebuked and forbidden to sit in the House of Commons. Although Elizabeth eventually relented, she left upon Wentworth an indelible impression that she was no respecter of free speech.

When Commons reconvened in 1576, Wentworth delivered himself of an oration on free speech that had been simmering in his Puritan soul for at least three years. In one of the great specimens of parliamentary discourse, Wentworth argued that if Parliament was to be Parliament, it must be accorded the freedom to express itself about everything "beneficial for the prince or state" — and that included religion. He complained particularly of "rumours and messages" — rumors that the queen disliked this or that, messages from the queen to the speaker of the House of Commons, all inhibiting free discourse. Included in Wentworth's oration was the blunt little statement that "her majesty has committed great faults." It was enough to make the members of the House suck in their breath. Shocked at such indiscretion, the House itself caused Wentworth to be arrested, as Elizabeth looked on impassively. Committed to the Tower, Wentworth stewed in his own righteousness for four weeks but made apologies to no one.

In the Parliament of 1581, Wentworth was uncustomarily subdued. He did not sit in the Parliament of 1584–85. In the session of 1586–87, however, he operated again at full throttle, as the Puritans renewed their demands on behalf of Presbyterianism. Anthony Cope, a member of Commons, introduced "a bill and a book," in which he proposed to abolish all laws touching the establishment of religion, including the Book of Common Prayer, and to introduce instead the Puritan standards of worship and discipline, which were presented to Parliament in the form of a book. Elizabeth promptly quashed the bill and the book, whereupon Wentworth proposed ten articles for debate, arguing that as Parliament was necessary to the realm for the making of laws, free speech was necessary to Parliament for its deliberations. Wentworth cursed all abridgers of free speech as enemies of God, the prince, and the state. Impudence! Elizabeth lost no time consigning both Cope and Wentworth to the Tower. It was Wentworth's last disquisition on the freedom of speech, yet he lives in the annals of Western society as one of the very greatest protagonists of that privilege.

THE DUTCH REVOLUTION

MEANWHILE, troublesome matters of foreign policy engaged Elizabeth's attention. In the Netherlands, the Dutch revolution, which had begun in 1572, proceeded stubbornly against the Spanish preponderance in the Low Countries. Prince William of Orange, leader of the Dutch rebels, held tenaciously to the provinces of Holland and Zeeland and looked to Elizabeth for moral and material support. Elizabeth knew that if she was indifferent to Orange, the Dutch would simply seek help from the French. From the English perspective, a French Netherlands would be worse than a Spanish Netherlands.

In France, the French Protestants, called Huguenots, began to revive in the 1570s, following the Massacre of St. Bartholomew (August 24, 1572), in which some seventy thousand Huguenots, including leaders, were slaughtered in Paris and other Protestant centers at the instigation of Catherine de' Medici. Later in the seventies, the Huguenots sought new leadership in two members of French royalty — Henry of Navarre, a Protestant betrothed to Catherine's daughter, Margaret, and Francis, duke of Alençon, Catherine's youngest son.

In 1578, when the Dutch were especially hard-pressed by the Spanish and when Elizabeth was reluctant to intervene on the Dutch side, Orange turned to Alençon, whose highest ambition was to achieve a kingdom for himself. The following year, as part of his general strategy, Alençon resumed his courtship of Elizabeth, which had been begun in 1576 but allowed to languish. Although she was now forty-five, the queen was deemed still fecund by her councillors, some of whom urged her to take Alençon's suit seriously. Just as ardently did Catherine de' Medici encourage her son to seek Elizabeth's hand. In the Netherlands, meanwhile, the revolution wore on, with Elizabeth, Alençon, and Orange now pitted against a relentless campaign of reconquest by the Spanish under two Spanish governors — Don John of Austria (d. 1578) and Alexander Farnese of Parma.

To dally with Elizabeth, Alençon first sent as proxy Jean de Simier, whom Elizabeth referred to affectionately as her ape. In August 1579 Alençon arrived in person for three weeks of strenuous courtship; Elizabeth called him her frog — not entirely unbefitting his scrofula and misshapen body. Never mind: love was in bloom, and a marriage seemed imminent. England, however, was not amused. The Privy Council was the scene of more than one tumultuous encounter between queen and council. When the Puritan printer John Stubbs published an attack against the marriage,

138. Francis, duke of
Alençon, portrait by
F. Clouet

both he and his apprentice lost their right hands in a public excision before a crowd of spectators thoroughly unsympathetic to her majesty. The apprentice pointed to his severed hand and offered the observation that that was the hand of an honest Englishman, while Stubbs shouted, "God save the queen!" as he fainted away.

The prospect of marriage disappeared almost as quickly and mysteriously as it began. Alençon reappeared in England again in 1581, when he was needed to help stave off Spanish successes in the southern provinces of the Netherlands; although Elizabeth showed some public affection for him, in private she had eschewed the marriage. As the 1580s wore on, Alençon was undone by political misfortunes in the Netherlands, suffering both defeats at the hands of the Spanish and disastrous quarrels with the Dutch themselves. He died in May 1584. The following month, the Dutch revolution suffered an even greater loss: an assassin took the life of William of Orange.

Misfortune also dogged Elizabeth in Scotland. In 1578 the regency of the pro-English Morton was undone. James VI, at twelve, became king in his own right, but effective control of the Scottish government passed to two pro-French members of the Stuart family — Esme Stuart, the earl of Lennox, and James Stuart, the earl of Arran. Morton was arrested in 1580 and executed the next year.

Resolved to uproot Protestantism in England and seat Mary Stuart on the throne of the combined realms of England and Scotland, Lennox imported two Jesuits whose activities in the north of England were timed to coincide with a French invasion of England across the Channel. Walsingham's secret service caught wind of these plans. Alerted, the Protestant lords of Scotland abducted King James at Ruthven in August 1582 and proceeded to harry both Lennox and Arran out of the country. The boy-king showed no great zeal to shower favor on either his mother (Mary Stuart) or her kin; he operated already out of enlightened self-interest. Arran did manage a brief return to power in Scotland in 1583, but with the assistance of a clever politician, the master of Gray, the English were able to oust the French party from Scotland once for all in October 1585 — a maneuver in which King James concurred. The Treaty of Berwick, concluded the following year, settled the relationship between England and Scotland and prepared the way for the eventual union of the two realms at Elizabeth's death.

The key to Lennox's scheme was an invasion of England across the Channel by the duke of Guise, in collaboration with Mary Stuart, the pope, and Philip II of Spain. The plot came to light in 1583, when Walsingham, by means of torture, broke the confidence of Francis Throckmorton, an English Catholic who carried secret intelligences between Mary Stuart and Mendoza, the Spanish ambassador accredited to Elizabeth. The year 1584 was a year of gravity in England. In January, Mendoza was expelled, Alençon died in May, and Orange was shot in June. Even to the pacificist Elizabeth, it had become plain that Rome meant to bring her down and finally crush the English Protestantism she had come to represent. Even to Elizabeth, the prospect of war was real.

During the last two decades of Elizabeth's reign, the English waged war in four perimeters against a loose confederacy of Catholic powers — (1) in defense of the island against the Spanish Armada, (2) on the high seas against Spanish shipping, (3) in the Netherlands as an ally of the Dutch rebels, and (4) in Ireland against Irish nationalists. It was a risky undertaking on the part of a small race (then half the population of Spain), with no standing army, an economy ungeared for war, and few commanders of any experience or ability, all led by a queen made even more cheap and indecisive by age. As the war began, the final episode in the drama of Mary Queen of Scots unfolded, including the execution of that Catholic monarch in 1587.

The beginning of England's war with the Catholic powers occurred in 1584, with the death of Alençon, the assassination of William of Orange, the rout of the Dutch rebels by Parma (of which the fall of Antwerp in 1585 was a major catastrophe), and the boozy incompetence of Henry III of France, which enabled the Guise family, ardently Catholic and pro-Spanish, to regain control of that nation in 1585. All of these developments put England and English Protestantism under enormous pressure. In 1585, the year Antwerp fell, English commerce was further inflicted by the Spanish seizure of English ships in Spanish harbors. It took Elizabeth only several months after such provocation to strike an alliance with the Dutch rebel, agreeing to maintain an expeditionary force in the Netherlands at her own expense. For their part, the Dutch ceded to England Flushing and Brill as "cautionary towns" — safe ports of entry for English supplies and reinforcement. In December, Leicester sailed with an army of seven thousand. The war was on.

While Leicester's campaign in the Low Countries proved a disaster, albeit a showy one, full of sound and fury signifying nothing, the English fortunately began to realize their fighting mettle on the high seas. The age of English sea power and the English naval hero had begun. In September 1585, in retaliation for Spanish seizure of English vessels several months before, Sir Francis Drake set sail for the West Indies with thirty ships and some two thousand men to harass Spanish shipping. In a series of amphibious assaults, Drake sacked the capitals of Cuba (San Domingo) and the Spanish Main (Carthagena) and so crippled Spanish naval power in the region that Philip II of Spain was forced to divert resources from the Netherlands to cover his losses in the Caribbean.

Meanwhile, Mary Stuart remained at the center of Catholic intrigue in England, aided and abetted by the Guises of France (her relatives) and by that evermore fanatical Catholic, Philip II of Spain. As 1585 began, Mary was consigned to Tutbury Castle, into the custody of a none-too-sweet-spirited Puritan, Sir Anyas Paulet, who saw none of Mary's graces but only her wickedness. Through the shadowy activities of a certain Dr. William Parry, who was executed for conspiracy against the Crown in March 1585, Walsingham and his secret service became convinced that a plot was being laid to kill

Elizabeth and release Mary. What remained unsubstantiated, however, was Mary's own complicity. Walsingham proceeded to trick Mary into disclosing her own guilt. In December 1585 he caused her to be removed to Chartley Manor, where, although the surveillance was ironclad, he managed to persuade Mary to think that she could pass letters to and from France without being detected. Every letter, of course, passed directly beneath Walsingham's nose, including the infamous letter of July 1586, in which Anthony Babington revealed to Mary the narrowest details of the projected assassination of Queen Elizabeth and asked for Mary's approval. When Mary finally signed her acknowledgment of the Babington Conspiracy, she effectively signed her own warrant of execution. Still Elizabeth hesitated. In September 1586 all of the conspirators were executed; in the following month, Mary's guilt was firmly ascertained by a judicial hearing. In spite of all that, it was not until February 1 in the following year that Elizabeth was finally moved to sign the warrant for Mary's death. Even then, she would not allow it out of her hands. Her council literally had to steal the warrant in order to serve it, and when the execution was completed, she at least feigned anger.

Mary Queen of Scots was beheaded at Fortheringay Castle on February 7, 1587, as Elizabeth waited in anguish. "I shall die," said Mary, "in the true and holy Catholic faith." And indeed she did. Clutching her crucifix, she besought God to be gracious to England and merciful to Elizabeth. Then she let fall her black velvet dressing gown to reveal the brilliant scarlet costume in which she chose to die. She would go to God dressed in the red of martyrdom. As she knelt over the block, she commended her soul to God. The executioner struck twice. When he stooped to pick up her severed head, he came up instead with a fistful of Mary's auburn wig, which, awkwardly, he held aloft, shouting, "Long live the queen!" Meanwhile the gray-haired head of Mary Queen of Scots rolled unceremoniously to the edge of the platform.

There was fury in Scotland. France moved closer in its alliance to Spain. The Spanish Armada was being fitted out. In England, however, an extraordinary and long-lasting national predicament had been removed.

SEA WAR WITH SPAIN

THE DEATH of Mary Queen of Scots led inexorably to England's great enterprise — its engagement with the Spanish Armada. As early as 1585 Philip II had become convinced that there would be no victory in the Netherlands, no Catholic triumph anywhere, without the fall of the Protestant Elizabeth, and that such an outcome depended upon a stunning invasion of England. Upon Mary Stuart's death, Philip asserted his own claims to the throne of England, saying that Mary Tudor had willed it to him and maintaining that James of Scotland, already associating with the Scottish Presbyterians, was a heretic and could not lawfully succeed. A year earlier, Pope Sixtus V had blessed Philip in his English endeavors and had given him some small portion of the papal treasury to underwrite his crusade.

The original Spanish plan called for a direct invasion of England from the south, supported by a great army and a great fleet under the admiralty of the marquess of Santa Cruz. As that plan proved too expensive, the Spanish decided instead to send a fleet to secure the English Channel, giving Parma an opportunity to cross over from the Netherlands with three thousand seasoned troops. During 1586 and 1587, the western coast of Spain became the staging area of a great armada, as men, ships, and supplies were assembled for the campaign against England. Such a large-scale operation did not go undetected by Walsingham, and England itself began to prepare.

Meanwhile Leicester was sent on a second expedition to the Netherlands (June–November 1587), which he bungled no less ostentatiously than he did the previous, increasing Elizabeth's frustration and depleting her treasury. She would likely have sought some accommodation with Parma if she could have, but intelligence of the Spanish buildup in Spain's west-coast harbors brought greater and greater alarm to England as the months passed. In April 1587 Sir Francis Drake was allowed to sail into Spanish waters to do as much damage as he could. In the harbor of Cádiz, he destroyed thirty ships; at Sagres, he interrupted Spanish shipping for two months, seriously curtailing the provisioning of the armada. It is probable that England gained a year's delay from Drake's harassment. It proved to be an auspicious year: in February 1588 Santa Cruz died, leaving Philip II without a competent officer to direct the armada.

A very reluctant Medina Sidonia became commander of the Spanish Armada in 1588; his utmost dedication was matched by a trivial knowledge of the seas and of ocean warfare. On the English side, command of her majesty's fleet was entrusted the same year to the lord admiral, Howard of Effingham, a commander of great stature and experience; in his company were three seasoned captains: Francis Drake, John Hawkins, and Martin Frobisher. Drake, passionately Protestant, had become nothing less than a national hero for all of his derring-do on the high seas, especially in the Caribbean, in harassment of Spanish shipping. Hawkins, beginning in 1569, had been almost single-handedly responsible for rebuilding the royal navy against the distant day when the Spanish might sail against England. The English captains could scarcely be constrained from sailing off and attacking Spain in Spanish waters, but Elizabeth was far too timid to countenance such a thing, so the English waited. By July 19, 1588, favorable winds had brought the Spanish Armada north into English waters off Plymouth. On the twentieth, the English fleet left Plymouth harbor to engage the armada.

The battle was to be fought by a concentration of some 130 ships, equally divided between the contestants, of which perhaps fifty were capital ships; the Spanish vessels were larger and more heavily armed, the English less formidable but more maneuverable and with guns of longer range. The Spanish naval tactic was the "crescent moon," a line-abreast formation, while the English tactic involved the concentration of fire on a single target by ships moving forward in a single line. Medina Sidonia's objective was to effect a linkage between the armada and Parma's army. Such an objective, however, implied the existence of suitable anchorage in Netherlandish waters, but no such anchorage had been agreed on. For nine days, the armada sailed northward in the English Channel, as if in search of a safe harbor, the more nimble English fleet giving chase.

By July 27 the great Spanish beast had reached the sandy harbor of Calais, virtually unscathed by its skirmishes with the English. Howard dropped anchor offshore, effectively penning the Armada into the shallow harbor of Calais. On the night of the twenty-eighth, the English sent in six fire ships, which broke up the crescent moon formation, scattering Spanish ships in all directions. The following day there occurred the battle of the Gravelines, in which English guns raked the disorganized armada, sinking four ships and rendering many others unfit for battle. In the rain squall that ended the battle, Medina Sidonia made his escape northward, with Howard in pursuit. As the armada came around the northern coast of Scotland and met the gales of the Atlantic Ocean, what remained of the great Spanish engine of war was hurled against the rocks or swamped in midocean. No more than half of the Spanish Armada managed to straggle back to Spanish ports in 1589. History interprets the defeat of the Spanish Armada as an English victory. It was not thought so at the time. The armada had not sunk under English bombardment, but under the wind of God. "Afflavit Deus," said the English — "God blew!" (And the God who blew was no doubt Protestant.) Elizabeth grumbled that so few spoils were taken; even Drake depreciated what the English had done, while the common person shuddered lest the Spanish were still there somewhere. It is probably an instance in which Divine Providence is given too much credit. If the battle of Gravelines was the first modern naval battle, it was also an English victory.

Already by the end of 1588 the English had resolved to counterattack. An English Armada, led by Drake and Sir John Norris (rebuilder of Elizabeth's army), was commissioned to undertake the so-called Portugal Expedition, designed to cripple Spanish power at one fell swoop. The expedition was poorly underwritten and poorly supplied from the start. When it finally departed in April 1589, it was already two months behind schedule. Having reached Lisbon, the English were surprised that the Portuguese did not rise in revolution against Spain — the linchpin of the English strategy — which left the English with nothing better to do than pack up and leave. At the end of June 1589, what remained of the great fleet made its way back to Plymouth with absolutely nothing to show for its cost or its efforts.

The war at sea continued. It was waged not so much by armadas or governments as by privateers — individuals who, having been given credentials by the Crown, put to sea to work as much havoc on Spanish shipping as possible. Beginning in 1585, as many as two hundred such expeditions left England in a single year, supported chiefly by London merchants who made handsome profits from the spoils.

In France, meanwhile, the assassination of Henry III in 1589 had brought a Huguenot to the French throne — Henry of Navarre. If he was utterly unappealing to the Catholic party in France, of which the Guise family were the principal members, he was quite the darling of Elizabeth, who responded with alacrity to his cries of help. She sent twenty thousand pounds in loan and an expeditionary force for Henry's purposes. But Henry of Navarre's military successes incurred nothing more than the increased wrath of Spain and induced two invasions of France by Spanish forces — first by Parma from the north, then by a Spanish army into Brittany. Elizabeth sent Henry two more expeditionary forces, one commanded by the experienced soldier John Norris, the other led by Robert Devereux, earl of Essex, a dazzling young charmer of twenty-six. Elizabeth was quite taken with Essex, to whom she had uncommon difficulty saying no. Essex, unfortunately, was given to exuberant and unprofessional gestures with his army and returned to England in January 1592, his army having been wasted by the siege of Rouen, to meet Elizabeth's withering displeasure. In the end, Henry of Navarre turned Catholic in 1593, a conversion that brought an end to the conflict in France. Within two years, all English troops were withdrawn from France (1595); within another two years (1597),

England, France, and the Netherlands had concluded an alliance of mutual assistance against Spain.

The war at sea, however, continued unabated. In 1595 Drake and Hawkins teamed up again (Frobisher having died in battle the previous year) and set sail for the Caribbean to raid Spanish shipping and installations. The outcome this time was dismal. Hawkins died at sea. After a series of failures, Drake too was stricken at sea and died at Porto Bello at the age of fifty-five. So ended the lives of the two greatest English sea captains of the Elizabethan era. In 1596 Essex, Howard of Effingham, and Francis Vere laid plans for an English attack on Spain, to which Elizabeth uncharacteristically gave consent. The expedition embarked in April 1596, with the best equipment of the Spanish war. Some 150 ships and 6,000 soldiers and sailors set sail under the direction of the three commanders and Sir Walter Raleigh. In a brief, brilliant campaign, Cádiz was taken and reduced. The difficulties of supply, however, soon forced the English to break off the campaign and return to England. Philip II stood humiliated before the world — not simply for the Spanish rout at Cádiz, but because of the fearsome prospect of English sea power.

Philip, however, refused to be undone. It took him less than three months after the debacle at Cádiz to hurl a new armada at the English. In this instance, however, the armada represented a Spanish intrusion into Ireland, in support of the Irish revolution against England that was then underway. Once again the Spanish mischief foundered in the storms and rocks of the Atlantic Coast, in this case off Cape Finisterre in northern Spain. Essex immediately began an agitation for another decisive stroke against Spain — as decisive, perhaps, as the campaign of 1596. Elizabeth agreed. The expedition of 1597, which was led by Essex, Howard, Vere, and Raleigh, was dispatched by Elizabeth with orders to demolish the remains of the most recent armada, which lay scattered in the harbors of northern Spain. That done, the English expedition was directed to attack the Spanish treasure fleet — its *flota* — in the Azores. But through a combination of disruptive storms and sheer incompetence, the English neither demolished the remains of the armada nor prevented the *flota* from reaching the safety of Spanish waters. The *flota* was a vast convoy of Spanish ships that operated once a year from Vera Cruz to Cádiz, transporting the production and treasures of Spanish America to Spain. To have intercepted the *flota* would have been a decisive English blow to Spanish revenues and thus to the war-making energies of Spain. The English fleet returned empty-handed and dispirited. Whipped by gales and partially dispersed, the fleet encountered a makeshift Spanish Armada, hastily refitted from the previous armada, for yet another attempt upon England. The island lay virtually undefended. The fear engendered by that episode, coupled with the failure of the expedition of 1597, were enough to convince both Elizabeth and her subjects that the age of naval expeditions should be brought to an end. Essex came home in disgrace. Three events of the following year (1598) brought the Spanish wars to an inconclusive end: (1) Henry IV of France sued for peace with Spain; (2) Philip II of Spain died (within weeks of Burghley's death); and (3) Maurice of Nassau began the final, five-year phase of the capture of the northern Netherlands from their Spanish overlords.

THE CONQUEST OF IRELAND

IF Elizabeth was partially responsible for the appearance of the Netherlands as a nation-state, she was also partially responsible for the deepening of Irish nationalism and of Irish Catholicism. The conquest of Ireland was a Tudor enterprise. Henry VIII had been the first English monarch to assert control over Ireland, but his grip had been allowed to slip badly after Thomas Cromwell's death. Thus, when Elizabeth became queen, the English stake in Ireland consisted simply of the Pale (that is, the English sphere in eastern Ireland from roughly Dundalk to Dublin and as far west as Athlone) and the southeastern and western towns of Waterford, Younghal, Cork, Limerick, and Galway. The rest of Ireland was Irish; it consisted of four provinces — Leinster, Munster, Connaught, and Ulster — each under the tribal authority of chiefs, slightly disguised to appear as English earls. The provinces in the south and west may have been affected by English influence, but Connaught and Ulster were Irish to the core, and Ulster was the very seat of Irish resistance to English rule. There was no telling what one might find beyond the Pale. Irish Ireland could be wild and was accustomed to war. Not even the Catholic religion was much of a pacifier in Ireland; the Irish were somewhat indifferent to the Irish Catholicism in which they had been raised and utterly disgusted by the Protestantism being advocated in England. Irish Catholicism probably blossomed because Elizabeth had the effrontery to throw the pope out of England. Wrote G. R. Elton: "At the beginning of [Elizabeth's] reign, Ireland was virtually ungoverned and heathen; by the end it was firmly under English control and Roman Catholic."

The Tudor policy in Ireland was conquest — including the establishment of English civil administration and the introduction of the Church of England. Conquest was not an elaborate affair; the English simply had to crush the power of the chiefs in battle wherever they made an uproar. Nothing so difficult was ever intended as crushing the whole nation at one time. Even at that, it took most of Elizabeth's reign to accomplish the conquest of Ireland.

The first contest pitted Elizabeth against the fierce chief of the Clan O'Neill, Shane O'Neill, who had seized control of most of Ulster and who saw the advantage of treating with both France and the Church of Rome against the English. When Ulster had at last been pacified (1566), Elizabeth turned her attention to Munster, where James Fitzmaurice Fitzgerald had raised virtually the whole province in rebellion. He too looked abroad for succor; when none came, he finally succumbed to English power in 1572. James Fitzmaurice left Ireland in 1575 and proceeded to Rome and Madrid to plead the Irish cause. An invasion of Ireland was actually attempted in 1579, but it failed. Nevertheless, the Irish were sufficiently stimulated to rise in rebellion under the leadership of the earl of Desmond. Elizabeth was therefore required to wage a third campaign in Ireland (1579–83) in which the Desmond rebellion was eventually suppressed. The last rebellion with which Elizabeth dealt has been called the Great Rebellion (1594–1603). It was led by the formidable Irishman Hugh O'Neill, earl of Tyrone, whose political ambitions apparently extended beyond Ulster to all of Ireland. With an army of six thousand, and with the stout support of a vigorous young chief, Hugh Roe O'Donnell, the rebellion of Tyrone opened in 1593 and endured until 1603, the year of Elizabeth's death, when O'Neill gave himself up. After the disgrace of the second Spanish expedition Essex was sent to lead a well-equipped army to Ireland in April 1599. It took Essex slightly more than four months to squander his fine army, sue for peace, and rush home to the lap of his queen. It was the end of his career.

By 1603 the conquest of Ireland was complete. The cost was paid mainly by the Irish in the form of death, destruction, and a burned-over land. Paradoxically, Ireland gained something for itself from this grisly experience — a heightened sense of nationhood and a rebirth of Irish Catholicism.

THE DECLINE OF PURITANISM

PURITANISM was in poor estate throughout the 1590s, its party spirit and party machinery having been broken by John Whitgift, its intellectual vitality having been sorely challenged by Richard Hooker. Certainly the greatest piece of theological literature to appear in the latter part of Elizabeth's reign was Hooker's monumental work *Of the Laws of Ecclesiastical Polity*, written to affirm the Church of England as an Anglo-Catholic institution against its Puritan detractors.

"Judicious" Hooker — so called because of the great comprehensiveness and balanced cadences of his thought — was born in Exeter in 1554 of a poor, Protestant, even Puritan family. Given the patronage of Bishop John Jewel, young Hooker was admitted to Corpus Christi College, Oxford, where, having attained the credentials of a scholar, he was eventually ap-

139. Richard Hooker

661

pointed a fellow of the college. Bashful and retiring, Hooker passed his life as an obscure don and rector. A controversy with Walter Travers, however, the Puritan intellectual with whom he successfully contended for the position of master of the temple, brought Hooker into the public eye and attracted the attention of Whitgift, Burghley, and even Elizabeth herself. He had become the principal propagandist of a new Elizabethan Anglicanism.

The first four books of Hooker's *Ecclesiastical Polity* appeared in 1593, the fifth in 1597. Hooker died in 1600 in Bishopsbourne, Kent, where he was vicar; "judicious" was carved into his grave-marker and was not, as some have thought, the invention of John Locke. The remaining three books of the *Polity*, although completed before Hooker's death, were not published until the period 1648–62, and only then in a haphazard form.

Hooker's *Polity* was the supremely important theological work of the late Elizabethan period for at least three reasons. First, it was a vast, complex, and comprehensive work, reminiscent of the great systems-books of the Middle Ages, in which such important issues as church and state, reason and revelation, Scripture and tradition, Protestant and Catholic were laid out in one orderly system for the inspection of the intellect. Second, no doubt inspired by the author's contest with Walter Travers, Hooker's book presented Anglicanism positively, comprehensively, and competitively. Young scholars in the universities had at last a fascinating body of Anglican divinity to challenge their wits, alongside the ponderous material coming from Rome, Wittenberg, or Geneva. Third, as he assayed and rejected the exaggerations of both Roman Catholicism and Protestantism, Hooker carved out an Anglo-Catholicism that was, as Elizabeth wanted: a middle, or third, way.

Ecclesiastical Polity begins with three prefatory notices, including an excursus on the touchy question of justification and a preface in which the dangers of Puritanism are recounted. In the second book, Hooker comments critically on the Puritan assumption that Scripture is the sole authority, not only for salvation, but for virtually all human affairs. If Rome finds Scripture "unsufficient," and if the Puritans find Scripture sufficient for "all things simply," Hooker prefers to say that some truth is opened by Scripture, some by nature, some by fresh spiritual insight, some by experience and reason. It ill behooves human beings to belittle any of those means chosen by Wisdom to disclose herself. While Hooker does not doubt that Scripture is an essential and even exclusive authority where issues of salvation are at stake, he is equally certain that Scripture requires the confirmation of human

662

"capacity and judgment." "The authority of man is, if we mark it, the key which openeth the door of entrance into the knowledge of the Scripture."

In book 3, Hooker challenges the Puritan assumption that the Scripture prescribes an exact blueprint for the constitution of the church from which no person may deviate in any particular, as if Puritan Presbyterianism were "a part of the Gospel." Hooker denied the necessity of any one form of church polity. It seemed to him that the same Holy Ghost who inspired the Scriptures might still be able to inspire human beings, directing them to legitimate, God-given forms of church government consonant with reason. It must also be noted that Hooker avoided the more conservative Anglican position, which asserted that episcopacy was *de jure divino,* that is, according to the law of God.

While Hooker challenged Puritanism intellectually, Whitgift sorely tried what remained of its organization. A dogged campaigner, the archbishop used the High Commission against the Puritans whenever and wherever he could. By 1580 the High Commission had become a court devoted to the suppression of religious pluralism throughout Elizabeth's realm. As grist for the High Commission, Whitgift published twenty-four articles in 1583, in which such sensitive issues as ecclesiastical dress, subscription to the Book of Common Prayer, adherence to Archbishop Parker's *Advertisements,* and the cessation of prophesyings were all firmly clamped on the consciences of Puritans, like it or not. So fiercely, so ruthlessly did Whitgift assail the Puritans that even members of Elizabeth's Privy Council were moved to protest. Elizabeth herself was conspicuously silent. Whitgift kept right on going until Tudor Puritanism was a shambles, its presbyterian structures smashed, its pamphleteers suppressed, its ministers squeezed into whimpering conformity. Seldom before or since has the Church of England seemed so ferocious.

The death of Leicester, Puritanism's chief advocate in the council, and of Field, its chief organizer — both in 1588 — cost the movement dearly. Old Cartwright persisted, spent 1590–92 in jail, issued a last hurrah (his *Apology*) in 1596, and faded away to Guernsey, where he expired in 1604. The Puritan choir in Commons fell silent, except for an occasional outburst, such as the one in 1593 against the tyranny of the High Commission. The year 1593 also saw the execution of three separatists — Henry Barrow, John Greenwood, and John Penry. Barrow's London congregation saw fit to flee to Amsterdam, where they all had a good sectarian quarrel; a remnant made it all the way to Plymouth Rock.

Thus by the end of Elizabeth's reign, the Church of England had become, in fact, the Church of England. And who can deny that it was in large measure the queen's own doing?

Meanwhile the English Catholics were also made to suffer under the oppressive machinery of the Tudor state. An act of 1593 restricted Catholics to a distance of five miles from their domicile. The recusancy laws (laws pertaining to the Catholics' refusal to attend Anglican worship) were so severe that Catholics faced exile if they could not afford the stiff recusancy fines. The war with Spain had created a dilemma for English Catholics. Could they possibly perceive of Philip II as an instrument of God, as the Jesuits proposed? Could they possibly acknowledge a Spanish succession to the throne of England in preference to a Stuart succession? A pamphlet by the Jesuit Robert Parsons (1594) advocated no less. Questions such as those rent the Catholic constituency, the Jesuits generally affirming Spanish interests, while the diocesan clergy remained fiercely English and Elizabethan.

In the midst of this crisis, Cardinal Allen died (1594). At Jesuit insistence, the pope appointed a diocesan priest, George Blackwell, to rule the English Catholics, knowing that Blackwell was a crypto-Jesuit, that is, convinced of Jesuit ideals and committed to Jesuit aims. For six years the diocesan priests of England resisted Blackwell, until an exasperated papacy finally abandoned the whole lot of them, leaving them to the Jesuits or Elizabeth's agents, whichever may have been worse. Exactly at that point Elizabeth might have reconciled the preponderance of English Catholics if she had conceded freedom of worship. She would not. At the very end of the reign, in November 1602, Elizabeth's government went to the length of expelling all Catholic priests except those diocesan clergy willing to swear loyalty. Thirteen did. Thus was English Catholicism divided and left anomalous.

THE ELIZABETHAN RENAISSANCE

THE REIGN of Elizabeth, already conspicuous for its longevity and grand achievements, came to a close with a brilliant Renaissance of letters. The Elizabethan Renaissance ought not to be dissociated from the greater Renaissance that began in Italy in 1300 and sweetened all of European experience in the several centuries that followed. The so-called New Learning began in England with the importation of Italian humanism by Erasmus, Colet, and More at the start of Henry VIII's reign. In the beginning, it consisted of such diverse intellectual strands as Italian classicism and Florentine Neoplatonism; the biblical scholarship of Colet, Erasmus, and Tyndale; the ethical idealism of More and Erasmus; the disgust expressed by such as Erasmus and Tyndale toward medieval piety and Scholasticism; and the introduction of Greek into the English universities by William Grocyn and Thomas Linacre. It produced a manifestation of new colleges and schools — Jesus (1496), Christ's (1505), St. John's (1511), Magdalene (1542), Trinity (1546), and Emmanuel (1584) at Cambridge; Brasenose (1509), Corpus Christi (1517), Christ Church (1525), and Jesus at Oxford, not to mention Eton, Westminster, and Harrow, which appeared in the same era.

Many of those colleges were associated with the English Reformation, and some, such as Trinity and Emmanuel, were remarkably Puritan in their sympathies. Despite the connection between the English universities and the English Reformation, a new definition arose during the Tudor era of both the client and curriculum proper to education. The client of education was no longer exclusively the curate, but increasingly the citizen. In other words, education was not simply at the service of someone seeking clerical orders but was deemed just as useful, if not more so, to a would-be gentleman, a person of letters, specifically secular in calling, someone who saw the purpose of his education and of his career to be citizenship — that is, service to the state and to society.

The great exemplar of the New Learning was Cicero — or, to use the Petrarchian synthesis, the exemplars were Cicero and Christ. At any rate, the English humanists looked to Cicero, whose Latinity, ethics, and educational philosophy were deemed exemplary. It was the Ciceronian premise that, in order to become fully human, in order to exercise all of the formidable intellectual power and moral purpose that attaches to human nature, one must become learned in the arts and letters, in the classics specifically, and that the chief end of such education was a secular calling — citizenship. According to G. R. Elton: "By combining classical learning with medieval knighthood, [the Ciceronian tradition in England] created the ideal of the gentleman, that powerful civilising influence of the next two hundred years: of that ideal, Sir Philip Sidney, who fused knightly 'courtesy' with humanistic learning and the Elizabethan courtier's love of poetry, stands as the first English embodiment."

Educational opinions of that sort acquired some reputable advocates in sixteenth-century England, including two royal tutors — John Cheke (1514–57), who taught Edward VI, and Roger Ascham (1515–68), who taught Elizabeth. Both were Greek scholars. As Cheke was indebted to Sir Thomas Elyot's *Governour* (1531), in which the education of a gentleman was discussed, Ascham was indebted to Cheke; Ascham's *Scholemaster* (1570) informed the educational philosophy of most of Elizabeth's reign.

Given the encouragement afforded by the printing industry, which began in 1476 when William Caxton (1422–91) set up shop, the Tudor era became one of significant publication. Modern English historical writing began with the appearance of Polydore Vergil's *Anglica historia*. It was modern in the sense that, by being based on historical sources, it overcame some of the disreputable characteristics of the chronicles that were produced in the later Middle Ages. Vergil (1470–1555), an Italian humanist and papal collector assigned to England, used the historical-critical tools of scholarship developed in Italy. The tradition began by Vergil reached its consummation in William Camden's *Annales regnante Elizabetha* (1615). Meanwhile, both Edward Hall and Richard Holinshed had popularized Vergil, and history generally, for English consumption; from Holinshed's voluminous chronicles, the Elizabethan dramatists drew much of their historical matter. If Vergil was the father of modern English history, Thomas More was the father of modern English biography. His standard-setting *History of Richard III* (1514) was followed by George Cavendish's *Life of Wolsey* (1557) and Francis Bacon's *Henry VII* (1622). The first collection of Bacon's *Essays*, on moral and philosophical subjects, also appeared in Elizabeth's reign (1597), as did Hooker's *Ecclesiastical Policy*.

As far as the fine arts were concerned, the Tudor age was deficient — except for exuberant costumes. The only major painter of the early Tudor period was an outsider — Hans Holbein the Younger, a citizen of Switzerland. The only Renaissance artist of any reputation who worked in England was Torrigiano from Florence; he built the tomb of Henry VII at Westminster. Most new architecture was perpendicular Gothic and therefore not of the Renaissance at all. The Elizabethan era produced only two painters of any prominence — George Gower, a court painter, and Nicholas Hillyard, who excelled at miniatures.

The Elizabethan Renaissance expressed itself chiefly in the English language — that heretofore plain and ungainly vehicle — to some extent in prose, handsomely in poetry, incomparably in drama.

The first to give style to English prose was John Lyly (1554–1606), whose two romances, *Euphues* (1579) and *Euphues his England* (1580), provided the name of a distinct (and disagreeable) style of prose — euphuism, distinguished by overwrought flourishes, including artful antitheses, lots of alliteration, and so on. Sir Philip Sidney, although a better craftsman than Lyly, partook of euphuism, in witness of which is his romance *Arcadia*, first published posthumously in 1590. The best English prose of the Elizabethan age is thought to have been the translations of ancient classics or Renaissance texts made in that period. Perhaps one should not invoke the Bible in the same sentence with Boccaccio and Machiavelli, but no piece of prose did more to establish English as a literary language than the *Authorised Version,* which was a translation of the Scriptures made in 1611.

The Renaissance of English poetry was begun toward the end of Henry VIII's reign by two poets who were well represented in *Tottel's Miscellany* (1557), an important anthology of English poetry; they were Sir Thomas Wyatt (1503–42) and Henry Howard, earl of Surrey (1517–47). Theirs is the distinction of having introduced the sonnet to English literature, principally in imitation of Italian and French Renaissance poets. Wyatt, for example, was greatly taken by the sonnets of Petrarch, and established an English sonnet tradition that peaked in the 1580s and 1590s. The poetic tradition begun by Wyatt and Surrey was not a mere imitation of Italian and French works: new meters and verse forms more suited to the English language were developed. Increasingly in the Elizabeth's reign, the conviction developed that English could be a literary language: the poets of *Tottel's Miscellany* felt a need to apologize for using English, by the end of the reign this was no longer the case.

Elizabethan poetry attained its highest expression in the works of Sir Philip Sidney (1554–86) and Edmund Spenser (1552–99). Sidney's *Defense of Poesy* (1582–83) showed the influence of Horace and continental Renaissance scholars in its valorization of poetry. The works of Spenser included *The Shepherd's Calendar* (1579), a series of twelve pastoral poems; the *Faerie Queene* (1589ff.), a lengthy allegorical poem that the poet saw as his chief work, akin to Virgil's *Aeneid; Mother Hubberd's Tale* (1595) and *Colin Clout Come Home Again* (1595), satires that made fun of contemporary poetry and loathsome people at court. Spenser's works raised English poetry to an exalted state, considering both its imagery and its language. In addition to his *Arcadia,* Sidney composed a sequence of sonnets — *Astrophel and Stella* (1584) — that encouraged a succession of sonnet-makers, including William Shakespeare, who produced an incomparable cycle of 154 sonnets.

It is for its theater that the Elizabethan Renaissance is chiefly remembered today. Here the application of "Renaissance" is particularly apt, for the chief antecedent for English drama was the classical tradition. English humanists preferred to sharpen their students' use of Latin by encouraging them to perform Latin plays, many of which were taken from ancient Roman originals. Latin plays were presented at Cambridge and Oxford on the

140. William
Shakespeare

occasion of royal visits. If plays were popular at the university, they also came into vogue at the Inns of Court, where dramas were produced after classical or Italian Renaissance models.

Two developments at the middle of Elizabeth's reign were prerequisite to the era of Shakespeare — the court play and the public stage. Both had the effect of removing the theater from university incubation, where it had begun, and of transferring it to places that could contribute to its development and to its popularity. John Lyly, whose euphuistic novels we have noted, was partially responsible for the growing delight taken in the theater by the court. Lyly wrote for the assorted fops and dandies, not to mention clergy and statesmen, who surrounded Elizabeth. His plays, based on classical mythology and ancient history, portrayed such stuff as captured maidens whose affections were contested for by powerful men. Small wonder that the court was titillated. By 1575 the office of revels had taken on the characteristics of a booking agency, an actual theatrical company in its own right — which may explain how the lord chamberlain became an officer of censoring and licensing.

At almost the same time, the public theater began in England, as companies of actors sought out the patronage of people of means and began to perform in public theaters built to their specifications. The first such stage in England was the theater in Shoreditch, built in 1576 by James Burbage, father of the famous Elizabethan actor Richard Burbage. The next was the Curtain. When opposition arose toward the theatrical crowd, the companies took the expedient of crossing over to Bankside, where a succession of theaters was built, including the Swan (1594) and the Globe (1598). Theaters, performers, patrons, Renaissance precedents, royal approval — even the bluenoses who protested — all existed; it was time for the playwright. The first major playwright was Thomas Kyd (1558–95), who was long on plots and short on poetry, and whose plays, beginning with the *Spanish Tragedy* (1585), were preoccupied with sudden death and terrible revenge. When copious bloodletting and the pileup of corpses exhausted the known supply of such plots, playwrights were driven to history, and more precisely, to the chronicles — that inexhaustible supply of such stuff, whether from the distant past (e.g., Henry V) or from the immediate past (e.g., Thomas Cromwell, Thomas More, and Foxe's *Book of Martyrs*). Frequently, these historical plays were used to comment indirectly on contemporary affairs.

Christopher Marlowe's (1564–93) four major plays — *Tamburlaine the Great* (1590), *The Jew of Malta* (1590), *Edward II* (1591), and *The Tragical History of Doctor Faustus* (1592) — were conspicuously clumsy in story but written in sublime poetry, without equal except in Shakespeare. Working at the same time, but of lesser rank, were the university wits — Robert Greene (1560–92), George Peele (1558–97), and Thomas Nash (1567–1601) — who left Cambridge to work in the London theater. Above all other playwrights was William Shakespeare (1564–1616), whose thirty-seven plays represent the greatest achievement in English drama. Others in the English dramatic tradition — Ben Jonson (1573–1637) was the most prominent — belong more appropriately to the succeeding reign.

EPILOGUE

NOT MANY of us are prescient enough to anticipate the death of a statesman or the transition from one order to another. Yet the last decade of Elizabeth's reign was filled with signs of transition. The people who managed England — members of the Privy Council and such — were generally people of lesser stature. By 1598, Leicester, Walsingham, and Burghley were all gone. Gone too were the great sea heroes, except for Raleigh. In the Church of England, the Presbyterian Puritans had been quite smartly put down, while the Catholics in England were badly divided and just as badly embarrassed. In Anglicanism itself, the older Calvinist basis had been supplanted by a new Anglo-Catholicism, of which Lancelot Andrewes and Richard Bancroft were prominent advocates.

In the 1590s the rights of Parliament became an issue again — this time over the question of succession. On this issue Peter Wentworth found his voice again. In speeches to the Commons and in his "Pithy Exhortation to Her Majesty for Establishing the Succession" (never published), he argued that unless the succession was established at once on Protestant terms, England might have to suffer yet another Catholic monarch. In 1591 the council sent him to prison on account of his vexations, and the Commons suspended him. He died in the Tower in 1597, as stubborn at seventy-three as he was in his youth. Wentworth was a consistent and formidable advocate of free speech.

What made Parliament's squabbles with Elizabeth credible in the nineties was the queen's paltry exchequer, left in a miserable estate by the drains of war. Battles over subsidies raised serious issues, not simply between queen and Parliament, but between the Commons and the Lords. The issue became, Whose initiative was it to propose legislation governing finance? In short, who held the purse strings of England? When the Commons was found to hold the line on expenditures, Elizabeth attempted to work her will through the House of Lords; she thought she could get more by using the leverage of the Lords. That maneuver, however, set off a fierce debate over whose privilege it was to initiate and regulate subsidies. The outcome was that, while Elizabeth managed to get most of what she needed, the Commons also managed to protect its prerogative of initiating money bills.

That issue was hardly out of the way before Elizabeth again clashed with Parliament — this time over monopolies. Elizabeth could create monopolies by the simple device of issuing letters patent. Elizabeth liked monopolies because they enabled her to pay debts and win favors without any real cost to herself. If a monopoly worked to raise prices, what of it? A little inflation would not hurt. Rather more loathsome was the fact that an aggrieved party to an unfair monopoly had no redress in court. Indeed, the *non obstante* ("notwithstanding") version of a monopoly enabled the monarch to dispense with laws governing the import, export, or trade in specified goods. As early as 1597, Parliament complained to Elizabeth about the abuses attached to monopolies and proposed to abolish them. Elizabeth, as usual, sent up a shower of words without saying much, if anything. The growing anger in Parliament over the evils associated with monopolies increasingly poisoned the atmosphere of the queen's final decade. As the century turned, Elizabeth finally caught on to the disfavor in which she was being held. In one last, magnificent stroke, she explained to Parliament how aghast she was at suddenly having discovered how many bad monopolies oppressed the people; she issued a royal proclamation forthwith, abolishing some monopolies and putting others under the regulation of law. In what was to be her last reception of her subjects, Elizabeth received a delegation of the Commons on November 30, 1601, come to thank her for giving remedy to the monopoly system, and in a "golden speech," made her farewell: "This I count the glory of my crown, that I have reigned with your loves."

One final, ugly scene remained to be played out. The chief player was Essex, whose arrogance and whose hold over the popular imagination made him a genuine danger to the realm. Despite the affection in which the queen held him, Essex mocked Elizabeth as having taken leave of her senses and of having become, like the rest of her government, an unwanted encumbrance. (Generally speaking, it was Essex's custom to despise almost everyone.) In September 1599, after the debacle in Ireland, Essex was committed to the custody of Sir Thomas Egerton and kept under house arrest for approximately a year, while the remnant of his Irish army, officers especially, assembled in London and clamored for his release and his return to power. The people of London became mesmerized by such agitation and fell into a similar mood, rallying around Essex and demanding his ascendancy. The popular appeal of Essex soon became very appreciable.

In 1600 Elizabeth moved decisively against Essex — not by a public trial as she had at first wanted, but in a private hearing that began in June. Five charges were brought against him, none of them even touching on treason, but all of them having to do with his conduct of the Irish campaign. Eschewing a defense, Essex threw himself on the queen's mercy and was stripped of his offices, removed from the Privy Council, and put under house arrest. He expected Elizabeth to relent and forgive. She did not. In September she refused to renew his monopoly on sweet wine, on which his fortunes depended. His talk against the queen grew ugly. From Essex House, where he was confined, manifold plots were hatched bearing both upon a Protestant succession and upon Essex's own delivery. Elizabeth's council, taking note of such activities, ordered Essex to appear in February 1601. When on

February 8, four of Elizabeth's privy councillors appeared at Essex's lodgings to summon him, Essex arrested them; then he and a crowd of some two hundred hotheads sallied forth into London to arouse the city to rebellion, yet not precisely to overthrow Elizabeth, but to exalt Essex. "For the queen, for the queen; there is a plot against my life!" Such was the formula of the insurrection. It amounted to very little. Essex and his colleagues were arrested; within nine days he was tried, convicted, and executed. "Sweet England's pride is gone — welladay, welladay." So ran the popular lament over the passing of Essex. The Tudor monarchy had begun with the necessity of suppressing the overweening arrogance of nobles who had set their own ambitions above crown and state, and so the Tudor monarchy had ended.

On March 24, 1603, as she approached her seventieth year, Elizabeth died quietly. The Tudor era was over; there were no more Tudors. It had been a remarkable dynasty. Where there had been civil war, the Tudors had brought domestic peace and unity; where there had been depression, the Tudors had brought enterprise and a rising prosperity; where there had been a dilapidated government, unfit to manage well either at home or abroad, the Tudors had brought a new state and the possibility of world-power status; where there had been skepticism and indifference toward religion, the Tudors had brought a new Anglicized version of organized religion.

EXCURSUS

Foxe's *Book of Martyrs*

FOXE'S *Book of Martyrs* WAS ONE OF THE MOST SUCCESSFUL BOOKS OF THE Elizabethan age. Published in 1563, it quickly took its place alongside the English Bible and the English prayer book as part of the indispensable library in every pious, Protestant English home. If it confirmed the English in hostility toward Roman Catholicism, that was merely part of its purpose. Treating as it did the whole sweep of Christianity as a history of martyrdom, Foxe's *Book of Martyrs* also managed to inculcate a philosophy of history that owed its existence to Augustine's *City of God*. Such a philosophy of history had at least these eleven particulars.

First, in spite of what the ancient philosophers, poets, and historians may have thought, history is not an endless cycle of chance and change, a cyclic ebb and flow ascribed to the inconstancy of Fortuna. At the end of his account of the Norman Conquest, for example, the Italian humanist Polydore Vergil wrote: "And thus do all human events ebb and flow, so that nothing is so certain as uncertainty itself and continual change into better or into worse." Polydore's conception of history was emphatically out of favor with the line of historical interpreters from Augustine to Foxe.

Second, history moves in a succession of ages, and so on and on to a concluding age always more or less imminent. Or, to change the figure, history moves in successive waves, to break finally upon a predestined shore when the end of history will come and the Creator's ultimate purposes for history will be achieved.

Third, within history, God is Providence. As Augustine said, The affairs of earthly history are "ruled and governed by one God as he pleases." History is thus primarily not cycles but sequence or succession, not fate or Fortuna but Providence.

Fourth, the ages become corrupt as human beings who live in them become corrupt — through disobedience. The ages are renewed, actually replaced, by the intervention of God. Therefore the ages of history are all characterized by the same story — the disobedience of men and women owing to their fallen state and the reestablishment of Judeo-Christian values through a small remnant of faithful people who are obedient to God, even though they must suffer in order to be obedient.

Fifth, therefore the history of martyrs is an important index to the world's history. When one hears the deaths of Latimer and Ridley recounted, one is hearing yet another important chapter in the providential character of history.

Sixth, history therefore is a work of creation, not the result of "evolution" or "progress," as if history had its own source of energy.

Seventh, Augustine thought that the providential care of history had devolved upon two agencies — the City of God, which was approximate to the Catholic Church, although never definitively identified with it, and the City of Earth, approximate to the civil order and, although often corrupt, useful to society and therefore never to be despised. In Augustine's characterization, the heavenly city rests on the love of God, and the people live "according to God." The earthly city, in contrast, rests on the love of self, worldly goods, and pride of power, and the people live "merely according to man." Both cities are destined to endure until the end of human history, each city having its own continuity. The earthly city owes its existence to the fact of the fall of Adam. The victims of the Fall huddled together to form a city, "earthly both in its beginning and in its end." It has a good of its own — an earthly peace that is itself a gift of God.

Eighth, using the analogy of the creation in seven days, Augustine divided history into seven ages, of which, he thought, his own age was the last. In this "Christian era," Christ reigned in his church, the gods of Rome having been driven, not simply out of their temples, but out of the heart of worshipers.

Ninth, Foxe was forced to recalculate the epochs of history, simply because of the passage of time. By Foxe's era, Augustine's description of things had been utterly transfigured by historical circumstances themselves. The Catholic Church, for example, so far from being approximate to the City of God, had, in Foxe's opinion, taken on the characteristics of Antichrist, while the earthly city, namely, Elizabethan England, was none other than the Elect Nation, to be used by God to bring history to its fulfillment.

Tenth, Foxe's *Book of Martyrs* may have been the first time, but by no means the last time, that Puritans referred to an "Elect Nation" and a "New Jerusalem" — namely, the serving of God's providential will in history through national purposes.

Finally, printing, as Foxe understood it, was an invention of God himself through his agent Gutenberg to consolidate the Reformation and thus bring history to its end.

A Select Bibliography of Works
on the Renaissance and Reformation

I. BIBLIOGRAPHIES AND GUIDES

Bibliographie Internationale de l'Humanisme et de la Renaissance. Geneva: Droz, Annual.

Brady, Thomas A. *Handbook of European History, 1400–1600: Late Middle Ages, Renaissance and Reformation.* Leiden and New York: E. J. Brill, 1994.

Kohl, Benjamin G. *Renaissance Humanism, 1300–1550: A Bibliography of Materials in English.* New York: Garland, 1985.

Ozment, Steven E. *Reformation Europe: A Guide to Research.* St. Louis: Center for Reformation Research, 1982.

II. GENERAL AND BACKGROUND WORKS

Baron, Hans. *The Crisis of the Early Italian Renaissance: Civic Humanism and Republican Liberty in an Age of Classicism and Tyranny.* Princeton: Princeton University Press, 1966.

Burckhardt, Jacob. *The Civilization of the Renaissance in Italy.* 2 vols. Translated by S. G. C. Middlemore. New York: Harper & Row, 1958.

Counter-Reformation and the Price Revolution, 1559-1610, The. Vol. 3 of *The New Cambridge Modern History.* Cambridge: Cambridge University Press, 1968.

675

Dannenfeldt, Karl H. *The Renaissance: Medieval or Modern?* Boston: Heath, 1959.

The Economy of Expanding Europe in the Sixteenth and Seventeenth Centuries. Vol. 2 of *The Cambridge Economic History of Europe.* Cambridge: Cambridge University Press, 1967.

Eisenstein, Elizabeth L. *The Printing Press as an Agent of Change.* 2 vols. Cambridge: Cambridge University Press, 1978.

Ferguson, Wallace K. *Europe in Transition 1300–1520.* Boston: Houghton Mifflin Company, 1962.

———. *The Renaissance.* New York: Holt, 1940.

———. *The Renaissance in Historical Thought.* Boston: Houghton Mifflin Company, 1948.

Ginzburg, Carlo. *The Cheese and the Worms.* Translated by John and Anne Tedeschi. New York: Penguin, 1982.

Green, V. H. H. *Renaissance and Reformation: A Survey of European History between 1450 and 1660.* London: Arnold, 1952.

Hale, J. R. *Renaissance Exploration.* London, 1968.

Hay, Denys. *Europe in the Fourteenth and Fifteenth Centuries.* New York: Holt, Rinehart & Winston, 1967.

———. *The Renaissance Debate.* New York: Holt, Rinehart & Winston, 1965.

Highet, Gilbert. *The Classical Tradition: Greek and Roman Influences in Western Literature.* London: Oxford University Press, 1967.

Houston, R. A. *Literacy in Early Modern Europe.* London: Longman, 1988.

Huizinga, Johan. *The Waning of the Middle Ages.* Translated by F. Hopman. Harmondsworth: Penguin, 1968.

Kerrigan, William, and Gordon Braden. *The Idea of the Renaissance.* Baltimore: Johns Hopkins University Press, 1989.

Mattingly, Garrett. *Renaissance Diplomacy.* Harmondsworth: Penguin, 1965.

Nowell, Charles E. *The Great Discoveries and the First Colonial Empires.* Ithaca: Cornell University Press, 1954.

Parry, John H. *The Age of Reconnaissance.* Cleveland: World Publishing Co., 1963.

Penrose, Boies. *Travel and Discovery in the Renaissance, 1420–1620.* Cambridge, Mass.: Harvard University Press, 1967.

Phillipps, J. R. S. *The Medieval Expansion of Europe.* New York: Oxford University Press, 1988.

Porter, Roy. *The Renaissance in National Context.* Cambridge: Cambridge University Press, 1992.

Reformation, 1520-1559, The. Vol. 2 of *The New Cambridge Modern History.* Cambridge: Cambridge University Press, 1958.

Renaissance, 1493-1520, The. Vol. 1 of *The New Cambridge Modern History.* Cambridge: Cambridge University Press, 1957.

Roeder, Ralph. *The Man of the Renaissance.* New York: Meridian Books, 1960.

Spitz, Lewis W. *The Renaissance and Reformation Movements.* Chicago: Rand McNally, 1971.

Symonds, J. A. *The Renaissance in Italy.* New York: Capricorn, 1964.

III. RENAISSANCE ART

Ackerman, James S. *The Architecture of Michelangelo.* Middlesex, England: Penguin, 1961.

Argau, Giulio Carlo. *The Renaissance City.* New York: Braziller, 1969.

Baxandall, Michael. *Painting and Experience in Fifteenth Century Italy.* Oxford: Clarendon, 1972.

Berenson, Bernard. *Italian Painters of the Renaissance.* 2 vols. London and New York: Phaidon, 1968.

Berti, L. *Masaccio.* University Park, Penn.: Pennsylvania State University Press, 1967.

Bertram, Anthony. *Florentine Sculpture.* New York: Dutton, 1969.

Blunt, Anthony. *Art and Architecture in France 1500–1700.* 4th ed. Harmondsworth: Penguin, 1980.

Chastel, Andre. *Italian Art.* New York: Harper & Row, 1963.

Christiansen, Carl C. *Art and the Reformation in Germany.* Athens: Ohio University Press, 1979.

Clark, Kenneth M. *Leonardo da Vinci: An Account of His Development as an Artist.* Harmondsworth: Penguin, 1975.

————. *Piero della Francesca.* 2nd ed. New York: Phaidon, 1969.

Cole, Bruce. *Italian Art, 1250–1550: The Relation of Renaissance Art to Life and Society.* New York: Harper & Row, 1987.

Freedberg, S. *Painting in Italy, 1500–1600.* Harmondsworth: Penguin, 1975.

Friedlaender, Max J. *From Van Eyck to Bruegel.* 2 vols. New York: Phaidon, 1969.

Gilbert, Creighton. *Renaissance Art.* New York: Harper & Row, 1970.

Hartt, Frederick. *History of Italian Renaissance Art: Painting, Sculpture, Architecture.* 3rd ed. Englewood Cliffs, N.J.: Prentice-Hall, 1987.

Huse, Norbert, and Wolfgang Wolters. *The Art of Renaissance Venice: Architecture, Sculpture and Painting, 1460–1590.* Chicago: University of Chicago Press, 1990.

Janson, H. W., ed. *Brunelleschi in Perspective.* Englewood Cliffs, N.J.: Prentice-Hall, 1974.

Lieberman, Ralph. *Renaissance Architecture in Venice, 1450–1540.* New York: Abbeville, 1982.

Lowrey, Bates. *Renaissance Architecture.* New York: Braziller, 1969.

Martindale, Andrew. *The Rise of the Artist.* New York: McGraw Hill, 1972.

————, ed. *The Complete Paintings of Mantegna.* Notes and catalogue by Niny Garavaglia. London: Weidenfield & Nicolson, 1971.

Martineau, Jane, ed. *Andrea Mantegna.* London: Royal Academy of Arts, 1992.

Murray, Peter. *The Architecture of the Italian Renaissance.* New York: Schocken Books, 1965.

————. *Architecture of the Renaissance.* New York: Abrams, 1971.

Oertel, Robert. *Early Italian Painting to 1400.* New York: Praeger, 1968.

Panofsky, Erwin. *Albrecht Durer.* Princeton: Princeton University Press, 1948.

————. *Early Netherlandish Painting: Its Origins and Character.* 2 vols. New York: Harper & Row, 1971.

————. *Idea, A Concept in Art Theory.* Columbia: University of South Carolina Press, 1968.

————. *Renaissance and Renascences in Western Art.* New York: Harper & Row, 1972.

————. *Studies in Iconology: Humanistic Themes in the Art of the Renaissance.* New York: Harper, 1939.

Pope-Hennessy, John. *Italian Renaissance Sculpture.* 3rd ed. New York: Vintage, 1985.

————. *The Portrait in the Renaissance.* New York: Bollingen Foundation, 1966.

Smart, Alastair. *The Assisi Problem and the Art of Giotto.* Oxford: Clarendon, 1971.

Steer, John. *A Concise History of Venetian Painting.* New York: Praeger, 1970.

Stokes, Adrian. *The Quattro Cento: A Different Conception of the Italian Renaissance.* New York: Schocken Books, 1968.

Tapie, Victor L. *The Age of Grandeur: Baroque Art and Architecture.* New York: Praeger, 1966.

Vassari, Giorgio. *The Lives of the Artists.* A selection translated by George Bull. Harmondsworth: Penguin, 1972.

Venturi, Lionello, ed. *Botticelli.* New York: Phaidon, 1961.

Wethey, Harold E. *El Greco and His School.* 2 vols. Princeton: Princeton University Press, 1962.

Wethey, Harold. *The Paintings of Titian.* 3 vols. London: Phaidon, 1969–75.

White, John. *Art and Architecture in Italy, 1250–1400.* 2nd ed. Harmondsworth: Penguin, 1987.

Wilde, J. *Venetian Art from Bellini to Titian.* Oxford: Clarendon, 1974.

Wittkower, Rudolf. *Architectural Principles in the Age of Humanism.* 4th ed. New York: St. Martin's, 1988.

————. *Gian Lorenzo Bernini: The Sculptor of Roman Baroque.* 3rd ed. Ithaca: Cornell University Press, 1981.

————. *Palladio and English Palladianism.* London: Thames and Hudson, 1974.

Wölfflin, Heinrich. *Renaissance and Baroque.* Translated by Kathrin Simon. Ithaca, N.Y.: Cornell University Press, 1966.

IV. RENAISSANCE PHILOSOPHY AND HUMANISM

Artz, Frederick B. *Renaissance Humanism.* Kent, Ohio: The Kent State University Press, 1966.

Bainton, Roland H. *Erasmus of Christendom.* New York: Scribner's, 1969.

Baron, Hans. *From Petrarch to Leonardo Bruni.* Chicago: University of Chicago Press, 1968.

Bush, Douglas. *The Renaissance and English Humanism.* Toronto: University of Toronto Press, 1939.

Cassirer, Ernst. *The Individual and the Cosmos in Renaissance Philosophy.* New York: Barnes & Noble, 1963.

Cassirer, Ernst, Paul Oskar Kristeller, and John Herman Randall, Jr. *The Renaissance Philosophy of Man.* Chicago: University of Chicago Press, 1948.

Copenhaver, Brian P., and Charles B. Schmitt. *Renaissance Philosophy.* New York: Oxford University Press, 1992.

Dresen, Sem. *Humanism in the Renaissance.* Translated from the Dutch by Margaret King. World University Library. London: Weidenfeld and Nicolson, 1968.

Gilmore, M. P. *Humanists and Jurists: Six Studies in The Renaissance.* Cambridge, Mass.: Harvard University Press, 1963.

————. *The World of Humanism 1453–1517.* New York: Harper, 1951.

679

Gleason, John B. *John Colet.* Berkeley: University of California Press, 1989.

Huizinga, Johan. *Erasmus and the Age of Reformation.* New York: Harper, 1957.

Kristeller, Paul Oskar. *The Classics and Renaissance Thought.* Cambridge, Mass.: Harvard University Press, 1955.

————. *Eight Philosophers of the Italian Renaissance.* Stanford: Stanford University Press, 1964.

————. *The Philosophy of Marsilio Ficino.* New York: Columbia University Press, 1943.

————. *Renaissance Thought II: Papers on Humanism and the Arts.* New York: Harper & Row, 1965.

————. *Studies in Renaissance Thought and Letters.* Roma: Edizion: di storia e letterature, 1969.

Lupton, J. H. *The Life of John Colet.* London: George Bell and Sons, 1909.

Phillips, Margaret Mann. *Erasmus and the Northern Renaissance.* London: Rowman and Littlefield, 1981.

Rabil, Albert J., ed. *Renaissance Humanism: Foundations, Forms and Legacy.* 3 vols. Philadelphia: University of Pennsylvania Press, 1988.

Skinner, Quentin, and Eckhard Kessler, eds. *The Cambridge History of Renaissance Philosophy.* Cambridge: Cambridge University Press, 1988.

Tracy, James D. *Erasmus, the Growth of a Mind.* Geneva: Droz, 1972.

Trinkaus, Charles. *In Our Image and Likeness: Humanity and Divinity in Italian Humanist Thought.* 2 vols. Chicago: University of Chicago Press, 1970.

Weiss, Roberto. *Humanism in England during the Fifteenth Century.* Oxford: Blackwell, 1957.

————. *The Spread of Italian Humanism.* London: Hutchinson, 1964.

V. RENAISSANCE LITERATURE

Forster, Leonard. *The Icy Fire.* Cambridge: Cambridge University Press, 1969.

Greenblatt, Stephen. *Renaissance Self-Fashioning: From More to Shakespeare.* Chicago: University of Chicago Press, 1980.

Greene, Thomas. *Light in Troy: Imitation and Discovery in Renaissance Poetry.* New Haven: Yale University Press, 1982.

Mazzotta, Giuseppe. *The Worlds of Petrarch.* Durham: Duke University Press, 1993.

Peterson, Douglas L. *The English Lyric from Wyatt to Donne.* Princeton: Princeton University Press, 1967.

Satterthwaite, Alfred W. *Spenser, Ronsard and DuBellay: A Renaissance Comparison*. Princeton: Princeton University Press, 1960.

Waller, Gary. *English Poetry of the Sixteenth Century*. New York: Longman, 1986.

VI. SCIENCE

Butterfield, Herbert. *The Origins of Modern Science, 1300–1800*. New York: Macmillan, 1957.

Crombie, Alistair C. *Augustine to Galileo*. Harmondsworth: Penguin, 1969.

Hall, Alfred R. *The Scientific Revolution 1500–1800*. 2nd ed. Boston: Beacon, 1966.

Kemp, Martin. *Leonardo da Vinci: The Marvellous Works of Nature and Man*. London: J. M. Dent, 1981.

Kuhn, Thomas S. *The Copernican Revolution*. Cambridge, Mass.: Harvard University Press, 1957.

Santillana, Giorgio de. *The Crime of Galileo*. Chicago: University of Chicago Press, 1976.

Wolf, Abraham. *A History of Science, Technology, and Philosophy in the Sixteenth and Seventeenth Centuries*. 3rd ed. Gloucester, Mass.: P. Smith, 1968.

VII. ITALY

Bentley, Jerry H. *Politics and Culture in Renaissance Naples*. Princeton: Princeton University Press, 1987.

Bouwsma, W. J. *Venice and the Defense of Republican Liberty: Renaissance Values in the Age of Counter Reformation*. Berkeley: University of California Press, 1968.

Brucker, Gene A. *Renaissance Florence*. Berkeley: University of California Press, 1985.

Burke, Peter. *The Italian Renaissance: Culture and Society in Italy*. London: Polity Press, 1987.

Chabod, Federico. *Machiavelli and the Renaissance*. Translated by David Moore. New York: Harper & Row, 1965.

Chamberlin, E. R. *The World of the Italian Renaissance*. London: G. Allen & Unwin, 1982.

de Grazia, Sebastian. *Machiavelli in Hell*. Princeton: Princeton University Press, 1989.

Gilbert, Felix. *Machiavelli and Guicciardini: Politics and History in Sixteenth-Century Florence.* New York: Norton, 1984.

Grendler, Paul F. *Schooling in Renaissance Italy: Literacy and Learning, 1300–1600.* Baltimore: Johns Hopkins University Press, 1989.

Guicciardini, Francesco. *The History of Florence.* Translated by Mario Domandi. New York: Harper & Row, 1970.

Hale, J. R. *Machiavelli and Renaissance Italy.* London: English Universities Press, 1961.

Hay, Denys. *The Italian Renaissance in Its Historical Background.* 2nd ed. Cambridge: Cambridge University Press, 1977.

Lane, Frederic. *Venice: A Maritime Republic.* Baltimore: Johns Hopkins University Press, 1977.

Martines, Laura. *Power and Imagination: City-States in Renaissance Italy.* New York: Knopf, 1979.

Neale, John E. *The Age of Catherine de Medici.* London, 1943.

Partner, Peter. *Renaissance Rome, 1500–1599.* Berkeley: University of California Press, 1976.

Plumb, J. H. *The Italian Renaissance.* New York and Evanston: Harper Torchbooks, 1965.

Ridolfi, Roberto. *The Life of Niccolo Machiavelli.* Translated by Cecil Grayson. Chicago: University of Chicago Press, 1974.

———. *Life of Girolamo Savonarola.* London: Routledge and Kegan Paul, 1959.

Rubinstein, Nicolai. *The Government of Florence under the Medici 1434–1494.* Oxford: Clarendon, 1968.

Ryder, A. F. C. *Alfonso the Magnanimous: King of Aragon, Naples and Sicily, 1396–1458.* Oxford: Clarendon, 1990.

Schevill, Ferdinand. *History of Florence: Founding of the City — Through the Renaissance.* New York: R. Ungar, 1961.

———. *The Medici.* New York: Harper, 1960.

Shaw, Christine. *Julius II, the Warrior Pope.* Oxford: Blackwell, 1993.

Villari, P. *Niccolo Machiavelli and His Times.* Translated by Linda Villardi. London, 1929. First published in 1878.

Weinstein, Donald. *Savonarola and Florence.* Princeton: Princeton University Press, 1970.

VIII. FRANCE

Denieul-Cormier, Anne. *A Time of Glory; the Renaissance in France, 1488–1559.* Garden City, N.Y.: Doubleday, 1968.

Greengrass, M. *The French Reformation.* Oxford: Blackwell, 1987.

Hornink, Henry. *Studies on French Renaissance.* Geneva: Slatkine, 1985.

Knecht, R. J. *Francis I.* Cambridge: Cambridge University Press, 1982.

Salmon, J. H. M. *Society in Crisis: France in the Sixteenth Century.* New York: St. Martin's, 1975.

Simone, Franco. *The French Renaissance.* New York: St. Martin's, 1970.

IX. SPAIN

Elliott, John H. *Imperial Spain 1469–1716.* New York: St. Martin's, 1963.

Fernandez-Armesto, Felipe. *Columbus.* New York: Oxford University Press, 1991.

Hillgarth, J. N. *The Spanish Kingdoms, Vol. II, 1410–1516.* Oxford: Clarendon, 1978.

X. NORTHERN AND CENTRAL EUROPE

Geyl, Pieter. *The Revolt of the Netherlands 1555–1609.* London: E. Benn, 1962.

Hoffmeister, Gerhart. *The Renaissance and Reformation in Germany: An Introduction.* New York: F. Ungar, 1977.

XI. ENGLAND

Elton, Geoffrey R. *England under the Tudors.* 3rd ed. London and New York: Routledge, 1991.

Fox, Alistair. *Thomas More: History and Providence.* Oxford: Blackwell, 1982.

Guy, John. *Tudor England.* New York: Oxford University Press, 1988.

Gwyn, Peter. *The King's Cardinal: The Rise and Fall of Thomas Wolsey.* London: Barrie and Jenkins, 1990.

Ives, E. W. *Anne Boleyn.* Oxford: Blackwell, 1986.

King, John N. *Tudor Royal Iconography: Literature and Art in an Age of Religious Crisis.* Princeton: Princeton University Press, 1989.

Loades, David. *The Reign of Mary Tudor.* 2nd ed. London and New York: Longman, 1991.

Marius, R. C. *Thomas More: A Biography.* New York: Knopf, 1984.

Rowse, A. L. *The Elizabethan Renaissance.* 2 vols. London: Macmillan, 1971–72.

Scarisbrick, J. J. *Henry VIII.* London: Methuen, 1968.

Smith, Lacey Baldwin. *Henry VIII: The Mask of Royalty.* London: Cape, 1971.

Starkey, David. *The Reign of Henry VIII: Personalities and Politics.* London: George Philip, 1985.

Tittler, Robert. *The Reign of Mary I.* 2nd ed. London; New York: Longman, 1991.

XII. PRE-REFORMATION STUDIES

Bartos, F. M. *The Hussite Revolution, 1424–1437.* Translated by J. M. Klassen. New York: East European Quarterly, 1986.

Black, Anthony. *Council and Commune: The Conciliar Movement and the Fifteenth-Century Heritage.* London: Burns & Oates, 1979.

Cameron, Euan. *The Reformation of the Heretics: The Waldenses of the Alps, 1480–1580.* New York: Oxford University Press, 1984.

Clark, James M. *The Great German Mystics: Eckhart, Tauler, and Suso.* Oxford: Blackwell, 1949.

D'Amico, J. *Renaissance Humanism in Papal Rome: Humanists and Churchmen on the Eve of the Reformation.* Baltimore: Johns Hopkins University Press, 1983.

Harper-Bill, C. *The Pre-Reformation Church in England, 1400–1530.* London: Longman, 1989.

Heath, Peter. *The English Parish Clergy on the Eve of the Reformation.* Toronto: University of Toronto Press, 1969.

Hudson, Anne. *The Premature Reformation: Wycliffite Texts and Lollard History.* New York: Oxford University Press, 1988.

McGrath, Alistair. *Intellectual Origins of the European Reformation.* Oxford: Blackwell, 1987.

McNeil, David O. *Guillaume Budé and Humanism in the Reign of Francis I.* Geneva: Droz, 1975.

Mollat, Guillaume. *The Popes at Avignon 1305–1378.* London: Nelson, 1963.

Oakley, F. *The Western Church in the Later Middle Ages.* Ithaca, N.Y.: Cornell University Press, 1979.

Oberman, Heiko A. *Forerunners of the Reformation: The Shape of Late Medieval Thought.* New York: Holt, Rinehart & Winston, 1966.

————. *The Harvest of Medieval Theology: Gabriel Biel and Late Medieval Nominalism.* Cambridge, Mass.: Harvard University Press, 1963.

Spinka, Matthew. *John Hus at the Council of Constance.* Translated from the Latin and Czech with notes and introduction. New York: Columbia University Press, 1965.

Swanson, R. N. *Church and Society in Late Medieval England.* Oxford: Blackwell, 1989.

Thomson, John A. F. *The Later Lollards 1414–1520.* New York: Oxford University Press, 1965.

————. *Popes and Princes, 1417–1517: Politics and Piety in the Late Medieval Church.* London: Allen & Unwin, 1980.

Tierney, Brian. *Foundation of Conciliar Theory.* Cambridge: Cambridge University Press, 1955.

Workman, Herbert B. *John Wyclif.* 2 vols. in one. Hamden, Conn.: Archon, 1966 (first published 1926).

XIII. THE REFORMATION — GENERAL

Bossy, John. *Christianity in the West, 1400–1700.* New York: Oxford University Press, 1985.

Cameron, Euan. *The European Reformation.* Oxford: Clarendon, 1991.

Dickens, A. G. *Reformation and Society in Sixteenth-Century Europe.* London: Thames and Hudson, 1966.

————. *The Reformation in Historical Thought.* Cambridge, Mass.: Harvard University Press, 1985.

Elton, Geoffrey R. *Reformation Europe 1517–1559.* New York: Harper & Row, 1963.

Gerrish, B. A., ed. *Reformers in Profile.* Philadelphia: Fortress, 1967.

Grimm, Harold J. *The Reformation Era 1500–1650.* New York: Macmillan, 1965.

Harbison, E. Harris. *The Christian Scholar in the Age of the Reformation.* New York: Scribner's, 1956.

Léonard, E. G. *A History of Protestantism.* Edited by H. H. Rowley and translated by J. M. H. Reid and R. M. Bethell. 2 vols. London: Nelson, 1965–67.

McGrath, Alister E. *Reformation Thought: An Introduction.* Oxford: Blackwell, 1988.

Oberman, Heiko. *The Dawn of the Reformation.* Grand Rapids, Mich.: Eerdmans, 1992.

Reardon, B. M. G. *Religious Thought in the Reformation.* London: Longman, 1981.

Spitz, Lewis W. *The Protestant Reformation, 1517–59.* New York: Harper & Row, 1985.

Whale, J. S. *The Protestant Tradition.* Cambridge: Cambridge University Press, 1959.

XIV. LUTHER AND THE GERMAN REFORMATION

Bainton, Roland H. *Here I Stand: A Life of Martin Luther.* New York: Abingdon-Cokesbury, 1960.

Bornkamm, Heinrich. *Luther's World of Thought.* St. Louis: Concordia, 1958.

Brecht, M. *Martin Luther: His Road to Reformation, 1483–1521.* 3 vols. Translated by J. L. Schaaf. Philadelphia: Fortress, 1985–93.

Fife, Robert H. *The Revolt of Martin Luther.* New York: Columbia, 1957.

Lohse, B. *Martin Luther: An Introduction to His Life and Thought.* Philadelphia: Fortress, 1986.

Lortz, Joseph. *The Reformation in Germany.* Vol. 1. Translated by Ronald Walls. New York: Herder and Herder, 1968.

Mackinnon, James. *Luther and the Reformation.* 4 vols. New York: Russell and Russell, 1962.

McGrath, Alister. *Luther's Theology of the Cross: Martin Luther's Theological Breakthrough.* Oxford: Blackwell, 1985.

Manschreck, Clyde. *Melanchthon: The Quiet Reformer.* New York: Abingdon, 1968.

Schwiebert, E. G. *Luther and His Times.* St. Louis: Concordia, 1950.

Scribner, Robert W. *For the Sake of Simple Folk: Popular Propaganda for the German Reformation.* Cambridge: Cambridge University Press, 1981.

———. *The German Reformation.* London: MacMillan, 1986.

Steinmetz, D. C. *Luther in Context.* Bloomington, Ind.: Indiana University Press, 1986.

Stupperich, Robert. *Melanchthon.* Philadelphia: Westminster, 1960.

XV. ZWINGLI, CALVIN, AND THE REFORMED CHURCHES

Bouwsma, William J. *John Calvin: A Sixteenth-Century Portrait.* New York: Oxford University Press, 1988.

Courvoisier, Jaques. *Zwingli: A Reformed Theologian.* Richmond: John Knox, 1963.

Eells, Hastings. *Martin Bucer.* New Haven: Yale University Press, 1931.

Gäbler, U. *Huldrych Zwingli.* Philadelphia: Fortress, 1986.

Höpfl, H. *The Christian Polity of John Calvin.* Cambridge: Cambridge University Press, 1982.

McGrath, Alister E. *A Life of John Calvin: A Study in the Shaping of Western Culture.* Oxford: Blackwell, 1990.

McNeill, John T. *The History and Character of Calvinism.* New York: Oxford University Press, 1954.

Potter, G. R. *Zwingli.* Cambridge: Cambridge University Press, 1976.

Stephens, W. P. *Zwingli: An Introduction to His Thought.* New York: Oxford University Press, 1992.

Wendel, François. *Calvin: Origins and Development of His Religious Thought.* New York: Harper & Row, 1963.

XVI. THE RADICAL REFORMATION

Littell, Franklin H. *The Anabaptist View of the Church.* Boston: Beacon, 1958.

Williams, George H. *The Radical Reformation.* Philadelphia: Westminster, 1962.

XVII. THE REFORMATION IN ENGLAND

Clebsch, William A. *England's Earliest Protestants, 1520–1535.* New Haven: Yale University Press, 1964.

Collinson, Patrick. *The Birthpangs of Protestant England: Religious and Cultural Change in the Sixteenth and Seventeenth Centuries.* New York: St. Martin's, 1988.

————. *The Elizabethan Puritan Movement.* Berkeley: University of California Press, 1967.

————. *The Religion of Protestants: The Church in English Society 1559–1625.* New York: Oxford University Press, 1982.

687

Dickens, A. G. *The English Reformation.* 2nd ed. London: Batsford, 1989.

Haller, William. *The Rise of Puritanism.* Philadelphia: University of Pennsylvania Press, 1972.

Hopf, Constantin. *Martin Bucer and the English Reformation.* Oxford: Blackwell, 1961.

Knappen, M. M. *Tudor Puritanism.* Chicago: University of Chicago Press, 1970.

Lake, Peter. *Moderate Puritans and the Elizabethan Church.* Cambridge: Cambridge University Press, 1982.

O'Day, Rosemary. *The Debate on the English Reformation.* London: Methuen, 1986.

Pollard, A. F. *Wolsey.* London: Fontana Library, 1965.

Ridley, Jasper. *Thomas Cranmer.* Oxford: Clarendon, 1962.

Rupp, E. G. *Studies in the Making of English Protestant Tradition.* Cambridge: Cambridge University Press, 1949.

Scarisbrick, J. J. *The Reformation and the English People.* Oxford: Blackwell, 1984.

Smith, H. Maynard. *Henry VIII and the Reformation.* New York: Russell and Russell, 1962.

Smyth, C. H. *Cranmer and the Reformation under Edward.* Cambridge: Cambridge University Press, 1926.

Williams, C. H. *William Tyndale.* London: Nelson, 1969.

XVIII. THE REFORMATION IN SCOTLAND

Burleigh, J. H. S. *A Church History of Scotland.* New York: Oxford University Press, 1960.

Cowan, I. B. *The Scottish Reformation: Church and Society in Sixteenth-Century Scotland.* London: Weidenfeld and Nicolson, 1982.

Donaldson, G. *The Scottish Reformation.* Cambridge: Cambridge University Press, 1982.

Ridley, Jasper. *John Knox.* Oxford: Clarendon, 1968.

Wormald, J. *Court, Kirk and Community: Scotland, 1470–1625.* Toronto: University of Toronto Press, 1981.

XIX. THE CATHOLIC REFORMATION

Daniel-Rops, H. *The Catholic Reformation.* New York: Dutton, 1962.

Dickens, A. G. *The Counter Reformation.* New York: Harcourt, Brace & World, 1969.

Evennett, H. O. *The Spirit of the Counter-Reformation.* Edited by John Bossy. Cambridge: Cambridge University Press, 1968.

Friedrich, Carl J. *The Age of the Baroque 1610–1660.* New York: Harper, 1952.

Jedin, Hubert. *A History of the Council of Trent.* 2 vols. to date. Translated by E. Graf. St. Louis: Nelson, 1957–.

Mullett, Michael. *The Counter-Reformation and the Catholic Reformation in Early Modern Europe.* London: Methuen, 1984.

Permissions

BLACK-AND-WHITE PRINTS

1. The Cloister with the Pazzi Chapel and tower. Church of Santa Croce, Florence. Alinari/Art Resource, New York.

2. B. Rossellino, Monument to Leonardo Bruni. Church of Santa Croce, Florence. Alinari/Art Resource, New York.

3. Michelozzo, Library Interior. San Marco Museum, Florence. Alinari/Art Resource, New York.

4. Palazzo Ducale, Urbino. Alinari/Art Resource, New York.

5. Titian, Portrait of a Cardinal, allegedly Bembo. Barberini Gallery, Rome. Alinari/Art Resource, New York.

6. Giotto, *Boniface VIII between Two Cardinals and a Deacon.* Basilica di S. Giovanni in Laterano, Rome. Alinari/Art Resource, New York.

7. Edward Smith, *John Wyckliffe D.D.* Engraving after an original painting. The Bettmann Archive, New York.

8. Czech religious leader Jan Hus (1372 or 1373–1415) at the Council of Constance (1414). Undated illustration. The Bettmann Archive, New York.

9. Donatello and Michelozzo, Monument to Martino V. Basilica di S. Giovanni in Laterano, Rome. Alinari/Art Resource, New York.

10. Monument to Nicholas V. Basilica Vatican, Rome. Alinari/Art Resource, New York.

11. Bust of Pious II. Borgia apartments, Vatican, Rome. Alinari/Art Resource, New York.

12. Pinturicchio, *Pope Alexander.* Vatican, Rome. Alinari/Art Resource, New York.

13. Ignoto Lombardo, Portrait of Cesare Borgia. Palazzo di Venezia, Rome. Alinari/Art Resource, New York.

14. Raphael, Portrait of Pope Julius II. Uffizi, Florence. Alinari/Art Resource, New York.

15. Sebastiano del Piombo, Portrait of Clement VII. Gallerie Nazionale di Capodimonte, Naples. Alinari/Art Resource, New York.

16. Verrocchio, Equestrian Monument of Colleoni. Venice. Alinari/Art Resource, New York.

17. Donatello, *St. Anthony Healing the Feet of a Young Man.* Relief. Basilica of St. Anthony, Padua. Alinari/Art Resource, New York.

18. Andrea Mantegna, San Zeno Altarpiece. Chiesa di San Zeno Maggiore, Verona. Alinari/Art Resource, New York.

19. Ca'd'Oro (House of Gold) Venetian Palace, 1420–1440. Venice. SEF/Art Resource, New York.

20. Palazzo Ducale. Venice. Alinari/Art Resource, New York.

21. Sansovino, Palazzo Reale (Biblioteca). Venice. Alinari/Art Resource, New York.

22. Antonello da Messina, Self-portrait (?). National Gallery, London. Alinari/Art Resource, New York.

23. Titian, Self-Portrait. Gemaeldegalerie Dahlem, Berlin. Foto Marburg/Art Resource, New York.

24. Giovanni Bellini, *Pietà.* Brera, Milan. Alinari/Art Resource, New York.

25. Giovanni Bellini, Portrait of Doge Leonardo Loredano. National Gallery, London. Alinari/Art Resource, New York.

26. Titian, *Paul III and His Grandsons.* Museo Nazionale, Naples. Alinari/Art Resource, New York.

27. Bonifacio Bembo, Portrait of Francesco Sforza. Brera, Milan. Scala/Art Resource, New York.

28. Bernardino dei Conti, *Madonna Enthroned with Christ Child, Doctors of the Church, and Donors Lodovico Moro with His Wife and Children.* Pinacoteca, Milan. Alinari/Art Resource, New York.

29. Leonardo da Vinci, *The Last Supper.* Santa Maria delle Grazie, Milan. Alinari/Art Resource, New York.

30. Santa Maria delle Grazie. Milan. Scala/Art Resource, New York.

31. Leonardo and Verrocchio, *The Baptism of Christ.* Uffizi, Florence. Alinari/Art Resource, New York.

32. Leonardo da Vinci, *The Annunciation of the Virgin.* Uffizi, Florence. Alinari/Art Resource, New York.

33. Leonardo da Vinci, Study for the *Adoration of the Magi.* Drawing Department, Uffizi, Florence. Alinari/Art Resource, New York.

34. Leonardo da Vinci, *Adoration of the Magi.* Uffizi, Florence. Scala/Art Resource, New York.

35. Leonardo da Vinci, *Armored Chariot.* Reale Library, Torino. Scala/Art Resource, New York.

36. Leonardo da Vinci, *Mona Lisa.* Louvre, Paris. Alinari/Art Resource, New York.

37. Leonardo da Vinci, *Anatomical Study* (12281). Windsor. Alinari/Art Resource, New York.

38. Alberti, Facade of Santa Maria Novella. Florence. Foto Marburg/Art Resource, New York.

39. Facade of Palazzo Vecchio (1298–1314). Florence. Alinari/Art Resource, New York.

40. Martini Simona, Detail from a mural painting in the cloister of Santa Maria Novella in Florence, showing Boccaccio and various other personages. The Bettmann Archive, New York.

41. Bronzino, Portrait of Cosimo the Elder. Medici Museum, Florence. Scala/Art Resource, New York.

42. Brunelleschi, The portico of the Foundling Hospital. Piazza of SS. Annunziata, Florence. Alinari/Art Resource, New York.

43. Brunelleschi, Interior of the Church of San Lorenzo. Alinari/Art Resource, New York.

44. Michelozzo, Facade of Palazzo Riccardi. Florence. Alinari/Art Resource, New York.

45. Mino da Fiesole, *Piero de' Medici.* Meseo Nazionale, Florence. Alinari/Art Resource, New York.

46. Verrocchio, Bust of Lorenzo de' Medici. National Museum, Florence. Alinari/Art Resource, New York.

47. Fra Bartolomeo, Portrait of Savonarola. Museo San Marco, Venice. Alinari/Art Resource, New York.

48. Verrocchio, Bust of Piero de' Medici. National Museum, Florence. Alinari/Art Resource, New York.

49. Ciuffag, *Statue of Joshua under the Effigy of Gianozzo Manetti.* Cathedral, Florence. Alinari/Art Resource, New York.

50. Alberti, Facade of Palazzo Rucellai. Florence, 1146-1551. Foto Marburg/Art Resource, New York.

693

51. Leon Battista Alberti, Eastern view of the Malatestiano Temple. Rimini (Emilia). Alinari/Art Resource, New York.

52. Arch of Constantine. Rome. Foto Marburg/Art Resource, New York.

53. Interior of Sant'Andrea, 16th and 17th c. Mantua. Alinari/Art Resource, New York.

54. Niccolo Fiorentino, Medallions of Pico della Mirandola and the Three Graces. National Museum, Florence. Alinari/Art Resource, New York.

55. Cimabue, *Madonna Enthroned.* Uffizi, Florence. Alinari/Art Resource, New York.

56. Giotto, *Madonna Enthroned with Child and Angels.* Uffizi, Florence. Alinari/Art Resource, New York.

57. Lorenzo Ghiberti, *The Sacrifice of Isaac.* National Museum, Florence. Alinari/Art Resource, New York.

58. Lorenzo Ghiberti, North Doors. Baptistry, Florence. Alinari/Art Resource, New York.

59. Lorenzo Ghiberti, Gates of Paradise. Detail, Jacob and Esau panel. Baptistry, Florence. Alinari/Art Resource, New York.

60. Lorenzo Ghiberti, Gates of Paradise. Detail, Adam and Eve panel. Baptistry, Florence. Alinari/Art Resource, New York.

61. Donatello, *David.* Marble. Museo Nazionale, Florence. Alinari/Art Resource, New York.

62. Donatello, *David.* Bronze. Bargello, Florence. Giraudon/Art Resource, New York.

63. Donatello, Equestrian Statue of Gattamaleta. Padua. Alinari/Art Resource, New York.

64. Donatello, *The Magdalen.* Baptistry, Florence. Alinari/Art Resource, New York.

65. Michelangelo, *The Pietà.* St. Peter's, Rome. Alinari/Art Resource, New York.

66. Michelangelo, *David.* Accademia, Florence. Alinari/Art Resource, New York.

67. Raphael, *Madonna of the Grand Duke.* Pitti Palace, Florence. Alinari/Art Resource, New York.

68. Michelangelo, Slave from the tomb of Julius II. Louvre, Paris. Alinari/Art Resource, New York.

69. Michelangelo, *Moses.* S. Pietro in Vincoli, Rome. Foto Marburg/Art Resource, New York.

70. Raphael, Stanze of Raphael, detail of vault. *Original Sin.* Vatican Palace, Rome. Alinari/Art Resource, New York.

694

71. Raphael, *The Sistine Madonna.* Dresden. Alinari/Art Resource, New York.

72. Raphael, Portrait of Leo X. Galleria Palatina, Florence. Alinari/Art Resource, New York.

73. Michelangelo and Vasari, The staircase in the vestibule, Laurentian Library. Florence.

74. Michelangelo, Interior of the Sistine Chapel. Vatican, Rome. Alinari/Art Resource, New York.

75. Michelangelo, Palazzo Senatorio. Rome. Alinari/Art Resource, New York.

76. Michelangelo, *The Pietà.* Cathedral, Florence. Alinari/Art Resource, New York.

77. Michelangelo, *The Rondanini Pietà.* Rondanini Palace, Rome. Alinari/Art Resource, New York.

78. Raphael, *Jurisprudence.* Stanze of Raphael, Vatican Palace, Rome. Alinari/Art Resource, New York.

79. Michelangelo, Interior of the new sacristy of San Lorenzo. Florence. Alinari/Art Resource, New York.

80. Michelangelo, Monument to Lorenzo de' Medici. San Lorenzo, Florence. Alinari/Art Resource, New York.

81. Michelangelo, Tomb of Giuliano de' Medici. Medici Chapel, Florence. Alinari/Art Resource, New York.

82. Michelangelo, *Virgin and Child.* Medici Chapel, Florence. Alinari/Art Resource, New York.

83. Santi di Tito, Portrait of Niccolò Machiavelli. Palazzo Vecchio, Florence. Alinari/Art Resource, New York.

84. Portrait of Queen Isabella of Spain. Painting, 15th c., attributed to Baldome Bermejo. Palacio Real, Madrid. The Bettmann Archive, New York.

85. Napolitan School, 15th c. Bust of Ferdinand I of Aragon. Marble. Louvre, Paris. Alinari/Art Resource, New York.

86. Gonçalves, Polyptych of Saint Vincent. Panel of the Child: detail of the head of Henry the Navigator. Mus. Nac. de Arte Antiga, Lisbon. Giraudon/Art Resource, New York.

87. Anonymous, Presumed portrait of Vasco da Gama, 16th c. Mus. Nac. de Arte Antiga, Lisbon.

88. Portrait of Amerigo Vespucci. Gallerie Nazionali Capodimonte, Naples. Alinari/Art Resource, New York.

89. Hans Holbein the Younger, *Erasmus.* Louvre, Paris. Alinari/Art Resource, New York.

90. John Colet. The Bettmann Archive, New York.

91. Hans Holbein the Younger, Portrait of Thomas More. Villa Albani, Rome. Alinari/Art Resource, New York.

92. Guillaume Budé (1467–1540), French scholar. The Bettmann Archive, New York.

93. F. Clouet, Marguerite de Valois, Queen of Navarre, Sister of Francois I. Musée Conde, Chantilly. Giraudon/Art Resource, New York.

94. Lucas Cranach the Elder, Portrait of Luther in 1533. Giraudon/Art Resource, New York.

95. Lucas Cranach the Elder, Portrait of The Electorate Johann Friedrich. Formerly Schmidt Collection, Berlin. Foto Marburg/Art Resource, New York.

96. Lucas Cranach the Elder (workshop), *Melanchthon*. Berlin. Foto Marburg/Art Resource, New York.

97. Titian, *Charles V.* Prado, Madrid. Alinari/Art Resource, New York.

98. Anonymous, French 16th c. *Anthony Marcault presenting his translation of Diodore of Sicily to Francis I and Court,* c. 1532. Musée Conde, Chantilly. Giraudon/Art Resource, New York.

99. Martin Bucer (1491–1551), German Protestant reformer. Undated engraving. The Bettmann Archive, New York.

100. Heinrich Giebel, Portrait of Count Philip of Hesse after Cranach. Foto Marburg/Art Resource, New York.

101. Zwingli at age 48. Portrait medallion. Foto Marburg/Art Resource, New York.

102. Anonymous, French 16th c. Portrait of Calvin, called the Portrait of Rotterdam. Musée Boymans, Rotterdam. Snark/Art Resource, New York.

103. Bernini, *Ecstasy of St. Theresa.* Santa Maria della Vittoria, Rome. Alinari/Art Resource, New York.

104. Panorama with view of St. Peter's. Ministry of Aeronautics, Florence. Alinari/Art Resource, New York.

105. Reconstruction of the old St. Peter's Basilica. Petriano Museum, Rome. Alinari/Art Resource, New York.

106. Bronze statue of St. Peter. St. Peter's, Rome. Alinari/Art Resource, New York.

107. Architectural ground plans for St. Peter's by Bramante, Michelangelo, and Carlo Maderno. Foto Marburg/Art Resource, New York.

108. Leonardo da Vinci, *Two Architectural Studies.* Institute of France Library, Paris. Scala/Art Resource, New York.

109. Bramante, S. Pietro in Montorio. Rome. Alinari/Art Resource, New York.
110. *Removal of the Obelisk of the Circus of Nero to the Sacristry of St. Peter's.* Rome. Alinari/Art Resource, New York.
111. Carlo Maderno and Michelangelo, Interior of St. Peter's. Rome. Alinari/Art Resource, New York.
112. Bernini, Monument of Alexander VII. St. Peter's, Rome. Alinari/Art Resource, New York.
113. Pietro Torrigiano, *Henry VII.* Painted terracotta, 16th c. Victoria & Albert Museum, London/Art Resource, New York.
114. William Tyndale. Oil painting by an unknown artist. The Bettmann Archive, New York.
115. Hans Holbein the Younger, Portrait of Henry VIII. Corsini Gallery, Rome. Alinari/Art Resource, New York.
116. *Cardinal Wolsey.* Engraving after the painting by Hans Holbein the Younger. The Bettman Archive, New York.
117. The Holbein School, *Anne Boleyn.* The Bettmann Archive, New York.
118. Gerard Flicke, Portrait of Thomas Cranmer. National Gallery, London. Snark/Art Resource, New York.
119. *Thomas Cromwell, Earl of Essex.* Engraving after the painting by Hans Holbein the Younger. The Bettmann Archive, New York.
120. Hans Holbein the Younger, *John Fisher, Bishop of Rochester.* The British Museum. The Bettmann Archive, New York.
121. Hans Holbein the Younger, Portrait of Jane Seymour. Kunsthistorisches Museum, Vienna. Foto Marburg/Art Resource, New York.
122. Hans Holbein the Younger, Portrait of Anne of Cleves. Louvre, Paris. Alinari/Art Resource, New York.
123. Sebastiano del Piombo, *Cardinal Pole.* The Bettmann Archive, New York.
124. Hans Holbein the Younger, Portrait of Thomas Howard, Duke of Norfolk. Windsor. Alinari/Art Resource, New York.
125. Hans Holbein the Younger, Portrait of Catherine Howard, Queen of England, wife of Henry VIII ca. 1520-1542. The Bettmann Archive, New York.
126. Catherine Parr (1512–1548), sixth wife of Henry VIII of England. From a painting by Holbein. The Bettmann Archive, New York.
127. *Portrait of a Lady,* also called *Portrait of Mary, Queen of Scots (1542-1587).* Painting, French 16th c. Prado, Madrid. The Bettman Archive, New York.

128. Hans Holbein the Younger, *King Edward the Sixth*. The Bettmann Archive, New York.

129. *Edward Seymour, Duke of Somerset*. Engraving after the painting by Hans Holbein the Younger. The Bettmann Archive, New York.

130. *John Dudley, Duke of Northumberland*. Engraving after the painting by Hans Holbein the Younger. The Bettmann Archive, New York.

131. Pietro Martire Vermigli (1500–1562), Florentine religious. Undated engraving. The Bettmann Archive, New York.

132. Polish religious reformer John à Lasco (1499–1560). Undated engraving. The Bettmann Archive, New York.

133. Queen Mary I (Mary Tudor) of England (1516–1558). Portrait painting. The Bettmann Archive, New York.

134. Titian, Portrait of Philip II of Spain. Pitti Palace, Florence. Alinari/Art Resource, New York.

135. School of the Clouets, Portrait Bust of Lord Burghley, Bailiff, Knight of the Order of the Garter. The Bettmann Archive, New York.

136. John Knox (1505–1572). Facsimile after a copper engraving by Hendrik Hondius the Younger. The Bettmann Archive, New York.

137. *Archbishop Whitgift*. After an engraving by G. Vertue. The Bettmann Archive, New York.

138. F. Clouet, Portrait of the Duke of Alençon. Musée Conde, Chantilly. Giraudon/Art Resource, New York.

139. English theologian Richard Hooker (1553 or 1554–1600). Undated engraving after a painting. The Bettmann Archive, New York.

140. Shop Sign Portrait of William Shakespeare. Folger Shakespeare Library. Art Resource, New York.

COLOR PLATES

1. Brunelleschi, interior of the chapel of the Pazzi family. Santa Croce, Florence. Erich Lessing/Art Resource, New York.

2. Piero della Francesca, portrait of Federico da Montefeltro and Battista Sforza, Uffizi, Florence. Alinari/Art Resource, New York.

3. Raphael, portrait of Balthasar Castiglione, Louvre, Paris. Scala/Art Resource, New York.

4. Titian, portrait of Eleonora Gonzaga. Uffizi, Florence. Scala/Art Resource, New York.

5. Pinturicchio, *Submitting to the Pope Eugenius IV in the Name of Federico III.* Duomo, Siena. Scala/Art Resource, New York.

6. Melozzo da Forli, *Pope Sixtus IV and Bartolomeo Platina. Pope Charges Platina with the Administration of the Vatican Library.* Vatican Library, Rome. Erich Lessing/Art Resource, New York.

7. Andrea Mantegna, altar of San Zeno. Predella: *The Crucifixion.* Louvre, Paris. Scala/Art Resource, New York.

8. Andrea Mantegna, *Camera degli Sposi.* Ducal Palace, Mantua. Scala/Art Resource, New York.

9. Andrea Mantegna, *The Ceiling.* Ducal Palace, Mantua. Scala/Art Resource, New York.

10. Andrea Mantegna, *The Meeting.* Ducal Palace, Mantua. Scala/Art Resource, New York.

11. Andrea Mantegna, *The Return from Rome of Cardinal Francesco Gonzaga.* Palazzo Ducale, Mantua. Scala/Art Resource, New York.

12. Andrea Mantegna, *The Court.* Ducal Palace, Mantua. Scala/Art Resource, New York.

13. Piazza San Marco. Venice. Scala/Art Resource, New York.

14. Andrea Palladio, facade, Villa Barbaro. Maser. Scala/Art Resource, New York.

15. Antonello da Messina, *The Annunciation.* National Gallery of Sicily, Palermo. Scala/Art Resource, New York.

16. Gentile Bellini, *Procession in St. Mark's Square.* Accademia, Venice. Scala/Art Resource, New York.

17. Giovanni Bellini, *Madonna and Child with Saints.* Accademia, Venice. Scala/Art Resource, New York.

18. Vittore Carpaccio, *The Rulers,* detail of *The Arrival of the Ambassadors, the Legend of Saint Ursula.* Galleria dell'Accademia, Venice. Erich Lessing/Art Resource, New York.

19. Titian, *Assumption of the Virgin.* Chiesa dei Frari, Venice. Cameraphoto/Art Resource, New York.

20. Titian, portrait of Isabella d'Este (1474–1539), Margravine of Mantua. Kunsthistorisches Museum, Gemaeldegalerie, Vienna. Erich Lessing/Art Resource, New York.

21. Titian, *The Venus of Urbino.* Uffizi, Florence. Scala/Art Resource, New York.

22. Tintoretto, *The Crucifixion.* School of San Rocco, Venice. Scala/Art Resource, New York.

23. Veronese, *Feast in the House of Levi*. Accademia, Venice. Scala/Art Resource, New York.

24. Central nave from the door of the entrance towards the main altar. Church of Santa Maria delle Grazie, Milan. Scala/Art Resource, New York.

25. Leonardo da Vinci, *The Madonna of the Rocks*, c. 1483. Louvre, Paris. Scala/Art Resource, New York.

26. Leonardo da Vinci, *The Virgin and Child with St. Anne*, c. 1508. Louvre, Paris. Scala/Art Resource, New York.

27. View of the Duomo and panorama with the Palazzo Vecchio. Florence. Scala/Art Resource, New York.

28. Benozzo Gozzoli, *Procession of the Magi*. Detail of the Procession with the Patriarch of Constantinople and Giuliano de' Medici. Palazzo Medici Riccardi, Florence. Scala/Art Resource, New York.

29. Benozzo Gozzoli, *Procession of the Magi*. Detail of Emperor John Paleologus VIII. Palazzo Medici Riccardi, Florence. Scala/Art Resource, New York.

30. Benozzo Gozzoli, *Court of the Magi*. Court of Lorenzo de' Medici and Attendants. Palazzo Medici Riccardi, Florence. Scala/Art Resource, New York.

31. Benozzo Gozzoli, *Court of the Magi*. Court of Cosimo the Elder. Palazzo Medici Riccardi, Florence. Scala/Art Resource, New York.

32. Benozzo Gozzoli, *Adoration of the Magi*. Detail of the angels. Uffizi, Florence. Scala/Art Resource, New York.

33. Benozzo Gozzoli, *Procession of the Magi*. Detail of the Castle. Palazzo Medici Riccardi, Florence. Scala/Art Resource, New York.

34. Altichiero da Zevio, *Francesco Petrarca (1304-1374)*. Detail from the *Burial of Saint Lucia*. Oratorio di San Giorgio, Padua. Erich Lessing/Art Resource, New York.

35. Domenico Ghirlandaio, *Annunciation of Zachariah*. Detail of mural (1486): Angelo Poliziano, Christoforo Landino, Marsilio Ficino, and Gentile Bacci. Santa Maria Novella, Florence. Erich Lessing/Art Resource, New York.

36. Giotto, *Life of St. Francis. St. Francis Donating His Cloak*. Basilica of St. Francis, Assisi. Scala/Art Resource, New York.

37. Giotto, *Life of St. Francis. Expulsion of the Demons from Arezzo*. Basilica of St. Francis, Assisi. Scala/Art Resource, New York.

38. Giotto, *Life of St. Francis. Confirmation of the Rule*. S. Francesco, Assisi. Scala/Art Resource, New York.

39. Giotto, *Life of St. Francis. St. Francis Preaching to the Birds.* Basilica of St. Francis, Assisi. Scala/Art Resource, New York.
40. Giotto, *The Dream of Joachim.* Scrovegni Chapel, Padua. Scala/Art Resource, New York.
41. Giotto, *Nativity.* Scrovegni Chapel, Padua. Scala/Art Resource, New York.
42. Giotto, *Kiss of Judas.* Scrovegni Chapel, Padua. Scala/Art Resource, New York.
43. Giotto, *The Last Judgment.* Scrovegni Chapel, Padua. Scala/Art Resource, New York.
44. Masaccio, *Expulsion from Paradise.* Carmine Church, Florence. Scala/Art Resource, New York.
45. Masaccio, *St. Peter Baptizing the Neophytes.* Carmine Church, Florence. Scala/Art Resource, New York.
46. Masaccio, *St. Peter Curing the Sick.* Carmine Church, Florence. Scala/Art Resource, New York.
47. Masaccio, *Distributing Alms and Death of Ananias.* Carmine Church, Florence. Scala/Art Resource, New York.
48. Masaccio, *Tribute Money.* Carmine Church, Florence. Scala/Art Resource, New York.
49. Masaccio, *Resurrection of the Son of Theophilus and St. Peter Enthroned.* Carmine Church, Florence. Scala/Art Resource, New York.
50. Massacio, *Resurrection of the Son of Theophilus and St. Peter Enthroned.* Detail starting from far right: portraits of Brunelleschi, Alberti, Massacio, and Masolino. Carmine Church, Florence. Scala/Art Resource, New York.
51. Lorenzo Ghiberti, Gates of Paradise. Baptistry, Florence. Scala/Art Resource, New York.
52. Lorenzo Ghiberti, North Door. *Annunciation.* Baptistry, Florence. Scala/Art Resource, New York.
53. Fra Filippo Lippi, *Madonna of Humility.* Castello Sforzesco, Milan. Scala/Art Resource, New York.
54. Fra Filippo Lippi, *Madonna and Child with Angels.* Uffizi, Florence. Scala/Art Resource, New York.
55. Fra Angelico, *The Annunciation.* Muse Diocesano, Cortona. Scala/Art Resource, New York.
56. Fra Angelico, *The Deposition.* San Marco Museum, Florence. Erich Lessing/Art Resource, New York.
57. Fra Angelico, *Coronation of the Virgin.* San Marco Museum, Florence. Scala/Art Resource, New York.

58. Fra Angelico, *San Lorenzo Distributing Alms to the Poor.* Niccolina Chapel, Vatican, Rome. Scala/Art Resource, New York.

59. Sandro Botticelli, *Pallas and the Centaur.* Uffizi, Florence. Erich Lessing/Art Resource, New York.

60. Sandro Botticelli, *Primavera.* Uffizi, Florence. Erich Lessing/Art Resource, New York.

61. Sandro Botticelli, *The Birth of Venus.* Uffizi, Florence. Scala/Art Resource, New York.

62. Sandro Botticelli, *The Annunciation.* Uffizi, Florence. Alinari/Art Resource, New York.

63. Domenico Ghirlandaio, *The Adoration of the Shepherds.* S. Trinita, Florence. Scala/Art Resource, New York.

64. Raphael, *Portrait of a Man.* Palatina, Florence. Alinari/Art Resource, New York.

65. Raphael, *Portrait of Maddalena Strozzi-Doni.* Palatina, Florence. Alinari/Art Resource, New York.

66. Michelangelo, *Creation of Eve.* Sistine Chapel, Vatican.

67. Michelangelo, *Temptation and Expulsion.* Sistine Chapel, Vatican.

68. Michelangelo, *Creation of Adam,* Sistine Chapel, Vatican.

69. Raphael, *The Dispute of the Sacrament.* Stanze, Vatican. Scala/Art Resource, New York.

70. Raphael, *School of Athens.* Stanze, Vatican, Rome. Scala/Art Resource, New York.

71. Raphael, *Transfiguration.* Pinacoteca, Vatican. Scala/Art Resource, New York.

72. Raphael, *Parnassus.* Stanze, Vatican. Scala/Art Resource, New York.

73. Raphael, *Expulsion of Heliodorus in the Temple.* Stanze, Vatican. Scala/Art Resource, New York.

74. Raphael, *Mass at Bolsena.* Stanze, Vatican. Scala/Art Resource, New York.

75. Raphael, *Meeting of Attila the Hun and Leo the Great.* Stanze, Vatican. Scala/Art Resource, New York.

76. Christopher Columbus, discoverer (1451–1506). Portraitgalerie, Schloss Ambras, Innsbruck. Erich Lessing/Art Resource, New York.

77. Michiel Sittow, portrait of Catherine of Aragon (1485–1536). Portraitgalerie, Schloss Ambras, Innsbruck. Erich Lessing/Art Resource, New York.

78. Anonymous, *Saint Ignatius before Pope Paul III.* Church of Jesus, Rome. Scala/Art Resource, New York.

79. Peter Paul Rubens, *The Miracle of Saint Francis Xavier,* detail. Kunsthistorisches Museum, Gemaeldegalerie, Vienna. Erich Lessing/Art Resource, New York.
80. Central nave towards the altar, St. Peter's, Vatican. Scala/Art Resource, New York.
81. View from the left of the Basilica and Piazza. St. Peter's, Vatican. Scala/Art Resource, New York.
82. English School, portrait of Queen Elizabeth I of England (1533–1603). Portraitgalerie, Schloss Ambras, Innsbruck. Erich Lessing / Art Resource, New York.

Index

References in italics indicate pages with black-and-white prints.

704